The Edinburgh Companion to Nonsense

Edinburgh Companions to Literature and the Humanities

Published

The Edinburgh Companion to Virginia Woolf and the Arts
Edited by Maggie Humm

The Edinburgh Companion to Twentieth-Century Literatures in English
Edited by Brian McHale and Randall Stevenson

A Historical Companion to Postcolonial Literatures in English
Edited by David Johnson and Prem Poddar

A Historical Companion to Postcolonial Literatures – Continental Europe and its Empires
Edited by Prem Poddar, Rajeev Patke and Lars Jensen

The Edinburgh Companion to Twentieth-Century British and American War Literature
Edited by Adam Piette and Mark Rowlinson

The Edinburgh Companion to Shakespeare and the Arts
Edited by Mark Thornton Burnett, Adrian Streete and Ramona Wray

The Edinburgh Companion to Samuel Beckett and the Arts
Edited by S. E. Gontarski

The Edinburgh Companion to the Bible and the Arts
Edited by Stephen Prickett

The Edinburgh Companion to Modern Jewish Fiction
Edited by David Brauner and Axel Stähler

The Edinburgh Companion to Critical Theory
Edited by Stuart Sim

The Edinburgh Companion to the Critical Medical Humanities
Edited by Anne Whitehead, Angela Woods, Sarah Atkinson, Jane Macnaughton and Jennifer Richards

The Edinburgh Companion to Nineteenth-Century American Letters and Letter-Writing
Edited by Celeste-Marie Bernier, Judie Newman and Matthew Pethers

The Edinburgh Companion to T. S. Eliot and the Arts
Edited by Frances Dickey and John D. Morgenstern

The Edinburgh Companion to Children's Literature
Edited by Clémentine Beauvais and Maria Nikolajeva

The Edinburgh Companion to Atlantic Literary Studies
Edited by Leslie Eckel and Clare Elliott

The Edinburgh Companion to the First World War and the Arts
Edited by Ann-Marie Einhaus and Katherine Isobel Baxter

The Edinburgh Companion to Fin-de-Siècle Literature, Culture and the Arts
Edited by Josephine M. Guy

The Edinburgh Companion to Animal Studies
Edited by Lynn Turner, Undine Sellbach and Ron Broglio

The Edinburgh Companion to Contemporary Narrative Theories
Edited by Zara Dinnen and Robyn Warhol

The Edinburgh Companion to Anthony Trollope
Edited by Frederik Van Dam, David Skilton and Ortwin Graef

The Edinburgh Companion to the Short Story in English
Edited by Paul Delaney and Adrian Hunter

The Edinburgh Companion to the Postcolonial Middle East
Edited by Anna Ball and Karim Mattar

The Edinburgh Companion to Ezra Pound and the Arts
Edited by Roxana Preda

The Edinburgh Companion to Elizabeth Bishop
Edited by Jonathan Ellis

The Edinburgh Companion to Gothic and the Arts
Edited by David Punter

The Edinburgh Companion to Literature and Music
Edited by Delia da Sousa Correa

The Edinburgh Companion to D. H. Lawrence and the Arts
Catherine Brown and Susan Reid

The Edinburgh Companion to the Prose Poem
Mary Ann Caws and Michel Delville

The Edinburgh Companion to Nonsense
Anna Barton and James Williams

Forthcoming

The Edinburgh Companion to Charles Dickens and the Arts
Edited by Juliet John and Claire Wood

The Edinburgh Companion to Virginia Woolf and Contemporary Global Literature
Edited by Jeanne Dubino, Catherine W. Hollis, Paulina Pajak, Celise Lypka and Vara Neverow

The Edinburgh Companion to Irish Modernism
Maud Ellmann, Sian White and Vicki Mahaffey

The Edinburgh Companion to Modernism and Technology
Alex Goody and Ian Whittington

The Edinburgh Companion to the Brontës and the Arts
Amber Regis and Deborah Wynne

The Edinburgh Companion to the Essay
Mario Aquilina, Nicole B. Wallack and Bob Cowser Jnr.

The Edinburgh Companion to Science Fiction and the Medical Humanities
Gavin Miller, Anna McFarlane and Donna McCormack

The Edinburgh Companion to W. B. Yeats and the Arts
Tom Walker, Adrian Paterson and Charles Armstrong

The Edinburgh Companion to Women in Publishing, 1900–2000
Nicola Wilson, Elizabeth Gordon Willson, Alice Staveley, Helen Southworth, Daniela La Penna, Sophie Heywood and Claire Battershill

https://edinburghuniversitypress.com/series/ecl

The Edinburgh Companion to Nonsense

Edited by Anna Barton and James Williams

EDINBURGH
University Press

Edinburgh University Press is one of the leading university presses in the UK. We publish academic books and journals in our selected subject areas across the humanities and social sciences, combining cutting-edge scholarship with high editorial and production values to produce academic works of lasting importance. For more information visit our website: edinburghuniversitypress.com

Edinburgh University Press Ltd
13 Infirmary Street, Edinburgh, EH1 1LT

Typeset in 10/12 Adobe Sabon by
IDSUK (DataConnection) Ltd

A CIP record for this book is available from the British Library

ISBN 978 1 4744 2384 7 (hardback)
ISBN 978 1 3995 5738 2 (paperback)
ISBN 978 1 4744 2385 4 (webready PDF)
ISBN 978 1 4744 2386 1 (epub)

Contents

List of Illustrations

Acknowledgements

Our sincere thanks to all those friends and colleagues whose advice, friendship and inspiration we have drawn upon at different points in the planning, commissioning, writing and editing of this book. Thanks to Ersev Ersoy and the team at Edinburgh University Press for their expert guidance and patience. We are also indebted to Marco Graziosi for his swift and generous response to requests for help obtaining a number of the illustrations included in this volume. And thanks, as ever, to our families, especially Brian King and Iain Kee Vaughan, for their care and support.

Every effort has been made to trace the copyright holders, but if any have been inadvertently overlooked, the publisher will be pleased to make the necessary arrangements at the first opportunity.

This book is dedicated to students of nonsense,
past, present and future, at the Universities
of Sheffield and York.

Introduction: Companionable Nonsense

Anna Barton and James Williams

> The Red Queen shook her head. 'You may call it "nonsense" if you like,' she said. 'But I have heard nonsense compared with which that would be as sensible as a dictionary!'[1]

Most people, most of the time, want to make sense. We wish, by our words and actions, to be understood; to be clear and rational; to communicate with others; and to answer, in some way, to the realities of the world around us. But most people some of the time – and perhaps some people most of the time – desire the opposite: to eschew sense; to refuse, in speech or behaviour, to accept or conform to the responsibilities of clarity, relevance and coherence. This refusal might be merely confused, petulant, obtuse or escapist. At other times, though – sometimes even within the same gesture – it can be creative, liberating or opaquely pregnant with implication. Sometimes it can even seem more meaningful, paradoxically, than the sensible alternative. Nonsense, for want of a better catch-all term for this refusal (and 'refusal' too is an imperfect description of the range of motivations at work) can create the conditions for imaginative connections and forms of oblique self-expression: it forms the basis for modes of literary art that channel the latent pre-semantic pleasures of sound, rhythm and pattern, without the obligations of rational communication or consistency. It can free us up to tell stories that are not indebted to or bound by rules of coherence and causality. It can articulate that part of our humanity that does not make sense even to ourselves, and it can dare, with varying degrees of justice and success, to speak to and for those who, for whatever reason, have been viewed as not fully participant in their society's shared game of sense-making: children, the insane, dreaming sleepers, slaves, women, inspired poets, queer people, animals. It can even help us question the idea of 'sense' as such, and the assumptions on which this seemingly neutral and inoffensive concept rests. It is this kind of creative nonsense that is the subject of this *Companion*.

The literature that most embodies this affirmative (as opposed to merely dismissive) use of the word 'nonsense' has often been seen as emerging in a particular place and time: Victorian England. And, more narrowly still, it has been inseparably associated with the writings of Edward Lear and Lewis Carroll, authors whose work was and is aimed primarily at children (while speaking, as good children's literature always does, to a much wider readership). For the early admirer G. K. Chesterton, the emergence of nonsense in the nineteenth century was a development of absolute and astonishing novelty, to be eulogised in language that just a few decades later might have come from the lips of an Italian Futurist: '"The Dong with the Luminous Nose", at least, is original, as the first ship and the first plough were original.'[2] A later and very different writer, Noel Malcolm, while attaching a much earlier date to the origin of nonsense, nonetheless insisted on the same fundamental fact that it had appeared at a specific historical moment and in a particular place: 'nonsense poetry sprang, almost fully armed, out of [Sir John] Hoskyns's head [in 1611]'.[3] But against this understanding of nonsense as a historically, geographically or culturally delimited genre there has always been another view which, while often taking Lear and Carroll as exemplary, sees in Victorian nonsense merely a new consolidation or manifestation of a playful tendency inherent in all literature, perhaps all human language, extending outwards into French surrealism, German *Galgenlieder*, and Russian *zaum* poetry, backwards through the likes of Swift and Rabelais, medieval *fatrasie* and Aristophanic drama, and forward into writers as bewilderingly different as James Joyce, Gertrude Stein and Ogden Nash. This view can often be found implicitly or explicitly underpinning the work of anthologies of nonsense, whose editors seek to draw together as diverse and interesting a span of samples as possible. For Geoffrey Grigson, '[t]he moment literature develops, nonsense literature must be expected'; for Hugh Haughton, nonsense is 'less a genre than a possibility, a dimension, a boundary which poetry touches more frequently than we usually imagine'.[4]

This volume, in its organisation and its scope, implicitly aligns itself with the latter view, although we have made no attempt as editors to police the views or positions of our individual contributors on such matters. Few would deny, in any case, there is something particularly energetic and self-aware about the nonsense of Victorian England, whatever claims of uniqueness we do or do not make for it, and that in some way (to borrow Haughton's phrase) nonsense 'came into its own'[5] in works like Carroll's 'Jabberwocky':

'Twas brillig, and the slithy toves
  Did gyre and gimble in the wabe:
All mimsy were the borogoves,
  And the mome raths outgrabe.[6]

This is nonsense of an especially acute and self-aware variety, and indeed so odd and startling is this verse that when Carroll first shows it to his reader it is printed in mirror writing: he goes out of his way to 'other' this kind of language, to set it apart as strange, as if cast in its own back-to-front language and script. And of course, no sooner does 'Jabberwocky' appear in print than Alice, the poem's first reader, grapples with what to make of it. 'Somehow it seems to fill my head with ideas – only I don't exactly know what they are!'[7] Alice, so often the book's voice of common sense, wants to know what it means (later on Humpty Dumpty obliges her with a parodic exegesis that some readers have taken rather over-seriously), and immediately she illuminates one of the inbuilt paradoxes of nonsense: that, in the words of the critic Wim Tigges, 'nonsense must at the same time invite the reader to interpretation and avoid the suggestion that there is a deeper meaning which can be obtained'.[8] Little if any nonsense, after all, is completely without meaning of any kind – what, for a semantic animal like *Homo sapiens* would that really mean anyway? – the apparatus of cogency, even if only at the level of phonology and grammar, underlies and infuses nonsense, and nonsense catches flashes of sense obliquely, as a gem held up to the light.

To shift from asking about 'meaning' to wanting to know '*the* meaning' of a nonsense text, however, seems to risk committing some kind of basic error. So perhaps it is a mistake to ask 'what does nonsense *mean*?' But the fact that nonsense forestalls certain kinds of explanatory question is not, we think, good grounds for shutting down others: how has the understanding of nonsense changed over time, and across different languages and cultural traditions? What are the boundaries of nonsense? Do questions of sense and nonsense end where language ends, or are there forms of nonsense – or forms analogous to nonsense – in other, non- or semi-verbal, art forms? Above all, *why make nonsense?* What kinds of things can we say or feel when we make nonsense that we cannot when we make sense? Nonsense, one might argue, has many localised and contingent cultural uses, from filling a gap where the name of an object should be ('pass me the thingummy-bob') to conjuring spells and controlling spirits ('*abracadabra!*') to the free play of song refrains ('the jingle-jangle morning'; 'a wop-bop-a-loo-bop')[9] to memorising the patterns of Latin metre ('down in a deep, dark ditch sat an old cow munching a beanstalk').[10] To this handful of examples might be added a whole array of other purposes: jokes, riddles, encryptions and parlour games.

A long-standing critical tradition has attempted to root out and set aside these purposes in the service of distinguishing false or merely *apparent* nonsense from 'true' nonsense, which supposedly has no kind of point or purpose at all. This view is at least as old as 1901, the year of Carolyn Wells's essay 'The Sense of Nonsense'. The rhyme 'Eena, meena, mona, mi', she writes,

> is not strictly a nonsense-verse, because it was invented and used for 'counting out' [. . .] also, in the case of the nonsense-verses with which students of Latin composition are sometimes taught to begin their efforts, where words are used with no relative meaning [. . .] It is only nonsense for nonsense's sake that is now under our consideration.[11]

Wells's phrase 'nonsense for nonsense's sake' – and it is surely no accident that her article appeared hot on the heels of the *fin-de-siècle* enthusiasm for 'art for art's sake' – makes clear that this kind of purism about nonsense has often gone hand in hand with other kinds of defence of the artistic self-sufficiency. But the anxiety that any kind of 'purpose' or 'use' for nonsense within a shared 'form of life'[12] is enough to rule something out of the sphere of 'true' nonsense has never gone away. And indeed, the question of what we may call 'nonsense' – how wide or narrow a semantic net the term casts – goes back beyond critics like Wells, into the Victorian literature that was the primary point of reference for almost all twentieth-century theorising. In *Through the Looking-Glass and What Alice Found There*, for instance, the Red Queen implies that we are free to apply the term as we see fit ('You may call it "nonsense" if you like . . .') and that the distinction between sense and nonsense is a matter of taste, or, at least, a question of perspective. At the same time, the Queen points to higher and stronger forms of nonsense known to the aficionado or the elect ('but I have heard nonsense compared with which . . .'). The 'as you like it' definition has always struggled to co-exist with the equally powerful preconception that the only real nonsense is, in the words of Edward Lear, 'pure and absolute'.[13] The purity of nonsense offers a different sort of freedom: a freedom from, rather than a freedom to. It suggests a kind of activity secure from the demands and responsibilities of the sensible, the rational and the real. It promises to recreate the innocent free play of childhood; but it also rebuffs critical interrogation by suggesting that nonsense is either above or beneath intellectual concerns.

Discussions of nonsense tend to lean towards one or other of these approaches to their subject. At the turn of the twentieth century, contemporary with Carolyn Wells, essays by Edward Strachey, G. K. Chesterton and Aldous Huxley propose nonsense as a special or sacred undertaking. Nonsense is 'a true work of the imagination, a child of genius'; it represents part of 'that eternal struggle between the genius or the eccentric and his fellow beings'; it can be compared to religious faith.[14] At the same time, psychoanalysis offered another approach (often resented by British defenders of nonsense, but in some ways parallel) that viewed the dream worlds of nonsense texts as manifestations of the underground of the mind, the anarchic realm of the subconscious. Freud describes jokes as ways to enjoy 'the liberation of nonsense' without giving up the commitment to 'the serious life'.[15] He associates this pleasure with the minds of children, writing that the child is gradually denied this kind of pleasure as he grows into rational consciousness. In the 1950s the purist approach to nonsense took on a new theoretical rigour in the work of Elizabeth Sewell. Writing with a sense of affinity to the traditions of logical philosophy, Sewell describes nonsense as 'a carefully limited world, controlled and directed by reason, a construction subject to its own laws [. . .] concrete, clear and wholly comprehensible'.[16] For her, true nonsense is not to be found in the anarchic, the chaotic or the dreamlike, but in a self-enclosed and self-sustaining form of literary play in which words, detached of their obligations to reference and relevance, are moved around like pieces on a chessboard. Sewell's version of nonsense is the opposite of the nonsense proposed by Freud; yet both agree on the purity of nonsense, its essential separateness from the (for Sewell) unclear and incomprehensible or (for Freud) stiflingly rational business of living in the real world.

As the twentieth century progressed, this absolutist version of nonsense, put under pressure by the rise of post-structuralist theory, began to give way to more relativist accounts. At the end of the 1970s, Susan Stewart's landmark study of nonsense proposed a dynamic relationship between nonsense and common sense: 'acts of common sense will shape acts of nonsense and acts of nonsense will shape acts of common sense'.[17] For Stewart, the value of nonsense can be found in the way it exposes common sense as 'an only partial reality, an ideology'.[18] The concept 'nonsense' seems to presuppose an understanding of 'sense', but 'sense' continually defines and reasserts itself against this shadowy Other. Mutually dependent, mutually producing, common sense and nonsense are neither fixed nor given; both play their part in the 'ongoing accomplishment of social life'.[19] Jean-Jacques Lecercle echoes Stewart's understanding of what is at stake in the production and identification of nonsense when he writes that nonsense might also be understood as 'metasense', a kind of writing particularly alert to its own forms and functions, one that can therefore be employed in different kinds of hermeneutic enquiry.[20] Homi K. Bhabha's discussion of 'colonial nonsense' is one example of this kind of enquiry. For Bhabha, nonsense exposes the tenuous and provisional nature of colonial subjectivity. He writes that in Western accounts of colonised subjects, 'the articulation of nonsense is the recognition of an anxious contradictory place between the human and the non-human, between sense and nonsense'.[21] For Bhabha, as for Stewart and for Lecercle, the identification of nonsense involves drawing a line that divides nonsense from its opposite. Nonsense becomes an important object of study, not just as a thing in itself, but for what it reveals about the subject who encounters and names it.

As with the earlier question of whether or not nonsense is historically and geographically specific, this *Companion* inevitably aligns itself with one position in its scope and selection while making no attempt to police the opinions of individual authors. As editors, we take the view that, however ingenious and illuminating theoretical defences of 'pure nonsense' like Sewell's may be, they come at a heavy cost: a narrowing and diminishing of the scope of nonsense as a field of enquiry. We are, in the end, closer to Stewart in our understanding that nonsense exists pervasively in our shared life as semantic animals, and in a dazzling array of relationships to 'sense', some of them 'purer' than others. We are sceptical about the move that would rule out of consideration the counting-out rhyme or the magic spell, the utopian language or the literary parody, because we do not see 'nonsense' as a precisely boundaried genre of writing but rather, or at least to an equal degree, as a shifting, context-sensitive and endlessly inventive mode of *reading*. We are even receptive to the thought that there might be modes of nonsense that move outside of language (the proper domain of 'sense') altogether, that other art forms might generate their own forms of 'nonsense'. This view animates our conviction that our understanding of nonsense is enlarged by bringing together the wide spread of approaches and the diverse set of examples that a volume like this one makes possible. At the same time, however, we know that our contributors take a range of principled positions on the question of definitions, and we have not censored essays which rule this or that example out as failing to meet the criteria of 'true' nonsense. A *Companion* makes its case in the aggregate.

* * *

With this in mind, a few words on the shape of the volume. The essays that follow each try to walk a line between surveying different aspects of nonsense in a way that would be helpful to the relative newcomer, and developing original arguments; between, in other words, the introductory and the exploratory. Sometimes the nature of the chapter's subject matter has demanded an approach that leans more one way or the other, but we hope that, taken as a whole, this *Companion* will serve both as a Baedeker for those new to the subject and as a stimulus to reconsideration and revaluation for those more familiar with the field.

Part I, 'Notes Towards a History of English Nonsense', takes as its point of departure the familiar understanding of nonsense as a genre of English literature. At the same time, however, it consciously avoids the familiar priority given to the Victorian, instead taking a long view, from the medieval to the late modernist. Jordan Kirk argues that medieval nonsense is a rich tradition that can be understood on its own terms, apart from the modern iterations that follow later. His chapter explores the topsy-turvy worlds and nonsense neologisms that appear in the literature of medieval England, Germany, France and Italy. Discussing the significance of nonsense for medieval linguistic theory and philosophy, Kirk demonstrates nonsense's central role in the work of education and interpretation during the period. Rebecca Fall considers the place of nonsense in early modern England. Her chapter looks at 'fustian' nonsense games, a common feature of life at the universities and inns of court in the sixteenth and seventeenth centuries, which employed nonsense to navigate and challenge the hierarchical social structures of these exclusive, rule-bound worlds. Demonstrating how fustian nonsense employs the materials of the rarefied culture it seeks to challenge, Fall goes on to explore how this tradition makes its way into the dramas of Johnson and Shakespeare, where it functions as a powerful form of frivolity.

Freya Johnston picks up the thread in the eighteenth century, the so-called 'Age of Reason', showing how nonsense was in fact woven into the literary cultures of the Enlightenment not only as a diversion or a sideshow but as a major focus for questions about literary creativity and the place of the imagination. Peter Swaab's chapter approaches the question of nonsense and Romanticism via the genre of the quest poem, in which he finds a major bridge between the voyaging and escapist narratives of the early nineteenth century and the works of Lear and Carroll. Nonsense literature is often understood as both a peculiarly Victorian phenomenon and one that is characterised by its oppositional relationship to Victorian art and culture. Martin Dubois challenges this counter-cultural view of Victorian nonsense by identifying its 'kinships' with other aspects of Victorian literary and print culture: literary parody, nursery literature and baby talk. His chapter, which reads Edward Lear and Lewis Carroll alongside Dickens, Christina Rossetti, Tennyson and Ruskin, draws new connections between the traditional 'founding fathers' of nonsense and their historical context.

Moving into the twentieth century, Noreen Masud uncovers the affinities between nonsense and modernism, showing how the strategies of Victorian nonsense hold particular appeal for writers responding to the seismic cultural shifts that occurred in the wake of the First World War. Masud demonstrates the ways that modernism learns from nonsense literature's off-kilter perspectives, its interest in ephemera, in the opportune and the happenstance, in order to cause its readers to doubt their critical faculties and confound their search for meaning. Adam Piette's discussion of nonsense and mid-century modernism explores the darker side of nonsense's twentieth-century legacy. Focusing on the work of Rebecca West and Samuel Beckett, Piette argues that nonsense is a spectre of Victorian patriarchy and colonialism that haunts the literature of the mid-twentieth century, and he explores the ways in which West and Beckett seek to exorcise it. These essays, between them, chart something of the variety of forms in which nonsense animates and influences the literary culture of the times immediately prior to our own.

Thus far our volume has remained in the tradition of literature written in English. Part II, 'Global Nonsenses', seeks both to expand and question this Anglocentric account of nonsense by taking samples of nonsense literature from a number of other major world languages and traditions. Sara Chiarini poses the question of whether nonsense writing can be found in ancient Greek: taking a strict definition of nonsense she concludes that only a handful of tantalising and suggestive fragments constitute nonsense by the familiar Victorian standard, but in the process uncovers a rich host of texts that exhibit nonsense features and fall within a more copious understanding of the term. Sumanyu Satpathy surveys the nonsense traditions of the many languages of India, both those which emerge in response to English models and those which exist as manifestations of indigenous literary cultures. In Satpathy's account, nonsense appears both as a dimension of the sophisticated linguistic self-awareness of Indian literatures, and as an illuminating way to approach questions of cultural colonialism and its responses. James Rann explores nonsense literature produced in the turbulent first decades of twentieth-century Russia. Focusing on the *zaum* poetry of Aleksei

Kruchenykh and Kornei Chukovsky's controversial children's literature, Rann considers how Russian nonsense seeks to establish new relationships between language, church and state, experimenting with kinds of writing that might provide temporary or permanent freedom from the burden of history.

Two final chapters bring us back to Western European traditions which closely parallel and are entangled with English. Alexandra Lukes focuses her discussion of French nonsense on Carroll's influence on the surrealist movement. She explores the work of Antonin Artaud, which displaces sense by insisting on the bodily experience of language, and the surrealist glossaries of Michel Leiris, which take their meanings from sound rather than etymology. Her readings open up larger questions about the Englishness of nonsense, its relationship to *non-sens* and *délire* and the nature and import of translation. Alessandro Giammei traces the relatively short history of Italian nonsense, which developed in spite of Italy's 'no-nonsense' literary tradition and as a deliberate disavowal of the fascistic nationalism of Mussolini. Focusing on the concrete poetry of Giulia Niccolai, the nonsense songs of Fosco Maraini, and the illustrated texts of Toti Scialoja, Giammei describes Italian nonsense as a cosmopolitan, anti-totalitarian tradition, one that draws on a global set of influences, from the neo-avant-garde of the New York School to the culture of post-war Japan.

The final section of the volume, Part III, 'Contexts and Connections' aims to set nonsense in a range of contexts both familiar and unfamiliar as a way of testing and exploring the limits and limitations of the term. Hugh Roberts invites consideration of the relationship between nonsense and translation in his exploration of adaptations of Rabelaisian nonsense in early modern England. Roberts takes examples from John Eliot's language guide, *Ortho-Epia Gallica* (1593) and *Coryat's Crudities* by Thomas Coryate (1611), to show how nonsense and linguistic play were used to come to terms with the new multilingual possibilities of the early modern world, as trade and travel led to greater opportunities for encounters between speakers of different tongues. Michael Heyman's chapter explores the possibility of nonsense beyond the strictly linguistic sphere by considering the relationship between nonsense and music. Beginning with a discussion of nonsense songs, in which nonsensical lyrics play against the formal sense of melody and rhythm, Heyman moves on to discuss nonsense scores and nonsensical performance. His chapter culminates in an examination of John Hoskyns's early modern experiments with multimodal texts that layer different musical and linguistic systems on top of the other, baffling the reader into a new awareness of how sound can make and unmake meaning.

Anna Barton's essay explores the sympathetic affinity between nonsense and femininity. Focusing on the work of Christina Rossetti and Stevie Smith, it considers how women writers participate in nonsense games in order to both express and escape gendered identity. Hugh Haughton moves the focus from gender to sexuality, seeking to account for 'the magical charge of Lear-style nonsense' for modern gay writers. Tracing the shifting resonance of the term 'queer' from the nineteenth to the twentieth century, Haughton offers an alternative genealogy of nonsense and modernism, considering the queer individuals and couples that populate Lear's poems and letters and Carroll's assaults on the boundary between the natural and the unnatural as models for writers including W. H. Auden, Gertrude Stein, John Ashbury and Joe Orton. Cassie Westwood offers a different perspective on matters of constructed identity and natural kinds by considering the ways that nonsense might allow us to re-imagine our relations to non-human animals. Taking in works from Aristophanes to Elizabeth Bishop, from Edward Gorey to D. H. Lawrence, Westwood explores the capacity nonsense has to disrupt the Aristotelian understanding of the human as the 'speaking animal', and proposes nonsense as a compensatory response to the problem of the unknowable animal interiority of others.

In two final essays, nonsense is read as a site of reflection on questions of meaning, truth and the divine. Michael Potter's chapter offers an analytic philosopher's perspective on nonsense as a term both inside and outside philosophy. Considering the linguistics of Chomsky alongside the logical philosophy of Frege and Wittgenstein, Potter tracks the fault lines between nonsense and impossibility, grammar and semantics, sense and tone and argues that, for philosophy, nonsense is an idea that contributes to debates about whether language is best understood as a means of describing or as a means of constructing truth. Finally, James Williams takes philosophical reflections on the limits of meaning and signification as a point of departure for exploring the roles played by nonsense within theological and religious traditions, taking in both Christian discourse on the nature of God, Jewish and Islamic traditions of mysticism and didacticism, and the complex nonsense-tradition of Zen Buddhism.

* * *

The title of Elizabeth Sewell's 1952 study, *The Field of Nonsense*, indicates something of her prologomenous purpose. Like many an academic pioneer, Sewell felt the need to establish definitions and boundaries, to ask first *what* she was studying before she could study it. Whatever the successes of her book (and they are many, and continue to be felt in these pages), nearly seventy years later the 'field' of nonsense remains contested and unstable. The reader of this book may be surprised to see how many different understandings of and approaches to nonsense are on display. As editors we cannot but be aware of the polyphonic nature of our *Companion*, even as we celebrate it. If a 'companion' should be the reader's friend, this book is more like consulting a group of friends than being guided by a single wise confidante. This experience can leave doubts pending, yet it is this same variety of opinion that makes nonsense such a dynamic, engaging and exciting area of study. We hope that newcomers to the topic will find a place for themselves within a lively conversation.

We are aware, too, of the provisional nature of an undertaking of this kind. To go back once more to Sewell's metaphor of the 'field', it is inevitable that some readers will think we have set the boundaries of our field far too narrowly, others, unjustifiably widely. There are certainly topics that we had hoped – in some cases intended – to cover, which the complications and constraints of a large edited volume in the end rendered impossible. The account given here of the history of nonsense writing in English is necessarily partial, a series of soundings rather than a continuous narrative, and it leaves largely unaddressed the ways in which nonsense might be refracted by the global plurality of Englishes into particularly African, American, Australian, Canadian, Indian, New Zealand or other forms. Part II, on Global Nonsenses, is still more inevitably a sampling, as opposed to a magisterial conspectus. We believe that important statements on nonsense in languages and cultures from Africa and South America to Scandinavia and China remain to be written (though others, as we have noted, have principled doubts about how universal a category nonsense is) and we suspect that, in some cases, the scholars best placed to write them have not yet emerged or remain unknown to the sometimes inward-looking world of Anglo-American academia. Part III is designedly eclectic and reflects the interests and commitments of scholars already invested in the subject rather than exhausting the limits of the range of possible approaches and contexts. The possibilities for nonsense in a wider range of media (visual arts, film, choreography . . .) remain, in our view, open questions deserving of further answers, even if many scholars would see nonsense as *by definition* only possible in literature, the art form whose medium is inherently semantic.

We think it well for editors to address such matters directly when placing a book into readers' hands, but we offer these observations as reflections rather than as regrets: we are excited and impressed by the range of angles from which the essays in this *Companion* approach their subject, the ingenuity and freshness of vision with which some chapters breathe new life into familiar themes, just as much as the creative leaps taken by others as they strike out into uncharted territory. Any edited collection is provisional in nature, and if the debates around the limitations and applications of the term 'nonsense' render this more so than most, that only serves to shed light on how much remains to be brought to the party.

Speaking of parties – and since we are writing at a moment when sociable gatherings are cruelly curtailed – it seems as good a way as any to end these introductory remarks by noting that a *Companion* is an especially apt kind of volume for nonsense. Nonsense has always been among the most companionable of art forms, just as it has always been preoccupied with the tensions between loneliness and sociability. The history of nonsense is one of solitaries, from Lear's Dong with a Luminous Nose roaming his island uttering his 'silvery squeaks',[22] to Eliot's Prufrock wishing he were 'a pair of ragged claws' and throwing up his hands in frustration that 'it is impossible to say just what I mean!'[23] But it is also one of adventurous gatherings, from the medieval trope of the 'Ship of Fools' (periodically reborn, as the nursery rhyme of the 'three men in a tub', or Peacock's 'wise men of Gotham' – 'In a bowl to sea went wise men three . . .'[24] – or Lear's 'Jumblies') to the happily chaotic gathering of the 'Quangle-Wangle's Hat'[25] or the 'wild rumpus' of Sendak's land of the Wild Things.[26] Misery isn't the only thing that loves company: nonsense does, too, because just as meaning is an interpersonal game that requires at least two to play (as Wittgenstein argued)[27] so is its shape-shifting alter ego. The maker of nonsense needs companions to turn what might be a private hell into a shared sociable game, and perhaps for this reason the speakers of nonsense texts, whether implied or fully realised characters, have been great and incessant talkers, driven by a need to communicate that runs every bit as deeply in nonsense as it does in sense (in the words of an anonymous seventeenth-century nonsense poem, 'Oh that my lungs could bleat like butter'd pease!').[28] We hope this volume serves to suggest a range of ways of companionable listening.

Notes

1. Lewis Carroll, *Through the Looking-Glass*, in *Alice's Adventures in Wonderland and Through the Looking-Glass*, ed. Hugh Haughton (London: Penguin, 1998), p. 140.
2. G. K. Chesterton, 'A Defence of Nonsense', in *The Defendant*, 2nd edn (London: R. Brimley Johnson, [1901] 1902), 42–50, p. 43.
3. Noel Malcolm, *The Origins of English Nonsense* (London: HarperCollins, 1997), p. 3.

4. Geoffrey Grigson, in *The Faber Book of Nonsense Verse* ed. Geoffrey Grigson (London: Faber and Faber, 1979), p. 11; Hugh Haughton, in *The Chatto Book of Nonsense Poetry* ed. Hugh Haughton (London: Chatto and Windus, 1988), p. 8.
5. Haughton, *Chatto Book*, p. 16.
6. Carroll, *Looking-Glass*, p. 132.
7. Ibid. p. 134.
8. Wim Tigges, 'An Anatomy of Nonsense', in *Explorations in the Field of Nonsense* (Amsterdam: Rodopi, 1987), p. 27.
9. Respectively, of course, from Bob Dylan's 'Mr Tambourine Man' and Little Richard's 'Tutti Frutti'.
10. The line is a mnemonic: its stressed and unstressed syllables stand in for the heavy and light syllables that make up (one permissible variant of) a line of Latin hexameter: – ∪ ∪ | – – | – ∪ ∪ | – – | – ∪ ∪ | – ∪. Verses of this kind were once commonplace pedagogical tools in the teaching of classical prosody (as attested by Carolyn Wells in the quotation referenced in the following note). Along with its companion pentameter, this appears in *The Faber Book*, ed. Grigson, p. 237.
11. Carolyn Wells, 'The Sense of Nonsense', *Scribner's Magazine* 29 (1901), 239–48, pp. 239–40.
12. We borrow here Ludwig Wittgenstein's term *Lebensform* used, among other places, in *Philosophical Investigations* and *On Certainty*, without claiming to use it in the precise sense intended there. See *Philosophical Investigations*, trans. Elizabeth Anscombe et al., 4th edn (Oxford and Malden, MA: Blackwell, [1953] 2009), §19, p. 11/11[e].
13. Edward Lear, *More Nonsense: Pictures, Rhymes, Botany, etc.* (London: Robert John Bush, 1872), p. vi.
14. Edward Strachey, 'Nonsense as Fine Art', *Little's Living Age* 64 (1888), 515–31, p. 515; Aldous Huxley, 'Edward Lear', in *On The Margin: Notes and Essays by Aldous Huxley* (New York: George H. Doran Co., 1923), 162–7, p. 163; Chesterton, 'A Defence of Nonsense', in *The Defendant*, pp. 42–51.
15. Sigmund Freud, *The Joke and Its Relation to the Unconscious*, ed. John Carey, trans. Joyce Crick (Harmondsworth: Penguin, 2002), pp. 133–4.
16. Elizabeth Sewell, *The Field of Nonsense* (London: Chatto and Windus, 1952), p. 5.
17. Susan Stewart, *Nonsense: Aspects of Intertextuality in Folklore and Literature* (Baltimore, MD: Johns Hopkins University Press, 1989), p. vii.
18. Ibid. p. 49.
19. Ibid. p. viii.
20. Jean-Jacques Lecercle, *The Philosophy of Nonsense: The Intuitions of Victorian Nonsense Literature* (London: Routledge, 1994), p. 2.
21. Homi K. Bhabha, *The Location of Culture* (London: Routledge, 2004), p. 178.
22. Edward Lear, *The Complete Nonsense and Other Verse*, ed. Vivien Noakes (London: Penguin, 2006) p. 424.
23. T. S. Eliot, 'The Love Song of J. Alfred Prufrock', in *The Complete Poems and Plays* (London: Faber and Faber, 1969), pp. 15, 16.
24. In *Chatto Book*, ed. Haughton, p. 199.
25. Lear, *Complete Nonsense*, pp. 391–2.
26. Maurice Sendak, *Where the Wild Things Are* (New York: Harper and Row, 1963), n.p.
27. For example, 'Can I say "bububu" and mean "If it doesn't rain I shall go for a walk"? – It is only in a language that one can mean something by something.' Wittgenstein, *Philosophical Investigations*, p. 18e.
28. *Chatto Book*, ed. Haughton, p. 105.

Part I:

Notes towards a History of English Nonsense

1

Buba, Blictrix, Bufbaf: Medieval Theory and Practice of Nonsense

Jordan Kirk

Figmenta poetarum, que ranis loquacibus comparantur.

Peter Comestor[1]

TO SPEAK ABOUT medieval nonsense would be exactly as wrongheaded as to speak about medieval homosexuality, and for all the same reasons. For neither of these Victorian categories was known to the people who lived between the end of the Roman Empire and the advent of the capitalist one. As Friedrich Kittler declares, it is 'our epoch' that is 'the epoch of nonsense'.[2] But if it is fitting to avoid referring too blithely to premodern homosexuality, this is not of course because before Krafft-Ebing women did not sleep with women or wish to do so, or men with men. So too with nonsense. It is scarcely to be imagined that medieval people never wrote or spoke for reasons other than to make sense; and indeed, it so happens that traces of such writing and speaking have survived in not insignificant quantities. If it is well to hesitate before assigning these texts to the category of nonsense, in order that gross anachronism might be avoided, faced with them it is also difficult to avoid the conclusion that something very like modern nonsense was in fact already familiar in the Middle Ages.

Nor is it necessary to conclude, on this basis, that nonsense must be a kind of ahistorical phenomenon that irrupts of its own accord given certain propitious causes and conditions. It is a curious fact that many of the most influential modern writers to experiment with nonsense also took an interest in medieval thought and literature. What, after all, is 'Jabberwocky' but some 'stanzas of Anglo-Saxon poetry'?[3] Not to mention the extensive medievalising of Knut Hamsun's *Hunger*, whose description of the 'discovery' of the meaningless word 'kuboa' would be cited in an important *zaum* manifesto; the fact that Christian Morgenstern was reading Meister Eckhart at the same time as writing 'Das große Lalula'; the fascination, on the part of the author of the great 'Sonnet allégorique de lui-même', with manuscripts and with medieval English alliterative poetry; James Joyce's manifest knowledge of medieval culture, as evidenced in *Finnegans Wake* in particular; and his sometime secretary's too, notably in *Molloy*, with its famous description of words as 'the buzzing of an insect'.[4]

Moreover, the Continental philosophers who have done the most to draw attention to the question of linguistic non-signification turn out themselves, many of them, to have been crypto-medievalists.[5] Jacques Lacan's most important discussion of *lalangue* is in Seminar XX, built around an account of courtly love; Roland Barthes's hermeneutics of the *bruissement de la langue* is indebted to medieval models (and Barthes even belonged to a group named after the *Miracle de Theophile*, a play that includes lines of nonsense that will be discussed below); Martin Heidegger, philosopher of the call that '"says" *nothing* which could be talked about', wrote his *Habilitationsschrift* on medieval speculative grammar; and Walter Benjamin undertook his dismantling of the 'bourgeois conception of language' only a few months after he had composed the fragment 'On the Middle Ages'.[6] Rather than a properly modern phenomenon of which dim medieval anticipations might be assembled, in short, or a universal possibility instantiated to varying degrees in different times and places, the theory and practice of nonsense as they emerge in modernity might themselves be the result of transmissions from the Middle Ages.

To demonstrate as much would be the task of another, more elaborate and no doubt more speculative inquiry. The purpose of this chapter is simply to establish the grounds on which a specifically medieval theory and practice of nonsense might be identified and interpreted on its own terms. It consists of three parts. The first is an overview of medieval texts that scholars have understood, or might profitably understand, as nonsense: notably, instances of the trope of *mundus inversus*, the world turned upside down. The second focuses in on medieval meaningless words on the order of Hamsun's *kuboa* or the neologisms of 'Jabberwocky', which have been comparatively neglected. The third turns to the linguistic disciplines of grammar, logic and rhetoric to establish that non-signification mattered not only to medieval poets but also to medieval theorists of language. This fact – that there was a scholarly tradition of thinking about language in its capacity to mean absolutely nothing – has been largely forgotten today. The suggestion of the essay as a whole, then, is that nonsense was widespread in the Middle Ages; that it took the form not only of comic inversion but of experiments in absolute non-signification; and that medieval literary nonsense should be understood in the light of the linguistic theory with which it was contemporary.

World Up-So-Doun

Noel Malcolm wrote in 1997 that there was 'no overall history of nonsense poetry in medieval and Renaissance European literature'.[7] These two decades later, the chapter of his *Origins of English Nonsense* in which he gestures in such a direction remains far and away the most comprehensive work of its kind. It is fortunate, then, that Malcolm's 'short history' of nonsense accomplishes so much. In its wake, and notwithstanding that 'many of the details remain very obscure', there can be no question that there existed a great number of high and late medieval texts that will answer to any modern description of nonsense.[8] These texts had of course been known to specialists, and some of them had been included in anthologies such as Hugh Haughton's important *Chatto Book of Nonsense Poetry*, but Malcolm undertook a complete survey of the relevant materials, proposed for them various filiations, and situated them with respect to a later, seventeenth-century nonsense corpus. He also insisted, rightly, on a certain way of approaching them – namely, as products of a high literary rather than organic folk tradition. This last point will bear further consideration below.

Malcolm traces the origin of the medieval nonsense tradition to a German poem written toward the beginning of the thirteenth century, whose first stanza reads:

Blatte und krone wellent muot willik sin,
so waenent topfknaben wislichen tuon,
So jaget unbilde mit hasen eber swin,
so ervliuget einen valken ein unmehtik huon,
Wirt danne der wagen vür diu rinder gende,
treit danne der sak den esel zuo der müln,
wirt danne ein eltiu gurre z'einem vüln:
so siht man'z in der werlte twerhes stende.

[Breastplate and crown want to be volunteer soldiers,
Boys playing with a top think they are acting wisely,
The boar hunts with hares, setting a poor example,
A feeble hen flies up and catches a falcon.
Then the cart goes in front of the oxen,
The sack drags the donkey to the mill,
An old nag turns into a filly:
This is what one sees in the world turned upside-down.][9]

The most straightforward, and indeed most adequate, way of categorising the works proper to the tradition thus inaugurated is as instances of the topos that the poet himself names in the final line just quoted: that of the *mundus inversus*, or world turned upside down.[10] The topos already appears in the work of the great twelfth-century romancier Chrétien de Troyes, who invokes 'les choses a envers': wolves fleeing lambs, lions stags, and the peasant his hoe.[11] And it is of course much more ancient than that. Its 'basic formal principle', Ernst Robert Curtius says, 'is the "stringing together of impossibilities" (ἀδύνατα, *impossibilia*)' and dates back to Archilocus – a somewhat arbitrary point of origin, given that traces of the rites, invocations and iconographies of the 'inverted world' are found throughout the ancient world and recede into prehistory.[12] However that may be, the Latin West inherited the literary topos most directly from Virgil and from the Bible, and it began to take on a new amplitude and independence in the works written in the train of the German poem just cited.[13]

Many such works survive, written in the various vernacular languages of Western Europe (French, Occitan, Italian, Spanish, English), and related to one another through a complex network of influences and affiliations. In German, some nine instances of the *Lügendichtung* or Lying Quodlibet survive, the earliest from the end of the thirteenth century and the latest from the fifteenth.[14] They consist of what Sarah Westphal-Wihl calls 'short, unrelated statements, whose syntax does not correspond to the couplet unit' and which 'contain fantastic adynata', often involving animals: cakes grow on trees, millstones fly, and – as she dryly summarises –'an old vinegar mug sets out to attend a tournament'.[15]

This German genre gave rise directly to a number of fifteenth-century English nonsense poems, among them 'The Cricket and the Grasshopper' and 'The Moon in the Morning'.[16] And generally speaking the *mundus inversus* topos was widespread in English letters, appearing in the early fourteenth-century 'Land of Cockaigne'[17] (where milk flows in the rivers and the abbeys are made of pudding) and in such 'lying ballads' as the one that begins:

I sawe a dog sethyng sowse
And an ape thechyng an howse
And a podyng etyng a mowse

I saw a dog cooking sauce,
And an ape thatching a house
And a pudding eating a mouse[18]

Or consider a stanza of the song whose refrain is 'News, News, News, News':

A cowe had stolyn a calfe away
And put her in a sake;
Forsoth, I sel no puddynges today;
'Maysters, what doo youe lake?'

A cow had stolen a calf away
And put her in a sack;
Forsooth, I sell no puddings today,
'Masters, what do you lack?'[19]

Examples of such poems – short works made up entirely of *impossibilia* – could be multiplied.[20] The *mundus inversus* topos also appears in the midst of longer works, including those by the Ricardian poets whose names are still remembered today. William Langland makes use of it; so does John Gower, on more than one occasion.[21] A great number of *impossibilia* can be found throughout the works of Geoffrey Chaucer, the so-called father of English verse: notably the thought experiment of dividing a fart into thirteen equal parts in the 'Summoner's Tale', Criseyde's invocation of eagles who mate with doves and rocks that move themselves in the *Troilus*, and most extendedly the 'up-so-doun' world of 'Lak of Stedfastnesse'.[22] Nor, in this connection, should his 'Nun's Priest's Tale' be overlooked: a dialogue on dream interpretation carried out by two chickens that ends with an extended evocation of a meaningless clamour, its reflections on language do not pale beside Lewis Carroll's.[23]

Nonsense was written in the romance vernaculars as well. In France there flourished a series of related forms: the *fatrasie*, *fatras*, *resverie* and *derverie*, as well as the *sotte chanson* and *sottie*.[24] A thirteenth-century *fatrasie* reads as follows:

Uns saiges sans sens
Sans bouche et sans dens
Le siecle mangea
Et uns sors harens
Manda les Flamens
Qui les vengera;
Mais tout ce no lor vaura
La plume de deus mellens
Qui quatre nés affondra.

Mais je ne sai que je pens:
De murder les apela.

[A senseless prof
Without teeth or mouth
Ate the era
And a red herring
Summoned the Fleming
To act as avenger.
But all this is no better
Than two whiting's feather
Causing four ships to sink.
I don't know what I think:
The charge was murder.][25]

In fourteenth-century Italy, this tradition blossomed into the *motto confetto*, the *frotolla* and the burlesque poetry of Sacchetti, Orcagna and Burchiello; and in Spain, in the next century, into the *dispartes* of Juan del Encina and his followers.[26]

Moreover, growing up alongside the genres already mentioned, and cross-pollinating with them, were a great number of other forms of absurdity, both in the vernaculars and in Latin. There were mock prophecies (e.g. of the past), mock prescriptions (recommending death as the remedy for fever, or the shadow cast by a ditch as the remedy for baldness), mock testaments (of an ass, or a piglet), mock sermons (on the topic of nothing), even mock masses (of drunkards or, again, asses).[27] There were Tales of Nothing at All,[28] absurd children's rhymes,[29] and 'nonsense centos'[30] collaging together fragments of scripture into new, incoherent narratives:

Postquam autem Alexander percussit Darium [1 Mcc 1.1], stravit Abraham asinum suum [2 Sm 17.23], et ascendit in arborem sicomorum [Lc 19.4], et traxit rete in terram [Jo 21.11], plenum quadratis rusticis. Piscatores autem [Lc 5.2] calefaciebant se [Mc 14.54] ad glacies, ne forte tumulus fieret in [Mt 26.5] piscibus.

[Moreover, after Alexander overthrew Darius, Abraham saddled his ass, and climbed up into a sycamore tree, and drew the net to land, full of sturdy peasants. The fishermen, moreover, warmed themselves at the ice, lest perhaps there should be a tumult among the fish.][31]

In short, nonsense was by no means unusual in medieval literature. Indeed, it should be affirmed that it was present at, and that it was the very source of, the new, properly medieval modes of song that emerged in eleventh-century Occitania and soon spread throughout the Latin West. William IX, the so-called first troubadour, announced at the turn of the twelfth century that he would sing a song about nothing at all:

Farai un vers de dreit nien:
non er de mi ni d'autra gen,
non er d'amor ni de joven,
ni de ren au,
qu'enans fo trobatz en durmen
sus un chivau.

[I'll make a verse about absolutely nothing:
it won't be about me or about other people,
it won't be about love or about youth,
nor about anything else,
because it was found while asleep
on a horse.][32]

This is the primal scene of post-classical European vernacular literature: the poet asleep on his horse, singing his song of nothing at all.

Jargon Absolu

In an influential attempt to categorise such materials, the medievalist Paul Zumthor distinguished two modes by which discourse is subjected in them to processes of dissociation. He calls these two modes relative and absolute nonsense.[33] Relative nonsense consists in a paratactic accumulation of sentences or propositions, each of which seems comprehensible enough when taken individually but bears no relation to what precedes or follows it. Absolute nonsense, for its part, rather than introducing its disjunction between successive sentences or propositions, introduces it into the individual propositions, by bringing together incompatible subjects and predicates. That is, incommensurability can inhere in a linguistic construction either at the level of the statement or at that of the series of statements. But, as Zumthor mentions in passing, there is also another kind of nonsense of which medieval instances can be found, obtaining at the level not of the argument and not of the sentence but at that of the word: unintelligible gibberish, or what has been called 'nonsense neologism'. Zumthor refers to this phenomenon as *jargon absolu*.[34]

Medieval instances of *jargon absolu* are by no means rare. It suffices, indeed, to remain with the 'first troubadour' to find one. In his fifth song, William IX declares that, meeting two women on the road, he responds to their greeting in the following manner:

anc no li diz ni 'bat' ni 'but',
ni fer ni fust no ai mentagut,
mas sol aitan:
'Babariol, babariol
babarian'.

[I said neither 'baf' nor 'buf',
I named neither metal nor wood,
but only:
'Babariol, babariol,
babarian'.] [35]

The utterance of 'babariol, babariol, | babarian' – articulate, versifiable and unintelligible – makes up the crucial moment in the events narrated in the poem: the two women, thinking him incapable of communication, take the poet with them and have their way with him. It also makes up the crucial moment of its reflection on the being of language. What William provides here are materials for a taxonomy of ways of saying *dreit nien*, nothing at all: for it is not simply a matter of either signifying or not signifying. In the phrase 'neither "baf" nor "buf"' what is established is that 'baf' is irreducible to 'buf'; in the following lines both of these are made distinguishable from utterances that would 'mention' things in the world (metal, wood); and finally all of these possible utterances are distinguished from what the poet says that he did, in fact, say aloud: namely, the sequence 'babariol babariol | babarian', which manages, by its near resemblance to words that refer to babbling, to mean meaninglessness even as it is itself strictly without meaning. In this stanza, in short, various modes of saying nothing are distinguished and, at the same time, coordinated together. 'Verse' is, for the first troubadour, a place in which speaking can be about nothing at all and yet be subject to linguistic differentiation.

This poetics of *jargon absolu* was not abandoned by the vernacular poets who wrote in William's wake. In the *Inferno*, written a decade into the fourteenth century, Dante describes an encounter with the giant Nimrod. The giant, suffering the punishment of Babel, says only 'Raphèl maì amècche zabì almi'.[36] This famous line, alongside that of Pluto ('Pape Satàn, pape Satàn aleppe'), has defied the efforts of interpreters to identify it as an instance of Arabic or Hebrew, Basque or Greek. It is composed in no particular language, serving rather as an instance of barbarolexis, a form of speech that cannot be assimilated to any known idiom.[37] As Virgil explains to the pilgrim, the giant's speech is unintelligible to all who hear it, just as the giant himself can understand no one else's speech.[38] 'Raphél maì amèche zabì almi' thus announces a condition of absolute linguistic incomprehension, in which the experience of unintelligibility cannot be overcome by means of translation, explanation or learning.

As Peter Dronke and others have indicated, Nimrod's 'convincing line of spoken Babelese' participates in a wider medieval tradition of invented languages.[39] Nor is the hellish location of the giant's utterance incidental to its incomprehensibility: the demonic, necromantic and heathen realms were associated, immemorially, with meaningless incantations and illegibile inscriptions. The phenomenon is evident not least on the stage. A century before the composition of the *Inferno*, Jean Bodel included in his *Jeu de Saint Nicolas* a golden statue that comes to life long enough to say,

Palas aron ozinomas
Baske bano tudan donas
Geheamel cla orlaÿ
Berec .he. pantaras taÿ[40]

– which means nothing at all. The other play invariably cited in this connection is Rutebeuf's *Miracle de Theophile*, from about 1261, in which Salatin conjures the devil with the following invocation:

bagahi laca bachahé
lamac cahi achabahé
        karrelyos
lamac lamec bachalyos
cabahagi sabalyos
        baryolas
lagozatha cabyolas
samahac et famyolas
        harrahya[41]

Incomprehensible incantations of this sort exist also in Latin liturgical drama, and appear widely in late medieval English plays.[42] In the Towneley *Judicium*, for example, the demon Tutivillus announces himself in a macaronic speech that combines English, Latin and sheer nonsense:

Mi name is Tutiuillus,
My horne is blawen.
Ffragmina verborum,
Tutiuillus colligit horum
Belzabub algorum
Belial belium doliorum[43]

Likewise, in *Mankynd*, the character Mischief reads aloud a writ copied out in an untidy hand, saying, 'Here ys blottybus in blottis | Blottorum blottibus istis'.[44] And in the N-Town *Adoration of the Shepherds*, a shepherd, having heard the phrase *Gloria in excelsis Deo,* explains that he has understood it perfectly:

I have that songe ful wele inum.
In my wyt weyl it is wrought,
It was 'Gle, glo, glas, glum.'[45]

These lines of dog Latin include words that sound like they would belong to a certain language, without being lexically recognisable; words uttered in one language as though they belong to another; words represented as in a game of telephone. They constitute a kind of grammelot, as Dario Fo will call his 'method of producing the semblance of a given language without adopting real or identifiable words from that language'.[46]

Such phonoaesthetic parody is not limited to works written for the stage. Chaucer's Parson, in the *Canterbury Tales*, says the following: 'But trusteth wel, I am a Southren man; | I kan nat geeste "rum, ram, ruf", by lettre'.[47] Here, a 'Northern', alliterative form of verse is evoked by means of a nonsensical series of utterances. Neither does Chaucer restrict his use of non-signifying words to cases in which he is depicting human speech. Certain vocalisations in his verse operate, indeterminately, as both the mere empty sound of an animal and a particular significative word in a human language. "For example, in the 'Manciple's Tale' – and it is by no means incidental that the prologue of that tale invokes, like William IX's *vers de dreit nien*, the figure of a rider asleep on his horse – the avian cry *cuckoo* doubles, to much effect, as the English word 'cuckold'. In his *Parliament of Fowls* – and in the bird debate form more generally, for example in *The Owl and the Nightingale* – this question of the proximity between bird noise and poetic speech is staged to great effect.[48] Throughout the *Parliament*, its avian characters appear to speak no differently than humans would – except for at a single moment, when:

The goos the cokkow and the doke also
So cryede kek kek kokkow quek quek hye
That thourgh myne eres the noyse wente tho.[49]

The status of these words is not explicitly addressed by the poem, and these same animals go on to speak in what is recognisably English. Does the poet mean to suggest that all the other lines of recorded bird speech have been silently translated, as it were, from bird language into human? Do these birds sometimes squawk and sometimes speak? However these and the many other questions that arise from this line are answered, or not answered, *kek kek kokkow quek quek* remains unmistakably the kernel around which the poem as a whole is formed.

Medieval examples of *jargon absolu*, like those of *mundus inversus*, could be multiplied, especially if the scope of the inquiry were expanded beyond the realm of straightforwardly literary works. For related phenomena appear in other contexts as well: in music, there are the incomprehensible words of the motet;[50] in the liturgy, the braying of the congregation in the so-called asinine masses;[51] in medicine, the nonsensical syllables of verbal charms against disease.[52] It is clear, in short, that the capacity of words to signify nothing whatsoever was a matter of interest among medieval people. What is less clear is the nature of that interest. Why did they see fit to record meaningless words with such frequency? Perhaps the explanation nearest to hand, given current habits of thought, is that barbarolexis would have functioned as a signifier of sociological or indeed interspecies alterity. For it will not have escaped notice that the meaningless utterances in question here are attributed, in the texts from which they are extracted, to inhabitants of more or less distant regions, to demons, to someone suffering in hell, to a (very vaguely construed) Muslim, to a rustic, and to various kinds of non-human animals. It is tempting to conclude that *jargon absolu* represents the projections of a dominant culture's fears and misunderstandings of a repressed other, or again (depending on one's emphases) the more or less triumphal returns of that repressed other. That is, either learned discourse would be attempting to relegate various groups of beings to a subhuman, non-linguistic realm by ascribing to them not speech but meaningless babble; or in that seeming babble those groups would be leaving an inassimilable trace of their resistance to the attempt to silence them.

But such an interpretation would only make sense if the dominant culture in question – official, learned, human, Latinate Christendom – understood itself in opposition to *jargon absolu*. For it is difficult to see how nonsense could have served as a mark of antinomian otherness unless that culture was itself committed to maintaining the primacy of sense.

Vox Non-Significativa

The idea that medieval learned discourse was, as a matter of fact, committed precisely to maintaining the primacy of sense was promulgated by one of the leading investigators of modern nonsense. Like many other writers on the subject, Elizabeth Sewell is noticeably resistant to *jargon absolu*, which she calls 'neologism' or 'nonsense neologism'. What is peculiar about this term is that – insofar as a neologism is of course a word newly assigned a meaning – to use it would seem to rule out in advance the possibility that the seemingly meaningless utterance to which it refers might, in fact, be meaningless.[53] So much is in keeping, however, with Sewell's larger project of trying to shield nonsense from the apparent danger of non-signification:

> Nonsense does not deal in any kind of physical or metaphysical nothingness, one needs to remember. It deals in words. Where these are normal and are acting normally, there cannot be a nothingness in so far as they are concerned, for words have reference to experience. 'Word implies relation to creatures' (*Summa*, Pt. I, Q. 34, Art. 4).[54]

One might be forgiven for starting at this reference, in a discussion of Victorian nonsense, to Thomas Aquinas. Recurring to an *auctoritas* in what is itself a medievalising gesture, Sewell would enlist the very thinker who stands for the Middle Ages generally to ground her account of language as essentially – or indeed compulsorily – meaningful.[55] The question is whether medieval linguistic thought will actually provide such a ground – or whether nonsense and non-signification might have had a place in medieval learning after all.

According to the educational schema that the Middle Ages inherited from late antiquity, the seven liberal arts (that is, non-instrumental disciplines) fell into two groups, the trivium and the quadrivium. The latter comprised the four, more advanced, disciplines of number: arithmetic, geometry, music and astronomy. These were only to be learned after the student had mastered the more elementary disciplines of the trivium – grammar, logic and rhetoric – which had as their object not number but speech: or, to be precise, what was called *vox*. The choice of the word *vox* as a technical term might seem surprising – for, depending on context, it can mean voice, or utterance, or word, or noise – but its imprecision had certain advantages. Among them was the fact that it made explicit that what the scientists of language were concerned with was not, at the most basic level, meaningful speech but rather something that was in itself capable both of sense and of nonsense, which they called *aer ictus*, 'struck air'. Each of the three arts of the trivium approached this same bare auditory event from a different angle: grammar concerned itself with the correctness of *vox*, logic with its truth, and rhetoric with its persuasiveness.

In the field of grammar, the most important *auctoritas* or textbook throughout the Middle Ages was the *Institutiones* of Priscian of Caesarea, written in Constantinople around the year 520. It famously begins by distinguishing *vox* into four kinds and giving examples of each kind: meaningful and writable (*arma virumque cano*, the opening words of the *Aeneid*); meaningful but not writable (hisses and groans); not meaningful but still writable ('ribbit', 'caw'); neither meaningful nor writable (creaking and lowing). The first thing to notice about this fourfold schema is that it provides an authoritative attestation of the existence of meaningless *voces*, a conceptual means of distinguishing them from other utterances, and a technical vocabulary with which to discuss them. And while it might be imagined that its purpose will be to restrict the focus of grammar to what is both meaningful and writable, this is not in fact the case.

For although grammar (as its name indicates) concerns itself only with writable *voces*, it does not fail to consider those of them that are without meaning. In fact, it might even be said to do so characteristically. For it is of course the discipline to which prosody belongs – that is, the analysis of syllables as such – and, as Priscian makes explicit, 'a syllable in itself can never signify anything'.[56] (Unlike the word 'king', for example, on Priscian's account the syllable *-king* in the word 'smoking' would be entirely devoid of signification.) Nor was grammar's interest confined to those syllables that make up already existing words, lines of verse, or sentences – meaningful or otherwise. In actual practice, a major part of what went on in the elementary classroom was the rote memorisation, recitation and inscription of isolated syllables. From at least the seventh century BCE until the nineteenth century of the present era, a fundamental aspect of grammatical instruction was something called the syllabary.[57] Students were asked to copy out, chant aloud and memorise, combinatorially, all of the possible syllables: *ba, be, bi, bo, bu; ca, ce, ci, co, cu*; and so forth; and then *bab*, *beb*, *bib*, *bob*, *bub*, and on and on in like fashion. Raffaella Cribiore draws attention to an extant record of syllabic training that includes the sequence *bras-bres-bris-bros-brus*, pointing out that such an exercise would be of only the most questionable use in learning to read actual words.[58] But the grammarians, it seems, were fully committed to this practice of nonsense. As Quintilian put it: 'they must all be memorised thoroughly and there must be no putting off the most difficult of them'.[59] To have been taught to write was to have passed through this regime, and it is to its particular inanities that the first troubadour will refer with the phrase *ni baf ni buf*, so crucial to his poetic taxonomy of *jargon absolu*.[60]

The discipline of logic, too, turned its attention to *baf* and *buf*, though for a somewhat different reason. Logicians continually invoked what they called *vox non-significativa*, non-significative utterance, for the purpose of distinguishing their own concerns from those of grammarians. Given that ours is the science specifically of the truth of *vox*, they explained, we do not and cannot deal with *voces non-significativae*: for when a meaningless word appears in a proposition (e.g. *every buf is mortal*), the truth or falsity of that proposition cannot be ascertained. This exclusion of nonsense words from the field of logic and their relegation to grammar, announced notably by the sixth-century scholar Boethius in an important commentary on Aristotle's *De interpretatione*, was to be repeated by the schoolmen down the centuries.[61]

Two things must be noted about this repetition. In the first place, of course, it has the effect not only of banning *voces non-significativae* but of proliferating them. To study logic was to encounter, on the very first page of its treatises and textbooks, *baf* and *buf* – and not only them. Boethius had invoked Stoic nonsense words in this connection – *blityri* and *skindapsos* – and invented his own, as well: *hereceddy*.[62] These examples mutated and were supplemented in the twelfth- and thirteenth-century logical textbooks: the *Ars emmerana* adduces *blictrix* and *sindiarsis*; the *Ars burana* has *blictrix* alone. In the *Introductiones parisienses* the pertinent example is *buba*. The *Logica 'ut dicit'* gives *buba* and *plectrix*; the *Ars meliduna* mentions *biltrix* and *buba*; and various manuscripts of the *Logica 'Cum sit nostra'* have *bon*, *bau* and *beltrix*; *buba* and *bultrix*; *bon*, *bau* and *bletrix*; *bou*, *bau* and *beltrix*; and *bu*, *ba* and *buf*.[63]

In the second place, despite their protestations the logicians found themselves having to pay further attention to these nonsense words after all. The problem arose in the case of what they called *suppositio materialis*, which is what takes place in a proposition such as *man is a monosyllable*. If *man is a monosyllable* can appear within the field of logic, if its truth can be evaluated and known, on what basis should *buf is a monosyllable* be excluded? The problem was debated at length, and various solutions were proposed. At stake was the very nature of the discipline: whether it could actually be distinguished from grammar at all. And, at the beginning of the fourteenth century, Walter Burley made the case forcibly that there could indeed be a very logic of nonsense, one that would be fully capable of analysing propositions on the order of *buba is buba* and *buba is bisyllabic*.[64]

Moreover, medieval logicians were exercised not only by the question of *jargon absolu*, but by that of absolute and relative nonsense as well. Indeed, their discipline was exactly the realm in which the incompatibility of subject and predicate (absolute nonsense) and the breakdowns of the syllogistic machinery (relative nonsense) were thought through most rigorously. Training in logic involved disputation of *impossibilia*, *insolubilia* and *sophismata*, the proving and disproving of absurd problems stemming from propositions on the order of *there is a donkey that every man sees*; or *the dead man is alive*; or *god does not exist*.[65] The resemblance between these *impossibilia* and the *impossibilia* of the *mundus inversus* literature is plain, obtaining even at the level of their common preoccupation with donkeys. As D. Vance Smith has indicated, the hermeneutic practices and assumptions of educated readers in the later Middle Ages were determined by developments in the logical curriculum.[66] Neither is it perhaps without importance in this connection that the famous mnemonic device developed in the thirteenth century for memorising the valid moods of the syllogism is itself a bit of nonsense verse:

> Barbara celarent darii ferio baralipton
> Celantes dabitis fapesmo frisesomorum
> Cesare cambestres festino barocho darapti
> Felapto disamis datisi bocardo ferison.[67]

As for the remaining linguistic art, it is of course the case that, as a topos, the *mundus inversus* belongs by rights to rhetoric, and should be understood in the terms of the rhetorical tradition, that is, with reference to the ways that it affects its audience. The texts that recur to the topos sometimes appear to do so for the sake of bemoaning the modern world, in the mode of *o tempora o mores*; sometimes in order to bring about amusement; sometimes for less easily categorised reasons.[68] But where the medieval rhetorical tradition took up the question of nonsense most essentially was in its theory of reading. For example, in what has rightly been described as being 'as close to a vernacular *art poétique* as the High Middle Ages produced',[69] the twelfth-century poet Marie de France developed a sophisticated hermeneutics of incomprehension. 'The ancients wrote obscurely', she explains, and thus what is called for in reading them is a mode of interpretation that is adequate to that obscurity, one that does not explain it away but preserves it – and, still more, transmits it in further writing.[70]

Marie's theory is itself an elaboration of the so-called 'redeemed rhetoric' or Christian hermeneutics that St Augustine develops in his massively influential *De doctrina christiana*. This treatise contains, as if in passing, a remarkable dictum: 'Nothing is better to commit to memory than those types of words and phrases of which we are ignorant.'[71] That the memorialising of unknown words is not simply a matter of retaining them until such time as their meanings might be discovered becomes clear when this passage is compared with one in the *De trinitate* where Augustine discusses the word *temetum*, which is found in scripture. An outmoded word (*vocabulum emortuum*) for wine, *temetum* reduces its readers to incomprehension and befuddlement.[72] Giorgio Agamben, drawing attention to this passage on multiple occasions, has shown it to be crucial to Augustine's thought overall. As Agamben summarises:

> In this passage, the experience of the dead word appears as the experience of a word uttered (a *vox*) insofar as it is no longer mere sound (*istas tres syllabas*), but not yet a signification – insofar as it is the experience, that is, of a sign as pure meaning and intention to signify before and beyond the arrival of every particular signification. For Augustine, this experience of an unknown word (*verbum ignotum*) in the no-man's-land between sound and signification is the experience of love as will to know.[73]

What Agamben will go on to underscore is the fact that the experience undergone by a person who happens to hear a *vocabulum emortuum* serves Augustine as the very model of contemplative devotion. The love of God, as conceived by the thinker whom the schoolmen could refer to simply as *theologus*, the Theologian, has nothing to do with understanding what is meant by the word 'God', or by any other, but takes place in incomprehension. His redeemed rhetoric is a discipline according to which the highest capacity of language is not to communicate meaning, or information, or doctrine, or anything else, but to empty itself to the point of death; and for which the highest capacity of the human psyche is to accede to the state of unknowing that would be the only adequate apprehension of the incomprehensible fact of *vox*.

Where medieval poetry descends into absurdity and gibberish, then, it would not be abdicating its role within a system of obligatory signification, nor channelling the inarticulable complaints of that system's discontents, but much rather fulfilling its most characteristic, and indeed most characteristically medieval, task: that of absolute kerygma.

The argument of Noel Malcolm's *Origins of English Nonsense*, the present chapter's point of departure, is in part polemical. Medieval and early modern nonsense, Malcolm maintains,

> was a highly literary phenomenon: it was the product of particular literary milieux, subject to development and transmission just like other literary genres, and intimately related (above all through the procedures of parody) to other literary forms and conventions. Nonsense poetry is not, in other words, something spontaneously produced by anarchic forces bubbling up from below – whether in the subconscious (dreams, madness) or in society and popular culture (folklore, carnival).[74]

The argument is entirely convincing. It is clear, from Malcolm's analysis, that the *fatrasie*, the *Lügendichtung*, the *frotolla* and their like have a history, and that a Bakhtinian recourse to notions of an irrepressible folk culture can only confuse matters.

But if these obscure verses are to be restored to their proper place in the history of letters, it will be necessary to expand the scope of the inquiry beyond works of literature in the narrow sense. For the learned culture in which these experiments in nonsense took place was not unfamiliar with questions of non-signification and absurdity, nor did it treat them only as problems to be overcome. To the contrary: throughout the Middle Ages, the capacity of *vox* to be uttered, analysed and contemplated in the absence of its bearing any meaning played a crucial role in basic linguistic instruction, in logical training and in the theory of interpretation. As modern poets would do after them, medieval poets took this non-significative capacity of *vox* as the very matter of their art.

Notes

1. Cited in Alastair Minnis, *Medieval Theory of Authorship* (Philadelphia: University of Pennsylvania, 1988), p. 11.
2. Friedrich Kittler, *Gramophone, Film, Typewriter*, trans. Geoffrey Winthrop-Young and Michael Wutz (Stanford: Stanford University, 1999), p. 86.

3. What would become, ten years later, the first four lines of 'Jabberwocky' originally appeared under the title 'A Stanza of Anglo-Saxon Poetry' in Carroll's self-published *Mischmasch* in 1855. Neither of course is the medievalising of *Looking-Glass* restricted to these stanzas: cf. above all the sequential chapters treating of the 'Lion and the Unicorn and those queer Anglo-Saxon Messengers' and of the Red and White Knights (Lewis Carroll, *Through the Looking-Glass*, ed. Hugh Haughton (Harmondsworth: Penguin, 1998), Chapters 7 and 8).
4. For *kuboa*, see Knut Hamsun, *Hunger*, trans. George Egerton (New York: Knopf, 1920), pp. 87–9, with Viktor Shklovsky, 'On Poetry and Trans-Sense Language', trans. Gerald Janacek and Peter Mayer, *October* 34 (1985), 3–24, p. 11; on Mallarmé's medievalism, R. Howard Bloch, 'Augustine, Mallarmé, and the Medieval Roots of Modernity', *Modern Language Notes* 127.6 (2012), S6–S22; on Joyce's, e.g. Umberto Eco, *The Aesthetics of Chaosmos: The Middle Ages of James Joyce*, trans. Ellen Esrock (Cambridge, MA: Harvard University Press, 1989); on Beckett's, Jonathan Ullyot, *The Medieval Presence in Modernist Literature: The Quest to Fail* (New York: Cambridge University, 2016) which can also be consulted on modernist medievalism generally, along with Simone Celine Marshall, and Carole M. Cusack, *The Medieval Presence in the Modernist Aesthetic: Unattended Moments* (Leiden: Brill, 2017).
5. On the medieval roots of twentieth-century Continental philosophy, see Bruce Holsinger, *The Premodern Condition: Medievalism and the Making of Theory* (Chicago: University of Chicago Press, 2005); Amy Hollywood, *Sensible Ecstasy: Mysticism, Sexual Difference, and the Demands of History* (Chicago: University of Chicago Press, 2001); and the essays in *The Legitimacy of the Middle Ages*, ed. Andrew Cole and D. Vance Smith (Durham, NC: Duke University Press, 2010).
6. See Jacques Lacan, *Seminar XX*, ed. Jacques-Alain Miller, trans. Bruce Fink (New York: Norton, 1998), e.g. 138f with Erin Felicia Labbie, *Lacan's Medievalism* (Minneapolis: University of Minnesota Press, 2006); Roland Barthes, *The Rustle of Language* (New York: Macmillan, 1987) with Helen Solterer, *Medieval Roles for Modern Times: Theater and the Battle for the French Republic* (University Park: Pennsylvania State University Press, 2010); Martin Heidegger, *Being and Time*, trans. Joan Stambaugh (Albany: State University of New York, 1996) with Ethan Knapp, 'Medieval Studies, Historicity, and Heidegger's Early Phenomenology', in *Legitimacy*, ed. Cole and Smith, 159–94; Walter Benjamin, *Early Writings: 1910–1917*, trans. Howard Eiland (Cambridge, MA: Harvard University Press, 2011).
7. Noel Malcolm, *The Origins of English Nonsense* (London: Fontana, 1998), pp. xiv–v. Readers of this book will recognise how closely the current section of this essay hews to it, though with different examples and emphases.
8. Ibid. p. 52.
9. Ibid. p. 53; the translation is Malcolm's.
10. See Ernst Robert Curtius, *European Literature and the Latin Middle Ages*, trans. Willard Trask (Princeton: Princeton University Press, 1990), pp. 94–8.
11. Chrétien de Troyes, *Cligès*, in *Romans* (Paris: Livre de poche, 1994), II, 3798–3806. Curtius refers in this connection also to the *Carmina burana*, the *Speculum stultorum*, the *Anticlaudianus*, the *Architrenius*, and the songs of Arnaut Daniel.
12. Curtius, *European Literature and the Latin Middle Ages*, p. 95. See for example Hedwig Kenner, *Das Phänomen der verkehrten Welt in der griechisch-römischen Antike* (Klagenfurt: Geschichtsverein für Kärnten, 1970); A. Basson, 'Two Instances of Mundus Inversus in Psalm 113', *Verbum et Ecclesia* 30.1 (2009), 1–14; *The Reversible World: Symbolic Inversion in Art and Society*, ed. Barbara A. Babcock (Ithaca, NY: Cornell University Press, 1978), Introduction.
13. See Malcolm, *Origins*, 78f with *Aeneid*, XI. 405 and e.g. Isaiah 2: 6–7.

14. Sarah Westphal-Wihl, 'Quodlibets: Introduction to a Middle High German Genre', in *Genres in Medieval German Literature*, ed. Hubert Heinen and Ingeborg Henderson (Göppingen: Kümmerle, 1986), 158–60.
15. Ibid. p. 158.
16. See Malcolm, *Origins*, pp. 58–62. The former will be found under the title 'The Insects and the Miller' in Rossell Hope Robbins, *Secular Lyrics of the XIVth and XVth Centuries* (New York: Oxford, 1955), p. 104; the latter in Thorlac Turville-Petre, 'Some Medieval English Manuscripts in the North-East Midlands', in *Manuscripts and Readers in Fifteenth-Century England: The Literary Implications of Manuscript Study*, ed. Derek Pearsall (Cambridge: Brewer, 1983), 125–41, pp. 137–8.
17. J. A. W. Bennett, and G. V. Smithers, *Early Middle English Verse and Prose* (New York: Oxford University Press, 1968), pp. 136–44; modernised in *The Chatto Book of Nonsense Poetry*, ed. Hugh Haughton (London: Chatto and Windus, 1988), pp. 41–5.
18. Richard Leighton Greene, *The Early English Carols* (New York: Oxford University Press, 1977), p. 289; lightly modernised in *Chatto Book*, ed. Haughton, p. 59.
19. Green, *Early English Carols*, p. 290.
20. Not to be overlooked in this connection are e.g. 'My Lady went to Canterbury' in Greene, *Early English Carols*, p. 290; 'Hearken to my Tale' and 'By God and Saint Hilaire', in *Reliquiae antiquae*, ed. Thomas Wright and James Halliwell, 2 vols (London: William Pickering, 1841–3), I, pp. 81–2 and 259–60; and 'When Nettles in Winter' in Robbins, *Secular Lyrics*, p. 103.
21. William Langland, *Piers Plowman: The B Version*, ed. George Kane and E. Talbot Donaldson (London: Athlone, 1988), Passus 4, ll.113–15; John Gower, *The Complete Works*, ed. G. C. Macaulay, 4 vols (London: Oxford, 1899–1902), II, p. 2 and IV, p. 278.
22. On these and the many other *impossibilia* in Chaucer, see Jean Klene, 'Chaucer's Contributions to a Popular Topos: The World Upside-Down', *Viator* 11 (1980), 321–34.
23. *Pace* Wim Tigges, *An Anatomy of Literary Nonsense (*Amsterdam: Rodopi, 1988). On the 'Nun's Priest's Tale', see especially Peter Travis, *Disseminal Chaucer: Rereading the Nun's Priest's Tale* (Notre Dame, IN: University of Notre Dame Press, 2009).
24. Martijn Rus has edited the *fatrasies* and *resveries* under the title *Poésies du non-sens*. See Robert Garapon, *La fantaisie verbale et le comique dans le théâtre français du Moyen Âge à la fin du XVIIe siècle* (Paris: A. Colin, 1957); Paul Zumthor, 'Fatrasie et coq-à-l'âne', in *La Fin du moyen âge et renaissance. Mélanges de philologie française offerts à Robert Guiette* (Antwerp: Nederlandsche Boekhandel, 1961), 5–18; and Patrice Uhl, *La Constellation poétique du non-sens au moyen âge: Onze études sur la poésie fatrasique et ses environs* (Paris: L'Harmattan, 1999). For the *sottes chansons*, see Eglal Doss-Quinby, Marie-Geneviève Grossel and Samuel N. Rosenberg, *'Sottes chansons contre Amours': parodie et burlesque au Moyen Âge* (Paris: Champion, 2010); for the *sottie*, Heather Arden, *Fool's Plays: A Study of Satire in the Sottie* (New York: Cambridge, 1980) and Olga Anna Dull, *Folie et rhétorique dans la sottie* (Geneva: Droz, 1994).
25. *Chatto Book*, ed. Haughton, p. 50. Four of the *fatrasies* are translated in that volume; see also the appendix to Gordon Douglas McGregor, *The Broken Pot Restored:* Le Jeu de la Feuillée *of Adam de la Halle* (Lexington, KY: French Forum, 1991).
26. See Malcolm, *Origins*, pp. 67–74.
27. On mock prognostications, see Jelle Koopmans, 'Rabelais et la tradition des pronostications', in *Editer et traduire Rabelais à travers les ages*, ed. Paul J. Smith (Amsterdam: Rodopi, 1997), 35–65; on prescriptions, Hugh Roberts, 'Medicine and Nonsense in French Renaissance Mock Prescriptions', *The Sixteenth Century Journal* 40.3 (2009), 721–44 and Denton Fox, 'Henryson's "Sum Practysis of Medecyne"', *Studies in Philology* 69.4 (1972), 453–60; on testaments, Jan Ziolkowski, *Talking Animals: Medieval Latin Beast Poetry, 750–1150* (Philadelphia: University of Pennsylvania Press, 1993), p. 40; on

sermons, Malcolm Jones, 'The Parodic Sermon in Medieval and Early Modern England', *Medium Aevum* 66.1 (1997), 94–114 and on both sermons and masses, Martha Bayless, *Parody in the Middle Ages: The Latin Tradition* (Ann Arbor: University of Michigan Press, 1996).

28. See Lisa Cooper, 'Nothing Was Funny in the Late Middle Ages: The "Tale of Ryght Nought" and British Library, MS Egerton 1995', *Journal of Medieval and Early Modern Studies* 47.2 (2017), 221–53.
29. See Nicholas Orme, *Medieval Children* (New Haven, CT: Yale University Press, 2001), Ch. 4.
30. See Bayless, *Parody*, pp. 157–67.
31. Quoted from Bayless, *Parody*, p. 162 with her bibliographical annotations and translation.
32. Guglielmo IX, *Poesie*, ed. Nicolò Pasero (Modena: STEM Mucchi, 1973), p. 92. As Agamben has emphasised, William is alluding here to an 'ancient exegetical tradition of the Gospel of St. John', in which *logos* is said to ride on the horse of *phonē*, that is, thought is expressed by vocal utterance. In this case, though, in which the poet is asleep on his horse, speech goes on while thought is suspended (Giorgio Agamben, *Idea of Prose*, trans. Michael Sullivan and Sam Whitsitt (Albany: State University of New York), 1995). This observation is developed crucially in Daniel Heller-Roazen, 'The Matter of Language: Guilhem de Peitieus and the Platonic Tradition', *Modern Language Notes* 113.4 (1998), 851–80.
33. Zumthor, 'Fatrasie', pp. 11–12.
34. Ibid. p. 9. The terminology is drawn from Robert Garapon, *La fantaisie verbale et le comique dans le théâtre français du Moyen Âge à la fin du XVIIe siècle* (Paris: A. Colin, 1957), 19f.
35. Guglielmo IX, *Poesie*, p. 126. For a history of the debates over this extremely troublesome passage, see Gerold Hilty and Federico Corriente, 'La Fameuse *cobla bilingue* de la Chanson V de Guillaume IX', *Vox Romanica* 65 (2006), 66–71. On William's 'ni "bat" ni "but"' and its variants see Gerald A. Bond, 'Philological Comments on a New Edition of the First Troubadour', *Romance Philology* 30.2 (1976), 343–61, pp. 352–3.
36. Dante, *Commedia*, XXXI. 67. On this passage, see Peter Dronke, *Dante and Medieval Latin Traditions* (London: Cambridge University, 1989), pp. 43–9; Henri Guiter, 'Sur deux passages obscurs de Dante et de Jehan Bodel', *Revue des langues romanes* 77 (1967), 179–86; Roger Dragonetti, 'Dante face à Nemrod: Babel mémoire et miroir de l'Eden', *Critique* 387–8 (1979), 690–706. The poet also speaks of Nimrod and the confusion of tongues in *De vulgari eloquentia*, ed. and trans. by Steven Botterill (Cambridge: Cambridge University Press, 1996), p. 15.
37. On barbarolexis, see Paul Zumthor, *Langue et techniques poétiques a l'époque romane* (Paris: Klincksieck, 1969), pp. 83–111 and Alexandre Leupin, *Barbarolexis: Medieval Writing and Sexuality* (Cambridge, MA: Harvard University Press, 1989).
38. 'a lui ciascun linguaggio | come 'l suo ad altrui, ch'a nullo è noto'. *Inferno*, XXXI. 80–1.
39. Dronke, *Dante*, p. 49. On medieval jargons and invented languages, see Garapon, *La fantaisie*; Lorenzo Renzi, 'Un aspetto del plurilinguismo medievale: dalla lingua dei re magi a papè satan aleppe', in *Omaggio a Gianfranco Folena* (Padua: Editoriale Programma, 1993), 61–73; Theodor Elwert, 'L'Emploi des langues étrangères comme procédé stylistique', *Revue de littérature compare* 34 (1960), 409–37; Jeffrey Schnapp, 'Between Babel and Pentecost: Imaginary Languages in the Middle Ages', in *Modernité au Moyen Âge: le défi du passé*, ed. Brigitte Cazelles and Charles Méla (Geneva: Droz, 1990).
40. Jehan Bodel, *Le Jeu de Saint Nicolas*, ed. Albert Henry (Brussels: Presses Universitaires de Bruxelles, 1965), p. 178. A parallel passage will be found in the Middle English *Romaunce of Richard Coer de Lion*, as noted by Suzanne Akbari, *Idols in the East: European Representations of Islam and the Orient, 1100–1450* (Ithaca, NY: Cornell University Press, 2012), p. 212 n. 25.
41. Rutebeuf, *Il Miracolo di Teofilo* (Alessandria: Edizioni dell'Orso, 2000), ll. 160–8.

42. See Bodel, *Le Jeu de Saint Nicolas*, p. 275 n. 1512. Adam Zucker explores this phenomenon in the centuries after the end of the Middle Ages in '*Twelfth Night* and the Philology of Nonsense', *Renaissance Studies* 30.1 (2016), 88–101.
43. Martin Stevens and Arthur C. Cawley, *The Towneley Plays*, 2 vols, EETS 13 (Oxford: Oxford University Press, 1994), XXX. 249–52. On this passage, see Margaret Jennings, 'Tutivillus: The Literary Career of the Recording Demon', *Studies in Philology* 74.5 (1977), 1–95; Michael Peterson, '"Fragmina Verborum: The Vices" Use of Language in the Macro Plays', *Florilegium* 9 (1987), 155–67.
44. Mark Eccles, *The Macro Plays: The Castle of Perseverance, Wisdom, Mankind* (London: Oxford University Press, 1969), pp. 680–1.
45. This passage is discussed in Janette Dillon, *Language and Stage in Medieval and Renaissance England* (New York: Cambridge University Press, 1998), p. 41.
46. Cited in Erith Jaffe-Berg, 'Forays into Grammelot: The Language of Nonsense', *Journal of Dramatic Theory and Criticism* 2 (2001), 3–16. For a treatment of the prehistory and theory of grammelot, cf. Alessandra Pozzo, *Grr . . . grammelot: parlare senza parole, dai primi balbettii al grammelot di Dario Fo* (Bologna: CLUEB, 1998).
47. Geoffrey Chaucer, *The Riverside Chaucer*, ed. Larry Benson (Boston: Houghton Mifflin, 1987), Prologue, ll.42–3, p. 287. Cf. the eagle's cry of *awak* in the *House of Fame*, with Leonard Michael Koff, '"Awak!": Chaucer Translates Bird Song', *The Medieval Translator* V, ed. Roger Ellis and Rene Tixier (Turnhout: Brepols, 1996), 390–418; and the utterance *ocy ocy* in John Clanvowe, 'The Boke of Cupide, God of Love', in *Chaucerian Dream Visions and Complaints*, ed. Dana Symons (Kalamazoo, MI: Medieval Institute Publications, 2004), p.123f.
48. On the 'language of the birds' see for example Réné Guénon, *Symbols of Sacred Science*, trans. Henry D. Fohr (Hillsdale, NY: Sophia Perennis, 2002), Chapter 7.
49. Chaucer, *Riverside*, ll. 498–500, p. 392.
50. See Emma Dillon, *The Sense of Sound: Musical Meaning in France, 1260–1330* (New York: Oxford University Press, 2012), pp. 6, 33, 173; Christopher Page, *Discarding Images: Reflections on Music and Culture in Medieval France* (New York: Oxford University Press, 1997), p. 85; and, on a related later phenomenon, David Rattray, 'In Nomine', *How I Became One of the Invisible* (New York: Semiotext(e), 1992).
51. Both Bakhtin and Jung took an interest in these bizarre masses, with their whinnying priest and congregation: Mikhail Bakhtin, *Rabelais and his World*, trans. Hélène Iswolsky (Bloomington: Indiana University Press, 1984); Carl Jung, 'On the Psychology of the Trickster Figure', in *The Archetypes and the Collective Unconscious*, trans. R. F. C. Hull (Princeton: Princeton University Press, 1969), 255–74, p. 258f. For an interpretation more in line with current scholarly allegiances, see Max Harris, *Sacred Folly: A New History of the Feast of Fools* (Ithaca, NY: Cornell University Press, 2011).
52. See for example Edina Bozoky, *Charmes et prières apotropaïques* (Turnhout: Brepols, 2003), p. 61 and Lea Olsan, 'Charms in Medieval Memory', *Charms and Charming in Europe*, ed. Jonathan Roper (New York: Palgrave, 2004), p. 74. Julie Orlemanski discusses the connections among poetry, birdsong and medical jargon in particular in 'Jargon', making specific reference to their nonsensicality ('Jargon and the Matter of Medicine in Middle English', *Journal of Medieval and Early Modern Studies* 42.2 (2012), 395–420).
53. Tigges, who adopts it even so, is for his part explicit about the shortcomings of this term: 'Strictly speaking, "neologism" is not quite a correct term' (*Anatomy*, p. 68).
54. Elizabeth Sewell, *The Field of Nonsense* (Victoria, TX: Dalkey Archive, 2015), p. 124.
55. Sewell does not fail to anticipate that neo-Thomism might seem strange as a lens through which to examine her particular object of inquiry: 'the Schoolmen seem to be the only people who can help in this enquiry into Nonsense, just because they are so logical [. . .] The conjunction of Scholasticism and Nonsense is not a piece of whimsy' (*Field of Nonsense*, p. 45).

56. 'Numquam syllaba per se potest aliquid significare' (Priscian, *Institutionum grammaticorum libri XVIII*, ed. Martin Hertz (Leipzig: Teubner, 1855), I, p. 53).
57. See William Johnson, 'Teaching the Children How to Read: The Syllabary', *Classical Journal* 106.4, 445–63; Raffaella Cribiore, *Gymnastics of the Mind: Greek Education in Hellenistic and Roman Egypt* (Princeton: Princeton University Press, 2001), pp. 172–6.
58. Ibid. p. 173.
59. *Orator's Instruction*, 1.1.30, cited in Johnson, 'Teaching the Children', p. 447.
60. On the currency of the phrase *ni baf ni buf*, see J. J. Beylsmit, 'Un Moyen d'exprimer "ne dire/savoir absolument rien." Pour le commentaire de ne bu ne ba', *NphM* 60 (1959), 334–47.
61. Boethius, *Commentarii in librum Aristotelis Peri hermeneias, pars posterior, secundam editionem continens*, ed. Carl Meiser (Leipzig: Teubner, 1880), p. 32.
62. Ibid. pp. 5, 59. On *blityri* and *skindapsos* generally, see Wolfram Ax, *Laut, Stimme und Sprache: Studien zu Drei Grundbegriffen der Antiken Sprachtheorie* (Göttingen: Vandenhoeck & Ruprecht, 1986), pp. 195–9; Stephan Meier-Oeser and W. Schröder, 'Skindapsos', *Historisches Wörterbuch der Philosophie* (Basel: Schwabe, 1971–2007).
63. These texts are collected in Lambert-Marie de Rijk, *Logica Modernorum: A Contribution to the History of Early Terminist Logic* (Assen: Van Gorcum, 1967); the *voces non-significativae* appear in their opening sections.
64. See Walter Burley, 'Walter Burley's Middle Commentary on Aristotle's Perihermeneias', ed. Stephen Brown, *Franciscan Studies* 33 (1973), 45–134, I.07; Ana María Mora-Márquez, 'La ontología realista de Walter Burleigh y su relación con las teorías del significado y de la suposición', in Walter Burleigh *Sobre la pureza del arte de la lógica: Tratado breve*, trans. Ana María Mora-Márquez (Bogota: CESO, 2009), 173–227; on the aspects of Burley's treatise mentioned here, see Jordan Kirk, 'Walter Burley on the Time of Unknowing', in *Time: Sense, Space, Structure*, ed. Nancy van Deusen and Leonard Michael Koff (Leiden: Brill, 2016), 177–200.
65. See for example Sten Ebbesen, 'The Dead Man Is Alive', *Synthese* 40.1 (1979), 43–70; Olga Weijers, *La 'disputatio' dans les Facultés des arts au moyen âge* (Turnhout: Brepols, 2002); Stephen Read, 'Paradoxes of Signification', *Vivarium* 54.4 (2016), 335–55.
66. D. Vance Smith, 'Medieval Forma: The Logic of the Work', in *Reading for Form*, ed. Susan Wolfson and Marshall Brown (Seattle: University of Washington Press, 2007), 66–79, p. 79.
67. Numerous versions of this mnemonic were in circulation; the one cited is from Dov M. Gabbay and John Woods, *Handbook of the History of Logic (Volume 2) Mediaeval and Renaissance Logic* (Amsterdam: North Holland, 2008), p. 331, where there will also be found a brief explanation of its use.
68. On the rhetoric of *mundus inversus* see Dull, *Folie et rhétorique*.
69. R. Howard Bloch, *The Anonymous Marie de France* (Chicago: University of Chicago, 2003), p. 25.
70. Marie de France, *Lais*, ed. Jean Rychner (Paris: Champion, 1973), Prologue.
71. 'Nulla sane sunt magis mandanda memoriae quam illa verborum locutionumque genera quae ignoramus', Augustine, *De doctrina christiana*, ed. and trans. R. P. H. Green (New York: Oxford, 1995), pp. 78–80. On the *De doctrina* as instruction in a hermeneutics of incomprehensibility, see Kirk, 'What Separates the Birth of Twins'.
72. Augustine, *The Trinity*, trans. Edmund Hill (Hyde Park: New City Press, 1991), p. 287.
73. Giorgio Agamben, *The End of the Poem: Studies in Poetics*, trans. Daniel Heller-Roazen (Stanford: Stanford University, 1999), p. 64; see also his *Language and Death: The Place of Negativity*, trans. Michael Hardt (Minneapolis: University of Minnesota, 1991), p. 33.
74. Malcolm, *Origins*, pp. 109–10; on this point, see also Bayless, *Parody*, p. 2.

2

'The Best Fooling': *Every Man Out of His Humour*, *Twelfth Night* and Early Modern English Nonsense Games

Rebecca L. Fall

Here they continue their game of vapours, which is nonsense: every man to oppose the last man that spoke, whether it concerned him or no.[1]

So reads a marginal annotation in the fourth act of Ben Jonson's wild, satirical comedy *Bartholomew Fair* (first performed 1614, printed 1631). Highlighting the nonsensicality of the scene, this note aptly glosses the 'game' it describes. A group of drunken ne'er-do-wells at Bartholomew Fair are huddled inside the 'pig-woman' Ursula's booth, engaged in a ludicrous mess of discursive contradiction. Their conversation goes nowhere, and it is impossible to tell what exactly they are talking about. The only guiding logic to their verbal 'game' is the principle of contradiction: '*every man to oppose the last man that spoke, whether it concerned him or no*'. 'If he have reason, he may like it, sir', a second-rate horse trader called Knockem observes, referring to Wasp, the servant of a landed buffoon, who has just insisted that he'll 'say nay' to 'anything, whatsoever it is, so long as I do not like it' (IV. 4. 32, 24–6). In response, an Irish pimp named Whit interjects, 'By no meansh, captain, upon reason, he may like nothing upon reason.' Wasp himself cuts in: 'I have no reason, nor I will hear of no reason, nor I will look for no reason, and he is an ass that either knows any, or looks for't, from me.' When Val Cutting, a 'roarer', chimes in to agree that ''Tis true, thou hast no sense indeed', Wasp remains insistently and appropriately contrary: ''Slid, but I have sense, now I think on't better, and I will grant him anything, do you see?' (33–5; 41–3).

What any of this signifies is quite unclear. The entire conversation is a mess of contradiction and confusion, the basic topic of discussion essentially unidentifiable. The antecedent of the 'it' that Knockem insists Wasp 'may like' if he has 'reason', for instance, may be 'anything' at all, 'whatsoever it is, so long as I do not like it' (IV. 4. iv, 26–7). And the direction of the conversation that follows this vague point of contention only twists and turns itself into knots, ultimately going nowhere. All in all, the scene's dialogue is neither semantically significant nor discursively meaningful. Rather, it operates according to the logic of the 'game' described in the marginal annotation – 'which is nonsense'.

Understanding that this scene stages a nonsensical 'game of vapours' relieves us of the hermeneutic obligation (though hardly the impulse) to suss out its meaning. But then we are confronted with the question of the function of the game itself. What is it doing here? How and why does it work? What did it mean to play games of nonsense in early modern England?

This essay aims to answer these questions by examining two plays from the period that feature nonsense jests and pranks: Jonson's *Every Man Out of His Humour* (first performed c. 1599, printed 1600) and Shakespeare's *Twelfth Night* (first performed c. 1601, printed 1623). I take these examples as case studies because they are closely contemporaneous, but also – more importantly – because they both draw their nonsense jests from a specific tradition of 'fustian' nonsense play that flourished in communities of educated, socially ambitious men at the universities, around London, and especially at the Inns of Court (early modern law schools). Anchoring my readings of the plays in this historical context, this essay investigates the stakes of instrumentalising nonsense in early modern England, especially on the stage, as a form of competitive or recreative play. Both cases suggest that however silly or senseless or pointless the 'game' of nonsense may be, it is nonetheless useful in that it offers an appealing, pleasurable, and low-risk method for navigating (and potentially destabilising) precarious social hierarchies.

In staging scenes that explicitly recall the 'fustian' revels of the Inns of Court, I argue, *Every Man Out of His Humour* and *Twelfth Night* show that early modern nonsense games create crucial space – linguistic, imaginative and political – for players to question or even reinvent social logic. They accomplish this by crafting a recreative moment deliberately and conscientiously free from the obligation to speak in a semantically cogent way, while simultaneously attempting to draw in non-players who are not aware that a game is being played. The stakes are thus low for the nonsense players, since after all it's only a game – and what's more, a game that is deliberately silly, eschewing semantic meaning. They can enjoy the process of 'playing' nonsense no matter the outcome, and risk little. Yet the rewards for players are potentially very high because they have the opportunity to 'baffle' or best the unwitting participants, typically authority figures.[2] By using *play* to temporarily suspend the discursive rules that govern social relations while also enlisting the interpretive participation of interlocutors who are not aware that there is a game at all, nonsense players might at best advance their positions in the social landscape, and at worst have a pleasant time enjoying their rhetorical recreations.[3]

The Purpose of Playing with Nonsense

Before discussing the specific examples that Jonson and Shakespeare provide, however, it is worthwhile to offer a brief introduction to a deliberately baffling topic.

When I say *nonsense* in the context of late sixteenth- and seventeenth-century England, I mean a form of unreasonable, absurd expression that usually adheres to select grammatical or prosodic rules but self-consciously avoids communicating any logical objective or coherent meaning. This is not to say, however, that nonsense has no meaning. Early modern nonsensical discourse approximates sense in many ways but ultimately refuses interpretability; resembling meaningful discourse while undermining its semantic principles generates the mode's expressive but non-communicative power. For instance, Knockem's observation during *Bartholomew Fair*'s 'game of vapours' that if Wasp has 'reason, he may like it, sir', would seem entirely sensical in and of itself, but the conversation in the aggregate is roundly meaningless. In this way, it accords with what Paul Zumthor terms 'relative' nonsense, wherein each phrase, sentence, 'line or couplet makes sense in itself, and it is only the juxtaposition of them in the verse that is without meaning'.[4] To put it another way, we can describe nonsense from the period, but cannot readily paraphrase it. This care to approximate and yet sidestep overall semantic sense is what distinguishes early modern English nonsense from either coded or frankly *bad* speech, and is ultimately what makes it socially useful.

Early modern nonsense was hardly limited to flashes of boisterous absurdity in otherwise sensical plays, either. Rather, from the late 1500s through the end of the next century, nonsense remained a broadly popular mode of writing across England. It appears in a variety of period media, from cheap-print pamphlets and broadside ballads to commercial plays and manuscript miscellanies shared among elite coterie audiences. And while literary critics rarely acknowledge this substantial history,[5] early modern nonsense represents an important line in the genealogy of modern literary forms, especially theatre and drama.

As Martin Esslin notes in his landmark 1962 study of post-World War II avant-garde theatre, seventeenth-century nonsense writing is central to the history of what he famously termed 'Theatre of the Absurd'. Mapping its kinship with the dominant tracks of theatrical history, he directly quotes one of the most widely circulated nonsense poems of the period, Richard Corbett's 'A Mess of Nonsense' (c. 1610–30): 'Like to the mowing tones of unspoken speeches | Or like two lobsters clad in logic breeches', begins the version he cites.[6] Even as he highlights the literary historical significance of early modern English nonsense, however, Esslin neglects the social historical contingencies of its production and circulation. Like most twentieth-century critics, he follows Freud's view of nonsense as a universal expressive form that offers access to the pre-social, extra-discursive realm of the unconscious, claiming that '[v]erbal nonsense is in the truest sense a metaphysical endeavour, a striving to enlarge and to transcend the limits of the material universe and its logic'.[7] Accordingly, for Esslin, Corbett's 'Mess' is representative of what he sees as the fundamental principle of nonsensicalism: 'it is precisely the desire [. . .] to hear the tones of the unspoken speeches of mankind, that lies behind the impulse to speak nonsense'.[8]

It is possible that such an impulse animated Corbett's practice as a nonsense poet. This certainly seems to have been the case for some nonsensicalist writers in the nineteenth and twentieth centuries.[9] Yet early modern nonsense writing was consistently and insistently *social*, often emerging within intimate community spaces (including, as this essay shows, at the Inns of Court) and serving to bond participants or collect new ones together. Corbett's 'Mess of Nonsense' was widely circulated in manuscript among coterie groups at the universities, networking the readers who shared it with each other and functioning as an 'in-joke' among those who could appreciate its parodic nonsensicality. Meanwhile, the 'Water Poet' John Taylor's 1648 pamphlet *Mercurius Nonsencicus* channelled nonsense to lambaste Parliamentarian factions during the English Civil War, rallying like-minded supporters while safeguarding readers (and the author) from political censure by never making quite enough sense to be seditious – and calling attention to this protective manoeuvre by bookending the pamphlet with an adaptation of Corbett's 'Mess': 'Like to th'embrodered Meadowes of the Moone, | Or like the houres 'twixt six and seven at Noone', the concluding stanza intones, 'Such is this pamphlet, writ with such advisement, | As troubles not the State, or what the Wise meant'.[10] Rather than a universal unconscious impulse to 'transcend the material universe', then, early modern English nonsense was a historically peculiar phenomenon that leveraged playful incoherence, inside jokes, and mocking tricks to facilitate social advancement and challenge authority in distinctly 'material' ways.

Even as it delights in the frivolous pleasure of pointless speech, early modern nonsense also aims to lure unsuspecting (or arrogant) audiences into attempting to discover meaning where, by design, none is available, in order to diminish their assumed authority by laughing at their futile attempts at interpretation. To offer one example I have discussed elsewhere,[11] John Taylor's 1620 pamphlet *Jack-a-Lent* concludes with a nonsense poem entitled 'Certaine blanke Verses, written of purpose to no purpose, yet so plainely contriv'd, that a Childe of two yeeres old may understand them as well as a good Scholler of fifty'. The absurdly and delightfully senseless poem ends with a challenge to the reader: 'he that of these lines doth make a doubt, | Let him sit downe and pick the meaning out.'[12] In daring readers to 'pick the meaning out' where there is none, Taylor's 'Certain blanke Verses' illuminate the power source of early modern nonsense: its capacity to make fools of those who insist on interpreting it seriously. Nonsense, in other words, reorients social logic by turning interpretive authorities – those who wield intellectual, rhetorical and hermeneutic power – into 'contemplative idiot[s]', as Maria puts it in *Twelfth Night* (II. 5. 16).

The development of 'fustian' style provides another example. Scholarly jargon, an exclusive verbal enclave for small but powerful groups of educated elites, inspired this particular form of nonsense, which evacuates learned idioms of semantic power by haphazardly mixing together erudite terminology and invented gibberish words without regard to meaning or usage.[13] Taylor again offers a case in point. His 1622 pamphlet *Sir Gregory Nonsence* opens with a mock dedication that deploys fustian expressly to ridicule scholarly jargon: 'Most *Honorificicabilitudinitatibus*, I having studied the seven Lubberly Sciences (being nine by computation) out of which I gathered three conjunctions foure mile Asse-under, which with much labour, and great ease, to little or no purpose, I have Noddicated your gray grave and graveled Prateection'.[14] While 'fustian' did sometimes refer to bombastic but ultimately sensical jargon, it also could – and frequently did – function as a synonym for nonsense in the period, as Hugh Roberts has thoroughly documented.[15] And while fustian nonsense might be written off merely as an easy way to mock dense, pretentious jargon, its resemblance to sensical speech is key to its ludic and social force. It is evident that such power – as well as the delight that speakers and audiences derived from talking foolishly on purpose – made senseless verbal play immensely appealing among educated, fashionable affiliates of Cambridge, Oxford and the Inns of Court, for whom fustian games remained a well-beloved custom throughout the late sixteenth and seventeenth centuries.

Remnants of this custom abound in manuscript and print miscellany collections of the period. Poems like Corbett's 'Mess of Nonsense' pepper manuscripts associated with educational institutions at the time, indicating that coteries of young men commonly passed nonsense verse among their friends. Clubs and fraternities around the universities and in London met regularly at taverns to improvise nonsense for each other in competitive 'wit-combats', during which club members judged each other's verbal dexterity and organised themselves according to a hierarchy based on those judgements.[16] From a 1633 legal deposition concerning one James Smith, for instance, we know that members of a club called the Order of the Fancy met regularly to 'drinke excessively, and to Speake non sence' competitively. The member deemed to have improvised the 'best non sence' during a given evening's game was 'Counted the best man' and offered the 'Cheifest place at the meetinge'.[17]

Other records show that members of the Inns of Court in London likewise incorporated nonsense games into their regular holiday celebrations. During the winter of 1597–8, the Middle Temple at the Inns of Court hosted its annual Christmas 'revels'. According to Benjamin Rudyerd's record of the season, which survives in at least one seventeenth-century manuscript as well as a 1660 print miscellany entitled *Le Prince d'Amour*, the festivities lasted two weeks and involved a variety of feasts, pranks and nonsense games. On one evening of celebration, several 'officers' of the revels' make-believe 'Court' offered bombastic speeches and toasts, many of which were nonsensical in some way or another. One, 'a prognostica*cion* w*hi*ch with greater skil foretold many things th*a*t were past', mangled chronology; its 'predictions', recorded in *Prince d'Amour*, veer into absurdity and nonsensicalism. Rudyerd reports that this literally preposterous prophecy was followed by 'a neate tuftaffety Oration' (probably delivered by Charles Best), which the well-known wit John Hoskyns 'answered in a handsome fustian speech'.[18]

Although the 'tuftaffety Oration' appears to be lost, Hoskyns's apparently 'extempore' speech survives in *Le Prince d'Amour* as well as at least four manuscript sources.[19] Its 'handsome fustian' manifests in abstruse esotericism and over-the-top rhetoric stretched to the point of nonsense: 'since the estates of Europe Have soe manye momentall inclinations and the Mathematicall confusion of theyre dominions is like to ruinate theyre subversions', he confusingly observes, 'I see noe reason why men sholde addicte themselves to take Tobacco in Ramus method'.[20] Here and throughout the speech, Hoskyns draws on ornate, Latinate language, mashing together multi-syllabic bits of scholarly jargon until they no longer make sense, while invoking learned philosophies like the pedagogical method of Petrus Ramus, an influential French humanist, in impressively illogical ways. This was part of a playfully nonsensical game of tit-for-tat that involved caking 'troopes of Tropes, and Centuries of Sentences' on each other: 'for your Tuffaty [*sic*] speech yow shall receve but a fustian answer', Hoskyns warns at the outset, anticipating the deliberate nonsensicalism to come.[21]

The fustian play of the Middle Temple revels celebrated rhetorical excess, signalling the broader vogue for nonsense emerging in the period. And while Rudyerd's account of 1597–8 offers the most detailed record of the nonsense games that occupied Inns of Court communities, there is evidence that the tradition carried on beyond that particular year. Indeed, throughout the long seventeenth century, Inns of Court holiday festivities regularly staged fustian improvisations and other pleasantly pointless games – as well as theatrical performances.

Like nonsense, theatre was a regular and beloved part of the revels. John Marston's *Histriomastix*, for instance, featured during the 1598–9 Middle Temple Christmas season. On some occasions, plays were expressly incorporated into broader gaming contexts, too. When Shakespeare's *Comedy of Errors* played at the 1594 Gray's Inn revels, it functioned as a formal part of the evening's nonsense games such that 'that Night was begun, and continued to the end, in nothing but Confusion and Errors; whereupon it was ever afterwards called *The Night of Errors*'.[22] Beyond finding venues for their works at the festivities, though, playwrights also honoured the witty absurdity of the revels in their work – including Jonson in *Every Man Out of His Humour* and Shakespeare in *Twelfth Night* – suggesting that the nonsense games of the community formed a key context for dramatic production.

Low Risk and Little Reward in *Every Man Out*

Jonson's intimate relationship with the Inns of Court is well documented, and *Every Man Out of His Humour* evinces an especially close connection to that community. The version of the play printed in Jonson's 1616 *Workes* is dedicated to the 'noblest nourceries of humanity, and liberty, in the kingdome: The Innes of Court'; his dedicatory epistle to the community reminisces fondly about the 'friendship' he enjoyed with 'divers in your societies' and alludes to the fact that the play found 'first favour' at the law schools, probably in performance.[23] Moreover, as Helen Ostovich notes in her introduction to the play, *Every Man Out of His Humour* in many respects 'models itself on the form and content of the revels'. Among other points of similarity, its dramatic structure, which builds a 'gradual assembly of self-displaying characters engag[ed] in various rhetorical games as members of competitive, ever-expanding, and shifting groups', as well as its '"ragging" revels tone', link the play to the festivities.[24] This stylistic and structural affinity makes sense considering Jonson's close literary relationship with that master of nonsense oration, John Hoskyns, who was regarded in the seventeenth century as the playwright's 'intellectual "father"'.[25]

In addition to the biographical connection between Jonson and the social circles in which fustian games were traditionally enjoyed, nonsense plays a key role in *Every Man Out of His Humour*. In terms of both structure and spirit, 'fustian' sits at the very centre of the play. At the beginning of the third act, we encounter Clove and Orange, two 'twins of foppery'. According to the play's prefatory characterological introductions, these 'coxcombs' live to 'feast players, and make suppers; and [. . .] enforce their ignorance most desperately to set upon the understanding of anything' while 'in company of better rank' (Characters, 95–102). We thus know from the start that navigating social 'rank' or hierarchy is the characters' prime concern in the play, and that their modus operandi involves mistaking and frustrating semantic 'understanding'. They are, in other words, quintessential figures of fustian nonsense.

Everything about Clove and Orange leans toward the nonsensical. As Ostovich observes, their names allude to 'aromatic delicacies' that were 'imported [. . .] to perfume the air and inhibit infection from foul odours' (note to Characters, 94). Their names, then, are airy and insubstantial. They 'suggest men's affectation, effeminacy, and irrelevance to native English manhood', Ostovich notes. However, the names also evoke a quality that Jonson elsewhere associates explicitly with nonsense games: vapour.

Appropriately enough, the two airy 'coxcombs' bring no dramatic, intellectual or poetic substance to the play. Like *Bartholomew Fair*'s 'game of vapours, which is nothing', their basic existence within the structure of *Every Man Out of His Humour* is based on the principle of non sequitur. When Clove and Orange appear at the top of Act 3, the scene has moved to Paul's Walk in London, and the bulk of the play's characters are strolling around the stage, highlighted variously in comic conversation. Clove and Orange appear as if from nowhere; they have not been introduced in the previous two acts, nor will they appear beyond this single scene. In a play with a large cast and tangled network of interlocking, overlapping story lines, Clove and Orange are remarkably isolated, and their singular appearance underscores the game-like, recreative nature of the nonsense they import. They function as a release from the plot order of the rest of the play.

Just as *Bartholomew Fair*, via a marginal note in the printed text, explains the logic (or lack thereof) of the game of vapours for the reading audience, *Every Man Out of His Humour* also acknowledges outright the disconnected nature of Clove and Orange's turn on stage. Cordatus, a member of the play's onstage audience who offers wry meta-commentary about its plot and performance throughout the show, observes that they are 'a couple, sir, that are mere strangers to the whole scope of our play – only come to walk a turn or two i' this scene of Paul's by chance' (III. 1. 38–40). In the play's vast set of characters, Clove and Orange have really nothing to do with anything. Certainly they represent a particular character type that Jonson might take satirical aim at – the fop who aspires to elite status and reveals himself to be a fool – but they do not contribute to the plot and have the same effect as a couple of figures dropped in by mere 'chance'.

Beyond their near-non sequitur of an entrance, the vapourous interlopers go on to *speak* nonsense, as well. As various characters promenade around Paul's Walk, Clove pulls his companion Orange aside. 'Monsieur Orange', he whispers, 'yond gallants observes us. Prithee, let's talk fustian a little and gull 'em, make 'em believe we are great scholars.' 'O Lord, sir!' Orange replies (III. 1. 168–71). Clove's 'fustian' certainly does not disappoint. 'Now, sir', he pronounces to his companion:

> whereas the ingenuity of the time and the soul's *synderisis* are but *embryons* in nature, added to the paunch of Esquiline and the *intervallum* of the zodiac, besides the ecliptic line being optic and not mental, but by the contemplative and theoric part thereof, doth demonstrate to us the vegetable circumference and the ventosity of the tropics; and whereas our intellectual or mincing capriole (according to the *Metaphysics*) as you may read in Plato's *Histriomastix* – You conceive me, sir?

In this wave of textbook fustian, Clove throws together a seemingly random assortment of scholarly jargon, including terms from theology (such as 'synderisis' or *synteresis*, referring to the faculty of guilt or conscience), biology (e.g. 'embryons'), scatology ('ventosity', or flatulence; 'paunch of Esquiline', or a latrine), and contemporary culture (*Histriomastix*, not a great work of Plato's but a satire by John Marston associated with the 1598–9 Inns of Court revels). Altogether it is a thoroughly senseless disquisition, and in reply Orange can only gasp with desperate hilarity, 'O Lord, sir!'

Senseless and bombastic, Clove's style is also remarkably similar to Hoskyns's 'Fustian Oration'[26] and therefore reminiscent of nonsense games played offstage by real historical figures. And like Hoskyns's 'fustian' Christmastide game, Clove's absurd tangle of language goes nowhere semantically and is ultimately uninterpretable. It thus accords with John Taylor's 1622 definition of nonsense: language '[w]ritten on purpose, with much study to no end [. . .] very fitly for the understanding of Nobody'.[27]

Although Clove's language may have no semantic 'end', it does have a social purpose. He intends to talk nonsense to 'gull' or trick any listeners – particularly any elite 'gallants' in the vicinity – into believing their conversation is meaningful. Orange's responses to Clove's nonsense talk suggest that he too is delighted by the possibility of luring someone into taking seriously a meaningless mess of fustian. While an actor might interpret his repeated exclamations of 'O Lord, sir!' in any number of ways – as desperation or confusion, for instance – it's likely that these interjections express hilarity and amusement. Orange is in on Clove's fustian game, and is equally eager to 'gull' the nearby 'gallants' by inspiring them to dig for sense where none exists, thereby making them the butt of the joke. Moreover, Clove repeatedly asks whether Orange 'understand[s]', as if to draw in listeners who might, foolishly, *try* to understand (III. 1. 178).

The fustian game may immediately serve to bring its players simple delight, but the potential reward is much higher. In talking nonsense just for fun, Clove and Orange might be able to deceive a nearby listener into taking them seriously and advancing their social status – 'make 'em believe we are great scholars'. Of course, the fustian players are not successful in their effort. Clove and Orange's onstage audience fail to be 'gull[ed]' by their nonsense game: 'Let us return to our former discourse, for they mark us not', Clove eventually concedes (III. 1. 200–1). This failure does not particularly matter, though. Clove and Orange are not chastised or punished for attempting to nonsensify their way into higher status – not even by the 'envious' and 'impatient' Macilente, who takes harsh revenge on anyone who so much as mildly irritates him (Characters, 9, 11). He is the only character who overhears Clove and Orange's fustian conversation, but dismisses it as unworthy of attention, merely muttering to himself 'O, here be a couple of fine tame parrots' (181–2). Even the play's most unforgiving character gives Clove and Orange's nonsense game a pass because it's nothing more than senseless chatter in the end.

The stakes of their game are therefore low, even as the (unachieved) potential reward could have been high. At best, Clove and Orange might convince some unsuspecting soul, one who does not recognise their nonsense *as* nonsense, that they are gentlemen. At worst, they simply give up the game after enjoying a pleasurably pointless chat. The worst comes to pass, and no harm is done. The nonsense players simply 'return to their former discourse' and go on their way, disappearing from the plot as quickly as they entered.

Fustian Jests in *Twelfth Night*

Though *Bartholomew Fair* and *Every Man Out of His Humour* offer particularly interesting examples of the practice, Jonson was not the only writer to import nonsense games onto the stage. Shakespeare's *Twelfth Night* stages a fustian game at the centre of its plot. Whereas Clove and Orange's effort to instrumentalise the game for social advancement falls flat, though, I argue that *Twelfth Night* sees its successful execution, offering a clear representation of the powerful potential in playing nonsense games.

Like *Every Man Out of His Humour*, *Twelfth Night* is circumstantially associated with Inns of Court revels, suggesting that its allusions to nonsense games are rooted in historical reality. John Manningham described watching it at the Middle Temple during Candlemas festivities in 1602:

> At our feast we had a play called 'Twelve Night, or What You Will' [. . .] A good practise in it to make the Steward beleeve his Lady Widdow was in love with him, by conterfeyting a letter as from his Lady in generall termes, telling him what she liked best in him, and prescribing his gesture in smiling, his aparaile, &c, and then when he came to practise making him beleeve they tooke him to be mad.[28]

Manningham's account suggests that for at least one Inns of Court affiliate, the central distinguishing feature of *Twelfth Night* is the prank that Maria, Toby, Andrew and

Fabian play on Malvolio – one designed to take his authority down a peg or two, which involves 'conterfeyting a letter [. . .] in generall termes'.

What Manningham means by 'generall termes' is unclear. We might reasonably assume he is referring to the broad strokes of Maria's letter. And yet its 'good practise' also lines up with the exercise of nonsense play elsewhere in the period – drawing in unwitting would-be interpretive authorities only to laugh at them when they fail to unlock some meaning that is not there: as Taylor taunts, 'he that of these lines doth make a doubt, | Let him sit downe and pick the meaning out'.[29] In other words, Manningham's description of the 'generall termes' of Maria's letter might refer to a text so vague and unclear as to be nonsensical. After all, her letter contains a 'fustian riddle' (II. 5. 92) – a bit of nonsense play that serves to delight her fellow players, but which is also designed to rearrange social hierarchies within the household.

Whatever Manningham's own take on it, *Twelfth Night* does entertain all manner of nonsensical recreation. The play is filled with fustian jests. Sir Andrew Aguecheek, for example, delights in a puzzling exchange with Feste in Act 2: 'In sooth, thou wast in very gracious fooling last night', Andrew remarks to the fool, 'when thou spok'st of Pigrogomitus, of the Vapians passing the equinoctial of Queubus. 'Twas very good, i'faith: I sent thee sixpence for thy leman; hadst it?' (II. 3. 19–22).

It is challenging to make much sense of the 'gracious fooling' Andrew reports here, which is often brushed off as 'mock learning'.[30] And certainly that is a component of what is happening. But the exchange goes on, extending well beyond mere 'mock learning' into something more confusing that involves other members of the household. Feste responds: 'I did impeticos thy gratillity: for Malvolio's nose is no whipstock; my lady has a white hand, and the Myrmidons are no bottle-ale houses.' 'Excellent!' Sir Andrew cries, 'Why this is the best fooling, when all is done' (II. 3. 23–6).

This exchange offers a prime example of Inns of Court-style fustian nonsense. We can identify the general topic of conversation: Andrew is complimenting Feste's skills as a fool – a job that comes with a professional imperative to entertain, which affords him special licence to test the boundaries of both decorum and sensicality – and has tipped him appropriately.[31] Expressing admiration for Feste's 'gracious fooling', Andrew inquires whether Feste received the 'sixpence' he sent for the fool's 'leman', or sweetheart. The initial phrase of Feste's reply is likewise intelligible enough, if bombastic. 'Impeticos' is likely a ludicrous way of saying 'put in my pocket', while 'gratillity' is a 'perversion of 'gratuity' that 'emphasise[s] its smallness'.[32] Feste is affirming, in amusingly over-the-top terms, that he received Andrew's tip from the previous evening. Beyond that, however, things become rather more perplexing. Whatever the pallor of '[m]y lady['s]' hand (Olivia's, presumably) has to do with either Malvolio's nose or Andrew's 'gratillity', let alone with Myrmidons (who are emphatically *not* 'bottle-ale houses') is quite unclear.[33]

Although we can discern the general topic of Andrew and Feste's conversation, it is more challenging to figure out what exactly they are saying *about* it. What does it mean to speak of 'Pigrogomitus, of the Vapians passing the equinoctial of Queubus'? What does it mean that 'the Myrmidons are no bottle-ale houses', and how does that relate to the act of 'impeticos[ing]' Andrew's 'gratillity'? I argue that it does not mean much of anything. This is an instance of nonsense, drawn from the tradition of the Inns of Court revels and other recreations among 'clubs' of intellectual aspirants at the universities and beyond. It echoes the 'wit-combats' and games of nonsense improvisation popular in those environments. Feste's lines, both reported and direct, sound as if they could be lifted directly from Hoskyns's 'Fustian Oration'. And in fact, they resemble in style another of Hoskyns's nonsense pieces:

> Even as the waves of brainlesse butter'd fish,
> With bugle horne writ in the Hebrew tongue,
> Fuming up flounders like a chafing-dish,
> That lookes asquint upon a Three-mans song:
> Or as your equinoctiall pasticrust
> Projecting out a purple chariot wheele,
> Doth squeeze the speares, and intimate the dust,
> The dust which force of argument doth feele:
> Even so this Author, this Gymnosophist,
> Whom no delight of travels toyle dismaies,
> Shall sympathize (thinke reader what thou list)
> Crownd with a quinsill tipt with marble praise.[34]

First printed in the prefatory material to Thomas Coryate's *Crudities* (1611), this nonsense poem is headed 'Cabalisticall verses, which by transposition of words, syllables, and letters make excellent sense, otherwise none.' To my knowledge, no scholar has yet managed to 'transpos[e]' the 'words, syllables, and letters' of Hoskyns's 'Cabalisticall' poem in a way that makes much 'sense' at all beyond gentle mockery of Coryate ('this Author [. . .] Whom no delight of travels toyle dismaies'). Its promise of 'excellent sense' seems only to be a witty ruse designed to confound a reader who is not in on the joke and doesn't understand how to play the nonsense game.

Twelfth Night in performance and print preceded the publication of *Crudities* and 'Cabalisticall Verses' by about a decade, though it is roughly contemporaneous with Hoskyns's 'Fustian Oration'. Yet the precise direction of influence does not really matter for my purposes. What does matter is that these connections suggest *Twelfth Night* belongs in key ways to the world of nonsense improvisation and fustian wit-combats.

This is significant because it demonstrates that a play as canonical as *Twelfth Night* not only participated in an emergent nonsense tradition, but imported specific elements of that tradition onto the stage, as well. The nonsense games and fustian wit-combats of Inns of Court affiliates and others of their ilk involved out-bombastifying one another, but also incorporated an element of (sometimes aggressive) mockery. While most scholars have assumed that the object of parody or mockery in these moments is the jargon of scholarship itself, the butt of the joke is ultimately those who attempt to interpret nonsense as if it were meaningful: would-be authorities of language who don't share the fustian crew's comic frame of reference. The point is to laugh at those who would presume to find authoritative meaning in what is deliberately uninterpretable.

Feste's exchange with Andrew is not the only time that nonsense creeps into *Twelfth Night*, either. As both Stephen Booth and Adam Zucker have shown, the play is replete with moments of unintelligibility and incoherence.[35] But the prime nonsense example in *Twelfth Night*, I contend, is the moment that so captivated Manningham when he watched the play at the Middle Temple Candlemas feast of 1602: 'A good practise in it to make the Steward beleeve his Lady Widdow was in love with him, by conterfeyting a letter [. . .] in generall termes.'

With her forged letter, Maria arranges with Toby, Andrew and Fabian to 'practise' a trick upon Malvolio. Her aim is clear: to diminish the steward's authority. She articulates this goal explicitly: 'Observe him, for the love of mockery, for I know this letter will make a contemplative idiot of him. Close, in the name of jesting! Lie thou there [*Drops a letter*]; for here comes the trout that must be caught with tickling' (II. 5. 15–19). The trap that Maria and her co-conspirators lay for Malvolio is a prop in a game – an act of play staged 'in the name of jesting' and 'for the love of mockery'. The initial objective is to 'make a contemplative idiot of him', suggesting that the game's immediate goal is to damage his authority (make him appear an 'idiot') by enticing ('tickling') him to interpret ('contemplate') foolishly. The game thus centres on the act of misplaced interpretation – specifically, the interpretation of a piece of writing that looks as if it should be meaningful but is not.

While the whole letter Maria writes contributes to the prank on Malvolio, my particular interest is in the nonsensical riddle at its core:

I may command where I adore,
But silence, like a Lucrece knife,
With bloodless stroke my heart doth gore;
M.O.A.I. doth sway my life.

(II. 5. 88–91)

Although Andrew swiftly identifies these lines as a form of nonsense play – 'A fustian riddle!' he claps delightedly (92) – the verse would initially appear to conceal some coded meaning. That's how Malvolio takes it, after all. Yet it is nonsensical, designed to frustrate interpretation; there is no real meaning in it. And the fact that it does look to Malvolio (and has appeared to many scholars across the centuries)[36] like a solvable riddle is entirely in keeping with the qualities of early modern English nonsense play. Indeed, what Hoskyns's 'Cabalisticall Verses' or Taylor's 'Certain blank verses' do explicitly, this verse does implicitly: it dares Malvolio to 'pick the meaning out', to try to 'make excellent sense' of what is in the end only 'fustian' nonsense. The initials 'M.O.A.I.' are tantalisingly close to the steward's own name, and the first line implies that the speaker has authority over her beloved, as Olivia has over Malvolio. Both elements impel Malvolio to rehearse an act of futile interpretation: 'Why, [Olivia] may command me', he reasons, 'she is my lady. Why this is evident to any formal capacity. There is no obstruction in this' (98–100). Malvolio's grandiose exegetical language ('this is evident to any formal capacity') marks him as victim of the nonsense game. He presumes to wield hermeneutic authority over a text with no meaningful content as a group of insiders watch and jeer. And ultimately, the failure of his interpretive authority provides them the opportunity to overtake him socially.

Twelfth Night's nonsense players chafe at Malvolio's status as well as his pretensions to virtue and intellectual supremacy: he is 'an affectioned ass', Maria complains, who is 'crammed (as he thinks) with excellencies' and 'cons state without book and utters it by great swarths' (II. 3. 124–7). In other words, he asserts authority by making a sweeping exhibition of rote learning in decorum, comportment and language. But Maria sees through him, and so decides to rearrange the contours of his authority by 'mak[ing] him a common recreation' – that is, by playing a game that serves as a form of shared recreation for her companions while also 're-creating' him as a more 'common' or lower-status figure (115). And she enables this rearrangement by entrapping him in a nonsense game that serves to test her wit, like a nonsense player at the Inns of Court, with Toby and Andrew. 'If I do not gull him', she insists, establishing the stakes of her game, 'do not think I have wit enough to lie straight in my bed' (114–16). She plans to 'gull' him and damage his status by making him over-reach in authority, and she uses fustian as bait. This is how early modern nonsense operates: it entices or 'tickles' would-be authorities into an interpretive posture in order to laugh at the failure of their efforts – and, importantly, mark them as outsiders. The victims of nonsense games are not in on the joke, and their failures of interpretation serve to bond nonsense players through a mutual understanding that there is nothing to understand.[37] The potential social rewards of nonsense games are thus high. They might diminish interpretive authorities enough to rewrite the social order.

This is certainly true of the fustian prank in *Twelfth Night*. It enables Maria not only to damage Malvolio's authority, but also to rearrange her own social situation advantageously. Her superior wit, occasioned by a brief and senseless verse, proves her desirability to the male players in her nonsense game, and her status is elevated as a result. 'I could marry this wench for this device', Toby remarks as they watch Malvolio mistake the fustian letter for an interpretable riddle (II. 5. 150). 'So could I, too', echoes Andrew (151). Toby is even moved by the display of her nonsensical wit to advance her economic status: he would 'ask no other dowry but such another jest', he insists (152). This is not idle talk, either; he does in the end actually marry her, elevating her status by making her the wife of a knight who is kin to a countess. Ultimately, the 'fustian riddle' has no meaning at all (like Hoskyns's 'Cabalisticall Verses', 'M.O.A.I.' has no semantic content, hidden or otherwise), but it does have a very useful function: to rewrite the social landscape of Maria's household and help her negotiate a higher position.

At the same time, this fustian prank is safe. It offers the players the opportunity to forge new alliances and diminish the presumed authority of outsiders like Malvolio without exposing themselves to censure. It's all just nonsense, after all. Even after the trick comes to light and Olivia learns that Malvolio 'hath been most notoriously abused' (V. 1. 356), Fabian is able to dismiss the game as a joke that ought not be taken seriously: it '[m]ay pluck on laughter [rather] than revenge', he insists (345). It's only a bit of foolish fustian, in the end, a silly game. There are no negative consequences beyond Malvolio's brief threat to be 'revenged', but the rewards are substantial: 'In recompense' for the delights of the nonsense game, Toby marries Maria and the irritating authority figure of the steward disappears from her newly consolidated purview.

Conclusion

If, as Martin Esslin suggests in *The Theatre of the Absurd*, English nonsense writing from this period plays a crucial role in the history of twentieth-century literature and theatre – influencing such canonical playwrights as Samuel Beckett, Eugène Ionesco and Jean Genet – then it is important to understand how it was created, shared and received in the long seventeenth century. It is important, in other words, to account for nonsense's social uses. Rather than (or in addition to) expressing some pre- or extra-conscious meaning, early modern nonsense approximated familiar rhetorical patterns while evacuating them of semantic value in order to take advantage of would-be authorities' presumed expertise. It functioned, as Elizabeth Freund writes of Maria's fustian letter, as a 'booby trap' for interpreters to 'dig [their] own hermeneutic grave[s]'.[38] Nonsense was in this way a productive and valuable form of play – not despite but precisely *because* of its pleasantly frivolous pointlessness, which held the power to undercut presumed authority while protecting the player from rebuke and further social damage. Acknowledging this historical context can help us better understand what is at stake in the works of Shakespeare and Jonson, and better calibrate how we encounter their jokes, oddities and plot manoeuvres. Perhaps more significantly, though, it can save us from falling victim to the nonsense game ourselves. For unless we acknowledge the valuable function of 'the best fooling', the delightful, dumb, possibly potent and certainly silly joke is on all of us. As the history of early modern nonsense shows, we either play the game of vapours, or fall victim to its confusions.

Notes

1. Ben Jonson, *Bartholomew Fair*, ed. John Creaser, in vol. 4 of *The Cambridge Edition of The Works of Ben Jonson*, 7 vols, ed. David Bevington et al. (New York: Cambridge University Press, 2012), stage direction at IV. 3. 10. Subsequent *Bartholomew Fair* citations are to this edition and will appear in text.
2. Upon discovering a confused and abused Malvolio at the end of *Twelfth Night*, Olivia cries 'Alas, poor fool, how have they baffled thee!' (William Shakespeare, *Twelfth Night*, ed. Elizabeth Story Donno (New York: Cambridge University Press, 2003), V. 1. 438); subsequent citations to *Twelfth Night* are to Donno's edition and will appear in text. Adam Zucker has written eloquently on nonsense and the interpretive politics of 'baffling' in the play; see Zucker, '*Twelfth Night* and the Philology of Nonsense', *Renaissance Studies* 30.1 (2016) 88–101, esp. p. 89 and pp. 99–101.
3. I use 'game' here as a broad term encompassing a range of recreative or otherwise playful activities, from 'sportive action, prank[s], [and] frolic' to 'trick[s] played in sport' and 'practical joke[s]' (*OED*, 'game, *n.*,' 7). Although Gina Bloom and others have demonstrated the value of rigourously theorising game-play, especially in the context of English theatrical history, this essay takes inspiration from the 'game of vapours' in *Bartholomew Fair* to deploy the concept in a looser, more flexible way: see Bloom, *Gaming the Stage: Playable Media and the Rise of English Commercial Theater* (Ann Arbor: University of Michigan Press, 2018). On games in traditional English holiday pastimes, see Leah Marcus, *The Politics of Mirth: Jonson, Herrick, Milton, Marvell, and the Defense of Old Holiday Pastimes* (Chicago: University of Chicago Press, 1986); and on Renaissance sport, see Gregory M. Colón Semenza, *Sport, Politics, and Literature in the English Renaissance* (Newark: University of Delaware Press, 2003). While the activities I examine in *Every Man Out* and *Twelfth Night* are not explicitly called games, they do possess game-like qualities in that they are forms of recreation which temporarily suspend the governing logic of ordinary life in the service of delighting their participants, according in key ways to definitions of play proposed by Roger Caillois, *Man, Play, and Games*, trans. Meyer Barash (New York: Free Press, 1961); and J. Huizinga, *Homo Ludens: A Study of the Play Element in Culture* (London: Routledge & Kegan Paul, 1980).
4. Paul Zumthor, 'Fatrasie et coq-à-l'âne', in *La Fin du Moyen âge et renaissance. Mélanges de philologie française offerts à Robert Guiette* (Antwerp, Nederlandsche Boekhandel, 1961), 5–18; English translation is from Noel Malcolm, *The Origins of English Nonsense* (London: Fontana, 1998), p. 65.
5. As far as I know, the only published long-form study of early modern English nonsense to date is Malcolm's *Origins of English Nonsense*. Emily Butterworth and Hugh Roberts recently edited a special issue of *Renaissance Studies* 30.1 (2016) dedicated to 'Gossip and

Nonsense in Renaissance France and England', which includes Adam Zucker's valuable 'Philology of Nonsense'. See also *Nonsense and Other Senses: Regulated Absurdity in Literature*, ed. Elisabetta Tarantino and Carlo Caruso (Newcastle upon Tyne: Cambridge Scholars, 2009), which offers an eclectic account of nonsense across time. Despite these few exceptions, however, most critics have tended to treat nonsense as if it originated with Edward Lear and Lewis Carroll in the nineteenth century. See, for example, Wim Tigges, *An Anatomy of Literary Nonsense* (Amsterdam: Rodopi, 1988), who claims that 'nonsense is a relatively recent phenomenon in literature, originating in Britain in the Romantic or post-Romantic era' (p. 2).

6. Corbett's 'Mess of Nonsense' – sometimes entitled 'Nonsense', 'Pure Nonsense', or even 'Sense' – was probably composed around 1620, and was widely circulated in print and manuscript. It appears in at least fifteen editions of three distinct seventeenth-century print miscellanies, and survives in at least twenty-five manuscripts. Structurally, 'Mess' parodies another widely circulated poem in the period attributed to Francis Quarles, beginning 'Like to the damask rose you see' (c. 1600–20).
7. Martin Esslin, *The Theatre of the Absurd* (New York: Bloomsbury, [1962] 2014), p. 284. Esslin is hardly alone in this perspective. Since Freud's *Jokes and their Relation to the Unconscious* (1905), prevailing scholarly opinion has held that nonsense represents a spontaneous and natural form of expression that offers access to the pre-social, extra-discursive realm of the unconscious. This view has fundamentally coloured twentieth-century theories of the mode; see, for instance, Hugh Haughton's important introduction to *The Chatto Book of Nonsense Poetry* (London: Chatto and Windus, 1988), which insists that nonsense is 'a kind of underground language – something to do with the unconscious, the rich world of sleep, slips of the tongue, and literary rejection slips' (p. 8), if not also an expression of the 'universal' experience of 'childhood' (p. 5).
8. Esslin, *Theatre of the Absurd*, p. 284.
9. It has been well documented that various post-World War II artists embraced nonsense in response to what they saw as a violent, meaningless world, and that it fulfilled their search for asemantic modes of expression that might transcend (or radically devalue) logocentric modes of communication. See, for example, Tristan Tzara's *Dada Manifesto 1918*, trans. Ralph Manheim, in *The Dada Reader: A Critical Anthology*, ed. Dawn Ades (Chicago: University of Chicago Press, 2006): 'abolition of logic, which is the dance of those impotent to create: Dada' (p. 42).
10. John Taylor, *Mercurius Noncsencicus* (London: [n. pub.], 1648), Wing T482A, p. 7.
11. Rebecca L. Fall, 'Popular Nonsense according to John Taylor and Ben Jonson', *SEL* 57.1 (2017), 87–110.
12. John Taylor, *Jack a Lent* (London: Printed [by G. Purslowe] for I. T., 1620), STC 23765.5, sig. C4v.
13. On fustian, see Hugh Roberts, 'Comparative Nonsense: French galimatias and English fustian', *Renaissance Studies* 30.1 (2016), 102; and his 'Performing Nonsense in Early Seventeenth Century France: Bruscambille's Galimatias', in *Nonsense and Other Senses*, ed. Tarantino and Caruso, 127–45. On fustian as rhetorical style, see Eleanor Clark, *Ralegh and Marlowe: A Study in Elizabethan Fustian* (New York: Fordham University Press, 1941); and Cynthia Lewis, '"A Fustian Riddle"?: Anagrammatic Names in *Twelfth Night*', *English Language Notes* 22.4 (1985), 32–7.
14. John Taylor, *Sir Gregory Nonsence His Newes from No Place* (London, Printed by N[icholas] O[akes], [1622]), STC 23795, sig. A3r.
15. Roberts, 'Comparative Nonsense'; cf. Malcolm, *Origins*, p. 30.
16. On club 'wit-combats', see Timothy Raylor, *Cavaliers, Clubs, and Literary Culture: Sir John Mennes, James Smith, and the Order of the Fancy* (Newark: University of Delaware Press, 1994), p. 21; and Michael Strachan, 'The Mermaid Tavern Club: A New Discovery',

History Today 17.8 (1967), 34. On the relationship between the Inns of Court and other clubs, Michelle O'Callaghan, 'Tavern Societies, the Inns of Court, and the Culture of Conviviality in Early Seventeenth-Century London', in *A Pleasing Sinne: Drink and Conviviality in Seventeenth-Century England*, ed. Adam Smyth (Cambridge: D. S. Brewer, 2004); and O'Callaghan, *The English Wits: Literature and Sociability in Early Modern England* (New York: Cambridge University Press, 2007), pp. 10–34.

17. UK National Archives MS SP 16/240, fos. 80–1.
18. British Library MS Harley 1576, fo. 248v. In early modern English, both 'tuftaffety' and 'fustian' referred to overblown, nonsensical or near-nonsensical rhetoric. On these textile metaphors and nonsense, see Malcolm, *Origins*, pp. 30–51.
19. Benjamin Rudyerd, *Le prince d'amour* (London: Printed for William Leake, 1660), Wing R2189, pp. 37–40. Manuscript sources include Bodleian Library MS Malone 16, pp. 74–5; Huntington Library MS HM 1338, fos. 146r-v.rev; BL MS Add. 25303, fos. 184v–185v; and Folger Shakespeare Library MS V.a.162, fos. 68r–69r.
20. BL MS Add. 25303, fo. 184v–185r. 'Tak[ing] tobacco' possibly alludes to Sir Walter Raleigh, who made tobacco fashionable in England and 'may have been present at the revels' (Roberts, 'Comparative Nonsense', p. 111).
21. BL MS Add. 25303, fo. 184v. On the nonsensicality of this text see Malcolm, *Origins*, pp. 9–11; and Roberts, 'Comparative Nonsense', pp. 111–13.
22. [Francis Bacon?], *Gesta Grayorum* (London: Printed for W. Canning, 1689), Wing C444, p. 22.
23. Ben Jonson, *The Workes of Benjamin Jonson* (Imprinted at London by Will Stansby, 1616), STC 14751, sig. G3r.
24. Helen Ostovich, ed, 'Introduction' to *Every Man Out of His Humour* (New York: Manchester University Press [Revels], 2001), p. 32. Unless otherwise noted, subsequent citations to *EMO* are to this edition and will appear in text.
25. Ibid. p. 28.
26. Ostovich likewise cites Clove's fustian talk as a 'tribute to Hoskyns's manipulation of rhetorical sound over substance of argument', but characterises both examples as 'satirical description[s] of law students' rather than positioning them within a larger history of nonsense games ('Introduction', p. 35). Yet Clove's language reflects other examples of nonsense from the period, as well, which suggests it is connected to a larger nonsense tradition. Taylor's *Sir Gregory Nonsence* (1622), for example, adopts a similar vocabulary and tone: 'With nine butter Firkins in a flame, | Did coldly rise to Arbitrate the cause: | Guessing by the Sinderesis of wapping' (sig. A6v).
27. Taylor, *Sir Gregory Nonsence*, title page.
28. John Manningham, *Diary*, quoted in *Twelfth Night*, ed. Donno, p. 1.
29. Taylor, *Jack a Lent*, sig. C4v
30. Scholars who brush off Feste's language here as mere 'mock-learning' include but are not limited to Maurice Charney, *Shakespeare's Style* (Madison, NJ: Fairleigh Dickinson University Press, 2014), p. 89; Donno, editorial notes to *Twelfth Night*, II. 2. 20–1; and Gustav Ungerer, 'The Equinoctial of Queubus', *Shakespeare Studies* 19 (1987), 101–10. Ungerer makes a valiant but ultimately inconclusive effort to 'unravel[. . .]the meanings' of Feste's so-called 'mock learning', despite acknowledging that it is 'unintelligible' (p. 101) and 'reminiscent of the traditional nonsense talk' (p. 102).
31. For further discussion of professional fools and clowns in this period, see (among others) Richard Preiss, *Clowning and Authorship in Early Modern Theatre* (New York: Cambridge University Press, 2014); Robert Bell, *Shakespeare's Great Stage of Fools* (New York: Palgrave MacMillan, 2011); and David Wiles, *Shakespeare's Clown: Actor and Text in the Elizabethan Playhouse* (Cambridge University Press, 1987).
32. Donno, editorial notes to II. 3. 23.

33. The *OED* gives two definitions for 'myrmidon *n.*': '1. Usu. in form Myrmidon [. . .] with reference to the Homeric story: a member of a warlike people inhabiting ancient Thessaly, whom Achilles led to the siege of Troy'; and '2. A member of a bodyguard or retinue; a faithful follower; one of a group or team of attendants, servants, or assistants.'
34. This poem appears in the vast prefatory apparatus to Thomas Coryate, *Coryats Crudities* (London: Printed by W[illiam] S[tansby for the author], 1611), STC 5808, sig. e6r.
35. See Stephen Booth, *Precious Nonsense: The Gettysburg Address, Ben Jonson's Epitaphs on His Children, and* Twelfth Night (Berkeley: University of California Press, 1998), esp. pp. 122–213; and Zucker, 'Philology of Nonsense', *passim*. Zucker does delve into a brief editorial history of one of these nonsense moments: 'What, wench, *Castiliano vulgo*' (I. 3. 41–2). This phrase, Zucker observes, is 'entirely nonsensical': 'Nobody, and I mean nobody, has ever been able to figure out precisely what "Castiliano vulgo" means, or even, for that matter, what language Toby is speaking when he says it', though Shakespeareans have 'done their best to explicate the phrase'. Zucker shows that despite the efforts of these 'explicators', asking what the phrase means is simply the wrong question: 'In some very simple, ordinary sense, the exact translation of these words is entirely irrelevant for the action of *Twelfth Night*, and especially in performance. They serve their point simply in their explosive, meaningful noise' (pp. 90–1). On other misplaced editorial tendencies to impose meaning on moments of Shakespearean unintelligibility, see Stephen Orgel, 'The Poetics of Incomprehensibility', *Shakespeare Quarterly* 42.4 (1991), 431–7.
36. For a survey of critics who have attempted to solve Maria's fustian riddle over the decades, see Peter J. Smith, 'M.O.A.I. "What should that alphabetical position portend?": An Answer to the Metaphoric Malvolio', *Renaissance Quarterly* 51.4 (1998), 1199–1224. By contrast, Lewis, '"A Fustian Riddle?"' does argue that the riddle is meant to be uninterpretable; whereas Catherine Belsey argues that the letter is emblematic of the play's broad interest in the 'riddle' of gender ('*Twelfth Night* and the Riddle of Gender', in *Why Shakespeare?* (Baskingstroke: Palgrave Macmillan, 2007), 129–48). I am most aligned with Adam Zucker, who forcefully argues that the fustian riddle 'is a radioactive version of nonsense, or even anti-sense: it dashes into jumbled bits all reasonable discourse', and observes that Malvolio's 'triumphant close reading [. . .] should send fear into the heart of every [literary] critic' ('Philology of Nonsense', p. 98); as well as Elizabeth Freund, for whom Maria's fustian letter is a 'booby trap' that prompts interpreters to 'dig[their] own hermeneutic grave[s]' ('*Twelfth Night* and the Tyranny of Interpretation', *ELH* 53.3 (1986), 471–89, p. 481).
37. See Bloom, *Gaming the Stage*, on the bonding function of games (p. 15).
38. Freund, '*Twelfth Night* and the Tyranny of Interpretation', p. 481.

3

Nonsense in the Age of Reason

Freya Johnston

The Irish writer and lawyer Matthew Concanen made a strictly no-nonsense claim about the spirit of 1725: 'we live in an Age where Sense, good Sense, and Nothing but Sense is required, and nothing else will be received'.[1] Concanen may not have been the best authority on the subject – he went on to attack Alexander Pope's *Peri Bathous, or the Art of Sinking in Poetry* (1727) and earned himself a place in *The Dunciad* (1728–43) as 'True to the bottom [. . .] | A cold, long-winded, native of the deep!' – but his view of the age turned out to be persistent.[2] 'The eighteenth century was, perhaps, all over Europe, the period when Nonsense was least appreciated', wrote Emile Cammaerts, discouragingly, almost one hundred years ago, 'no doubt because Wit was so much in the fashion. For Wit and Nonsense are arch-enemies.'[3] It is true that many authors of the period defined wit and nonsense as opposing impulses; but this does not mean that nonsense failed to thrive.[4]

Before the 1720s, nobody had felt that something best summarised as nonsense had gained enough purchase on the collective imagination to warrant a 'Dissertation' embracing its 'critical History, Philosophy, and singular Use [. . .] in all Articles and Professions of human Life' (another 'Dissertation upon Nonsense', consciously reviving the Scriblerian atmosphere of the 1720s, appeared sixty-five years later).[5] Glossing nonsense as the negation of truth, John 'Orator' Henley also registered its variety and fertility, central characteristics of what eighteenth-century writers meant when they identified anything as nonsensical. That said, as a personified Nonsense tells one votary in 1760, 'In me, whate'er by nature is disjoin'd, | All opposite extremes involved you find';[6] in other words, fertility in this perpetually shifting terrain also necessarily evokes its opposite number, the absolute dead end:

> Truth is one and the same, but the Sense of it in the Understandings of Persons is different; and there are certain Causes of that Difference; Diversity in the Brain, Blood and Spirits; in Education, Climate, Custom, Habit, Passion, Accidents, the Air and Elements, any Turn, or Circumstance of Life. These, or any of them, will produce a various Impression of the same Thing, not only in several, but in the same Persons. Hence it is that *Nonsense* is so very copious; for what is at a certain Time, or Place, Sense to one, is frequently *Nonsense* to another, and to himself also in another Place, or at another Juncture.[7]

Even if the aim of his oration is parodic, Henley also recognises with an entirely straight face that truth will always vary in how it is received and interpreted by different human beings. A further implication of his argument is that those people – any people – cannot but change many times in the course of their lives. In so doing, they may cease with alarming rapidity to make sense of themselves to themselves, let alone to each other. Education is despatched as a piece of nonsense, or as one major cause of it, in the 'Dissertation'. But that claim is itself quickly turned into a potentially subtler consideration of the various ways in which everyone learns about the world. Such differences are bound to produce a range of responses to the same thing within a group of different individuals at any one time, and indeed within the same person across time.

An internalised, individuated conception of nonsense develops in the course of the eighteenth century alongside the persistence of an older, learned and mock-learned genre of (sometimes apocalyptic) paradox: light is dark, night is day, legless men run, the sleeping are awake, the dead are the living, and so on. One example of this older strain's continuing influence is John Dunton's 'Asserting Rational Nonsense' (1707), a sonnet that appears to tire of its own oxymorons when the first-person voice enters. It is as if the cack-handed attempt at scholarly wit then palls, the author registering instead, at some level, the emergence of a new kind of nonsense – one that has more to do with lapses in perception and self-recognition than with a parade of classical lumber:

O monstrous, hideous Troops of Dromedaries,
How Bears and Bulls from Monks and Goblins varies!
Nay would not *Charon* yield to *Cerberus*,
But catch'd the Dog, and cut his Head off thus:
Pluto enrag'd, and *Juno* pleas'd with Ire,
Sought all about, but could not find the Fire:
But being found, well pleas'd, and in a spite
They slept at *Acharon*, and wak'd all Night:
Where I let pass to tell their mad Bravadoes,
Their Meat was tosted Cheese and Carbonadoes.
Thousands of Monsters more besides there be
Which I, fast hoodwink'd, at that time did see;
    And in a word, to shut up this Discourse,
    A Scholar's Whip is good to spur a Horse.[8]

Dunton is no medieval dreamer awaking from a vision, although his lines build on that tradition; rather, he poses as one allowing himself to entertain the coexistence of mutually exclusive states (this possibility is itself phrased as a paradox, the 'hoodwink'd' or blind man who 'at that time did see'). The whole piece exemplifies a mode of being at odds with reality; within that frame, as a paradoxical catalogue, it plays with individual creatures or items that are additionally at variance with one another. 'Bears and Bulls' clearly belong together: both are animals, each also starts with the letter 'b' ('bull' having the additional, highly pertinent meaning of 'A self-contradictory proposition; [. . .] an expression containing a manifest contradiction in terms or involving a ludicrous inconsistency unperceived by the speaker').[9] They vary, then, as a couple, from 'Monks and Goblins', but the extra joke intended here is that we might not think that 'Monks and Goblins' are natural bedfellows. A monk, after all, is human; a goblin is not. Dunton expects us to do a slight double take at this, and then to accept the joke that here we *are* in fact looking at a couple just as like one another as bears and bulls are – that is, if we accept that monks and goblins are both embodiments of superstition. Catholicism, in other words, is of the same order of reality as folklore, and neither monks nor goblins are to be trusted (boom boom). Spelling it out like this makes a tiresome piece of doggerel all the more tiresome, but that is the nature of such overstretched humour; the point is that even a nonsense poem as rough and ready as Dunton's toys with sameness and difference, and with the ways in which they may change places. 'Asserting Rational Nonsense' therefore has a kinship with Henley's formally very different 'Dissertation' in that both of them acknowledge and rehearse 'a various Impression of the same Thing'.

The fearful intimation that we may temporarily or permanently cease to sympathise with or even comprehend our own minds – that we may harbour seemingly mutually exclusive versions of ourselves within ourselves – is woven into the fabric of John Locke's *Essay concerning Human Understanding* (1689), as it is into Adam Smith's *Theory of Moral Sentiments* (1759). This is partly down to the proliferating meanings of and implications arising from the capacious term 'sense', an object (as Concanen implies) of close philosophical and literary enquiry from the late seventeenth century onwards. Like sense, its sometime mirror image, nonsense fosters self-division and faction – internal and external varieties of more or less fruitful strife. Nonsense gives birth to further nonsense, and fast; it is ruinously attractive, and not only because its productions – as *The Dunciad* is at pains to stress – are so often abortive. 'It hath been observed', George Campbell noted, 'that in madmen there is as great a variety of character, as in those who enjoy the use of their reason. In like manner, it may be said of nonsense, that, in writing it, there is as great scope for variety of style, as there is in writing sense.' The collocation of insanity with nonsense ('In like manner') does not quite amount to a warning, but nor is it exactly an invitation to authors to revel in such siren-like variety.[10] Many eighteenth-century readers of Pope recognised that the most nonsensical result of *The Dunciad*, a poem contrived to wipe out its mediocre targets, was that it spotlighted and ended up preserving the variegated landscape of nonentity that it had set out to destroy. Without Pope's help, the dunces' names would not have survived.

One key property of eighteenth-century nonsense writing is the startling, life-giving and death-dealing action of making inert language, or what is often termed 'cant', appear to be 'sensible' again, as if a skeleton had suddenly been made to dance – but with the sole intention of finishing it off properly this time, once and for all.[11] Henry Fielding's 'modern Glossary' (1752), a lexicographical sample of fashionable language includes (for instance) 'COXCOMB. A Word of Reproach, and yet, at the same Time, signifying all that is most commendable.'[12] This definition, like that of many words in the glossary, has a double character shared with that of nonsense itself, which, as Henley says, is 'the contrary to what is right, just, or proper in Things themselves, and yet is often embrac'd and advanc'd as right, just and proper'.[13] Fielding also includes in his list the narrower definition of 'nonsense', as parried about by the beau monde. It is the repudiation of ancient sense: 'NONSENSE. Philosophy, especially the Philosophical Writings of the Antients, and more especially of Aristotle.' Alongside that narrowing of the horizons of nonsense is another kind of talk that should mean more than, or something very different from, what it does, and in which diametrically and vitally opposing qualities are collapsed into the same thing; namely, chatter: 'VIRTUE. / VICE. } Subjects of Discourse'.[14]

Arthur Lovejoy argued in 1924 that once a word has come to indicate one thing and its opposite at the same time, as well as a number of things in between, it has essentially lost its meaning: 'The result is a confusion of terms, and of ideas [. . .] The word "romantic" has come to mean so many things that, by itself, it means nothing.

It has ceased to perform the function of a verbal sign.'[15] But this cannot be quite right, or we would have long ago ceased to find everyday use for words that play host to one meaning and its mirror image, and which seemingly thrive on self-division. Such words, known as contronyms or antagonyms, have often to do (as in the cases of 'let' or 'sanction') with the dividing line between the permitted and the not permitted, where there is sometimes great advantage to being in two diametrically opposed minds at once. One step on from that, these words may embody the experience of being in two minds, and even be in two minds about that (the word 'cleave', for instance, means either being divided from or united with someone or something). Contronyms and antagonyms might have been particularly useful in an age that was exercised by taxonomies – by putting things in their places, and consequently by a sense of whatever could not or should not be put in its place, or would have to be left out of the best-made list. Still, what Lovejoy proceeded to argue about how to approach a term such as 'Romanticism' applies equally plausibly to 'nonsense'. The only coherent method of analysis, in both cases, involves attention to individual 'strains' rather than to a single entity:

> A belief in progress and a spirit of reaction were, paradoxically, twin offspring of the same idea, and were nurtured for a time in the same minds. But it is just these internal incongruities which make it most of all evident [. . .] that any attempt at a general appraisal even of a single chronologically determinate Romanticism – still more, of 'Romanticism' as a whole – is a fatuity. When a Romanticism has been analyzed into the distinct 'strains' or ideas which compose it, the true philosophic affinities and the eventual practical influence in life and art of these several strains will usually be found to be exceedingly diverse and often conflicting. [. . .] What will [. . .] appear historically significant and philosophically instructive will be the way in which each of these distinguishable strains has worked itself out, what its elective affinities for other ideas, and its historic consequences, have shown themselves to be.[16]

One obvious place in which to locate and separate a few of the rival strains of nonsense is Samuel Johnson's *Dictionary of the English Language* (1755), the work of a man who once aspired to write a poem called 'The Palace of Nonsence a Vision'. Going by its definitions in the *Dictionary*, nonsense by the mid-eighteenth century was licensed to negate only a very limited kind of sense. In particular, it could make no inroads on the 'sense' that is synonymous with 'reason'. Johnson confines nonsense to 'Unmeaning or ungrammatical language' and 'Trifles; things of no importance'. Yet the examples he cites in support of those definitions (from Samuel Butler, John Dryden, Alexander Pope and James Thomson) suggest a more unruly and invasive beast, with the potential both to create and to destroy. Nonsense is further associated, in the first group of his citations, with questionable literature: tales that are neither true nor false (Butler); works that do not sell (Dryden); and editions that misrepresent their authors (Pope).[17] That last variety of nonsense also governs some lines by Pope's shady co-conspirator on *The Dunciad*, Richard Savage, in *Fulvia. A Poem* (1737):

> She tells my story, and repeats my wit.
> With mouth distorted, thro' a sounding nose
> It comes, now homeliness more homely grows.

With see-saw sounds and nonsense not my own,
She skrews her features, and she cracks her tone.[18]

Fulvia's brand of nonsense entails accidentally or deliberately misrepresenting another person, especially a writer; indeed, the verb 'To nonsense', in use since at least the late seventeenth century, seems mostly to have applied to the havoc wreaked on one writer's words by another.[19] In the age of the scholarly variorum, 'How easy it is', as Pope observed in a letter of 1711, 'to any one to give [. . .] a new nonsense, to what the author intended.'[20] The labour and self-regard of editors and learned commentators – and the whole combative business of their discerning in such works 'what the author intended' – triggered a lengthy counter-blast of mock-scholarship from the Scriblerians, whose own intentions were far from stable or transparent and therefore easy to countermand and misrepresent. For all his attacks on Grub Street and professional editors, Pope delighted in their productions; they always unleashed his creative energies. Eighteenth-century tales of tubs, cock-and-bull stories, farragoes, and hodge-podges have a generic association with nonsense, a quality associated in this period not so much with the absence of rationality as with an affront to property, subordination and decorum – an affront which may, admittedly, make an author go mad in the end. Nonsense is understood to lay siege to the coherence and integrity of a literary work, as to the stylistic and moral cohesiveness of its originator, and it may well annihilate a writer in the process.

Pope's dunces are traced in their mock-epic poem from early efforts in 'new-born Nonsense' to their mature involvements in confusion, theft, vice and decay.[21] In the *Epistle to Arbuthnot* (1734), Pope depicts a dunce as one 'who now to sense, now nonsense, leaning, | Means not, but blunders round about a meaning'.[22] Johnson's definition of nonsense as 'Unmeaning or ungrammatical language' is here anticipated as a kind of insult to the necessary demarcation of sense from its opponents. Pope flirts with what it might feel like to mean nothing at all, to have no real purpose or intention, no loyalty to or affiliation with one side or another; in doing so, he is also flirting with the idea of his own lack of commitment to a cause. The tidy parcel of a closed heroic couplet seems both offended and enlivened by the refusal of a dunce to identify himself with any one side or party. To 'blunder round about' something might involve an escape from responsibility; it is a liberation from the confines of adulthood, perhaps, as well as a missed opportunity to belong somewhere you would want to be, and to make sense.

Nonsense is bound up with children in this period (as it more obviously is in the nineteenth century), but without exhibiting any obvious interest in children themselves. Rather, eighteenth-century nonsense as we might follow it from (say) Alexander Pope to Laurence Sterne keeps children in view primarily in terms of botched succession. It must be partly down to the influence of *The Life and Opinions of Tristram Shandy, Gentleman* (1759–67) that it became quite popular to characterise nonsense as a family with its own history and genealogy.[23] But just as most characters in the nineteenth-century card game Happy Families look gruesome and miserable, this is no merry nonsensical clan. Offspring in eighteenth-century nonsense writing tend to be invoked in relation to a line gone wrong, or fertility displayed to no avail – perhaps in some early instances alluding to Queen Anne, who endured seventeen pregnancies but died without surviving issue. Pope's dunces produce multiple, short-lived, incomplete and abortive works, while Tristram Shandy has a vivid sense of himself as an impotent, ailing family memorialist, the final member of his tribe. Forms of generation and intergeneration are frequently made, in this context, to issue only death, or if not death then an offensive or sickening sort of hybridity:

> Round him much Embryo, much Abortion lay,
> Much future Ode, and abdicated Play;
> Nonsense precipitate, like running Lead,
> That slip'd thro' Cracks and Zig-zags of the Head;
> All that on Folly Frenzy could beget,
> Fruits of dull Heat, and Sooterkins of wit.[24]

'Sooterkins', Johnson's *Dictionary* tells us, citing Pope's friend Swift, are 'A kind of false birth fabled to be produced by the Dutch women from sitting over their stoves' (Swift's image was striking enough for Lord Chesterfield to recall it in a letter of 1749 to his son, touching on the effects of fumigation versus inspiration).[25] Cibber's diseased, womb-like brain is sexually overheated and hyper-productive; playing host to the coupling of Folly and Frenzy yields only a gaggle of deviant and thwarted literary children. (He is something of a male counterpart to Mary Toft and her claim in 1726 to have given birth to a deformed animal whose heart and lungs grew outside its body, thence to a rapid succession of dead rabbits.)[26] Pope's reference, in this context, to 'abdicated Play' is oddly sad, as if he has in mind not only disinherited dramas but also infant games that had to be abandoned or could never hope to thrive. The depiction of Cibber's works suggests, too, the fitness of the miscellany as an eighteenth-century repository of nonsense, a ragbag of the mixed-up and the indecorous. Miscellanies could, after all, be the work of one author as well as of several, their jumbled variousness applying to a single individual's range of complete and incomplete productions across a more or less coherent lifetime as well as to a publication by various hands.[27]

David Hume sounded a cautionary note to anyone trying to pin down nonsense in the eighteenth century, asking Hugh Blair in 1761 'Does a man of sense run after every silly tale of hobgoblins or fairies, and canvass particularly the evidence? I never knew anyone, that examined and deliberated about nonsense who did not believe it before the end of his enquiries.'[28] A 'man of sense' might be tempted to differentiate himself as starkly as possible from nonsense, but the endeavour to do so is ill advised. The pursuit of evidence 'particularly' for nonsense – which here, as often in the eighteenth century, is equivalent to the kind of superstition on show in Dunton's 'Monks and Goblins' – risks fostering a belief in, even a love of, what you are pursuing. Running after nonsense, as Shakespeare was said by Johnson to chase quibbles – only for Johnson to be accused of demeaning himself by attending so closely to Shakespeare's littleness – makes a nonsense of the pursuer.[29] The assertion of disparity results, nonsensically, in the opposite of what it set out to achieve: a sense of equality and a consequent affront to hierarchy (as is generically the case in mock-epic, with its alternate efforts to prise apart and to equalise the high and the low).

* * *

Around 1760, William Cowper assumed the voice of an owl called Madge. Addressing 'a bird of paradise' and fellow member of the 'Nonsense Club' – a group of seven

Westminster men who dined together every Thursday – Madge admitted to some distress. Being short of her usual ink, she says,

> I am forced to dip my beak in the blood of a mouse, which I have just caught; and it is so very savoury, that I think in my heart I swallow more than I expend in writing. A monkey who lately arrived in these parts, is teaching me and my eldest daughter to dance. The motion was a little uneasy to us at first, as he taught us to stretch our wings wide, and to turn out our toes; but it is easier now. I, in particular, am a tolerable proficient in a horn-pipe, and can foot it very nimbly with a switch tucked under my left wing, considering my years and infirmities. [. . .] We have had a miserable dry season, and my ivy-bush is sadly out of repair. I shall be obliged to you if you will favour me with a shower or two, which you can easily do, by driving a few clouds together over the wood, and beating them about with your wings till they fall to pieces.[30]

Many ingredients in this letter anticipate Edward Lear's better-known recipes for nonsense: Cowper rustles up his bird in order to express some human quirks and anxieties and to suggest, in lightly agonised terms, the pains of art ('True Ease in Writing comes from Art, not Chance, | As those move easiest who have learn'd to dance').[31] This night owl, like many of Lear's characters, is a melancholy creature who frets about ingestion and expenditure and who seeks consolation and companionship. Both writers mingle, in the shape of a bird, a certain predatory quality with solicitude, discomfort and valetudinarianism. Perhaps the most striking difference between the two men is that Cowper's nonsense, unlike Lear's, appears to be code that a small group of initiates will readily understand. In his 'Defence of Nonsense', G. K. Chesterton inclined to think 'that no age except our own could have understood that the Quangle-Wangle meant absolutely nothing, and the Lands of the Jumblies were absolutely nowhere'.[32] The recipient of Cowper's nonsense, on the other hand, would most likely have been able to convert much of it directly into sense. Lance Bertelsen points out that Madge (a name meaning 'barn owl') invokes a bush, the sign of a tavern;[33] Charles Ryskamp tells us that 'to look like an owl in an ivy-bush' was a proverbial phrase for appearing ridiculous (which perhaps sheds some light on the opening lines of Thomas Gray's *Elegy Written in a Country Churchyard* (1751)).[34] Nineteenth-century nonsense, in Chesterton's reading, was not like this, because it entailed the sheer absence of symbolism:

> It is true in a certain sense that some of the greatest writers the world has seen – Aristophanes, Rabelais and Sterne – have written nonsense; but unless we are mistaken, it is in a widely different sense. The nonsense of these men was satiric – that is to say, symbolic; it was a kind of exuberant capering round a discovered truth. There is all the difference in the world between the instinct of satire, which, seeing in the Kaiser's moustaches something typical of him, draws them continually larger and larger; and the instinct of nonsense which, for no reason whatever, imagines what those moustaches would look like on the present Archbishop of Canterbury if he grew them in a fit of absence of mind. [. . .] We fancy that if the account of the knave's trial in *Alice in Wonderland* had been published in the seventeenth century it would have been bracketed with Bunyan's *Trial of the Faithful* as a parody on the State prosecutions of the time. We fancy that if *The Dong with the Luminous*

> *Nose* had appeared in the same period everyone would have called it a dull satire on Oliver Cromwell.[35]

Eighteenth-century nonsense is really, in this reading of it, a form of satire; as in Cowper's letter, it means or stands for something. It is not-sense only in that it serves so clearly as the flipside of sense, pointing (as in older topsy-turvy or paradoxical or world-upside-down varieties of nonsense) directly to 'A discovered truth' that is its opposite. Chesterton's 'discovered' hovers between a truth that has been uncovered to the world (as if on a stage) and a truth that has been found out by the inquirer (as if on a quest). That double sense of 'discovery' flourishes in the eighteenth century, perhaps, because writers and readers of the period needed to move between impersonal and personal senses of revelation, perhaps also to fudge or skate over the matter of how reason relates to religion. Or, broadly speaking, this may have been a period in which it suited many people to remain in two minds (officially or unofficially) about whether the world yields up its own truths or requires of us that we hunt them out.

We might read Cowper's letter as nothing more or less nonsensical than a modestly pitched plea from one friend to another to go out for a drink. But you would have to notice alongside that potentially straightforward request the odd concern about swallowing; why does Cowper have Madge compose her letter in the blood of a mouse she has just killed and wants to eat, and therefore in some way set his own capacity to survive against his capacity to write? The owl is consuming the means by which she might otherwise be nourished in the longer run – ink – if it could indeed be shown that anyone might live by their pen. The fact that Madge thinks about this 'in my heart' shows that it is not just an idle concern, or indeed only a thought. A heartfelt desire for literary independence (as well as the desire to buck against prudence and convention) was, as Bertelsen demonstrates, the *raison d'être* of the Nonsense Club. During the early 1760s, the period in which Cowper impersonated Madge, he was facing the prospect of working in some sort of public office – a prospect that made him feel 'like a man borne away by a rapid torrent into a stormy sea from which he sees no possibility of returning, and where he knows he cannot subsist'.[36] Although he was already trying to console himself by tracing the semblance of his misery in another's case, Cowper's eventual response was to attempt suicide, a course of action which certainly secured his permanent escape from a conventional career, as indeed from marriage, and which might itself be classed as nonsensical. In 1774, William Kenrick described two other members of the Nonsense Club, the poets Charles Churchill and Robert Lloyd, as possessing a 'suicide genius' – by which he partly meant their wish to exempt themselves from the common fate of humanity.[37]

'Suicide genius' overlaps with 'the genius of nonsense', as it is hailed in a musical extravaganza of that name towards the end of the century, produced by another member of the club.[38] Cowper's retirement from the world into a routine of therapeutic composition, reading and gardening could be classed as a form of 'suicide genius', too. In 1764, Charles Careless had this to say on the subject of retirement, in an introductory piece of 'SERIOUS NONSENSE':

> your Hermits and Misanthropes may pride themselves in their erroneous notions of things, and in endeavouring to make the world believe that peace and happiness are only to be found in a retreat from it; yet their own examples, and their own

> histories, are sufficient to invalidate their assertions. For if we attentively contemplate their behavior, and minutely scrutinise into the secret springs of actions, we shall find, that none of them ever secluded themselves from the chearful face of society, till pushed by despair. But how odious, and how contemptible, is such a conduct! Suicide itself is scarcely more criminal.--------As suicide proceeds from the very height of cowardice, a fear of braving the dangers of life; so a seclusion from the community, arises from the same cause, and is, in effect, the same thing. For, regardless of the ends for which he was sent into the world, and removing himself from the station his great Creator had placed him in, he counter-acts and disobeys his orders; and, ceasing to be a member of society, commits a kind of self-slaughter.[39]

To be nonsensical could thus entail either voluntarily or involuntarily not being in your senses or right mind, whether through drink or the rejection of custom or convention. It might mean the wish no longer to live, or the pursuit of an existence unrecognised by most people as worthy of the name (as in *The Tatler*'s prosecution of those it dubbed 'Metaphorically Defunct').[40] The association of nonsense with death, or with the not-living – people who in the judgement of others do not deserve to be alive, or those who wish to be dead, or those whose animation we are unable to gauge – has a vibrant comic history. To lack sense (that is, to be without physical motion or feeling) is one way of describing someone who is no longer alive; a dead person might therefore reasonably be classified as non-sensical, and good jokes can spring from that. When Jonathan Swift launched his attack on the astronomer and almanac-maker John Partridge he insisted, very effectively, that his antagonist was dead. Partridge protested, naturally enough, that he wasn't; Swift's proof that, on the contrary, he must be arose from the fact that it was commonly said that '*no Man* alive *ever writ such damned Stuff*' as Partridge apparently had. So if Partridge had indeed produced his own works, he was not alive; therefore he was a dead man, a piece of nonsense. It was a stroke of genius on Swift's part to animate that cliché or dead metaphor (as Donald Davie or Christopher Ricks might describe it, the deadness in this case being that of a flogged horse) about '*no Man* alive [. . .]' by yoking it, irretrievably, to authorship, and in so doing to annihilate his opponent's life in print.[41]

Much that is summarised and dismissed as nonsense in the eighteenth century is religious enthusiasm, as for instance in *Fanatic Blunders faithfully collected from their books, sermons, and prayers; containing a Gallimaufry of enthusiastic zeal, farce and nonsense.*[42] This text was originally printed in 1710, but reappeared in an enlarged version in 1789, clearly because it was thought to have renewed purchase in the year of the French Revolution. The secular version of such nonsense is singularity, or the affectation of it, always one of Johnson's chief targets and the reason for his dismissing *Tristram Shandy* as a merely 'odd' book that seemingly 'did not last'.[43] Nonsense is also a form of unripeness, an unproven claim whose truth or untruth cannot yet be determined. It is a childish thing because it has not yet been in the world long enough for us to know what it is or how to value it. Burke invokes the word in that sense in his *Reflections on the Revolution in France* (1790), referring to the spurious notion that British kings are somehow elected by popular vote as a 'doctrine' which may well be 'nonsense, and therefore neither true nor false'.[44] George Campbell had made a similar suggestion in 1776, arguing that it is 'justly allowed to be the best criterion of nonsense' that it will 'contain nothing, but either an identical proposition, which conveys no knowledge, or a proposition of that kind, of which one cannot so much affirm, that it is either true or false'.[45] If nonsense describes something that is (as yet) neither true nor false, then it must also be in some way synonymous with literature itself, which in Philip Sidney's celebrated formulation neither affirms nor denies anything; as Samuel Butler writes in the third part of *Hudibras*, 'till th' are understood all Tales | (Like Nonsense) are nor *True*, nor *False*'.[46] Nonsense might therefore be construed as a claim that is waiting to be tested and comprehended before it can be classified as truth or falsehood, like a child waiting (perhaps in vain) to reach maturity, or like a savage or primitive society that has yet to become civilised.[47]

Fictions of the monstrous and unnatural kind bulk as large in Burke's *Reflections* as they do in Pope's *Dunciad*, both writers being concerned with affronts to and disruptions of ancient customs and privileges, succession, and subordination. When Burke reviewed the first two volumes of *Tristram Shandy* in the *Annual Register* for 1760, he nicely captured Sterne's combination of up-to-the-minuteness with concern for the past, praising the work as 'so happy an attempt at *novelty*' and calling the 'principal figure' of the fiction '*old* Shandy' – presumably intending Walter Shandy to be understood as a sort of Old Hamlet. Burke's identification of the old alongside the new is related to what he meant in the same review when he brilliantly described *Tristram Shandy* as 'a perpetual series of disappointments'.[48] It is not only pleasure but continuity and succession that are repeatedly broken off in Sterne's narrative – although this lack of fruition went on to be tempered, perhaps even countered, by the serial or successive form in which the book appeared. Over the course of its seven-year series of appearances, it was repeatedly a brand new thing as well as a continuation of what had gone before. Burke noted the 'little regard to any connexion' evinced by Sterne, and this absence of 'connexion' would have disturbed a writer for whom, as Seamus Perry notes, 'nothing is more important to his thinking'.[49] To someone so compelled by the intricate joined-up-ness of human life, relationships, writing and politics, the absence or disruption of such connexion was interesting, even alluring, as well as a fearful prospect:

> It must be observed that the cessation of pleasure affects the mind three ways. If it simply ceases, after having continued a proper time, the effect is *indifference;* if it be abruptly broken off, there ensues an uneasy sense called *disappointment;* if the object be so totally lost that there is no chance of enjoying it again, a passion arises in the mind, which is called *grief.*[50]

Decades after he wrote these lines, Burke lost his own son and heir. 'Had it pleased God to continue to me the hopes of succession', as he wrote with sad dignity in *A Letter to a Noble Lord* (1796), 'I should have been, according to my mediocrity, and the mediocrity of the age I live in, a sort of founder of a family.'[51]

Those same hopes of succession manifested themselves in the eighteenth-century 'genius of nonsense', as it is hailed in a musical confection of that name – 'original, whimsical, operatical, pantomimical, farcical, electrical, naval, military, temporary, local'. The origins of this work lie with the quack doctor James Graham, who promised relief from sterility to those who hired his 'celestial bed', a contraption 'supported by forty pillars of brilliant glass of the most exquisite workmanship' and engraved with the legend, 'Be fruitful, multiply and replenish the earth.' Graham had his bed linked up to magnets and electrical machines and charged £50 a night for the privilege of using it. The temple in which it lay drew large audiences, ladies visiting 'incog'. Horace Walpole, having pranced along with the crowd, remarked on 23 August 1780 that Graham's was 'the most impudent puppet-show of imposition I ever saw, and the mountebank himself the dullest of his profession, except that he makes the spectators pay a crown apiece'.[52] And so Graham became a celebrity, while on 2 September 1780 George Colman the elder produced at the Haymarket Theatre his *Genius of Nonsense*, in which John Bannister appeared as Emperor of the Quacks. The farce had received twenty-two performances by July 1781, suggesting that nonsense will always find people to appreciate it, even in an age of remorseless good sense.

Notes

1. Matthew Concanen, 'Of modern poetry', in *The Speculatist. A Collection of Letters and Essays, Moral and Political, Serious and Humorous: Upon Various Subjects* (London: J. Watts, 1730), 37–41, p. 41.
2. Alexander Pope, *The Dunciad*, II. 299, in *The Twickenham Edition of the Poems of Alexander Pope*, gen. ed. John Butt, 11 vols (London: Methuen & Co.; New Haven: Yale University Press, 1940–69), V: *The Dunciad*, ed. James Sutherland (1943, repr. 1965), p. 137.
3. Emile Cammaerts, *The Poetry of Nonsense* (London: Routledge, 1925), p. 82.
4. Not everyone thought nonsense and wit were mutually exclusive. In one historical-allegorical account, Nonsense is said to be 'a great favourite at court, where she was highly caressed on account of her wit'. '*The history of Nonsense*', in *The Annual Register, or a View of the History, Politics, and Literature, for the Year 1767* (1768), 201–4, p. 202.
5. John Henley, 'A Dissertation Upon Nonsense', in *Oratory Transactions. No. II*, 3rd edn (London: Mrs. Dodd, Mrs. Nutt, Mrs. Turner, Mr. Green and Mrs. Graves, 1729), 5–30, p. 6; 'Dissertation upon Nonsense. Transcribed from the original MSS of Martinus Scriblerus', in *The European Magazine and London Review*, VIII (1786), 175–6.
6. Thomas Blacklock, 'The Genealogy of Nonsense', in *A Collection of Original Poems by Scotch Gentlemen* (Edinburgh: A. Donaldson, 1760), p. 10.
7. Henley, 'A Dissertation Upon Nonsense', pp. 10–11.
8. John Dunton, 'Paradox XIX: Asserting Rational Nonsense', in *Athenian Sport: or, Two Thousand Paradoxes merrily argued, to amuse and divert the age* (London, B. Bragg, 1707), p. 140. On the medieval and Renaissance traditions of nonsense writing and their persistence into later periods, see e.g. Noel Malcolm, *The Origins of English Nonsense* (London: HarperCollins, 1997); Rosalie Colie, *Paradoxia Epidemica: The Renaissance Tradition of Paradox* (Princeton: Princeton University Press, 1966).
9. See 'bull, *n. 4*', sense 2a (*OED*).
10. George Campbell, *The Philosophy of Rhetoric*, 2 vols (London: W. Strahan and T. Cadell; Edinburgh: W. Creech, 1776), II, p. 77.
11. On the definition and properties of 'cant', see e.g. *Boswell's Life of Johnson: together with Boswell's Journal of a Tour to the Hebrides and Johnson's Diary of a Journey into North Wales*, ed. G. B. Hill, rev. and enlarged L. F. Powell, 6 vols (Oxford: Clarendon Press, 1934–50), IV, pp. 220–1 [15 May 1783].
12. Henry Fielding, 'A modern Glossary', in *The Wesleyan Edition of the Works of Henry Fielding*, 15 vols in 16 (Oxford: Clarendon Press, 1967–2011), *The Covent-Garden Journal and A Plan of the Universal Register-Office*, ed. Bertrand A. Goldgar (1988), *The Covent-Garden Journal* 4 (14 January 1752), 33–8, p. 36.

13. Henley, 'A Dissertation Upon Nonsense', pp. 9–10.
14. Fielding, 'A modern Glossary', pp. 37, 38.
15. Arthur O. Lovejoy, 'On the Discrimination of Romanticisms', *PMLA* 39 (1924), 229–53, p. 232.
16. Ibid. pp. 252–3.
17. Samuel Johnson, *A Dictionary of the English Language*, 2 vols (London: W. Strahan, for J. and P. Knapton; T. and T. Longman; C. Hitch and L. Hawes; A. Millar; and R. and J. Dodsley, 1755). On his unrealised 'The Palace of Nonsence a Vision', the last of five titles listed under 'Poetry, and Works of Imagination', see *Samuel Johnson's 'Designs': A Facsimile of the Manuscript, with a New Transcription & an Introductory Essay*, ed. and introd. Paul Tankard (New York: The Johnsonians, 2008), Leaf 16 Recto.
18. Richard Savage, *Fulvia. A Poem*, in *The Works of Richard Savage, Esq. Son of the Earl Rivers. With an Account of the Life and Writings of the Author, by Samuel Johnson, LL.D.*, 2 vols (London: T. Evans, [1775]), II, p. 189.
19. 'To nonsense' (sense 1, *trans.*): 'To make nonsense of; to describe or represent as nonsense' (*OED*, first example 1681).
20. *The Correspondence of Alexander Pope*, ed. George Sherburn, 5 vols (Oxford: Clarendon Press, 1956), I, p. 122 [25 June 1711].
21. Pope, *The Dunciad Variorum* (1729), book i, l. 58, in *The Dunciad*, ed. Sutherland p. 67.
22. Pope, *An Epistle from Mr. Pope, to Dr. Arbuthnot*, ll. 185–6, in *The Twickenham Edition of the Poems of Alexander Pope*, IV: *Imitations of Horace with An Epistle to Dr Arbuthnot and the Epilogue to the Satires*, ed. John Butt (corrected edn, 1961), p. 109 and n. As Butt notes, in the source poem for *Arbuthnot*, Pope's 'Fragment of a Satire', this description of blundering was pegged to one author in particular: Charles Johnson, who wrote a musical farce, *The Cobbler of Preston* (1716).
23. See e.g. '*The history of Nonsense*', pp. 201–4.
24. Pope, *The Dunciad in Four Books* (1742), book i, ll.121–6, in *The Dunciad*, ed. Sutherland, p. 278.
25. Swift includes a '*Sooterkin*' in the poem 'To Doctor Delany, on the Libels Writ Against Him' (1730), l. 118. See Jonathan Swift, *Poetical Works*, ed. Herbert Davis (London: Oxford University Press, 1967), p. 439.
26. On Toft's notorious hoax and its literary implications, see Dennis Todd, *Imagining Monsters: Miscreations of the Self in Eighteenth-Century England* (Chicago and London: University of Chicago Press, 1995).
27. See e.g. the range of ages, experiences and places, as well as of genres, mentioned on the title page of Thomas Chaloner, *The Merriest Poet in Christendom: or, Chaloner's miscellany, being a salve for every sore. By Tho. Chaloner, Gent. during his Residence in the Excise, as also whilst School-Master at New Shoreham, and Little Hampton in Sussex: Containing all his Extempore Flights, Satyrs, Songs, Turns of Fancy and Humours, both in his Minority and since, for upwards of Ten Years past. Publish'd and recommended to the world by Robert Hartley, a sincere Friend to the Author, and an Encourager of Art and Ingenuity* (London: Henry Bulley and George Lee, 1732).
28. David Hume to Hugh Blair [1761], in *The Letters of David Hume*, ed. J. Y. T. Greig, 2 vols (Oxford: Oxford University Press, 1932), I, p. 360.
29. Samuel Johnson, 'Preface to Shakespeare' (1765), in *The Yale Edition of the Works of Samuel Johnson*, 23 vols (New Haven and London: Yale University Press, 1958–2018), VII–VIII: *Johnson on Shakespeare*, ed. Arthur Sherbo and Bertrand H. Bronson (1968), VII, p. 74.
30. *The Letters and Prose Writings of William Cowper*, ed. James King and Charles Ryskamp, 5 vols (Oxford and New York: Clarendon Press and Oxford University Press, 1979–86), I: *Adelphi and Letters 1750–1781* (1979), p. 88.

31. Alexander Pope, *An Essay on Criticism* (1711), ll. 362–3, in *The Twickenham Edition of the Poems of Alexander Pope*, I: *Pastoral Poetry and An Essay on Criticism*, ed. E. Audra and Aubrey Williams (1961), p. 281.
32. G. K. Chesterton, 'A Defence of Nonsense', in *The Defendant* (London: Dent, [1901] 1907), 61–70, p. 65.
33. Lance Bertelsen, *The Nonsense Club: Literature and Popular Culture, 1749–1764* (Oxford: Clarendon Press, 1986), p. 94.
34. Charles Ryskamp, *William Cowper of the Inner Temple, Esq.* (Cambridge: Cambridge University Press, 1959), p. 196. The third stanza of Gray's *Elegy* has an 'ivy-mantled tow'r' and a 'moping owl'.
35. Chesterton, 'Defence', pp. 64–5.
36. William Cowper, *Adelphi: An Account of the Conversion of W. C. Esquire* (written in 1766 or 1767), in *The Letters and Prose Writings of William Cowper*, I, p. 16.
37. *The Poetical Works of Robert Lloyd, A.M. To which is prefixed an account of the life and writings of the author. By W. Kenrick, LL.D.*, 2 vols (London: T. Evans, [1774]), I, p. xxii.
38. [George Colman], *Songs, Duetts, Trios, &c. in The Genius of Nonsense: an original, whimsical, operatical, pantomimical, farcical, electrical, naval, military, temporary, local extravaganza. Performed at the Theatre-Royal in the Hay-Market* (London: T. Cadell, 1780).
39. Charles Careless, *The Amours and Adventures of Charles Careless, Esq.*, 2 vols (London: James Fletcher and Co., 1764), I, p. 5.
40. See e.g. *Tatler* no. 46 (26 July 1709) and no. 118 (10 January 1710), in *The Tatler*, ed. Donald F. Bond, 2 vols (Oxford: Oxford University Press, 1987), I, 326–34, p. 331; II, 200–5, pp. 200–3.
41. See the 'Partridge Papers' in *The Prose Works of Jonathan Swift*, ed. Herbert Davis, 14 vols (Oxford: Basil Blackwell, 1939–68), II: *Bickerstaff Papers and Pamphlets on the Church*, ed. Herbert Davis (1966), 139–65, p. 162.
42. See *OED* 'enthusiasm' sense 3: 'Fancied inspiration; "a vain confidence of divine favour or communication" (Johnson). In 18th c. often in vaguer sense: Ill-regulated or misdirected religious emotion, extravagance of religious speculation.'
43. *Boswell's Life of Johnson*, II, p. 449 [20 March 1776].
44. Edmund Burke, *Reflections on the Revolution in France*, ed. L. G. Mitchell (Oxford: Oxford University Press, [1790] 2009), p. 14.
45. *The Philosophy of Rhetoric*, II, p. 76.
46. *Hudibras the Third Part*, canto i, ll. 237–8 (slightly misquoted in Johnson's *Dictionary* under 'NONSENSE'), in Samuel Butler, *Hudibras*, ed. John Wilders (Oxford: Oxford University Press, 1967), p. 198.
47. See the discussion of 'nonsense' in relation to 'savage life' and the arguments put forward in its favour by Rousseau and Lord Monboddo in *Boswell's Life of Samuel Johnson*, II, pp. 73–5 [30 September 1769].
48. [Edmund Burke], *The Annual Register, or a View of the History, Politics, and Literature, for the Year 1760* (1761), '*Life and Opinions of* Tristram Shandy, *&c.* Dodsley, Pall-mall, *octavo*', 247–9, p. 247 (my emphases).
49. Seamus Perry, 'Complex to the Core', *Times Literary Supplement*, 24 October 2014, 3–5, p. 3.
50. Edmund Burke, *A Philosophical Enquiry into the Origin of our Ideas of the Sublime and the Beautiful* [1757], ed. James T. Boulton, rev. edn (Oxford: Basil Blackwell, 1987), p. 37.
51. Edmund Burke, *A Letter to a Noble Lord* [1795], in *Further Reflections on the Revolution in France*, ed. Daniel E. Ritchie (Indianapolis: Liberty Fund, 1992), p. 307.
52. *The Yale Edition of Horace Walpole's Correspondence*, ed. W. S. Lewis, 48 vols (New Haven: Yale University Press, 1937–83), p. xxxiii, p. 217.

4

'The Light of Sense | Goes Out': Romantic Poetry and Victorian Nonsense Poetry

Peter Swaab

It seems natural to ask what was Victorian about nonsense poetry, but this essay will take the slightly different approach of asking what was Romantic about it.[1] Various thematic and generic links suggest themselves as possible approaches. First, we might say that nonsense brings a cooling comic self-consciousness to many of the dramas of Romanticism – for instance those involving childhood, isolation, utopian dreams, travel and empire. In exploring topics of such sublimity, nonsense always grounds it in absurdity, chiefly the absurdity of love in Edward Lear, and of meaning in Lewis Carroll. Second, the links between nonsense writing and children make it an inheritor of Romantic debates about the twin states of innocence and experience. Third, if Romanticism can be seen, as Harold Bloom once proposed, as the 'internalisation of quest-romance',[2] then nonsense writing is its re-externalisation. It is an externalisation in the mock-heroic mode, with the rider that the mock-heroic does not only mock the heroic but re-imagines it too. Fourth, as a departure from our norms, nonsense is always a form of travel literature. In setting out from the normal world nonsense is a genre in which, as Wordsworth wrote in *The Prelude*, 'the light of sense | Goes out'. However, it goes out not completely but 'in flashes that have shewn to us | The invisible world'.[3] William Empson suggested in his seminal essay on 'sense' in *The Prelude* that the metaphor implied a lighthouse's intermittences of illumination: 'Wordsworth induces his baffling *sense* to become a lighthouse occasionally flashing [. . .] The ecstasy both destroys normal sense and fulfils it.'[4] Fifth and lastly for now, nonsense writing is sceptical about the entire project of making sense. It assumes that we may be up to something important and worthwhile when we stop making sense.

Romanticism and nonsense are each large, disputable and multiform categories. This essay is an attempt at relating the two, at thinking about some of the dimensions and implications of a rich area of affinity and influence. We might from this perspective see nonsense writing as an escalation of Keatsian negative capability, 'when man is capable of being in uncertainties, Mysteries, doubts, without any irritable reaching after fact & reason –'.[5] Nonsense resides in uncertainties, mysteries and doubts, it makes these its imaginative ground. It is a genre that acknowledges by its name that its capability in relation to sense is a negative one. It doesn't make a song and dance about these limitations on understanding except by making them the matter of song and dance. Nonsense writing, to conclude these opening thoughts, should not be seen as the opposite or abolition of sense but as a negotiation about where and how far we can get with being sensible. Ambivalences around that idea enrich nineteenth-century writing across the sometimes unhelpful period bridge dividing Romanticism and Victorianism. This essay will look at many of the ways in which ideas and methods of the Romantic period were carried over to the heyday of nonsense writing. My discussion will be grounded on a range of representative instances from major writers of the Romantic period, and then focus on a comparison of Wordsworth and Edward Lear before some concluding thoughts.

The first example comes from William Blake, from one of the songs in the early 'An Island in the Moon', in which the baby of 'old corruption' is imagined giving some kind of monstrous incestuous birth:

And as he ran to seek his mother
He met with a dead woman
He fell in love & married her
A deed which is not common[6]

The 'Marriage hearse' of Blake's 'London' is in prospect here, a nightmare world of generation turned upside down.[7] When so much of what governs the world is against the rules of sense in such ways, then a rude overturning of conventional moral norms can be progressive as well as contrary. Blake sometimes imagines such reversals in exuberant and comic spirit, most notably in *The Marriage of Heaven and Hell*. When we hear of Ezekiel who 'eat dung, & lay so long on his right & left side' and Isaiah who went 'naked and barefoot three years', we are not far from the world of Edward Lear's limericks.[8] In the penultimate 'Memorable Fancy' of the poem the angel conducts the narrator on a journey of revelation that also turns the world upside down: 'down the winding cavern we groped our tedious way till a void boundless as a nether sky appeard [*sic*] beneath us. & we held by the roots of trees and hung over this immensity'.[9]

The second instance comes from the other end of the period, from Felicia Hemans's anthology piece 'Casabianca' (1826):

The boy stood on the burning deck,
  Whence all but he had fled;
The flame that lit the battle's wreck,
  Shone round him o'er the dead.

Yet beautiful and bright he stood,
  As born to rule the storm;
A creature of heroic blood,
  A proud, though childlike form.

The flames rolled on – he would not go,
  Without his father's word;
That father, faint in death below,
  His voice no longer heard.[10]

Spike Milligan was one of many goaded into adapting or parodying the poem. 'The boy stood on the burning deck | Whence all but he had fled – | Twit'.[11] What sense is there, the poem wonders, in adhering to a code of conduct when it leads to death? Is it glory or idiocy? This is a question that will echo into such Victorian works as '"Childe Roland to the Dark Tower Came"', 'The Charge of the Light Brigade' and *The Hunting of the Snark*. The fourth stanza of the poem, indeed, sounds like an exchange from *Alice in Wonderland*'s 'Father William'. First Hemans:

He called aloud – 'Say, father, say
 If yet my task is done?'
He knew not that the chieftain lay
 Unconscious of his son.

And then Carroll:

'You are old, father William,' the young man said,
 'And your hair has become very white;
And yet you incessantly stand on your head –
 Do you think, at your age, it is right?'

'In my youth,' father William replied to his son,
 'I feared it might injure the brain;
But, now that I'm perfectly sure I have none,
 Why, I do it again and again.'[12]

These are a couple of father-son exchanges that are going nowhere. Hemans's questions about heroism and absurdity linger on into *The Hunting of the Snark* (1876), in which all the crew members, as if adhering dutifully to the alliteration of the boy on the burning deck, begin with the letter B (Bellman, Baker, Beaver, Butcher, etc.). A further but more direct afterlife of Hemans's poem comes in 'Casabianca' by Elizabeth Bishop, one of the twentieth-century poets most interestingly inspired by nonsense, along with Auden and Stevie Smith. Her version deepens Hemans's by seeing the story of grand compulsion as a story of love:

Love's the boy stood on the burning deck
trying to recite 'The boy stood on
the burning deck.' Love's the son
  stood stammering elocution
  while the poor ship in flames went down.

Love's the obstinate boy, the ship,
even the swimming sailors, who
would like a schoolroom platform, too,
  or an excuse to stay
  on deck. And love's the burning boy.[13]

A brief example from Shelley, at the end of 'The Sensitive Plant', supplies a perspective from which the story that comprised the poem was all nonsense:

but in this life
Of error, ignorance and strife –
Where nothing is – but all things seem,
And we the shadows of the dream,

It is a modest creed, and yet
Pleasant if one considers it,
To own that death itself must be,
Like all the rest, – a mockery.[14]

Nonsense sometimes overlaps with such truths of wisdom literature, in which human life is seen as a mockery. The modesty of the creed can be heard through the modesty of Shelley's rhyme 'and yet | Pleasant if one considers it', with a feeling of what a relief it can be to let it all go, to relax into mockery.

Byron, the great comic poet of the Romantic period, shared some of Shelley's high and dry mockery of human life, but his imagination was more often social. Like Lewis Carroll, he relished the absurdities of systems of knowledge and the character of professional deformation. In Canto X of *Don Juan*, at the court of Catherine the Great, Juan is ailing, and the doctors are called in:

But here is one prescription out of many:
 'Sodae-Sulphat. 3 vi. 3. s. Mannae optim.
Aq. fervent. F. 3. ifs. 3ij. tinct. Sennae
 Haustus' (And here the surgeon came and cupped him)
'*R*. Pulv. Com. gr. iii. Ipecacunahae'
 (With more beside if Juan had not stopped 'em).
'Bolus Potassae Sulphuret. sumendus,
Et Haustus ter in die capiendus.' (Canto X, st. 41)[15]

Byron gives us medicine as learned nonsense. The stanza mixes English and Latin, words and numbers, and scrambles its own metrics by the overload of abbreviations; it makes a brilliant display of its own absurdity. The editors tell us that 'The prescription seems to indicate a rigorous purge, a sweat, and an emetic to mend or end the patient; it does not appear to be a remedy for any specific disease.' Juan was wise to stop 'em.

More introspectively and psychologically, Byron's poems think about the absurdities discoverable in our own selves. Remembering the days of his childhood in Scotland in *Don Juan*, he at once celebrates and ironises patriotic idealisations around place and nostalgic idealisations across time.

As 'Auld Lang Syne' brings Scotland, one and all,
 Scotch plaids, Scotch snoods, the blue hills, and clear streams,
The Dee, the Don, Balgounie's Brig's *black wall*,
 All my boy feelings, all my gentler dreams
Of what I *then dreamt*, clothed in their own pall,
 Like Banquo's offspring; – floating past me seems
My childhood in this childishness of mine:
I care not – 'tis a glimpse of 'Auld Lang Syne'. (Canto X, st.18)

Wordsworthian insights into the permanence of early influences become vertiginous here. The 'boy feelings' and 'gentler dreams' take us on a receding journey from the present to the past to the imaginings of the past, and back to the present in which such thoughts and feelings persist uncertainly – the phrase 'Auld Lang Syne' 'brings' Scotland, but what it brings seems to be 'floating past'. The evocation of Scotland comes from a series of alliterations, sometimes faintly over-emphatic ('Scotch plaids, Scotch snoods', 'Balgounie's Brig's *black wall*'). Byron conveys the power by which these things coalesce 'one and all' into a sense of 'Scotland'; but he also looks quizzically at the way such a construction of nationhood (richly underway in the novels of Walter Scott) gathers together the worlds of clothing, landscape, geography, engineering and personal association. The scepticism and the warmth of feeling are richly entangled. If Byron feels patriotism and nostalgia as 'this childishness of mine', still it's not a childishness that he cares to wish away.

Romanticism sometimes offered an invitation to visit places in which the sense of something far more deeply interfused could sound like no sense at all. 'The Child is father of the Man', wrote Wordsworth.[16] 'Really?', answered Hopkins:

> 'The child is father to the man.'
> How can he be? The words are wild.
> Suck any sense from that who can:
> 'The child is father to the man.'
> No; what the poet did write ran,
> 'The man is father to the child.'
> 'The child is father to the man!'
> How *can* he be? The words are wild.[17]

The charm of Hopkins's poem lies in how it preserves a respect and affection for the original (albeit misquoting it slightly). The joke works both ways; sturdy common sense has its own preposterousness converting everything to its own optics. 'No; what the poet did write ran, | "The man is father to the child"'. It did not take Nabokov to show that textual editors can run mad too. What most often gets called nonsense has no monopoly on the ridiculous.

William Hazlitt was prompted by 'Kubla Khan' to write that 'Mr Coleridge can write better *nonsense* verses than any man in England.'[18] Other critics, too, had recourse to the idea of 'nonsense' in relation to his poetry. Charles Lamb, for instance, also on 'Kubla Khan': 'I am almost afraid that Kubla Khan is an owl that wont bear daylight, I fear lest it should be discovered by the lantern of typography & clear reducting to letters, no better than nonsense or no sense.'[19] Or the author of the unsigned review of 'Christabel' in the *Monthly Review*: 'It is grand, in a word, it is sublime, to be lawless; and whoever writes the wildest nonsense in the quickest and newest manner is the popular poet of the day!'[20] These critics register a range of responses, which include admiration but also convey a reluctance to engage with the poems on the terms they seem to the critic to propose. What is there in Coleridge's poetry to provoke these references to 'nonsense'? J. C. C. Mays makes the illuminating suggestion that Coleridge 'like his early models, Chatterton and Macpherson, withdrew into a separate, protective world in order to speak without constraint'.[21] How 'separate' is the world of Coleridge's poetry, how far from the norms of 'sense' and 'day light' (to use Lamb's terms), and what freedoms from constraint did he fashion for himself?

One of Coleridge's early poems, 'To a Young Jack Ass' (1794), imagines two possibilities that are integral to the world of Victorian nonsense writing, namely the overthrow of hierarchies and the possibility of a magical communion between humans and other animals. The poem is prompted by the sight of 'a Young Jack Ass in Jesus Piece. Its mother near it chained to a log.'[22] Coleridge later called it a 'ludicro-splenetic' piece,[23] with the hyphen indicating but not analysing the connection between the anger and the humour. The poem tries out various poetic modes to lament the situation, including making the creature a sort of Hamlet by speculating on its having 'prophetic fears' and thoughts of 'the thousand aches | "Which patient merit of the unworthy takes"'.[24] We are in the world, then, of 'The oppressor's wrong, the proud man's contumely',[25] and the poem ends in denunciation of 'a scoundrel Monarch's Breast' (line 40). The Hamlet allusion is risky in this context, but, as Empson noted, 'the young Coleridge was brave about being laughed at',[26] seeing this as a dimension of political provocation and religious humility, and he writes defiantly that 'I hail thee Brother – spite of the fool's scorn!' The conservative *Anti-Jacobin* magazine duly provided the scorn Coleridge anticipated, making tears over donkeys one of its recurrent tropes for emotional affectation and humanitarian folly. Byron, too, was to call Coleridge 'the bard who soars to elegise an ass'.[27]

In the poem Coleridge expands his feelings for the young ass into a utopian vision of life in a pantisocracy:

And fain I'd take thee with me, to the Dell
Where high-soul'd Pantisocracy shall dwell!
Where Mirth shall tickle Plenty's ribless side,
And smiles from Beauty's Lip on sunbeams glide,
Where Toil shall wed young Health that charming Lass!
And use his sleek cows for a looking-glass –
Where Rats shall mess with Terriers hand-in-glove
And Mice with Pussy's Whiskers sport in Love!
How thou wouldst toss thy heels in gamesome play,
And frisk about, as lamb or kitten gay! (26–36)

This continuation exemplifies Mays's helpful idea that Coleridge wrote 'a poetry of ever-renewed beginnings'.[28] First there is 'Plenty's ribless side', a stark phrase from the hungry 1790s; the side only appears 'ribless' because it is not so painfully thin as to make the ribs visible. Then as the personifications continue Coleridge shifts from the humanitarian realism evoked by 'ribless' to the personifications of 'Beauty', 'Toil' and 'Health', which might be figures from Georgian porcelain miniatures of pastoral felicity. And next comes the moment most relevant to this discussion, as the poem modulates into lines that closely prefigure nonsense verse:

And use his sleek cows for a looking-glass –
Where Rats shall mess with Terriers hand-in-glove
And Mice with Pussy's Whiskers sport in Love!

The voice of political protest and humanitarian sensibility has turned into an articulation of animal magic. The rats and terriers mess together, like the wolf and the lamb in

Isaiah 11: 6, and both species are unzoologically imagined for a moment with hands and even with gloves. Coleridge's mice and cats, like Lear's owl and pussy-cat (who also have hands), sport in love and not in the hunt. The prefiguring of nonsense is important, but so too is the fact that Coleridge felt enough unease about the proto-nonsensical mode that he left out these three lines when he published the poem in the *Morning Chronicle*.

Coleridge's friend Lamb pointed out that 'Burns hath his mouse and his louse; Coleridge, less successfully, hath made overtures of intimacy to a jackass.'[29] We could also think of such poems of the extended Romantic period as Anna Letitia Barbauld's 'The Mouse's Petition' (c. 1769) and Cowper's 'Epitaph on a Hare' (1783). These Romantic explorations of affinities across the human-animal divide are often experiments in tone as well as theme, and they have a momentous afterlife in the greatest such poem of the age, Coleridge's 'Rime of the Ancient Mariner'. The mariner's story turns on the moment when his heart goes out to the 'water-snakes':

> Within the shadow of the ship
> I watch'd their rich attire:
> Blue, glossy green, and velvet black,
> They coil'd and swam; and every track
> Was a flash of golden fire.
>
> O happy living things! no tongue
> Their beauty might declare:
> A spring of love gusht from my heart,
> And I bless'd them unaware:
> Sure my kind saint took pity on me,
> And I bless'd them unaware! (1798 text, lines 279–89)[30]

The phrase 'living things' suggests a paradox – if they are 'living' are they really 'things'? – hence perhaps the awkward little internal rhyme, a rhyme however that gets taken up and resolved later in the stanza by 'spring of love'. The beauty of these creatures lies beyond what 'tongue [. . .] might declare', beyond the reach of what is 'aware' and speakable, but not beyond the reach of love. Although the mariner himself makes sense of this outpouring of love by invoking his 'kind saint', this may be one of the moments when Coleridge's readers in 1798 are prompted to mistrust the theology of the pre-Protestant narrator. A remark recorded in Coleridge's *Table Talk* suggests the author had reservations about moral interpretations of the story:

> It ought to have had no more moral than the Arabian Nights' tale of the merchant's sitting down to eat dates by the side of a well, and throwing the shells aside, and lo! a genie starts up, and says he *must* kill the aforesaid merchant, *because* one of the date shells had, it seems, put out the eye of the genie's son.[31]

This Arabian Nights version sees the mariner's culpability as a matter of absurd bad luck. Are there other absurdities from which 'The Ancient Mariner' might be thought a nonsense poem? The voyage, whose purpose is never explained, proceeds into a world of unknown powers, rules and prohibitions. Two figures in what the marginal gloss calls 'the skeleton-ship' play at dice to decide the mariner's fate. The wedding guest at first expects he will be hearing a 'laughsome tale';[32] he gets more than he counted on, and so do the readers of the poem, but that doesn't mean it lacks elements that could be described this way – in the skeleton-ship, for instance, the two dice-playing figures who 'therein sate merrily', or the pilot's boy on the rescue boat 'Who now doth crazy go' and 'Laugh'd loud and long' (1798 text, lines 190, 610–11). The marginal glosses that Coleridge added in 1817 interpret the story into theological intelligibility, but the narrating voice of the poem is more unstable and unreliable. It would diminish the scope of 'The Ancient Mariner' to think of it mainly as a nonsense poem but its afterlife even so includes the example it gave to Lear and Carroll of a questing voyage into strange seas and incomprehensible encounters.

The rest of this chapter focusses not on Coleridge but on the pre-eminently influential figure of Wordsworth, looking at the bearings of his poetry on Victorian nonsense writing, and especially on the poems of Edward Lear.[33] One way to see Wordsworth's 'Idiot Boy', Johnny, is as a hero of nonsense, asserting a world turned upside down as he makes answer to his mother's questioning:

And thus, to Betty's question, he
Made answer, like a traveller bold,
(His very words I give to you),
'The cocks did crow to-whoo, to-whoo,
And the sun did shine so cold.' –
Thus answered Johnny in his glory,
And that was all his travel's story.[34]

'And that was all his travel's story': we can hear 'that was all' in two ways, the glory and integrity of 'that was the whole thing' or the shrugging concession of 'that's your lot'. The turn of phrase comes back a generation later at a moment comparably suspended between revelation and disappointment:

Thou shalt remain, in midst of other woe
Than ours, a friend to man, to whom thou say'st,
'Beauty is truth, truth beauty', – that is all
Ye know on earth, and all ye need to know.[35]

Is Keats's 'Grecian Urn' uttering the achievement of knowledge or its frustration? And is there a hint of something absurd about a vocalising pot, as there would be forty years later in FitzGerald's *Rubáiyát of Omar Khayyám*, where we overhear a group of pots philosophising by night?

Shapes of all Sorts and Sizes, great and small,
That stood along the floor and by the wall;
And some loquacious Vessels were; and some
Listen'd perhaps, but never talk'd at all.
[. . .]
Whereat some one of the loquacious Lot –
I think a Súfi pipkin – waxing hot –
'All this of Pot and Potter – Tell me then,
Who is the Potter, pray, and who the Pot?'[36]

That's the 1879 version; in 1868 what FitzGerald called the 'Pot-theism' of the 'Súfi pipkin' had sounded more exasperated, more urgent, and perhaps more nonsensical: 'Who makes – Who sells – Who buys – Who *is* the Pot?'[37] The poet as pot, perhaps.

Alongside 'The Idiot Boy' Wordsworth's other great comic poem of 1798 is 'Peter Bell'. If the Idiot Boy narrator could be teasing, then, David Bromwich suggests, the narrator of 'Peter Bell' appears to 'fret very little about the needs of an audience'; he is 'a dotard teller whose hints we must screen out to read through'.[38] The absence of fretting is a rhetorical method of a kind; the poem is an experiment in insouciance. And some of the time we need not read *through* this narrator; his mode is his message. Telling the story so simply, helplessly, unhurriedly to the poem's audience of children is a way of giving permission to fantasy. It might really for instance make little folks merry.

> There was an old Derry down Derry, who loved to see little folks merry,
> So he made them a Book, and with laughter they shook
> At the fun of that Derry down Derry.[39]

There's happiness to be had and given in taking such leave of your senses, as Lear's drawing shows (Figure 4.1). This was a permission Wordsworth afforded himself for a short time in such poems as 'The Two Thieves', 'The Idiot Boy' and 'Peter Bell'.[40]

The prologue to 'Peter Bell' begins by seeming to bring the poet back from his sky balloon, back down to earth and a village scene, from a deep romantic land that this poem calls 'fairyland':

> There was a time, a time indeed,
> A time when poets lived in clover.
> What boots it now to keep the key

Figure 4.1 Edward Lear, 'There was an old Derry down Derry', *A Book of Nonsense* (London: Frederick Warne and Co., 1846; 18th edn, 1866), title page.

Of Fairyland? for, woe is me!
Those blessed days are over.

There is a party in the Bower,
Round the stone table in my garden;
The squire is there, and as I guess,
His pretty little daughter Bess,
With Harry the church-warden.

They were to come this very evening,
They know not I have been so far,
I see them there, in number nine,
All in the bower of Weymouth pine,
I see them, there they are.

And there's the wife of Parson Swan,
And there's my good friend Stephen Otter.
And, ere the light of evening fail,
To them I must relate the tale
Of Peter Bell the Potter.[41]

With Parson Swan and Stephen Otter in the party we might be forgiven here for thinking we are in the world not of Peter Bell but Beatrix the Potter. Like Coleridge's 'To a Young Jack Ass', this story also features an ass – a donkey ass not a silly ass – and the telling conjures a magical human kinship with the world of animals. Although it leaves behind 'those blessed days' and affirms the solid claim 'I see them, there they are', the prologue does not simply renounce the world of the sky balloon. Instead, it changes one kind of enchanted world for another, at least until 'the light of evening fail', a phrase eloquent of the knowledge in such poems that the illumination they shed is temporary.

Wordsworth continued but tempered the visions of a comic world he offered in 'The Idiot Boy' and 'Peter Bell' within a sequence of comic narratives spanning the decade from the *Lyrical Ballads* to the first drafting of *Benjamin, the Waggoner* in 1806 (like *Peter Bell*, it remained unpublished until 1819). Among the most interesting is 'The Blind Highland Boy'. This poem, which is very seldom discussed by critics, was published in 1807 in *Poems, in Two Volumes*. It tells in forty-one five-line stanzas the story of a blind boy, blind from birth, who sets out on the dangerous waters of Loch Leven in a washing tub. He is rescued and brought home. Wordsworth's Fenwick note tells us that 'The story was told me by George Mackereth for many years parish-clerk of Grasmere. He had been an eye-witness of the occurence [sic]. The vessel in reality was a washing-tub which the little fellow had met with on the shores of the loch.'[42] Like 'Peter Bell', it starts with a prologue, though this time an abbreviated one of just two stanzas establishing it as 'A Tale told by the Fire-side':

Now we are tired of boisterous joy,
We've romped enough, my little Boy!
Jane hangs her head upon my breast,
And you shall bring your Stool and rest,
   This corner is your own.[43]

How does the setting differ from 'Peter Bell'? First, the narrator is female not male, a mother as against the 'Peter Bell' narrator whose family ties the poem leaves unmentioned. Second, she is more recognisably instructive. 'Now we are tired of boisterous joy' is something parents say to children who show no sign at all of being tired of boisterous joy, but need a reminder that they *ought* to be. The 'we' is wishful and didactic. 'Wisdom doth live with children round her knees'[44] here; the parental bond was a wilder thing in 'The Idiot Boy'. Where Betty Foy sent Johnny out on his perilous journey for mysterious loving reasons of her own (a little like Aunt Jobiska in Lear's 'Pobble who has no Toes'), the mother here offers a safer home.

The voyage away from land, safety and sense is figured as a compensatory joy for the blind boy, answering his yearning to go to the far places he's heard of in stories. His rescuers pursue him:

> With sound the least that can be made
> They follow, more and more afraid,
> More cautious as they draw more near;
> But in his darkness he can hear,
> And guesses their intent
>
> *'Lei-gha-Lei-gha'* – then did he cry
> *'Lei-gha-Lei-gha'* – most eagerly;
> Thus did he cry, and thus did pray,
> And what he meant was, 'Keep away,
> And leave me to myself!'[45]

Wordsworth resorts uncannily to italics and repetition and a word from Erse to convey a fierce aliennness within the boy's desire. The first manuscript version of the Erse word in his Commonplace Book had been 'Lega, Lega' (*Poems, in Two Volumes*, p. 498). He had consulted Walter Scott about the word for what he called 'a highland story told me by an eye witness; the man was an Englishman and the Erse word sounded in my ears like Lega [. . .] signifying – "beware", keep away, let me alone'.[46] The gloss by the poem's narrator leaves out the meaning of 'beware', which would have conferred an admonitory power on the boy, as in the lines from Coleridge's 'Kubla Khan' – 'And all should cry, Beware! Beware! | His flashing eyes, his floating hair!' The emphasis here lies not on his inspired authority but on the needy and wishful aspects of his uttering of a cry and a prayer.

It is the link in this poem between a crazy voyage and somebody finding their sole self that especially anticipates some of Edward Lear's figures. Many of the nonsense selves are wedded to self-sufficiency. His loners have no love interests, no sons and daughters, no visible relations. They like it that way and guard their isolation fiercely. This is the other side of Lear's delight in pretended extended families, something we see in such poems as 'The Scroobious Pip' and 'The Quangle Wangle's Hat' and in many of the limericks.

> There was a Young Lady whose bonnet, came untied when the birds sate upon it;
> But she said 'I don't care! all the birds in the air
> Are welcome to sit on my bonnet!'

Figure 4.2 Edward Lear, 'There was a Young Lady whose bonnet', *A Book of Nonsense* (London: 1861), p. 5.

Figure 4.3 Edward Lear, 'There was an Old Person of Bree', *More Nonsense: Pictures, Rhymes, Botany, Etc* (London: 1872), n.p.

> There was an Old Person of Bree,
> Who frequented the depths of the sea;
> She nurs'd the small fishes, and washed all the dishes
> And swam back again into Bree.[47]

As against these visions of harmony, the limericks often show us undivided selves, perversely untouchable and strangely triumphant. In this respect they are

Figure 4.4 Edward Lear, 'There was an Old Man of Kildare', *A Book of Nonsense* (London: 1855), n.p.

cousins to such self-sufficing Lewis Carroll figures as Humpty Dumpty and Father William.

> There was an Old Man of Kildare,
> Who climbed into a very high chair;
> When he said, 'Here I stays,
> Till the end of my days,'
> That immovable Man of Kildare.[48]

The situation seems permanent partly because the 'When' that starts the third line leads, ungrammatically, nowhere. The semicolon after 'high chair' promises a fresh start and prospect but what the Old Man finds in the situation is the promise and prospect of stasis. But this Old Man looks contented enough, with his pipe and his jauntily crossed legs and immobility and his distance from the telescope-using watcher below. Some of the other limerick figures also take self-sufficiency to extremes that are both adroit and grotesque.

> There was an Old Person of Spain, who hated all trouble and pain;
> So he sat on a chair, with his feet in the air,
> That umbrageous Old Person of Spain.[49]

Gazing at his own kneecaps, this mysterious person comprises his own support, backrest and outlook.

Figure 4.5 Edward Lear, 'There was an Old Person of Spain', *A Book of Nonsense* (London: 1871), p. 90.

One way the light of sense may go out is in blindness. 'The Blind Highland Boy' is one of several Wordsworthian alignings of blindness and insight – 'in his darkness he can hear' – often in relation to Homer and Milton, and most grandly in the passage about the blind beggar in *The Prelude* (1805 text, VII.111–40). Lear's figures, too, sometimes look blind, or at least differently visioned, like the Old Person of Grange.

There was an Old Person of Grange,
Whose manners were scroobious and strange;
He sailed to St Blubb, in a waterproof tub,
That aquatic Old Person of Grange.[50]

Perhaps the Person of Grange found the waterproof tub on the shores of Loch Leven.[51] A helper animal can steer the limerick hero safely away when he seems unsighted himself.

There was an Old Man whose despair
Induced him to purchase a hare:
Whereon one fine day, he rode wholly away,
Which partly assuaged his despair.[52]

Figure 4.6 Edward Lear, 'There was an Old Person of Grange', *More Nonsense: Pictures, Rhymes, Botany, Etc* (London: 1872), n.p.

Figure 4.7 Edward Lear, 'There was an Old Man whose despair', *More Nonsense: Pictures, Rhymes, Botany, Etc* (London: 1872), n.p.

Figure 4.8 Edward Lear, 'There was an Old Man of Messina', *More Nonsense: Pictures, Rhymes, Botany, Etc* (London: 1872), n.p.

This smiley backward-glancing hare seems a kindly attentive creature, a counterpart to the little dog who seems to understand the blind boy in a way beyond everybody else in the poem.[53] Sometimes the protagonist can see but has no wish to look in the right direction.

There was an Old Man of Messina,
Whose daughter was named Opsibeena;
She wore a small wig, and rode out on a pig,
To the perfect delight of Messina.[54]

Lear's nonsense allows this perspective to be a 'perfect delight' widely shared whereas for Wordsworth's blind boy 'the triumph of his joy' is temporary.

The conjuring in 'The Blind Highland Boy' of the boy's wished-for distance from terrestrial human life often echoes Wordsworth's 'Elegiac Stanzas on Peele Castle', but it does not end in the highland boy's drowning:

Thus, after he had fondly braved
The perilous Deep, the Boy was saved;
And, though his fancies had been wild,
Yet he was pleased, and reconciled
To live in peace on shore.[55]

Is nonsense poetry an art of being 'reconciled'? or even of being 'pleased, and reconciled'? It has sometimes been conceived in opposite terms, as a poetry of protest, for instance by Aldous Huxley and George Orwell.[56] But this is only one possible emphasis. Nonsense often articulates protest while also narrating or implying acquiescence. In Lear, for instance, there are several stories in which getting away from it all leads to getting back to it all. The man of Dunluce goes out to sea, for reasons undisclosed, and then returns, also for reasons undisclosed.

There was an Old Man of Dunluce,
Who went out to sea on a goose;
When he'd gone out a mile, he observ'd with a smile,
'It is time to return to Dunluce.'[57]

That seems to do the trick. The Jumblies go to sea in a sieve, they do, but twenty years later they all come back. 'The Table and the Chair' go to town for a walk, which is difficult because their legs are stiff, but then get lost and go back home (*Complete Nonsense*, pp. 253–6, 277–8). Are they pleased and reconciled to be back? Maybe. Has a deep distress humanised their souls?[58] Unlikely, because they're pieces of furniture. The stoicism of nonsense can be lighter in tone than the elegiac stanzas because the stories are further from the world of all of us. Possibly the Man of Dunluce and the Table and the Chair realise, like Dorothy in *The Wizard of Oz*, that there's no place like home. That may of course have been exactly why they wanted to get away from it. 'No place' is somewhere you can *think* of getting to and it can become like home to the imagination. 'No place' could translate into Greek as 'utopia', with the prefix ou (οὐ) meaning

Figure 4.9 Edward Lear, 'There was an Old Man of Dunluce', *More Nonsense: Pictures, Rhymes, Botany, Etc* (London: 1872), n.p.

'not' followed by topos (τόπος) meaning 'place'. We could say of nonsense poetry what Maddalo says to Julian in Shelley's poem: 'You talk Utopia'.[59]

These comparisons, in conclusion, might lead us to see a Romanticism in which self-critique and scepticism were quite robustly in place from the start. They might also illuminate the awareness in writings of the Romantic period that obstacles to sense can at times be experienced not just as perplexity but as enjoyment shared with an audience, uncovering a mutuality in limitation and producing a comedy of forbearance in the recognition of ordinary levels of creaturely incompetence. The comparison might also point us to a further appreciation of some of the less canonical works by the most canonical writers. For Blake, 'An Island in the Moon' alongside *The Marriage of Heaven and Hell*; for Wordsworth, a line that goes from 'Peter Bell' and 'The Idiot Boy' through to *Benjamin, the Waggoner*; for Coleridge, a perspective on the self-referential, jocose and fantastical in his work; for Shelley, more salience to the poems that Donald Davie once discussed and admired under the heading of 'Shelley's Urbanity', including 'Julian and Maddalo', 'Peter Bell the Third' and 'The Sensitive Plant';[60] for Keats, some of the comic verse together with 'Lamia' and 'The Cap and Bells'. And the larger picture could give more centrality to Byron, with his Popeian conviction that man in all his absurdity is 'the glory, jest and riddle of the world', and that poetry should aim above all else for the state of being 'a moment merry'.[61]

In a 1948 essay T. S. Eliot proposed a line of influence and affinity from Poe to Valéry, from American Romanticism to the waning days of French symbolism.[62] A parallel line, Anglocentric as against Franco-American, might be from Blake to Lewis Carroll, or Wordsworth to Lear. The destination of Romanticism might then resemble not the faded Shelleyanism that Stephen Dedalus has to reject before he can become a properly Joycean modernist artist, but something more coolly and steadily self-conscious – not a dispensable *fin de siècle* lassitude but instead a further flourishing of Romantic traditions in figures such as Housman, Eliot and Auden, for whom romantic aspiration is usually linked to the possibility of absurdity.

Notes

1. This chapter enlarges and revises my article 'Romantic Poetry and Victorian Nonsense Poetry: Some Directions of Travel', in *Romanticism* 25 (2019), 90–102.
2. Harold Bloom, 'The Internalization of Quest-Romance', in *Romanticism and Consciousness: Essays in Criticism*, ed. Harold Bloom (New York: W. W. Norton & Co., 1970), 3–24.
3. 'In such strength | Of usurpation, in such visitings | Of awful promise, when the light of sense | Goes out in flashes that have shewn to us | The invisible world, doth Greatness make abode': William Wordsworth, *The Prelude* (1805 text), VI. 532–6, in *The Major Works*, ed. Stephen Gill (Oxford: Oxford University Press, 2008).
4. William Empson, *The Structure of Complex Words* (London: Chatto and Windus, 1951), pp. 294–5.
5. *The Letters of John Keats*, ed. Hyder Rollins, 2 vols (Cambridge, MA: Harvard University Press, 1958), I, p. 193 [to George and Tom Keats, 21, 27 December 1817].
6. William Blake, *The Complete Poems*, ed. Alicia Ostriker (Harmondsworth: Penguin, 1977), p. 64.
7. 'But most thro' midnight streets I hear | How the youthful harlots curse | Blasts the new-born Infants tear | And blights with plague the marriage hearse' (Blake, *Complete Poems*, p. 128).

8. Blake, *Complete Poems*, p. 187.
9. Ibid. p. 190.
10. Felicia Hemans, *Selected Poems, Letters, Reception Materials*, ed. Susan J. Wolfson (Princeton: Princeton University Press, 2010), pp. 428–9.
11. Spike Milligan, 'Casabazonka', *The Magical World of Milligan*, ed. Norma Farnes (London: Virgin Books, 1999), p. 99.
12. Lewis Carroll, *Jabberwocky and Other Nonsense: Collected Poems*, ed. Gillian Beer (London: Penguin, 2012), pp. 703, 709. The editorial note is quoted from *Don Juan*, ed. T.G. Steffan, E. Steffan and W. W. Pratt (Harmondsworth: Penguin, 1982), p. 687.
13. Elizabeth Bishop, *Poems* (New York: Farrar, Straus and Giroux, 2011), p. 7.
14. *Shelley's Poetry and Prose*, ed. Donald H. Reiman and Sharon B. Powers (New York: Chatto and Windus, 1977), p. 218.
15. Lord Byron, in *Don Juan*, *The Major Works*, ed. Jerome J. McGann (Oxford: Oxford University Press, 1986), pp. 703, 709. The editorial note is quoted from *Don Juan*, ed. T.G. Steffan, E. Steffan and W. W. Pratt (Harmondsworth: Penguin, 1982), p. 687.
16. Wordsworth, 'My heart leaps up when I behold', in *William Wordsworth: The Major Works*, p. 246.
17. Gerard Manley Hopkins, 'A Trio of Triolets. No 3 – "The Child is Father to the Man" (Wordsworth)', in *Gerard Manley Hopkins: A Critical Edition of the Major Works*, ed. Catherine Phillips (Oxford: Oxford University Press, 1986), 157–8.
18. William Hazlitt, *The Examiner*, 2 June 1816; cited in J. C. C. Mays, *Coleridge's Experimental Poetics* (New York: Palgrave Macmillan, 2013), p. 84.
19. Charles Lamb, *The Letters of Charles and Mary Anne Lamb*, ed. Edwin J. Marrs, 3 vols (Ithaca: Cornell University Press, 1975–8), III, p. 215.
20. Unsigned, *Monthly Review*, January 1817, in *Coleridge: The Critical Heritage,Vol I, 1794–1834*, ed. J. R. de J. Jackson (London: Routledge & Kegan Paul, 1970), p. 246.
21. Mays, *Coleridge's Experimental Poetics*, p. 81.
22. This is the title in Coleridge's manuscript version dated 24 October 1794, from which I quote; the poem was first published as 'To a Young Ass, its Mother being Tethered Near it' in the *Morning Chronicle* on 30 December 1794. *The Collected Works of Samuel Taylor Coleridge: Vol. 16, Part 1: Poetical Works: Part 1. Poems (Reading Text)*, ed. J. C. C. Mays (Princeton, NJ: Bollingen Press, 2001), p. 84.
23. *Letters of Samuel Taylor Coleridge, III: 1807–1814*, ed. Earl Leslie Griggs (Oxford: Oxford University Press, 1959), p. 433; to Robert Southey, 8 February 1813. Cited in Paul D. Sheats, 'Young Coleridge and the Idea of Lyric', *Coleridge Bulletin* New Series 20 (2002), p. 22.
24. 'To a Young Jack Ass', ll. 9, 11–12; 'Oh my prophetic soul', *Hamlet* I. 5. 40; 'the spurns | That patient merit of the unworthy takes', III. 1. 80–1.
25. *Hamlet* III. 1. 78.
26. *Samuel Taylor Coleridge: Selected Poetry*, ed. William Empson and David Pirie (Manchester: Carcanet Press, [1972] 1989), p. 39.
27. Lord Byron, *English Bards and Scotch Reviewers*, in *Selected Poems,* ed. Peter Manning (London: Penguin, 2005), p. 17 (line 262).
28. Mays, *Coleridge's Experimental Poetics*, p. 82.
29. *The Letters of Charles and Mary Lamb*, I, p. 165.
30. See the helpful presentation of texts in *Coleridge's* Ancient Mariner*: An Experimental Edition of Texts and Revisions 1798–1828*, ed. Martin Wallen (New York: Station Hill, 1993) pp. 44–5.
31. *Specimens of the Table Talk of Samuel Taylor Coleridge* (London: John Murray, 1836), p. 82; entry dated 31 May 1830.
32. The *OED* records this as the first usage of the word for its second sense, of something 'that causes laughter; amusing'. It records a single earlier use of the word in its primary

meaning of 'inclined to laughter; mirthful': this comes from Shelton's 1612 translation of *Don Quixote*: 'No more good Sir, quoth Sancho, for I confesse I haue beene somewhat too laughsome.'

33. Wordsworth is more frequently juxtaposed with Lewis Carroll, prompted by the parodic relation to 'Resolution and Independence' of the White Knight's song 'I'll tell thee everything I can'; see *Jabberwocky and Other Nonsense*, ed. Beer, 215–7.
34. William Wordsworth and Samuel Taylor Coleridge, *Lyrical Ballads*, ed. Michael Mason (London: Longman, 1992), p. 169.
35. 'Ode on a Grecian Urn', in *Keats: Complete Poems*, ed. Miriam Allott (London: Longman, 1970), p. 537.
36. Edward FitzGerald, *The Rubáiyát of Omar Khayyám*, ed. Daniel Karlin (Oxford: Oxford University Press, 2009), p. 86; 1879 version, stanzas LXXXIII and LXXXVII.
37. 'Pot-theism' is FitzGerald's coinage, in a note he added to the poem in 1872; see Karlin's notes in *Rubáiyát*, p. 92.
38. *Disowned by Memory: Wordsworth's Poetry of the 1790s* (Chicago: University of Chicago Press, 1998), pp. 127, 126.
39. Edward Lear, *A Book of Nonsense* (London: Frederick Warne and Co (1846); 18th edn, (1866)), title page. The standard modern edition of Lear's nonsense is *Edward Lear: The Complete Nonsense and Other Verse*, ed. Vivien Noakes (London: Penguin, 2006). In modern editions such as Noakes's the drawings usually appear smaller in proportion to the text than in the Victorian editions reproduced here; modern editions also tend to standardise the limericks as four-line poems, whereas those Lear saw through the press variously use three, four and five lines, reproduced accordingly here.
40. For valuable discussions of Wordsworth's comic mode see Donald Davie's essay 'Dionysus in "Lyrical Ballads"' in *Wordsworth's Mind and Art*, ed. A. W. Thomson (Edinburgh: Edinburgh University Press, 1969), 110–39, more recently in Matthew Bevis's wide-ranging and imaginative exploration of *Wordsworth's Fun* (Chicago: Chicago University Press, 2019).
41. *Wordsworth: The Major Works*, ed. Gill, p. 95.
42. William Wordsworth, *'Poems, in Two Volumes' and Other Poems, 1800–1807*, ed. Jared Curtis (Ithaca: Cornell University Press, 1983), p. 420.
43. Wordsworth, *Poems, in Two Volumes*, p. 221. Wordsworth first added the subtitle 'A Tale told by the Fire-side' to the manuscript versions of the poem for its 1807 publication in book form.
44. See Wordsworth's sonnet, 'I grieved for Buonaparte, with a vain', line 9; *Wordsworth: The Major Works*, ed. Gill, p. 267.
45. Wordsworth, *Poems, in Two Volumes*, p. 227.
46. *The Letters of William and Dorothy Wordsworth: The Middle Years, Part 1, 1806–1811*, ed. Ernest de Selincourt, rev. Mary Moorman (Oxford: Oxford University Press, 1969), pp. 123–4 [to Walter Scott, 20 January 1807].
47. Lear, *A Book of Nonsense* (London: 1861), p. 5; *More Nonsense: Pictures, Rhymes, Botany, Etc* (1872), n.p.
48. Lear, *A Book of Nonsense* (London: 1855), n.p. I draw some of the comments on Lear in this paragraph and the previous one from my essay '"Some think him . . . queer": Loners and Love in Edward Lear', in *Edward Lear and the Play of Poetry*, ed. James Williams and Matthew Bevis (Oxford: Oxford University Press, 2016), 89–114.
49. Lear, *A Book of Nonsense* (1871), p. 90.
50. Lear, *More Nonsense: Pictures, Rhymes, Botany, Etc* (1872), n.p.
51. Wordsworth, *Poems, in Two Volumes* p. 225 ('A Household Tub'), p. 421. Wordsworth bowed to Coleridge's pressure and replaced the washing tub in later editions with an exotic 'Turtle-shell'. Lear may have re-enlisted Wordsworth's turtle-shell for 'The Courtship of the

Yonghy-Bonghy-Bò': 'Through the silent-roaring ocean | Did the Turtle swiftly go; | Holding fast upon his shell | Rode the Yonghy-Bonghy-Bò' (*Complete Nonsense*, p. 327).

52. Lear, *More Nonsense*, n.p.
53. Wordsworth, *Poems, in Two Volumes*, p. 222, p. 228; lines 36–40, 186–90.
54. Lear, *More Nonsense*, n.p.
55. Wordsworth, *Poems, in Two Volumes*, p. 228.
56. Aldous Huxley, 'Edward Lear', in *On the Margin* (London: Chatto and Windus, 1923), 167–172; 'Nonsense Poetry', in *The Collected Essays, Journalism and Letters of George Orwell*, 4 vols, (Harmondsworth: Penguin, 1970), IV, 64–8.
57. Lear, *More Nonsense*, n.p.
58. 'A deep distress hath humanized my Soul': 'Elegiac Stanzas on Peele Castle', line 36.
59. Shelley, 'Julian and Maddalo', *Shelley's Poetry and Prose*, p. 117; line 179.
60. Donald Davie, *Purity of Diction in English Verse* (London: Chatto & Windus, 1952), pp. 133–59.
61. Alexander Pope, *An Essay on Man*, Epistle II, line 18 in *The Poems of Alexander Pope*, ed. John Butt (London: Methuen and Co., 1963), p. 516; *Don Juan*, IV. 5. 39.
62. T. S. Eliot, 'From Poe to Valéry' (1948), in *To Criticize the Critic* (London: Faber & Faber, 1965), 27–42.

5

Victorian Nonsense and Its Kinships

Martin Dubois

Discovering that Little Nell and her grandfather are not at home, Dick Swiveller in Charles Dickens's *The Old Curiosity Shop* (1840–1) asks to leave them a message:

> 'You'll mention that I called, perhaps?' said Dick.
>
> Mr Quilp nodded, and said he certainly would, the very first time he saw them.
>
> 'And say', added Mr Swiveller, 'say, Sir, that I was wafted here upon the pinions of concord, that I came to remove, with the rake of friendship, the seeds of mutual wiolence and heart-burning, and to sow in their place, the germs of social harmony. Will you have the goodness to charge yourself with that commission Sir?'[1]

This is classic Swiveller. 'Great draughts of words are to him like great draughts of wine', G. K. Chesterton observed, 'pungent and yet refreshing, light and yet leaving him in a glow'; this 'unerring instinct for the perfect folly of a phrase' evinces what Chesterton called 'a lonely literary pleasure in exaggerative language'.[2] Such flights of language recur in Dickens's fiction. They are attached most obviously to characters identified with verbal folly or excess, such as Sam Weller of *The Pickwick Papers* (1836–7), with his stream of so-called 'Wellerisms', or Mr Grimwig of *Oliver Twist* (1837–9), who in a strange turn upon the phrase 'I'll eat my hat' is led continually to repeat 'I'll eat my head!' when stating that he thinks something is unlikely to happen ('We are at a loss to perceive what point and meaning there is in these words, and the constant repetition of them; and such peculiar, inane foolishness is very rarely found in real life', sighed one reviewer).[3] Beyond the talk of his characters, the same pleasure in verbal exuberance can also be witnessed in the way Dickens's '[e]xcessive metaphors bring before the mind grotesque fancies', in the words of the French critic Hippolyte Taine.[4] Taine gives as examples of Dickens's extravagance in description the moment in *David Copperfield* (1849–50) when Mr Mell is remembered to have taken up his flute and blown at it, David says, 'until I almost thought he would gradually blow his whole being into the large hole at the top, and ooze away at the keys', and also Tom Pinch's feeling in *Martin Chuzzlewit* (1842–4) upon finding that his master Pecksniff, in whom he had trusted, is actually a scoundrel: 'Tom had so long been used to steep the Pecksniff of his fancy in his tea, and spread him out upon his toast, and take him as a relish with his beer, that he made but a poor breakfast on the first morning after his expulsion.'[5] In these examples, hallucinatory vision runs away with itself. They operate in the same way as the metaphor that Susan Stewart describes as no longer able to be '"rescued" from nonsense by contextualization': a figure of description that 'instead of having its causality rooted in everyday life situations, becomes itself a kind of causality'.[6]

Why begin a chapter on Victorian nonsense with Dickens? The obvious place to start would be with the two masters of the nonsense tradition, Edward Lear and Lewis Carroll. My point in doing otherwise is to highlight that the category of 'Victorian nonsense' can be expanded beyond this familiar but often isolated pairing. For although we no longer tend to believe that nonsense is peculiarly Victorian, with Lear and Carroll heralded as the creators of 'a new literature' (as Chesterton once had it),[7] the impression remains that, among the Victorians, nonsense techniques were largely peculiar to Lear and Carroll. This is partly a legacy of the purist view of nonsense as an autonomous game of language removed from external reference; it is also a product of the emphasis on Lear and Carroll's nonsense as 'the true inversion or underside of its culture' (as Stephen Prickett argues) and as 'remarkably anti-normative writing' (as John Bowen describes it).[8] What such a view tends to obscure are the many currents of nonsense flowing through Victorian writing more broadly. To take again the example of Dickens: the nonsense similes Lear included in his letters ('I suppose everything will come right some day, as the Caterpillar said when he saw all his legs fall off as he turned into a Chrysalis' is one memorable example) share common ground with the cockney 'Wellerisms' of *The Pickwick Papers*, such as Sam Weller's answer as to if he minds the rain when travelling – 'Wotever is, is right, as the young nobleman sveetly remarked ven they put him down in the pension list 'cos his mother's uncle's vife's grandfather vunce lit the king's pipe vith a portable tinder-box' – and also his remark upon neatening items set out for a wedding breakfast: 'There; now ve look compact and comfortable, as the father said ven he cut his little boy's head off, to cure him o' squintin'.'[9] Likewise, the strangeness found in the description of Coketown in Dickens's *Hard Times* (1854), when 'the piston of the steam-engine' is said to have 'worked monotonously up and down, like the head of an elephant in a state of melancholy madness', also comes close to the manner of Lear's similes.[10] We see here what Garrett Stewart, writing of Dickens, calls a recognition of 'the laughable just around the corner from the habitual'.[11]

Making this type of connection reminds us that while nonsense came into its own in the Victorian period, it was not out on its own in the literary culture of the time. We can see this more fully by observing the exchanges of nonsense with three forms of writing that also achieved new prominence in the period: parody, nursery rhymes, and baby talk. In considering such exchanges, this chapter proposes that the affinities and interactions Victorian nonsense holds with its near relatives enables it to be seen as more than a special case, existing only on the margins of dominant literary traditions and practices. Its cast of actors extends beyond Lear and Carroll to others who borrowed and echoed the techniques of nonsense in less familiar ways.

Parody

For all that certain theorists insist on their difference, it is evident that nonsense often originates in parody. A famous example is Lewis Carroll's poem 'Jabberwocky'. 'Jabberwocky' appears early in the second of the *Alice* books, *Through the Looking-Glass and What Alice Found There* (1871), where it is discovered by Alice printed in mirror writing. She admires the poem but is confused by its meaning: '"It seems very pretty," she said when she had finished it, "but it's *rather* hard to understand! [. . .] Somehow it seems to fill my head with ideas – only I don't exactly know what they are!"'[12] This was not the poem's first outing. The first stanza of 'Jabberwocky' had a previous existence as a 'Stanza of Anglo-Saxon Poetry' printed in one of the family magazines Carroll produced with his siblings, where it appeared appended with a series of bizarre definitions and proposed origins for the stanza's words; this piece of mock scholarship poked fun at the etymological speculations familiar to the Victorian historical study of language. Extended from a single stanza to a full poem, 'Jabberwocky' in *Through the Looking-Glass* evokes the manner of the Anglo-Saxon epics but is no longer obviously directed towards a single or specific target. Instead, in Humpty Dumpty's later explanation to Alice of the poem's meaning, 'Jabberwocky' becomes a spur to speculations about language and meaning, and the nature of the relation between words and concepts. Even in changed form, however, it remains possible to recognise that the origins of the poem are in parody. Indeed, in being formed of an invented language whose words are traced with Anglo-Saxon, 'Jabberwocky' engages the concern of Victorian philology with how English is intimately tied to other languages in a history that stretches beyond national borders.[13]

'Jabberwocky' is typical of the way Carroll's nonsense is parodic in inspiration and orientation. This is true at a number of levels, as may in fact be characteristic of nonsense more generally.[14] The *Alice* books include numerous parodies in the narrow sense of the exaggerated imitation and inversion of earlier texts, of which perhaps the most famous is Alice's inadvertent misrendering of Isaac Watts's instructional verse 'Against Idleness and Mischief' (1715) as 'How doth the little crocodile' (Watts's praise for the diligent industry of a 'busy bee' is turned in Alice's jumbled recitation into admiration for a crocodile who 'welcomes little fishes in | With gently smiling jaws').[15] But Carroll's nonsense is also parodic in the broader sense that it mocks social and institutional conventions and attitudes. Sometimes the object of the parody is relatively precise. The caucus-race in Chapter 3 of *Alice's Adventures in Wonderland*, for instance, clearly sends up competition between political parties (in being organised by a dodo who insists that '*Everybody* has won, and *all* must have prizes' it also cheerfully upends a main lesson of evolutionary theory).[16] On other occasions the target is larger and more diffuse. We see this particularly in Alice's determined but futile attempts to comprehend Wonderland by the habits and precepts of her own society, in which (among other possibilities) is contained an extended mockery of the pressure to conform to societal expectation felt by a child of her sex and class.[17] Such mockery is present throughout both *Alice* books. Even at the banquet near to the end of *Through the Looking-Glass*, when Alice has had enough success in adapting to her new surroundings to be crowned 'Queen Alice', she finds herself perplexed not just by the fantastical character of what she experiences, but by the pointed reversal of the custom she attempts to follow:

> 'You look a little shy: let me introduce you to that leg of mutton', said the Red Queen. 'Alice – Mutton: Mutton – Alice'. The leg of mutton got up in the dish and made a little bow to Alice: and Alice returned the bow, not knowing whether to be frightened or amused.
>
> 'May I give you a slice?' she said, taking up the knife and fork, and looking from one Queen to the other.
>
> 'Certainly not', the Red Queen said, very decidedly: 'it isn't etiquette to cut any one you've been introduced to. Remove the joint!'[18]

As the Red Queen's chiding makes apparent, Alice has in fact committed a double faux pas: the pun on 'cut', which can mean both the making of an incision and 'to affect not to see or know (a person) on meeting or passing him' (*OED*), has her getting it wrong by standards that are at once morally serious (the infliction of pain upon a living creature, something Carroll, as a passionate anti-vivisectionist, personally abhorred) and merely polite (it is rude deliberately to ignore an acquaintance). That such a lapse should have come about from a misguidedly routine effort to show good manners – 'May I give you a slice?' – reveals the inflexibility bred in Alice by the habits of conduct in which she has been instructed. This is a running theme in the *Alice* books, and it means that many of Carroll's parodies in the narrow sense tend also to have broader significance. 'How doth the little crocodile' is typical in this respect: as well as sending up Watts's poem specifically, it also ridicules the custom of compelling children to memorise and recite moralistic verse, and the emphasis on discipline and rote learning which dominated much educational practice of the period.[19]

The success of the *Alice* books was achieved in the context of a thriving culture of parody. Comic magazines such as *Punch*, to which Carroll himself submitted some early verses, catered to the Victorian taste for the lampooning of social fashion, institutional authority, and literary practice both old and new.[20] Victorian parody often had a flavour of nonsense, not least when the parody was literary and drew attention to the tendency for verbalism in Victorian poetry. Thus C. S. Calverley, perhaps the most popular parodist of the period, mocked the inconsequence of the refrains found in Pre-Raphaelite ballads by giving his parody 'Ballad' (1872) a banal refrain exaggeratedly free of any relation to what surrounds it in other lines of the poem: '*Butter and eggs and a pound of cheese*'. The poem ends with disdain for the praise of what is meaningless: 'And this song is consider'd a perfect gem, | And as to the meaning, it's what you please'.[21] Likewise, W. S. Gilbert's 'Oh, Hollow! Hollow! Hollow!', from the Gilbert and Sullivan opera *Patience* (1881), satirises in the empty musicality of its words the aestheticist pretensions of its speaker. The first stanza of the poem runs:

What time the poet hath hymned
The writhing maid, lithe-limbed,
  Quivering on amaranthine asphodel,
How can he paint her woes,
Knowing, as well he knows,
  That all can be set right with calomel?[22]

'Well, it seems to me to be nonsense', declares one of those who hears the poem. 'Nonsense, yes, perhaps', says another, 'but oh, what precious nonsense!'[23] Part of the joke is that language so dreamily opaque is also scatological. Calomel was a preferred Victorian laxative, meaning that the 'writhing maid' is twisting around in pain of constipation rather than the erotic excitement that might be expected from the poem's overblown language. What the parody shows, as Carolyn Williams says, is that 'beautiful forms can lie': drawn to interpret what is represented by the woman's body, we find that 'even this tried-and-true signifier can turn out to be hollow or, even worse, the opposite of hollow – yet a near equivalent – full of shit'.[24]

This nonsensical send-up of an aestheticist absorption in beauty is a traditional type of parody, offering conservative ridicule of new artistic fashions. More unusual is that nonsense parody was also a way for Victorian writers to make light of criticisms of their work. One of the likely targets of Gilbert's 'Oh, Hollow! Hollow! Hollow!' was Algernon Charles Swinburne, a poet who was himself a brilliant parodist, not least of his own writing. Swinburne included as the last poem in his collection of parodies *Heptalogia, or The Seven Against Sense* (1880) the self-parody 'Nephelidia', of which these are the opening lines:

> From the depth of the dreamy decline of the dawn through a notable nimbus of nebulous moonshine,
> Pallid and pink as the palm of the flag-flower that flickers with fear of the flies as they float,
> Are they looks of our lovers that lustrously lean from a marvel of mystic miraculous moonshine,
> These that we feel in the blood of our blushes that thicken and threaten with throbs through the throat?[25]

This is an absurdly exaggerated rendering of Swinburne's distinctive manner, in which some of his favourite devices – including heavy alliteration, long incantatory lines, propulsive anapaestic rhythms, and melodious language – are pressed to the extremes habitually identified by his critics in their censure of his writing. In such self-ridicule is contained both Swinburne's recognition of what might be contrived and formulaic about his familiar style, and also a humorous reproach to his critics: if one were to believe their censure, this self-parody is the kind of poem he would be producing in sincerity, when the reality is actually nothing so excessive. Like Carroll, then, Swinburne uses nonsense parody to hold different kinds of convention up to comic scrutiny, often showing them to be insubstantial or arbitrary.

Lear's nonsense is differently angled. In private, he could employ similar methods to Carroll. The parody found in his letters of the first two stanzas of a poem addressed to him by Alfred Tennyson, 'To E. L., on His Travels in Greece' (1853), has been shown by Anna Barton to represent 'at once a self-effacing refusal to accept the compliment paid by Tennyson's poem and an arch critique of it', in which 'the parodic words and phrases [. . .] hold on to a semblance of sense that in turn discovers a want of sense within their model'.[26] In the nonsense which he chose to publish, however, Lear rarely keeps his literary models entirely at an ironic distance. 'Calico Pie', first published in *Nonsense Songs, Stories, Botany, and Alphabets* (1871), echoes in its refrain the lines 'But the tender grace of a day that is dead | Will never come back to me' from Tennyson's 'Break, break, break' (1842):

> Calico Pie,
> The little birds fly
> Down to the calico tree,
> Their wings were blue,
> And they sang 'Tilly-loo!'
> Till away they flew, –
> And they never came back to me!
> They never came back!
> They never came back!
> They never came back to me!

As is typical of Lear, these lines are at once absurd and poignant, a combination all but impossible in most kinds of literary parody. There are elements that might be expected to puncture the sadness, not least the illogical pairings made with Calico, 'plain white unprinted cotton cloth' (*OED*), which is joined in the opening stanza with 'Pie' and 'tree', and elsewhere in the poem, via the chances of rhyme, with 'Jam', 'Ban' and 'Drum'. The surprise is that they do not: the poem's nonsense lyricism twists Tennysonian melancholy in such a way that Lear is able to call into play opposite emotions of sorrow and laughter.

This is in the nature of Lear's nonsense songs, which, as Hugh Haughton suggests, 'though they include elements of parody, generate uniquely anomalous forms of their own': 'Unlike Carroll who remained structurally dependent on parody as a stimulus to his nonsense poetry, Lear devised a medium with its own logic.'[27] Or as Sara Lodge puts it: Lear 'teeters between sincere echo and parody, exposing the nature of reprise as always potentially melancholy and funny at the same time'.[28] His mode of writing is thus paradoxical in a way that is itself difficult to parody (unlike Carroll's 'Jabberwocky', which was frequently parodied from the moment of its first appearance in print). We need to look elsewhere to discover the literary affinities Lear keeps.

Nursery Rhymes

If one main basis for nonsense exists in the parody of literary culture, the other lineage traditionally suggested for nonsense lies in popular and folk culture, in which it is seen to derive from sources including drinking songs, street and playground games, comic ballads, folk tales and nursery rhymes. This type of culture increasingly made its way into print in the eighteenth and nineteenth centuries. In particular, fairy tales and nursery rhymes which had previously existed chiefly in oral tradition and in chapbooks were collected and set down as part of 'the early nineteenth-century rediscovery of juvenile readers', in which such texts were now 'marked [. . .] specifically as works for children'.[29] One landmark here is the publication in 1823 of an English translation of fairy tales gathered by the brothers Grimm; another is James Orchard Halliwell's pioneering volume *Nursery Rhymes of England* (1842), whose success went a long way to ensuring that the nursery rhyme tradition was a well-established feature of middle-class childhoods by the time Lear and Carroll were publishing their nonsense works. The split in early nineteenth-century children's publishing, which saw a tussle between those who saw children as 'inheritors and future transmitters of a traditional oral repertory' and those who envisioned 'child readers raised solely on improving modern children's books',[30] had by this time become less obvious, in part because of the appearance of new fairy tales (such as John Ruskin's *The King of the Golden River*, from 1851) which combined the moral and the fantastical. Thus, while the association of Victorian nonsense with popular and oral forms may suggest that it existed in contrast or even in opposition to high literary culture – just as might its basis in the parody of established writers and texts – it is also the case that such forms were by this time enjoying an improved status because of their prominence in print culture, where they were increasingly seen as acceptable reading matter for the children of well-to-do families.[31]

The combination of linguistic play and imaginative topsy-turviness found in nursery rhymes helped to place nonsense for its Victorian readers. A notice of Lear's *A Book of Nonsense* (1846, enlarged 1861) in the magazine *Once A Week* is typical in prefacing its praise for Lear ('Never was a book published that so exactly hit the child's mind as this one') with remarks about the appeal and 'universality' of nursery rhymes.[32] Lear himself made drawings for nursery rhymes including 'Hey diddle diddle' and 'Goosy goosy gander'. His friend Marianne North testified that when Lear performed his own settings of music for Tennyson's poetry, 'putting the greatest expression and passion into the most sentimental words', he would 'continue the intense pathos of expression and gravity of face, while he substituted Hey Diddle Diddle, the Cat and the Fiddle, or some other nonsensical words to the same air'.[33]

Lear's nonsense has strong affiliations with popular culture and oral tradition more generally. His first nonsense publication, *A Book of Nonsense* (1846), comprised of limericks, was published under the pseudonym 'Derry down Derry', a name derived from one of the fools who feature in the folk tradition of mummers' plays, as well as a refrain found in early English folk songs.[34] By his own account, Lear was drawn to the limerick form by his discovery of a copy of *Anecdotes and Adventures of Fifteen Gentleman* (c. 1821), attributed to Richard Scrafton Sharpe, a collection intended to compete with *The History of Sixteen Wonderful Old Women*, the earliest known book of limericks, which had appeared a year earlier from a rival children's publisher specialising in books based on fairy tale and nursery rhyme material from oral tradition.[35] There Lear discovered the following limerick:

There was a sick man of Tobago,
Who liv'd long on rice-gruel and sago;
But at last, to his bliss,
The physician said this –
'To a roast leg of mutton you may go!'[36]

In truth, this example of the form is more interesting for its difference from Lear's own limericks than for any similarity. The contrast with a Lear limerick such as 'There was an Old Man of Cape Horn', from his *A Book of Nonsense* (1846), helps to reveal something of the distinctiveness of Lear's methods:

There was an Old Man of Cape Horn,
Who wished he had never been born;
So he sat on a chair,
Till he died of despair,
That dolorous Man of Cape Horn.[37]

Of the two limericks, Lear's is in all ways much the more startling. The narrative of 'There was a sick man of Tobago' may be brief, but it is reasonable; likewise, the earlier limerick only partially submits to the logic of rhyme, which mediates rather than defines the events unfolded in the poem – hence the strained phrasing apparent in the odd syntax of 'To a roast leg of mutton you may go!', a product of the effort to align rhyme and metre with description. By contrast, in 'There was an Old Man of

Figure 5.1 Edward Lear, 'There was an Old Man of Cape Horn', Edward Lear, *A Book of Nonsense,* 25th edn (London: Frederick Warne & Co., 1885), p. 54.

Cape Horn', rhyme is more inevitable, and appears to have at least equal charge of the poem's direction, so that we do not know how to take the limerick's sad and puzzling story. Can the chances of verbal correspondence really be relied upon to reveal something authentic about old age and depression, or are these instead an opportunity to take the poem's events more whimsically? By virtue of their brevity and organisation by rhyme and repetition, Lear's limericks have fun with our desire to see a story go somewhere, often ending up back precisely where they started – a type of inversion that suggests the truth of T. S. Eliot's well-known observation that Lear's nonsense 'is not vacuity of sense: it is a parody of sense, and that is the sense of it'.[38] The same characters recur across the limericks (the Old Man, the Young Lady, the Old Person, the Young Person, and the 'They' by whom they are often viewed antagonistically), as do many of the same behaviours and actions, but even when the limericks are read together it is hard to have confidence in interpretations of their thematic meaning. Characterisations of the 'They' – such as that given by George Orwell, in which '"They" are the realists, the practical men, the sober citizens in bowler hats who are always anxious to stop you doing anything worth doing' – identify a pattern which can only ever be loose, since it is not present across the board.[39] In addition, as in the case of the oddly misshapen figure drawn for 'There was an Old Man of Cape Horn', there are obvious exceptions to Thomas Byrom's rule that in the interaction between Lear's text and drawing, 'the image calms the word': the frequent discrepancy between image and word is only sometimes a means for Lear 'to make life look strange and more joyful'.[40]

What is certain is that, like nursery rhymes, Lear's limericks are joyously attuned to the child's delight in patterns of sound as their understanding of language develops. The same applies to Carroll's nonsense. Modern theories of child language acquisition posit that during acquisition 'children's language use [. . .] is most daring and most advanced when it is used in a playful setting', and that games with words, sounds and meanings, in which language is treated as an object to be exploited and manipulated, are crucial to what is called 'metalinguistic awareness'.[41] The way the *Alice* books highlight the potential for a tiny change of sound to transform meaning is part of their emphasis on the metalinguistic. 'Did you say "pig", or "fig"?', says the Cheshire Cat to Alice after she has informed him of the fate of the baby in the 'Pig and Pepper' chapter of *Alice's Adventures in Wonderland*, a question which hints at how accidents of speech reveal the importance held by particular elements in language ('Freedom there is in language, but order comes first' is how Jean-Jacques Lecercle describes the linguistic intuition of Victorian nonsense).[42] That it is given to a child still early in her literacy to make such discoveries allows the book to remain close to our first experience of discovering the complex structures of language. As Gillian Beer remarks, 'The *Alice* books do not simply *address* a child reader but share that moment of learning to read, in which words still have insecure edges and a nimbus of nonsense blurs the sharp focus of terms.'[43]

It helped that both Lear and Carroll first conceived their nonsense in friendship with children. In Lear's case, the children were those of his artistic patron, the Earl of Derby; in Carroll's case, they were the children of the Dean of his Oxford college. But the divergence in Lear's and Carroll's language play indicates an important difference between their nonsense. In the *Alice* books, games of language (including puns, riddles, dislocations, non sequiturs and visual jokes) have a more intellectual quality than does Lear's play with coincidences of sound and incongruous meanings. Behind the hyper-correct language practices which cause Alice such difficulty in the Mad Tea-Party chapter in *Alice's Adventures in Wonderland* can be seen a fascination with the logic of discourse which is removed in kind from Lear's nonsense, and also contrary to the old impression of Charles Dodgson (mathematician and logician) and Lewis Carroll (pseudonymous writer of nonsense) as separate and distinct identities. We see at play here and elsewhere in the *Alice* books a professional interest in syllogism and paradox quite unlike Lear's creation of loopy semantic incongruities from similarities of sound.

Lear and Carroll were not alone in deriving inspiration for nonsense from the nursery rhyme tradition. Christina Rossetti's collection of nursery rhymes, *Sing-Song* (1872), also has an acute sensitivity to the way children discover the structures of language. The nursery rhyme which begins 'What are heavy?' is one among a number in the collection to tease its readers with the possibility that meaningful connections exist between a word's literal and metaphorical uses:

> What are heavy? sea-sand and sorrow:
> What are brief? to-day and to-morrow:
> What are frail? Spring blossoms and youth:
> What are deep? the ocean and truth.[44]

In both its catechistic form and in its proverb-like concision, 'What are heavy?' has a look of profundity which leads us to expect that its pairings are joined semantically, even when – as in the case of sea-sand and sorrow, or the ocean and truth – what may instead be shown is how wide the gulf can be between the literal and the figurative. Elsewhere in *Sing-Song*, Rossetti inhabits this same difference between literal and metaphorical meanings to surreal effect, as in the riddle which begins 'A pin has a head, but has no hair', a series of fourteen lines all composed according to the formula 'an *x* has *y*, but no *z*', including 'Needles have eyes, but they cannot see', 'A boot has a tongue, but is no singer', and ending 'And baby crows, without being a cock.'[45] Here the formula invites us to envisage that which it negates (a needle with sight, a boot that sings, and so on), with the result for the child reader that, as Constance W. Hassett observes, 'language itself becomes temporarily less transparent, and "that's the fun"'.[46]

What Rossetti shows of the difference between literal and metaphorical meanings she also reveals of rhyme. *Sing-Song* includes riddles and mnemonics that, whether concerned with measures of time ('How many seconds in a minute?') or with colour ('What is pink?'), trace a path through their subject by means of rhyme, only to show, at the last, that its resources are not infinite. Having asked and answered a series of questions on the model of lines such as 'How many months in a year? | Twelve the almanack makes clear', 'How many seconds in a minute?' ends with the lines 'How many ages in time? | No one knows the rhyme'.[47] 'What is pink?', having asked and answered in the manner of 'What is blue? the sky is blue | Where the clouds float thro'', ends stumped by the lack of a rhyme for its final colour: 'What is orange? why, an orange, | Just an orange!'[48] These ploys are a way of unpicking the idea that rhyme is always either shaped by or else shapes deep connections of sense. The logic of rhyme proves to be less circumspect, and the linkages it makes are zanier, as shown by another of the nursery rhymes in *Sing-Song*, 'If a mouse could fly':

> If a mouse could fly,
>   Or if a crow could swim,
> Or if a sprat could walk and talk,
>   I'd like to be like him.
> If a mouse could fly,
>   He might fly away;
> Or if a crow could swim,
>   It might turn him grey;
> Or if a sprat could walk and talk,
> What would he find to say?[49]

This spry piece of nonsense at once celebrates rhyme's capacity to create meaning and belies the idea that such meaning tends to be sensible or even consequential. As elsewhere in *Sing-Song*, we are brought to realise both the importance of a feature or structure of language and to notice the arbitrariness with which it can function.

The nonsense of *Sing-Song*, which is often phrased in the conditional (as in '*If* a mouse could fly'), is never as wholly fantastic as that of Lear and Carroll – a difference suggested to be part of Rossetti's effort to distance her writing for children from that of Carroll.[50] Where she joins with Carroll and Lear, however, is in playing with language in a way that requires her readers (as Roderick McGillis observes of *Sing-Song*) to engage with poetry as 'a form of communication that differs from statement'.[51] In this respect, as an education in what is special to poetry, nonsense is not a minor element in

Rossetti's oeuvre, but a track by which we can approach patterns of words, sounds and rhythms in her writing generally. Reading her most famous work for children, 'Goblin Market' (1862), or the enigmatic 'My Secret' (also 1862, and later 'Winter: My Secret', a poem which in Rossetti's notebook had the title 'Nonsense'), we encounter poems which heighten our awareness of the workings of language in being so much more than the sum of their paraphrasable content. '[M]y secret's mine, and I won't tell', says the speaker of 'My Secret', before venturing a different reason for its remaining unknowable: 'Or, after all, perhaps there's none: | Suppose there is no secret after all, | But only just my fun.'[52] To look to extract a determined meaning may be to get the poem's logic all wrong. Instead, what is foregrounded is verbal play – play that, in enabling the reticence which is the hallmark of Rossetti's style, suggests another impulse in nonsense which resonates widely in Victorian culture at large: its manifestation of the impossible desire for privacy in language. The presence of this desire in the Victorian fascination with nonsensical baby talk is the subject of the next section.

Baby Talk

The *Alice* books have never been out of print; Carroll's nonsense epic *The Hunting of the Snark* (1876), though nowhere near as popular, is still very well known. By contrast, his late nonsense novel *Sylvie and Bruno* (1889) and its second volume *Sylvie and Bruno Concluded* (1893) sold disappointingly in Carroll's lifetime and rest for the most part neglected even now.[53] One cause of this neglect is the odd mix of elements combined in the books, which are made up (among other things) of fairy tale, romance, theological pronouncement and mathematical discussion, all split between parallel plots. Another factor is their cloying sentimentality. The latter is nowhere more in evidence than in the baby talk Carroll gives to the fairy child Bruno, of which a representative example is the report Bruno and Sylvie offer of one of the characters they encounter in the fairy world, the Professor:

> 'He's got a curious machine – 'Sylvie was beginning to explain.
>
> 'A *welly* curious machine', Bruno broke in, not at all willing to have the story thus taken out of his mouth, 'and if oo puts in – somefinoruvver – at *one* end, oo know – and he turns the handle – and it comes out at the uvver end, oh, ever so short![54]

This representation of childish mispronunciation may seem to us unbearably syrupy, but what is hard to swallow for readers now was much in fashion then. Such mispronunciation used as a private language of endearment has a long history, of which a famous example is the 'little language' that Jonathan Swift creates in his *Journal to Stella* (written 1710–13; published 1766, 1768). The late nineteenth century saw the phenomenon made emphatically public, with a gush of baby talk appearing both in poetry for children as well as in child novels such as John Habberston's *Helen's Babies* (1876) and Mary Louisa Molesworth's *Carrots: Just a Little Boy* (1876). The fashion for baby talk was long-lasting enough that it made an appearance in Rudyard Kipling's *Just So Stories* (1903) soon after the turn of the century.

In the case of *Sylvie and Bruno*, Bruno's baby talk shows how Carroll's intense feeling for childhood could turn mawkish. The *Alice* books have long been held to evoke an ideal of childhood derived partly from Romantic writing, in which the child is celebrated as naturally perfect, innocent and spiritual, and as embodying creative imagination, qualities seen in contrast with the concerns and corruptions of the adult world. This may be too simple an impression both of the *Alice* books and of the Victorian 'cult of childhood' as it is manifested in children's literature of the period. In Marah Gubar's recent revision of familiar arguments about Carroll and childhood, the character of Alice is recognised to be thoroughly socialised, and the *Alice* books seen to represent as much an exploration of the child's agency as a dream of childhood arrested in time so as to remain pure and naïve.[55] In the case of *Sylvie and Bruno*, however, the traditional view of the appeal of childhood to Carroll still has validity, which in turn raises familiar and troubling questions about the extent to which the innocent child functions in Carroll's work as a blank space on to which can be projected adult desires.[56]

The baby talk of *Sylvie and Bruno* is worth remarking because it suggests another way in which Victorian nonsense was far from an activity pursued only on the margins of the period's culture. Baby talk was not just a feature of late Victorian poetry for children and child novels. When used in private correspondence, it offered a nonsense outlet for Victorians who in their public personas appear to have had little overlap with Lear and Carroll. The context for such talk was often romantic. The painter Clementina ('Kit') Anstruther-Thomson was in the habit of addressing her lover and collaborator Vernon Lee using infantile language ('just one or two words to say you aren't ill, weeny, weeny', 'I blow you a kiss, little Beloved', 'My little weeny Vernon, I blow you a kiss').[57] Marie Corelli, the bestselling novelist, likewise employed baby talk in the letters she wrote to Arthur Severn in the course of their romantic friendship early in the twentieth century ('When is 'oo tumin? 'Oo must turn Thursday').[58] Such baby talk touches nonsense when it assumes the character of what William Empson, writing of Carroll's 'Jabberwocky', calls 'a code language': 'the language with which grown-ups hide things from children or children from grown-ups' – and, we might add in the case of baby talk used between adults, grown-ups from other grown-ups, in simulating the mispronunciations of children.[59]

The letters from the art and social critic John Ruskin to his cousin Joan Agnew, later Severn (after her marriage to the recipient of Marie Corelli's baby talk, Arthur Severn), are a case in point. Here is a letter from Ruskin to Joan Severn from 1871, signed 'St C.', one of Ruskin's preferred signatures to his intimates:

> Pease – Pease – Pease get
> well and ite poo Cuzzie but [fay]
> one wordie – me so sad – me
> so welly sad – me dont know
> fott _ tt tt tt tt tt to do.
> – Arfie writes me nice etties
> but I cant do without just
> a pencil scratch – me fitened.
> – Me send oo all the kisses
> I've got – me ove oo so much
> so much – Pease come back
> pussie.
> Ever oos voted St C.[60]

As here, Ruskin and Joan Severn's idiolect commonly involved the slurring of words; it included not only baby talk but also what Ruskin named as 'Tottish', the imagined tongue of Scottish toddlerdom. Much of the letter is easily comprehended, but there are signs here of the impulse to secure intimacy by the making of private significance that will come to the fore as the baby-talk correspondence progresses. 'I never write my letters for any peepies to understand but you', Ruskin wrote to Joan in 1886, even if – with Joan's knowledge – he was also to initiate his friend Francesca Alexander in the baby-talk idiom, and use a version of it in his conversations with another friend, Marie Schmidlin, the 'Marie of the Giesbach' of one of the projected chapters of Ruskin's autobiography *Praeterita*.[61] What is noticeable is that Ruskin's desire for special closeness to Joan manifests itself in the wish to arrive at a form of language that in its privacy and distinction from common speech can be truly their own and no other's. This wish is likely to be what lies behind the strange 'Mexican' turn taken in their correspondence in 1876, whereby (as Ruskin tells Joan) '"I love oo." is ni-mits-tsika-waka-thasolta – and a Kiss is a tetenamiquilitzli' – a turn which is only the most extreme instance of a more general disposition to elaborate and opaque ritual in the baby-talk, ritual even Joan herself on occasion sometimes struggled to understand.[62]

This playful and knowing fascination with the dream of a special language that escapes social function is also seen in Lear and Carroll and represents another way in which their nonsense has kinships with the wider culture of their day. In Carroll, it appears most obviously in 'Jabberwocky' and in Humpty Dumpty's claim in *Through the Looking-Glass* that 'When *I* use a word, [. . .] it means just what I choose it to mean – neither more nor less.'[63] In Lear, we see it in a letter written to his friend Evelyn Baring in 1862:

> Thrippsy pillivinx,
>
> Inky tinky pobblebockle abblesquabs? – Flosky! beebul trimble flosky! – Okul scratchabibblebongibo, viddle squibble tog-a-tog, ferrymoyassity amsky flamsky ramsky damsky crocklefether squigs.
>
> Flinkywisty pomm,
> Slushypipp.[64]

The letter mimics epistolary convention in such a way that many elements are recognisable. There is here the form of an opening salutation ('Thrippsy pillivinx') and closing ('Flinkywisty pomm'), as well as the appearance of familiar types of sentences, especially in the initial enquiry and its succeeding exclamation. What results is partly parodic, in that the ease with which we can determine these elements even in a nonsense letter shows how empty or clichéd they can become, but it is also a game with language similar in manner to the 'Mexican' turn of Ruskin's baby-talk letters. 'If language represents our ineluctable publicness', writes Adam Phillips, 'then language as free association is the closest we can get to speaking that contradiction in terms, a private language, a language of desire.'[65] Lear's letter apes the kind of free association seen in Ruskin, whereby private meanings create intimacy, highlighting in the process our reliance on conventional forms and structures, and so emphasising the inevitable public and social nature of all language.

Ruskin described his 'play-letters' as 'the only relief I have for a moment in the day', and in the difference between what he termed his languages of 'Professorial'

(Ruskin was at the time Slade Professor of Fine Art at Oxford) and 'Pessy-wessorial' he evidently found necessary breathing space from the demands of his public life.[66] To assume a lack of connection between these identities, however, would be to repeat the same mistake that leads to the assumption that Carroll and Dodgson were entirely separate personalities. It would be to suppose that the inversions and reversals seen in nonsense occur only on the periphery of culture and in opposition to prevailing forms of thinking and writing. In fact, in Ruskin's case, the baby-talk nonsense is a companion to the inwardness seen in many of his later publications, in which a tendency to make mythology out of personal relations results in the embedding in public writing of obscure private symbols and references.[67]

For Ruskin, then, as it was for Swinburne and his self-parody, and indeed for Rossetti and her nursery rhymes, nonsense is not an outlier, but instead joins with some of the main currents of a writer's work. This should in turn alter how we conceive of the two Victorian masters of nonsense, Lear and Carroll. Their achievements in nonsense remain unparalleled, but the prevalence of nonsense elements in the literature of period more generally means they are not like the misfits of Lear's 'The Daddy Long-legs and the Fly' (1870), a lone pair who, feeling outcast, travel 'Far, and far away' in order to discover a world in which they can make their own fun.[68] Within Victorian culture, Lear and Carroll were in good company.

Notes

1. Charles Dickens, *The Old Curiosity Shop*, ed. Elizabeth Brennan (Oxford: Clarendon Press, 1997), p. 112.
2. G. K. Chesterton, *Charles Dickens: A Critical Study* (New York: Dodd Mead, [1903] 1906), p. 124.
3. S. F. Williams, 'Dickens's Works: A Series of Criticisms', in *The Rose, the Shamrock, and the Thistle* 4.20 (1863), 145–57, p. 156.
4. Hippolyte Taine, 'Charles Dickens: son talent et ses œuvres', *Revue des deux Mondes*, trans. H. Van Laun, repr. in *Charles Dickens: The Critical Heritage*, ed. Philip Collins (London: Routledge, [1856] 1971), 337–42, p. 338.
5. Charles Dickens, *David Copperfield*, ed. Nina Burgis (Oxford: Clarendon Press, 1981), p. 69; and *Martin Chuzzlewit*, ed. Margaret Cardwell (Oxford: Clarendon Press, 1982), p. 556.
6. Susan Stewart, *Nonsense: Aspects of Intertextuality in Folklore and Literature* (Baltimore: Johns Hopkins University Press, 1978; repr. 1989), p. 35.
7. G. K. Chesterton, *The Defendant*, 2nd edn (London: R. Brimley Johnson, 1902), p. 47.
8. Stephen Prickett, *Victorian Fantasy* (Hassocks: Harvester, 1979), p. 126; John Bowen, 'Comic and Satirical', in *The Cambridge History of Victorian Literature*, ed. Kate Flint (Cambridge: Cambridge University Press, 2012), 265–87, p. 280.
9. Edward Lear, *The Complete Nonsense and Other Verse*, ed. Vivien Noakes (London: Penguin, 2002), p. 466; Charles Dickens, *The Pickwick Papers*, ed. James Kinsley (Oxford: Oxford University Press, 1998), pp. 641, 344.
10. Charles Dickens, *Hard Times*, ed. Paul Schlicke (Oxford: Oxford University Press, 2006), p. 26.
11. Garrett Stewart, *Dickens and the Trials of the Imagination* (Cambridge, MA: Harvard University Press, 1974), p. 7.
12. Lewis Carroll, *Alice's Adventures in Wonderland* and *Through the Looking-Glass*, ed. Hugh Haughton (London: Penguin, 1998), p. 134.

13. See James Williams, 'Lewis Carroll and the Private Life of Words', *The Review of English Studies* 64.266 (2012), 651–71.
14. M. R. Haight comments that the 'characteristic effect' of nonsense 'is parody of a playful, fantastic kind, carried out at several linguistic levels', including parody of the operation of language per se: see Haight's 'Nonsense', *The British Journal of Aesthetics* 11.3 (1971), 247–56, p. 255.
15. Carroll, *Wonderland*, p. 19.
16. Ibid. p. 26.
17. For an alternative reading of Alice's insistence on viewing Wonderland through the norms and values of her own society, see Daniel Bivona, 'Alice the Child-Imperialist and the Games of Wonderland', *Nineteenth-Century Literature* 41.2 (1986), 143–71. Bivona proposes that 'Alice has an imperial penchant for producing her own self-justifying evidence as well as an exasperating (although understandably human) tendency to rationalize her own failures of comprehension' (p. 149).
18. Carroll, *Looking-Glass*, pp. 229–30.
19. On the educational function of poetry memorisation and recitation in the period, see Catherine Robson, *Heart Beats: Everyday Life and the Memorized Poem* (Princeton: Princeton University Press, 2012).
20. On affinities between the *Alice* books and *Punch*, see Gillian Beer, *Alice in Space: The Sideways Victorian World of Lewis Carroll* (Chicago: University of Chicago Press, 2016), pp. 75–101.
21. C. S. Calverley, 'Ballad', from *Fly Leaves* (Cambridge: Deighton, Bell, and Co., 1872), p. 50, ll. 39–40.
22. W. S. Gilbert, *The Complete Annotated Gilbert and Sullivan*, ed. Ian Bradley (Oxford: Oxford University Press, 1996), p. 287.
23. Ibid. p. 287.
24. Carolyn Williams, *Gilbert and Sullivan: Gender, Genre, Parody* (New York: Columbia University Press, 2011), p. 179.
25. Algernon Charles Swinburne, 'Nephelidia', in *Major Poems and Selected Prose*, ed. Jerome McGann and Charles L. Sligh (New Haven: Yale University Press, 2004), p. 204, ll. 1–4.
26. Anna Barton, 'Delirious Bulldogs and Nasty Crockery: Tennyson as Nonsense Poet', *Victorian Poetry* 47.1 (2009), 313–30, p. 319.
27. Hugh Haughton, 'Edward Lear and the "Fiddlediddlety of Representation"', in *The Oxford Handbook of Victorian Poetry*, ed. Matthew Bevis (Oxford: Oxford University Press, 2013), 351–69, p. 351.
28. Sara Lodge, *Inventing Edward Lear* (Cambridge, MA: Harvard University Press, 2019), p. 84.
29. Katie Trumpener, 'The Making of Child Readers', in *The New Cambridge History of English Romantic Literature*, ed. James Chandler (Cambridge: Cambridge University Press, 2009), 553–77, p. 554.
30. Trumpener, 'The Making of Child Readers', p. 574.
31. As Michael Levy and Farah Mendlesohn observe of traditional tales, 'In the mid century, fairy tales transmuted into both the subject of antiquarian study and a vehicle for moral guidance. The book market in the nineteenth century was structured in such a way that the new type of fairy tale [. . .] aimed to resonate with the previously disregarded nursery tales and raise them to be suitable parlour fare for both children and adults of the middle classes' (*Children's Fantasy Literature: An Introduction* (Cambridge: Cambridge University Press, 2016), p. 31).
32. 'A. W.', 'Nursery Tales and Toy Books', *Once a Week* 3.53 (1867), 25–7, p. 27.

33. Marianne North, *Recollections of a Happy Life: Being the Autobiography of Marianne North*, ed. Mrs. John Addington Symonds, 2 vols (London: Macmillan and Co., 1892), I, p. 29.
34. Derry Down Derry [Edward Lear], *A Book of Nonsense* (London: Thomas McLean, 1846).
35. The rival publisher was John Harris, who in 1805 had published to great success Sarah Catherine Martin's *The Comic Adventures of Old Mother Hubbard*; Harris would follow this with *Original Ditties for the Nursery* (c. 1805), which included the first appearances in print of 'Little Polly Flinders' and Tweedledum and Tweedledee. See 'Harris, John' in *The Oxford Companion to Children's Literature*, ed. Daniel Hahn, 2nd edn (Oxford: Oxford University Press, 2015), 263–4.
36. 'There was a sick man of Tobago', from *Anecdotes and Adventures of Fifteen Gentleman* (c. 1821). Available at <http://www.nonsenselit.org/Lear/limbooks/fg04.html> (last accessed 24 August 2017).
37. Lear, *Complete Nonsense*, p. 97.
38. T. S. Eliot, 'The Music of Poetry' (1942), in *On Poetry and Poets* (London: Faber and Faber, 1957), 26–38, p. 29.
39. George Orwell, 'Nonsense Poetry' (1945), repr. in *Essays* (London: Penguin, 2000), 324–8, pp. 326–7.
40. Thomas Byrom, *Nonsense and Wonder: The Poems and Cartoons of Edward Lear* (New York: Dutton, 1977), pp. 123, 128.
41. J. S. Bruner, 'Language, Mind, and Reading' in *Awakening to Literacy*, ed. Hillel Goelman, Antoinette A. Oberg and Frank Smith (Exeter, NH: Heinemann, 1984), 193–200, p. 196.
42. Jean-Jacques Lecercle, *Philosophy of Nonsense: The Intuitions of Victorian Nonsense Literature* (London: Routledge, 1994), p. 68.
43. Beer, *Alice in Space*, p. 77.
44. Christina G. Rossetti, *Sing-Song: A Nursery Rhyme Book* (London: George Routledge and Sons, 1872), p. 34.
45. Ibid. pp. 54–5.
46. Constance W. Hassett, *Christina Rossetti: The Patience of Style* (Virginia: University of Virginia Press, 2005), p. 126.
47. Rossetti, *Sing-Song*, pp. 46–7.
48. Ibid. pp. 51–2.
49. Ibid. p. 72.
50. See U. C. Knoepflmacher, *Ventures into Childland: Victorians, Fairy Tales, and Femininity* (Chicago: University of Chicago Press, 1998), pp. 350–77.
51. Roderick McGillis, 'Simple Surfaces: Christina Rossetti's Work for Children', in *The Achievement of Christina Rossetti*, ed. David A. Kent (Ithaca: Cornell University Press, 1987), 208–30, p. 219.
52. Christina Rossetti, 'My Secret', in *Poems and Prose*, ed. Simon Humphries (Oxford: Oxford University Press, 2008), pp. 6–9.
53. An exception here is Gilles Deleuze, who claims that *Sylvie and Bruno* is 'a masterpiece which, in comparison with *Alice* and *Through the Looking-Glass*, displays a set of entirely new techniques'. See his *The Logic of Sense*, trans. Mark Lester, ed. Constantin V. Boundas (London: Athlone Press, 1990), p. 43.
54. Lewis Carroll, *Sylvie and Bruno* (London: Macmillan, 1889), p. 227.
55. Marah Gubar, *Artful Dodgers: Reconceiving the Golden Age of Children's Literature* (Oxford: Oxford University Press, 2010), pp. 93–124.
56. These desires, when seen in the context of Carroll's child friendships, have been controversially suggested to be erotic in nature: see especially James R. Kincaid, *Child-Loving: The Erotic Child and Victorian Culture* (New York: Routledge, 1992). More recent perspectives have tended to be in the nature of Robert Douglas-Fairhurst's view that in respect of children

'Carroll's strongest feelings were sentimental rather than sexual.' See his *The Story of Alice: Lewis Carroll and the Secret History of Wonderland* (London: Harvill Secker, 2015), p. 138.

57. Anstruther-Thomson's baby talk is cited in Burdett Gardner, *The Lesbian Imagination, Victorian Style: A Psychological and Critical Study of Vernon Lee* (New York: Garland, 1987), p. 206.
58. Correlli's baby talk is cited in Teresa Ransom, *The Mysterious Miss Marie Corelli: Queen of Victorian Bestsellers* (Thrupp: Sutton, 1999).
59. William Empson, *Some Versions of the Pastoral* (London: Penguin, [1935] 1995), p. 214.
60. *John Ruskin's Correspondence with Joan Severn: Sense and Nonsense Letters*, ed. Rachel Dickinson (London: Legenda, 2009), p. 136 [2 June 1871].
61. Ruskin, *Correspondence with Joan Severn*, p. 225. 'I've been sending some mewys letters to Francesca too', Ruskin writes to Joan in 1887 (p. 244).
62. Ibid. p. 183.
63. Carroll, *Looking-Glass*, p. 186.
64. Lear, *Queery Leary Nonsense: A Lear Nonsense Book*, ed. Lady Strachey (London: Mills & Boon, 1911), p. 5.
65. Adam Phillips, *Side Effects* (London: Penguin, 2006), p. 70.
66. Ruskin, *Correspondence with Joan Severn*, pp. 98, 115, 177.
67. See Dinah Birch, *Ruskin's Myths* (Oxford: Clarendon Press, 1988).
68. Lear, 'The Daddy Long-legs and the Fly', in *Complete Nonsense*, p. 248.

6

Shady Pleasures: Modernist Nonsense

Noreen Masud

Writing 'Some Notes on my Own Poetry' in 1957, Edith Sitwell describes the public reaction to her dizzying early poems: 'Their apparent gaiety caused them to be suspect. They were useless. They were butterflies. They were spivs.'[1] Her early-career poems in *Façade* (1918–23) offer themselves as butterflies, glistening in an enchanted childhood space. Colours and images flicker, the text folding blithely along the centreline of its own arbitrary rhyme:

> That hobnailed goblin, the bob-tailed Hob,
> Said, 'It is time I began to rob.'
> For strawberries bob, hob-nob with the pearls
> Of cream (like the curls of the dairy girls . . .) ('Country Dance')[2]

The rhymes pop up at the end and in the middle of lines; the butterfly flits around the garden, flashing a new side of its wing each time. Pretty, frivolous, fluttering to a point of nonsense where sound takes precedence over meaning. When Sitwell performed these poems by shouting them out through her papier-mâché 'Sengerphone' – dissolving into nervous laughter, inconsistently audible – meaning drained away even further. The *Daily Graphic* headlined their review 'Drivel They Paid to Hear'.[3] Virginia Woolf wrote to her sister Vanessa on 20 February 1922 to report that Violet Dickinson had described a recital as 'sheer nonsense'.[4] This dismissive set phrase, as James Williams notes, positions nonsense as 'glassy and impenetrable', a cliffside without intellectual footholds.[5] Woolf herself couldn't quite relax into this dismissal. She wrote in her diary, after hearing Sitwell perform in June 1923, 'I kept saying to myself "I dont really understand . . . I dont really admire." [*sic*] The only view, presentable view that I framed, was to the effect that she was monotonous.'[6] *Façade*'s dance between sense and nonsense nags at Woolf, just skirting her understanding and admiration. One 'presentable view' (of Sitwell's monotony) manages to emerge. Others – unpresentable? Unformed? – simmer below the surface, escaping the uneasy critical conversation Woolf holds with herself.

Is this the poetic 'spivviness' that Sitwell mentioned? Something seedy, not quite realised, but definitely suspect or shady? She explains her word in 'Some Notes on my Own Poetry': 'The gaiety of some [of the poems] masks darkness – the see-saw world in which giant and dwarf take it in turns to rush into the glaring light, the sight of the crowds, then, with a terrifying swiftness, go down to the yawning dark.'[7] Sitwell is writing after the see-saw world of the 1940s, when the figure of the spiv rose to cultural prominence. War left human detritus in its wake – deserters and draft-dodgers, living on their wits – who nevertheless filled gaps in the market, supplied unobtainable goods and services for those who could pay.[8] Osbert Lancaster immortalised these spivs in his *Daily Express* cartoons as the fancy-suited, natty-moustached figures loitering on street corners with their suitcases of nylons.[9] On one level, spivs seemed harmless and even lovable. They weren't 'really' criminals, just contact men for a darker underworld,[10] and – the reasoning ran – they got one over on the government to supply the common man.[11] On another level, though, you still needed to be on your guard. That smooth-talking, sleekly dressed character was fundamentally looking out for himself at the expense of others. He might be slipping you coloured water in place of contraband whisky; useless rubbish instead of substance.[12]

The spiv's illicitly fine clothes give him butterfly colour and vibrance – he is highly visible – but he originates in, and stands in for, a darker world for which he acts as messenger. Sitwell's giant and dwarf in 'Some Notes on my Own Poetry' cross over between light and dark, visibility and concealment, lovability and sinisterness. Their mobility between worlds – they are agile, adaptive, fugitive – makes them spivvy. To illustrate her point, Sitwell quotes the original ending of her poem 'Said King Pompey':

> Said the Bishop,
> Eating his ketchup:
> 'There still remains Eternity
> Swelling the diocese,
> That elephantiasis,
> The flunkeyed and trumpeting sea.'[13]

This nonsensical ending, Sitwell suggested, suited 'the moronic cackling of the 1920's over ruin, over their bright-coloured hell'. In response to a spiteful, inane social and literary environment, '[t]he poem', she writes, 'deliberately guttered down into nothingness, meaninglessness'.[14] Nothingness and meaninglessness seemed – to this poet at least – well suited to the period: gleeful, cackling, inane, hellish. What Sitwell implies here is, on one level, that nonsense offers a form which meets the demands of modernist art. More deeply, she suggests that this mode of nonsense is particularly amoral and self-interested: empty in its vibrant patterns. Spivvy, in short. The word hadn't even gained popular currency in the 1920s. But for Sitwell, this emerging model of decorative, opportunistic, smooth-talking wickedness offered a key both to the rise of modern literature, and to its nonsense strategies. Balancing between shows of innocent prettiness and of shady wickedness, nonsense moments in modernism pose a question: how seriously should we take their straightfaced promises to supply us with 'sense'? Engaging fully and rewardingly with modernist nonsense might in fact involve positioning it as a certain kind of playful, creative scam – to which, in some cases, the reader may choose to submit.

Modernism and Nonsense

What kinds of deals did modernist writing strike with nonsense? If the world is nonsensical, ruined, moronic, suggests Sitwell, you need a writing style which matches: which brings together the incongruous, juxtaposes rubbish alongside the precious, arranges objects in a game which has no end and refuses to resolve into a single consoling meaning. Much is familiar in this account of the modernist text. In it, however, we may also recognise Elizabeth Sewell's definition of nonsense – a fixed field in which objects may be rearranged – as well as Wim Tigges's: 'the simultaneous presence and absence of rules, the feeling that arbitrary rules are meticulously adhered to, but might be abandoned at any moment [. . .]'[15] The relationship between authority and rebellion is complex for modernism, as it is for nonsense. When Jean-Jacques Lecercle described nonsense as 'on the whole a conservative-revolutionary genre [. . .] deeply respectful of authority in all its forms', he might easily have been describing the decorous misbehaviour of high modernist literature.[16] Modernist literature does not attend to what we feel it ought to. It dwells on a bar of lemon soap, on a plane tracing advertisements in the sky, on earworms and snatches and rubbish: the base and the ephemeral. And yet it maintains dialogue with the monuments of tradition. T. S. Eliot's *The Waste Land* stages the breakdown of language, even as its footnotes (claim to) preserve and track back to origins; Joyce's great novels take the frames of mythical structures, and position invented words and endlessly punning constructions within them. Crimes are being committed, then, against literature and tradition and the bones of good language, but their scale and gravity are hard to gauge. Both nonsense and high modernism may cooperate with the police when it comes down to it.

Modernism absorbs nonsense structurally, then, but also locally: in its motifs and metaphors. T. S. Eliot loved Edward Lear and was indebted to Lewis Carroll; his poetry ventriloquises music hall, popular song, jokes.[17] The 'HOO HOO HOO' of his hooting characters in *Sweeney Agonistes* (1926–7) echoes the primitive, drum-beating stereotypes which recur in Dadaist nonsense.[18] A nonsense sensibility runs through Wallace Stevens's 'Emperor of Ice Cream'; the elephants dancing through Beethoven in E. M. Forster's *Howards End* (1910); the room crammed floor to ceiling with furniture in Dylan Thomas's *Adventures in the Skin Trade* (1938). And yet we hesitate to agree with Woolf's letter to her sister that some modernist literature might be 'sheer nonsense'. The judgement runs the risk of ignorance. It looks foolish and conventional, perhaps primly Victorian, to deem something nonsense which might turn out to be sense.[19] Hugh Kenner acknowledges this response in *The Pound Era*, and deflects the same phrase on to some useful scapegoats: 'Those Georgian readers [. . .]'[20] To Those Georgian Readers, he suggests, Eliot's 'patient etherized upon a table' in *Prufrock* would have seemed, once again, 'sheer nonsense'.[21] Kenner explains this response in terms of emotions which do not fit one other: '*evening* and *sky* carry feeling in one direction, but the *etherized patient* in another'.[22] Eliot's metaphor involves elements which cannot cohere. It yokes together the incompatible like Lewis Carroll's walrus and carpenter.[23]

How do we talk about these moments of nonsense without rehabilitating them into sense?[24] Modernism's nonsense necessarily has a concealed order which we can access, feels Alison Rieke. She argues that writers like Joyce, Stein, Stevens and Zukofsky 'put [nonsense techniques] to work as hidden sense, the kind of sense or meaning that is only uncovered after considerable digging'.[25] Marnie Parsons twists away from this laborious approach. Sitwell's work, for instance, 'is neither nonsense or not-sense', but does not fully emerge into sense: in her dancing, rhythmic verse, 'the reader is caught in the struggle between meaning and movement, the struggle of meaning *as* movement'.[26] We are back to Woolf's struggle, to drag meaning to the surface from the roil of image and sensation in poems like Sitwell's 'Country Dance', to have a 'presentable view' instead of revolving unease: 'I dont really understand . . . I dont really admire.'

But this revolving unease matters to nonsense writing, and particularly to the nonsense of modernism. Reading modernist literature, we are unsure of when to dig and when to dance along; when to try and understand and when to give up on rationalisation. The problem is that modernism fibs constantly to us about where we ought to stand. Eliot's footnotes in *The Waste Land* promise decodability, but behave in the end as a red herring, leading us to references of limited interpretative value; Eliot himself branded the notes 'bogus scholarship' in 1956.[27] Whether or not we altogether trust Eliot's later verdict, the notes lure us into interpreting where it is possibly inappropriate to do so – taking the joke cerebrally – and the joke therefore rebounds on us. Notoriously, James Joyce made a similar gesture explicit. Reluctant to show the mythical schema underpinning *Ulysses* to a translator, he jokingly explained that he had 'put in so many enigmas and puzzles that it will keep the professors busy for centuries arguing over what I meant, and that's the only way of insuring one's immortality'.[28] Even if Joyce is faking his cynical bid for academic immortality entirely, for laughs, he has clearly considered the point. His brag compounds our injured suspicion, as readers, that we are being cheated: coerced into finding meaning where there might only be 'sheer nonsense'. When we protest in this way – when we call Sitwell's *Façade* or Joyce's *Ulysses* or Wallace Stevens's 'The Emperor of Ice Cream' sheer nonsense – we are really saying: you have sold us a sham product; you are a spiv; you claimed it was whisky but it is really just coloured water.

Ulysses flirts with a status as nonsense, with its coined words, nonsense phrases and topsy-turvy assignation of value to snotgreen seas and lingering bowel movements. *Finnegans Wake* (1939) relaxes further into the mode, becoming what Hugh Haughton calls 'our great nonsense epic':[29]

> I have met with you, bird, too late, or if not, too worm and early: and with tag for ildiot repeated in his secondmouth language as many of the bigtimer's verbaten words which he could balbly call to memory that same kveldeve, ere the hour of the twattering of bards in the twitterlitter between Druidia and the Deepsleep Sea [. . .][30]

Finnegans Wake brings us up to the edge of interpretation: every neologism is packed so densely with connotation that they proliferate out of cohesion. A successful reading, as Michael Wood suggests, must permit much of the text to remain 'sheer nonsense' – 'making deals with surpluses of meaning [. . .] ignoring some of them, converting some of them [. . .] enjoying some of them precisely as surplus'.[31] To read in this way, we have to become both utterly streetwise and freely naïve: to be suspicious and taken in and interrogative and heedless all at the same time. We must buy the whisky in the awareness that it may be coloured water; suspiciously pass up a genuine offer of Scotch; and only occasionally find that our gambles pay off. We cannot trust the spiv shifting his wordy goods on this literary street corner, or our own responses to them. The nonsense of modernism revolves around anxieties about just what we are being sold, and why.

Spectacle in Modernist Nonsense

When she ventriloquises critique of her early nonsense poems as 'useless [. . .] butterflies [. . .] spivs', Edith Sitwell stands up for butterflies and spivs as well as her own work. The spiv is enjoyable as a kind of urban butterfly, flashy in his fashionable suits and distinctive moustache. His role is above all to display. Yet he is also flimsy, shadowy, intangible: vanishing at a touch, or the sight of a policeman, like a butterfly's crumbling wing. He offers a form of spectacle which tantalises because of its fugitivity. Many of the key moments in modernist nonsense have this same quality: of extravagant spectacle which nevertheless crumbles easily away, is lost to the future. The Dadaists' use of meaningless sounds and absurd juxtapositions place them firmly as the most clearly 'nonsense' movement, or movements, of the early twentieth century. But much of their work, such as it was, existed only as ephemera. When the Dadaist Hugo Ball ascended the stage in 1916 to recite his 'abstract poems':

> *gadji beri bimba glandridi laula lonni cadori*
> *gadjama gramma berida bimbala glandri galassassa laulitalomini* [. . .][32]

only a small audience witnessed his startling performance of nonsense. Ball was dressed in a costume of blue cardboard tubes and a gold cardboard collar: the detritus of the everyday made flashy. Yet we have only descriptions and (colour-free) photographs to testify to the scene, and the inert nonsensical syllables on the page. Similarly, Sitwell designed *Façade* as experience as much as poetic text, with elaborate, vividly coloured staging, musical settings, and a system of curtains and megaphones. Reconstructions could be attempted; less easy to stage without parody is Sitwell's inaudible voice and amateurish giggling. These spectacles of modernist nonsense are startling but short-lived: losable, discardable, temporary. After these performances end, their texts can be restaged, but no longer observed in their original form.

Even those privileged to witness these spectacles did not feel fully present with them. On stage, as Sitwell's audience lamented, the poems of *Façade* were even more nonsensical than they were on the page. The work frustrates because, as Woolf's puzzled critique in her diary suggests, it hovers on the edge of comprehensibility, sliding in and out of focus. Susan Stewart's description of nonsense as 'a failed event' resonates here.[33] *Façade* represents a spectacle that has gone wrong. Presented with the markers of event, significance and ceremony which seem to promise value, possessing apparent meaning for Sitwell and her associates,[34] the work nevertheless resists understanding, even as it insists on its own comprehensibility. Like a fuzzing TV, it slides, barely, out of interpretative view.

It is this sense of sense-just-missed, of something almost witnessed but ultimately elusive, which informs the nonsense of Gertrude Stein's *Tender Buttons* (1914). Stein exerted a clear influence on Edith Sitwell, though Stein's nonsense is largely linguistic and Sitwell's has more in common with the fairytale.[35] *Tender Buttons* presents lists of Objects, Food and Rooms, described in deliberate, careful sentences. Within their often accurate syntax, however, inappropriate or maladapted words squat; they transform lines which seem to mimic a guide to etiquette, or a guide to aesthetics, into nonsense:

> COLORED HATS.
> Colored hats are necessary to show that curls are worn by an addition of blank spaces, this makes the difference between single lines and broad stomachs, the least thing is lightening, the least thing means a little flower and a big delay a big delay that makes more nurses than little women really little women.

> [. . .]
> A FEATHER.
> A feather is trimmed, it is trimmed by the light and the bug and the post, it is trimmed by little leaning and by all sorts of mounted reserves and loud volumes. It is surely cohesive.[36]

'[A] spectacle and nothing strange', Stein observes, smoothly and opaquely, in the first paragraph of the poem.[37] Nothing strange? Marjorie Perloff describes how the simplicity of Stein's grammar and observations can initially mask the text's strangeness.[38] But what is strange about *Tender Buttons* is precisely the spectacles that it stages, deflecting their visibility in the same gesture. As far as halfway into the first clause of 'COLORED HATS', interpretation seems unproblematic: beautiful objects are being displayed to view. Coloured hats set off a curled hairstyle. But when we reach 'blank spaces', the scene being sketched suddenly blurs. It resists being imagined, let alone interpreted.

What is so striking about Stein's deployment of nonsense here is that the sensation remains of meaning just missed. She tweaks meaning imperceptibly out of sight, brushing it barely below the surface of comprehension. This is not Edward Lear's physically broad nonsense, where Old Men get smashed, Seven Young Parrots fluffle and guffle and bruffle each other to death, and a Shovel and Broom square off threateningly on a daytrip which turns sour.[39] In Stein's nonsense, the body does not absorb itself in dramatic, liberating movements: the fights and dance and acrobatics which feature heavily in Lear's poetry, limbs and noses expanding gaily to their fullest (im)possible extents. With Stein, we find ourselves in the realm not of gross but of fine motor skills. A feather is trimmed; a 'least thing is lightening'; a 'little flower' is set with a dainty flourish on the top of an impossible-to-envisage situation. These tiny, almost imperceptible movements – fulfilling the 'necessary' and the 'least thing' – seem purposeful and feminine. They might adjust the edges of a charming spectacle: a becoming hat or nicely arranged tablecloth, brought together into a feast for the eyes by a thoughtful finishing touch. Instead, Stein's elaborations on her initial statements ('A feather is trimmed') result in something which cannot in fact be visualised, which lurks just out of sight and resists being grasped. Meticulous, perfected grooming comes to seem shady: a suspect gaiety, which deceives rather than clarifying.

Stein's spectacular nonsense had a wide impact. Walter Conrad Arensberg, of the New York Dadaists, published 'For "Shady Hill," Cambridge, Mass.' in the July 1917 edition of the Dadaist magazine *391*; its style bears an obvious debt to Stein. 'The clothes are on the parlor. They are acted by buttons. To extract the meet, invert as if to the light, registering the first position at half. The passage is in time.' We are drawn ourselves into the same realm of careful adjustment: we extract, we invert, we register, with a perfumer's delicate touch. Abruptly, however, the poem's final line explodes in outrage: 'INTERFERE IN ORDER TO MORrow was once upon a timePIECE OF MY MInd you do not'.[40] We have misjudged something, somewhere – we have 'INTERFERE[d]' one time too many – and receive a sharp scolding (getting a 'PIECE OF MY MInd'). Something has gone too far, in this delicate scheme of adjustments, and the result is outrage. Edith Sitwell's 'En Famille' shows the same interest in the transgressive nonsense of excessive orderliness, as it adjusts sense finely out of sight:

In the early spring-time, after their tea,
Through the young fields of the springing Bohea,
Jemima, Jocasta, Dinah, and Deb
Walked with their father Sir Joshua Jebb –
An admiral red, whose only notion
(A butterfly poised on a pigtailed ocean)
Is of the peruked sea whose swell
Breaks on the flowerless rocks of Hell.[41]

'En Famille' is not exactly nonsense, and yet it is pure Edward Lear. All the parts are in place. Jemima, Jocasta, Dinah and Deb assemble like Lear's broom, shovel, poker and tongs, or like his Violet, Slingsby, Guy and Lionel; they go out to 'take the air' like Lear's table and chair.[42] The 'springing Bohea' has the poker-faced portent of 'the great Gromboolian plain' and the 'Hills of the Chankly Bore' in 'The Dong with a Luminous Nose'.[43] The Chankly Bore is part of Lear's well-trodden landscape – it hoves again into view in 'The Jumblies' – and so is 'Bohea' for Sitwell.[44] Between different poems, 'bohea' morphs between being a dainty afternoon tea and being a place: the dwarfs 'are drinking their bohea' in part 21 of *The Sleeping Beauty*.[45] Sitwell underlines the sophisticated evocativeness of the Bohea by doubling its meaning, making it impossible to imagine as a discrete entity. Aristocratic nicety becomes associated with a nonsensical resistance to vision. Sir Joshua Jebb personifies this tendency: he is another locus where Sitwell assembles a spectacle slipping just out of sight. He becomes a kind of butterfly: not only are his thoughts butterflies, 'poised' on a nicely coiffed sea, but he is an 'admiral red', a reversed echo of 'red admiral'. We wonder: are the girls walking with a formally dressed sailor, or a gravely oversized lepidopteran? In Jebb's very displaying and butterflying, there is a shady invisibility. The lines heap on detail and modification, overadjusting and ornamenting him into a figure who defies visualisation.

Though he frustrates a focusing eye, display matters to this shadowy butterfly-father. When his daughters long to call on the beautiful, 'preened' Myrrhina, he insists that she is too scandalous:

'She gets down from table without saying "Please,"
Forgets her prayers and to cross her T's,
In short, her scandalous reputation
Has shocked the whole of the Hellish nation [. . .]
For Hell is just as properly proper
As Greenwich, or as Bath, or Joppa!'[46]

It is precisely Myrrhina's lack of finish – her refusal to put perfecting touches on things ('please', the crossbar of a T) – that Sir Joshua Jebb deplores. Sitwell invoked hell as a site of ruin and chaos in 'Some Notes on my Own Poetry'; here, the environment of the 'Hellish nation' contrasts absurdly with Jebb's finickiness. It is like Lear's Mrs Discobbolos worrying about finding socially acceptable matches for her children, while they all huddle absurdly atop the wall which is their only home.[47]

Myrrhina does not perform spectacle properly. She sits, highly visible and exquisite, at her window, but does not attend to other daintinesses of social behaviour. Yet, emphasising his very meticulousness of display, Sitwell renders Sir Joshua Jebb himself as suspicious. His finickiness is laughable – his objections echo the smash-happy 'They' of Lear's limericks, who disapprove of unruly conduct – but is there something suspect about his extreme coiffed-ness? Already half-butterfly, his neat behaviour threatens to tip into flimsy ornament rather than military orderliness. The significance of this becomes clear when we remember that, when the spiv attends meticulously to the width of his lapels and the trim of his moustache, the result – as Richard Hornsey notes – is not the fulfilment of duty but suspect masculinity, bordering on an illicit queerness.[48] Too much fine-tuning, as in Arensberg's poem, becomes an offence against society's structures, including those which govern the rules of sense.

What we see, then, in the nonsense of both Stein and Sitwell, is carefully curated spectacle presented as both good and bad behaviour: neat and dainty, but also a kind of over-tinkering of detail that shifts the text away from meaning into chaos. Minute interventions and modifications add up to a whole submerged just below the surface of meaning: like a painting which was finished about eight strokes before the painter finally stopped, and remains irreversibly spoiled. We are left with the sense that we did not fully witness the nonsense text. It happened just out of our reach, in an intangible pass: a response to a situation which was quickly over.

Opportunism and Opportunity

> He believed that it was for the man of letters to record these epiphanies with extreme care, seeing that they themselves are the most delicate and evanescent of moments. He told Cranly that the clock of the Ballast Office was capable of an epiphany. Cranly questioned the inscrutable dial of the Ballast Office with his no less inscrutable countenance.
>
> – Yes, said Stephen. I will pass it time after time, allude to it, refer to it, catch a glimpse of it. It is only an item in the catalogue of Dublin's street furniture. Then all at once I see it and I know at once what it is: epiphany.
>
> [. . .]
>
> Having finished his argument Stephen walked on in silence. He felt Cranly's hostility and he accused himself of having cheapened the eternal images of beauty. For the first time, too, he felt slightly awkward in his friend's company and to restore a mood of flippant familiarity he glanced up at the clock of the Ballast Office and smiled:
>
> – It has not epiphanised yet, he said.[49]
>
> (James Joyce, *Stephen Hero*)

Modernist literature roves around, picking up the everyday scraps it comes across, making them serve some purpose or dissolving them into mere sound. It is opportunistic: it makes the most of unprepossessing materials, and reacts promptly to sudden finds or chances, like the singing woman in Woolf's *Mrs Dalloway*, the chance meeting on London Bridge in Eliot's *The Waste Land*, the rainbow at the end of Lawrence's novel – indeed, like Carroll's Bread-and-butterfly, shaped out of a nursery-tea, and the sieve which Lear gives his Jumblies to use as a boat.[50] Even Stein's *Tender Buttons* alights, one after another, on the objects which surround members of any household. In *Stephen Hero*, then, the clock balances on the edge of epiphany – a high moment of modernist seriousness, where ultimate revelation might manifest itself – and also on the edge of nonsense. It is poised to commit to some antic, like the dish running away with the spoon, or Edward Lear's broom and shovel taking a drive in the park.[51] Therefore small, irrelevant, cheap things come to stand in for a lot in modernism; in the same moment, we suspect that they cannot bear everything being heaped on them. These expectations assume the scale of nonsense. The clock cannot epiphanise, any more than it can go for a drive in the park or run away with a spoon. It is that failed overextension of function, that arbitrary and absurd selection (we know Stephen used the clock as an example because it was right there) which allows Stephen to brush off his own words with a laugh; to implicitly dismiss them as nonsense or just a bit of fun.

This modernist capacity to respond to an occasion, to use chance occurrences as stimulus and produce a text or an extrapolation out of thin air, is nonsense's bread and butter (and indeed its Bread-and-butterfly). When he met some children on holiday, Edward Lear wrote alphabets to amuse them. He created the texts on the discarded scraps of paper he had to hand, leaving them one by one on the children's luncheon plates.[52] Other kinds of letters – those sent in the post – offered occasions for nonsense and fooling. Lear used a letter to Lady Duncan to describe how 'two considerate Frogs' had come to visit him, bringing their tadpoles along on this social call.[53] In the twentieth century, T. S. Eliot followed suit in using the occasional, the incidental, the intimate as an excuse for nonsense. He developed his Practical Cats through correspondence with the Tandys, only later gathering these moments of play with various children into a book.[54] In the same vein, he liked to replace addresses on envelopes with nonsense verse:

> My good friend Postman, do not falter,
> But hasten to Sir Arthur Salter,
> And then enquire for LESLIE ROWSE,
> Who's hidden somewhere in the house [. . .][55]

Lear's influence surfaces here: the disposable opportunity of the letter offers a chance to play (imagining the eminent Rowse as stowaway) without the weight of having to matter, to work properly. These verse addresses do not plan ahead, but simply take their opportunities where they appear, and improvise and invent as they go.[56]

Opportunism, improvisation, slapdash playfulness: these characterise most overtly the instincts of Dada. Placing nonsense at the centre of its practice, Dada emphasises the joy that a spivvy sensibility can offer: the excitement of showing off, sleight-of-hand and bluff. Looking back on the movement, the founder of Berlin Dada, Richard Huelsenbeck, calls its practitioners – not without approval – 'literary jobber[s]'.[57] His own dream, he suggests, had been '[t]o be something like a robber-baron of the pen [. . .] that was my picture of a Dadaist'.[58] Huelsenbeck elaborates on this picture:

> A Dadaist is the man who rents a whole floor at the Hotel Bristol without knowing where the money is coming from to tip the chambermaid. A Dadaist is the man of chance with the good eye and the rabbit punch. He can fling away his individuality like a lasso, he judges each case for itself [. . .] The motley character of the world is welcome to him but no source of surprise.[59]

This is someone who acts first and thinks later, who takes large flamboyant risks and deals with matters as they arise: reckless, slightly dangerous, ultimately admirable. The Dadaists were charming spivs, in other words, before the idea of the spiv gained full currency: spotting opportunities, pouncing on available resources,[60] redistributing and rearranging goods rather than producing anything new,[61] making big claims only meagrely borne out in the art they produced, and all with a knowing delight. In his *Dada Fragments* (1916–17), accordingly, Hugo Ball calls Dada 'a play with shabby debris'.[62] Tristan Tzara, one of Swiss Dada's key figures, advised, tongue perhaps in cheek, that making a Dadaist poem was merely a question of reshuffling sense. We recognise in his instructions an early version of William Burroughs's 'cut-up' technique:

> Take a newspaper.
> Take some scissors.
> Choose from this paper an article of the length you want to make your poem.
> Cut out the article.
> Next carefully cut out each of the words that makes up this article and put them all in a bag.
> Shake gently.
> Next take out each cutting one after the other.
> Copy conscientiously in the order in which they left the bag.[63]

This reorganisation of objects, suggests Elizabeth Sewell, underpins the mechanic of nonsense. She views nonsense as a game which constructs a universe of logical discourse, selected and controlled: 'within this playground the mind can then manipulate its material, consisting largely of names of things and numbers'.[64] In light of this serious play, Tzara's word 'conscientiously', in his Dadaist poem instructions, is good. The cut-up poem is labour without being work: unproductive copying, which does not plan ahead, has no useful product and even undermines other work, by breaking down reliable language. Nonsense tends to be idle in this key way: in the Dadaists' hands, it sails closer to the wind, titillating its readers with an idleness which flirts with transgression. When Sitwell imagined her audience calling her poems 'spivs', one of the qualities she invokes is the type's laziness. It is, Robert Murphy suggests, through his very lounging and gossiping that the spiv acquires his comprehensive knowledge of the underworld and its various players.[65] Strategic laziness was an important Dadaist tactic; they continually insisted on their own importance, wrote manifesto after manifesto on what their work was or would do. Nevertheless, they produced comparatively little work. As David Hopkins points out, Duchamp built up his myth as much via magazines as via exhibitions of his 'relatively meagre output'.[66] Instead, Tzara's manifesto offers a recipe for a larky swizz: how to produce Dadaist art without any work, by simply rearranging and reacting to what is already available at hand.

Dada's playful spivviness simply magnifies a tendency which runs through nonsense, in which chance is key to the text's pleasure. W. H. Auden wrote, in 'Notes on the Comic', that the words in a comic rhyme '[take] charge of the situation' on the basis of their 'auditory friendship', so that 'instead of an event requiring words to describe it, words had the power to create an event'.[67] In one of Edward Lear's limericks, for instance, a man must dance with a raven because he comes from Whitehaven.

The same determination of narrative by rhyme happens, decades later, in Edith Sitwell's 'Popular Song':

> Lily O'Grady,
> Silly and shady,
> Longing to be
> A lazy lady [. . .][68]

Edith Sitwell recalled that *Façade* began as a dare: Richard Greene quotes her as saying that William Walton gave her rhythms and said, 'There you are, Edith, see what you can do with that.' Walton remembers the beginnings differently – he thought that Edith had suggested collaboration – but this performance of opportunism is instructive.[69] It plays out in the rhyme here: 'O'Grady' produces 'shady', or perhaps 'lady' produces both. Sitwell likes the feminine rhymes which often dominate nonsense verse, and when she gets a good one she keeps deploying it. 'Lady' and 'shady' appear also in Poem 18 in the Sleeping Beauty sequence:

> She fled, and changed into a tree, –
> That lovely fair-haired lady. [. . .]
> And now I seek through the sere summer
> Where no trees are shady.[70]

Shady lady, lady shady: as in Joyce's *A Portrait of the Artist as a Young Man*, where Stephen allows the nonsense-image of ivy that 'whines and twines upon the wall' to play through his brain, Sitwell's swapping rhyme threatens to numb meaning.[71] The words behave reversibly, empty units to be played with. But 'shady' retains the shadow of its meanings.[72] To be 'shady' is to be just a little bit suspect, not fully trustworthy. But more, calling someone 'shady' absolves one from the responsibility of spelling out what one finds just a little bit 'not quite right' – like the impropriety that Sir Joshua Jebb suspects of Myrrhine in 'En Famille'. Myrrhine is shady, beyond the pale, but Jebb has nothing to go on but flimsy nursery signifiers of decorum (saying please, crossing Ts). So the word 'shady' is enough: an insinuation which needs no elaboration.

Sitwell's love of the word 'shady' says a lot. Her most nonsensical poems are shady – not quite right; not offering themselves up easily to sense though we feel they ought to be legible – but it is hard to put one's finger on why. That spiv-sourced whisky might not even be something as harmless as coloured water: sewage, perhaps, or poisonous tincture of iodine. A great deal of nonsense, of course, has that feeling of 'not-quite-right'-ness, of the world sent askew. The difference with modernist nonsense is that it starts to feel 'shady' – often pleasurably, sometimes frustratingly – because of the promises it makes to the reader about what it is and what it is doing.

Conclusion: Advertising and Charlatanry

> Dada is the world soul, dada is the pawnshop. Dada is the world's best lily-milk soap.[73]

Dada is good at making promises to its audience. In Hugo Ball's 1916 manifesto, he makes three typically grandiose promises – grandiose, in two cases, precisely because of their startling meagreness. Dada is the world soul, but also the pawnshop, and the world's best lily-milk soap: vast and small and implausibly over-egged all at the same time. Dada is nonsense which is going to change everything in its revitalisation of base and tiny things – as soon as its practitioners get round to it.

Making promises which can't be achieved is itself a well-established sort of nonsense. Noel Malcolm describes how the genre of medieval impossibilia imagines the basic physical features of the world transformed into tempting foods. In the medieval English poem 'The Land of Cockaygne', rivers flow with oil and wine, and ready roasted geese call out 'Hot geese, hot geese' as they fly, advertising themselves as wares.[74] Later, Lear's nonsense recipes promised Amblongus Pies and Gosky Patties, so long as one followed the impossible instructions scrupulously:

> Procure some strips of beef, and having cut them into the smallest possible slices, proceed to cut them still smaller [. . .][75]

Dada situates itself knowingly within this nonsense lineage. When Ball advertises the movement as 'the world's best lily-milk soap', he promises purity, whiteness, reliability. Framed within the image of Dada-as-pawnshop, however, we suspect we will get something altogether grubbier and seedier. Dada's advertisements offer something which isn't really there, and it revels in that fact. In *New York Dada* (April 1921) for instance:

> Dada is a new type; a mixture of man, naphthaline, sponge, animal made of ebonite and beefsteak, prepared with soap for cleansing the brain. Good teeth are the making of the stomach and beautiful teeth are the making of a charming smile. Halleluiah of ancient oil and injection of rubber.[76]

The mixture that is Dada could come out of Lear's recipe for Gosky Patties, but makes even wilder and more insistent promises: beautiful teeth, charming smile, clean brain. Lear, we remember, never claims that Gosky Patties are any good to eat. This is turn-of-the-century nonsense, based around the untrustworthy claims of charlatan advertising. Such claims turn up in A. E. Housman's nonsense poetry, as metrically cooperative final phrase and as punchline:

> The shades of night were falling fast,
>   And the rain was falling faster,
> When through an Alpine village passed
>   An Alpine village pastor:
> A youth who bore mid snow and ice
>   A bird that wouldn't chirrup,
> And a banner with the strange device –
>   'Mrs Winslow's soothing syrup.'[77]

Parodying Henry Wadsworth Longfellow's 'Excelsior', Housman replaces the earlier poet's grand and mysterious banner proclaiming 'Excelsior' with one advertising domestic medicine.[78] The poem goes on, in the pleasingly uneventful way that nonsense does, not amounting to very much or bearing out the dramatic opening with substantive plot. An old man tells the youth to bring his umbrella (the youth replies that he has galoshes); a young woman solicits him (he replies 'Unhappily

I'm married'). Anticlimax follows that Messiah-like entrance, on a dark and stormy night, bearing the two miracles of 'a bird that wouldn't chirrup' and a banner promising the divine cure of 'Mrs Winslow's soothing syrup'. Mrs Winslow's Soothing Syrup proves irrelevant to the plot. It cures no one. And indeed this was always the case. A mixture of morphine, soda ash and ammonium, the American Medical Association had it on its list of 'Nostrums and Quackery' by 1911.[79] Housman's crucial first stanza terminates on a piece of quackery, and that is what this nonsense poem proves to be: making big, spivvy claims at the outset which do not bear out over the course of time.

This is what Dada does, with its endless manifestos and unkept promises, and it does not trouble to hide this affiliation to the quack advertisement. *New York Dada* goes on to warn: 'Therefore, Madam, be on your guard and realize that a really dada product is a different thing from a glossy label.'[80] If there is little more to Dada than the glossy labels of manifestos, the warning to be on our guard seems sound. The advertiser does not trouble to hide the implausibility of his own claims. He is only one rung up from the spiv selling nylons on the street corner, who, when challenged, assures you on one hand that his nylons are the best, and in the same breath asks you how you could expect the best nylons for this price. We know Dada's claims for its nonsense may well be nonsense, but we understand the category error of trying to argue back.

It is this spivvy doubleness which exemplifies the dilemma of modernist nonsense. There is clearly some kind of pretence going on – but in what direction? Is nonsense more sensical than it seems (we accept that *Finnegans Wake* is not nonsense but sense, for instance, and the fragmentation of *The Waste Land* is serving an interpretative purpose), or less? Tristan Tzara declares in 'Monsieur Antipyrine's Manifesto', another key Dada text, 'while we put on a show of being facile, we are actually searching for the central essence of things [. . .]'[81] Don't be fooled by the foolery, he advises. There is sense at the bottom of all this – and not just sense, but 'the central essence of things'! The Dadaists perform their emptiness, but within that performance, they claim, there is a vital significance. Modernism uses nonsense, argues Holly Laird, to unsettle settled meanings, so that its writers might establish the seriousness of their own work, and that of the new structures of meaning they sought to make available.[82] Nonsense, in other words, might make space for a new scale of value. That was, anyway, the hope and the promise.

Along these lines, Hugh Haughton describes how, after Freud organised the apparent meaninglessness of dreams into interpretability, nonsense threatened to get above itself: to become 'a very serious place indeed', in the hands of movements like surrealism.[83] Dreams and free association and startling juxtapositions were put to useful work, serving up insights into the human unconscious. Can we put writers like Stein and Sitwell and Tzara to work in this way? Or might they already be working: a kind of literary black market, trading in unfamiliar currencies? These nonsense writers shift value into surfaces rather than depths, opportune moments rather than lofty eternities, promises rather than pay-offs. And yet they insist, often grandly, on their legibility and significance. That shadiness – caught between clarity and opacity, spectacle and invisibility, arbitrariness and suggestion – preserves them in their own, spivvy, strand of modernist nonsense. But more: it alerts us to the wheeling-dealing, the bluff and nonsense, which might be going on more broadly, behind the most respectable of literary modernist closed doors.

Notes

1. Edith Sitwell, 'Some Notes on my Own Poetry', in *Collected Poems* (London: Sinclair-Stevenson, 1993), xv–xlvi, xvii.
2. Sitwell, *Collected Poems*, p. 130.
3. Quoted in Victoria Glendinning, *Edith Sitwell: A Unicorn Among Lions* (London: Phoenix, 1981), p. 79.
4. Virginia Woolf, *The Question of Things Happening: The Letters of Virginia Woolf, Volume II: 1912–1922* (London: Hogarth Press, 1976), p. 506.
5. James Williams, *Edward Lear* (Liverpool: Liverpool University Press on behalf of Northcote House, 2018), p. 10.
6. Virginia Woolf, *The Diary of Virginia Woolf: Volume II, 1920–1924*, ed. Anne Olivier Bell (London: Penguin, 1981), p. 246.
7. Sitwell, 'Some Notes on my Own Poetry', xviii.
8. Roy Ingleton, *The Gentlemen at War: Policing Britain 1939–45* (Maidstone: Cranborne Publications, 1994), p. 283.
9. Richard Hornsey, *The Spiv and the Architect: Unruly Life in Postwar London* (London and Minneapolis: University of Minnesota Press, 2010), pp. 19–20.
10. Robert Murphy, *Realism and Tinsel: Cinema and society in Britain 1939–1948* (Routledge: London and New York, 1989), p. 150.
11. David Hughes, 'The Spivs', in *Age of Austerity: 1945–1951*, ed. Michael Sissons and Philip French (Harmondsworth: Penguin, 1964), 86–105, p. 90.
12. Donald Thomas, *Villains' Paradise: Britain's Underworld from the Spivs to the Krays* (London: John Murray, 2005), p. 61.
13. Sitwell, 'Some Notes on my Own Poetry', p. xviii.
14. Ibid.
15. Elizabeth Sewell, *The Field of Nonsense* (London: Chatto and Windus, 1952), p. 55; Wim Tigges, *An Anatomy of Literary Nonsense* (Amsterdam: Rodophi, 1988), p. 54.
16. Jean-Jacques Lecercle, *Philosophy of Nonsense: The Intuitions of Victorian Nonsense Literature* (London and New York: Routledge, 1994), p. 2.
17. On T. S. Eliot's connections with Lewis Carroll, see Elizabeth Sewell, 'Lewis Carroll and T. S. Eliot as Nonsense Poets', in *T. S. Eliot: A Symposium for His Seventieth Birthday*, ed. Neville Braybrooke (London: Rupert Hart-Davis, 1958), 49–56; on his relationship with Edward Lear, see Anne Stillman, 'T. S. Eliot Plays Edward Lear', in *Edward Lear and the Play of Poetry*, ed. James Williams and Matthew Bevis (Oxford: Oxford University Press, 2016), 260–80.
18. On Dada's use of African stereotypes, see David Hopkins, *Dada and Surrealism: A Very Short Introduction* (Oxford: Oxford University Press, 2004), p. 7.
19. See, for instance, Alice's uptight declaration that Wonderland's courtroom proceedings are simply 'Stuff and nonsense'. Lewis Carroll, *Alice's Adventures in Wonderland and Through the Looking-Glass*, ed. Roger Lancelyn Green (Oxford: Oxford University Press, 1998), p. 108.
20. Hugh Kenner, *The Pound Era* (London: Faber and Faber, 1975), p. 131.
21. Ibid. p. 132.
22. Ibid.
23. Carroll, *Looking-Glass*, p. 162.
24. On the critical instinct to allegorise nonsense into sense, see, further, Michael Holquist, 'What is a Boojum? Nonsense and Modernism', *Yale French Studies* 96 (1999), 100–17.
25. Alison Rieke, *The Senses of Nonsense* (Iowa: University of Iowa Press, 1992), p. 2.
26. Marnie Parsons, *Touch Monkeys: Nonsense Strategies for Reading Twentieth-Century Poetry* (Toronto: University of Toronto Press, 1994), pp. 147–8.

27. John Whittier-Ferguson, *Framing Pieces: Designs of the Gloss in Joyce, Woolf and Pound* (Oxford: Oxford University Press, 1996), pp. 7–8.
28. Quoted in Richard Ellman, *James Joyce* (London: Oxford University Press, 1966), p. 535.
29. Hugh Haughton, 'Introduction', in *The Chatto Book of Nonsense Poetry*, ed. Hugh Haughton (London: Chatto and Windus, 1988), 1–32, p. 30.
30. James Joyce, *Finnegans Wake*, ed. Robbert-Jan Henkes, Erik Bindervoet and Finn Fordham (Oxford: Oxford University Press, 2012), p. 37.
31. Michael Wood, 'Distraction Theory: How to Read while Thinking of Something Else', *Michigan Quarterly Review* 48.4 (Fall 2009), n.p.
32. Quoted in Hans Richter, *Dada: art and anti-art*, trans. David Britt (London: Thames and Hudson, 1965), p. 42.
33. Susan Stewart, *Nonsense: Aspects of Intertextuality in Folklore and Literature* (London: Johns Hopkins University Press, 1989), p. 4.
34. See Marlene Dolitsky, *Under the Tumtum Tree: From Nonsense to Sense* (Amsterdam: John Benjamins, 1984), p.11, on nonsense as 'a phenomenon of reception; its problematic lies in attributing a meaning to an opaque text which is presumed, however, to have meaning for the emitter'.
35. On the poets' relationship, see Gyllian Phillips, '"Glittering like the wind": Edith Sitwell's Female Poetry' in *The Many Facades of Edith Sitwell*, ed. Allan Pero and Gyllian Phillips (Gainesville: University Press of Florida, 2017), 121–39.
36. Gertrude Stein, *Tender Buttons* (New York: Haskell House, 1970), pp. 24–5.
37. Ibid. p. 9.
38. Marjorie Perloff, *Wittgenstein's Ladder: Poetic Language and the Strangeness of the Ordinary* (Chicago and London: The University of Chicago Press, 1996), pp. 106–7.
39. Edward Lear, *The Complete Nonsense and Other Verse*, ed. Vivien Noakes (London: Penguin, 2006), pp. 172, 197, 242.
40. *391 5* (July 1917), 4.
41. Sitwell, *Collected Poems*, p. 128.
42. Lear, *Complete Nonsense*, p. 277.
43. Ibid. p. 422.
44. Ibid. p. 255.
45. Sitwell, *Collected Poems*, p. 99.
46. Ibid. pp. 128–9.
47. Lear, *Complete Nonsense*, pp. 430.
48. Hornsey, *The Spiv and the Architect*, p. 19.
49. James Joyce, *Stephen Hero*, ed. Theodore Spencer (London: Jonathan Cape, 1956), pp. 216–18.
50. Carroll, *Looking-Glass*, p. 154; Lear, *Complete Nonsense*, p. 253.
51. Lear, *Complete Nonsense*, p. 241.
52. Vivien Noakes, *Edward Lear* (Glasgow: Fontana, 1979), p. 252.
53. Lear, *Complete Nonsense*, p. 191.
54. T. S. Eliot, *The Poems of T. S. Eliot: Volume II: Practical Cats and Other Verses*, ed. Christopher Ricks and Jim McCue (London: Faber and Faber, 2015), p. 40.
55. Ibid. p. 159.
56. Hughes, 'The Spivs', p. 88.
57. Richard Huelsenbeck, extract from *En Avant Dada: A History of Dadaism* (1920), in *Modernism: An Anthology*, ed. Lawrence Rainey (Oxford: Blackwell, 2005), 462–77, p. 464.
58. Huelsenbeck, *En Avant Dada*, p. 465.
59. Ibid.
60. On hijacking commodities as spivs' work, see Hornsey, *The Spiv and the Architect*, p. 107.

61. On the spivviness of this tendency, see Penny Legg, *Crime in the Second World War: Spivs, Scoundrels, Rogues and Worse* (Sevenoaks: Sabrestorm Publishing, 2016), p. 43.
62. Hugo Ball, 'Dada Fragments (1916–17)', in *Modernism: An Anthology*, ed. Rainey (Oxford: Blackwell, 2005), 477–9, p. 477.
63. Tristan Tzara, *Seven Dada Manifestos and Lampisteries*, trans. Barbara Wright (London: Alma Classics, 2011), p. 39.
64. Sewell, 'Lewis Carroll and T. S. Eliot as Nonsense Poets', p. 49.
65. Murphy, *Realism and Tinsel*, p. 150.
66. Hopkins, *Dada and Surrealism*, p. 32, p. 46.
67. W. H. Auden, 'Notes on the Comic', in *The Dyer's Hand* (London: Faber and Faber, 2012), 265–75, p. 271.
68. Sitwell, *Collected Poems*, 146.
69. Richard Greene, *Edith Sitwell: Avant-Garde Poet, English Genius* (London: Virago, 2011), p. 152.
70. Sitwell, *Collected Poems*, p. 94.
71. James Joyce, *A Portrait of the Artist as a Young Man*, ed. R. B. Kershner (Boston and New York: Bedford Books, 1993), p. 157.
72. On the racist implications of 'shady', see Marsha Bryant, 'Sitwell beyond the Semiotic: Gender, Race, and Empire in *Façade*', in *The Many Facades of Edith Sitwell*, ed. Allan Pero and Gyllian Phillips (Gainesville: University Press of Florida, 2017), 94–120, p. 114.
73. Hugo Ball, 'Dada Manifesto', in *Flight out of Time: A Dada Diary by Hugo Ball*, ed. John Elderfield (London and Berkeley: University of California Press, 1996), 219–21, pp. 220–1.
74. Noel Malcolm, *The Origins of English Nonsense* (London: HarperCollins, 1997), p. 82.
75. Lear, *Complete Nonsense*, p. 250.
76. Tristan Tzara, 'NEW YORK DADA', in *New York Dada* (April 1921).
77. A. E. Housman, *Collected Poems and Selected Prose*, ed. Christopher Ricks (London: Penguin, 1988), p. 235.
78. An echo of Lear's 'Uncle Arly', who sold 'Propter's Nicodemus Pills', is also audible here. Lear, *Complete Nonsense*, p. 456.
79. American Medical Association, *Nostrums and Quackery* (Chicago: American Medical Association, 1911), p. 318.
80. Tristan Tzara, 'NEW YORK DADA', in *New York Dada* (April 1921).
81. Tzara, *Seven Dada Manifestos*, p. 1.
82. Holly Laird, 'Laughter and Nonsense in the Making and (Postmodern) Remaking of Modernism', in *The Future of Modernism*, ed. Hugh Witemeyer (Ann Arbor: University of Michigan Press, 1997), 79–100, p. 95.
83. Haughton, *Chatto Book*, p. 22.

7

Mid-Century Nonsense and Destructive Mockery

Adam Piette

Nonsense comes in many shapes and forms but two main types need foregrounding when thinking about modernist comedy: nonsense as a deliberate derangement of ordinary sense-making as in mad anarchistic joyful play; and nonsense as the sarcastic slur used to control those who are less powerful or deemed deviant ('That's nonsense!' as domineering put-down). The Dada-Surrealist wing of European modernism found destructive energy in the organised derangement of the senses associated with Edward Lear and Lewis Carroll – David Gascoyne in his 1935 *A Short Survey of Surrealism* names them as surrealist writers.[1] Carroll features in the first surrealist manifesto, Breton and Aragon write essays on his work, and his nonsense appears in Breton's black humour anthology. Nonsense in this tradition is a gainsaying of bourgeois virtues and power systems through anarchic language gaming. At the same time, a troubling paradox remains at the heart of modernist nonsense. Breton had theorised black humour as a fusion of Hegelian objective humour with more subjective Freudian gallows humour: the object as internalised by the Romantic narcissist retains its social meanings and externality, mimicking the cold heartless superego when the self is threatened by death.[2] This pastiching of cold powerplay inherent in wit (black humour being the enemy of sentimentality for Breton) draws much of its power to overthrow convention from imitation of forms of victimisation. Mireille Rosello critiques Breton's black humour as a miming of pitiless mockery which draws upon 'reactionary masculinity and self-aggrandising disdain for the poor or for women, upon whose bodies many of the cruelties of such humour are played out'.[3] The raillery written into the logic of nonsense can be celebrated for its childlike affectivity, for its subversive political potential, and for its powers to generate wild form and language. But this positive reading skates over the flipside to wit, namely the investment in superego dominance written into the role-playing of nonsense. As Freud put it, 'the humorist acquires his superiority by assuming the role of the grown-up, identifying himself to some extent with the father, where he reduces the other people to the position of children'.[4] This chapter will explore the flipside to wit in modernist nonsense, particularly in the work of Rebecca West and Samuel Beckett, where patriarchal violence and derangement of the mind shape the play of language and the ways of resistance.

The surrealist adopted Victorian nonsense as a style best able to capture the unconscious of culture, deploying both Freudian theories of child sexuality and unconscious fabulations and Marxist-satirical attacks on bourgeois power structures. Lewis Carroll in particular was read as scripting dreamwork as resistance to adult manipulation, signifying freedom as such: 'Alice's freedom begins with the absence, in Wonderland, of Mrs Mother or any delegate of parental authority.'[5] Yet, from another perspective, the only creatures Alice meets are nothing other than a series of pseudo-adult authorities. The nonsense of the books merges the absurdity of adult rules with a 'surrealist' parody of their grotesque (and childish) irrationality. Humpty-Dumpty's language games have a bullying edge that rhymes in sinister ways with the vicious lethal laws commanded by the royal chess pieces. Carroll for the surrealists, then, exemplified the double nature of nonsense as both an unconscious means of disturbing the rigid laws of culture and as the bullying comic procedures of those who have power to hurt.

Comparably, Joyce from the beginning of his career as a writer explored the ways subjects internalise, from childhood on, tyrannical authorities as scarily nonsensical dream forces within the secrets of the psyche. As Stephen muses in *Ulysses*, seeing his former self in a cowed student: 'My childhood bends beside me [. . .] Secrets, silent, stony sit in the dark palaces of both our hearts: secrets weary of their tyranny: tyrants willing to be dethroned.'[6] Importantly, the tyranny has such power in the dark places of the heart because it works there as language. Language acquisition, as Joyce demonstrated superbly in the opening chapters of *Portrait of the Artist as a Young Man*, entails the acquisition of cultural tyrants in the mind concealed in the language learnt. Joyce took notice of the rise of surrealism in the 1930s through his friendship with Eugène Jolas: *transition*, Jolas's avant-garde journal, published the first instalments of *Finnegans Wake*. Both Jolas and Joyce were interested in the philosophy of language with relation to surrealist experiments in child dream language – in particular, they were drawn to the ways such dreams stage the tyranny of family control as revealed in the distortions to language, as with Freudian slips of the tongue, or telling disturbances to syntax. Jean-Michel Rabaté has written well on their reading of the influential work on language signs and symbols, Ogden and Richards' 1923 *The Meaning of Meaning*, which explored the multiple forms of interference which distorted the logic of sense-making in utterances.[7] Ogden and Richards reflect on the treachery of ordinary understanding: 'We may fail to recognize a word qua sound, both when the word is spoken to us and when we are about to utter it ourselves'; 'the context required for the understanding of a word may lapse' – due to aphasia, amnesia, emotional interference.[8] Those lapses, they argued, may be symptoms of social control in the symbol-situation that is generating disruptive and warping effects in the symbolisation, disturbed attitudes to referent and listener, strange promotion of effects, difficulties of expression.[9] The extraordinary deployment of nonsensical procedures of language-distortion in the *Wake* is clearly aiming to capture the psychoanalytic plasticity of the language of dream at night-time; it has also to do with the disturbing factors brought about by individual and collective emotions, memories and failures/lapses of speakers and listeners within difficult controlling contexts. These factors are forms of power relations: 'the power to confuse and obstruct [. . .] is largely due to the conditions of communication'.[10] Ogden and Richards think through symbolisation as a network of treacherous relations and pun on the family complex this implies: 'the relation [. . .] between symbol and referent' is compared to indirect 'family relations'.[11] This family complex colours the ways ordinary language is understood to construct meaning and shapes the misprisions threatening all communications: 'the familiar ways in which language may be used to deceive'.[12] Joyce explores the familial treacheries of sense-production through a compositional choice to infect the graphic shape of words with sound distortions so that nonsense is being generated at the level of the individual phoneme. These distortions mime the psychoanalytic pressure on child language acquisition in dream experiences and mimic the ways all utterances are subject to lapses and failures due to saturation by emotional and cultural interference.

Nonsense is a minor word in the *Wake:* it appears a handful of times, notably in the distortion of 'nursery rhymes' to become the 'nonsery reams' Anna Livia wears to meet her sweetheart,[13] neatly bringing together the child language games that help children move from nonsense to sense in processing language, but also hinting at the ways nursery songs become trivialising piles of paper that oppress, worn by Anna Livia to transform her into self-infantilising paramour. Much more systemic to the book is the distortion of and play on the word 'sense', with over forty overt uses, most often in conjunction with sound, as in the 'sound of Irish sense' (*FW* p. 13), 'soundest sense', 'sound sense', 'soundsenses and sensesound' (p. 121). Joyce skews the reasons understood in language ('sound sense' as sense that is appropriate and logical) with the arbitrary chances of sound effects, thereby subverting the clarities of daytime sense-production: 'socioscientific sense is sound as a bell' (p. 112) implies it is only as reliable as the arbitrary phoneme, so subject, always, to the failure 'to recognize a word qua sound'. 'Common sense' (p. 292) is subject to the disturbing factors of subjectivity, even and especially in post-Freudian childhood: 'innersense' (p. 229) and 'inasense' (p. 391) fuse 'innocence' with 'inner sense', which at night mutates into the ways the child 'sabcunsciously senses' (p. 394).

The sounds of the words generate and signal the lapses and failures generated by multiple contexts of desire; but they are also symptoms of the family relations governing the child and all language acquisition. The dream logic combines innersense with 'no sense at all' (p. 454) and multicultural trans-temporal 'oversense' (p. 378) to create the peculiar nonsense of the *Wake:* and that logic stages an epic series of stories about the nuclear family under dissolution, tales of broken patriarchy and child resistances. At the end of the study period chapter (II.2), the children write a nightletter to their parents which runs:

> With our best youlldied greedings to Pep
> and Memmy and the old folkers below and
> beyant, wishing them all very merry Incar-
> nations in this land of the livvey and plenty
> of preprosperousness through their coming
> new yonks
> from
> jake, jack and little sousoucie
> (the babes that mean too)
> (p. 308).

The letter both obeys nonsensical family law by producing text under parental injunction (as in 'write a Christmas letter to your Pop and Mummy, children!') at the same time as it unpicks that law with unconscious wishes – that both parents will die from their own rapacity (Yuletide becomes 'youlldied' at a time of 'greedings'), that their prosperity in the New Year indicates how preposterous they are, that their future in the New Year signals their outmoded pastness ('yonks'). The nonsense disturbs the communication with infectious sounds that reveal other meanings: the children 'mean too'. As Ogden and Richards argue:

> In all the child's experience, words mean [. . .] joy in using words and in expressing itself in frequent repetition, or in playing about with a word [. . .] reveals the active nature of early linguistic use. And it would be incorrect to say that such a playful use of words is 'meaningless.' It is certainly deprived of any intellectual purpose, but possesses always an emotional value.[14]

Joyce's radical nonsense unpicks the Freudian/Jungian patriarch and his family complex by deploying the language of distortion, verbally introjecting lapses and failures into the phonemic surface, to make a form of soundsense that is an emotional language of child parody of adult forms of control.

Rebecca West, in her 1928 essay 'The Strange Necessity', famously criticised Joyce for narcissistic reactionary sentimentality with *Ulysses*, though she believed it a great book. One of the ways she considered his late work deeply flawed was in its staged incoherence, the broken form implying that consciousness begins understanding the world by way of isolated words and phrases. Not so: consciousness understands the world by way of 'wordless sentences' that language acquisition supplies with verbal form, filling the ghostly preverbal form of syntax.[15] West explicitly attacks Joyce's 'idea of nonsense as a primary state of language' from which sentences emerge: the mistake lies in believing sentences '[represent] sense constructed out of nonsense' (*SN* p. 34); nonsense, rather, is a weapon deployed by the jester; rhyme, jingle, assonance mocking language's 'highest uses' (p. 39). Bloom is one of literature's best court jesters, and it is clownishly that he fulfils his purpose as 'Universal Father': he talks a lot of nonsense, his gibberish a way of saving his children from unlucky belief in the ideal (pp. 42–3).

West's critique of Joyce turns, then, on a redefinition of Joycean nonsense not as a primary state of language but as a mode of clownish patriarchy. This she developed in her 1956 semi-autobiographical novel, *The Fountain Overflows*, where a poltergeist rules the roost at Number 475, Knightlily Road.[16] West's autobiographical child-narrator avatar, Rose, goes to the house with her mother Clare, alarmed at the domestic situation where her cousin Constance lives with her daughter Rosamund, both forced to work long hours because Jock, the husband and father, will not give them enough money; the symptom of which is clearly the poltergeist. The supernatural creature is a thing that haunts and breaks down domestic objects in domestic space; it is also a menace made of nonsense. When Clare and Rose try to stop Constance making any luncheon, she replies, 'Nonsense, I must make a meal for Rosamund and me anyway' and is about to go the kitchen. As though triggered by the word and the move into female domestic space, the poltergeist begins its work:

> A few yards from the house there was a clothesline, on which there were hanging four dishcloths. Three heavy iron saucepans sailed through the air, hit the dishcloths, and fell to the ground. Evidently they had taken to the air without due preparation, for their lids were scattered on the ground below them. I put down the poker, for I realised the nature of the violence raging through this house.
>
> 'Is this what you call a poltergeist?' I asked Mamma. We had read about them in books by Andrew Lang. (*FO* p. 91)

Lang had written the article on 'poltergeist' for the eleventh edition of the *Encyclopaedia Britannica* featuring a famous Worksop poltergeist case of 1883, examined also in the poltergeist appendix to *The Making of Religion* (1898).[17] It features a medium, a young girl called Eliza Rose, whose presence in the house triggers poltergeist destruction of flying domestic objects: 'all day many things kept flying about and breaking themselves', basin, cream jug, clock, 'a miscellaneous throng of objects'[18] – recalling Edward Lear's staging of animate crazy kitchen and dining-room objects. Poltergeist cases, Lang argued, more often than not featured a young girl 'suffering from nervous malady or recent nervous shock'.[19] In West's novel, Rosamund has been traumatised by her father's ill treatment; Jock is a Scottish brute who treats both wife and daughter to savage raillery. That he is Scottish is telling – the mother of Cicely Fairfield (Rebecca West) was Scottish, and had to counteract a Scottish Calvinist-patriarchal upbringing. And it is Scottish folklore which is most useful when thinking about West's staging of the poltergeist as spirit of nonsense. The Scottish Lang gives the story:

> The Highlanders attribute many poltergeist phenomena [. . .] to taradh, an influence exerted unconsciously by unduly strong wishes on the part of a person at a distance. [. . .] We may call this kind of thing telethoryby, a racket produced from a distance.[20]

For West, the telethoryby, or racket at a distance, is generated by the patriarchal pressures internalised by the women of the house as paranoia, as animate uncanny domestic objects, as violent nonsense. The Worksop case as fictionalised in *The Fountain Overflows* draws much of its strange comedy from allusion to Lewis Carroll – the cook throwing kitchen and domestic appliances at the Duchess, baby and Alice in 'Pig and Pepper': 'the fire-irons came first; then followed a shower of saucepans, plates, and dishes'.[21] The saucepans and dishcloths in *The Fountain Overflows* are followed by a smashed jug, a cooking-pot sailing through the air into the garden 'just as the saucepans had done', wrenched curtains ejected through sash windows and trampled into the ground of the garden, etc. (*FO* pp. 91–4). The allusion implies a correlation between the poltergeist and Rosamund's repressed anger about women under patriarchy as servants, kitchen creatures, mothers of pig-babies.

Rose is scared of the 'pack of demons', the 'spectral monsters' who stand 'between my Mamma and me' (pp. 95–6). The poltergeist is also plural, a 'They' who force mother and daughter to live a life of female slave-drudgery: 'They never hurt us. They just break things and spoil things, so that we have to spend our lives mending and washing' (p. 95). Rosamund is not scared of them, and her stoicism and resistance gives heart to Rose. Eventually, Clare and Rose help Rosamund and her mother exorcise the poltergeist simply by the four of them being together in the same room:

> There they lay and stirred no more, nor were ever to stir again in all the known history of that house. To drive out the evil presence it had needed simply that we four should be in a room together, nothing more. (p. 96)

The racket-making spirit returns, however, but in human form, as Jock the husband/father – first announced by 'noises which made me frightened in case the horrible things had come back' (p. 100). But these are thuds and 'an insane amount of noise' made at the door, sounds 'meant to be heard and to distress' (p. 100) – Rose knows that her father is 'on their side' (p. 102), i.e. the same side as the poltergeists, because he makes the same noises as they do.[22] The bullying fact is confirmed when Jock appears and subjects them to dark sarcasm, comic routines, annihilating humour. Jock pretends to be a simpleton to act being secretly 'much cleverer than educated people and [. . .] laughing at them all the time' (p. 101). It is clear, from the consonance of the two names, Rose-Rosamund, that Rosamund is a lightly allegorised version of Rose, as are the two mothers who 'met when they were about as old as we are' (p. 95). Rose and her Mamma also have to suffer a father/husband, Piers, who is reckless with family income, treats his wife and children as secondary to his work as a political thinker, forces the women in the house to extremes of anxiety over their economic fate as dependents without funds. The Scottish Jock is alter-ego to the Anglo-Irish father who is based closely on West's father, Charles Fairfield, who deserted his family when she was eight years old.

The cruel raillery is aimed at the women's domestic routines his own indulgence in patriarchy forces them to undergo – a wit characterised by 'clownishness' (the term used by West to describe Bloom and his nonsense), 'the bow-legged stride of the Scottish comedian, the pointless leer' (p. 296). Mamma challenges him on these contradictions: '"Jock, why must you play the clown?"' And Jock answers: '"Life is so terrible. There is nothing to do but break it down into nonsense"' (p. 305). Nonsense is, then, being analysed by West as a spirit of post-Victorian patriarchy, a remnant of the thinking that enclosed women in the domestic sphere, returning as mockery and buffoonery which mocks little girls as slaves and fools. The wit is destructive of the domestic space by forcing women and girls apart as female agents, and subjecting them to the drudgery of fixing the broken things of the nonsense-beggared home. Jock's raillery issues out of Calvinist disciplinary procedures, but is looser, more anarchic and dangerous than that: for it aims at mind control through bullying verbal and gestural violence, larded with Philistine routines, a teasing misogyny which destroys.

But just as the solidarity of the four women and girls exorcises the ghosts, so does feminist language remove the late Victorian menace of the patriarch. Rosamund tells Rose about the likely future: 'She broke into laughter that was malicious but only gently so. "Oh, the papas will seem such fuss-and-botherers then"' (p. 308). It is an astonishing moment, and Rose is rocked by the words – what surprises her is Rosamund's use of comedy:

> Rosamund had laid an axe at the roots of a tree which I did not care to identify; and I was displeased too because she mocked at what angered her. [. . .] She had not spoken as if she hated my father or her father; she only laughed at them, lying on her bed among her spilled golden hair. (p. 308)

Rosamund is using her father's raillery against him: taking the destructive nonchalance of nonsense and using its telethorybic agency to disable the pretentions of the men who laid the dark trap for the new women of the post-Victorian era. For West, nonsense at mid-century is the ghost of Victorian patriarchy lording it over the naughty little girls of feminist modernism, a ghost which enacts patriarchal sneers and leers at girlish insolence at the same time as it maliciously expresses the trauma of the domestic sphere it constructs and destroys. Yet nonsense can become a weapon of quiet laughing resistance;

possibly because, like the poltergeist, the wit aimed against women has so clearly to inhabit their neuroses, must adopt, though only theatrically, the female household things and words. Rosamund's daring vision of a feminist future beyond patriarchy is a riposte, but also a light act of raillery too, that manages to inhabit the subject position of the Papas with the same gentle maliciousness of the nonsense-wielding comedian.

Nonsense displays the machinery of the father-daughter relationship as symptom, joke and destructive power. For West it also displays, as a modernist form of comedy, the absent presence of the father as source of the daughter's imagination – it haunts the house as poltergeist even when the male is not there; but the ghost still retains a semblance of energy after exorcism, before being spectacularly broken down into nonsense by the feminist artwork that is the daughter's raillery and the feminist mid-century novel. West reveals, in other words, the double nature of nonsense, as at once the mode often taken by patriarchy to ridicule and control the women within the domestic sphere; and as a mode of resistance, of comic counter-raillery.

Samuel Beckett had defended Joyce against West's perceived attack on *Ulysses* in 'Dante . . . Bruno. Vico . . . Joyce', his contribution to the 1929 collection *Our Exagmination Round His Factification for Incamination of Work in Progress* – he mocks West for the Pavlovian theory of aesthetics as well as for buying hats in Paris while attacking Joyce's narcissism. Yet his own work reveals a deeper affinity with West, especially the force of her critique of Joycean nonsense, that assumes nonsense is a primary linguistic state from which sense can be made, therefore devaluing sentence structure, or syntax. And, equally, Beckett has his own version of the Universal Father in his sights too. Beckett's *Watt* features a Victorian patriarch, Mr Knott, who is hardly ever seen outside his quarters, occupying a house that embodies the dead culture of the Anglo-Irish Big House, now ghostly, enigmatic, a zone of radical nonsense.

Watt's entry into Knott's house is scripted as a dissolution into a kind of mad house in that all servants of Mr Knott suffer what Arsene, the previous incumbent of the post Watt is applying for, describes as a sudden imperceptible change in perception of the world. What this change entails is hard to define; in Arsene's words:

> The change. In what did it consist? It is hard to say. Something slipped. There I was, warm and bright, smoking my tobacco-pipe, watching the warm bright wall, when something somewhere some little thing slipped, some little tiny thing. Gliss–iss–iss–STOP! I trust I make myself clear.[23]

The little tiny thing has an effect on the language, not only making it difficult to say, but also infiltrating its slippages into the attempts to say it: Arsene's English goes a little tiny bit strange, with the s-run ('something somewhere some little thing slipped') jostling with the awkward 'some'-repeats and l-string in 'little thing slipped' to create a little structure curiously unpunctuated, only held together by arbitrary sound-repetitions, marking a tiny shift away from logical sequence but maddeningly enough to change the whole world: 'so changed that I felt transported, without my having remarked it, to some quite different yard, and to some quite different season, in an unfamiliar country' (*W* p. 42). Becket's own shift from Ireland to France is being activated here: just as Watt's own train journey seems to situate Mr Knott's house in Foxrock, Beckett's family home, and yet the French-sounding Arsene and his changed language gives translatory evidence that this is Knott-Ireland, another country.

Watt is already a very strange man when he travels to Mr Knott's house, as the opening sequence with Hackett and the Nixon couple demonstrates. His body and mind is on its way to collapse of some kind – perhaps precisely because Watt is a fanatic of order to the point of indulging in permutation games (or as one might say empty formal exercises in syntax) to soothe his spirits. Mr Knott's house turns the logic that soothes him into a form of mania – by taking Watt's love of abstract syntactical form and order and transforming this into nonsense as the most radical turn towards non-sense, no meaning.

The incident of the Galls father and son, piano-tuners is the mystery that triggers Watt's little change with its very absence of meaning, its strong negativity, its nothingness: 'What distressed Watt [. . .] was not so much that he did not know what had happened, as that nothing had happened, with the utmost formal distinctness, and that it continued to happen, in his mind' (p. 73). The sequence of events plays itself out in Watt's mind as an increasingly abstract film:

> the complex connexions of its lights and shadows, the passing from silence to sound and from sound to silence, the stillness before the movement and the stillness after, the quickenings and retardings, the approaches and the separations, all the shifting detail of its march and ordinance, according to the irrevocable caprice of its taking place. (p. 69)

It is as though Watt is discovering the beauty of abstract modernism, but as arbitrary and meaningless parade of visual and acoustic forms, close to West's wordless sentences. The rage to discover what the incident means makes Watt turn to Mr Knott and engage in interrogation of his rituals in the Big House. This little tiny shift – in logical relations between words and things, between things, between bodies and objects and the perception of them – constitutes a shift from sense to nonsense. It is a reversal of the terms of West's critique of Joyce, for the nonsense starts with the syntax then moves in on the isolated words and phrases, fusing the lapses and failures of communication analysed by Ogden and Richards into the very core syntax of apperceptive experience. The Galls incident 'in a sense' resembles other incidents in Mr Knott's house, 'and in a sense not' (p. 69). Everything in the house resembles everything else that occurs, in a sense, i.e. in a sense that can be made into a system. But then 'in a sense not', in a not-sense, all incidents are crazy *puncta* which wound and mock the mind with their singularity. The sense of things in Mr Knott's house is at once a commonly held abstracting of words from things, bodies from perceptions, events from significances, and at the same time a nonsensical swirl of negativities with nothingy, indecipherable, impossible presence-absence. Modernist art at this pitch is abstract because its very syntax is nonsensical; its nonsense a symptom of a schizoid/schizophrenic experiencing of one's own empty life events as obscurely not one's own. The step into nonsensical unreason leads to three modes of madness in Watt's stories: the uncanny nature of objects in the house; the refusal of routines to generate anything more than aporia; and the reduction of the human to the level of the machinic-melancholic, under the compulsion of a radical form of comedy. Objects, like the pot in the kitchen, become uncanny because they lose any connection with their names, and thus lose power even to syntactically connect to anything else, to any other word beyond nonsense strings of sound. Routines become aporetic because they cannot be made to conform to the strict analytic logic Watt believes is the only cure to incomplete epistemological control of the stifling environment of the Big House. And humans are reduced to things because the language has fallen down and can no longer signal affect, only the not-affect of extreme comedy.

But there are limits to the nothing that Beckett's art of nonsense is breaking down: and it is at that limit that Knott as patriarch re-emerges. Ellen Wolff, in her excellent study *An Anarchy in the Mind and in the Heart*,[24] reads Watt as a story about the 'enigmatic landlord-master' of the Anglo-Irish Big House. The estrangements and destructiveness of independence and civil war, followed by the establishment of Eire and the shift into neutrality during the World War, have made the landlord-master a memory-formation, a ghost in the house of Irish fiction and Irish fiction-making. The Big House has become, Wolff argues, 'a slippery dream-product'.[25] Watt with his 'tortured attempt to understand' the Galls and Knott is equivalent to the Irish writer dislodged from country and tradition attempting to interpret Irish history.[26] For Watt, the Galls, as stranger invaders of the house, reconfigure colonisation, Wolff argues.[27] Knott is the landlord-master of Irish fiction, and it is as subject to this enigmatic, crazily immaterial/mental lord and master that Watt's sense of things is dispossessed of sense.

The Galls father and son figure the unbearable vision of a blind continuity from Victorian imperial subject father to post-Independence Free State son in the service of the same old patriarchal and radically absent(ee) landlord that motivates Watt's dismay:

> The mice have returned, [Mr Gall junior] said.
> The elder said nothing. Watt wondered if he had heard.
> Nine dampers remain, said the younger, and an equal number of hammers.
> Not corresponding, I hope, said the elder.
> In one case, said the younger.
> The elder had nothing to say to this.
> The strings are in flitters, said the younger.
> The elder had nothing to say to this either.
> The piano is doomed, in my opinion, said the younger.
> The piano-tuner also, said the elder.
> The pianist also, said the younger. (p. 69)

The fact that this incident develops 'a purely plastic content, and gradually lost, in the nice processes of its light, its sound, its impacts and its rhythm, all meaning even the most literal' (p. 69) is not, then, due entirely to the nothingy nature of the exchange; but because the exchange stages a form of patriarchal anxiety that has a destructive effect on creativity (the ruined piano) and on life (the doomed masters and servants as pianist and piano-tuner). The elder and younger generations signify a father-son relationship that is in bondage, still, to the Anglo-Irish master; and the bondage continues to pertain because of the father-son form of subjection which reproduces it in little. Their only hope is that the piano is properly destroyed – 'Not corresponding, I hope' – signifying self-destruction. The mental death of being the master's servant is being transmitted across the Independence faultline to the new Eire-generation: 'It resembled them in the sense that it was not ended, when it was past, but continued to unfold' (p. 69). 'Nothing had happened, with the utmost formal distinctness, and [. . .]

it continued to happen, in his mind' (p. 73): the 'nothing' is the sign of censorship in the Free State, the censorship of the continuing internalised subjection after the Big House has fallen down. The nonsense that is the post-imperial slave mentality suffered in Mr Knott's house is a symptom, then, of the fact that the estrangement from one's own country that the Big House imposed on the Irish continues to pertain as a ghost of an Anglo-Irish inferiority complex – Eire is still 'an unfamiliar country'.

To become a post-Independence citizen means properly exorcising the poltergeist spirit of the old enemy:

> Watt considered, with reason, that he was successful, in this enterprise ['foisting a meaning where no meaning appeared'], when he could evolve, from the meticulous phantoms that beset him, a hypothesis proper to disperse them, as often as this might be found necessary. There was nothing, in this operation, at variance with Watt's habits of mind. For to explain had always been to exorcize, for Watt. (pp. 74–5)

The meticulous phantoms are generated by the phantasmal persistence of the Big House mentality in Ireland. They are the old patriarchs still there despite being NOT. The exorcism is performed by Watt, as it was by the women and girls in *The Fountain Overflows*, simply by assuming a commonly held view ('with reason') where there is nonsense, meaning where there is no meaning, against the grain of the destructive energies of the phantoms. These phantoms do not throw pots and pans, but dissolve even the very meaning of 'pots' and 'pans', the very meaning of meaning, combining poltergeist estrangement of the object with the 'same destruction' that defaces the subject under the compulsion of the patriarch. But Watt discovers a new subjectivity as subject to Mr Knott, a subjectivity that denies the lethal nonsense of the regime's reification, dehumanisation, and comedic violence, and discovers, like Rosamund's laughter at the Papas, a counter-nonsensical nonsense which is surreal freedom – in a new mad language of one's own, in an unfamiliar country beyond the meticulous master-phantoms and father-elders.

Joycean nonsense as child resistance to the normative feeds off the destructive mockery bourgeois culture reserves for deviants and misfits, and stages that dissolutional, mutational resistance at the level of the phoneme. West's analysis of that mockery as 'poltergeist' domestic ideology and Beckett's sense of the irrational as symptom of the meaning-bleaching effects of arbitrary rule post-Independence show how subversive nonsense plays out the nonsense of power through alter-semantic manoeuvres. All three demonstrate the doubleness of nonsense as symptom of patriarchal control systems, and as anarchic resistance to it through parody and then extreme bids for freedom. As if to return these measures to their origin in Dada and surrealist poetry, work by Jack Spicer stages a childlike writing as comparable nonsense resistance in the avant-garde poetics of mid-century. In a letter to Allen Joyce when he moved to New York from his home in San Francisco, he lamented the city's lack of nonsensical bohemian anxieties he was familiar with out west:

> Like most primitive cultures, New York has no feeling for nonsense. Wit is as far as they can go. That is what I miss the most, other than you, and what is slowly pulling my identity apart. No one speaks Martian, no one insults people arbitrarily,

> there is, to put it simply, no violence of the mind and of the heart, no one screams in the elevator.[28]

Heavily influenced by the nonsense verse of Carroll and Lear, he fused their child verses with Rimbaud, Dickinson, Dada, modernist art as well as the looser idioms borne of New York School-camp attachment to popular culture. The 'Martian' writing speaks in alienated play of the violence of mind and heart as symptom of the greater violence of US culture at mid-century. It was through brave defence of gay relations in the monolithic homophobia of the States that his own brand of nonsense emerges. In his 1956 Unvert Manifesto, nonsense is the mode of queer art and sexual bonding: 'Non-sense is an act of friendship' (*JS* p. 75). That act merges modernist art (here Schwitters and Dada) with surrealist Carroll and Lear as queer camaraderie and hedonism that makes a non-sense of the Christian ideology structuring legal homophobia: 'Nonsense. Mertz, Dada, and God all go to the same nightclubs' (p. 75).

In the 1959 sequence 'Apollo Sends Seven Nursery Rhymes to James Alexander', Spicer moved more darkly to the roots of his child-intimacy with nonsense. Apollo is scripted as a violent god, 'Savage | As the god of plague', destructive and madly playful, figured, for instance, in the third poem as a mouse destroying a chessboard, a principle of violence of mind and heart attacking the gameplay of parental law, its power to play out and command the syntax of subjection in language. The child in this zone is 'a child of the mirror', Alice who dares defy Apollo – the fifth poem recalls his boy self with eyes full ('Of tears? of visions? of trees?'), thinking of game and toy, but maddened by contradictions of desire:

> So close to nonsense that the mind shuttles
> So full of nonsense
> That there could be a hand, a throat, a thigh
> So close to nonsense that the mind shuttles
> Between
> The subway, station of what would'
> Nt. (p. 221)

The eyes are full of the mind's own otherness and unreadable desires, censored before born, yet operating as anguished lust that shuttles the mind to and fro – or is it fear of violence, the hand at the throat? Nonsense here is a symptom of a lethal authority under Apollo (the lord of poetry demanding obeisance to its own radical nonsense-destruction of all 'other' games) at the same time as it figures forth the queer affects that will force this poem we read into being out of the violent contradictions of desire. It takes a great deal of nonsense to split the law of patriarchal syntax that denies deviant desire in two, to mean too against the nonsensically destructive splitting imposed by homophobic culture, to find a sub-way out of the double bind of non-meaning and destructive effacement of illegal desire. Spicer finds a form to deny denial and assert not only the desire forbidden by superego, family and state, but also, in the same breath, articulate the contradictions operating within the language of the body and heart: 'station of what would' | Nt'. Jack Spicer here unleashes a symptomatic non-sense poetry that enacts the radical language-resistance to the patriarchy that we have seen at work in the spirited nonsense of the late modernists.

Notes

1. David Gascoyne, *A Short Survey of Surrealism* (London: Routledge, 1935), p. 132.
2. André Breton, *Anthologie de l'humour noir* (Paris: Jean-Jacques Pauvert, 1966), pp. 12–13.
3. Doug Haynes, 'The Persistence of Irony: Interfering with Surrealist Black Humour', *Textual Practice* 20.1 (2006), 25–47, p. 27. Paraphrasing Mireille Rosello, *L'Humour noir selon André Breton* (Paris: Jose´ Corti, 1987).
4. 'Humour' (1927), in *The Standard Edition of the Complete Psychological Works of Sigmund Freud*, ed. James Strachey and Anna Freud, trans. James Strachey, 24 vols (London: Hogarth Press, 1958), XXI, 159–66, p. 163.
5. 'Lewis Carroll en 1931' (my translation), *Le Surréalisme au service de la Révolution* 3 (1931). Available at <http://melusine-surrealisme.fr/site/Surr_au_service_dela_Rev/Surr_Service_Rev3.htm> (last accessed 1 May 2021).
6. James Joyce, *Ulysses*, ed. Hans Walter Gabler (New York: Vintage, 1986), p. 172.
7. C. K. Ogden and I. A. Richards, *The Meaning of Meaning* (Harcourt and Brace, [1923] 1968), discussed by Jean-Michel Rabaté, 'Joyce and Jolas: Late Modernism and Early Babelism', *Journal of Modern Literature* 22.2 (1998), 245–52.
8. Ogden and Richards, *The Meaning of Meaning*, p. 219.
9. Ibid. pp. 223–7.
10. Ibid. p. 12.
11. Ibid. p. 119.
12. Ibid. p. 16.
13. Joyce, *Finnegans Wake* (London: Penguin, 1992), p. 619. Hereafter referenced in the main text as *FW*.
14. Ogden and Richards, *The Meaning of Meaning*, p. 321.
15. Rebecca West, 'The Strange Necessity', in *The Strange Necessity: Essays and Reviews* (Frome: Butler and Tanner, 1928), 13–198. Hereafter referenced in the main text as *SN*.
16. Rebecca West, *The Fountain Overflows* (London: Virago, [1957] 1984). Hereafter referenced in the main text as *FO*.
17. Andrew Lang, 'Poltergeist', *Encylopaedia Britannica*, 11th edn, ed. Franklin Hooper and Hugh Chisholm, 29 vols (Cambridge: Cambridge University Press, 1910–11), XXII, 14–17. 'The Poltergeist and His Explainers', appendix B, *The Making of Religion*, 3rd edn (London: Longmans, Green: 1909), 324–39. Cf. also Lang's *Cock-Lane and Common-Sense* (London: Longmans, Green, 1894). Rebecca West's sister, Laetitia Fairfield, was 'a member of the Society for Psychical Research and an expert on exorcism', Victoria Glendenning's introduction to *The Fountain Overflows*, p. ix.
18. Lang, 'Poltergeist', p. 15.
19. Ibid. p. 15.
20. Ibid. p. 16.
21. Lewis Carroll, *Alice's Adventures in Wonderland and Through the Looking-Glass, and What Alice Found There*, ed. Hugh Haughton (London: Penguin, 1998), p. 53.
22. Jock's only serious passion is attending seances: soldering the connection between the poltergeist's destruction and his own wit.
23. Samuel Beckett, *Watt* (London: Calder and Boyars, [1953] 1963), p. 41. Hereafter referenced in the main text as *W*.
24. Ellen Wolff, *An Anarchy in the Mind and in the Heart: Narrating Anglo-Ireland* (Lewisburg, PA: Bucknell University Press, 2006).
25. Ibid. p. 158.
26. Ibid. p. 161.
27. Ibid. p. 160.
28. Quoted introduction, *'my vocabulary did this to me': The Collected Poetry of Jack Spicer*, ed. Peter Gizzi and Kevin Killian (Middletown, CT: Weskeyan University Press, 2008), p. xvi. Hereafter referenced in the main text as *JS*.

Part II:
Global Nonsenses

8

In Search of Ancient Greek Nonsense

Sara Chiarini

It is generally assumed that nonsense is an achievement of modern European cultures, but this is true only in part. It is true that the Graeco-Roman civilisation does not offer anything comparable to Victorian nonsense literature as a genre centred on the systematic overturning of those shared and communicable notions about reality and logic that Susan Stewart called 'common sense'.[1] On the other hand, ancient Greek philosophers from the Sophists onwards developed a debate about human language and its functions, which led them to reflect on the capacity of language to convey both truth and falsehood. In that context some philosophers dealt with issues of meaninglessness (Plato) and incongruity (Aristotle). Neither Plato nor Aristotle had any poetic or elaborate form of nonsense in mind but were rather concerned with the kinds of mistakes and misunderstandings that occur within linguistic communication. Plato's ethical approach to language and its function means that to him any untrue statement, regardless of whether it is the product of ignorance, deceit or delirium, does not say anything and is therefore to be considered vacuous.[2] Conversely, Aristotle's analytical approach focuses on the inner flaws of human language and the mechanisms by which communication can fail.[3] In both cases it is clear that in antiquity there was a deep awareness of the capacity of language to bewilder its audience and to describe non-existent or impossible people, places and events.

There have been several scholarly attempts to chase after nonsense in classical literature, and in each case ancient Greek comedy has been seen as the most promising hunting ground. This chapter follows this path and culminates in an examination of a fragment from a Greek comic playwright whose work bears a close resemblance to more modern examples of nonsense. But first, I will tackle a crucial issue of method that can be summarised in two main questions: (1) Is the assessment of a passage or scene as nonsense only possible from the reactions it arouses, be they intra-textual (expressed by a character within the text) or extra-textual (stemming from the audience or the reader)? Are we able to say something about the purpose(s) of the authors in writing those lines? (2) Are all instances of nonsense in ancient literature to be classified as simple tropes, as rhetorical devices for the purpose of humour, laughter, parody, ethical reflection and so on, or is nonsense ever pursued as the ultimate goal of a piece of writing, as in the Victorian period?

Aristophanes' *Birds* as Nonsense Comedy

The first modern scholar to draw an analogy between Victorian nonsense and ancient Greek comedy was Cédric Whitman. In his series of Martin Classical Lectures at

Oberlin College in 1968 he used the category of nonsense to interpret the *Birds* by Aristophanes. The greatest playwright of Old Comedy is well known for his play with linguistic registers, fanciful coinages and hilarious dialogues based on incomprehension between characters.[4] However, it is with reference to the structure and overall content of the comedy Ὄρνιθες (*Órnithes*) that Whitman invokes the analogy with nonsense poetry. The play follows a middle-aged Athenian called Pisthetaerus (that is 'Trustyfriend'), accompanied by his fellow Euelpides (that is 'Goodhope'), who persuade the birds to build a new city between heaven and earth, thereby gaining control over all communications between men and gods. Once the city is built, Pisthetaerus and his bird comrades must fend off the undesirable humans who want to join them in their new utopia. Eventually he is himself miraculously transformed into a bird-like god figure and replaces Zeus as the pre-eminent power in the cosmos.

According to Whitman, Aristophanes' goal was to portray, not some sort of moral or political allegory, but rather 'nothing', in its 'positive meaning of the articulable conception "nothing" or "nothingness", [. . .] as useful to thought and criticism as zero is to a mathematician'.[5] Whitman argues that the *Birds* celebrates the demiurgic power of words over factual reality, especially through the figure of Pisthetaerus, who is able to persuade the population of the birds to build an airy city from which to rule over mankind in place of the gods. The whole process of construction of the new city-state Νεφελοκοκκυγία (*Nephelokokkygía*, that is 'Cloud-cuckoo-land') and the celebration of the primate of the birds over the Olympian gods is read by Whitman as a series of repeated contradictions or, as he puts it, a 'dissociative circularity':

> The equations of the *Birds* cancel out. In order to evade the imperial metropolis [Athens], the imperial metropolis must be rebuilt; in order to achieve reality, reality must be denied existence; in order to find meaning, language must be handed over to its most limitless ambiguities; the return to nature, with its songs and pastures, becomes a return to the city, with its laws and conventions. But what does it all mean? Is it that the *Birds* is meaningless and without relevance apart from its fine artistry? Hardly so; but it is about meaninglessness, the circle of inscrutable nature again, the absurdity which calls for the heroic act of individual freedom and self-transformation.[6]

Whitman's identification of the *Birds* as a nonsense play raises two issues: a hermeneutic and a conceptual one. Is the underlying narrative pattern of the *Birds* – the eternal cycle of rejection and re-establishment of the same values and social structures, as it is brilliantly highlighted by Whitman – best defined as nonsense? Might it be, rather, a beautiful instance of comic reversal in a carnivalesque sense? A confusion between the concepts of nonsense and parodic reversal on the one hand and between nonsense and fictional imagination on the other seems to affect Whitman's analysis. Although we may well agree that Aristophanes had in mind no concrete political situation to be allegorically lampooned while composing this comedy and dealt with broader human behavioural matters, it is hard to maintain that the actual subject of the *Birds* is meaninglessness, even if we view it, along with Whitman, as the exaltation of the inexhaustible resources of linguistic creativity. The plot of the *Birds* does follow a comprehensible order of events and does not challenge the audience with inexplicable inconsistencies. Aristophanes' skilful combination of real and imaginary elements, rightly stressed by Whitman, is the essence of fiction, and this alone does not produce nonsense.[7]

Among all passages from the *Birds* quoted by Whitman, the cosmogony sung by the chorus of birds in the first *parabasis* of this comedy is labelled as a peak of nonsense lyricism by the scholar (ll. 685–704):

ἄγε δὴ φύσιν ἄνδρες ἀμαυρόβιοι, φύλλων γενεᾷ προσόμοιοι,
ὀλιγοδρανέες, πλάσματα πηλοῦ, σκιοειδέα φῦλ' ἀμενηνά,
ἀπτῆνες ἐφημέριοι ταλαοὶ βροτοὶ ἀνέρες εἰκελόνειροι,
προσέχετε τὸν νοῦν τοῖς ἀθανάτοις ἡμῖν τοῖς αἰὲν ἐοῦσιν,
τοῖς αἰθερίοις, τοῖσιν ἀγήρῳς, τοῖς ἄφθιτα μηδομένοισιν,
ἵν' ἀκούσαντες πάντα παρ' ἡμῶν ὀρθῶς περὶ τῶν μετεώρων,
φύσιν οἰωνῶν γένεσίν τε θεῶν ποταμῶν τ' Ἐρέβους τε Χάους τε
εἰδότες ὀρθῶς, Προδίκῳ παρ' ἐμοῦ κλάειν εἴπητε τὸ λοιπόν.
Χάος ἦν καὶ Νὺξ Ἔρεβός τε μέλαν πρῶτον καὶ Τάρταρος εὐρύς·
γῆ δ' οὐδ' ἀὴρ οὐδ' οὐρανὸς ἦν· Ἐρέβους δ' ἐν ἀπείροσι κόλποις
τίκτει πρώτιστον ὑπηνέμιον Νὺξ ἡ μελανόπτερος ᾠόν,
ἐξ οὗ περιτελλομέναις ὥραις ἔβλαστεν Ἔρως ὁ ποθεινός,
στίλβων νῶτον πτερύγοιν χρυσαῖν, εἰκὼς ἀνεμώκεσι δίναις.
οὗτος δὲ Χάει πτερόεντι μιγεὶς μύχιος κατὰ Τάρταρον εὐρὺν
ἐνεόττευσεν γένος ἡμέτερον, καὶ πρῶτον ἀνήγαγεν ἐς φῶς.
πρότερον δ' οὐκ ἦν γένος ἀθανάτων, πρὶν Ἔρως συνέμειξεν ἅπαντα·
συμμιγνυμένων δ' ἑτέρων ἑτέροις γένετ' Οὐρανὸς Ὠκεανός τε
καὶ Γῆ πάντων τε θεῶν μακάρων γένος ἄφθιτον. ὧδε μέν ἐσμεν
πολὺ πρεσβύτατοι πάντων μακάρων ἡμεῖς. ὡς δ' ἐσμὲν Ἔρωτος
πολλοῖς δῆλον· πετόμεσθά τε γὰρ καὶ τοῖσιν ἐρῶσι σύνεσμεν.[8]

[You humans, creatures of the darkness, whose nature is as weak as that of leaves, moulded of clay, ephemeral race with the appearance of shadow, unwinged, living only one day, miserable, dreamlike mortals: listen to us, who are immortal, eternal beings, ethereal, never aging and dealing only with imperishable matters, so that you can learn everything from us about the celestial things. Once you have learned about the nature of the birds, the birth of the gods, of the rivers, of Erebus and Chaos, then you call tell Prodicus on our behalf that he can go weep for the rest of his life.

At the beginning there was Chaos, Night, dark Erebus and wide Tartarus. Neither earth nor air or heaven existed yet. First, black-winged Night laid an egg as light as the wind in the infinite bosom of Erebus. After the revolution of long ages sprang from it the desirable Eros, his back sparkling with golden wings, resembling the swirls of wind. He mated in deep Tartarus with winged and dark Chaos and hatched forth our race, the first to be brought to the light. The race of the immortals did not exist until Eros had mixed together all the ingredients: from the combination of the ones with the others heaven, ocean, earth and the imperishable race of the blessed gods came into being. Thus we are by far the oldest among all the blessed creatures. We are the offspring of Eros, it is clear from many proofs: we can fly and we lend assistance to lovers.][9]

The chorus claims the superiority of birds over all the creatures and divine entities according to an original genealogy that places their birth even before the creation of earth, air and sky, as the offspring of Chaos and Eros. The whole account is an explicit parody of Hesiod's *Theogony* and some descriptions given by the birds do indeed sound bizarre, like the 'egg as light as the wind' (ὑπηνέμιον ᾠόν, l. 695) laid by Night, from which Eros sprang (l. 696). Nevertheless, Whitman's assessment of this image as an 'image of pure nothingness, [. . .] the central image of absurdity, dream, illusion, concentrating in a word all the other images of nothingness' seems rather overstated.[10] This and other details occurring in the passage and across the play look odd and unlikely, but cohere with the plot and do not arouse that alienating effect which is typical of many forms of nonsense. They surprise rather for their extravagance, and contribute to the type of humour pervading the whole play that is based on the parodic reversal of shared notions and beliefs.[11]

Flashes of Nonsense in Old Comedy

Although neither the *Birds* nor any other extant work of ancient comedy can be considered, in its entirety, an example of the formal genre of 'literary nonsense', many elements of such works recall the sorts of linguistic experimentation and play with communicative frames on which modern nonsense poetry is based. Recently, a systematic attempt to explain certain dramatic solutions in ancient comedies with the help of the category of nonsense has been undertaken by Stephen Kidd.[12] His use of the term is instrumental (that is, related to specific rhetorical devices employed by the comic playwright) rather than functional (that is, meant to define the literary scope of a piece or the author's goals).

Kidd links nonsense to two emerging contexts: play and delirium.[13] These are both present in Greek comedies and their respective outputs are categorised as 'positive' and 'negative', despite being eventually unified by the common reaction of disapproval they arouse in the audience – be it in the stalls or on stage. For Kidd, the abstention from interpretation or judgement of a given assertion is the key identifying mark of nonsense in ancient comedy. This implies that nonsense cannot be defined by means of specific and objective features, but only via its reception, so that it should be understood as an 'irreducibly subjective' phenomenon.[14]

Among the positive forms of nonsense are those playful sequences which either convey some symbolic content that lacks a reference, or mock real individuals in a particularly aggressive tone but without the intention to be taken seriously by the people concerned.[15] Negative nonsense on the other hand is generated by a few rhetorical tools typical of comedy, such as iteration, rambling speech, wordplay and coinages, whenever they threaten to obstruct the progress of the plot.[16] That is why purposeless (and apparently foolish) exchanges are usually brought to an end by accusations of nonsense expressed by characters playing the role of the 'straight scolder'.[17] These elements make up the non-serious part of comedies, that part which may or may not arouse laughter, but does not carry any deep political, ethical or religious message.

One type of nonsense, according to Kidd's taxonomy, is verbal aggression against a living person: a subgenre categorised by ancient scholars with the term ὀνομαστὶ κωμῳδεῖν (*onomastì kōmōideîn*). To exemplify this, Kidd chooses an extreme case of satiric persecution, namely the Athenian dithyrambic poet Cinesias, who was made the object of a series of jibes by Aristophanes and other playwrights of Old Comedy.[18] Kidd wonders how such insistent attacks might have affected Cinesias and argues that the only way to 'survive' such verbal aggression would have been to laugh at it together with the rest of the audience.[19] This results in an overlap between sense and seriousness on the one side and nonsense and humour on the other. According to this 'ethical' approach, which recalls a Platonic understanding of nonsense, any statement that does not convey a truthful message falls into the category of nonsense.[20]

Kidd's exploration of humorous comic experimentation with language touches on a more familiar understanding of literary nonsense. Kidd examines tropes such as neologisms, non-aggressive puns and wordplay, and identifies 'abuse' or 'excessive amplification' in terms of their nonsense effect: whenever a pun or wordplay lacks an allusion to a real situation or person, that is it seems to have been composed for the fun of juggling with words, it passes the boundary from sense into nonsense. For instance, the series of gags studding the scene from Aristophanes' *Birds* in which Euelpides, Pisthetaerus and the Hoopoe – the leader of the birds' community – observe the arrival of the birds summoned to assembly, is viewed by Kidd as an anti-climax from referential (what Kidd terms, 'successful') to non-referential (described by Kidd as 'feeble') puns (ll. 267–309). The main characters have a joke ready for each type of bird appearing on stage; Kidd considers a series of puns based on the Greek term for 'crest' (λόφος) exemplary of a 'degradation' of humour towards nonsense (since the attribution of these lines to any of the three characters involved in the scene is debated, I have left them unmarked):

ὦ Πόσειδον, ἕτερος αὖ τις βαπτὸς ὄρνις οὑτοσί.
τίς ὀνομάζεταί ποθ' οὗτος;
οὑτοσὶ κατωφαγᾶς.
ἔστι γὰρ κατωφαγᾶς τις ἄλλος ἢ Κλεώνυμος;
πῶς ἂν οὖν Κλεώνυμός γ' ὢν οὐκ ἀπέβαλε τὸν λόφον;
ἀλλὰ μέντοι τίς ποθ' ἡ λόφωσις ἡ τῶν ὀρνέων;
ἢ 'πὶ τὸν δίαυλον ἦλθον;
ὥσπερ οἱ Κᾶρες μὲν οὖν
ἐπὶ λόφων οἰκοῦσιν ὦγάθ' ἀσφαλείας οὕνεκα (ll. 287–94)

– By Poseidon, another colourful bird here. What is this one called?
– This here is a 'gluttonous'.
– Does any other 'gluttonous' exist beside Cleonymus?
– And why, if he is Cleonymus, hasn't he thrown away his crest?
– And what is all this being crested of the birds? Have they come for the hoplite race?
– Well, actually they inhabit the crests for the sake of safety, like the Carians.

The butt of this series of jokes is Cleonymus, a general and political ally of Cleon, and a frequent target of Aristophanes' jibes. While the identification of Cleonymus with a bird eating with its head down to the ground – the literal meaning of κατωφαγᾶς – hints at his gluttony, and the dropping of the (crested) helmet alludes to his cowardice in battle, the two following puns abandon the link with Cleonymus and simply expand the wordplay around λόφος/crest. The 'point' of the last two jokes is merely the homophony between the crests of birds, helmets and mountains. Kidd writes:

> The devolution of sense in this pun series can be seen, not so much as an inadvertent decrease in joke quality, but as an attempt to push language, in play, to a certain volatile boundary. That is, the crescendo or climax that is being created over these eight lines is not one of sense – indeed, the jokes become less and less 'pointed' through these lines – but rather a crescendo of meaninglessness, of lines becoming increasingly senseless. It is as if, in this larger stretch of wordplay, the perception of nonsense is actually being aimed at.[21]

This same observation applies to Aristophanes' coinages and repetitions,[22] whose occasional exaggeration stops just short of bewildering the audience. Language play in ancient Greek comedy is always subordinate to the chief purpose of amusing the audience. It is not driven by the intellectual desire to explore (and cross) the limits of the communicable or the comprehensible, but rather to provide that comic framework within which significant contents can be conveyed.[23]

A last group of sources seems to be the most promising material in which to look for more advanced forms of literary nonsense in antiquity. It consists of metaphorical language that lacks its tenor, as Kidd defines it.[24] Two types of texts are included in this category: allegories and metaphors on the one side and riddles on the other. While metaphors and, above all, allegories built around characters that symbolise someone or something else, tend to operate across the entire play, puzzles occur rather as autonomous local units. As in the case of jokes and wordplay, it is the expansion of the allegory or metaphor to include apparently purposeless details that makes nonsense seep into such passages. Kidd's example of a nonsense metaphor comes from *Peace*, a play written during the Peloponnesian War between Athens and Sparta, which describes a farmer who flies to heaven on a monstrous dung beetle in search of the lost goddess Peace, only to discover that the God of War has buried her in a pit. With the help of a chorus of farmers, the farmer Trygaeus rescues Peace, Theoria and Oporia, and the play ends with a joyful celebration of marriage and fertility. Trygaeus conceals the sexual fantasies of the Athenians from the beautiful Theoria (personification of the Festival), now released from her captivity, beneath a series of athletic metaphors:

> ἔπειτ' ἀγῶνά γ' εὐθὺς ἐξέσται ποεῖν
> ταύτην ἔχουσιν αὔριον καλὸν πάνυ,
> ἐπὶ γῆς παλαίειν, τετραποδηδὸν ἑστάναι,
> [πλαγίαν καταβάλλειν, εἰς γόνατα κύβδ' ἱστάναι,]
> καὶ παγκράτιόν γ' ὑπαλειψαμένοις νεανικῶς
> παίειν, ὀρύττειν, πὺξ ὁμοῦ καὶ τῷ πέει.
> τρίτῃ δὲ μετὰ ταῦθ' ἱπποδρομίαν ἄξετε,
> ἵνα δὴ κέλης κέλητι παρακελητιεῖ,
> ἅρματα δ' ἐπ' ἀλλήλοισιν ἀνατετραμμένα
> φυσῶντα καὶ πνέοντα προσκινήσεται,
> ἕτεροι δὲ κείσονταί γ' ἀπεψωλημένοι
> περὶ ταῖσι καμπαῖς ἡνίοχοι πεπτωκότες. (ll. 894–905)[25]

> Now that you have her, you can organise already tomorrow a beautiful contest: wrestling her on the ground, getting her on all fours, throwing her on the flank, pushing her down on her knees, then, rubbed with oil, striking her vigorously while you wrestle, digging her with fist and penis at the same time.
>
> After all this, you shall run a horse race on the third day, where horse will ride side by side with horse and – the chariots overturned one on top of the other – will rush whinnying and panting, while other drivers will lie down with their penises in plain sight, having fallen next to the turning posts.

Here, Kidd notices a progression similar to that in the series of the 'crest' puns in the *Birds*, with the allusion to sexual practices gradually fading along with the succession of athletic contests. While the double entendre is particularly manifest in the wrestling scenes, not all the details and actions of the horse race seem to have an evident sexual meaning. However, two remarks must be added: first, the reference to male genitals is particularly conspicuous in the second part of this sequence, so that there is no risk that the audience might lose the 'point'; second, we should not expect every detail of a comic metaphor or allegory to match with a corresponding element of its object; that is to say, we should not expect the same accuracy found in the metaphors and allegories of philosophical or theological treatises. I would therefore scale down Kidd's claim that 'reference-free' expansions of allegories or metaphors like those in *Peace* would have had such an alienating and confusing effect on the audience. The inherent link between sport and sex is well discernible throughout the passage and even if Aristophanes did insert details without caring too much about the precise correspondence of every element, to maintain that this would have aroused an uncomfortable feeling of nonsense in the audience seems exaggerated.

All in all, Kidd's study succeeds very well in illustrating the main components of Aristophanes' comedies that are neither functional to the progression of the plot nor conveyors of serious content. While his warning not to read Old Comedy too seriously should be welcomed, the application of the concept of nonsense to all the disruptions, incongruities and teasing happening on stage seems too widely extended. Can these parts of a comic play be called nonsense, just because they do not provoke the same kind of laughter a pointed joke does? After all they also concur – together with the more refined satirical passages – to the chief goal of comedy, namely humour and fun. The distinction drawn by Kidd seems therefore to be of a rather qualitative kind, that is between more or less skilfully elaborated jokes and plays on words. The off-topic expansions of Old Comedy discussed so far, despite displaying several of the features of the nonsense genre, do not reach the same kind of autonomy as in some European literatures of the modern age. They are rather parenthetic deviations placed within meaningful passages to increase their comic effect.

The fact that the Greeks did not develop a nonsense genre independent from other literary forms was not caused by a lack of awareness about the complex relationship between reality and language. The philosophical reflections on linguistic relativism and on the epistemological issue of communication, as formulated by Gorgias and other Sophists in the fifth century BCE, had laid theoretical foundations that could have potentially encouraged a systematic poetic engagement with the arbitrariness of language and meaning. Aristophanes might have been influenced by the sophistic relativism in his playful experimentation with language,[26] but the closest to the modern understanding of nonsense that ancient literature gets was composed by a later generation of comic playwrights, more precisely by an author called Antiphanes, who seems to have pushed some of his plays beyond the limits of sense and coherence. But before turning to this playwright, it is worth making a brief digression on the barely known author of the most nonsensical fragment of Old Comedy.

Crates

We know very little of the Athenian poet Crates, who was among the earliest composers of Attic comedies and was already celebrated by his rival Aristophanes.[27] Only ten titles and sixty short fragments from his plays are preserved, so that it is extremely hard to reconstruct any of his plots. This loss is indeed regrettable, especially considering the fragment under discussion here. It belongs to a play entitled Σάμιοι (*Sámioi,* that is *The Men of Samos*), about which we know nothing beyond the assumption that the members of the chorus performed the roles of Samian men. The passage I wish to add to Kidd's collection of nonsense texts is reported by Athenaeus, a Greek rhetorician and grammarian who lived between the end of the second and the beginning of the third century CE and left many quotations from ancient Greek comedies in his monumental Δειπνοσοφισταί (*Deipnosophistaí*, that is *Philosophers at Dinner*). It is only five lines long, but manages to conflate so much nonsense in such a short space that one regrets not to be able to read more from this play:

σκυτίνῃ ποτ᾽ ἐν χύτρᾳ τάριχος ἐλεφάντινον
ἧψε ποντιὰς χελώνη πευκίνοισι κύμασι,
καρκίνοι ποδάνεμοί τε καὶ τανύπτεροι λύκοι
†υσοριμαχειν† ἄνδρες οὐρανοῦ καττύματα.
παῖ᾽ ἐκεῖνον, ἄγχ᾽ ἐχεῖνον. ἐν Κέῳ τίς ἡμέρα;[28]

[Once upon a time a sea turtle cooked ivory salted fish
in a leathern pot with waves of pinewood,
wind-swift crabs and long-winged wolves
[. . .] men, the soles of the sky.
Strike him! Choke him! What day is it in Keos?]

Most commentators agree that the first four lines belong to a riddle, and indeed the story-like beginning and the abundance of animal characters point to this. This however adds little to our comprehension of the scene portrayed, especially given the corrupt beginning of line 4, which most likely deprives us of the predicate of the second clause. The blending of unrelated concepts in the noun phrases ('ivory salted fish', 'leathern pot', 'pinewood waves', 'wind-swift crabs', 'long-winged wolves', 'the soles of the sky') and their arrangement in grammatically correct patterns recalls the Chomskyan nonsense sentence 'colorless green ideas sleep furiously'.[29] Matters are complicated further by the last line, which does not seem to belong to the riddle, but rather to be addressed by the speaker to another character on stage, and not to have any link with the preceding text. If lines 1–4 are a nonsense riddle, then line 5 can be hardly classified as a reply to it. Moreover, the closing interrogative sentence is not as absurd as it may first appear: we know from the ninth-century CE scholar and

Patriarch of Constantinople, Photius, that 'what day is it in Keos?' was a common saying (or perhaps a joke) in antiquity, inspired by the fact that the inhabitants of the Aegean island of Keos did not have a shared calendar.[30] Whichever way the audience might have perceived this jumble of words, Crates' creative freedom in the experimentation with language emerges so plainly, that it seems to have even overcome the humorous purpose. This passage attests to a form of nonsense that seems to enjoy a certain autonomy from both its fictional context and the prevailing humorous aim of its genre.[31] This 'pseudo-riddle' is indeed not funny, not even in the 'funny-strange' way pinpointed by Kidd in his overview, but rather very challenging for the audience and potentially alienating.[32]

It is no coincidence that Crates' fragment has been identified as a riddle, or a riddle fragment. This playful form of linguistic expression owes its own existence to the human interest in the manipulation of language and in the complicated relationship between word and world. It is unsurprising, therefore, that the riddle offered a fruitful terrain on which to compose nonsense texts in antiquity. Both this and the following passage from a later comedy by Antiphanes are structured as riddles, although only in their formal appearance, since they completely miss the supposed target of a riddle, namely, to conceal a certain content behind linguistic twists and reversals.

Antiphanes

Antiphanes is one of the few authors of the Middle Period of Attic Comedy for whom a significant number of fragments are preserved. Ancient and medieval scholars used the term μέση (*mésē*) to denote the period of transition and experimentation between the two 'poles' of Attic comedy embodied by the leading figures of Aristophanes and Menander and chronologically situated in the late fifth and late fourth century BCE respectively. While Aristotle mentioned the key terms that define the two poles of Attic comedy, namely αἰσχρολογία (*aischrología*, that is 'foul language, obscenity') for Old Comedy[33] and ὑπόνοια (*hypónoia*, that is 'guess, insinuation') for New Comedy, an author of the early second century CE named Platonius provides us with the first witness of a transitional phase between the extremes of the ἀρχαία (*archáia*) and the νέα (*néa*).[34] During this time, features that were characteristic of Old Comedy, such as personal mockery, political satire and foul language, still survive, although reduced in frequency. At the same time those elements that mark New Comedy, such as stereotyping (the braggart soldier, the slave parasite, the swindling cook, the *hetaira*, the peevish old man . . .) and stock motifs (for example, feast and sex) already emerge. The scarcity of textual sources available for the μέση (*mésē*) and the lack of distinctive features prevent us from a full appreciation of the actual achievements of this 'hybrid' production. As Nesselrath puts it, it is precisely the blend of surviving motifs from the ἀρχαία (*archáia*) with emerging novelties (*Merkmalkombination*) – in other words its transitional nature – that led already ancient critics to regard the Attic comedy of the first half of the fourth century as a distinct phase in the history of the genre.[35]

Riddles in ancient Greek literature have featured at least since Hesiod and, in drama, also occur in tragedies and satyr-plays.[36] They are of course by no means meaningless or absurd: they simply convey or, better, conceal their content in an elusive and convoluted way. Middle Comedy seems to have exploited this rhetorical device to a great extent, even at the cost of the linearity of the plot.[37] Athenaeus drew most of the riddles quoted in Book 10 of the *Deipnosophistaí* from Middle Comedy. In particular, the deception of the other by means of unsolvable riddles seems to have been a central topic in the dialogues of Antiphanes' comedies, together with a broader exploration of the deceptive power of language. This is the reason why Kidd briefly leaves Old Comedy to make an excursus on Antiphanes in the section of his study devoted to riddles as evidence of his first subcategory of nonsense, namely 'language without reference'.[38] In this final section I will argue that one fragment by Antiphanes presents us with a second ancient source of elaborated nonsense along with the passage from Crates' *Sámioi* illustrated above.

The fragment under scrutiny belongs to a comedy significantly entitled *Próblema*: the Greek word πρόβλημα (*próblema*) indicates a task or question put forward – from the verb προβάλλειν (*probállein*), 'to throw forward' – in order to be solved. Since the only extant fragment from this play contains a series of riddles, it is likely that the title was intended as a synonym for γρῖφος (*grîphos*) or αἴνιγμα (*aínigma*) and that riddles played a central role in the plot.[39] As Konstantakos aptly puts it, riddles in this piece seem to have evolved from occasional diversions from the events portrayed on stage into a 'major constituent of the play'.[40] Here is the surviving text from the *Próblema*:

(A.) ἰχθύσιν ἀμφίβληστρον ἀνὴρ πολλοῖς περιβάλλειν
οἰηθείς, μεγάλη δαπάνῃ μίαν εἵλκυσε πέρκην·
καὶ ταύτην ψευσθεὶς ἄλλην κεστρεὺς ἴσον αὐτὴν
ἦγεν. βουλομένη δ'ἕπεται πέρκη μελανούρῳ.
    (B.) κεστρεύς, ἀνήρ, μελάνουρος, οὐκ οἶδ'ὅ τι λέγεις·
    οὐδὲν λέγεις γάρ. (A.) ἀλλ'ἐγὼ σαφῶς φράσω.
ἔστι τις ὃς τὰ μὲν ὄντα διδοὺς οὐκ οἶδε δεδωκὼς
οἶσι δέδωκ' οὐδ' αὐτὸς ἔχων ὧν οὐδὲν ἐδεῖτο.
    (B.) διδούς τις οὐκ ἔδωκεν οὐδ'ἔχων ἔχει;
    οὐκ οἶδα τούτων οὐδέν. (A.) οὐκοῦν ταῦτα καὶ
    ὁ γρῖφος ἔλεγεν· ὅσα γὰρ οἶσθ'οὐκ οἶσθα νῦν
    οὐδ'ὅσα δέδωκας, οὐδ'ὅσ' ἀντ'αὐτῶν ἔχεις.
    τοιοῦτο τοῦτ'ἦν. (B.) τοιγαροῦν κἀγώ τινα
    εἰπεῖν πρὸς ὑμᾶς βούλομαι γρῖφον. (A.) λέγε.
(B.) πίννη καὶ τρίγλη φωνὰς ἰχθῦ δύ'ἔχουσαι
πόλλ'ἐλάλουν, περὶ ὧν δὲ πρὸς ὅν τ'ᾤοντο λέγειν τι,
οὐκ ἐλάλουν· οὐδὲν γὰρ ἐμάνθανεν, ὥστε πρὸς ὃν μὲν
ἦν αὐταῖς ὁ λόγος, πρὸς δ'αὐτὰς πολλὰ λαλούσας,
αὐτὰς ἀμφοτέρας ἡ Δημήτηρ ἐπιτρίψαι.[41]

[(A.) A man who was resolved to cast a net at many fish, caught only one perch after a great effort. Indeed a grey mullet, disappointed about the perch, led it [and] at the same time another one [into the net?]. A perch willingly follows a saddled bream [?].

(B.) Grey mullet, sir, saddled bream [?], I have no clue what you are talking about. You are talking nonsense.

(A.) Then I will speak more plainly. There is someone who, having given what belongs to him, is unaware that he has given it to those he has given to, nor does he know not to have what he does not need at all.

(B.) Someone who gave what he did not give and has what he does not have? I do not understand a word of all this.

(A.) Well, this is precisely what the riddle says. Indeed you do not know what you know, nor what you have given or what you have in return for that. That's what it was about.

(B.) Alright, now I want to tell you a riddle.

(A.) Go ahead.

(B.) A fan mussel and a mullet – two fish that have voices – were having a long conversation, but they were talking neither about what nor to whom they believed to be saying something. [This person] did not understand anything, so that they directed their speech to him, but in truth they were just chatting between each other. May you, Demeter, crush them both!]

Any attempt to make sense out of this exchange is pointless: although single elements could have indeed been inspired by widespread idioms or proverbs, it is their juxtaposition that empties the passage of intelligible meaning. As in the case of the fragment from Crates' *Sámioi*, unrelated concepts have been arranged into a syntactically acceptable frame. To begin with the fishing fable-like episode recounted at ll. 1–4, three unconnected actions are juxtaposed: the meagre capture of a perch by a man, some sort of revenge or hostility between a grey mullet and a perch and a closing γνόμη (*gnómē*) perhaps alluding to the common fellowship between wicked people.[42] This muddle of events is then made even more obscure by the two following 'explanations' of the alleged riddle, ironically introduced by the paradoxical clause 'I will speak more plainly' (ἀλλ'ἐγὼ σαφῶς φράσω). Lines 7–8 and 11–13 feature the usual riddle technique of ascribing the subject of the riddle both some quality or activity and its contrary and relying on the confusing effect of the iteration of the same verb.

Although Konstantakos cannot resist the temptation to provide some solution for the riddle of ll. 1–13,[43] he rightly insists on the actual aim of the whole passage, namely, to write 'a piece of nonsense cast in riddle-form'. His assessment of the final riddle of ll. 15–19 on the other hand is appealing: the character who until that moment had been the recipient of the riddle now wants to take revenge for having being fooled, and counteracts with a new puzzle.[44] From the formal point of view, the last part of the fragment consists of a hotchpotch of elements from the previous riddles, namely the imagery of fish and the tale-like form from the first, and the accumulation of affirmative and negative forms from the other two. Two garrulous sea creatures keep on speaking to someone, who does not understand anything of what they are talking about, so that the two animals end up just prattling between each other. The situation described here however does seem to have some overall purpose, since it portrays the scene happening on stage. The anonymous addressee of the two chatterers symbolises the character telling the riddle, while the mussel and mullet stand for the first speaker or speakers who initiated the foolery.[45]

This passage can be considered a high point of ancient Greek nonsense literature. Its composition seems to have been motivated by a desire to play with language, regardless of the comic effect the scene might or might not have aroused. The final lines confirm the impression that the whole passage is at the same time a celebration and a parody of the power of language.[46] In this regard it brings to mind one of the most famous passages from Carroll's *Alice's Adventures in Wonderland*:

> 'Why is a raven like a writing-desk?'
> 'Come, we shall have some fun now!' thought Alice. 'I'm glad they've begun asking riddles – I believe I can guess that,' she added aloud. [. . .]
> 'Have you guessed the riddle yet?' the Hatter said, turning to Alice again.
> 'No. I give up,' Alice replied. 'What's the answer?'
> 'I haven't the slightest idea,' said the Hatter.
> Alice sighed wearily. 'I think you might do something better with time than waste it in asking riddles that have no answers.'
> 'If you knew Time as well as I do' said the Hatter, 'you wouldn't talk about wasting it. It's him.'[47]

The Mad Hatter's riddle 'Why is a raven like a writing desk?' arouses, not only in Alice but also in many readers, the same sense of frustration that the audience of Crates' and Antiphanes' riddles must have experienced. The analogy between the sources can also be extended to the authors' deliberate choice to devise a riddle without answer.[48]

While most scholars have focused on the reactions of the audience or readership in order to identify nonsense in literature, looking for more or less explicit rejections of the nonsense text or refusals to engage in a hermeneutic effort to 'understand' it, I would suggest that we reverse the perspective and look for the clear purpose of an author to create a text that is meant not to convey any real content – to be distinguished from the purpose of being obscure – and simply displays the author's delight in playing freely with words, letters and grammar as the essence of a poetry of nonsense. According to this reading, the autonomy of the nonsense text is a crucial feature that keeps apart actual pieces of nonsense from other similar techniques like coinages, iterations and expansions that are the standard armoury of the comic poet.

Notes

1. Susan Stewart, *Nonsense: Aspects of Intertextuality in Folklore and Literature* (Baltimore: Johns Hopkins University Press, 1979), p. vii.
2. See Sara Chiarini, 'Οὐδὲν λέγειν/*nihil dicere*. A Lexical and Semantic Survey', *Mnemosyne* 72 (2019), 114–49, pp. 128–33.
3. See for instance Aristotle's considerations concerning the limits of dialectic and the *reductio ad absurdum* (*Physics* 4.1); his analysis of the phenomenon called ἀδολεσχεῖν (*adoleschein*), that is, to be forced by argument to over-repeat a word and thereby make it meaningless (*Topics* 6.3; *Sophistical Refutations* 13 and 31; *Metaphysics* 6.4); and, more broadly, his classification of thirteen types of fallacies in the construction of a logical argument, which is the subject of the *Sophistical Refutations*.
4. See for instance the dialogue between Mnesilochus and Cleisthenes in Aristophanes' *Thesmophoriazusae* (ll. 584–634), staging a series of nonsense claims, which range from rambling utterances to protracted bewildering speech.
5. Cédric H. Whitman, *Aristophanes and the Comic Hero* (Cambridge, MA: Harvard University Press, 1964), p. 172.
6. Ibid. p. 198.

7. 'All this is nonsense, of course, but in the sense of nonsense poetry, which, at its best, regularly juxtaposes real and imaginary things or words in such a way as to exploit the real in favour of the imaginary' (Whitman, *Aristophanes*, p. 171). This statement is followed by a rather obscure analogy with Edward Lear's 'The Pobble who has no Toes'.
8. This and subsequent quotations from the play follow the text in *Aristophanes: Birds* ed. Nan Dunbar (Oxford: Clarendon Press, 1995).
9. This and all subsequent translations are mine.
10. Whitman, *Aristophanes*, p. 184. From the attribute given to the egg Whitman deduces that the egg must be 'incapable of hatching', and thus 'a contradiction in terms, a big joke, a hoax'.
11. For the distinction between nonsense and humour in Aristophanic comedy see James Robson, *Humour, Obscenity and Aristophanes* (Tübingen: Gunter Narr Verlag, 2008), pp. 22–9. As Robson points out, nonsense does not arouse laughter, but rather 'irritation' for the 'misunderstanding of frame' in the communication, while humour presupposes an 'ideal context of mutual understanding and communicative cooperation between speaker and listener' (p. 34).
12. Stephen Kidd, *Nonsense and Meaning in Ancient Greek Comedy* (Cambridge and New York: Cambridge University Press, 2014). Several scholars over the past years have resorted to the term 'nonsense' to describe passages from Greek comedies or even whole plays, but without the critical awareness in the usage of the term that Kidd displays. See for instance Kenneth J. Reckford, *Aristophanes' Old and New Comedy: Six Essays in Perspective* (Chapel Hill: University of North Carolina Press, 1987), and Gregory W. Dobrov, 'Winged Words/Graphic Birds: The Aristophanic Comedy of Language' (unpublished doctoral dissertation, Cornell University, 1988).
13. On the relationship between nonsense and joke see Kidd, *Nonsense and Meaning*, pp. 124–37, and on play and mental impairment as the two contexts in which nonsense can be produced, pp. 29–51.
14. Ibid. p. 14.
15. Ibid. pp. 52–117.
16. Ibid. pp. 118–60.
17. Ibid. pp. 161–86; see also Chiarini, 'Οὐδὲν λέγειν/*nihil dicere*', pp. 120–8.
18. Aristophanes, *Birds* ll. 1372–400; *Ecclesiazusae* l. 330; *Lysistrata* l. 860; *Frogs* ll. 153, 1437; also fragment 156.10 in *Poetae Comici Graeci*, ed. Rudolf Kassel and Colin Austin, 8 vols (Berlin: De Gruyter, 1983–2001), in which see also Pherecrates, fragment 55, Strattis, fragments 14–22.
19. Kidd, *Nonsense and Meaning*, pp. 87–119.
20. See Chiarini, 'Οὐδὲν λέγειν/*nihil dicere*', pp. 128–33.
21. Kidd, *Nonsense and Meaning*, pp. 146–7.
22. Simplicius of Cilicia, in his commentary on Aristotle's *Categories* (1a16), distinguished between proper speech utterances and other non-linguistic sounds. The notion of nonsense does not arise from vocal noises without linguistic value but only from the aberrant juxtaposition of real words or parts of them. It is however significant that Aristophanes' pseudo-words, when put in the mouth of some character, never arouse an accusation of talking nonsense as reaction among the interlocutors in the play (on this see Chiarini, 'Οὐδὲν λέγειν/*nihil dicere*', pp. 144–6).
23. Towards the end of the chapter devoted to nonsense as 'no-sense', Kidd seems to slightly reframe his argument when he states that, in comedy, the boundary of nonsense is never fully transgressed, since in such case the fun would be sacrificed: Kidd, *Nonsense and Meaning*, pp. 155–7.
24. Ibid. pp. 52–86.
25. Following the text in *Aristophanes: Peace* (Oxford: Clarendon Press, 1998), ed. S. Douglas Olson.

26. Sophists indeed figured and were satirised in various plays of Old Comedy: see Christopher Carey, 'Old Comedy and the Sophists', in *The Rivals of Aristophanes: Studies in Athenian Old Comedy*, ed. David Harvey and John Wilkins (London: Duckworth 2000), 419–36, pp. 427–31 for Aristophanes' interest, in *Clouds*, in the individual profiles of particular Sophists.
27. Crates began his theatrical career as an actor performing for Cratinus and only later started composing his own plays. Aristophanes mentions him in the *Knights* (ll. 537–40) and Aristotle says that he was the first to abandon the ἰαμβικὴ ἰδέα (*iambikē idéa*, that is the mere deriding of existing individuals) in order to create more cohesive plots. See Kassel and Austin, *Poetae Comici Graeci*, IV, pp. 83–5, and Kenneth W. Dover, Geoffrey Arnott, Nick Lowe and David Harvey, 'Biographical Appendix', in *The Rivals of Aristophanes: Studies in Athenian Old Comedy*, ed. David Harvey and John Wilkins (London: Duckworth, 2000), 323–33, pp. 326–7.
28. Crates fragment 32, in Kassel and Austin, *Poetae Comici Graeci* (preserved in Athenaeus, *Deipnosophistae*, III 117 b).
29. Noam Chomsky, *Syntactic Structures* (The Hague: Mouton, 1957), p. 15.
30. See Photius, *Lexicon* ε 972: ἐν Κέωι τίς ἡμέρα· Εὔπολις Φίλοις· 'οὐδεὶς γὰρ οἶδεν ἐν Κέῳ τίς ἡμέρα'· οὐχ ἑστᾶσι γὰρ παρ᾽αὐτοῖς αἱ ἡμέραι, ἀλλ᾽ἕκαστος ὡς βούλεται ἄγει. *Photii Patriarchae Lexicon: Volumen II: E-M*, ed. Christos Theodoris (Berlin and New York: De Gruyter, 1998), p. 98.
31. See Ioannis M. Konstantakos, 'A Commentary on the Fragments of Eight Plays of Antiphanes' (unpublished doctoral dissertation, University of Cambridge, 2000): riddles are 'incidental elements amusing the audience but bringing the action to a standstill [. . .]; they are expanded for their own sake' (p. 150).
32. Konstantakos takes a halfway position: 'Krates 32 [. . .] strings together a series of absurdities (non-existent objects (σκυτίνη χύτρα, τάριχος ἐλεφάντινον), proverbial ἀδύνατα (καρκίνοι ποδάνεμοι, τανύπτεροι λύκοι (cf. App. *Prov.* 3.45, Diogenian. 6.4)) in the form of a *griphos* [. . .], perhaps intends to parody riddles and riddle-scenes: Krates composes a piece of nonsense and has it propounded as a *griphos* in order to ridicule riddles as nonsensical and silly', 'Commentary', p. 152.
33. On this see Jeffrey Henderson, *The Maculate Muse: Obscene Language in Attic Comedy* (New Haven and London: Yale University Press, 1975).
34. γεγόνασι δὲ μεταβολαὶ κωμῳδίας τρεῖς· καὶ ἡ μὲν ἀρχαία, ἡ δὲ νέα, ἡ δὲ μέση ['comedy underwent three changes: one called *archáia*, one called *néa*, and one called *mésē*']: *Prolegomena de Comoedia* III.7–8 in *Scholia in Aristophanem. Pars I: Prolegomena de Comoedia. Scholia in Acharnenses, Equites, Nubes*, ed. Willem J. W. Koster (Groningen: Bouma's Boekhuis, 1975).
35. See Heinz-Günther Nesselrath, *Die attische Mittlere Komödie: Ihre Stellung in der antiken Literaturkritik und Literaturgeschichte* (Berlin and New York: De Gruyter, 1990), pp. 331–40, p. 336. See also Athina Papachrysostomou, *Six Comic Poets: A Commentary on Selected Fragments of Middle Comedy* (Tübingen: Gunter Narr Verlag, 2008), pp. 10–23.
36. See *Fragmenta Hesiodea*, ed. Reinhold Merkelbach and Martin L. West (Oxford: Clarendon Press, 1967), fragment 266, and *Tragicorum Graecorum Fragmenta*, 5 vols (Göttingen: Vandenhoeck and Ruprecht, 1981–2009), III: *Aeschylus*, ed. Stefan Radt (2009), fragment 116; IV: *Sophocles*, ed. Stefan Radt (1999), fragment 395; V: *Euripides*, ed. Richard Kannicht (2004), fragment 83.
37. On the possible reasons for the popularity of riddles in Middle Comedy see Konstantakos, 'Commentary', p. 156, and Gregory W. Dobrov, 'Μάγειρος ποιητής: Language and Character in Antiphanes', in *The Language of Greek Comedy*, ed. Andreas Willi (Oxford: Oxford University Press, 2002), 169–90, pp. 176–7.
38. Kidd, *Nonsense and Meaning*, pp. 57–65.

39. Konstantakos suggests a combination of riddles and satire on philosophical disputations, given Antiphanes' preference for a semantically broader term for 'riddle' in the title: 'Commentary', p. 181. We know from another fragment that the mockery of philosophers was within Antiphanes' repertoire (see Antiphanes fragment 120 in Kassel and Austin, *Poetae Comici Graeci*).
40. Konstantakos, 'Commentary', pp. 182–3.
41. Antiphanes, fragment 192 in Kassel and Austin, *Poetae Comici Graeci*, (preserved in Athenaeus, *Deipnosophistaí*, X 450c-e).
42. This proverb is also attested in Athenaeus, *Deipnosophistaí*, VII 319c, but we have no explanation concerning its metaphorical meaning. The likely interpretation provided in the main text is argued exclusively on a stylistic basis, that is, by analogy with other sayings in the form 'A willingly associates with B'. Kidd has fittingly highlighted the explanatory function of δέ in the proverbial sentence, which paradoxically emphasises the inconsequentiality between the three statements: see *Nonsense and Meaning*, p. 62.
43. Apart from the several textual emendations he proposes, Konstantakos believes that both the grey mullet and the saddled bream symbolise the fisherman of the first sentence and represent him as the prototype of an empty-belly: see Konstantakos, 'Commentary', pp. 189–96. The point is that all such exegetic efforts do not lead to an answer of the riddle.
44. Ibid. pp. 96–201.
45. In my opinion this is the strongest clue in support of Konstantakos's thesis that the fragment requires the presence of three characters on stage (two riddlers and one 'riddlee'), although his distribution of ll. 1–4 (A), 6b–8 (B) and 10b–13a (B) between the two riddlers seems to me unnecessary. It is more reasonable to assume that only one of the riddlers leads the conversation, while the others just witness it without taking the floor. See Konstantakos, 'Commentary', pp. 183–4.
46. Antiphanes' attitude towards language is confirmed by a passage that celebrates the pastime of telling riddles. Antiphanes fragment 122 in Kassel and Austin, *Poetae Comici Graeci* contains a monologue about the 'hermeneutics' of riddles. It begins with a sceptical statement about the uselessness of riddling during symposia: ἐγὼ πρότερον μὲν τοὺς κελεύοντας λέγειν | γρίφους παρὰ πότον ᾤόμην ληρεῖν σαφῶς | λέγοντας οὐδέν, ὁπότε προστάξειέ τις | εἰπεῖν ἐφεξῆς ὅ τι φέρων τις μὴ φέρει, | ἐγέλων νομίζων λῆρον, οὐκ ἂν γενόμενον | οὐδέποτέ γ', οἶμαι, πρᾶγμα παντελῶς λέγειν, | ἐνέδρας δ' ἕνεκα (ll. 1–7a) ['Once I used to believe that those who urge to tell riddles while drinking were plainly drivelling and talking nonsense. Whenever someone commanded (us) to guess one after the other what someone does not carry while carrying it I laughed, thinking that it was rubbish and that he was certainly telling something that can never happen, I guess, just to trick us']. However, it ends by re-evaluating riddles, via a belated but successful guessing of a riddle that had first appeared without solution: νυνὶ δὲ τοῦτ' ἔγνωχ'ὅτι | ἀληθὲς ἦν· φέρομεν γὰρ ἄνθρωποι δέκα | ἔρανόν τιν', οὐ φέρει δὲ τούτων τὴν φορὰν | οὐδείς. σαφῶς οὖν ὅ τι φέρων τις μὴ φέρει, | τοῦτ'ἔστιν, ἦν θ'ὁ γρῖφος ἐνταῦθα ῥέπων (ll. 7a–11) ['Now, however, I have realised that it was true: we ten people are carrying some meal, but no one of us is carrying the burden (of it). This is clearly a case of someone carrying nothing despite carrying something. This is what the riddle was hinting at']. Most commentators, including Kidd (*Nonsense and Meaning*, pp. 58–61) and myself ('Οὐδὲν λέγειν/*nihil dicere*', p. 127) have focused on the first part of the fragment, without considering that (1) a plausible solution of the riddle is, after all, given and (2) the closing remarks redirect the blame against a morally reprehensible way of manipulating language, aimed at avoiding payment of a debt: καὶ τοῦτο μὲν δὴ κἄστι συγγνώμην ἔχον· | ἀλλ'οἷα λογοποιοῦσιν ἐν τῷ πράγματι | οἱ τἀργύριον μὴ κατατιθέντες (ll. 12–14) ['And this is at least excusable, but all the stories those who do not pay the money invent in their business . . .']. While riddles are harmless, it is the purpose of cheating the other that makes the play with language reproachable.

47. Lewis Carroll, *Alice's Adventures in Wonderland and Through the Looking-Glass*, ed. Peter Hunt (Oxford: Oxford University Press, 2009), pp. 60–2.
48. Dodgson explains, in the 1896 Preface to *Alice's Adventures in Wonderland*, that he had originally created the riddle without solution, but since he received many letters from frustrated readers requesting an answer, he felt compelled to provide one. He suggests 'Because it can produce a few notes, though they are very flat; and is nevar put with the wrong end in the front!', adding that 'This, however, is merely an afterthought: the Riddle, as originally invented, had no answer at all' (Carroll, *Wonderland*, p. 6). While reading, one tends automatically to correct 'nevar' to 'never'. However, this is a significant part of the answer, as 'nevar' is 'raven' backwards. Ultimately, as is the frustrating nature of nonsense, Dodgson's answer is exactly as stated above: there is no answer. For the Hatter to have had an answer would have undermined his nonsensical nature.

9

Traditional Moorings, Modern Practices: Indian Literary Nonsense

Sumanyu Satpathy

It is not hard to compose difficult verse
[But] it is not that easy to write *ja-ta* ('nonsense')
Rabindranath Tagore (Prefatory verse from *Khapchhada*, my translation).[1]

THE FIELD OF nonsense in multilingual India is both fascinating and complex. It demands not only mutual translation into diverse regional languages, but also, enabled by such translations, the recalcitrant archive cries out for subtle theorisation.[2] It is only through collaborative and sustained enterprises of translation and theorisation that any coherent history of Indian nonsense can be charted. Until recently not much work had been done by scholars on literary nonsense, a tradition which is over a century old in the Indian subcontinent.[3] Modern Indian pioneers, such as Rabindranath Tagore (Bangla, 1861–1941), Nandakishor Bala (Odia, 1875–1928), Sukumar Ray (Bangla, 1887–1923), Sri Prasad (Hindi, 1932–2012), Kalindi Charan Panigrahi (Odia, 1901–91), Ramakrushna Nanda (Odia, 1906–94), and Mangesh Padgaonkar (Marathi, 1929–2015) often alluded to and drew on indigenous tales of fantasy, mantras, riddles and children's rhymes in discussions of the subject in their respective languages. The lineages connecting the indigenous body of oral and written texts with modern literary nonsense forge what might amount to a tradition of Indian nonsense. A composite Indianness that one encounters in literary nonsense of the region grew out of such imbrications.[4] In this chapter, I offer a brief narrative of Indian nonsense for the anglophone reader. The chapter seeks to map the ways in which the genre began to be hybridised across Indian literary languages through colonial contact, and acquired an identity of its own. But, before I begin, it might be salutary to consider the question: how is nonsense understood in the disconcertingly heterogeneous subcontinental culture?

What's in a Name?

Many Indian writers of nonsense are at a loss to find respectable equivalent names for the genre in their respective languages. In common parlance, the term signifies what is conceptually and empirically untenable. The Sanskrit word *udbhat* ('absurd' or 'bizarre') is perhaps the most widely used alternative, but there are also etymologically intractable words which are themselves nonsense terms. Such terms are used to designate common utterances which are non-connotative or are inflected by connotative as well as denotative confusion/imprecision. The equivalent terms in Bangla, for example, are *ja-ta* and *ajgubi*. Equivalents in Urdu, Hindi and Punjabi are *ajab*, *und-sund*, *be-matlab* and *bakwas*. In Malayalam (which might itself sound like palindromic nonsense to non-Malayalis) the word for nonsense is *asambandham*, or *aprasangika*. *Asambandham*, therefore, refers to a signifier without any logical signified. Vaikom Muhammad Basheer (1908–94) uses the Malayalam nonsense word *hunthrappibusatto*, which is entirely his coinage, as the title of a story. In one of his essays in *Literature and Culture*, U. R. Anantamurthy (1932–2014) refers to the fifteenth-century mystic poet Purandara's use of the word *lola lotte*. In Kannada, *lotte* refers to the unintelligible children's babble, and *lola* further emphasises the word, the very sound of which conveys the sense that it is nonsense.[5]

As a term for the literary genre of nonsense, *gadbadjhala* is quite popular in Hindi and Marathi. Sukumar Ray used and popularised the term, *abol-tabol* in Bangla. After Nandakihor Bala, the term *nanabaya* has gained popularity among Odia people. However, it covers a wide range of writing from sensible nursery or game rhymes to nonsense 'pure and absolute'.[6] Other Odia writers have offered such terms as *asangata sahitya* (Kalindi Charan Panigrahi), *alukuchi-malukuchi* (J. P. Das (1936–)), *anabana* (Das Benhur (1953–)). Niranjan Behera (1938–2015) suggests *bai-jhaia* as an Odia equivalent of nonsense. For, as he points out, a tribe known as the Bathudi call naughty and obstinate children *bai-jhaia*. The word *bai* refers to madness or whim, and tagged to the meaningless *jhaia*, the resulting term, *bai-jhaia* is indeed closest to the idea of nonsense.[7] Behera's persuasive argument has not had many takers. To conclude, apart from the currency of Ray's term *abol-tabol*, no consensus seems to exist among writers in different Indian languages. In obvious exasperation, authors often revert to the English term, nonsense, in vernacular transcript.

Another aspect of literary nonsense in India is that even when aware of the genre in the West, many writers ignore, sometimes deliberately, its generic attributes. For them, all meaningless children's jingles constitute nonsense literature. Generally, however, verbal play, puns, puzzle, absurd logic with or without a hint of meaning are taken as a few of the characteristic techniques of nonsense in Indian languages. Of course, the extent to which such nonsense succeeds in appealing to the young readers will depend on the balance between meaning and non-meaning. For many others, nonsense is self-consciously 'nonsense' in the tradition of Lear and Carroll. Yet, while incorporating certain traits of European nonsense, or even while translating them, they remain quintessentially Indian. What Satyajit Ray says of Sukumar Ray's work is equally true of many other modern writers of nonsense: 'nothing could be more quintessentially Bengali than the latent spirit of this topsy-turvy world [of Sukumar Ray]'.[8] While examining Indian nonsense texts one notices how the practitioners invariably breathe the spirit of local traditions.

The Spirit of Indigenous Traditions

John Beames (1837–1902), the feted colonial administrator and philologist, who spent a few years in the Odia-speaking regions of Eastern India, was one of the first to try and make sense of local folk nonsense. Beames selected and translated a few mantras (literally, sacred sounds), and called them 'human nonsense'.[9] In the course of his work, he encountered many nonsense words, observing that '"*sankat, kikat, killi*" are nonsense words, which though [. . .] untranslatable are stated to be used here in some mystic sense'.[10] He went on to say that 'human nonsense, like human sense, is very much the same everywhere, and it is only because in ruling men one must take their nonsense into consideration quite as earnestly as their sense'.[11] Beames's impatience with 'rubbish' leads him to ignore the intricate traditions that bind Buddhist and Hindu tantric practices, which had spread widely across South Asia by the seventh century CE. This tradition of tantric practices can be traced to Nepal, with its integral feature of hermetically sealed verses supposedly carrying therapeutic powers. The mantras were believed to empower practitioners and believers, and cure them of everything – from snake bites to impotence.

This is one of the many instances of how nonsense in Indian culture exists in its intersecting matrices of folk, literary, religious and secular domains. Whether the intentions behind obfuscation of meaning in these mantras, are questionable or not is moot. But let us look at a few Odia samples that are part of a long tradition in Odisha, from the sixteenth-century poet-seer Achyutananda Das (1510–1631) to the nineteenth-century blind, tribal poet, Bhima Bhoi (1850–95), often thought of as a crypto-Buddhist. I cite two examples from their work. The first one is from one of the numerous *malikas* (Hindu eschatological verse) by Achyutanada:

Waves billow in the dry pond
The birdie has flown away
leaving the unhatched egg behind.[12]

This apparent piece of nonsense is often interpreted as a way of comprehending and defining the god Vishnu in terms of *sunya*, that is, as *sunya purusha* (*sunya* is 'void' and *purusha* is 'person'). The reality of *sunyavad* is presented as a series of utterances that might appear to be nonsense to the unconverted but could signify reality to the believer in the sect. Bhima Bhoi's philosophy draws on 'Alekh Dharma', a nineteenth-century dissident Hindu sect.[13] In his numerous supplications to the formless *guru*, Alekh Mahima, the incongruous world is made evident:

There's no land to farm,
but the ploughshare ploughs up the soil
No seeds are sown, but crops are reaped
There's no barn, nor any labourer
But paddy is threshed.[14]

The seeming paradoxes, verging on nonsense are more obvious in the original Odia than here in translation. As is the case with the following verse:

Sons are as yet unwed
But daughters-in-law
are aplenty in the family
Grandsons are begotten too
without any carnal intercourse.[15]

These apparently hermeneutically sealed propositions are often subjected to elaborate exegeses by the faithful followers of the *Mahima* sect.[16] One of the explanations is that the lines capture the attempt to articulate the shift from dualism to monism. There is a serious challenge here for the logic-seeking reader. Such verses of apparent nonsense are usually cast in coded forms, and go by different names in what was often called *ulti bhasa*, *sandhya bhasa*, or in Kannada-speaking regions a *bedagu*,[17] that is, an incomprehensible idiom. The idea perhaps was to deliberately keep the system beyond the reach of the uninitiated. Absurd propositions like these are seen either as deeply meaningful or utter nonsense depending on who is reading them. Calling such verses 'nonsense', even now, would be tantamount to sacrilege for a believer.

From Folk Nonsense to Literary Nonsense

Lest one be surprised by the textual overlaps among diverse linguistic traditions, one ought to remember that the present-day language-based borders were either fluid or non-existent in pre-colonial times. For centuries, multiple liminal spaces around major linguistic zones allowed cultural transactions across regions. I invoke the older traditions since some of the common techniques of nonsense literature include the inversion of logic and language, the creation of peculiar collocations, and experiments with size and scale.

Along with the proliferation of nationalist discourses, one of the consequences of the colonial disciplinary practices was a new desire to textualise the oral traditions. As a result of the resulting scholastic enquiries, many oral verses and tales were compiled, and are now available in print. Among these are the 'thorn' tales,[18] which display common features across different linguistic cultures of South Asia. Each begins with a fallacious proposition about, typically, three entities, out of which two are stated to be in a similar state, and the third one as being in a different state. That is, in each case various alternatives are given which *sound* logical even when they are tautological. This strategy can be seen in many languages across India. For example, there are three houses in a village, out of which two are 'broken down', and the third has no roof; or that three potters, two of whom are 'sulking' and the third one is in a bad mood, or out of three earthen pots, two are 'broken' and the third one has no bottom.

The formula of the thorn tales made its way beyond specific languages into authored texts such the sixteenth-century *Shikarnama* by Khawaja Banda Nawaz Gesu Daraz:

> We four brothers were only from the countryside. Three were without clothes, and the fourth one was absolutely naked. The brother who was naked had money in his aasteen. All four went to the market to buy bows and arrows. Death came, and all four died. But twenty-four came back to life and stood up. Just then four bows came into view. Three of them were broken and were quite useless. The fourth one had neither any end nor a bowstring. The naked brother who had money in his aasteen bought the bow with neither any end nor a bowstring. Now the thought of the arrow was worrying. Four arrows came into view [. . .] Three were dead, and the fourth one was lifeless.[19]

The narrative follows a similar semantic trick to the one described above. The variation here is that the number is four and three instead of the typical three and two.

As above, the narrator introduces the further illogic of the brothers digging a hole to 'raise' a platform and a *tak* ('shelf') on a wall-less wall.

An extract from a verse by Kabir, a medieval Sufi poet, can be cited as an example of a similar but more recent tradition:

> A legless man runs in all directions,
> A blind man surveys the world.
> The rabbit whips round and swallows the lion.
> Such marvels! Who knows what they mean?[20]

Like the other users of *ulti bhasa*, Kabir conceives of reality as being ineffable and mysterious. These instances derive from a blend of *bhakti* and Sufi traditions. In the former case, belief can be *shagun* and *nirgun*; and the latter, the Islamic, *mufti* and *sufi*. For those who believe in a God without form or attribute (*nirgun/sufi*), reality might be topsy-turvy, which is somewhat unacceptable to those who believe in a substantiate God (*shagun/mufti*) tradition.

An English Tale Called *Alice in Wonderland*

Edward Lear and Lewis Carroll travelled to India in two different ways: the former, both in person and through his works; and the latter, through his works alone. Much to Lear's own surprise, his work appeared in schools in India not long after publication.[21] Nevertheless, it was Carroll's *Alice* books which achieved a greater cultural impact. The first Gujurati translation of *Alice's Adventures in Wonderland* appeared in 1917. The first Bangla translation appeared, surprisingly belatedly, seventeen years later, in 1934. Tamil, one of India's oldest languages, did not see its own *Alice* translation until 1957. Many others followed in due course. The way the various translators dealt with crucial passages of nonsense is in itself a curious story, which I have told elsewhere.[22] But such works of translation and adaptation played a major role in introducing Indian readers to Western literary nonsense. In fact, one of the earliest adaptations of *Alice* appeared in Bangla in the form of Trailokyanath Mukhopadhya's (1847–1919) fantasy *Kankabati* (1892), a story describing an Alice-like Indian girl, who runs away from home and experiences a fantastic dream. In the course of her voyage down the river, Kankabati, like her Western counterpart Alice, meets strange creatures. *Kankabati* was followed by Tagore's 'Ekti Ashadhe Galpa' ('An Absurd Tale'). Tagore's story had all the ingredients of a traditional Indian tale of fantasy.[23] That Tagore was familiar with *Alice* is beyond doubt as his tale appeared in the same issue of the Bengali journal, *Sadhana* (*Meditation*), where he had noted that Trailokyanath's fantasy reminded him of 'an English tale called "Alice in the Wonderland"' [*sic*].[24] Tagore drew on Carroll's influence a second time when, in 1932, he turned the plot of the short story into a dance drama, *Tasher Desh*, or *The Land of Cards*.[25]

Critics and historians like Partha Mitter and Sankho Ghosh suggest that Sukumar Ray knew Lear's work.[26] The combination of verbal and visual media that defined Lear's nonsense was unprecedented in Bangla or even Indian culture prior to Sukumar's time. Nor was, for that matter, intentional nonsense 'pure and simple', nonsense written for non-didactic, satirical purposes, a recognised practice. Sanskrit aesthetic theory does not mention anything that comes close to what one might call nonsense. This leads one to conjecture that the source of the new rasa may have been the anglophone nonsense of Lear and Carroll. As Satyajit Ray wrote in his Introduction to his father's collected works:

> Sukumar named this special vein of nonsense the *rasa* or spirit of whimsy [in Sukumar's original Bangla, *kheyal ras*]. Needless to say, it is not one of the nine *rasas* of Indian dramatic theory [. . .] But authentic literary nonsense masks its caprice beneath an apparent gravity in an urbane and sophisticated manner unknown in popular rhyme.[27]

Ray goes on to say that 'there has been wit and humour in Bangla literature, both poetry and prose, from the earliest times, but there is little or no nonsense'.[28] Had there been any such conscious use of the rasa of whimsy, if one were to follow Satyajit or Sukumar's Ray's argument, it would have been mentioned in the *Natyasastra* by Bharata, or those who followed him.[29] But there was neither any such formulation of a rasa of whimsy nor any instance of intentional nonsense in the works of earlier writers. As Satyajit Ray says, Sukumar Ray's nonsense tale, *Haw-jaw-baw-raw-law* is 'the finest piece of nonsense in Bengali prose', adding that it is 'obviously influenced by *Alice in Wonderland*'.[30] By juxtaposing successive soft and hard consonants of the Bangla alphabet, Sukumar Ray creates his nonsense title. Furthermore, Sukumar's borrowings from Carroll are clear in his illustrations of the cat with a peculiar name ('A Tree-Cat'), conjured up from a handkerchief, speaking nonsense, and engaging in nonsensical conversation with a crow in a scene that recalls the exchanges between the Mad Hatter and the Dormouse. However, there is a new dimension to the Indian nonsense of Tagore and Sukumar Ray, in which politics plays a role.

Sukumar Ray and the Politics of Nonsense

Elsewhere I have considered the way some of Lear's verses, especially those composed around his Indian visit, can be read in terms of colonial ideology.[31] In a way, Sukumar's nonsense sets up a counter-discourse by treating the white European as the other. His 'Ashambhab Naye' ('It's not Impossible') is a case in point. Lear's limericks featured a number of long-nosed characters.[32] Likewise Sukumar cocks a snook at the Englishman with a long nose, using the format of the traditional children's tale of '*Ek je chhilo*' ('There once was . . .', a phrase that recalls Lear's stock-in-trade limerick openings: 'There was a . . .'): '*Ek je chhilo Saheb, tahar | Guner maddhey naker bahar*' [lit., 'There was once a sahib, whose most outstanding feature was his protruding nose']. In order to make his obstinate donkey go the way he desired, the sahib ties a radish to his enormous nose and dangles it before him. There is more to be said about the way Sukumar's nonsense engages in several battles on different ideological fronts. For the purposes of this introductory overview it is enough to say that, in appropriating the methods of English nonsense, Sukumar does not sacrifice the specificities of Bangla linguistic devises: puns and the macaronic both play a role. But more interestingly, in place of Lear's use of Hobson-Jobson words is Sukumar's use of English words, such as 'cricket', 'club', 'Monday', 'nonsense', etc.

Sukumar's anti-colonial politics was not restricted to his writing. Sukumar also established 'The Nonsense Club' in 1905 in Calcutta.[33] He parodies English club culture by establishing 'Monda Sammelan' (it is both a Monday Club and also a *monda* eating club, *monda* being a festival delicacy of Bengalis and Odias alike). Just as the mathematician Lewis Carroll subverted logic and reason in his *Alice* books, Sukumar, who travelled to England to pursue scientific study, also critiqued the rational and 'Western' or modern discourses of law, science and philosophy. Carroll's influence on Sukumar be seen in such nonsense as 'Article Twenty-One' and 'Drighanchu':

Disastrous laws rule the land
Blessed by Shiva's loving hand!
If by chance you slip and fall
Guards appear grim and tall,
Drag you to court at a run [34]

'Article Twenty-One' can be seen as a satirical take on the draconian and often meaningless laws prevalent in British India. The whimsical idea of punitive action ruled by the number twenty-one is perhaps a jibe at both the arbitrariness of the legal system and the unfairness of punishment disproportionate to the 'crime'. This is certainly indebted to Carroll's Queen of Hearts. In his masterpiece, 'Drighanchu', the King orders the executioner to chop off the head of the 'one who made that horrible noise'. But the most celebrated and oft-quoted nonsense lines are from the politically incorrect verse passage in the same story. It runs thus: '*Holde sabuj, orangutan | Int patkal chit patang | mushkil ashan udey mali | Dharamtala karamkhali*' [lit., 'Yellow-green orangutan | Brick-stone, upside down | difficult, easy | Odia gardener | Dharamtala only work'].[35] Thus, the actual birth, flowering and maturation of modern Indian nonsense per se, can be seen in the works of Sukumar Ray, partly through his adaptation and Indianisation of nonsense techniques borrowed from Lear and Carroll, and partly through the modernisation of indigenous modes and materials. Though Tagore evinced interest in nonsense and children's verse early in his career, he was to attempt serious nonsense verse much later, in the late 1930s. Therefore, we accord Sukumar the pride of place in the pantheon of Indian writers of nonsense, including his senior, Tagore. But, unlike most Tagore scholars, who tend to highlight his politics and neglect his nonsense, I wish to focus on the latter.

Playing Nonsense with Words and Cards

Tagore's short story 'An Absurd Tale', mentioned earlier, in spite of the title, had little nonsense and less politics. Best described as a tale of fantasy, its similarity with the card people in *Alice* is also superficial. But, in *Tasher Desh*, Tagore's adaptation of Carroll runs much deeper.

There are a number of parallels between the *Alice* books and Tagore's dance drama. Like the Queen of Hearts crying out 'off with his/her head' in *Alice*, the King in Tagore's play yells 'banishment!' at the drop of a hat. Prince and Merchant in *Tasher*

Desh are amused to see the card people not only calling each other by their pip numbers, but also engaged in completely meaningless acts that recall the repainting of the Queen's roses undertaken by the card-gardeners in Chapter 8 of *Alice's Adventures in Wonderland*. Tagore's cards enter singing the following chorus:

> Pick it up, put it back.
> back and forward,
> Left and right.
> Don't want't, don't want't.
> Sit down, stand up.
> Throw it away, pick it up.
> Up down, down up
> Spin and move
> Enough! enough![36]

When the Prince and his merchant friend laugh watching their meaningless movements, the three card people ask them why they did so. The Prince replies, 'At least my laughter has some meaning. What you were doing is absolutely meaningless.' Card One replies, 'Meaning? What is meaning needed for? [We need] only rules.' He goes on to call the Prince mad. The Prince asks him how he could make out that he was mad. Card One replies that he could do so by observing a person's manners (*chal-cholon*); and that, though his *cholon* was OK, his *chal* was not. The reduplicative phrase in its entirety refers to manners; but Tagore breaks the term into its components and ascribes meaning to each independently, turning the utterance into nonsense. *Chal* means both gait and the turn for each player of dice or cards to cast their dice or cards (as in 'hand' in English). It also means to play a trick on someone. In itself, *cholon* might connote either a way of life or a walk. By breaking up the hyphenated term, Tagore is able to play around with various punning possibilities, in a way that recalls Carroll's wordplay. But, unlike Carroll, he uses the tale for didactic purposes. So the whimsicality of the Queen in *Alice* becomes a political instrument for Tagore. Unsurprisingly, most Tagore critics have paid attention to this dance drama for its topical politics. But, in my view at least, in *Tasher Desh*, Tagore's nonsense triumphs over his sense.

The other aspect of the dance drama that I wish to highlight here is that, though Tagore borrows the idea of the card people from Carroll, he frames the narrative around the prince and merchant sailing to a distant land, following the indigenous tradition of folk narratives. As we saw earlier, Carroll's Alice had been relocated to quintessentially Bengali contexts in Traikolyanath and Sukumar. Thus, in the works of these masters, whether it is Trailokyanath, Tagore or Sukumar, there is a loss of innocence about Indian Nonsense; and both the indigenous and the modern European tradition of literary nonsense combine to give a new character to the genre in Indian languages. Yet, many Indian writers continued to write children's verse oblivious of the work of Lear and Carroll. Rephrasing Edward Lear's response on seeing the Taj Mahal, one might say of India, 'Henceforth, let the writers of nonsense be divided into two classes – them as has read Lear and Carroll, and them that hasn't' [*sic*].[37] Before I consider post-Tagore-Sukumar nonsense, I will briefly discuss how the genre is theorised by Indian writers.

Indigenising Nonsense

We have discussed the way Indian writers of nonsense struggled with the terminology for the genre. Given that the term is used pejoratively, and even as a minor literary genre somewhat infra dig, when writers do write nonsense they often offer an apologia of sorts.

To begin with, we go back to *Khapchhada* (1937),[38] and notice that Tagore offers two elaborate explanations for his belated attempt to write nonsense. Addressing his instigator, Rajshekhar Basu, better known by the pen name Parashuram,[39] he invokes the high-canonical traditions with numerous allusions to *puranic* myths, and explains why the reader must accord high seriousness to nonsense:

> Should you see that the outer cloak has come off the old man.
> [. . .]
> If his utterances do not have any bearing on sense
> and his mind is crazy,
> Or, that it has reached the furthest limits of caprice,
> and you blame it all on his education,
> Then shall I speak of why Brahma has four faces.[40]

The outer cloak is a reference to the identity of the poet as a serious-minded poet-philosopher, which he has discarded in favour of the rasa of whimsy. Should he be ridiculed for having become quite whimsical and capricious, he would like to remind the reader of the four faces of Brahma. These verses thus connect the two major works of nonsense by Tagore, *Tasher Desh* and *Khapchhada*. We recall that one of the cards, Pip number Six in *Tasher Desh*, after mocking the Prince and Merchant for their lack of any identity in terms of class, race, caste, etc., boasts of his own origin thus: 'We are the world famous *tashbongshiyo* [of the Tash Dynasty] [. . .] After creating the universe, by afternoon, Brahma was so exhausted that he yawned; and we were created from that sacred yawn.' 'Precisely for this reason', Pip Five adds, 'We are also known as the Yawn Dynasty.' At the auspicious moment of twilight, he continues, 'the Lord let out four yawns simultaneously through his four faces [. . .] out of which popped out Clubs, Diamonds, Hearts and Spades [. . .]'.

Similarly, in the apologia for *Khapchhada*, Tagore alludes to the myth of Brahma's creation, but gives it a serious twist. He recounts the functions of the four faces of Brahma, the first one showers profound philosophy; the second resounds in the utterance of the Vedas; in the third one he creates poetry steeped in rasa; but,

> In the fourth, waves of excitement
> break the dam of sanity.
> From such an impact,
> p'haps nonsense swirls up.
> Thus, the disciple of Brahma, the poet says,
> No matter how much you laugh at me
> It will be on record
> That imagination plays with creativity
> But it is no less crazy about miscreation![41]

This attempt on Tagore's part to infuse an element of high seriousness in the discussion of nonsense can be read as an attempt to bring respectability to the genre. Though critics give credit to Sukumar Ray for starting the Nonsense Club and coining the term *kheyal rasa*, it was Tagore who had set up Kham-kheyali Sabha (or the Whim-wham Club) and practised nonsense by serving fish curry without a single piece of fish at lunches to which he invited his guests through whimsical invitations.[42]

In 1921, in neighboring Odisha, a group of young students of Ravenshaw College of Cuttack set up another 'Nonsense Club' made up of writers who aspired towards a new aesthetic.[43] The autobiography of one of the founding members, the Odia poet Panigrahi, records that five friends, all students from Ravenshaw College, set up the club to discuss literature. They borrowed the term, Panigrahi recalls, from an edition of the letters of William Cowper prescribed in their syllabus.[44] Possibly, Annada Sankar Ray (who began his writing career as an Odia writer before switching over to Bangla, and who was a founding member of the Club), knew of Sukumar Ray's 'Nonsense Club'. He was instrumental in choosing the name. Panigrahi says nothing of the contents of the magazine published by the club, the editorship of which he was entrusted with, except that they brought out a mouthpiece of the club through a handwritten journal called the *Nonsense Club Magazine* in three languages; Odia, Bengali and Hindi. Panigrahi, however, outlines the scope of nonsense in very broad terms. Years later, Annada Sankar wrote numerous nonsense verses in Bengali under the rubric of *chhoda*. It is possible that he had published a few of his juvenile nonsense verses in the magazine. Since nothing more is known about this so-called Nonsense Club, this episode of literary culture is of interest if only for the retrospective formulations of the genre by Panigrahi.

Panigrahi himself also addressed questions concerning the definition of nonsense. In English literature, he says, 'one notices a genre called nonsense'. He then proceeds to define the literary genre from *Cassell's Encyclopedia of Literature*, which he quotes at some length. Translating most part of this into Odia, Panigrahi says, this pleases us, not by a sequence of sweet-sounding word patterns or syntax, but through contradiction and paradox, or incongruence or absurdity. He calls those literary creations 'nonsense' which draw their inspiration from the traditional Odia *nanabaya geeta* or those children's rhymes and folk tales which fill the young and old alike with the kind of rasa described above. Though the name 'Nonsense Club' was inspired by this ideal, its main aim was to create 'ever-fresh strangeness and impart new sensations'.[45] I invoke this episode in Odia's cultural history because it happens to be one of the rare extended discussions of nonsense in any Indian language (other than Bangla) by a mainstream writer.

Ramakrushna Nanda, who wrote numerous pieces for children and ran Odia children's magazines, also drew connections between Odia *nanabaya* and nonsense. He said:

> Unintelligibility or irrelevance does not reduce the value of *nanbaya*. The rhythm and style is unique. Sometimes the meanings are unclear or impossible to ascertain. In English, some of these rhymes are called 'nonsense' or meaningless rhymes. By defying the metrical prescriptions and grammatical conventions, the spontaneity of these rhymes endear themselves to children.[46]

Nanda further refers to Lear's limericks in the context of humour in nursery rhymes. After providing the Odia reader with some metrical details regarding the form of the limerick, and quoting Lear's 'Old man with a beard' as an example of the form, he says that 'Lear's humorous rhymes are enjoyed by both children and adults. In Odia no such accepted forms or purely humorous compositions exist.'[47]

Reworking of Traditions

There is no evidence of any direct influence of English nonsense on the Odia, Assamese and Hindi writers of the late nineteenth and early twentieth century. But developments in literary culture of Bengal presidency, of which certain Odia-speaking regions were a part, made an impact on the newly educated Odia. Nandakishor Bala, one of the most eminent of Odia writers for children, a contemporary of Sukumar, reworked traditional rhymes and wrote many of his own. A good example is his famous Odia rhyme *teenimanjika*, a term he uses to rhyme with the reduplicative *kunchikunchika* ('curled-curled'). The word is not entirely meaningless: the word *teeni* means three, *manjika* means prostitute, or layers/curls; but the composite word is a nonsense coinage. Loosely translated the couplet would read, 'The high mountains are curled curled | on which is seated the thrice-gnarled.'[48]

The bilingual (Odia/Bangla) writer, Annada Sankar reworked traditional *chhoda* into high quality nonsense, but tended to give it a satirical slant. Yet, his nonsense ensures the continuation of the Tagore-Sukumar legacy.

Agartala's Aga Khan
Sundarban's Bagha Khan
But the heads of both the brothers
Will be broken by our own
A year and half old Naga Khan[49]

Here he moves from the normative Aga Khan to the non-normative Khans, Bagha (a tiger, Sundarban being a tiger reserve) and Naga (the poisonous cobra).

By the middle of the twentieth century, modern literary nonsense had gained greater visibility and currency in the subcontinent. *Alice* had by now been translated into, and was now available in, many of the Indian languages. Even Lear had become domesticated. Bengali writers continue to dominate in the field of Indian nonsense. Between 1930 and 1960, as many as ten, if not more, Bengali writers adapted Lear's limerick, 'There was an old man with a beard'. Satyajit Ray was one of them. Along with many other limericks by Lear, Ray also translated Carroll's 'Jabberwocky'. His translations involved much that can also be seen as instances of cultural translation as he drew the cultural content out of the original. Gone were the signifiers of English culture. His lines were now suffused with the terms from the familiar world of the target language, Bangla, such as *hutum pyancha* and *handi chanchha*. More importantly, Satyajit Ray used Lear's illustrations as well as the form of the limerick even as he subverts them. The well-known limerick of the old man with a beard becomes a very Bangla affair, complete with a *budho* ('old man') and '*hutum pyancha, ekta bodhhai handi chanchha* [. . .]' ['a night owl, and scrounger of the cooking pot, etc.'] He translated another line from 'There was an old man with a nose' to '*Ek jey saheb | tar jey chhilo nak*'. Lear and Carroll continued to cast their spell on writers until decades later.

In Hindi, Harindranath Chattopadhya (1898–1990) became known for many nonsense rhymes, such as *rail gadi* and *naniki nao chali*; Sri Prasad wrote 'Amrud' ('Guava') and 'Jamun' ('Black Berries');[50] and Sarveshwar Dayal Saxena wrote the hugely popular 'Batuta Ka Joota'. All these nonsense verses in Hindi, however, written mostly for children, are best grouped under the rubric of *gadbarjhala*. One can include Navakant Barua, the Assamese poet in this list too. His 'Nagaon' ('Ninepur') is modelled on Sukumar's 'Article Twenty-One', except that the number twenty-one is imaginary and nine is a twist on the name, a real town. The name literally means nine villages. Both the poems are, however, about arbitrary laws around the two numbers. Such punning on a place name that has a numerical component is a common device adopted by many writers of nonsense. JP (J. P. Das) too seizes the opportunity with his poem 'Athagarhra Pila' ('The Boy of Athgarh') on the town, Athagadh (literally, 'a place with eight forts'), and allows his *kheyal rasa* to run riot.

In fact, of all the regional poets closer to our times, it is JP's Odia nonsense that, like all good nonsense, endears itself to readers of all ages. He is one of the few major Indian writers who has a significant body of genuine nonsense, with diverse techniques: puns, reworked or parodied folk rhymes, riddles, macaronic word play, limericks, clerihews, travesty of logic and so on. Though among the forefront of major Indian writers, he treated nonsense with as much seriousness as he did the other genres such as poetry, short fiction, the novel and plays. Cognisant of Indian and English nonsense writers, he is the author of five collections of Odia nonsense.

JP's understanding of the rules of nonsense can be gauged by the fact that he has himself directly drawn on or translated many nonsense English verses.[51] His successful translation of 'Jabberwocky' as 'Jabberbaka'[52] is a masterclass in the way difficult nonsense can be translated. He uses the same sense, but juxtaposes *Jabber* with the bird, *baka* or crane, but also evokes the mythical *bakasur,* a crane-headed monster supposedly killed by Bhim, or, in another version, by Krishna. After ensuring that the attention of the reader is drawn through this vaguely demonic creature, the rest of the poem includes all the ingredients of Carroll's original, such as nonsense words sounding like sense because of their clever syntactic positioning. Thus, JP, Niranjan Behera and Das Benhur have reinvented traditional rhymes in the course of developing their respective brands of nonsense.

Nonsense in Non-literary Popular Culture

Nonsense has travelled well in India and has adapted itself to the Indian reality and folk and literary traditions with remarkable resilience. It has carved an identity of its own, distinct from Western traditions, while accepting many Western techniques and strategies. Traditional Indian nonsense has now been collected and printed in book form in different Indian languages, but they are not museum pieces: they survive to this day mainly through regional oral and folk traditions, and continue to be part of the living tradition in rural India. They have also mutated through their appropriation by the stage, modern and postmodern arts, as well as cinema, radio, advertisements and television. As the inclusion of dialogues and songs from Bollywood shows, Indian nonsense is alive and well. The process started by Sukumar when he adopted nonsense for the stage farces, *Jhalapala* (*Cacophony*) and *Lakshmaner Shaktishel* (*The Magical Arrow of Lakshman*, which was a spoof of the *Ramayana*) has progressed to reach Indian theatre, cinema, and beyond. From folk theatre nonsense lyrics first entered the Hindi film world through the works of Shailendra (1923–66) and Harindranath Chattopadhyay, to name just a couple. Shailendra composed a few nonsense lyrics for the film *Masoom* (1960), such as 'Nani teri morni' ('Granny, your peahen is stolen by the peacock'), with stanzas containing non-sequitor lines. Chattopadhyay also composed the rap-like song, 'Railgaadi' ('Railway train') for the film *Aashirwad* (1968). But all these are mainly children's nonsense rhymes that continued the association of nonsense with children's rhymes. Adult nonsense in films is a more recent phenomenon, when nonsense was the chief source of (mostly adult) humour. Kader Khan excelled in writing such dialogues.

Literary Modernism and Nonsense

As was the case with English modernism, literary modernists in India used the tradition of nonsense while writing 'serious' literature. Literary modernism in India organised itself largely under the influence of James Joyce, T. S. Eliot, Ezra Pound, W. H. Auden and Wallace Stevens, to name a few, many of whom were keen readers of Lear and Carroll. Unsurprisingly, many Indian modernists, from Bishnu Dey to Kunjuni either wrote nonsense or made use of it in their works. A few leading Hindi and Urdu modernist writers (such as Shamser Bahadur Singh) translated *Alice's Adventures in Wonderland*, and many others who were exposed to literary nonsense used it to their advantage. The iconoclastic Urdu writer Sadat Hasan Manto wrote a short story called 'Toba Tek Singh', in which the following famous lines are repeated throughout the narrative with small variations: '*Upar di gur gur di annexe di bedhiyana di moong di daal* of *di* Pakistan and Hindustan of *di durr phitey mun*', which are all a mix of sensible Urdu and Hindi words and phrases, but in nonsense collocation: 'annexe [. . .] of Pakistan and Hindustan of [. . .]' are disconnected English words; '*Upar di gur gur di*', etc. are a collocation of Punjabi-sounding nonsense words. The sentence can be loosely translated as 'the inattention of the annexe of the rumbling upstairs of the dal of moong of the Pakistan and India of the go to bloody hell!' Though critics have tried to interpret it in the spirit of modernist exegesis, it is best seen as a strategic use of nonsense.[53] The madness of the eponymous character and his meaningless expressions can be interpreted as a metaphor for the meaninglessness of partition.

Gulzar, like many other Indian writers, has composed nonsense on the formula of topsy-turvy-dom. His 'One-Eyed Town' comprises lines such as the following:

Their rivers flowed on bridges
And trains ran on water, not land,
On bushy tails of apes grew
Thick grapes in bunches grand.[54]

Gulzar, Sri Prasad and other modern poets fall back on the well-established trope of the topsy-turvy world to compose nonsense. However, whereas the traditional verses of Achyutandanda Das, Bhima Bhoi and Kabir do so to invoke a world elsewhere that is incomprehensible to the ordinary man, modern-day writers use the trope as a by-product of the rasa of whimsy, nonsense. Also, all these examples point to a persistent attempt on the part of Indian nonsense writers to invoke traditional tropes and images, whether from folk, bhakti or epic traditions, and to recreate folk tales, riddles and children's rhymes with European models in mind. Creatures as in *Panchatantra* tales talk, and sometimes in a language that is illogical.

Among the other mainstream modernist writers who have used the tradition of nonsense are Basheer, M. D. Muthukumaraswami and Kunjunni. Though they sometimes aim to disrupt notions of sense and nonsense, one can still invoke them as practitioners of Indian nonsense. The former uses the stream-of-consciousness mode, which depends on the genre of nonsense. Kunjunni uses fallacy as logic in the following poem:

Because the *pappadum* is round
So, the milk is white.
Because the milk is white
So the pot's made of clay.[55]

Moving forward into the second half of the twentieth century, we encounter nonsense as an effective strategy of postmodernism. Salman Rushdie (1947–) has used oriental and European traditions and worked them into his narratives, *Haroun and the Sea of Stories* and *Luka and the Fire of Life*. Rushdie's usual knack of stretching the real world into the realm of the fantastic helps him to draw on techniques of nonsense while writing for children. In *Luka* especially he signposts his indebtedness to the tradition of nonsense in a way that confirms the long chain between nonsense, modernism and postmodernism. While drawing on William Blake's portmanteau term 'Nobodaddy' Rushdie not only introduces a conceptual category drawn from the eighteenth-century poet to the informed, adult reader, but he also introduces a comically named character that children familiar with nonsense literature can identify with. He continues to do so with the more expressive names Nobody and Nonsense, which happen to be the names of the two tickling hands of Luka's father.[56] While this is impressive and complex intertextuality, it is representative of the problem endemic to much Indian English nonsense, including those of Anushka Ravi Shankar. There is technical virtuosity, but, unlike the nonsense in the Indian vernaculars, it shows little knowledge of indigenous traditions of nonsense outlined above.

Conclusion

From the high seriousness of Tagore's formulations of nonsense to the craziness and crassness of Indian film lyrics, from the appropriation of the genre by modernists such as Manto to that of the postmodernist Rushdie, Indian nonsense is complex and diverse. All said and done, one must admit that the vast and disparate body of Indian nonsense is dominated by Bangla not only in terms of quality and quantity but also in terms the breadth and depth of scholarship, translation and circulation even after a century. No other South Asian language can match this.

Finally, though it is impossible to talk of a 'pure' indigenous tradition of modern nonsense, Indian nonsense is not the simple cross-breeding of two traditions (as in Sukumar Ray's 'Khichudi' or mish-mesh figures). Even direct imitations and translations of European models are not uncommon; and these are often acknowledged. The techniques too of the macaronic and forms such as the limerick may have been derived from anglophone traditions. Even so, Indian nonsense is always more Indian than

European in its essence. The jokes, puns, the natural and the phantasmagoric worlds of Indian nonsense invoke the familiar Indian ethos. Indian nonsense is thus a composite genre, but its many parts – indigenous as well as imported – are, like Tenniel's visual rendering of 'Jabberwocky', barely recognisable, the local inextricable from the foreign elements.

Adi Sankaracharya's formulation is worth invoking here in the Indian context. In his Sanskrit treatise *Mohamudgar* he says, '*Artham anartham bhabaya nityam*'. This is taken usually as an indictment of materialist aspirations: 'Remember always that *artha* (money) is the source of all *anartha* (calamity).' But it also could mean that *artha* (meaning) is the source of all *anartham* (trouble), that *artha* (meaning) is the source of all *anartham* (non-meaning), or even that meaning is contrary to its own self. The saying takes us back to what we started with about the category, 'Indian nonsense', that it is part of India's traditional epistemology; but also that nonsense, like parody, is caused as much through authorial intention as through readerly intervention.

Notes

1. Rabindranath Tagore, *Rabindra Rachanabali: Janma Shatabdi Edition* (Calcutta: Government of West Bengal, 1960), pp. 439–40.
2. The fifth schedule of the Indian constitutions recognises twenty-two languages as the official Indian languages, and nearly fifty other languages aspire to the same status. Numerous other languages, sidelined as dialects, add to the complexity of the linguistic culture of the subcontinent. George Abraham Grierson, a member of the Indian Civil Service and a linguist, had first surveyed these in his *Linguistic Survey of India* (LSI), which is a comprehensive survey of the languages of British India, describing 364 languages and dialects. The LSI was first published after decades of manual research, in 1928.
3. The situation remained unremedied until Michael Heyman, Anuska Ravishankar and I curated a large number of narratives and verses scattered in public memory as well as in private collections of printed nonsense in more than twenty-three Indian languages. In the three-part Introduction to the anthology, we grappled with the diversity and complexity of subcontinental nonsense. (See *The Tenth Rasa: An Anthology of Indian Nonsense with an Introduction and Notes*, ed. Sumanyu Satpathy, Michael Heyman and Anushka Ravi Shankar (New Delhi: Penguin India, 2007)).
4. I have only briefly proposed elsewhere how modern Indian nonsense grew out of the imbrication between what can be retrospectively identified as traditional Indian nonsense and European literary nonsense following colonial contact. See Sumanyu Satpathy, 'Edward Lear, India and the Politics of Nonsense', in *Children's Literature and the Fin de siècle*, ed. Roderick Mc Gill (New York: Greenwood Press, 2002), 73–81.
5. U. R. Anantamurthy, 'Tradition and Creativity', in *Literature And Culture* (Calcutta: Papyrus, 2002). p. 111.
6. Edward Lear, *More Nonsense: Pictures, Rhymes, Botany, etc.* (London: Robert John Bush, 1872), p. vi.
7. Behera's letters to the author, 2 February 2004–1 November 2004, quoted in Sumanyu Satpathy, *Tini Manjika: Eka Odia Nonsense Sankalan* (Bhubaneswar: Siksha Sandhan, 2010), p. 30.
8. Satyajit Ray, Introduction to *The Select Nonsense of Sukumar Ray*, trans. Sukanta Chaudhuri (New Delhi: Oxford University Press, 1987), n.p.
9. John Beames, 'Folklore of Orissa', *Essays on Orissan History and Literature*, ed. Kailash Pattanayak (Orissagarh: Prafulla, 2004), p. 119.

10. Ibid.
11. Ibid.
12. In Tandra Patnaik, *Sunya Purusa* (New Delhi: D. K. Printworld (P) Ltd, 2005), p. 31.
13. *Bhaktakavi Bhimabhoi Granthabali*, ed. Karunakar Sahu (Cuttack: Dharmagranth Store, 2011).
14. Ibid. p. 46.
15. Ibid. pp. 44–6.
16. One interpretation of Bhima Bhoi's verses might go as follows: *jiva* is nature or body; *param* is supreme soul; the body comprises five *pranas*, plus five *koshas* like children, and so on. At this philosophy's core lies the paradox that *sunya* or void is actually the fullness.
17. See *The Tenth Rasa*, ed. Satpathy et al., p. xivi.
18. So called by the editors of *The Tenth Rasa* because of the dominant image in the opening lines in many of these folk texts is that of the thorn. For further details and examples see *The Tenth Rasa*, pp. 180–2.
19. Khwaja Banda Nawaz Gesu Daraz (1320?–1422?) was a Sufi saint in Gulbarga (Deccan, now Andhra Pradesh). He went to Daulatabad (Deccan) from Delhi as a child with his father. After the death of his father, he returned to Delhi and became a disciple of Hazrat Nizamuddin Aulia. At the advice of his spiritual guide, he went to Gulbarga and lived there till his death. Gesu Daraz had a large number of followers. See Anwar Sadeed, *Urdu Adab ki Mukhtasar Tareekh* (*A Short History of Urdu Literature*) (Lahore: A. H. Publishers), 1996, pp. 49–50; Abu Bakar Abbad and Arjumand Ara Sayyid Ehtesham Husain, *Urdu Adab ki Tanqeedi Tareekh* (*A Critical History of Urdu Literature*) (New Delhi: National Council for Promotion of Urdu Language, 1983), pp. 27–8.
20. Kabir, *The Bijak of Kabir*, trans. Linda Hess and Sukhdeo Singh (Oxford: Oxford University Press, 2002).
21. John Lehman, *Edward Lear and His World* (New York and London: Thames and Hudson, 1977), p. 103.
22. Among the last Indian languages to translate Alice can be included Assamese (1980) and Nepali (1992). I have discussed this in some detail in *Alice in a World of Wonderlands*, ed. Jon Lindseth (New Castle, DE: Oak Knoll Press, 2015).
23. See Sumanyu Satpathy, 'What's in a Name: Fantasy and Nonsense', *An Anthology of Indian Fantasy Writing*, ed. Malashri Lal (New Delhi: Sahitya Akademi, 2016), 114–28.
24. Trailokyanath Mukhopadhyay, *Kankabati*, trans. Nandini Bhattacharya (New Delhi: Primus Books, 2016), p. 199.
25. Tagore, 'Ekti Asadhe Galpa', in *Sadhana* (Ashad/Summer, 1892).
26. Partha Mitter, *Art and Nationalism in Colonial India (1850–1922)* (Cambridge: Cambridge University Press, 1994), p. 135; Sankho Ghosh, *Kalpanar Hysteria* (Calcutta: Papyrus, 1984), p. 118.
27. Satyajit Ray in *The Select Nonsense of Sukumar Ray,* trans. Sukanta Chaudhuri (New Delhi: Oxford University Press, 1987), n.p.
28. Ibid.
29. Bharata Muni's formulation of the eight rasas was extended by other aestheticians; in the context of our discussion the 1000 CE scholar Abhinavagupta's contribution is crucial in the addition of the ninth rasa that is *shanta rasa* (serenity).
30. Satyajit Ray in *Select Nonsense of Sukumar Ray*, n.p.
31. Satpathy, 'Edward Lear, India, And The Politics of Nonsense'.
32. Lear was conscious of his own features which included 'a most elephantine nose'; he described himself thus in a letter to Charles Empson; see *Edward Lear: Selected Letters*, ed. Vivien Noakes (Oxford: Oxford University Press), p. 16.
33. See Debasish Chattopadhyay, 'Nonsense Club and Monday Club: The Cultural Utopias of Sukumar Ray', in *The Literary Utopias of Cultural Communities 1790–1910*, ed. Corporaal Marguérite and Jan van Evert (Leiden, Netherlands: Brill, 2010), 243–52.

34. See *The Tenth Rasa*, ed. Satpathy et al., p. 26. My translation here differs both from the one that appears in *The Tenth Rasa* and in Satyajit Ray's *The Select Nonsense*. Both the earlier translations drop the reference to Odia and the Muslim working class.
35. Mitter says that 'Both (Lear and Sukumar) eschewed sarcasm, malice and ridicule; both left out the cruel and the grotesque' (Mitter, *Art and Nationalism*, p. 135). But here we find Sukumar succumbing to the temptation. The juxtaposition of Orang Utang and Udey mali are not fortuitous, and does make some sense. Udia people are deprecatingly referred to as 'Udey', and also suggesting that the community is servile, acting only as gardeners; they are not only malis but primates as well, as the other folk rhyme already quoted would suggest.
36. *Tasher Desh* n.p. Available at <https://bangodarshan.com/ratan/stock/TASER_DESH.pdf> (last accessed 1 May 2021).
37. 'Henceforth, let the inhabitants of the world be divided into two classes – them as has seen the Taj Mahal; and them as hasn't' [*sic*] (*Indian Journal: Water Colours and Extracts from the diary of Edward Lear, 1873–1875*, ed. Ray Murphy (London: Jarrods, 1953), p. 79).
38. The Bangla title means incongruity or mismatch; but it is also a pun on *chhoda* (the nearest English equivalent of this Bangla term would be 'nursery rhyme', or 'children's verse', as I have already suggested). The Bangla term *chhele-bhulano chhoda* itself is an alliterative description and a nativisation of the Western genre of lullaby and nursery rhyme. Tagore was one of the first great modern Indian poets to realise the importance of such *chhoda*.
39. Rajshekhar Basu, better known by the pen name Parashuram (16 March 1880 – 27 April 1960), was a Bengali writer, chemist and lexicographer. Basu's knowledge of Sanskrit was legendary. He was chiefly known for his comic and satirical short stories, and is considered the greatest Bengali humorist of the twentieth century. He was awarded the Padma Bhushan in 1956.
40. Tagore, *Rabindra Rachanabali*, pp. 439–40.
41. The Bengali word that I translate here as 'nonsense' is *jaa-taa* which literally means balderdash, but the same is not being used here pejoratively. It is a 'non-semantic' equivalent of *abol-tabol* with the kind of *rasa* described above. More recently, Bengali poets and scholars like Sankho Ghosh and Shivaji Bandopadhyaya have dealt with the subject of nonsense in book-length studies. Ghosh entitles his book *Kalpanar Hysteria* (*Hysteria of the Imagination*), which in itself offers a view of nonsense as imagination run wild – not very different from Tagore's interpretation of the source of nonsense as torrential eloquence of 'miscreation'.
42. See Chattopadhyay, 'Nonsense Club and Monday Club'.
43. Kalindi Charan Panigrahi, *Ange Jaha Livaichi* (*What I have Experienced in Life*), (Cuttack: Cuttack Student's Store, [1973] 2006), p. 256.
44. Ibid. pp. 366–7.
45. Ibid. pp. 368–71.
46. *Odia Shishu Sangit Sankalan*, ed. Ramakrushna Nanda (Bhubaneswar: Orissa Sahitya Akademi, 1981), p. 3.
47. Ibid. p. 11.
48. See Sumanyu Satpathy, *Tini Manjika: Eka Odia Nonsense Sankalan*, p. 77.
49. Ibid. p. 179.
50. Available at <https://www.pitara.com/fiction-for-kids/hindi-poems-for-kids/अमरुद-बन-गये/> and <https://www.pitara.com/fiction-for-kids/hindi-poems-for-kids/जामुन/> (last accessed 1 May 2021).
51. I have translated a few of these for the National Book Trust of India, under the title *Nanasense*, by coining a portmanteau term ('nonsense' and *nanabaya*) to indicate the hybrid nature of such nonsense.
52. *Jabber* in Odia and Bangla is derived from the Urdu *jabber* meaning great and mighty. A recent translation of the poem in Hindi appeared in a blog under the title 'Bakarsuri',

which is exactly coined with the same logic as JP's. Available at <https://shailendra.me/blog/translation/jabberwocky-in-hindi/> (last accessed 1 May 2021).

53. 'Toba Tek Singh' translated from the Urdu by Frances W. Pritchett. The relevant nonsense line, untranslated by Prichett, is translated by me with the help of friends. Available at <http://www.columbia.edu/itc/mealac/pritchett/00urdu/tobateksingh/translation.html> (last accessed 1 May 2021).
54. For Behera and Gulzar, see *The Tenth Rasa*, ed. Satpathy et al. pp. 86–103.
55. *The Tenth Rasa*, ed. Satpathy et al., p. xxix.
56. Salman Rushdie, *Luka and the Fire of Life* (New York: Random House, 2010).

10

Signs and Wonders: Two Approaches to Nonsense in Russia

James Rann

The well-meaning person who, by merely studying the logical side of things, has decided that 'faith is nonsense', does not know how truly he speaks; later it may come back to him in the form that nonsense is faith.

G. K. Chesterton[1]

Nonsense gets everywhere. Even at the peak of the Russian realist tradition, in Anton Chekhov's grimly unfantastical novella *The Peasants* (1897), we are reminded that some words have nothing to do with communicating a message or representing the world but are no less important for that. The devout peasant Olga, whose life starts off bad and gets worse, takes comfort in the Bible precisely because it seems so divorced from reality:

> She read the Gospels every day aloud, like someone reading the lesson in church, not understanding much of them. But the holy words moved her to tears and she almost swooned with delight as she brought out such things as 'whosoever' or 'until I bring thee word' [. . .] When she said words from the Bible, even without understanding them, she looked compassionate, radiant and deeply moved.[2]

Olga is far from alone in preferring sublimity to sense. Many proponents of the Latin liturgy would argue that its beauty and sanctity is contingent on its obscurity, just as the Spanish-language pop songs that occasionally float to the top of the charts are best enjoyed in ignorance of the banality of their lyrics. Although Olga's gospel, like the Tridentine Mass or 'Macarena', means something to someone somewhere, to her it is an exquisite nonsense and, what is more, a transformative one. Words without meanings – be they screams, spells or snarks – are still powerful, and nowhere more so than in Russia.

This is not to say that the rhymes and riddles usually associated with 'nonsense' as a literary genre have not been marginalised and belittled in Russia as elsewhere in Europe, nor to deny that most of the many near-equivalents of the word 'nonsense' in Russian have connotations of worthlessness. But rivalling, and perhaps even underpinning, this dismissive attitude is a persistent and pervasive tendency to treat words unmoored from meanings with respect and even fear because of their uncanny force. This wary acknowledgement of the potential strength of nonsense has come to the surface in the many and varied sojourns away from sense dotted throughout Russian literature and history. Although these instances have rarely been thought to constitute a tradition and even more rarely given the collective title of 'nonsense', one can certainly identify a lineage of writers who flout not just the conventions of ordinary discourse but the very logic of communication itself. This heritage starts with anonymous folk poetry and takes in the absurdism of Nikolai Gogol in the nineteenth century and Daniil Kharms in the twentieth, the spoof aphorisms of hoax author Kozma Prutkov, and the postmodern game-playing of Dmitrii Prigov and Lev Rubinshtein.

As elsewhere in Europe, however, it was in the early twentieth century that the nonsensical undercurrents in Russian literature came closest to the mainstream. This period saw not only copious outpourings of modernist linguistic experimentation but also a new wave of publishing for children that, alongside more obviously character-building fare, gave an outlet to talented writers with a penchant for nonsense.[3] In this chapter, I will show how the different approaches to nonsense taken by two writers working in the decades before and after the 1917 revolution – one in the avant-garde, the other in children's literature – not only relate to the concerns of their era, but also reopen longstanding debates in Russia about the purpose and duties of language. Where do words come from: from our own minds or our hearts, from society or from God? Is the point of writing to represent the world or to change it? And if to change it, then how? Nonsense can be a serious business.

Two Species of Modern Nonsense

The first twentieth-century phenomenon I will explore is the expressionist, non-semantic poetic language known in Russian as *zaum* ('trans-sense'), invented not long before the revolution by radical poets of the modernist avant-garde and pioneered in particular by the Futurist Aleksei Kruchenykh. The second is Kornei Chukovsky's defence of his fantastical poems for children, which are now revered as classics, but which were criticised by the Soviet authorities in the 1920s and 1930s for being both unacceptably frivolous and dangerously subversive. Chukovsky's response was the much-reprinted *From Two to Five* (first published 1928), an apologia for nonsense by children and for children in which he explores and lauds the absurd linguistic inventions of infants.

At first sight, Kruchenykh and Chukovsky have quite a lot in common. They were both born in the 1880s in relatively humble circumstances, made a name for themselves before the revolution, and then lived on, surrounded by a number of mutual acquaintances, until the late 1960s. They shared an impish sense of humour but also both sought to use their rejection of convention to instigate significant changes in the world – a seriousness of intent that is, to be sure, typical of much Russian literature. Finally, they were both at once practitioners and theoreticians, producing a series of quite sensible texts which explicate their nonsense to readers and critics. That is where the common ground ends, however. Not only were their career paths very different, but the two writers were far from friends: Chukovsky once called Kruchenykh 'as dull as a post' and Kruchenykh accused Chukovsky of plagiarism.[4]

The dissimilarity between the two is further evident in the distinct forms of nonsense they advocated. Kruchenykh's 'transrational' *zaum* poetry uses words without any identifiable meaning. You could compare it to 'Jabberwocky', but this would not do justice to its deliberate impenetrability or its ambition. *Zaum* was supposed to be an utterly new and idiosyncratic idiom and was intended as a self-consciously provocative, utopian and at times aggressively chauvinist intervention into the esoteric debates about language that accompanied Russian modernist poetry. The totality of Kruchenykh's rejection of sense and signification in *zaum* has afforded him a certain cult status but limited his popular appeal. Chukovsky, by contrast, continues to be one of Russia's most widely read children's authors and his analysis of infants' linguistic inventions has proved to be of lasting value to both psychologists and theoreticians of nonsense, vindicating, it would seem, his stated desire to be of immediate practical use to society. What is more, while Kruchenykh's *zaum* rejects everyday meaning at a linguistic level, refusing to treat language as a system of stable arbitrary signs, Chukovsky's poetry departs from common sense at the level of plot and characterisation. *The Crocodile*, for instance, tells the long and somewhat convoluted tale of a certain Krokodil Krokodilovich Krokodil, an African reptile-about-town whose anthropomorphic trappings – using aeroplanes, smoking cigarettes, speaking Turkish – do little to dampen his enthusiasm for eating people.

There is, however, a more fundamental distinction between the nonsense of Kruchenykh and that of Chukovsky. The latter sees sense as ontologically prior to nonsense: nonsense may invert sense, but it is still determined by it and subordinate to it. Like most Russians, Chukovsky does not often use the bookish loanword *nonsens*, except in relation to English nonsense literature, but the words he does use share the same privative connotation of lack or opposition as 'nonsense'.[5] What is more, he argues in *From Two to Five* that although nonsense is powerful, it is powerful only as a tool for the consolidation of reality and sense, proposing that 'we can plant realism in [the child's] mind not only directly, by acquainting them with the realities in their surroundings, but also by means of fantasy'.[6] Kruchenykh, in contrast, conceptualises his work not as the opposite or underside of sense, but rather as something that transcends it. The root *um* means intelligence and the prefix *za* implies something which goes further, hence the translator Paul Schmidt's ingenious coinage 'beyonsense'.[7] For Kruchenykh, therefore, nonsense is neither a mirror to reality nor a holiday from it. Its otherness is not that of binary opposition but rather an indefinable absence of association.

Although the analogy is not perfect, the difference between the two Russians is similar to that which G. K. Chesterton detected between Lewis Carroll and Edward Lear. Chukovsky is like Carroll, for whom nonsense is above all an 'escape into a world where things are not fixed horribly in an eternal appropriateness' – a world which, even if it inverts reality, still remembers that there has been an inversion. On the other hand, Kruchenykh, at least when he is in *zaum* mode, enjoys the same 'completeness of [. . .] citizenship in the world of unreason' as Lear, inhabiting a realm where the mood music is not 'the pomp of reason, but [. . .] the romantic prelude of rich hues and haunting rhythms'.[8] And so, while Kruchenykh still often presents his rejection of conventional rationality as a superior version of reason and realism, he imagines it as historically and logically antecedent to sensible language.[9]

Closer to Chukovsky and Kruchenykh than Chesterton – in time and space at least – was Mikhail Bakhtin, the Russian philosopher whose concept of 'the carnivalesque', coined in 1940, colonised much academic writing from the 1980s onwards, including the study of nonsense.[10] While this overused term has occasionally been stretched beyond the point of elasticity, it is not insignificant that Bakhtin identifies in medieval feasts a distinction, similar to that of Chesterton, between different versions of temporary topsy-turviness. In true carnivals, he says, ordinary people briefly 'entered the utopian realm of community, freedom, equality, and abundance'; official church and state celebrations, in contrast, 'did not lead the people out of the existing world order and created no second life. On the contrary, they sanctioned the existing pattern of things and reinforced it.'[11] At the risk of being overly schematic, whereas Kruchenykh's *zaum* is nonsense of the former, carnivalesque type – a promise of an entirely different universe, Chukovsky's nonsense is presented as an escape valve for latent otherness which helps to support the status quo.

I draw this parallel not to suggest that, since Chukovsky frames nonsense as a departure that reinforces reality, he in some way sought to bolster the Soviet system. Far from it. Chukovsky began writing for children quite late in his career, turning with genuine enthusiasm to a genre that, for writers such as Kharms, offered something of a refuge from ideological persecution. But if this was Chukovsky's hope too, then he was to be disappointed and he ended up having to defend his nonsense from official attacks of life-threatening severity. Nevertheless, the way in which he mounted his defence shows that he shared with his detractors fundamental assumptions about nonsense and about literature as a whole. Even when talking about nonsense, he sought to play the Soviet game by its rules, honouring them in their breach. To invoke the axiology of the medieval church again, he was a sinner – conscious and unrepentant, but inside the system. Kruchenykh, on the other hand, was a born heretic – an advocate of an alternative cosmology, drawn to nonsense as a way of freeing himself from convention per se.[12]

This religious analogy is not accidental, but rather a reflection of the deep roots that debates about nonsense had in Russia's ecclesiastical culture. Bakhtin, writing in the officially atheist Soviet Union, posits a politically correct dichotomy between official church feasts and secular popular celebrations, but the proposed opposition between grass-roots anti-clerical fervour and top-down hieratic orderliness obscures the internal tensions that were typical of the history of the Russian Orthodox Church, which was often marked by bitter disputes about the relative virtues of hierarchy and spontaneity, of order and disorder. Orthodoxy has always put special emphasis on the church's role as the guarantor of continuity and community, the embodiment of an unbroken and unbreakable tradition of togetherness. The internal critics of the church hierarchy who emerged intermittently in the late medieval and early modern periods never questioned these conservative principles, but rather argued that the church had strayed from them. Fifteenth-century 'non-possessors', for instance, preached asceticism and condemned the alleged acquisitiveness of some monasteries as an abandonment of early Christian self-sufficiency. This movement was eventually defeated, as were a variety of later 'heresies', but right up until the revolution of 1917 the leadership of the church felt obliged to confront outbursts of self-consciously conservative nonconformism in the shape of individual eccentric holy men, ecstatic sectarians, and, most significantly, the schismatic 'Old Believers', who broke from the church in the seventeenth century and have not returned. The disputes surrounding these confrontations are important to the history of Russian nonsense, and to understanding the arguments that were used to prosecute and defend the experiments of Kruchenykh and Chukovsky, because, amongst other things, they were arguments about language, about whose words were sacred and whose profane.

Holy Nonsense

Let us return, then, to Olga's incomprehensible gospel. The two words Chekhov quotes are much more obscure than the translator's 'whosoever' and 'until I bring thee word'. *Ashche* ('if') and *dondezhe* ('until') are, in fact, barely even Russian, belonging more properly to Old Church Slavonic, the traditional liturgical language of the Russian Orthodox Church.[13] The long survival of this language in services, in popular devotion, and in the wider culture, even after Russian translations of the Bible were published in the mid-nineteenth century, exemplifies the church's commitment to conservatism, next to which even the Roman Catholic aversion to the vernacular seems half-hearted. When, a century after Martin Luther, the Russian church faced its own crisis of identity, it was not the challenge of innovative doctrines and popular appeal that precipitated a split in the church, but a tussle between competing versions of the authority of tradition. Patriarch Nikon and his reformist faction, who argued that religious texts and practices should be corrected to align with Greek examples, eventually emerged victorious against opponents who preferred to adhere to the texts and practices of their Russian ancestors. The latter group, first referred to by their opponents merely as 'schismatics' and only later as 'Old Believers', were so unwilling to yield to what they perceived as foreign infiltration that they preferred to face persecution in their own splinter church rather than accept the reversions that they perceived as innovations.

Such zealous commitment to tradition on all sides, promoting form over content, is fertile ground for gibberish. This process is familiar in Western Europe too – for instance in the uneducated Reformation-era parish priest's 'mumpsimus' mocked by Erasmus – but in early modern Russia such nonsense was especially widespread. The practice of *mnogoglasie* ('many voices'), in which different parts of the liturgy were sung simultaneously to reduce the length of the service, produced 'a chaotic din of sound that could not be sorted by any means'.[14] Similarly *khomoniia*, a misapplied adherence to outdated orthography, produced coinages that, according to a monk at the time, seemed 'foreign, uncharacteristic, and contradictory to the language in which we were brought up and learned Holy Scripture'.[15] Finally, over the years, the meaningless rhythm-matching words *ananaek* and *khabuvy* – something like the medieval equivalent of scat singing – had become so widespread that texts were unrecognisable, leaving the congregation 'all wallowing in darkness, no one knowing the truth, [since] it remains unknown from where this is taken and in what language it is being spoken'.[16]

What is surprising about these irruptions of nonsense is not that they occurred, but that they survived so long. This was largely because they found principled defenders who prioritised fidelity to established examples over clarity of communication. *Khomoniia* and *ananaek* are thus still the norm for certain Old Believer communities and, despite learned complaints, a church council in 1659 permitted *mnogoglasie* to continue in parish churches for several decades more.[17] Over and above traditionalism, a crucial factor in the persistence of this liturgical nonsense was the fact that the same longing for sublimity felt by Chekhov's Olga was experienced by ardent believers who, as a sceptical Soviet historian says, 'did not permit critical thinking in religious questions' and so 'when they heard this nonsense saw in it some mysterious sense hidden from their understanding'.[18] It did not matter that the congregation did not understand; what mattered was that God *did* understand. If anything was heretical, conservative opinion held, it was not nonsense but rather the proposed shift of emphasis from God's infinite comprehension to limited worldly perception.[19]

Although this conception of nonsense as the marker of a higher, divine sense was eventually excluded from official Orthodox religious practice, it continued to prosper on the margins. One of the unique features of pre-revolutionary Russian Christianity was the popular devotion afforded to so-called 'holy fools', men whose rejection of all social behavioural norms marked them out not as insane but rather as especially close to God.[20] Part of the holy fools' disavowal of common sense was a refusal to observe the usual rules of speech and instead to keep silent or, more often, to replace cogent sentences with 'incomprehensible expressions [. . .] shouts, exclamations and aphoristic phrases'.[21] Their supporters regarded the 'murky words' of medieval holy fools like Andrei Tsaregradskii either as a form of higher communication with God or as an expression of a depth of feeling that surpassed human understanding.[22] Even when used as a means of interpersonal communication, nonsense speech was perceived as a purer, more sacred medium: Tsaregradskii was said to have once held a conversation with a young admirer in 'Syrian', which is to say, the imagined common language of all mankind before God's polyglot punishment for the Tower of Babel. Holy glossolalia became a way for nonconformists to demonstrate their distinction from their enemies: at a dispute in Moscow in 1682, the Old Believer representatives spent hours shouting nothing but 'So, so! A-a-a-a!'[23] This display was dismissed by one of their ultimately triumphant modernising opponents as either demonically motivated or 'the disorderly cries of stupid peasants', cementing the association between incoherence and marginality. Sure enough, glossolalia continued to be most popular on the periphery of religious practice, particularly among the ecstatic cults which, despite persecution by church and state, flourished among the peasantry into the twentieth century, which would accompany their wild dancing with impenetrable shrieks and murmurs.[24]

Although not without parallel in other forms of Christianity such as Pentecostalism, these manifestations of religious nonsense demonstrate the evergreen vigour in Russian religion of apophatic theology, a strand in Christian thought that was particularly cherished in Orthodoxy. The apophatic tradition proposes that God is so great that he cannot be known or spoken of using the base means of our universe (kataphatically); he can only be understood in terms of what he is not (apophatically) – 'a kind of apprehension by supreme ignorance of Him'.[25] Nonetheless, divine nonsense was never comfortably endorsed by the church hierarchy, but remained a mystical, anti-authoritarian counter-discourse formed in opposition to the dominant doxa and practice and treated as a hostile threat to the authority of church and state, who exercised their power in part through the control of categories and meanings.

Aleksei Kruchenykh and *Zaum*

The same debates about language that accompanied tensions in the early modern Russian Orthodox Church – about the wisdom of ignorance, about submission and subversion, and about national identity – appear again in early twentieth-century Russia around the work of Kruchenykh and Chukovsky. While Chukovsky certainly does not dismiss nonsense, it is Kruchenykh who best maintains the traditions of the semi-heretic holy fools and sectarians – an inheritance that was very evident to contemporaries seeking to understand the strangeness and scandal of Futurism, such as the journalist who in a 1913 report on the Futurists demanded 'the confinement of all these holy fools to a madhouse'.[26] The poets deliberately invited such comparisons by disrespecting both literary decorum – their rabble-rousing debut manifesto 'A Slap in the Face of Public Taste' famously called for the ejection of the classics of Russian literature from 'the steamship of Modernity' – and the mores of polite society, gadding about with paint on their faces and wooden spoons in their buttonholes and, what is more, making sounds without identifiable meaning, or, as they called it, *zaum*.

The affinity between *zaum* and glossolalia was observed by the Futurists' earliest interpreter Viktor Shklovsky, whose article 'On Poetry and Trans-Sense Language' (1916) remains an excellent introduction to the topic.[27] Shklovsky argues that sectarians, children and Futurists all share a preference for the expressive and affective functions of language over its rational, communicative capabilities. Such functions are present in all language, it is suggested, but they are particularly prominent in poetry, which approximates the pure expressivity of music.[28] *Zaum* is the maximal realisation of this potential and, as such, the culmination of a quest to overcome the limitations of language that Shklovsky detects in both Russian Romanticism and in the dominant poetic school of the first decade of the new century, Symbolism.

The Futurists, like the admirers of the original holy fools, believe that this irrational aspect of language is superior to the common sense of everyday language.[29] Shklovsky cites Kruchenykh's 'The Declaration of the Word as Such' (1913), the manifesto which contains the first usage of the word *zaum*, as part of an argument that rationality is not our home, but our prison:

> Thought and speech cannot keep up with the experience of one who is inspired, and so the artist is free to express himself not only in shared language (concepts), but also in his private language (the creator is individual), and a language that has no definite meaning (it is not frozen), *zaum*. Shared language binds, free language allows you to express yourself more fully. (E.g. *go osneg kaid*, etc.).[30]

Of course, the Futurists' desire radically to extend the possibilities of both consciousness and the literary language was shared by an array of modernists in Russia and beyond. *Zaum* was in part a response to a thoroughgoing crisis of representation born from frustration with realism: how can conventional art capture all the complexity and mystery of the contemporary world? It is no coincidence that *zaum* emerged from the same milieu as the first Russian experiments in abstract art or that one of the first proper *zaum* poems, Kruchenykh's 'Dyr bul shchyl' (1913), was illustrated with an early Rayonist drawing by Mikhail Larionov. Both *zaum* and non-figurative art represented attempts to go beyond traditional means of rendering the world and the self. What is more, both manifested a widespread desire, more pronounced in Orthodox Russia than elsewhere, to make word and image iconic, so that they would not to reproduce the world mimetically, but rather, like a holy icon, offer a direct, transformative connection with intangible higher forces.[31]

What really distinguishes the Futurists' *zaum* from previous experiments in abstract language by, for instance, Stéphane Mallarmé or their compatriot Andrei Belyi is the emphasis on utter newness and their pointed polemic against Symbolism.[32] Despite their evident debt to Symbolists like Belyi, in their public rhetoric the Futurists condemned Symbolist poetry as out of touch, effeminate and hopelessly enervated by an obsessive merry-go-round of secret meanings. As another sceptic, Osip Mandelshtam, later put it: 'For the Symbolist [. . .] a rose is like the sun, the sun is like a rose, and a dove is like a girl and a girl is like a dove.'[33] The Futurists' response was to not only mock Symbolist pretension but also to shift attention back on to the word in and of itself, hence 'The Declaration of the Word as Such'. *Zaum* was the ultimate expression of this reorientation towards language as sound since it frustrated any attempts at symbolic interpretation and revelled in the articulatory jouissance of Russian consonants.

And they were self-consciously *Russian* consonants. In contrast to other post-Symbolists like Mandelshtam, the Futurists' plan for the literary language was deliberately nationalistic. They presented Futurist poetry in general and *zaum* in particular as a purgative cure for a Russian tongue bedevilled by effete alliteration and tired metaphors, urging readers not to 'use worn out images epithets and words – switch to *zaum*'.[34] Kruchenykh said of the infamous 'Dyr bul shchyl' (1913) that 'there is in these five lines more of the Russian national spirit than in all the poetry of Pushkin [. . .] not a voiceless languorous creamy smear of poetry (patience . . . pastille . . .) but tremendous bardry'.[35] I leave the title of the poem untranslated here for obvious reasons: by Kruchenykh's own admission, the words '*dyr bul shchyl*' 'have no fixed meaning' and so cannot be easily rendered in English.[36] This would have pleased the Futurists, who were unusually antipathetic to translation, which they disdained for ignoring the 'word as such' in favour of disembodied meaning.[37]

This hostility to translation became another fertile source of nonsense, particularly in the work of Vladimir Mayakovsky, a poet who liked *zaum* in principle if not in practice. In his poetry Mayakovsky quotes from languages like English or Georgian in the original, creating passages that defy understanding but, he thought, retain perlocutionary power. He performs a similar trick in his play *The Bathhouse*, in which the Englishman Pont-Kich speaks in a language that is recognisable as his native tongue, but which is constructed out of Russian words, in a manner reminiscent of Luis d'Antin van Rooten's homophonic nursery rhyme translations. An audience member who is both bilingual and a genius might thus be able to hear Pont-Kich saying both 'Ouch! Ivan howled at the door, but the beasts were dining. Ouch! A mannequin went to Paradise, but a raccoon went to Hindustan' – the literal meaning of the Russian words – and something a bit like 'I wonder very well, as very oh be dully. I shall rye mannequin and why not understand' – the 'English' interpretation of these same syllables.[38]

The isolationist bent of *zaum* is further evident in the Russian Futurists' valorisation of its apparent unsophistication. Unlike their Italian namesakes, the Russian Futurists' hostility to the achievements of European culture manifested itself not so much as a forward-looking adoration of technological progress as a neo-primitivist return to an imagined past of linguistic and cultural integrity, before 'everything was done to quash the primordial feeling of our native language, to strip the word of its fertile grain, to castrate it'.[39] Kruchenykh's *zaum*, with its preponderance of guttural consonants and paucity of grammatically feminine endings, strives to reconstruct the masculine energy of this imagined proto-language. This 'black language like that of wild tribes' possesses not only atavistic strength, but also prelapsarian purity, much like Andrei Tsaregradskii's 'Syrian': 'Words die, the world is eternally young. The artist has seen the world in a new way and, like Adam, gives everything its name.'[40]

The impermanence implied by this 'eternally young' world points to a more fundamental break with the past in Kruchenykh's *zaum*, one which hints at the scale of the Futurists' ambition. It is not enough to liberate language from the burdensome history of culture; the *zaum* poet's language must exist in a moment of pure presentness. It represents, in miniature, an irruption into a utopian time-outside-of-time that anticipates a still more thoroughgoing eschatological escape for all of mankind. All the Futurists celebrated ephemerality – they urged readers to tear up their books once they had finished reading – but Kruchenykh's insistence on *zaum* as a blink-and-you'll-miss-it outburst helps us to draw a distinction between his approach to nonsense and that of his early collaborators Elena Guro and, especially, Velimir Khlebnikov.[41] While he shares a preoccupation with primordial purity, Khlebnikov is much more concerned than his collaborator with making from *zaum* a coordinated and consistent system, one which could then serve as a universal language in the new world he felt was imminent.[42] Khlebnikov also eschews representation, but his *zaum* coinages are not presented as transitory expressionist flashes like those of Kruchenykh, but as constituents of a quasi-rational epistemology.

We can see in this distinction the ambivalent position of Futurist *zaum* in relation to later developments in literary and linguistic theory. The work of Khlebnikov, whose other main project was to produce a complete arithmetical rationale for predicting the future, resembles a prophetic fever-dream of the structuralist world view propagated by his friend and disciple Roman Jakobson. Khlebnikov is reminiscent of the eponymous hero of Jorge Luis Borges's story 'The Analytical Language of John Wilkins', the Enlightenment polymath who tries to create 'a general language that would organize and contain all human thought'.[43] The spurious and unwieldy taxonomies produced by such a totalising approach to human experience, parodied by Borges, later helped the post-structuralist Michel Foucault express his scepticism of universalism, not by furnishing him with a rational argument but rather by inspiring a fit of laughter that shattered

> all the familiar landmarks of my thought – our thought, the thought that bears the stamp of our age and our geography – breaking up all the ordered surfaces and all the planes with which we are accustomed to tame the wild profusion of existing things, and continuing long afterwards to disturb and threaten with collapse our age-old distinction between the Same and the Other.[44]

The anarchic spirit in Foucault's Dionysian, anti-structuralist laughter is also present in Kruchenykh. In his scandalous semi-*zaum* opera *Victory over the Sun* (1913), Futurist strongmen capture and imprison the sun, revoking Apollonian clarity and renewing the world by depriving it of its only source of light. Just as Kazimir Malevich's 'Black Square', which made its debut in *Victory over the Sun*, poses a challenge to all painting, so Kruchenykh's *zaum* seeks to transform the operation and scope of language by first destroying it, exposing the fragility of the scaffolds of sense and meaning that support it.[45] The liberatory obliteration offered is both figurative and literal: Kruchenykh's *zaum* offers an unwitting rebuke to one of the pillars of structuralist thought, the Saussurean dichotomy between *langue* and *parole*, by dispensing with *langue*, language as system, to produce language that is all utterance, pure *parole*, free from the constrictions engendered by history and society.

Such grandiose ambition might seem a little ridiculous when compared to the limited scale and significance of the textual legacy of Kruchenykhian *zaum*. Its alogical, unsystematic nature precluded Kruchenykh's antisemantic poetry from becoming anything more than an occasionalism. This is not to say, however, that *zaum* had no life outside of Kruchenykh and Futurism's *annus mirabilis* of 1913. Notable among the other experimental writers who continued to investigate *zaum*'s expressive and philosophical potential are Ilia Zdanevich, who later had close links with Dadaists and surrealists in France, and the late Soviet underground poets Rea Nikonova and Serge Segay. Kruchenykh himself broadened his definition of *zaum* after 1917 and updated his rhetoric to include greater emphasis on the creativity of the collective.[46] His interest in nonsense never waned but took on different forms reflecting a more recuperative but no less scandalous attitude to the past. Nevertheless, *zaum* had already lost its dynamism by the late 1920s and the beginning of a new, Stalin-dominated cultural era which exalted realism and tried to exclude anything as silly, slippery and subversive as nonsense. In fact, some critics even suggested that the game was already up in 1913, because, in taking Futurist poetics as far as they could go, Kruchenykh's 'Dyr bul shchyl' had forced *zaum* into a corner from which it could not escape.[47]

But maybe the brevity of *zaum*'s heyday does not matter. You only need to defeat the sun once, and such was the epochal impact of 'Dyr bul shchyl' that it came to be seen something bigger than just a poem. It became a symbol of its turbulent age, for some an ideal, for others an abomination. For Kruchenykh's fellow *zaumnik* Igor Terentev, writing in 1924, the poem is an 'alphabet of Futurism [. . .] a riddle, a challenge which was incomprehensible ten years ago' but which has now been revealed as 'a hole into the future'.[48] Terentev, like many avant-gardists eager to prove their movement's usefulness to the revolution, suggests that *zaum*'s explosion of the rules of language anticipated and accelerated political renewal. A similar position, with a negative valence, was taken by representatives of rival schools like Symbolism and Acmeism, whose antipathy to Futurism only increased after the revolution forced them into emigration while giving new opportunities to the Futurists. For them, the aggressive meaninglessness of 'Dyr bul shchyl' presaged the senseless violence of the Bolsheviks. Zinaida Gippius, the grande dame of émigré literature in Paris, described the poem as 'what happened to Russia' and in his 1929 novella *The Disintegration of the Atom* the poet Georgii Ivanov portrayed Kruchenykh as the epitome of a debased age.[49]

This grudging respect for Kruchenykh's representative power was anticipated by an equally hostile, but much more prescient, critic, who in a polemical article of 1913 said:

> For me there is a prophecy in him, a symbol of our future days. Sometimes it seems to me that if we all disappear and only he alone is left, then our whole era would be preserved in every detail for future centuries. It doesn't matter that he is a shallow, dim little figure; as a symptom he is enormous.[50]

That critic was Kornei Chukovsky.

Kornei Chukovsky

In the flurry of sardonic invective that is 'The Futurists' Chukovsky ridicules the idea that the unbridled destructive nonsense of Futurist *zaum* could ever reveal any higher sense:

> 'We will destroy the obsolete movement of thought according to the law of causality, toothless common sense, symmetric logic.' This is what the Futurists argued at their most recent meeting in Finland.

> Reason is overthrown, the whole world is irrational, but, of course, that's not enough for them. If we are going to have freedom, we want ultimate freedom. If we are going to destroy, let's destroy.
>
> Having overthrown the yoke of Reason, are we really going to remain in the fetters of Beauty? Shouldn't we overthrow Beauty at the same time? For too long the Petrarchs, Beethovens and Rembrandts have reigned over us! Beauty has enslaved the world and Kruchenykh is the first poet to save us from this age-old oppression.' [. . .] This is rebellion for the sake of rebellion, this is an ecstasy of destruction, and there's no way of stopping them now.[51]

We can contrast this attitude to the irrationality of *zaum* to Chukovsky's altogether more positive analysis of children's nonsense in *From Two to Five* (1928): 'children's literature from which all "nonsenses" are expurgated will fail to meet certain inherent needs of the three- to four-year-old child, and will deprive him of wholesome mental nourishment'.[52] The Futurists had also celebrated the linguistic creativity of children's nonsense, publishing children's naïve poems and drawings and eagerly comparing infants' fresh perspective on language with their own.[53] Chukovsky, however, was at pains to point out that in children nonsense is only a phase and that their irrationality exists only to serve rationality: 'nonsense [. . .] strengthens in his mind a sense of the real; [. . .] it is precisely in order to further the education of children in reality that such nonsensical verse should be offered to them'.[54]

In contrast to the mysticism of the holy fools and sectarians and the disruptive ambition of Kruchenykh, Chukovsky has a comparatively narrow and instrumental vision for nonsense as a temporary irrational furlough that reinforces the foundations of rationalism. Although this pragmatic approach to nonsense seems sincere, its repeated articulation in the different editions of *From Two to Five* can also be attributed to the pressure on writers, from the late 1920s onwards, to conform to the official expectation that literature should not only be realist (whatever that might mean) but also contribute to the promotion of Soviet values. More specifically, Chukovsky's functional, realism-through-fantasy defence of nonsense in *From Two to Five* is a strategic response to the hostility his fantastical poems for children inspired in officials. Nonsense had become a more serious matter than ever, but the key questions remained the same as those asked of both Kruchenykh's *zaum* and of early modern glossolalia. Is there in nonsense a path to a higher truth? Is nonsense inherently subversive? What is its relationship to national identity?

Chukovsky claimed that he began *The Crocodile*, his first poem for children, in 1915. It is not mentioned in his diary, however, until February 1917, shortly after its first instalment was published, and there is good reason to believe that he wrote much of it after the February Revolution and then backdated its composition in order to defuse the ongoing and widespread accusations that his children's poems were deliberately anti-Bolshevik.[55] In 1925 censors in Leningrad banned his poem *The Chatterbox Fly* because, among other things, the insect protagonists resembled a prince and princess, making the poem too similar to the traditional fairy tales that were suspected of being a Trojan Horse for counter-revolutionary values.[56] Chukovsky immediately condemned these accusations as 'a joke, because there are no grounds whatever for such a suspicion. It is tantamount to saying that the Crocodile is Chamberlain in disguise.'[57] His comparison was more apt than he knew and *The Crocodile* also soon fell victim to the Leningrad censors, who characterised his books as 'successful and acceptable in their light rhythmic verse, but ideologically completely unsatisfactory'.[58] Although Chukovsky's persistence and contacts meant that *The Crocodile* was eventually deemed suitable for publication, his optimism was ultimately dashed when, in February 1928, Nadezhda Krupskaya, Lenin's widow and head of children's publishing in the Soviet Union, placed a long and evidently heartfelt condemnation of *The Crocodile* in *Pravda*. Criticism from such a high-ranking source was as good as an official decree and Krupskaya's attack was soon followed by more from influential pedagogues and, allegedly, concerned citizens and parents – a trend which continued for another thirty years. *The Crocodile* remained out of print for most of this time, except for a window of surprising liberalism between 1932 and 1935, and Chukovsky faced a further wave of official castigation in the mid-1940s when his books *We Shall Overcome Barmalei* and *The Adventures of Bibigon* were also proscribed.

What was it about Chukovsky's seemingly innocent fantasies that inspired such bureaucratic animosity? Paradoxically, they were seen as simultaneously too meaningless and too meaningful. In the first place, their comical disengagement from reality was viewed by literal-minded readers as too distant from the practical needs of the first Soviet generation. Krupskaya recognises *The Crocodile*'s humour, but scolds the author for failing to satisfy Soviet children's burning curiosity about reptilian biology and instead giving them 'improbable gobbledy-gook'.[59] A review in *Izvestiia* in 1936 has a mixed opinion of Chukovsky's 'Brave Men', an adaptation of the English nonsense rhyme 'Four and Twenty Tailors', praising it for 'mocking cowardice' but chastising its unprovoked attack on unsuspecting gentlemen's outfitters: 'Is cowardice particularly common in people of that profession? Why encourage in children a bad attitude to people of a particular profession?'[60] Best of all, a correspondent in 1960 expresses dismay at Chukovsky's sympathetic portrayal of a fly, 'a harmful insect which', he notes with envy, 'has been completely eradicated in the People's Republic of China'.[61]

Not every reader had such practical concerns and official policy towards children's literature eventually became less obsessed with verisimilitude. Nonetheless, a critic in 1944 could still argue that 'artistic invention must have its logic and in theory respond at least vaguely to a possible reality. Otherwise fantasy becomes falsity, and the depiction ceases to be artistic.'[62] A more persistent and pernicious concern, however, was that such fantastical falsity was not just implausible but positively harmful since the years of infancy were crucial in the development of a child's personality. In the militarised atmosphere of Stalinism, childhood was imagined as a battleground in which 'our enemies are trying to tear our children from us using books'.[63] Nonsense was ideologically suspect not just because it was useless, but also because it was inherently un-Soviet. As Krupskaya warms to her theme in her *Pravda* letter, she deploys a barrage of synonyms for nonsense to express the inappropriateness of *The Crocodile*:

> Maybe it is acceptable to teach a child to speak such rubbish in bourgeois families, to read such claptrap, but it has nothing whatsoever to do with the education we want to give the generation that is now growing up. This blabbering disrespects the child. First he is lured in with some gingerbread – cheerful, innocent rhymes and comic images – but along the way the way he is given something murky to swallow, which won't go without consequences. I think that children should not be given *The Crocodile*, not because it's a fairy tale, but because it is bourgeois murkiness.[64]

Krupskaya, who uses the same root meaning 'murk', *mut*, as was used to describe the language of the holy fool Andrei Tsaregradskii, implies an equivalence between the indistinctness and instability of nonsense and the risk posed by the Soviet Union's enemies at home and abroad. This ideological intolerance of nonsense came to be fundamental to Stalinist aesthetics, as is evident in one of its classic documents, the denunciation in *Pravda* of Dmitrii Shostakovich's opera *Lady Macbeth of Mtsensk* in 1936. The article 'Muddle instead of Music' criticises Shostakovich for producing 'a disordered, muddled stream of sounds' that denies the audience the 'simplicity, realism and comprehensible imagery' that they allegedly desire.[65] Shostakovich repeats the sins of the discredited avant-garde – the article warns the composer against 'playing at *zaum*' – and, as such, can only satisfy a bourgeois foreign audience who do not share Soviet citizens' distaste for apolitical formal experimentation.

As so often, these dismissive condemnations of ideologically inadequate art reveal a deeper insecurity. Not only is the murk and muddle of Chukovsky and Shostakovich at once beneath contempt and perilously persuasive, but their works' apparent refusal of straightforward interpretation also serves as a rebuke both to the regime's explicit endorsement of ideological legibility and to its underlying epistemology.[66] Much as Gippius saw *zaum*'s refusal of linguistic logic as the first crack in the edifice of order before the earthquake of revolution, so the Soviet authorities feared nonsense because it did not fit in its strict, often binary, rules of categorisation.[67] Nonsense, like all ambiguous art, threatens those in power not so much because it is subversive, but because they cannot be sure that it is not subversive. That doubt is more of a challenge to authority than the most pointed critique or satire.

Early Soviet apparatchiks' instinctive intolerance of nonsense is not solely an outgrowth of a totalitarian desire to control discourse; it also has identifiable roots in the critical realist approach to art favoured by much of the Russian intelligentsia from the 1860s on. Readers brought up on the essays of nineteenth-century critics Vissarion Belinskii and Nikolai Chernyshevskii tended to locate the value of literature in its effectiveness in diagnosing and curing social ills. Content was king. Accordingly, to such readers, nonsense, with its tenuous connection to reality, was often strangely invisible: how else could a deeply unusual writer like Gogol have come to be seen as a prophet of social change?

What is more, since critical realist literature was often censored by the tsarist authorities, writers like the poet Nikolai Nekrasov, one of Krupskaya's idols, were obliged to smuggle in anti-authoritarian messages where possible using Aesopian language. This in turn cultivated among adepts a hypertrophic hermeneutics of suspicion, in which reading was a matter of peeling back layers of discursive concealment in order to reveal the hidden truth. This model of meaning is very different from the epistemology of apophatic theology that informed ecstatic nonsense, but the two are not incompatible, and are in fact sometimes found inhabiting the same space in mystic traditions like Kabbalah. Apophatic theology posits phenomena that exist beyond the realm of rational discourse (that is, the divine) and therefore beyond the reach of even the most incisive interpreter. Krupskaya and her fellow materialists, on the other hand, simply have no interest in the ineffable. On the contrary, the foundational tenets of socialist realism, which were beginning to crystallise in the late 1920s, presupposed that not only it is not the duty of the writer to go searching for the sublime, but also that there is no higher realm. Heaven is a place on earth, and that place is the Soviet

Union. Furthermore, the realist presumption that the writer can accurately reproduce the world, which is pushed to its extreme in socialist realism, narrows the gap between the word and the world, leaving little room for nonsense as anything other than empty formalism or a particularly tricky cryptogram.

Consequently, although Krupskaya's first instinct is to reject nonsense as an alien incursion into Soviet reality, her second is to treat it as code. Much of her *Pravda* letter is, somewhat bizarrely, devoted to a spirited defence of the aforementioned Nekrasov from slights she has detected in Chukovsky's typically sarcastic monograph about him. She accuses the upstart Chukovsky of inserting a parody of the great Nekrasov into *The Crocodile*, which she deems inappropriate both because parody is not suitable for children and because Chukovsky seems to mock Nekrasov's radical politics. The passage in question depicts the poem's child-hero Vania freeing animals from their cages: 'To your people | I give freedom | Freedom I give.'[68] Krupskaya insists that Chukovsky has a hidden agenda:

> What does this rubbish signify? Does it have some political meaning? It evidently has some meaning. But it is so carefully masked that it is quite hard to figure it out. Or is it just a selection of words? But it's not such an innocent selection of words.[69]

In a letter of rebuttal, Chukovsky insisted that, just as sometimes a cigar is just a cigar, sometimes a crocodile is just a crocodile:

> At that time [1916] the Crocodile wasn't taken for [White Army general] Denikin, but Kaiser Wilhelm II. [. . .] But, luckily when my *Crocodile* appeared in print (in January 1917), millions of children immediately realised that *The Crocodile* is just a crocodile, that Vania is just Vania, and that I am a writer of fairy tales and poems for children, not a scribbler of political pamphlets.[70]

As it happens, Chukovsky is being both inconsistent – elsewhere he argues that his tale *is* a political allegory and the emancipation of the zoo animals *is* a metaphor for the liberation of the revolution – and disingenuous. Igor Kondakov has shown convincingly that most of Chukovsky's children's poems really are Aesopian retellings of the Bolshevik personalities and policies that he found monstrous.[71] Krupskaya may be repulsive, but she is also right. And Chukovsky knows it. While he disagrees with Krupskaya on details of interpretation and on the acceptability of nonsense, both Chukovsky's deployment of nonsense as a stalking horse for political satire and his defence of it on instrumental grounds are much closer to the world view of Krupskaya than of Kruchenykh. In part, of course, this is a matter of pragmatism: a canny operator like Chukovsky would not do anything as reckless as admitting that his alligator on the banks of the Neva was in fact an allegory, and an anti-Soviet one at that, or defending nonsense on its own terms. Instead, he found a way to justify nonsense within the logic of Soviet aesthetics.[72]

An important strategy in Chukovsky's argument for nonsense is his appeal to the instinctive wisdom and authority of children, who love nonsense. In the Soviet Union the traditional presumption of children's innocence was further strengthened by the notion that these children, born after capitalism, were less burdened by its baleful influence. Chukovsky privileges the instinctive political correctness of the untutored masses, explicitly comparing his sensitivity to children's opinions with the nineteenth-century radicals who went out into the countryside to bask in the innate moral authority of the oppressed Russian peasantry and implicitly aligning himself with the twentieth-century recapitulation of this 'going to the people' among Soviet artists and writers who went out to factories and fields to learn from the working class.[73] Children are not the only ones who know better than common sense, however: Chukovsky makes a similar appeal to the authority of scientific vindications of nonsense. He aligns his endeavours to catalogue and analyse children's own nonsense with the empiricism and rationality which, in theory at least, also underpinned historical materialism, making reference along the way to Engels's *Anti-Dühring*, Lenin, Darwin, Francis Bacon and a professor of applied mathematics.[74]

Finally, Chukovsky strives to move nonsense away from its connotations of ecstatic, apophatic mysticism. As suggested above, he repeatedly argues that nonsense is only a tool to ensure Soviet children's linguistic and psychological vigour and to consolidate their grip on reality (and, therefore, to help perpetuate that reality). Moreover, the unreality of nonsense is subordinate to the reality of sense not just instrumentally, but also structurally, since they are, he suggests, mirror images. He describes the value of games of 'topsy-turvy' in which the order of things is inverted: 'the essence of the game is the deliberate reversing of normal positions' in which 'for every "wrong" the child realizes what is "right," and every departure from the normal strengthens his conception of the normal'.[75]

By so doing, Chukovsky manages to find a place within the Russian realist paradigm for material that seemed utterly unwelcome in both nineteenth-century critical realism and its new socialist incarnation. First, he presupposes that there is an authentic truth out there waiting to be discovered, and not just in some inaccessible higher realm; second, he suggests that the purpose of literature is both to reflect the world and to effect a change its readers. Kruchenykh agrees that nonsense should do something as well as be something, but the change he wants to see is much more fundamental and far-reaching and much less earthbound. He is not content, like Chekhov or Chukovsky, with trying to show our lives in all their rational and irrational glory, but aspires to something higher, the sublimity sensed by Olga in the Scripture, a holy nonsense spoken in the tongues not of men but of angels.

Notes

General Note: In the body of the text Russian names and words are transliterated according to the standard Library of Congress system, with the following modifications: first, the names of certain individuals with international reputations are presented in the form most familiar to English-language readers, hence Chukovsky, not Chukovskii; second, the Russian letter known as the soft sign, which marks the palatalisation of consonants, is not represented. These exceptions do not apply to the notes, unless an English translation published under a different form of the author's name is being cited.

1. G. K. Chesterton, 'A Defence of Nonsense' in *The Defendant*, 4th edn (London: J. M. Dent & Sons, 1914), 42–50, p. 50.
2. Anton Chekhov, 'Peasants', in *The Oxford Chekhov*, ed. and trans. Ronald Hingley (London: Oxford University Press, 1965), 193–222, p. 199.
3. On nonsense in Russian modernism, see Ol'ga Burenina-Petrova, *Simvolistskii absurd i ego traditsii v russkoi literature i kul'ture pervoi poloviny XX veka* (St Petersburg: Aletheia,

2005); on nonsense in twentieth-century Russian children's literature, see Ben Hellman, *Fairy Tales and True Stories: The History of Russian Literature for Children and Young People (1574–2010)* (Leiden: Brill, 2013), pp. 241–3, 324–34.

4. Kornei Chukovskii, 'Futuristy', in *Sobranie sochinenii* (Moscow: Khudozhestvennaia literatura, 1969), VI, 202–39, p. 220; Iurii Denisov, 'Leopard futuristicheskoi armii', in *Aleksei Kruchenykh v svidetel'stvakh sovremennikov*, ed. Sergei Sukhoparov (Munich: Otto Sagner, 1994), 153–60, p. 156.
5. Two of the many terms Chukovskii uses to denote children's nonsense are *nelepitsa,* with the approximate meaning of 'something absurd' and the etymological meaning of 'something not beautiful' and *bessmyslitsa* meaning 'something devoid of sense'.
6. Kornei Chukovsky, *From Two to Five*, trans. and ed. Miriam Morton (Berkeley: University of California Press, 1963), p. 90. Chukovskii is not the only student of nonsense to propose that it helps to shore up the edifice of common sense: see also, for instance, Richard A. Hilbert, 'Approaching Reason's Edge: "Nonsense" as the Final Solution to the Problem of Meaning', *Sociological Inquiry* 47.1 (1977), 25–31.
7. See Velimir Khlebnikov, *The King of Time: Selected Writings of the Russian Futurian*, ed. Charlotte Douglas, trans. Paul Schmidt (Cambridge, MA: Harvard University Press, 1985), p. 113. One might take inspiration from Schmidt and from contemporary gender terminology and propose that the hierarchised distinction between sense and nonsense be replaced with the different-but-equal categories 'trans-sense' and 'cis-sense'.
8. Chesterton, 'Defence', pp. 44–6.
9. Compare Aleksei Kruchenykh, *Vozropshchem* (St Petersburg: Svet, 1913), p. 9: 'You know at the end of the day, despite all its "nonsensicalness" the world of the artist is more rational and real than the world of the philistine even in a philistine sense.'
10. See, for instance, Kevin Shortsleeve, 'The Cat in the Hippie: Dr Seuss, Nonsense, the Carnivalesque, and the Sixties Rebel', in *The Oxford Handbook of Children's Literature*, ed. Lynne Vallone and Julia Mickenberg (Oxford: Oxford University Press, 2012), 189–209.
11. Mikhail Bakhtin, *Rabelais and His World*, trans. Hélène Iswolsky (Bloomington: Indiana University Press, 1984), p. 9.
12. Compare Susan Buck-Morss, *Dreamworld and Catastrophe: The Passing of Mass Utopia in East and West* (Cambridge, MA: MIT Press, 2000), p. 34: 'in the logic of medieval Christendom sinners are normal, safe enemies, whereas heretics who challenge the legitimacy of Christian dogma itself are the absolute enemy and cannot be tolerated even if they are peaceful, because heretics, by definition, cannot be peaceful'.
13. It should be noted that, although Old Church Slavonic is from a different branch of the Slavonic language family, its similarity to and long influence on the Russian literary language means that it is not as incomprehensible to a Russian speaker as, say, Latin is to an English or German speaker.
14. Johann Von Gardner, *Russian Church Singing, Vol. 2: History from the Origins to the Mid-Seventeenth Century*, ed. and trans. Vladimir Morosan (New York: St Vladimir's Seminary Press, 2000), p. 256.
15. The monk Evfrosin is quoted in Von Gardner, *Russian Church Singing*, p. 276.
16. Ibid. p. 287.
17. Ibid. p. 281, and Paul Bushkovitch, *Religion and Society in Russia: The Sixteenth and Seventeenth Centuries* (New York: Oxford University Press, 1992), p. 57.
18. N. D. Uspenskii, *Drevnerusskoe pevcheskoe iskusstvo* (Moscow: Muzyka, 1955), p. 205.
19. Compare Yuri Lotman and Boris Uspenskii, 'Binary Models in the Dynamics of Russian Culture (to the End of the Eighteenth Century)', trans. Robert Sorenson, in *The Semiotics of Russian Culture*, ed. D. Nakhimovsky and Alice Stone Nakhimovsky (Ithaca: Cornell University Press), 30–66, p. 56.

20. On holy fools, see, for instance, Ewa M. Thompson, *Understanding Russia: The Holy Fool in Russian Culture* (Lanham, MD: University Press of America, 1987).
21. A. M. Panchenko, 'Smekh kak zrelishche', in D. S. Likhachev, A. M. Panchenko and N. V. Ponyrko, *Smekh v Drevnei Rusi* (Leningrad: Nauka, 1984), 72–153, p. 94.
22. Ibid. p. 92.
23. Ibid. pp. 96–7.
24. See Aleksandr Etkind, *Khlyst: Sekty, literatura i revoliutsiia* (Moscow: Novoe literaturnoe obozrenie, 2013), pp. 48, 547, and Panchenko, 'Smekh kak zrelishche', p. 97.
25. Vladimir Lossky, *In the Image and Likeness of God* (London and Oxford: Mowbrays, 1974), p. 13.
26. *Moskovskii listok* 46, 24 February 1913.
27. Viktor Shklovsky, 'On Poetry and Trans-Sense Language', trans. Gerald Janecek and Peter Mayer, *October* 34 (Autumn, 1985), 3–24. For more detail on the relationship between *zaum* and glossolalia, see Gerald Janecek, *Zaum: The Transrational Poetry of Russian Futurism* (San Diego: San Diego University Press, 1996), pp. 26–31.
28. Shklovsky, 'On Poetry and Trans-Sense Language', p. 6.
29. In their debut manifesto 'A Slap in the Face of Public Taste', the Futurists express their disdain for 'the filthy stains of "common sense" and "good taste"'. See, *Manifesty i programmy russkikh futuristov*, ed. Vladimir Markov (Munich: Fink, 1967), p. 50.
30. Aleksei Krucenykh and Velimir Khlebnikov, 'Deklaratsiia slova kak takovogo', *Manifesty i programmy russkikh futuristov*, ed. Markov, 61–3, p. 63. Note that *zaum* is used here in its adjectival form *zaumnyi*. On the history of the word *zaum*, see Janecek, *Zaum*, p. 2.
31. Juliette Stapanian provides a subtle reading of the relationship between *zaum* and abstract art: see Juliette R. Stapanian, 'Universal War "Ъ" and the Development of *Zaum*': Abstraction toward a New Pictorial and Literary Realism', *The Slavic and East European Journal* 29 (1985), 18–38. See also: Sara Pankenier Weld, *Voiceless Vanguard: The Infantilist Aesthetic of the Russian Avant-Garde* (Evanston, IL: Northwestern University Press, 2014), p. 65; Charlotte Douglas, 'Victory Over the Sun', *Russian History* 8 (1981), 69–89; Nina Gurianova, *The Aesthetics of Anarchy: Art and Ideology in the Early Russian Avant-Garde* (Berkeley: University of California Press, 2012), p. 117. On iconicity of the word in Russian Futurism, see Janecek, *Zaum*, p. 138, and I. P. Smirnov, *Khudozhestvennyi smysl i evoliutsiia poeticheskikh sistem* (Moscow: Nauka, 1977), p. 134.
32. See Janecek, *Zaum*, p. 8.
33. Osip Mandel'shtam, 'O prirode slova', in O. E. Mandel'shtam, *O Poezii: Sbornik statei* (Leningrad: Academia, 1928), 26–45, p. 41.
34. Aleksei Kruchenykh, 'Tainye poroki akademikov', in *Manifesty i programmy russkikh futuristov*, ed. Markov, 82–5, p. 84.
35. Aleksei Kruchenykh and Velimir Khlebnikov, 'Slovo kak takovoe' in *Manifesty i programmy*, ed. Markov, 53–8, p. 55.
36. Aleksei Kruchenykh, *Pomada* (Moscow: Izdatel'stvo G. L. Kuz'mina i S. D. Dolinskogo, 1913), p. 13.
37. Kruchenykh took great delight in the handful of failed attempts to translate his poem that he lived to see. See *Pamiat' teper' mnogoe razvorachivaet: Iz literaturnogo naslediia Kruchenykh*, ed. Nina Gur'ianova (Oakland: Berkeley Slavic Specialities, 1999), pp. 243–4, and Viacheslav Nechaev, 'Vspominaia Kruchenykh', *Minuvshee: Istoricheskii al'manakh* No. 12 (Moscow: Atheneum Feniks, 1993), 377–86, p. 383.
38. Vladimir Maiakovskii, *Polnoe sobranie sochinenii v trinadtsati tomakh*, ed. V. A. Katanian, 13 vols (Moscow: Khudozhesvtennaia literatura, 1955–61), XI, p. 285. Maiakovskii engaged the translator Rita Rait-Kovaleva to construct a facsimile of English for the play, which nonetheless falls short of sense in English.

39. Aleksei Kruchenykh, 'Novye puti slova', in *Manifesty i programmy*, ed. Markov, 64–73, p. 65.
40. Kruchenykh, *Pomada*, p. 13; Aleksei Kruchenykh, 'Deklaratsiia slova kak takovogo', in *Manifesty i programmy*, ed. Markov, 61–3, p. 63.
41. Kruchenykh and Khlebnikov, 'Slovo kak takovoe', p. 57.
42. Janecek, *Zaum*, p. 138.
43. Jorge Luis Borges, 'The Analytical Language of John Wilkins', in *Other Inquisitions*, trans. Ruth L. C. Simms (London: Souvenir Press, 1973), 101–6, p. 102.
44. Michel Foucault, *The Order of Things: An Archaeology of the Human Sciences* (New York: Pantheon, 1970), p. xv. For a more detailed consideration of the similarities between *zaum* and poststructuralism, see Helen Palmer, *Deleuze and Futurism: A Manifesto for Nonsense* (London and New York: Bloomsbury, 2014).
45. See Douglas, 'Victory over the Sun', pp. 69–89.
46. See, for instance, Aleksei Kruchenykh, *Fonetika teatra* (Moscow: 41°, 1923), p. 5.
47. Compare Sergei Gorodetskii, 'Muzyka i arkhitektura v poezii', *Rech'*, 17 June 1913, p. 3, and Vladislav Khodasevich 'O formalizme i formalistakh', in O. A. Korostelev and N. G. Mel'nikov, *Kritika russkogo zarubezh'ia* (Moscow: Olimp, 2002), 319–25, p. 319.
48. Igor' Terent'ev, 'Kto Lef, kto Praf', *Krasnyi student* 1 (1924), 11–12. Terent'ev puns on the first word of the poem 'dyr', which sounds like a masculinised version of the word for 'hole' – *dyra*.
49. Gippius is quoted by Sergei Biriukov, in 'Poeticheskii masterklass: urok deviatyi, zaumnyi'. Available at <http://www.topos.ru/article/2306> (last accessed 15 August 2018). On Ivanov, see Justin Doherty, 'The Pushkin Contexts of Georgii Ivanov's Disintegration of the Atom', *Two Hundred Years of Pushkin. Volume 1. 'Pushkin's Secret': Russian Writers Reread and Rewrite Pushkin*, ed. Joe Andrew and Robert Reid (Amsterdam and New York: Rodopi, 2003), 121–34, pp. 127–8.
50. Chukovskii, 'Futuristy', p. 223.
51. Ibid. p. 234.
52. Chukovsky, *From Two to Five*, p. 105.
53. See Pankenier Weld, *Voiceless Vanguard*, pp. 76–91.
54. Chukovsky, *From Two to Five*, p. 90
55. I. V. Kondakov, '"Lepye nelepitsy" Korneia Chukovskogo: tekst, kontekst, intertekst', *Obshchestvennye nauki i sovremennost'* 1 (2003), 158–76, p. 159.
56. Kornei Chukovsky, *Diary, 1901–1969*, ed. Elena Chukovskaya and Victor Erlich (New Haven: Yale University Press, 2005), p. 171.
57. Ibid. p. 171.
58. Ibid. p. 171.
59. Nadezhda Krupskaia, 'O "Krokodile" Chukovskogo', *Pravda*, 1 February 1928, p. 5. On the wider debate around fantasy in children's literature in the Soviet Union, see Hellman, *Fairy Tales and True Stories*, pp. 357–65. A range of sources relating to the debate around *The Crocodile* can be found at <http://www.chukfamily.ru/kornei/pro-et-contra/borba-za-skazku> (last accessed 16 August 2018).
60. T. Chuguev, 'Plokhaia kniga khoroshego pisatelia', *Izvestiia*, 3 July 1936.
61. A. P. Kolpakov, 'V redaktsiu "Literaturnoi gazety"', *Literaturnaia gazeta* 99, 20 August 1960.
62. P. Iudin, 'Poshlaia i vrednaia striapnia K. Chukovskogo', *Pravda*, 1 March 1944, p. 3.
63. Parents of the Kremlin nursery, 'My prizyvaem k bor'be s Chukovshchinoi', *Doshkol'noe vospitanie* 4 (1929).
64. Krupskaia, 'O "Krokodile"', p. 5.
65. 'Sumbur vmesto muzyki', *Pravda*, 28 January 1936.
66. Compare Pedro Querido, 'From Kharms to Camus: Towards a Definition of the Absurd as Resistance', *Modern Language Review* 112.4 (2017), 765–92, p. 777.

67. Igal Haflin, *Red Autobiographies: Initiating the Bolshevik Self* (Seattle: University of Washington Press, 2011), p. 21: 'more than an applied ideology, Bolshevik discourse was a technique, a set of stratagems for describing and classifying people'.
68. Kornei Chukovskii, 'Krokodil' in *Stikhotvoreniia*, ed. M. S. Petrovskii (St Petersburg: Akademicheskii proekt, 2002), 63–80, p. 78.
69. Krupskaia, 'O "Krokodile"', p. 5.
70. Kornei Chukovskii, 'V zashchitu "Krokodila"', in Kornei Chukovskii, *Sobranie sochinenii v piatnadtsati tomakh*, ed. E. Chukovskaia, 15 vols (Moscow: Terra, 2001), II, 612–14, p. 612.
71. See Kondakov, '"Lepye nelepitsy" Korneia Chukovskogo', 158–76.
72. Compare D. I. Petrenko, 'Metapoetika K. I. Chukovskogo v kontekste polemiki o novoi detskoi literature (20–30 gody XX veka)', *Iazyk: Tekst: Diskurs* 7 (2009), 144–53. Like many Soviet writers, Chukovskii was sensitive to the fact that, in order to be effective forms of exculpation, texts needed to be altered to fit changing priorities and as such he continued to modify *From Two to Five* throughout its many different editions.
73. On the Soviet requirement for writers to engage with ordinary citizens, see Evgeny Dobrenko, *The Making of the State Writer: Social and Aesthetic Origins of Soviet Literary Culture*, trans. Jesse M. Savage (Stanford: Stanford University Press, 2001), p. 214. Chukovskii also praises the popular creativity of folk poetry, another genre which enjoyed official favour, as a good model for children's authors. See Chukovsky, *From Two to Five*, p. 144.
74. Chukovsky, *From Two to Five*, pp. 104, 117.
75. Ibid. p. 102.

11

'What's the French for fiddle-de-dee?': Nonsense in French

Alexandra Lukes

Nonsense and *Non-Sens*

LET US BEGIN with an exercise in translation: what is the French for the English term 'nonsense'? A cursory look at the *Oxford-Hachette French Dictionary* gives the following approximations: *absurdités* ('absurdities'), *balivernes* ('twaddle'), *n'importe quoi* ('guff'), *bêtises* ('stupidities'), *histoires* ('fibs'), *fantaisie* ('whim'), *petit rien* ('trifles'), *contradiction* ('contradiction'). While all of these terms or expressions reveal one or more aspects implied in the original, no single one of them seems to fit the bill entirely. The examples provided in the dictionary illustrate the problem: among them, we find the English 'to talk/write nonsense', translated in French as 'dire/écrire n'importe quoi', which, while accurate to a certain extent, does not have the same connotations as the English formulation may have for an English speaker, familiar with the nonsense writing of authors such as Lewis Carroll or Edward Lear, or the nonsense spoken by their fictional characters. Conversely, the sentence 'What utter nonsense!' is rendered as 'C'est complètement absurde!' ('It's completely absurd!'), an exclamation that may evoke the concept of 'the Absurd', arguably as much a cornerstone of French literary and philosophical tradition as 'nonsense' is of English.

Rather than looking to translate the term, then, let us instead *not* translate it. In so (not) doing, we can turn once more to a dictionary for guidance, but, in this case, a dictionary of untranslatables: Barbara Cassin's *Vocabulaire européen des philosophies: dictionnaire des intraduisibles*. Here, we find the following entry: 'NONSENSE (anglais) – fr. *non-sens*, *absurdité*'.[1] The entry is a lengthy piece on the history of the term, which combines an analysis of its philosophical meaning (through references to David Hume, Thomas Hobbes, Rudolf Carnap, Gottlob Frege, Bertrand Russell and Ludwig Wittgenstein) with a consideration of its poetic and comical uses (through Carroll's writing and Sigmund Freud's work on jokes). Throughout the article, the English term nonsense and the French *non-sens* co-exist with each other, variously used to refer to literary traditions, philosophical reflections, or psychoanalytic processes in either or both languages.

Without discussing the content of the entry, let us consider its title and look at the term *non-sens*, the first of the two words offered as French versions of the English term nonsense. Here we are faced with two contradictory messages: on the one hand, *non-sens* presents itself as the most obvious, straightforward and unproblematic translation of the English term nonsense and, on the other, given the context of untranslatability in which both terms appear, *non-sens* reveals itself to be the untranslatable other of 'nonsense'. As a result, it becomes apparent that *non-sens* not only fails to translate 'nonsense', but, more importantly, it raises problems in relation to the very practice of translation.

Reflecting on this issue, in an article on the incommensurability of French and English literary traditions, Antoine Compagnon considers different uses of the terms nonsense and *non-sens*. Compagnon observes that, in the French context, the term *non-sens* haunts every *lycée* student's memory of his or her Latin translations, because it indicated the worse possible translation mistake that a student could make: the error that makes no sense whatsoever. The reason that Compagnon gives for why *non-sens* was deemed to be the worst of the translation mistakes (worse than, say, *faux-sens* and *contresens*) is that, in his words, 'French petty rationality is more tolerant of a mistranslation that makes sense than of a mistranslation that doesn't, more tolerant of stupidity than of folly.'[2] Whether or not one agrees with this assessment, it becomes apparent from Compagnon's discussion that playing with sense involves differing degrees of danger. Thus, for instance, while Carroll's nonsense flirts (innocently or not) with the world of madness,[3] exercises in *non-sens* veer further away from the bounds of reason, as mistranslations misplace sense somewhere in the passage from one language to another.

Two lines of inquiry emerge from the above considerations. The first concerns the issue of (un)translatability between languages and cultures, and raises the question of whether nonsense (as a term, discourse, or genre) can be translated.[4] The second consists in a theoretical reflection on how notions of nonsense and *non-sens* (and the interaction between the two) offer literary and linguistic tools for thinking through the problem of language(s), exploring the limits of where playing with sense leads to troubling forms of madness. Both of these lines of inquiry will be followed below, intertwined, as we consider the theoretical questions within a framework that is mostly circumscribed to late nineteenth- and twentieth-century literary practices, with a focus on the French side of the Channel.

Our reading takes as its starting point what is commonly referred to as the *fin-de-siècle* crisis of language and considers Carroll as representative of nonsense writing, due to his direct and indirect influence on French literature, and in particular the surrealist movement. More specifically, we will examine two examples of French literary practice, both inspired by Carroll, which reveal a tension between nonsense and *non-sens*: Antonin Artaud's idiosyncratic translation of an episode of Carroll's *Through the Looking-Glass*, where nonsense devolves into *non-sens* by liberating the scream of the body that works to destroy language; and Michel Leiris's language games, influenced by Carrollian wordplay, that explore the line between private and public uses of language and the challenges of 'translating' between them.

The Depreciation of Language

Carroll's influence on the surrealist movement was both explicit and implicit. Hailed as one of the (many) precursors of surrealism by the leader of the group, André Breton,[5] Carroll was widely admired by the surrealist circle and his books became the object of a number of translations and adaptations. Among them, we find examples of interlingual translation, such as Louis Aragon's translation of *The Hunting of the Snark*,

Henri Parisot's translation of the *Alice* books, and Artaud's version of the episode of 'Humpty Dumpty' from *Through the Looking-Glass*; we also find intersemiotic translations or adaptations, such as Salvador Dalí's and Max Ernst's illustrations of Alice; and intralingual translations or interpretations, such as Raymond Queneau's work on the imaginary language of dogs, Frédéric Delanglade's 'magical' poem *A lys* (*To lily*), and Pierre Mabille's *Miroir du merveilleux* (*Mirror of the marvellous*). Carroll's influence is also visible in the fields of psychoanalysis, philosophy and literary criticism – in, for instance, works by Gaston Ferdière (noted psychoanalyst of the surrealists, and of Artaud in particular) on portmanteau words in mental patients, children, and poets; and Jacques Lacan's 'Homage to Lewis Carroll'.[6]

The surrealists' interest in Carroll, beyond certain shared themes such as childhood, dreamworld and unconventional settings, lies primarily in the question of language. Breton refers to this concern in an essay that reflects on the *fin-de-siècle* origins of the surrealist movement – 'Du surréalisme en ses œuvres vives' ('On Surrealism In Its Living Works') – and he draws a connection between France and England at the end of the nineteenth century on the basis of this issue: 'This need to counteract ruthlessly the depreciation of language, a need which was felt in France by Lautréamont, Rimbaud, Mallarmé, and at the same time in England by Lewis Carroll, has not ceased to be just as imperative since that time.'[7] A brief examination of Breton's choice of Carroll's French counterparts proves helpful for our discussion.

In an article on nonsense in France, Henri Grubbs describes the works by Lautréamont, alongside those by Alfred Jarry, as 'distinguished examples of Nonsense'.[8] Grubbs, however, never fully explains what he means by 'Nonsense literature of distinction',[9] assuming that his examples will speak for themselves. On these grounds, the famous image created by Lautréamont in *Les Chants de Maldoror* (*The Songs of Maldoror*), and which was adopted as the definition of the surrealist notion of beauty – namely, 'beautiful [. . .] as the chance encounter on a dissecting table of a sewing machine and an umbrella!'[10] – is touted by Grubbs as 'certainly Nonsense, though not of the type most frequently found in English Nonsense writers'.[11]

Maurice Blanchot's reading of Lautréamont offers some insight into why the latter's work may be considered comparable to, yet distinct from, English nonsense. Blanchot notes that the reader of *Les Chants de Maldoror* is unsettled because there seems to be a disconnect between reading and understanding. More specifically, the reader appears to understand the individual parts, but remains puzzled as to how they fit together as a whole: '*The Songs of Maldoror* remains one of the strangest works of all literature, because the meaning, always clear, of the details in no way announces the meaning of the whole.'[12]

This appears to be the exact opposite of what happens in English nonsense, where the tension between parts and wholes tilts towards the latter. Alice's reaction to reading the nonsense poem 'Jabberwocky' is indicative of this phenomenon: while she is unsure about the meaning of individual words, she is nevertheless satisfied that there is an overall sense, which she can sum up in a concise description – 'It seems very pretty [. . .] but it's *rather* hard to understand! [. . .] Somehow it seems to fill my head with ideas – only I don't exactly know what they are! However, *somebody* killed *something*: that's clear, at any rate.'[13] The distinction between parts and wholes in the process of understanding is significant, and it relates to how language is being disrupted; or, more precisely, which aspect of language is being affected, syntax or semantics.

Jean-Jacques Lecercle explores this idea by envisaging two possible readings of the poem 'Jabberwocky', depending on whether the reader is reading syntactically or semantically. The first reading is a syntactic one – Lecercle calls it 'a *langue* reading'[14] – whereby the reader understands the syntactic structure of the poem, temporarily passing over Carroll's coinages, for which there are no dictionary definitions. So, for instance, in the first two lines – ''Twas brillig, and the slithy toves | Did gyre and gimble in the wabe'[15] –, the reader will recognise that 'brillig' and 'slithy' are adjectives, 'toves' and 'wabe' are nouns, and 'gyre' and 'gimble' are verbs, even if he or she is not sure what these words actually mean. Such a reading is justified by the fact that nonsense as a genre, on the whole, respects syntax, retaining syntactic coherence while encouraging semantic confusion. This renders nonsense literature suitable for pedagogical purposes, because it teaches correct grammar rules by flouting them or putting them into question.[16]

The second reading of 'Jabberwocky', Lecercle argues, is a 'remainder reading' or 'a *lalangue* reading',[17] where words are liberated from their syntactic constraints and allowed to play freely. Lecercle calls this a 'poetic' reading, as it invites readers to free-associate and to create connections between words through alliteration and assonance – for instance, Carroll's invented word 'mimsy' may evoke 'flimsy', 'mime' and 'prim'.[18] Lecercle's argument is that nonsense is a 'conservative-revolutionary genre' because, while retaining a pedagogical function, it nevertheless has poetic ambitions, teaching us 'how to listen to language speaking on its own'.[19]

From this perspective, we can consider the poetic experiments on syntax that occur on the other side of the Channel. In the battle against the depreciation of language, respecting syntax could be thought of as constituting a limitation, to the extent that such a stance does not question the very structures on which language relies and the accompanying logical expectations.[20] Thus, the French counterparts to Carroll's nonsense literature cited by Breton (in particular Mallarmé) focus their attention on the problem of syntax. Rupturing syntactic norms is considered one of the chief defining characteristics of Mallarmé's famous hermeticism, charged with rendering language 'strange' by stretching it beyond its limits; and Rimbaud's famously agrammatical phrase 'JE est un autre' ('I is an other') questions notions of subjectivity and identity in relation to language use, by breaking conventional syntactic structures required for communication.[21]

With the manipulation of syntax comes the danger of losing not only the meaning of familiar words, as words become displaced within the sentence, but also, and perhaps as a result, the danger of losing one's mind. Mallarmé signals this risk, relating to his friend Henri Cazalis the consequences of coming close to encountering what he calls the 'pure work': 'I've almost lost my reason and the sense of the most familiar words.'[22] If the 'pure work' refers to Mallarmé's ultimate poetic project, which was intended to unlock the meaning of the universe, its creation entails experiments with syntax that have dangerous repercussions on subjectivity and language, liberating the play of words at the expense of the poetic voice:[23]

> The pure work of art implies the elocutionary disappearance of the poet who yields the initiative to words, set in motion by the clash of their inequalities; they illuminate each other with reciprocal lights like a virtual trail of fire on precious stones, replacing the perceptible breath of the old lyric or the individual enthusiastic direction of the sentence.[24]

Here, we have entered into a different territory, where 'quarrying out the lines'[25] of poetry – as Mallarmé puts it, 'en creusant le vers'[26] – has serious repercussions on both language and the speaker's ability to master it.[27]

While Carroll's nonsense aims to retain a balance between breaking rules and maintaining order, the French counterparts in the battle against the depreciation of language take one step further, into a territory where madness, language and literature come together. Here we find a typically French tradition and field of study that has come to be known as literary logophilia or *délire*, where critical and clinical discourses brush against each other, bringing literature into dialogue with linguistics, psychoanalysis and philosophy.

Literary Logophilia and *Délire*

A brief look at the terms used to refer to this tradition opens up some important considerations. Michel Pierssens's study of logophilia, *La Tour de Babil* (*The Tower of Babble*),[28] shows that the term logophilia (love of the word) embraces the semantic fields of fascination, passion and compulsion, extending into extreme and destructive forms of fervour. As such, it is never far removed from a certain form of madness, namely, the madness of language, which arises from compulsive practices of dismantling the linguistic sign, in order to exploit the arbitrary relationship between signifier and signified.

In Pierssens's reading, logophilia is considered both a science and a literary venture. This is visible by his inclusion, among others, in the logophilic tradition of the linguist Ferdinand de Saussure, as both the founder of modern linguistics and the delirious explorer of anagrams in Latin Saturnian verse;[29] similarly, the writer Jean-Pierre Brisset's work on French grammar is included in the tradition, as its serious scientific ambitions are conjoined with meticulous dismantling of the French language into component parts, which the author associates with the croaking of frogs.

Lecercle discusses an analogous phenomenon and corpus of texts but uses the term *délire*. In his reading, *délire* refers to both a discourse and a concept. As a discourse, Lecercle characterises it as embodying 'the shady aspect of the expression of instinctual drives' in opposition to 'the abstraction of language as an instrument of communication and rational argument';[30] and, as a concept, he defines it as the object of a conception of language that foregrounds 'the materiality of words and their relation to the subject's desire'.[31] Lecercle's corpus is both theoretical and literary: he analyses the philosophical and theoretical implications of a discourse that questions the nature of subjectivity, via the works of theorists such as Lacan, Julia Kristeva and Gilles Deleuze; and he investigates the languages of *délire* itself, in the works of the aforementioned authors (Brisset and Saussure), as well as Artaud, Raymond Roussel – the pre-surrealist practitioner of linguistic games based on subtle changes in spelling – and the American Louis Wolfson, who wrote in French and developed a multilingual translation practice in order to destroy his mother tongue, English.

The choice of the term *délire* is significant; but more significant is the fact that Lecercle chooses to retain the French term, untranslated, within his English language studies on the topic. Moreover, Lecercle explicitly draws attention to this fact and provides a series of justifications. The reasons he gives for this non-translation are varied. First, a straightforward admission that he cannot find a satisfactory English equivalent – the obvious translation, 'delirium', being too narrowly confined to the psychiatric context, and other translations ('delusion', 'frenzy', 'mania', 'raving', 'ranting') being inadequate for various reasons.[32] He then explains that this lack of equivalence depends, however, not on inherent difficulties of translation, but rather on the fact that choosing an English name for the concept would contradict the very idea of *délire,* insofar as *délire* is an 'experience of possession, of loss of control by the subject',[33] which casts doubt on the individual's ability to master language. Finally, Lecercle offers a historical reason for not being able to translate the term *délire*: because it refers to a tradition (linguistic, psychoanalytic, philosophical and literary) that is characteristically French.[34]

Reflecting on the untranslatability of the term *délire*, Lecercle notes that his choice to write in English a book on untranslatable French concepts and theories is in itself indicative of the very nature of the object of his study. By suggesting that the untranslatability of *délire* in some way defines the mode of relation that brings together, while keeping apart, the French and English languages, Lecercle raises questions about what it means to conceive of something as untranslatable – be it a text, a language, or a culture – as well as what is involved in attempting to bridge the translational gap.

These questions can be nuanced by taking a broader view of Lecercle's critical work, as his explorations into the French tradition of *délire* find a counterpart in detailed work undertaken on the English tradition of literary nonsense, and in particular, the work of Carroll. The implication is that the relationship between Carrollian nonsense and French *délire* is one of untranslatability, which, in placing in dialogue nonsense with *non-sens*, explores the limit where playing with sense devolves into madness.

This particular mode of relating Carrollian nonsense and French *délire* finds echoes elsewhere in the scholarship, in particular, in the title and contents of a symposium that took place in 1989 at the Whitney Museum of American Art in New York, entitled 'Nonsense: Culture Through the Looking-Glass', the contributions to which were published a year later in a special supplement to the journal *Art & Text* with the abridged title *Nonsense.*[35] The title of the symposium, in patently referring to Carroll, aims to establish a filiation between Carroll's fictional universe and twentieth-century literary culture. However, there are two points that qualify this assumption: the first is that Carroll's work remains, for the most part, absent throughout the collection; the second is that these essays cover a very particular slice of 'culture', which is represented by marginal forms of writing that belong to a predominantly (while not exclusively) French critical tradition. In this tradition, we find work on glossolalia (via the Swiss psychologist Théodore Flournoy's studies of Hélène Smith, a medium who supposedly spoke Martian), logophilic discourses, the untranslatability of nonsense into *non-sens*, Artaud's disruptive uses of language, Wolfson's schizophrenic phonetics, the linguistic 'remainder', and psychoanalytic work on language and babble, explored through different media (painting, sculpture, radio and film). 'Nonsense', therefore, appears to be a synonym for logophilia, *délire* and *non-sens*; more precisely, it is the umbrella term that comprises them all.

The opening lines of the volume explain how the term is being used:

> One of the principal features of modern and contemporary culture is to disrupt the order, codes and commonplaces of everyday life. What characterizes this project is the aspiration to express what cannot be said in ordinary language, and ultimately

> the desire to prohibit the totalisation of all semantic fields. The limit case of this enterprise is exemplified by nonsense – that which stands beneath or at the threshold of meaning in ordinary and theoretical discourse. In the 20th century tradition of experimentation in the arts, nonsense has operated as the very alteration of our languages. It is precisely the effects of this alteration on a variety of fields that was the concern of the symposium.[36]

This preface pits nonsense against ordinary language; more specifically, nonsense, by 'altering' language, allows individuals to 'express what cannot be said in ordinary language'. Conceiving of nonsense as 'the very alteration of our languages' implies that nonsense is the mechanism by which language becomes other (*alter* implies a choice between two); the opposition, though, is not between ordinary and what might be called non-ordinary language, but, rather, between ordinary language and not-language (language's *alter*). But what is the other of language? What form does this non-language take?

Artaud, *Non-Sens* and The Body

Artaud's work, and in particular his encounter with Carroll's nonsense, offers a place to explore these questions. In 1943, during his internment in the mental asylum of Rodez, under the care of doctor Ferdière, Artaud was encouraged to translate the episode of 'Humpty Dumpty' from *Through the Looking-Glass*, as part of an art therapy programme designed to encourage his creativity. Artaud's reaction to Carroll was visceral and uncompromising: after an initial appreciation of Carroll's discussion of the slippery nature of the relationship between language and meaning, Artaud condemned Carroll for what he saw as English snobbery and pusillanimity, a critique that could be understood, from Artaud's perspective, as Carroll not wanting to take the play with sense to its extreme conclusion, where language (and thought) is threatened with annihilation. Artaud's own text, which he called *L'Arve et l'aume: tentative anti-grammaticale à propos de Lewis Carroll et contre lui*, is precisely what the title intimates: an anti-grammatical attack against Carroll and his work. By rupturing grammar and mistranslating (or, mistreating) the original, Artaud veers from nonsense into the dangerous territories of *non-sens*.

Artaud's anti-grammatical attack consists of disrupting the fabric of the original work in two main ways: by producing a number of ungrammatical translations of Carroll's sentences and by inserting unrecognisable syllables into the text. An example of the former occurs towards the beginning of the episode, when Alice first sets eyes on Humpty Dumpty – 'she thought he must be a stuffed figure after all'[37] – which is rendered by Artaud as follows: 'elle pensa que ce lhomme pouvait bien n'être qu'être un insufflé pontin rum bourré après taim: un'.[38] This version is both syntactically incoherent and semantically obscure, containing words that do not belong to the dictionary – although it is possible to connect Artaud's invented words to Carroll's original meanings, by tying 'pontin' to 'pantin' ('puppet'), 'rum bourré' to 'rembourré' ('stuffed'), and 'après taim', to 'après tout' ('after all').[39]

An example of the second of Artaud's methods of disruption, namely, the insertion of mysterious syllables into the text, can be seen in his rendition of the word 'Jabberwocky', which he 'translates' by an entire stanza:

NEANT OMO NOTAR NEMO
'Jurigastri – Solargultri
Gabar Uli – Barangoumti
Oltar Ufi – Sarangmumpti
Sofar Ami – Tantar Upti
Momar Uni – Septfar Esti
Gonpar Arak – Alak Eli'[40]

Accompanying this 'translation', Artaud mischievously addresses the question of meaning and understanding, by adding a note which states the following: '*Si tout cela ne plaît pas on peut choisir comme titre une seule de ces phrases, par exemple: MOMAR UNI ou GONPAR ARAK ALAK ELI, qui veut dire: as-tu compris?*' ['If you do not like all of this, you can choose as a title one of these phrases, for instance: MOMAR UNI or GONPAR ARAK ALAK ELI, which means: have you understood?'][41]

Assuming that the reader would most likely answer the question in the negative, Artaud invites him or her to reformulate the question: 'Have you understood?' would become something along the lines of 'What do you understand by the question: have you understood?', ultimately asking the reader to think about what it means to understand something. But Artaud's note is even more subtle: in claiming that the reader is free to choose any one of the groupings of syllables above, Artaud offers a powerful critique of judgement because, while seemingly allowing the reader to make that judgement for him- or herself, he also states that there is no difference in meaning between the terms, thereby invalidating the act of judgement that differentiates between them, as well as the choice itself.

This is significant when we consider that nonsense as a genre relies on being able to retain the capacity to judge: to judge is to discern, and to pronounce a verdict; it implies assessing different possibilities and deciding which are correct and which are not. The nonsense in the *Alice* books remains within the world of judge and jury (hence, the genre's predilection for trial scenes),[42] where there is a right way and a wrong way to use language; and nonsense, while creating temporary havoc, nevertheless teaches us which one is the right way. Conversely, Artaud's foray into *non-sens*, in breaking grammatical norms and using ostensibly incomprehensible syllables, reconsiders what is involved in the act of judgement as well as what it means to understand.

In his correspondence on the topic of his translation of Carroll's text, where he addresses these and related questions, Artaud explains the nature and function of the syllables. Providing a series of examples – 'ratara ratara ratara | atara tatara rana | otara otara katara | otara ratara kana [. . .]'[43] – Artaud describes how the syllables are supposed to be read:

> they can only be read rhythmically, in a tempo which the reader himself must find in order to understand and to think [. . .] but this is worthless unless it gushes out all at once; pieced together one syllable at a time, it no longer has any value, written here it says nothing and is nothing but ash.[44]

Thinking and understanding occur through an act of rhythmic scansion – Artaud uses the term 'scandés'[45] – which relies upon the individual's ability to find his or her own breath rhythms in connection with the letters on the page. This requires an oral performance that takes place 'all at once', as opposed to a slow reading that decomposes each syllable into its component parts, in an attempt to find meanings that may or may not be attached to those parts. Such a practice goes against Humpty Dumpty's and Alice's patient parsing of the meaning of the portmanteau words in the 'Jabberwocky' poem, where seemingly incomprehensible words are elucidated, so that an 'understanding' of the poem can be produced, one that goes beyond Alice's initial assessment that '*somebody* killed *something*'.

Reading Artaud's writing differs radically from reading a nonsense poem. Whereas readers of the *Alice* books would, on the whole, agree with Alice's assessment of the 'Jabberwocky' that '*somebody* killed *something*: that's clear, at any rate',[46] readers of Artaud cannot make the same claim of clarity. Echoing Artaud's instructions on how to breathe his mysterious syllables to life, and taking them as suggestions for how to read his writing more generally, critical responses to Artaud's work typically refer to the 'unassimilable' or 'indigestible'[47] nature of the experience – terms that underline the physicality implied in the process of reading and, arguably, of understanding. Coming into contact with Artaud's words, attuning oneself to the rhythms of the text, produces powerful sensations that have the potential of obliterating logic and thought, bringing the reader close to Artaud's own painful state of mind: 'To find oneself again in a state of extreme shock, clarified by unreality, with, in a corner of oneself, some fragments of the real world.'[48]

What remains after the shock is, in Artaud's words, far more valuable than works, words or language: 'And I have already told you: no works, no language, no words, no mind, nothing. Nothing but a fine Nerve Meter.'[49] The image of the nerve-metre, which Artaud calls 'pèse-nerfs' and which dates from as early as 1925, long before his encounter with Carroll, is striking: the term brings together mind and body, by conjoining the act of weighing (physical or mental) with the image of connecting, via the transmission of impulses of sensation and movement between brain, spinal cord, muscles and organs. The associations implied in Artaud's choice of words, between 'peser' ('to weigh') and 'penser' ('to think'), in addition to the visual similarity of the two French words on the page, entail that thinking becomes primarily a physical activity.

Artaud's conception of thought and language is therefore inseparable from the relationship that he has with his body, namely, a deeply private experience that is based on pain and suffering – as he writes in his first published work, 'I do suffer, not only in the mind but in the flesh and in my everyday soul.'[50] As such, Artaud's language, especially visible in his later works, is at the limit of language, as the physical and mental pain that he endures shatters socially recognised and recognisable linguistic forms;[51] more significantly, language is used against itself, to impede critical thinking, judgement or the transmission of verbal content, becoming instead rhythm, movement and sensation.

Leiris, *Non-Sens* and The Senses

Leiris engages in a similar exploration of the personal or, indeed, private nature of language, by playing with sense and the senses, without however arriving at Artaud's extreme conclusions. Both Artaud and Leiris were members of the surrealist movement in its early days and, thus, participated in literary and poetic explorations of the nature of linguistic expression, developing what Breton saw as the battle to renew language that conjoined England and France at the end of the nineteenth century, in the wake of Carroll, Lautréamont, Rimbaud and Mallarmé. While for Artaud this practice led to the liberation of the cry of the body at the expense of verbal language, for Leiris it prompted a heightened awareness of the sounds of words, in an attempt to negotiate between the private and public dimensions of the act of communication.

This is apparent in Leiris's choice of format for his literary and linguistic experiments: a series of inventive and idiolectal glossaries, where common words are redefined according to networks of private associations. The first examples of these language games were published in instalments in the 1920s in the surrealist journal *La Révolution surréaliste* (*The Surrealist Revolution*), under the title *Glossaire j'y serre mes gloses* (*Glossary: My Glosses' Ossuary*, to use Lydia Davis's translation of the title); but Leiris's fascination with the practice endured for another sixty years, with the publication in 1985 of *Langage tangage ou Ce que les mots me disent* (*Language Anguish or What Words Say To Me*).

Leiris's practice belongs to a tradition of works that playfully appropriate the format of the dictionary,[52] such as Gustave Flaubert's *Dictionnaire des idées réçues* (*Dictionary of Received Ideas*) and Ambrose Bierce's *The Devil's Dictionary*, published in 1911 and 1906 respectively. The choice to critique the dictionary format is significant: as the locus for established meaning and as a didactic instrument for linguistic consensus, the dictionary is the emblem of socialised language and the definition of sense; using the format to undermine its purpose, therefore, constitutes an 'anti-academic' gesture,[53] which, in Leiris's hands, is intended to both combat the depreciation of language and reassess how individuals relate to words.

The following are some examples of Leiris's glosses, which simultaneously play on all aspects of the sign (signifier, signified, referent): 'ACADÉMIE – macadam pour les mites'[54] ['academy – macadam for mites']; 'CHANCE – pour l'enchâsser, on la pourchasse'[55] ['chance – to encase it, we chase it']; 'DÉFINIR, c'est Disperser. Dilemme De la Démence'[56] ['To Define, is to Disperse. Dilemma of Dementia']; 'FOLIE – la foi en de faux liens'[57] ['folly – faith in false links']; 'VOCABLES – vos câbles, pour échapper à vos caveaux'[58] ['vocables – your cables to escape from your caves']. Other examples exploit the visual play of the words on the page, such as, 'ô (étOnnée, la bOuche mOlle s'arrOndit, gObe l'ObOle de l'hOstie . . .)'[59] ['o (shOcked, the mOist mOuth rOunds, swallOws the Offering of the hOst . . .)'], and the entry entitled 'Le plongeoir de Narcisse'[60] ('Narcissus's diving board'), where the letters of Leiris's first and last names are displayed around an empty centre (see Figure 11.1).

The words included in the glossary are, for the most part, everyday French words, familiar to any French-language speaker. However, Leiris's idiosyncratic practice of definition produces, in the long run, an overall neologistic impression, through an echo-effect, or echolalia, between the word being defined and the words that are intended to constitute its definition. On the one hand, the gloss gives the illusion of opening up common words to an array of meanings that they presumably harbour; on the other, the echolalic string of words condenses into the original word, which, by this accordion-type movement, is transformed into a Carrollian portmanteau that, as such, requires the gloss in order to receive meaning.[61]

In this way, Leiris's anti-academic dictionary presents ordinary words as empty ciphers (an image that evokes the empty centre in 'Le plongeoir de Narcisse'), constructed

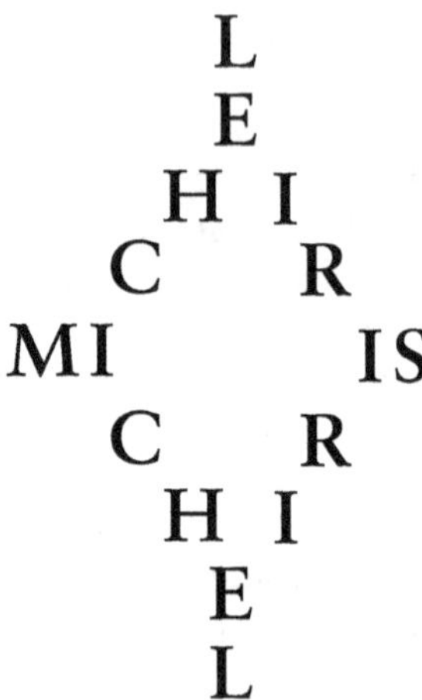

Figure 11.1 'Le plongeoir de Narcisse', *Mots sans mémoire. Simulacre. Le Point Cardinal. Glossaire j'y serre mes gloses. Bagatelles végétales. Marrons sculptés pour Miró* (Paris: Gallimard, 1969), p. 115.

according to private (or, indeed, narcissistic) networks of associations. This practice operates a reversal of the common-sense understanding of the opposition between idiolect and sociolect: words of everyday language are considered to be instances of private language, and the commentary of the gloss constitutes a practice of 'translation' that allows these words to enter into the common space of the dictionary. Such a shift in perspective is aimed to encourage readers to pay attention to how they use language; but doing so is not without its dangers, as Leiris intimates in a note to the *Glossaire*:

> The everyday meaning and the etymological meaning of a word can teach us nothing about ourselves, since they represent the collective part of language, which was made for all people and not for each of us individually. By dissecting the words we like, without bothering about conforming either to their etymologies or to their accepted significations, we discover their most hidden qualities and the secret ramifications that are propagated through the whole language, channeled by associations of sounds, forms, and ideas. Then language changes into an oracle, and there we have a thread (however slender it may be) to guide us through the Babel of our minds.[62]

The game, in dissecting words, transforms everyday language into Ariadne's thread, guiding us through our mental labyrinth. Significantly, this labyrinth is referred to by the term 'Babel', the founding myth of the dispersal of languages and the birthplace of translation. The redefined language of the glossary could therefore be thought of as a translation device that leads to a form of self-knowledge. However, insofar as this language is characterised as an 'oracle', it also poses a threat to the subject to whom it speaks: oracular language is a divinatory word, the meaning of which is often obscure, ambiguous and potentially dangerous for the addressee, because it is almost always misinterpreted. Playing with language, therefore, is a serious game that puts at risk the playing subject.

In this context we can understand the formulation that Leiris uses to describe his linguistic practice, a formulation that is implicitly inspired by Carroll: 'Curieusement donc, chercher du côté du non-sens ce dont j'ai besoin pour rendre plus sensible le sens' ['Curiously, then, looking towards non-sense to find what I need to make sense more perceptible'].[63] Leiris plays with meaning by playing on the senses. To an English ear, Leiris's sentence plays a further trick, by using the cognate 'sensible', which in French maintains a connection with the senses while in English adds a reference to meaning: Leiris's venture into the 'côté du non-sens' would thereby be an attempt to make sense both more perceptible and more sensible – and an English reader familiar with Carroll would be sensitive to the use of the adverb 'curieusement', which constitutes the only solecism in the *Alice* books, 'curiouser and curiouser'.[64] Turning towards *non-sens*, then, renders the reader more sensitive not only to the play of sense and of the senses, but also to linguistic difference and to the incommensurability of languages.

To complicate things further, Leiris's expression 'du côté du non-sens' echoes two other formulations that he uses in two different contexts: the first, to refer to the figure of the artist, as 'quelqu'un qui est passé de l'autre côté du miroir' ['someone who has gone through the looking-glass'];[65] the second, to describe the language used in certain indigenous cultures to conjure up the dead – 'une langue de l'autre côté' ['a language of the other side'].[66] These formulations, alluding to Carroll's phrase 'through the looking-glass',[67] evoke a practice of crossing the border between worlds (real or imaginary), which not only reveals a central aspect of Leiris's poetic inspiration, his conception of 'le merveilleux' ('the marvellous'),[68] but also relates to a specific event in his life: Leiris came close to experiencing both the passage 'de l'autre côté' and 'une langue de l'autre côté', following an attempted suicide in 1957, which put him in a coma and left him with temporary aphasia due to the emergency tracheotomy that saved him.

Leiris's language games – the practice of inflecting *non-sens* in order to heighten sense and the senses – create the conditions for literature to stage a passage 'de l'autre côté du miroir', by carefully negotiating between public networks of shared words and private labyrinths of linguistic associations. This tension, constantly at work in every act of communication, while allowing those very acts to take place, also threatens the integrity of the speaking subject, by the emergence of 'une langue de l'autre côté'. The Leirisian language game is thus more than mere wordplay; it is a serious activity that, playing with sense and the senses, between private and public, also crosses the border between life and death.

Nonsense, Madness and Translation

Our reflection on nonsense in France – or, more precisely, nonsense in French – has led us to think about the relationship between *non-sens*, logophilia and *délire*, through explorations of various literary practices that show the complexities inherent in language use across cultural and linguistic divides. The underlying thread is constituted by the question of translatability and the role that translation plays in the development of such practices, whether translation is considered as a movement between two distinct languages (as with Artaud), or as a tension between private and public uses within the same language (as with Leiris).

More specifically, our discussion on 'translating' English nonsense as French *non-sens* shows what happens in the attempt to cross the border between languages. The etymological definition of translation, as the act of carrying something across from one language to another, has typically produced debates that waver when it comes to identifying what that something is: Is it content? Is it form? And can the two be pried apart? These questions, which are at the heart of what translation does and is, return us to our previous reflection on the two forms of linguistic disruption – semantic or syntactic – practised on opposite sides of the Channel in the battle against the depreciation of language, and they raise important considerations about the nature of language and the conditions of literature.

Walter Benjamin's seminal contribution to the discussion warns that the distinction between form and content is, in itself, misleading. Opening his essay on the 'task' of the translator by stating that works of art communicate neither message nor information, Benjamin claims that any translation that aspires to reproduce a message is a grave misunderstanding of what translation is: 'a translation that aims to transmit something can transmit nothing other than a message – that is, something inessential. And this is also the hallmark of bad translations.'[69] Rather, Benjamin upholds the counter-intuitive position that translation should proceed syntactically, 'by conveying the syntax word-for-word'.[70] The end result of such a stance is the striking appraisal of Friedrich Hölderlin's 'monstruous' literal translations of Sophocles' plays, to the extent that, in these translations, 'the sense plunges from abyss to abyss until it threatens to become lost in the bottomless depths of language'.[71] Significantly, sense is not lost; rather, it (merely) 'threatens to become lost'.

As we have seen in our discussion, this threat lies on the horizon of translation as such, to the extent that, as a practice, it negotiates the hazardous territories of non-language that lie between languages. *Non-sens*, then, would refer not only to the production of mistranslations, as defined by Compagnon, but, more radically, to the dangerous yet compelling movement from one language to another, so that, as Shoshana Felman notes, in discussing the relationship between madness and literature, 'somewhere between languages, will emerge the freedom to speak'.[72] Our conjoined discussion of English nonsense and French *non-sens* shines a light on such an aspiration, by showing that moving between languages is a perilous yet exhilarating game, that calls language(s), identity, and the individual's ability to speak into serious play.

Notes

1. Barbara Cassin, *Vocabulaire européen des philosophies: dictionnaire des intraduisibles* (Paris: Éditions du Seuil, 2004), p. 859. The entry on nonsense is written by Sandra Laugier.
2. Antoine Compagnon, 'Somebody Will Always Get It', in *Nonsense*, ed. David B. Allison, John G. Hanhardt, Mark Roberts and Allen S. Weiss, (special issue of *Art & Text*, 37 (1990)), 71–3, p. 71. Compagnon proceeds to argue that, while in French there may not be a word to translate the English term 'nonsense', French literature nevertheless has a tradition of comedy and parody that plays with sense. Early experiments with language appear in the medieval *fatrasies* – short poems that produce what Paul Zumthor calls 'non-sens absolu' [absolute non-sense] (*Langue, texte, énigme* (Paris: Éditions du Seuil, 1975), p. 78) – and in the theatrical genre of the *sottie*, which foregrounds the figure of the 'sot' [fool]; examples of linguistic inventiveness can be found throughout French literature, from Rabelais's neologising to surrealist automatism and Oulipian rule-bound wordplay.
3. On the connection between nonsense and madness, Jean-Jacques Lecercle notes: 'Nonsense [. . .] is a constant effort towards mastery, towards blocking the emergence of the radically unmeant, the true or radical nonsense of possession or delirium' (*Philosophy of Nonsense:*

The Intuitions of Victorian Nonsense Literature (London: Routledge, 1994), p. 134); and, further: 'the game itself, in spite of its name, is not mad. Its constitutive strategy is one of last-ditch defence against the contagion of madness' (ibid. p. 204).

4. See Lecercle's 'Translate It, Translate It Not', *Translation Studies* 1.1 (2008), 90–102, and 'Modalities of Translating Nonsense', *Translation Studies* 12.1 (2019), 15–23, for a discussion of the relationship between nonsense and translation; see Warren Weaver's *Alice in Many Tongues: The Translations of Alice in Wonderland* (Madison: University of Wisconsin Press, 1964) and Jon Lindseth and Alan Tannenbaum's *Alice in a World of Wonderlands: The Translations of Lewis Carroll's Masterpiece* (New Castle, DE: Oak Knoll Press, 2015) for discussions of the numerous translations of the *Alice* books. In this context, it is worth noting that Carroll indirectly raises the issue of whether nonsense can be translated, by using the synonym 'fiddle-de-dee' in the Red Queen's question to Alice in *Through the Looking-Glass*: 'What's the French for fiddle-de-dee?' (Lewis Carroll, *Alice in Wonderland*, ed. Donald J. Gray (New York and London: W. W. Norton & Company, 1992), p. 195).
5. In listing the precursors of surrealism and their surrealist attributes, Breton describes Carroll as surrealist 'in nonsense' ('Surrealism: Yesterday, Today and Tomorrow', *This Quarter* 5.1 (1932), 7–44, p. 17). The list in which Carroll's name appears is supplementary to the original one in Breton's first manifesto of 1924 – see André Breton, *Manifestoes of Surrealism*, trans. Richard Seaver and Helen R. Lane (Ann Arbor: University of Michigan Press, 1972), pp. 26–7.
6. For more details on the above, and on other French translations or adaptations of Carroll, see Marie-Hélène Inglin-Routisseau, *Lewis Carroll dans l'imaginaire français: la nouvelle Alice* (Paris: L'Harmattan, 2006); Michel Remy, 'Surréalice? Lewis Carroll et les surréalistes', *Europe* 68: 736–7 (1990), 123–33; Elizabeth Sewell, *Lewis Carroll: Voices from France* (New York: Lewis Carroll Society of North America, 2008); and Jeffrey Stern, 'Lewis Carroll The Surrealist', in *Lewis Carroll, A Celebration: Essays on the Occasion of the 150th Anniversary of the Birth of Charles Lutwidge Dodgson*, ed. Edward Guiliano (New York: C. M. Potter, 1982), 132–53.
7. Breton, *Manifestoes*, pp. 297–8.
8. Henri Grubbs, 'Nonsense in France and in French Literature', *Modern Language Quarterly* 8.1 (1947), 21–9, p. 25.
9. Ibid. p. 25.
10. Comte de Lautréamont, *The Songs of Maldoror*, trans. R. J. Dent (Washington DC: Solar Books, 2011), p. 210.
11. Grubbs, 'Nonsense', p. 26.
12. Maurice Blanchot, *The Work of Fire*, trans. Charlotte Mandell (Stanford: Stanford University Press, 1995), p. 162.
13. Carroll, *Alice*, p. 118, italics in the original.
14. Jean-Jacques Lecercle, 'Nonsense and The Remainder', in *Nonsense*, ed. Allison et al., 75–80, p. 79.
15. Carroll, *Alice*, p. 116.
16. In relation to this point, Lecercle talks of 'hypersyntaxism' (*Philosophy of Nonsense*, p. 58): 'Syntax has logical precedence over semantics – the construction of coherent meaning presupposes the coherence of the syntactic organization of the utterance' (ibid. p. 57). See pp. 56–8 for an analysis of the only example of syntactic chaos in Carroll, 'the Duchess's sentence', and pp. 69–114 for a discussion of the pedagogical function of nonsense literature.
17. Lecercle, 'Nonsense', in *Nonsense*, ed. Allison et al., p. 79.
18. Ibid. p. 79.
19. Ibid. p. 80.

20. See George Steiner's critique of Carroll's nonsense on these grounds in *After Babel: Aspects of Language and Translation* (Oxford: Oxford University Press, 1992), pp. 196–7.
21. Arthur Rimbaud, *Poésies. Une saison en enfer. Illuminations* (Paris: Gallimard, 1999), p. 84.
22. Stéphane Mallarmé, *Selected Letters of Stéphane Mallarmé*, ed. and trans. Rosemary Lloyd (Chicago: University of Chicago Press, 1988), p. 84.
23. In the process, Mallarmé claims to have lost himself: 'I am now impersonal and no longer the Stéphane that you knew, – but a capacity possessed by the spiritual Universe to see itself and develop itself, through what was once me' (*Selected Letters*, p. 74).
24. Mallarmé, 'Crise de vers', trans. Rosemary Lloyd, in Rosemary Lloyd, *Mallarmé: The Poet and His Circle* (Ithaca: Cornell University Press, 1999), 227–33, p. 232.
25. Mallarmé, *Selected Letters*, p. 60.
26. Stéphane Mallarmé, *Œuvres complètes*, I (Paris: Gallimard, Bibliothèque de la Pléiade, 1998), p. 696.
27. Carroll's nonsense world may also stage the dangers to subjectivity inherent in this practice, but these dangers are for the most part reversible: such would be the case, for instance, with Alice's temporary loss of her name upon entering 'the wood [. . .] where things have no names' (*Wonderland*, p. 135), because she recovers the memory of who she is as soon as she emerges into the clearing.
28. Michel Pierssens, *La Tour de Babil. La Fiction du signe* (Paris: Éditions de Minuit, 1976).
29. See Jean Starobinski, *Words Upon Words: The Anagrams of Ferdinand de Saussure* (New Haven: Yale University Press, 1979).
30. Jean-Jacques Lecercle, *Philosophy Through The Looking-Glass* (La Salle, IL: Open Court, 1985), p. 11.
31. Ibid. p. 11.
32. Ibid. p. 8.
33. Ibid. p. 9.
34. The case of the American Louis Wolfson requires some qualification. His book, *Le Schizo et les langues* [The Schizo and Languages], written in French and published in 1970 by Gallimard with a preface by Deleuze, generated a cross-cultural and inter-linguistic dialogue between 'French theory' and North America – most notably, with the conference on 'Schizo-Culture' held at Columbia University in 1975, attended by, among others, Deleuze, Guattari, Foucault, Lyotard, Wolfson, John Cage and William Burroughs. This dialogue was shaped by the founding of a series of journals around those years: *Diacritics* (1971), *SubStance* (1971), *Semiotext(e)* (1974), *Critical Inquiry* (1974), *October* (1976) and *Social Text* (1979).
35. *Nonsense*, ed. Allison et al., 51–116.
36. Ibid. p. 51.
37. Carroll, *Wonderland*, p. 159.
38. Antonin Artaud, *Œuvres*, ed. Evelyne Grossman (Paris: Gallimard, 2004), p. 917.
39. For this analysis, see Anne Tomiche, 'Penser le (non)sens: Gilles Deleuze, Lewis Carroll et Antonin Artaud', in Anne Tomiche and Philippe Zard (eds), *Littérature et philosophie* (Arras: Artois Presses Université, 2002), 123–45, p. 131.
40. Artaud, *Œuvres*, p. 922, italics in the original.
41. Ibid. p. 922, italics in the original.
42. Lecercle remarks on the fondness for trial scenes in nonsense literature, owing to the genre's 'metalinguistic and pedagogic aims': 'Intuitions about language are often produced by encounters with the judiciary' (*Philosophy of Nonsense*, p. 88).
43. Antonin Artaud, *Antonin Artaud. Selected Writings*, ed. and with an introduction by Susan Sontag (Berkley and Los Angeles: University of California Press, 1988), p. 451, bold in the original.
44. Ibid. p. 451.

45. Artaud, *Œuvres*, p. 1015.
46. Carroll, *Wonderland*, p. 118.
47. Susan Sontag, 'Artaud', in Artaud, *Antonin Artaud. Selected Writings*, xvii–lix, p. lix.
48. Artaud, *Antonin Artaud. Selected Writings*, p. 81.
49. Ibid. p. 86.
50. Ibid. p. 44.
51. Elaine Scarry describes the effect of pain on language as a form of shattering in *The Body in Pain: The Making and Unmaking of the World* (Oxford: Oxford University Press, 1985), pp. 4–5; see also Virginia Woolf on the relationship between pain, illness and language in *On Being Ill* (London: Hogarth Press, 1930).
52. A glossary can be thought of as a particularised dictionary, one that carves out a linguistic subfield within the sociolect, insofar as it is generally attached to a given body of work to which it offers itself as an appendage, explaining the meaning of words that are either specialised or antiquated.
53. Leiris uses the term 'anti-academic' to underscore the revolutionary nature of the project: 'ce dictionnaire dont le projet même était une marque entre autres de l'esprit violemment antiacadémique dont nous étions animés, mes compagnons surréalistes et moi' ['this dictionary, the very project of which was a sign among others of the violently anti-academic spirit that animated my surrealist companions and me'] (Michel Leiris, *Langage tangage ou Ce que les mots me dissent* (Paris: Gallimard, 1985), p. 145). This sentiment is shared by Artaud in the following note, appended to the first publication of Leiris's glosses in *La Révolution surréaliste* (n.3, 15 April 1925): 'Yes, this is all that language is good for from now on, a means of going mad, eliminating thought, rupturing; a labyrinth of foolishness, not a DICTIONARY into which certain pedants from the environs of the Seine may channel their spiritual narrownesses' (in Michel Leiris, *Brisées: Broken Branches*, trans. Lydia Davis (San Francisco: North Point Press, 1989), p. 3).
54. Michel Leiris, *Mots sans mémoire. Simulacre. Le Point Cardinal. Glossaire j'y serre mes gloses. Bagatelles végétales. Marrons sculptés pour Miró* (Paris: Gallimard, 1969), p. 73.
55. Ibid. p. 78.
56. Ibid. p. 82.
57. Ibid. p. 90.
58. Ibid. p. 113.
59. Ibid. p. 100.
60. Ibid. p. 115.
61. Various critics have noted that Leiris's glosses resemble portmanteau words, drawing explicit comparisons with Carroll: Pierre-Henri Kleiber, *'Glossaire j'y serre mes gloses' de Michel Leiris et la question du langage* (Paris: L'Harmattan, 1999), p. 111; Jonathan Pollock, 'Les implications du titre *L'arve et l'aume* ou Comment Antonin Artaud transforme le legs de Lewis Carroll', in *Altérations, créations dans la langue: les langages depravés*, ed. Anne Tomiche (Clermont-Ferrand: Presses Universitaires Blaise Pascal, 2001), 145–56, p. 153; Michael Riffaterre, 'Pulsion et paronomase: sur la poétique de Michel Leiris', *Revue de l'Université de Bruxelles* 1–2, (1990), 179–200, p. 187.
62. Leiris, *Brisées*, pp. 3–4. The note originally appears in the first instalment of the *Glossaire*, published in aforementioned number of *La Révolution surréaliste*, p. 7.
63. Leiris, *Langage*, p. 90.
64. Carroll, *Wonderland*, p. 13.
65. Michel Leiris, *Fibrilles*, *La Règle du jeu*, III (Paris: Gallimard, 1966), p. 289.
66. Leiris, *Langage*, pp. 108–9.
67. Inglin-Routisseau draws attention to the fact that the French translation of Carroll's expression 'through the looking-glass' oscillates between 'de l'autre côté du miroir' and 'la traversée du miroir' (*Lewis Carroll*, pp. 235–78).

68. The notion of 'le merveilleux' is discussed abundantly in *Frêle bruit*, the last volume of Leiris's four-part autobiography, with explicit mentions of Carroll (*Frêle bruit*, *La Règle du jeu*, IV (Paris: Gallimard, 1976), p. 355ff.). Significantly, the original title for *Glossaire j'y serre mes gloses* was intended to be *Glossaire du merveilleux*.
69. Walter Benjamin 'The Translator's Task', trans. Steven Rendall, in *The Translation Studies Reader*, 3rd edn, ed. Lawrence Venuti (London and New York: Routledge, 2012), 75–83, p. 75.
70. Ibid. p. 81.
71. Ibid. p. 83.
72. Shoshana Felman, *Writing and Madness (Literature/Philosophy/Psychoanalysis)* (Palo Alto, CA: Stanford University Press, 2003), p. 19. Felman situates her discussion within the context of a dialogue between two languages and cultures, between French and English, France and the United States. She notes that some of the articles that make up her book were written in French while others were written in English; that the authors studied are split between both languages (Gérard de Nerval, Honoré de Balzac, Gustave Flaubert and Henry James); and that the theoretical framework is both French (Jacques Lacan, Jacques Derrida, Michel Foucault) and American (what she refers to as 'the Yale School' of critics, influenced by the Belgian émigré Paul de Man). As for her own voice, Felman seeks to write in such a way that her readers would not know which language she is writing from or what nationality she belongs to, whether she is French, American or, in fact, neither (pp. 17–18).

12

Italian Nonsense: Tradition, Translation, Translocation, Transcodification (and a Trinity)

Alessandro Giammei

As it is hardly possible to make these people understand ordinary Italian, a stranger might, if alone, be awkwardly situated in the event of any misunderstanding.

Edward Lear (1852)[1]

A No-Nonsense Tradition

Giuseppe Tomasi di Lampedusa, the Sicilian prince who wrote the bestselling Italian novel of all time, owned one of the most exquisite private collections of English books in the whole of the newborn Republic of Italy. In his palazzo, a few years after the fall of fascism, he gave private lectures on English literature to a group of ecstatic young boys, one of whom was destined to become the first professor of Literary Theory in Italy's ultra-philological academia.[2] Half a century later, right before leaving for New York to direct the Italian Cultural Institute, another disciple transcribed and published these fabled lectures, including one that is entirely dedicated to Nonsense.[3] The topic galvanised the prince's disdain for Italy's provincialism. In a time when even Shakespeare's name was customarily italianised into 'Guglielmo', Tomasi spoke about this unruly strand of Victorian literature – a yearning for adventure transported in the realm of pure language, as he defined it – using its anglophone terminology. He even composed a limerick in English on the spot to give his students an example of this special form of humour, which he considered a genre. In fact, he believed it to be the natural late modern culmination of British literary culture: a sophisticated, precise, even rigorous challenge to narrative logic and proper poetry that no Italian could possibly understand. Italian literature, he complained, is the most serious of all traditions, a tragic sequence of sombre poets and dramatists, and it trains Italian readers to be amused only by classical or moralising humour – from Ariosto's irony to Manzoni's sober social caricatures. He didn't believe there could be any Nonsense outside of English.

In fairness, the prince wanted to brush a dusty and nationalistic conception of literature off the shoulders of his pupils, who grew up under a regime that prohibited translation, reduced art to a vessel for spiritual and patriotic values, and ultimately lacked any sense of humour. The Italian canon, after all, started with a Comedy (albeit Divine), crowned Boccaccio's comedic tales as the primary model for prose, and includes gems of imaginative linguistic and narrative fun such as Luigi Pulci's chivalric giants, who literally explode because of their irrepressible laughter, or Teofilo Folengo's bodily epic in macaronic quasi-Latin. In the land of Ruzante, Aretino, Tassoni, Belli, Pirandello and Fo, comedic literature has also directly played with linguistic short-circuits, such as the terrifying and meaningless 'Papé Satàn aleppe' that resonates in Dante's *Inferno* at the beginning of Canto VII. Some of the most erudite and playful heirs of Petrarch's lyrical model, like the Florentine Burchiello, devoted their careers to lexical juggling and a stupefying deconstruction of established poetical norms: delirious songbooks in perfect metrics whose real meaning escaped most readers for centuries. However, as recent philological efforts of exegesis reveal,[4] they have (alas!) a meaning after all: they can be credibly explained, solved like an enigma, just like the demonic language invented by Dante. While Italian literature is not as serious as Tomasi lamented, its comedic texts (even the most bold and paradoxical ones) have invariably had the flaw of making sense. And those texts that really abjure sense altogether, studied by linguists and admired by post-structuralists,[5] are not fun at all.[6] The prince's envy for the nonchalant absurdity of the Brits (and in particular of Edward Lear and Lewis Carroll, whom he considered to be the masters of the genre) was, at least at the time he wrote his lecture, justified.

In order to develop an indigenous form of Nonsense comparable to that which Tomasi described to his students, Italy's literature had to wait for the end of modernity. Italian Nonsense is a postmodern phenomenon that stemmed from the experimentalism of the neo-avant-garde of the late sixties and seventies. While forms of irrationalism, obscurity and wordplay characterised many of the aesthetic trends and movements of Italian modernism, a truly nonsensical literature akin to English – appealing, if not editorially addressed, to children but aimed at readers of all ages – only appeared in Italian when authors like Carroll were fully received (and adequately translated) with the same cultivated enthusiasm expressed by Tomasi in the early fifties. However, as noted by many Italianists (including myself),[7] Alice had a hard time crossing the Alps to acclimate in the land of Pinocchio. Both the ages of national unification and of fascist nationalism, separated by World War I, dismissed Nonsense as a minor or immoral curiosity, and even those who appreciated its subtleties, like Tomasi, considered it to be irreducibly foreign.

Tomasi represented a rare case of Anglophile erudition, with a specific sensibility for refined comedy. Towering Italian experts of English literature and literary humour of the first half of the twentieth century, such as Mario Praz and Carmelo Previtera, shared the prince's passion for Victorian Nonsense, but also his belief that their compatriots could not really understand it. Praz wrote in 1935 that 'in England this genre is deemed worth of a great deal of respect: indeed, it seems that only the English language is capable of producing the sublime of the absurd'.[8] Previtera, four years later, stated that 'this humour is an exclusive property of the Englishmen, or at least of Anglo-Saxon peoples: a native plant that thrives in the mists of Albion'.[9] Despite the fact that Lear had a studio in Rome, travelled throughout the peninsula to draw landscapes and collect folkloric songs, and died in Sanremo where he is buried, limericks and other forms of nonsense-verse were long inaccessible to Italian readers. Lewis Carroll's *Alice* books, as well as his entire production in verse, remained equally unknown in Italy for a long time, so much so that popular authors were not afraid to plagiarise them by re-using their original illustrations up until the early twenties.[10]

While German and French translations of *Alice's Adventures in Wonderland* started circulating even before the publication of its sequel, *Through the Looking-Glass*, the first Italian version of the novel appeared only in 1872, and only because Carroll directly solicited it through his friend Dante Gabriel Rossetti.[11] It was printed at a modest scale, and it hardly circulated.[12] A more widely diffused translation was published at the beginning of the following century, when Lear's limericks were also translated for the first time as part of the Italian version of Arthur Meer's popular *Children's Encyclopædia*. In both cases, the sophisticated wit of the originals was mortified by translators: Carroll's novel became a girly fable, devoid of any clever wordplay,[13] and Lear's poems were qualified, opting for the most derogatory option to translate the word 'nonsense', as '*le sciocchezze di Edoardo Lear*' – literally: 'stupid things by Edoardo [*sic*] Lear'.

Interestingly, both these early translations were curated by women, Emma Cagli and Camilla Del Soldato. This is not to say that Italy's editorial world, in the first decade of the twentieth century, was particularly inclusive in terms of gender – in fact, it proves the opposite. Rather than works of literature, Carroll's and Lear's Nonsense texts were evidently perceived as unimportant *divertissements* for children by two respectable gentlemen who accomplished serious things in other fields, and the translation of children's literature was considered as a maternal, pedagogical occupation suitable for women. Benedetto Croce, the most influential literary critic of the century, banished all novels and poems for children from the realm of real art ('*arte vera*').[14] When they write for children, he declared in 1904, even the greatest authors (such as Luigi Capuana or Grazia Deledda, whom he otherwise admired) become just pedagogues or moralists, and those who only write for children are, at best, entertainers.[15] The authoritative stigma that Croce imposed on children's literature accompanied the masterpieces of Victorian Nonsense throughout their difficult Italian diffusion in the first half of the twentieth century – a story of misunderstanding and diffidence that I recounted in detail elsewhere.[16] Here, it is worth mentioning that some enthusiastic (if isolated) cases of reception took place in the interwar period. In the thirties, a young Fosco Maraini (destined to become a legendary orientalist, and one of Italy's greatest Nonsense poets a few decades later) used Lear's rhymes, which he knew by heart, to teach English to cadets of the Royal Navy on the Amerigo Vespucci ship.[17] In the same years Carlo Izzo started his solitary and passionate investigation of the *Book of Nonsense*,[18] which led to a series of translations (now considered classics) that, after the war, were put to music by Goffredo Petrassi.[19] Giuseppe Fanciulli's *Il castello delle carte*,[20] a comedic and uncanny illustrated story, was clearly inspired by Carroll, as were two novellas of the early twenties that openly challenged the claustrophobic limits of children's literature in Italy. The first, Massimo Bontempelli's *La scacchiera davanti allo specchio*,[21] is a rationally magical adventure that mixes the incongruous logic of *Through the Looking-Glass* with the metaphysical world-building of Plato's cave, Ariosto's moon and Abbott's *Flatland*. The second, Annie Vivanti's *Sua Altezza!*[22] is a surreal *Bildungsroman* that materialises metaphors and plays with literal interpretations of idioms and figurative language. Yet aside from these episodes of fruitful reception, early twentieth-century Italy tended to confine British Nonsense to the children's literature that Croce disdained. Within those boundaries, Lear was hardly read and Carroll was demonised by fascism.

As Caterina Sinibaldi and others have shown,[23] under Mussolini's regime Nonsense was considered a particularly nasty foreign weed to be condemned during the so-called *bonifica del libro* (roughly, 'decontamination, sanitation, or reclamation of books') enacted by the fascist ministries of education and popular culture. For a 1938 national conference on children's literature, fascist pedagogue Nazareno Padellaro gave a talk on *Alice in Wonderland*, stating that the novel is immersed in a 'nightmarish atmosphere' that deforms the rational vision 'that is the innate gift of all Italians'. 'Even if the Anglo-Saxon spirit loves such intoxications', he argued, 'one doesn't see why we should teach them to our children.'[24] Padellaro obviously expressed a nationalist, even autarchic position, but his core message (that Nonsense does not belong here, and Italians cannot appreciate its English spirit) converged with that of admirers of the genre. As a matter of fact, more respectful versions of the same ideas appear in post-war essays on children's literature by anti-fascist authors. Bruno Betta, for instance, admitted that Carroll's work is 'a masterpiece for the Anglo-Saxons', but cautioned Italian parents and teachers against giving it to their boys and girls ('never before they turn 10, and only if you cannot find books that are more suitable to our children!').[25] Catholic pedagogues like Lina Sacchetti, while acknowledging the global success of Alice's story, found it inferior to sensible and morally edifying tales like *Pinocchio*.[26]

Ultimately, Tomasi's dramatic complaints about the impenetrable seriousness of Italy's no-nonsense tradition made sense, and kept on faithfully describing Italian Nonsense (or better, the absence of it) up until the raucous years of contestation, when the genre attracted avant-garde authors precisely because it offered a way out of the cumbersome legacy of Italy's sensible, moral and stubbornly rational literary history.

Trailblazing Translations and Three Crowns

If tradition was the primary reason of rejection that Nonsense encountered in modern Italy, translation was certainly a major enduring obstacle. The two are, of course, interconnected. When the first complete Italian edition of Lear's *Book of Nonsense* was printed in Vicenza in 1946, in a modest edition of one thousand copies, the publisher decided to title it *Il libro delle follie* (the book of foolish things), refusing both the English term 'Nonsense' and its italianisation *Nonsenso* that the translator, Carlo Izzo, intended to use. For the second edition, which appeared eight years later in Venice, publisher Neri Pozza simply bought the many unsold copies of the first version and distributed them with a new cover.[27] Translations of Carroll's work circulated much more in the same years, but their literary quality was vastly inferior, justifying the perplexed comments of the pedagogues mentioned earlier. Still seen as stories for children, the *Alice* novels were not seen by their translators as containing complex linguistic challenges, and the creative morphology of Carroll's poems was basically ignored in the first half of the century. The eponymous monsters of 'Jabberwocky' and *The Hunting of the Snark* were tellingly turned into Giabbervocco and Snarco by early translators,[28] who italianised the spelling but not the dense semantics of the original titles – and other equally meta-semantic words in the texts received similar treatment.

In 1951, two years before Tomasi's lesson on Nonsense, Walt Disney presented his animated version of *Alice in Wonderland* at the Venice International Film Festival. When the Cheshire Cat materialises in the film, he sings a tune whose lyrics, in the original, correspond to the first quatrain of 'Jabberwocky' from *Through the*

Looking-Glass. The version that the audience in Venice (and, from the 6 December release, all over Italy) listened to is the following:

A destra ed a manca va, di qua, di su, di giù, di là
la luna sorge all'ólimon e i palmìpedon neppur.
Albeggia, ed il solleon a larghe falde sbianca il mar
la luna sorge all'ólimon e i palmìpedon neppur.

A literal English translation of these meaningless lines would sound, more or less, like this: 'To the right and to the left it goes, here, up, down, there | the moon rises on the holemon, and not even the mome raths. | It dawns, and the summer sun whitens the sea in large layers | the moon rises on the holemon, and not even the mome raths'. I render *ólimon*, an invented word that probably combines 'lemon' and 'horizon', with an equally awkward portmanteau, 'holemon'. Except for another portmanteau – *palmìpedon*, which directly translates Carroll's 'mome raths' by combining the Italian terms for 'hand-palms' and 'pedestrians' – the four lines share only a metrical cadence with 'Jabberwocky' (and the Jabberwock itself doesn't appear at all). They were written by a prolific adaptor of American films, Roberto de Leonardis: one of only five Italians, to date, to be honoured by the Disney Fan Club with the official rank of Disney Legend.[29] A recent documentary for the sixtieth anniversary of the film[30] reveals that Disney chose to cut a scene centred on Humpty Dumpty, the Jabberwock, and the other untranslatable chimeric creatures of the poem, opting instead for an animation of the ballad of the Walrus and the Carpenter. However, he still wanted 'Jabberwocky' to be featured in the film, and so decided to use it as the Cat's musical motif. While de Leonardis translated the lines of *The Walrus and the Carpenter* faithfully, the non-narrative and lexically inventive Nonsense of 'Jabberwocky' received, instead, a defusing, normalising treatment. It is particularly interesting that the first line directly quotes Dante, who described the chaotic movement of lustful souls with the same fast-paced sequence of monosyllables adopted by de Leonardis: 'di qua, di là, di su, di giù li mena' (*Inferno* V, 43).[31] An effective and influential hendecasyllable, this line was often reprised almost identically throughout the history of Italian poetry, most prominently by Ludovico Ariosto in the sixteenth century.[32]

Besides resorting to this ultra-Italian Dantesque trope, de Leonardis clearly avoided the challenge of directly translating the original, and opted instead for a reformulation of parts of the other poem by Carroll that he extensively translated for the film. The following lines of his version base their comedic incongruity on the paradoxical concurrent rising of both the moon (*luna*) and the *solleon* (an Italian expression for 'summer sun', which combines *sole* and *leone*). The idea did not come from 'Jabberwocky' of course, but from 'The Walrus and the Carpenter' ('The moon was shining sulkily, | Because she thought the sun | Had got no business to be there'), which starts with the same image of the sun shining on the sea that de Leonardis used for the Cat's tune. The poem about naïve oysters and their ill-intentioned hosts does not present the same linguistic challenges that made 'Jabberwocky' a primary case study for translatology.[33] De Leonardis was able to establish a formal equivalence with the first text: he translated its plot, not caring too much about the effect that its words were meant to achieve with the audience. In order to transmit the (non)sense of the second, he would have had to attempt a dynamic equivalence,[34] dealing with what happens in it at the level of semantics. Rather than going for an abstruse italianisation of the original (like the plain 'Giabbervocco' used by Silvio Spaventa Filippi and Giuliana Pozzo in the previous decades) or simplifying a rich blend of words into one Italian term (like Adriana Valori did with 'Tartaglione' in 1954), de Leonardis just threw in the towel.[35]

The deconstructive potential of Nonsense was fully understood and tackled by Italy's literary culture only between the end of the sixties and the beginning of the seventies, when, coincidentally, Disney's movie returned to Italian theatres. In 1970, Izzo's translations of Lear's poems were finally published with the title *Il libro dei nonsense*, and canonised in one of the most prestigious collections of Italy's editorial market: Giulio Einaudi's philologically curated and beautifully printed Millenni. Other major publishers such as Mondadori and Fabbri issued new versions of *Alice in Wonderland*, which was newly translated at least three times in the previous two years. In the same moment, Umberto Eco included Segal's and Civ'jan's formalist analysis of English Nonsense in one of his foundational contributions to semiology, offering a precise definition of the limerick as a poetic form.[36] The thirty-four paradoxes of Gilles Deleuze's *Logique du sens* strongly influenced an Italian academia that was heavily structuralist in inclination and rejuvenated by the turmoils of 1968, and the publisher Bompiani devoted an entire issue of his popular Almanacchi to playful forms of art such as *la letteratura nonsensica*.[37] In 1969, in the pages of the largest and most respected national newspaper, *Il Corriere della sera*, young literary critic Pietro Citati called Carroll 'the most exquisite philosopher of our times'.[38]

It was in this time of change[39] that new theoretical appreciation of nonsense on the most abstract and purist peripheries of Italy's neo-avant-garde, generated translations and poetic experiments that formed the first real Italian contribution to the genre. Since the canonisation of Dante, Petrarch and Boccaccio as the 'three crowns' of medieval literature, Italy's literary history has always had a penchant for poetic trinities (Boiardo, Ariosto and Tasso for chivalric epic; Leopardi, Foscolo and Manzoni for Romantic poetry; Carducci, Pascoli and D'Annunzio for Decadence, and so on). In homage to this tradition, one could say that the 'three crowns' of Italian Nonsense in the sixties and the seventies are Giulia Niccolai, Fosco Maraini and Toti Scialoja. I shall go on to discuss their different approaches to logic and semantics, but first it is important to list a few crucial characteristics that they share.

These 'three crowns' of Italian Nonsense were linked by three major characteristics. They were, in the most elevated sense of the word, dilettantes. They looked at the Italian language and literary tradition from the liminal point of view of multilingualism, translation, expatriation, nostalgia. They actively reacted against the recent legacy of fascist culture and its moralising, homogenising, rationalising prescriptions. Despite the fact that they were educated in the years of Croce's anathema against children's literature and fascist diffidence towards foreign literature in general (and *Alice in Wonderland* in particular), all three had known and loved Victorian Nonsense since their youth. Like Lear, the landscape artist, and Carroll, the mathematician, they approached writing as an initially collateral activity, a complement to a more official career. Maraini was an ethnologist and scholar of East Asian cultures and literatures, Niccolai travelled the world as a professional photographer before becoming an editor, publisher and translator, while Scialoja was an eminent abstract painter, art critic and professor at Rome's Academy of Fine Arts. Their poems stemmed from linguistic epiphanies experienced through these 'serious' occupations, investigating the logical incongruities and the revealing phonetic coincidences that occur while travelling, reproducing pictures, practicing action-painting, and trying to make sense of Western culture during a postmodern economic boom. The Italian Nonsense they produced was informed by the loss of meaning generated by an endless repetition of sounds and images, and by viewing the Italian language as an exotic architecture of resounding syllables. It was rooted in the theory of informal art and the phenomenology of abstract expressionism, as well as in a clash between photographic eye and literary subjectivity inspired by the coeval objectivism of French narrative.

Another important point of contact among the three authors is the perspective of linguistic displacement from which they accessed nonsense verse in Italian. Scialoja, one of the first European artists to visit the painters of the New York School, started composing illustrated limericks in Paris during a long artistic sojourn in which he didn't have many chances to speak Italian. According to him, it was a longing for his native tongue that inspired the nonsensical rhymes that he sent from his studio on Rue de la Tombe Issoire, to his five-year-old nephew James Demby, who would receive and read them in Rome.[40] Niccolai was the daughter of a Milanese engineer and a worldly American woman from a family of New England timber merchants. She grew up bilingual, and devoted much of her life to the translation of such untranslatable modernist authors as Gertrude Stein and Dylan Thomas.[41] Maraini, whose mother was a Hungarian writer of Anglo-Polish descent, grew up bilingual too, and in his youth taught English on a military ship, visiting North Africa and the Middle East. As an anthropologist he specialised in Tibet, where he travelled with Italian sinologists, and then migrated to Japan, where he lived and taught for many years before and after World War II.[42] Multilingualism helped these poets understand the semantic possibilities of Nonsense verse: just as English is the real protagonist of Lear and Carroll's works, Italian became the primary object of analysis and playful deconstruction for Maraini, Niccolai and Scialoja.

It is worth adding that all three poets nourished a profound disgust for totalitarianism. Their anti-fascist devotion to freedom explains the xenophile, anti-traditional poetic research that they undertook, and deeply influenced their lives. While in Japan, Maraini refused to adhere to Mussolini's Repubblica di Salò, and for this reason he was imprisoned in a concentration camp in Nagoya for two years with his wife and daughters.[43] Because of her mother's nationality, Niccolai was discriminated against as a child under Mussolini's regime, enduring the harassment of schoolmates and teachers in the village on the Como lake where she was evacuated during the bombings.[44] Scialoja participated in the anti-fascist resistance in Rome at the end of the war. Along with fellow painters Renato Guttuso and Mario Mafai, he joined a group of partisan fighters that started guerrilla actions against the Nazi-fascists.[45]

What's in a Place Name?

On a number of occasions – now preserved for posterity on YouTube – Gigi Proietti, one of Italy's most popular post-war comedians (he dubbed Robin Williams's genie in the Italian version of *Aladdin*), performed a hilarious sonnet titled *Il Lonfo* on national television. He did so to lovingly mock other great Italian actors, such as Vittorio Gasman, Piera degli Esposti or Carmelo Bene, who occasionally agreed to read classical masterpieces of Italian poetry, from Cavalcanti to Leopardi, for the cultural programs of the RAI TV broadcasting service. Proietti's performance of *Il Lonfo* became a cult. The actor's voice, his dignified and dramatic tone, and the pensive intensity of his academic elocution were worthy of the most serious and grand poetic recital. The perfect metrical cadence of the fourteen Petrarchan lines that he read – rhymed according to the Tuscan scheme that influenced the entirety of the Western lyrical canon – resonated exquisitely throughout the performance. What made it impossible not to laugh was the absurd language of the poem, uncannily similar to that of the great texts recited in serious readings and yet completely different:

Il Lonfo
Il Lonfo non vaterca né gluisce
e molto raramente barigatta,
ma quando soffia il bego a bisce bisce
sdilenca un poco e gnagio s'archipatta.

È frusco il Lonfo! È pieno di lupigna
arrafferia malversa e sofolenta!
Se cionfi ti sbiduglia e ti arrupigna
se lugri ti botalla e ti criventa.

Eppure il vecchio Lonfo ammargelluto
che bete e zugghia e fonca nei trombazzi
fa lègica busìa, fa gisbuto;

e quasi quasi in segno di sberdazzi
gli affarferesti un gniffo. Ma lui zuto
t'alloppa, ti sbernecchia; e tu l'accazzi.[46]

There is no way to translate *Il Lonfo* without rewriting it, because it is written in a nonsensical language that maintains the grammatical structures and phonetic characteristics of Italian without being Italian. It also perfectly uses the phonetic figures, rhythmical rules and rhetorical devices of Italy's traditional poetic language, which famously evolved independently from that of prose.[47] It makes it possible, for an Italian, to imagine what Dante would sound like to the ears of a Martian: to enjoy an Italian poem in the way that a foreigner might.

Proietti found *Il Lonfo* in Fosco Maraini's first (and only) book of poems, *Gnòsi delle Fànfole*. All the texts in the book are written in the same refined and estranging quasi-Italian, and form a nonsensical songbook. A small publisher, Di Donato, printed it in 1966, in 300 numbered copies, mostly given by the author to friends and colleagues. Maraini's Italian nonsense was a solitary attempt to import the elegant Victorian meta-semantics of Carroll and Lear into a tradition that had rejected them for almost a century (the influence of 'Jabberwocky', in particular, is noticeable). Through the years, the book acquired many admirers and became a cult, as the latest curator of the verses, Maro Marcellini, remembered in the foreword to his annotated edition.[48] It was reprinted, included in the complete works of the author,[49] and even put to music by popular jazz pianist Stefano Bollani[50] before gaining a vast mainstream audience thanks to Proietti's televised performances of *Il Lonfo*. 'Meta-semantics' is the term that Maraini used himself to describe the intransitive morphology, at once familiar and alien, of his rhymes, which have been recently defined more precisely 'peri-semantic'.[51] To explain the genesis of his *Fànfole*, Maraini described language as an ecological system in which a patient observer can find 'natural gems' (*gioielli di natura*) that mysteriously evolved into their current curious shapes and colours. Fruitful collections of such gems are topographical charts, atlases and train announcements. Lists of place names captivated Maraini's multilingual ear, and suggested to his pen how to form the domestic exoticism of a new, nonsensical Italian.[52]

While Maraini's represented an early and detached case of pure semantic experiment, the Nonsense of Scialoja and Niccolai germinated directly from the deconstructionist and neo-avant-garde re-evaluation of Carroll and Lear. Niccolai was one of the very few women who took part in Italy's most prominent neo-avant-garde movement, the Gruppo 63.[53] In 1969, with other poets interested in subverting linear textuality and experimenting with concrete and visual poetry, she abandoned the group and moved to Mulino di Bazzano, where she devoted her life to writing, editing and publishing edgy literature outside of the mainstream editorial market. Her first book of concrete poems, *Humpty Dumpty* (1969),[54] is a microscopic analysis of Carroll's nonsense novels: she extracted minimal portions from *Alice's Adventures in Wonderland* (sometimes just one or two words) to build visual comments on its plot, its challenge to logical assumptions, and the intrinsically nonsensical nature of language in general. Using a typewriter, Letraset typefaces and a Linotype machine, she crafted an entire book without writing one word herself: the entire text, shaped in various forms, is borrowed from Carroll, and becomes eloquent and understandable to Italian readers (in fact, to readers of any language) thanks to the visual arrangement of letters, syllables, and sentences (Figures 12.1–3).

Figure 12.1 Giulia Niccolai, 'Senses Do Sound!' and 'He Might Bite p. 121', from *Humpty Dumpty* (Turin: Geiger, 1969), pp. 13–4, artisanal Linotype on paper, 11x15cm.

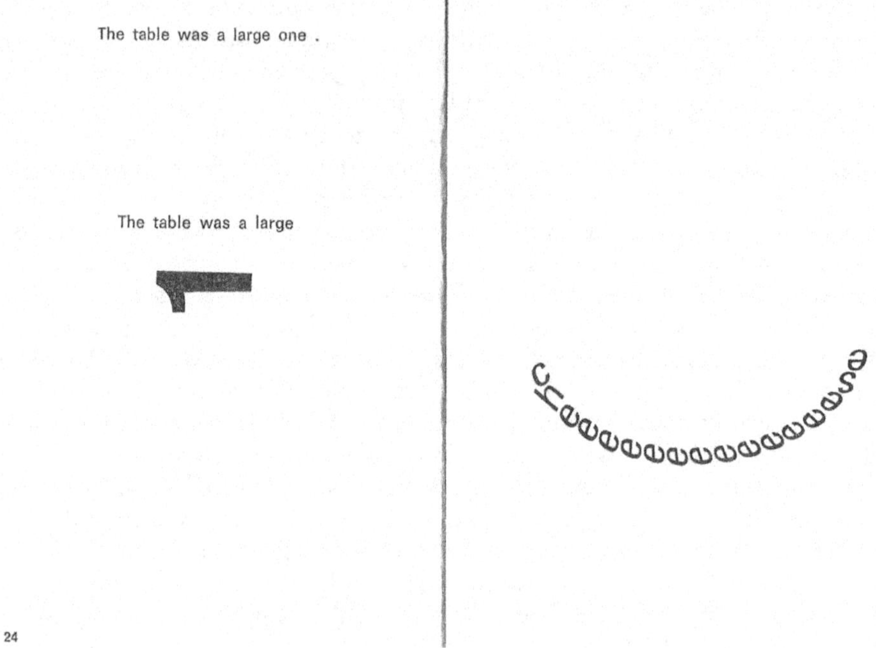

Figure 12.2 Giulia Niccolai, 'The Table Was a Large One p. 93' and 'The Cheshire Cat's Grin p. 83', from *Humpty Dumpty* (Turin: Geiger, 1969), pp. 24–5, artisanal Linotype and xeroxed Letraset print on paper, 11x15cm.

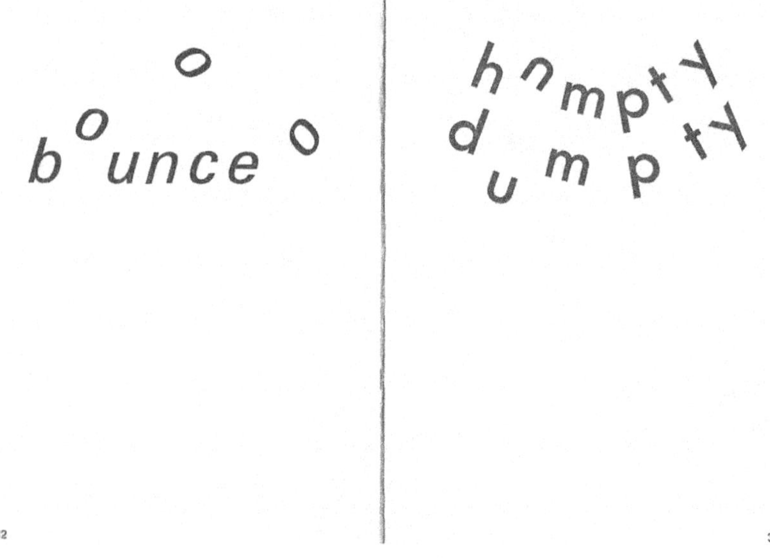

Figure 12.3 Giulia Niccolai, 'To Bounce p. 241' and 'Humpty Dumpty p. 261', from *Humpty Dumpty* (Turin: Geiger, 1969), pp. 31–2, xeroxed Letraset print on paper, 11x15cm.

Between 1970 and 1971, while reviewing the new translation of Lear's *Limericks* for the journal *Tam Tam*, Niccolai composed two books, *Greenwich* and *New Greenwich*, that synthesise her playful and rigorous contribution to Nonsense.[55] Like Maraini's *Fànfole*, the *nonsensi geografici* of these two collections are based on the intransitive and untranslatable familiarity of place names: every single word of each poem, except for conjunctions and prepositions, was taken from an atlas. The criteria adopted by Niccolai, explained in a seriocomic afterword, were proximity, rhythm and a teasing seduction of sense, which is just slightly out of reach in the geographical compositions. Since the words that compose each text come from the same atlas page, the poems approximate many different languages. Poems based on Italian place names for instance, like 'Como è trieste Venezia', sound Italian, while poems based on American place names, like *Utah*, sound English:

Utah
Strawberry strawberry
holden monroe
bountiful farmington
minnie plateau.
Emory upton
on devils side
washington terrace
oh enterprise!
Riverton vernon
elmo woodside
strawberry strawberry
lofgreen lakeside.

Nothing is more untranslatable than toponyms: ancient, powerful words that resist the natural evolution of language, crystallising ancient morphologies and semantics. Sometimes they even survive the places that they define, becoming, through time, vestigia of lost meaning. The poems in *Greenwich* that are based on Sardinian place names, for example, look like Latin *carmina*; those based on French toponyms from around Lyon seem like early modern ballads of the Romance tradition. With *Greenwich*, Niccolai flirted with the utopia of a universal poetic language while mocking the xenophobia of Italy's literary tradition. In the following decades she wrote books of poems that deconstructed dictionaries, mixed texts with objects and reflected on linguistic coincidences and wordplays.[56] She became a towering figure of Italy's experimentalism, studied all over the world, and at the turn of the twenty-first century began to merge her earlier nonsense poetics with the Buddhist philosophy that she learned from Tibetan monks.

Place names were a spark for Scialoja's Nonsense as well. His poems however, like Lear's limericks, are written in a readable language and look like nursery rhymes. They are multimodal texts, always accompanied by illustrations drawn by the author that complete the words, visualising their impossible or ridiculous content. As noted above, Scialoja started writing them to amuse his young nephew at the beginning of the sixties. He then continued to fabricate illustrated letters, with typed rhymes and sketches, for other children in his family, eventually collecting many illustrated texts in an artisanal book that circulated among friends. The book was noticed by an editor at Bompiani, who published a selection of the rhymes in 1971, under the title *Amato topino caro*. This beautiful edition, filled with Scialoja's elegant and colourful drawings – which were secretly inspired by Grandville's uncanny etchings[57] –became one of the favourite books of Italo Calvino's seven-year-old daughter Giovanna, who convinced her father to publish Scialoja's second book, *Una vespa! Che spavento*, with Einaudi in 1975. Already famous as a painter, Scialoja started a literary career that continued until his death.[58]

To present his second book, Calvino directly connected Scialoja's poems with Lear and Carroll, calling them 'the first true Italian example of a poetic amusement congenial to the extraordinary English tradition of limericks and nonsense verse'. As a matter of fact, Scialoja's early poems are based on a linguistic mechanism very close to that of Lear's limericks. Most of them play on the assonances between the name of an animal and that of a place (*cani* and Kenya for instance, or *marmotta* and Mar Morto) and keep building on the same sounds.[59] The resulting micro-stories are grammatically plausible, like those of Lear, but the author's absolute attention for the sounds makes the sense progressively disappear.[60] Walruses on tricycles, woodpeckers at picnics, rabbits on the Capitol hill: the poems are only justified by the phonetic associations of their words in Italian (*tricheco* and *triciclo*, *picchio* and *pic nic*, *coniglio* and *Campidoglio*). To truly translate them, one needs to rewrite them – and this is what I tried to do in the following example, keeping the central animal (*rondini*, swallows) and the rhythmic structure, but changing meanings in order to make sounds work.

Sotto la gronda gridano le rondini:
'Sono grandìni i chicchi della grandine!'[61]

['Six swift swallows, wallowing like whales,
bawl, whirl, wander and howl above the vales.']

Rather than playing with the enigmatic sound of toponyms and peri-semantic words, like Niccolai and Maraini, Scialoja mobilised the sounds of classical Italian poems. Many of his limericks are parodies of famous texts of the lyrical tradition. In this, he is close to the model of Carroll, who composed parodic versions of English Romantic poems and eighteenth-century didactic children's verse. However, while Carroll's parodies of authors such as Watts and Southey came to supercede the original texts, such that in some cases they are much less familiar today than Carroll's nonsensical versions, Scialoja played with a tradition that remains vivid in the memory of any Italian who attended elementary school. The authors that he parodied most often are Nobel Prize winners like Carducci, tragic symbolists like Pascoli, and poet-philosophers like Leopardi. The extremely serious texts of these masters are traditionally learned by heart by Italian children long before they are able to understand them. Scialoja's parodies, therefore, allow adult readers to recall the confusing repetition of grandiloquent words and constructions that they experienced as children: to live again, like Alice, in the strict and nonsensical rules of Wonderland, the impression that the meaning of things is just beyond their grasp.

Geography and philology are twin sisters, according to a passage from Ionesco quoted at the beginning of Niccolai's *Greenwich*.[62] Italian Nonsense mobilised these two unlikely muses to acclimate Victorian humour in the most serious of all traditions. It is time, now, to repatriate their senseless but meaningful rhymes in the mists of Albion, translating them with the same inventive enthusiasm that recent Italian masters of Nonsense translation, such as Ottavio Fatica,[63] and Milli Graffi[64] applied to Carroll and Lear, now loved and studied as classics by readers of all ages.

Notes

1. Edward Lear, *Edward Lear in Southern Italy: Journals of a Landscape Painter in Southern Calabria and the Kingdom of Naples*, ed. Peter Quennell (London: William Kimber, 1964), p. 152.
2. I am referring to Francesco Orlando, who recalled the Sicilian lectures in his *Ricordo di Lampedusa* (Milan: All'insegna del pesce d'oro, 1963).
3. Giuseppe Tomasi di Lampedusa, 'Nonsense', in *Opere*, ed. Gioacchino Lanza Tomasi (Milan: Mondadori, 1995), 1167–9.
4. See for instance Giuseppe Crimi, *L'oscura lingua e il parlar sottile: tradizione e fortuna del Burchiello* (Rome: Vecchiarlli, 2005). On the decryption of similar forms of Italian early modern Nonsense *à clef*, see the Renaissance and Baroque chapters of *'Nominativi fritti e mappamondi': Il nonsense nella letteratura italiana*, ed. Giuseppe Antonelli and Carla Chiummo (Rome: Salerno, 2007).
5. On texts that make no sense in the oeuvre of canonical authors such as Montale and Caproni, see Andrea Afribo, 'Approssimazioni al nonsense nella poesia italiana del Novecento' in Antonelli and Chiummo, *Nominativi fritti e mappamondi*, 289–306.
6. A typical example of unfunny Nonsense is Alfredo Giuliani's 1979 composition *Poema Chomsky*. Giuliani was a pre-eminent figure of Italy's neo-avant-garde, and was interested in the purely grammatical aspects of Nonsense. He composed a poem by repeating Chomsky's famous example of a nonsensical sentence ('colourless green ideas sleep furiously') in a variety of Italian translations. Despite this cold, purely structural approach to the concept, he appreciated Nonsense verse as a humorous literary genre, and was one of the first critics to map Italian approximations to it (including the ones attempted by Scialoja and Niccolai, on which I will insist in the last section of this essay). See Alfredo Giuliani, *Le droghe di Marsiglia* (Milan: Adelphi, 1977), pp. 396–7.
7. See for instance, *Quando Alice incontrò Pinocchio*, ed. Pompeo Vigliani (Turin: Trauben, 1988), and Alessandro Giammei, 'Nonsense-verse Made in Italy', *il verri* 60 (2016), 31–43.
8. 'In Inghilterra è un genere degno di gran rispetto: solo in lingua inglese, infatti, pare che sia possibile creare il sublime dell'assurdo'. Mario Praz, *Cronache Letterarie Anglosassoni II. Cronache inglesi e americane* (Rome: Edizioni di Storia e Letteratura, 1951), p. 56.
9. '[Quest]'humour è proprietà esclusiva degl'Inglesi o almeno dei popoli anglosassoni: una pianta indigena che vegeta fra le brume di Albione'. Carmelo Previtera, *La poesia giocosa e l'umorismo* (Florence: Vallardi, 1939), p. 36.
10. In his quintessentially Tuscan *La regina di cuori* for instance, Renato Fucini clearly draws on John Tenniel's classical illustrations of Carroll's work, which are directly reused in an early edition of his book *Il ciuco di Melesecche* (Florence: La Voce, 1922).
11. The translator was Rossetti's nephew, Teodorico Pietrocola Rossetti. The edition was printed by Loescher in Turin.
12. See *Quando Alice incontrò Pinocchio*, ed. Vigliani, p. 68.
13. The first Italian academic biography of Carroll, in 1968, utterly condemned the translation (published in 1908, with the title *Nel paese delle meraviglie*) in these terms ('non ha nulla a che vedere con l'astratto squisito nitore della vera Alice'). See Laura Draghi Salvatori, *Lewis Carroll* (Florence: Le Monnier, 1968), pp. 45–55.

14. 'l'arte per bambini non sarà mai arte vera' ['art for children will never be real art']. These considerations appeared in a 1904 essay on Luigi Capuana, which was then collected in an influential 1914 book. See Benedetto Croce, *La letteratura della Nuova Italia* (Rome-Bari: Laterza, 1929), III, pp. 101–18.
15. See Croce's comments on De Amicis in Benedetto Croce, *La letteratura italiana per saggi storicamente disposti*, ed. Mario Sansone, 4 vols (Rome-Bari: Laterza, 1960), III, p. 384.
16. Alessandro Giammei, *Nell'officina del nonsense di Toti Scialoja. Topi, toponimi, tropi, cronotopi* (Milan: edizioni del verri, 2014). See in particular the first chapter, 'Il nonsense vittoriano e l'Italia. Cronistoria di un difficile acclimamento', pp. 11–58.
17. Fosco Maraini, *Case, amori, universi* (Milan: Mondadori, 1999), p. 260.
18. His first, seminal study is Carlo Izzo, 'L'umorismo alla luce del Book of Nonsense', *Ateneo Veneto* 126.119 (1935), 211–19.
19. Goffredo Petrassi, *Nonsense: per coro a cappella da The Book of Nonsense di Edward Lear* (Milan: Suvini-Zerboni, 1953).
20. Giuseppe Fanciulli, *Il castello delle carte. Novelline bizzarre* (Florence: Bemporad, 1914).
21. Published in 1922 by Bemporad and reprinted many times, this novella was translated into English: Massimo Bontempelli, *The Chess Set in the Mirror*, trans. Estelle Gilson (Philadelphia: Paul Dry Books, 2007).
22. On this novella, see Maria Rosa Truglio, 'Annie in Wonderland: Vivanti's sua altezza! and children's literature during fascism', *Quaderni d'Italianistica* 1 (2004), 121–43.
23. See Caterina Sinibaldi, 'Tradurre Alice durante il ventennio fascista', in *I dilemmi del traduttore di Nonsense*, ed. Angela Albanese and Franco Nasi, special issue of *Il lettore di provincia* 138 (2012), 65–79; and Mariella Colin, *Les enfants de Mussolini. Littérature, livres, lectures d'enfance et de jeunesse sous le fascisme* (Caen: Presses universitaires de Caen, 2010).
24. Nazareno Padellaro, 'Traduzioni e riduzioni di libri per fanciulli', in *Convegno nazionale per la letteratura infantile e giovanile* (Rome: Stige, 1939), 35–42, p. 41.
25. 'Sempre non prima dei 10 anni e se non si trovano libri che per i nostri fanciulli riescono più adatti!' Bruno Betta, *La letteratura per l'infanzia. Che cosa leggere dall'infanzia alla gioventù. Guida pratica per l'educatore alla conoscenza della letteratura infantile* (Brescia: Vita Scolastica, 1952), p. 107.
26. Lina Sacchetti, *Letteratura per ragazzi* (Florence: Le Monnier, 1954), pp. 83–93.
27. For the editorial history of Izzo's translation, see his foreword to Edward Lear, *Il libro dei nonsense*, ed. Carlo Izzo (Turin: Einaudi, 2004), i–xxiii, p. xxii.
28. I am referring to Silvio Spaventa Filippi, who translated the *Alice* novels in 1914, and Cesare Vico Lodovici, who translated *The Hunting of the Snark* in 1945.
29. The prestigious title is confirmed on the official site of the Disney fan club, in which a curious biography of de Leonardis appears. Available at <https://d23.com/walt-disney-legend/roberto-de-leonardis/> (last accessed 1 May 2021).
30. The documentary, titled *Through the Keyhole: A Companion's Guide to Wonderland*, is included in the 2011 home-video '60th anniversary edition' of the film released by Disney.
31. Dante Alighieri, *The Divine Comedy: Inferno*, trans. and with a commentary by Charles Singleton (Princeton: Princeton University Press, 1989), pp. 48–9.
32. In his *Orlando Furioso* (1532), Ariosto reuses Dante's eight syllables (sometimes extracting the hemistichs 'di qua di là' or 'di su di giù') on dozens of occasions. For a sample, and a discussion of the bibliography on Dante in Ariosto, see the recent Lorenzo Bartoli, '«Solo e senza altrui rispetto» (*Orlando Furioso* XXIII, 122, 2). Nota sulla follia di Orlando', *Quaderns d'Italià* 22 (2017), 75–82, p. 78.
33. On the matter, see Daniela Almansi, 'Nonsensing Translation: How to turn the spotlight on the blind spots of interpretation', *Bookbird* 53.3 (2015), 56–65; Pilar Orero, *The Problems of Translating 'Jabberwocky': The Nonsense Literature of Lewis Carroll and Edward*

Lear and Their Spanish Translators (New York: Edwin Mellen, 2007); and Björn Sundmark, 'Some Uffish Thoughts on the Swedish Translations of Jabberwocky', *The European Journal of Humour Research* 5.3 (2017), 43–56.

34. I am borrowing the terms 'formal equivalence' and 'dynamic equivalence' from Eugene Nida's essays of biblical translation. See Eugene Nida, *Towards a Science of Translating* (Leiden: Brill, 1964).
35. On Italian translations of Jabberwocky see *I dilemmi del traduttore di Nonsense* ed. Albanese and Nasi. The volume includes a rich bibliography by the curators (pp. 173–82).
36. Umberto Eco, *I sistemi di segni e lo strutturalismo sovietico* (Milan: Bompiani, 1969), pp. 151–61.
37. The 1966 issue, which appeared with the title *Arte e Gioco* and included a section on Nonsense (pp. 107–12).
38. 'Il più squisito filosofo dei nostri tempi'. The article is now collected in a book that takes its title from Carroll: Pietro Citati, *Il tè del cappellaio matto* (Milan: Adelphi, 2012), 333–6, p. 334.
39. The re-evaluation of Nonsense continued throughout the seventies. In 1976, a monographic issue of the avant-garde journal *il verri* was devoted to the genre, and in 1977 Gianni Celati held a legendary seminar on Carroll's Alice at the DAMS in Bologna, see *Alice disambientata: materiali collettivi (su Alice) per un manuale di sopravvivenza*, ed. Gianni Celati, afterword by Andrea Cortellessa (Florence: Le Lettere, 2007).
40. On Scialoja's writing and formation, and on his relationship with writers and literature in general, see Giammei, *Nell'officina del nonsense di Toti Scialoja* (in particular Chapters 2 and 3, 59–168). See also Eloisa Moira, *Un allegro fischiettare nelle tenebre* (Macerata: Quodlibet, 2015).
41. For an intellectual and, in part, biographical portrait of Niccolai, see Rebecca West, 'Giulia Niccolai: A Wide-Angle Portrait', in *Neoavanguardia*, ed. Luca Somigli (Toronto: Toronto University Press, 2010), 212–30.
42. On Maraini's life, see Maraini, *Case, amori, universi*.
43. On this episode, see Dacia Maraini, *Bagheria* (Milan: Rizzoli, 1993).
44. An experience recalled in Giulia Niccolai, *Favole & Frisbees* (Milan: Archinto, 2018).
45. For a precise and rich chronology of Scialoja's life, see Giuseppe Appella, 'Vita, opere, fortuna critica', in *Toti Scialoja. Opere 1955–1963* (Milan: Electa, 2000), 127–216.
46. Fosco Maraini, *Pellegrino in Asia*, ed. Franco Marcoaldi (Milan: Mondadori, 2007), p. 1479.
47. During the Italian Renaissance, prominent humanists such as Pietro Bembo established Giovanni Boccaccio's *Decameron* as the standard linguistic model of prose, and Petrarch's *Rerum Vulgarium Fragmenta* (today known as *Canzoniere* or 'Songbook') as the standard model of poetic, and in particular lyrical, language. Petrarchan linguistic traditions remained particularly conservative: that is why, for instance, the language of opera, based on those conventions even in the twentieth century, sounds less decipherable to the ears of native speakers even in comparison to the language of pre-Petrarch poets, like Dante. On the morphology of Italian poetic language, see Luca Serianni, *La lingua poetica italiana* (Rome: Carocci, 2009).
48. Fosco Maraini, *Gnòsi delle Fanfole*, ed. Maro Marcellini (Milan: Baldini Castoldi, 2007).
49. Maraini, *Pellegrino in Asia*, pp. 1478–96.
50. The eponymous album was published by Universal Music in 1998.
51. Daniele Baglioni, 'Poesia metasemantica o perisemantica? La lingua delle Fànfole di Fosco Maraini', in *Studi linguistici per Luca Serianni*, ed. Valeria Della Valle and Pietro Trifone (Rome: Salerno, 2007), 469–80.
52. Maraini's discussion of his own creative process is in his preface to the *Fanfole*, now in Fosco Maraini, *Pellegrino in Asia*, pp. 1479–84.

53. On Niccolai's role and feminist stance within the Gruppo 63, see Alessandro Giammei, 'Desdemona, Noun: See Othello. Giulia Niccolai: Gender & Neoavanguardia', *Engramma* 145 (2017), 67–82.
54. All of Niccolai's book of poems, from 1969 to 2012, were collected in Giulia Niccolai, *Poemi & Oggetti*, ed. Milli Graffi (Florence: Le Lettere, 2012).
55. An early comment by Bulgheroni is still very illuminating on the ethos and method of Niccolai's first books of Nonsense. See Marisa Bulgheroni, 'Una geografia nonsensical', *Tam Tam* 6/7/8 (1974), 21–4.
56. For a detailed history of Niccolai's poetry, see Alessandro Giammei, 'La bussola di Alice. Giulia Niccolai da Carroll a Stein (via Orgosolo) fino all'illuminazione', *il verri* 51 (2013), 33–77.
57. The direct influence of Grandville's *Vie Privée et Publique des Animaux* (an 1842 disquieting social satire, not really suited for children) on Scialoja's drawings remained undetected until recently. See Alessandro Giammei, 'Disegni (con poesie) per bambini e connoisseurs', in *100 Scialoja Azione e Pensiero*, ed. Claudio Crescentini (Rome: De Luca, 2015), 88–93.
58. The complete poetic works are collected in two books, one of playful nonsense poems and one of more experimental, less comedic texts: Toti Scialoja, *Versi del senso perso* (Milan: Mondadori, 1989), and *Poesie 1978–1998*, ed. Giovanni Raboni (Milan: Garzanti, 2002).
59. Proposing an Italian version of Carroll's portmanteau words (the *parole melagrane* or pomegranate words), Scialoja described his process in Toti Scialoja, 'Come nascono le mie poesie', *il verri* 8 (1988), 9–20.
60. On the linguistic aspects of Scialoja's poetry, as well as his literary sources, see Luca Serianni, 'Il gioco linguistico nella poesia di Toti Scialoja', in *Nominativi fritti e mappamondi*, ed. Antonelli and Chiummo, 307–24.
61. Toti Scialoja, *Quando la talpa vuol ballare il tango* (Milan: Mondadori, 1997), p. 6.
62. In *La Leçon* (1951), the professor states that 'Géographie et philologie sont sœurs jumelles.' Eugène Ionesco, *Théâtre I*, ed. Jacques Lamarchand (Paris: Gallimard, 1954), p. 73.
63. Ottavio Fatica, an award-winning poet, curated a new version of Lear's poems in 1994. A prestigious edition was printed more recently: Edward Lear, *Limericks*, ed. Ottavio Fatica (Turin: Einaudi, 2002).
64. Graffi was a younger follower of Niccolai's avant-garde group. She published her translation of *Jabberwocky* in her debut book as a poet – Milli Graffi, *Mille graffi e venti poesie* (Parma: Geiger, 1979), pp. 43–4. She then curated an integral version of Carroll's novels for Garzanti, which is still in print. She also translated *The Hunting of the Snark* – Lewis Carroll, *La caccia allo Snualo*, ed. Milli Graffi (Matera: Edizioni del Labirinto, 1982). Her own experimental poetry, concerned with the limits of language and the power of performance, awaits a systematic study. Milli Graffi was a fearless beacon in the realm of Italy's neo-neo-avant-garde, a master in translating the untranslatable and the (not-so-fairy) godmother of any young scholar interested in nonsense and experimentalism. To her memory I dedicate this essay.

Part III:
Contexts and Connections

13

English 'hibber-gibber' and the 'jargon of France': Rabelaisian Nonsense in Translation

Hugh Roberts

Translation often results in miscommunication, misunderstanding, or indeed nonsense. The ways in which one makes sense of things may be shaken on encountering others who speak a different language or languages. Once burst, a monoglot bubble is much less stable and reassuring than might have been imagined, which is doubtless one of the underlying causes of xenophobia. Anyone who has attempted to learn another modern language is familiar with feelings of stupidity or inadequacy as one's best attempts sometimes result in gibberish. Moreover, while problems of understanding are of course amplified when two or more languages are involved, they also apply even within a single language, which will naturally have its own codes, dialects or languages within languages, as well as its own potential for ambiguity and confusion. Such broad issues of sense, nonsense and translation play out in particularly extraordinary ways in the writings of François Rabelais (1483/94–1553), as well as in the reception of his work in England at the turn of the seventeenth century.[1]

All of Rabelais's books in the sequence about the giants Gargantua and Pantagruel are marked by inexhaustible linguistic inventiveness, including prominent nonsensical episodes, especially the incomprehensible court case between Baisecul ('Kissebreech') and Humevesne ('Suckfist') in *Pantagruel* (1532), as well as the mock prophecies found in the 'Fanfreluches antidotées' ('Antidoted Fanfreluches') of *Gargantua* (1534/5).[2] Yet Rabelaisian nonsense is not restricted to these episodes, for his humour and verbal playfulness are always liable to spill into unreason of various forms. Following Noel Malcolm and taking my cue from Rabelais's own linguistic exuberance, I use 'nonsense' in a deliberately broad way, a 'cluster-concept' with examples on which everyone will agree and outlying areas which are less clear-cut.[3] Any stricter definition is liable to miss the very instances of incoherence or miscommunication that occur when languages and cultures intersect, which will be my focus. This in turn implies a broad understanding of translation itself, from the more or less literal to much freer adaptation. I shall however concentrate on works where Rabelais's influence is beyond doubt, namely two parodic English texts, John Eliot's language guide, the *Ortho-Epia Gallica* (1593), and a handful of the numerous 'Panegyircke Verses' that preface the travel memoir of Thomas Coryate (1577?–1617), *Coryats Crudities* (1611). This chapter will thus offer a detailed case study of the ways in which Rabelaisian nonsense was translated into English culture. What light do these works shed on the creation and dissolution of speech communities among London's cosmopolitan and multilingual merchants as well as the wits in the Inns of Court? Beyond such specific points, what does the translation of Rabelaisian nonsense tell us about the history of nonsense writing in Europe more generally, especially as it relates to modern foreign languages and those who speak them?

As will become apparent, works parodying late sixteenth-century language guides or mocking a man from Somerset who undertook a tour of Europe are scarcely the most radical contemporary religious, political or philosophical deployments of nonsense. In contrast to these later English works, Rabelais himself at times used nonsense to engage in satire of the papacy.[4] Similarly, the poet Clément Marot (1496–1544) who, unlike Rabelais, became a Protestant, invented a genre of nonsense verse, the 'coq-à-l'âne', which also features satire amidst overarching incoherence.[5] 'Coq-à-l'âne' was subsequently adopted for militant purposes by both sides in the long years of religious conflict in France, with dozens of examples over several decades.[6] Yet Eliot's work and the 'Panegyircke Verses' are not wholly apolitical for they engage, albeit in bizarre ways, with key contemporary concerns about unclear, excessive or duplicitous language.[7] Noel Malcolm's thesis that early modern English nonsense poetry is principally concerned with making a mockery of literature itself is not wholly convincing.[8] This is true even of the prefatory poems to *Coryats Crudities*, starting with what Malcolm considers to be the first piece of pure nonsense verse in early modern England, the 'Cabalisticall Verses, which by transposition of words, syllables, and letters make excellent sense, otherwise none, *In laudem Authoris*' by John Hoskins (1566–1638).[9] To illustrate some of the issues around modern foreign languages during the early modern period, and to give some essential background as to why Rabelais became an essential point of reference for English comic writing about such concerns, it will help briefly to look at a key episode in his fiction, namely Pantagruel's first encounter with his friend, the polyglot trickster Panurge.

Panurge's Languages

Walking outside the Paris city walls, Pantagruel, his servants and some scholars accompanying them see a dishevelled man approaching who nevertheless appears to the eponymous giant to have a noble bearing. Pantagruel decides to offer him help and asks a series of questions about who he is, where he has come from, and so forth, in mock epic fashion.[10] The stranger replies in fourteen different languages: German, Antipodean, Italian, Scottish, Basque, 'Lanternoys', Dutch, Spanish, Danish, Hebrew, Greek, Utopian, Latin, and, finally, French, which the stranger (soon named as Panurge) says is his mother tongue.[11] The companions are confounded by the languages they hear, including ones they could reasonably be expected to know or at least recognise, although the more learned in the group identify the Hebrew and the Greek, even though they do not decrypt it. Of the three made-up languages, Pantagruel has an impression of understanding the third, since it sounds like Utopian, and he is a native of Utopia, but this doubtless merely reinforces the tantalising quality of such made-up languages, which inevitably look or sound like other languages, hence Panurge's Utopian contains such simple French words including *dont* ('whose') and *vous* ('you'): 'Agonou dont oussys vous denaguez algarou: nou den farou zamist vous mariston ulbrou [. . .]'.[12] Rabelais makes the point all the more absurd by having

Pantagruel claim an impression of understanding of Panurge's made-up language because it reminds him of another invented one.

Such made-up languages or gibberish take nonsense writing to a logical extreme of sorts – they have the appearance of sense, and will often have recognisable elements within them for this very reason, but they ultimately frustrate the desire to find meaning, although this has not stopped some scholars from trying to translate them into sense.[13] Panurge's Utopian, which is of course inspired by the *Utopia* (1516) of Thomas More (1478–1535), boomerangs back to England in a poem 'In the Utopian tongue' by Henry Peacham (1578–1644?), one of the pieces of mock praise of Coryate, which in turn inspires similar pieces by the specialist of early modern nonsense writing in English, John Taylor (1580–1653), including two poems in Utopian and an 'Epitaph in the Barmooda tongue, which must be pronounced with the accent of the grunting of a hogge'.[14] More's, Rabelais's, Peacham's and Taylor's Utopias only resemble one another by looking like, but not actually being, languages. For instance, the opening couplet of More's quatrain in Utopian gives 'Utopos ha Boccas peula chama polta chamaan. | Bargol he maglomi Baccan soma gymnosophoan.'[15] The allusion to a gymnosophist at the end, for example, gives a hint of esoteric meaning, particularly tantalising to the scholarly types who would spot the allusion to these ascetic and mystical Hindu philosophers known to Alexander the Great. These made-up languages are therefore grist to Jacques Bouveresse's point that nonsense typically takes the form of an analogy of sense: a nonsensical expression looks like others that make sense, and we are provoked into seeking it.[16] The incomprehension of Pantagruel and his entourage is therefore performative in that it acts out the effects of nonsense, mirroring the impact on the reader. The tendency of scholars to find meaning in episodes which are specifically designed to deny it is therefore built into the very provocation of nonsense writing.[17] In other words, it might be professionally embarrassing for the critic to admit that the sense of an episode might ultimately be undecidable, and it certainly leaves the translator in a difficult position.[18]

Perhaps more unsettling than the nonsense languages is the way in which they cause Pantagruel and his followers to fail to react appropriately to, or even understand, the nine non-nonsense languages. Furthermore, in the latter Panurge always says the same thing, namely, that he is in need of sustenance before he can answer any questions. Given Panurge's appearance, the message of his different languages should be clear to Pantagruel and his companions even before he has spoken. Some sense goes without saying. The failure of Pantagruel and his followers to grasp Panurge's meaning is all the more disconcerting since this chapter immediately follows a much anthologised letter from Gargantua to his son, the eponymous giant, in which he lays out a humanist manifesto for language learning (of Greek, Latin, Hebrew, Chaldean and Arabic), having eulogised the invention of printing and the restoration of these ancient languages.[19] The humanist ideal is at the very least shown to be highly challenging in practice on this encounter with a polyglot like Panurge. His mastery, by implication, comes from travel and adventure, not book study, and the opposition between experience and scholarship underlies the chapter. The two co-exist awkwardly: it is not by accident that they encounter Panurge outside of the city walls, since this illustrates how he is not bound by the confines of academia. Panurge is furthermore a manifestation of the expanding boundaries of the early modern world. Rabelais thereby suggests that languages are best learned in interactions but also get mangled in them: nevertheless,

Panurge's approach has obviously been more effective than that of those who struggle to understand other tongues when away from their desks.

Panurge's multiple languages are moreover inspired by an episode in the most famous medieval French farce, *La Farce de Maistre Pierre Pathelin*, in which the eponymous hero speaks seven different languages to perplex a creditor.[20] However, as Terence Cave has pointed out in a major study of Rabelais's chapter within the context of modern language-learning in Renaissance Europe, Rabelais deliberately redraws the linguistic map in this episode.[21] While Pathelin speaks various dialects of French, especially of northern France, and some Latin, Panurge embraces European vernaculars of the kind that would have been heard among foreign students in the Latin Quarter in Paris.[22] By also having Panurge speak Hebrew and Greek, Rabelais alludes to the restoration of ancient languages that Gargantua mentions in his letter, and which had recently been put into practice by the creation in 1530 of the Collège Royal by François I (1494–1547), which included a professorship of Greek. The conclusion of the episode with French confirms contemporary decrees and manifestos for the language, including, famously, that of Villers-Cotterets (1539), which established French as the official language of administration within the kingdom, in opposition to the dialects spoken by Pathelin. For such reasons, Cave argues that, far from being a negative portrayal of the after-effects of Babel, the episode is in fact a celebration of the vernacular.[23] The chapter can thus be seen to champion national languages and even suggests, given the inclusion of Antipodean, the potential to extend these to the very ends of the earth.

Cave also shows that the episode in many ways resembles and indeed predicts manuals for learning modern languages, in which two or more vernaculars were presented side by side.[24] Yet the presence of nonsense and incomprehension in this chapter simultaneously suggest that this triumph of various national tongues, and even the study of them, was ambivalent. Language learning is always marked by the struggle to understand, which often feels like idiocy and/or is accompanied by the constant risk of losing face, while speakers of other tongues and dialects, including Panurge and Pathelin, are very often associated with vagrants, travellers, charlatans and merchants who have a tendency to befuddle their clientele. Other languages and those who speak them thereby pose various threats, which are very commonly exploited for comic purposes on the early modern English stage, not least in comedies at the turn of the seventeenth century in which nonsense Dutch often features. This in turn is a sign of London as a multilingual city in which peoples of different nations regularly struggled to understand one another.[25] It is in this context that Eliot's parodic language guide and the mock verses to *Coryats Crudities* appear, both making significant use of Rabelais and his nonsense.

John Eliot, *Ortho-Epia Gallica* (1593)

The *Ortho-Epia Gallica* is supposedly a guide to French pronunciation, as illustrated by its subtitle: *Eliots Fruits for the French: Enterlaced with a double new Invention, which teacheth to speake truly, speedily and volubly the French-tongue. Pend for the practise, pleasure, and profit of all English Gentlemen, who will endevour by their owne paine, studie, and dilligence, to atteaine the naturall Accent, the true Pronounciation, the swift and glib Grace of the noble, Famous, and Courtly Language.*[26] John

Eliot was a jobbing language teacher and translator.[27] Two points about his career are particularly important as far as his translation of Rabelaisian nonsense is concerned: first, he is mocking foreigners in London who set up shop around St Paul's in the late sixteenth century to teach modern languages, thereby taking clientele from their English counterparts; and, second, he was a translator of news from France – the *Ortho-Epia Gallica* contains numerous dialogues that involve the swapping of news and rumours about events across the Channel, including the opening of the dedicatory letter 'To the learned professors of the French tongue in the famous citie of London': '*Messires*, what newes from Fraunce, can you tell? Still warres, warres' (sig. A3r). Eliot's deployment of Rabelaisian verbal acrobatics is a carnivalesque release from both the seriousness of the conflict in France and from contemporary moralising language guides. In this way, Eliot predicts Lewis Carroll's nonsensical reworkings of moralising nineteenth-century verse for children. Although nonsense is by no means inevitably morally subversive – Eliot himself is somewhat conservative[28] – moral good sense, especially when didactically expressed, is clearly a tempting target for writers of nonsense.

Moreover, Eliot acknowledges and justifies his idiosyncrasy by claiming that he has written in 'a merrie phantasticall vaine [to] stir up the wit and memory of the learner' (sig. B1v). Humour might well form part of the art of memory, but nonsense goes a step too far for language learning for all but the most advanced learners. Alongside a reference to how the 'finest wits' (sig. B1r) read French, Eliot suggests a small circle of erudite readers who would be able to grasp his work, although the suggestion of just such a circle may itself be part of the highly Rabelaisian provocation of suggesting a higher, esoteric meaning to a serio-comic work. Nevertheless, only very advanced learners of French would be in a position to fully appreciate Eliot's jokes, not least given the highly challenging nature of Rabelais's language. What is true of Eliot is even more obviously the case of the 'Panegyircke Verses' to *Coryats Crudities*: deliberate mistakes and complex wordplay that spill into nonsense are perverse demonstrations of mastery that serve to reinforce the social bonds of the small groups that produce such works, and who share similar educational backgrounds.

The title page to the *Ortho-Epia Gallica* already indicates that this is not a wholly serious endeavour, from the absurdly learned Greek term 'orthoepy' ('correctness of diction') to the parodic allusion to the *First* (1578) and *Second Fruits* (1591), moralising and genteel Italian language guides by John Florio (1553?–1625), the famous translator of Montaigne into English.[29] The dedicatory letter, in Italian, to Robert Dudley mimics Florio's own dedication of the *Firste Fruites* to Robert Dudley, Earl of Leicester (1533–88), who had of course been dead for five years when the *Ortho-Epia Gallica* was printed, leaving the identity of the dedicatee of Eliot's work something of a mystery, if not a piece of nonsense.[30] Moreover, in his letter 'To the learned professors of the French tongue', Eliot draws attention to the difficulties of the enterprise of language learning, and especially of translation: 'I had some paine to make our English hybber-gybber jump just with the Jargon of Fraunce', he informs the reader, drawing on terms that suggest nonsense of various kinds, from gibberish to jargon (the cant language of thieves and travellers, also known as 'pedlar's French' in a typically xenophobic association between foreigners and criminality), thereby comically devaluing the vernacular and 'foregrounding the inarticulate speech that forms at the intersection of languages', as Carla Mazzio puts it.[31]

A particularly inspired representation of inarticulate speech, or rather incomprehension like that of Pantagruel and his followers, which may well have inspired Eliot, occurs in the dialogue 'La Bourse/The Exchange'.[32] This begins with just such a scene of misunderstanding. Men from England, Spain, Portugal and Italy all greet one another with terms of politeness in their native tongues, only for the perplexed Frenchman to miss the point of these phatic utterances and say 'Je n'entends pas Latin, monsieur' ['I do not understand Latin, Sir'].[33] Whereas Panurge's polyglot intervention on his first appearance in the giant tales takes place beyond the city walls with only one character mastering multiple languages, Eliot's reimagining of the episode suggests multilingual interactions were a very real part of everyday life in London, at least in such key places as the Exchange. Economic and multilingual exchange go hand in hand. Studying modern foreign languages was perhaps more the business of the merchant than the scholar, as Latin would still have been a lingua franca for the latter. Rabelais may already be playing on this point when the learned Epistemon claims to understand the Hebrew 'bien Rhetoricquement pronuncée' ['most Rhetorically pronounced'] after he has failed to understand Italian, for example.[34] Bilingual or trilingual dialogues in language manuals like those of Gabriel Meurier (1530?–1610), printed in another key centre of trade in the sixteenth century, namely Antwerp, are often presented with vim and wit and are specifically targeted at a readership of merchants.[35] Eliot takes the tendency to playfulness already present in such language guides beyond a heuristic technique to become a springboard for absurdity and nonsense. Again, only a linguistically advanced reader would get the joke – Eliot invites his readers who spot the Frenchman's mistake to join an elite group. Yet laughing at the witless Frenchman may be tinged with the worry that we may be inadvertently falling into the same trap ourselves. As critics we should not be too quick to assume that we are part of the circle of the initiated, or even that such a circle ever existed.[36]

Eliot's work thereby sheds an unusual light on ever-increasing encounters with other languages in the early modern world, especially in key locations such as London, and how these often result in incomprehension and nonsense. An early dialogue, 'De la dignité des Orateurs, et l'excellence des langues' ('Of the dignitie of Orators, and excellencie of tongues') is particularly important in providing this context. Eliot gives examples of extreme linguistic competence, including that of the great classical scholar Joseph Scaliger (1540–1609), who was apparently fluent in Hebrew, Greek, Latin, Spanish, Dutch, French, Italian, Numidian, Arabic, Assyrian, Persian, English and Chaldean (sig. F1r-v), in other words even more languages than Panurge (the insertion of Numidian, a lost language of Algeria, is however presumably a joke). There is nevertheless a marked sense of excitement in these dialogues about the possibility of learning multiple languages, and of a rapid growth of exposure to other languages as a corollary to voyages of discovery by Europeans. For example, one of the interlocutors discusses overhearing Japanese men speaking in Rome, describing their language as 'royal, foudroyant, superbe, glorieux, & magnifique à merveilles' ['princely, thundering, proud, glorious, and marvellous loftie', sig. H3r]. Similarly, in another inversion of European dominance, the languages of Mexico make Old World tongues seem like 'jargons barbares' ['barbarous prittle-prattle', ibid.].

Yet this dialogue is obviously hyperbolic to an extent that may cause the reader to question its eulogy of different tongues. There is a lingering concern that only a vanishingly small number of people can master multiple languages as Scaliger did, which is of course why he is presented as an exceptional case. Even when one of the interlocutors in the following dialogue, 'Le Voyageur' ('The Traveller'), praises Elizabeth I (1533–1603), who apparently knew eight languages (sig. L1r), Eliot is making an unacknowledged borrowing from Florio's *Firste Fruites* (1578), a work mocked throughout.[37] For mere mortals, such linguistic mastery remains a fantasy, not unlike the idea of Hebrew as the language of God, which expresses everything with perfect clarity, including the most secret matters of the heart (sig. F2r). Moreover, those who do master multiple languages may have a whiff of sulphur about them, as Panurge does: Coryate relates his encounter in Lyon with a Turk in the entourage of François Savary de Brèves (1560–1628), erstwhile French ambassador in Constantinople. The Turk is 'a great scholler in his kinde [who] spake sixe or seven languages besides the Latin, which he spake very well', yet he refuses baptism and is mentioned alongside Brèves's jester, 'a blacke Moore [. . .] a mad conceited fellow, and very merry', as if multilingualism were akin to folly.[38] The extraordinarily difficult yet somewhat suspicious nature of polyglot mastery indicates the impossibility of returning to the state before the fall of the Tower of Babel. Much of the time language learners are left floundering. Eliot's scene in the Exchange is much more representative of everyday life, making misunderstanding and nonsense the norm and competence the exception at least when speakers of different languages encounter one another, and possibly even beyond that.

Eliot constantly takes his readers down paths that lead to this conclusion. For instance, at an early stage of this supposed guide to French pronunciation, Eliot gives an impossible example of 'The volubilitie of the French tongue':

> The French use in one period (if a word end with a consonant, and the next following begin with an open vowell or dipthongue, no point or comma comming betweene) to pronounce three, foure, or five words with a swift voice together, as, *Prins en amour ardant embrassoit un image* ['Taken with burning love he embraced an image'], sound, *Preenzanamoorardantambrassoettewnneema*^{z}*ieh*, as if it were all but one word. (sig. C2v)

Mazzio claims this 'conglomerate "word"' is 'a veritable feast for the eye', yet it is above all a twist for the tongue, an alexandrine turned into a nonsensical neologism.[39] The line of French verse already discusses perverse desire for an image – a deliberate choice, no doubt, as Eliot's coining is itself an aberrant image of French pronunciation.

Among Eliot's numerous borrowings from Rabelais there are apparently none from the nonsensical court case between Baisecul and Humevesne and only one from the 'Fanfreluches antidotées' in *Gargantua*.[40] Nevertheless, the trend of the very frequent borrowings from Rabelais throughout the main part of the book, 'Le Parlement des Babillards' ('The Parlement of Pratlers'), is to portray language as so much chatter, gossip and illogicality veering into nonsense. For example, in the dialogue 'The Marriner', it is hard to know what a putative student of French pronunciation would have made of Eliot's transcription of Panurge's cries of fear during the storm in the *Quart Livre* (1552) – 'Bou, bou, bous, bous: paisch, bo-bo-bous: Be-be-be-bous: ho-ho-ho-zalas-helas!' – which are in turn translated or rather mistranslated in the parallel text with English onomatopoeia that seem to have less to do with fear than with the noise of the tempest: 'Dish, dash, plash, crack, rick-rack, thwack, bounce, flounce, rounce, hizze, pizze, whizze, sowze' (sig. o2v-o3r). Panurge's wails have changed into something else, as if Rabelais's original linguistic inventiveness gives Eliot licence to produce his own sound effects. In so doing, he gives the lie to the idea that onomatopoeia are invariably universal, pre-linguistic signs like animal cries, for even they seem to be culturally and linguistically inflected symbols.

In another episode, 'The Inne', Eliot borrows from *Gargantua*, XXXIX, 'Comment le Moyne fut festoyé par Gargantua, et des beaulx propos qu'il tient en souppant' ('How the Monk was feasted by Gargantua, and of the jovial discourse they had at supper'). In other words, this is a banquet scene, and the monk in question, Frère Jean, has licence to engage in repartee, including a nonsensical interlude in which he claims:

> De tous poissons fors la tanche, prenez l'aesle de la Perdrys, ou la cuisse d'une Nonnain, n'est ce falotement mourir quand on meurt le caiche roidde? Nostre prieur ayme fort le blanc de chappon.
>
> [Of all fishes, but the tench, take the wing of a Partridge, or the thigh of a Nunne; Doth not he die like a good fellow that dies with a stiff *Catso*? Our Prior loves exceedingly the white of a capon[.]][41]

Frère Jean is playing on a proverb, 'De tout poisson, fors la tanche, | Prens le dos et laisse la panche' ['Of all fish, except the tench, | Take the back and leave the belly'], which he turns into a piece of nonsense.[42] It is no coincidence that proverbs such as this one about fish, which already mean very little, should become one of the key building blocks of nonsense. As Stephen Booth puts it, a proverb like this is 'nonimporting pattern, pattern that fits the "nonsense" label because and only because it does not ordinarily signify anything', and it thereby 'takes the place of, does the job of, the ordinary, substantive, syntax-borne coherence that we expect, demand, and do not notice is absent'.[43] By juxtaposing such expressions in strange ways, writers like Rabelais as well as Clément Marot in his *coq-à-l'âne* bring out their innate nonsense, drawing their readers' attention to the underlying strangeness of everyday speech. Eliot follows suit:

> De tous oyseaux je n'ayme point l'oye ny l'oyson. / Of all birds I love not the goose nor the gosling.
>
> De tous poissons j'estime l'anguille poison. / Of all fishes I esteeme the Eele poyson.
>
> De tous poissons frais fors la tenche, prens l'aisle de la perdrix, ou la cuisse d'une nonnain. / Of all fresh fish except the tench, take the wing of a Partridge, or the buttocke of a Nunne.
>
> Je ayme fort le blanc d'un chapon. / I love wonderfully the white of the capon. (sig. p3v-p4r)

Proverbs are heavily deployed in language manuals, not least by Florio, to combine linguistic instruction with moral edification, a practice Eliot parodies through mock maxims like this one.[44] Yet Eliot is perhaps unwittingly even more nonsensical than Rabelais: the 'buttocke of a Nunne' is left hanging in the Englishman's version, although it is entirely clear why Frère Jean mentions it, given his comment about the joy of dying 'with a stiff *Catso*'.[45] Rabelais's ribaldry is too much for Eliot. Such bowdlerising shows how Eliot attempts to convey Rabelaisian culture with the nonsense, but without the obscenity, presumably because bawdiness would have offended the community of readers he addresses. Yet the ribaldry in Rabelais serves to bond the community together – jokes like these are emblematic of good fellowship. This male bonding is also a feature of nonsense, including the example of Frère Jean's parodic proverb about fish, because satirically coded or jokingly incomprehensible pieces serve to reinforce community ties, gesturing towards a common, shared knowledge and social standing. Despite his qualms about obscenity, Eliot offers no moral or didactic message, but instead suggests open-ended dialogue, which mocks earnestness and allows for other types of social bonding through linguistic play. Thus Eliot not only shows how language, and especially language learning, can lead to nonsense or incoherence, but also how idle talk may not be so idle after all, especially insofar as it can serve to reinforce social ties.

The 'Panegyricke Verses' to *Coryats Crudities* (1611)

The ways in which nonsense can reinforce social ties are particularly apparent among the group of over fifty young men of letters who gathered within and around the Inns of Court and taverns of London and who contributed parodic eulogies to *Coryats Crudities* (1611).[46] These mock encomia feature nonsense verse as well as other poetry in various ancient and modern languages, including French. The most developed of the French pieces is the twenty-six line 'Sonnet [*sic*] composé en rime à la Marotte' ('Sonnet composed in bauble rhymes') by Laurence Whitaker (1578?–1654), who was to become a distinguished parliamentarian.[47] Whitaker immediately places his work under Rabelais's banner. Coryate was from Odcombe in Somerset, something the wits play on constantly, and according to his fellow Somerset man Whitaker he is 'cet Heroique Geant Odcombien, nommé non Pantagruel, mais Pantagrue, c'est-à-dire, ny Oye, ny Oison, ains tout Grue' ['this heroic Odcombian giant, named not Pantagruel, but Pantagrue, that is to say, nither goose, nor gosling, but all crane [i.e. fool]']. Whitaker is playing on the Greek prefix 'panta-', meaning 'all', and the associations of the word 'grue', which not only designates a crane but also, according to Cotgrave, a 'sot, asse, goosecap, hoydon, lobcocke', presumably because this particular bird appears to be stupid.

Although less obviously nonsensical than Eliot's adaptation of Rabelais in 'The Inne', for example, Whitaker's so-called sonnet, and especially the notes in the margin, possibly by Coryate himself, stage deliberate mistakes and misunderstanding. For example, the first note claims that a 'marotte' refers to the other seminal writer of sixteenth-century French nonsense, Clément Marot, but it is in fact a fool's sceptre or bauble. Eliot also associates the French poet with folly, in the dialogue on languages, in which the interlocutors hesitate as to whether he was 'the Kings foole' or 'the Poet Roiall'.[48] Care needs to be taken here for 'artificial' folly, in other words a knowing performance that requires an effort of interpretation, as opposed to genuine mental incapacity, does not inevitably equate to nonsense, even if some instances, like those in *King Lear*, can come close.[49] As with Eliot's multilingual set piece at the beginning of his dialogue on 'The Exchange', the 'Panegyricke Verses' are designed to appeal a linguistically sophisticated *happy few* and, conversely, exclude the less knowledgeable. Coryate is a jester to the court of wits who gathered around the Inns of Court as well as local taverns, as he had earlier been at the household of the young Prince Henry.[50]

The mock learned notes perform error in a way that is reassuring to the reader who is pleased to spot deliberate mistakes. For example, returning to Whitaker's sonnet, a 'Badin' ('A foole, dolt, sot, fop, asse, coxcombe' according to Cotgrave) is glossed as 'Voyageur' ('Traveller'), supposedly from the Greek βαδίζειν ('to walk, go about, proceed'). This note encapsulates Coryate's role: he is both a learned fool and a not unlearned traveller who allows himself to be a willing object of mockery for the wits, not unlike Marot who is either the king's poet or his fool or perhaps both. Advanced language learners oscillate between the risk of error and foolishness on the one hand and demonstrating mastery on the other. Coryate thereby acts as a kind of safety valve for anxieties about mistakes that may lurk at the back of the minds of even highly competent practitioners of modern languages. Indeed, one of the contributors to the 'Panegyricke Verses', Ben Jonson (1572–1637), predictably makes mistakes and demonstrates a not very advanced grip of French when annotating his copy of Rabelais in private, including when he glosses the mock catalogue to the Library of the Abbaye de Saint Victor (*Pantagruel*, VII), which Whitaker also cites in the introduction to his sonnet.[51] Languages are not easy and Rabelais's French is particularly difficult. Allusions to Rabelais are simultaneously badges of learning and indications that one is beyond pedantry, given its mock scholarly content. Coryate thereby gives the wits licence to take pleasure in their learning and superiority while maintaining an appropriately ironic distance.

As Noel Malcolm points out, this kind of mock scholarship often comes very close to nonsense, another instance being a poem by 'Glareanus Vadianus' – probably the cleric John Sandford (1565?–1629) – in which a 'Bologna sawcidge' is glossed as a 'French *Quelque chose* farced with oilet holes and tergiversations, and the first blossoms of Candid Phlebotomie'.[52] The French and Latinate terms probably hide obscene content, especially given that the item being glossed is a sausage. Moreover, Malcolm considers such examples as evidence supporting his thesis that 'the real origins of nonsense writing are to be located' in 'precisely [this] sort of self-conscious literary or courtly milieu'.[53] The 'Panegyricke Verses' do undoubtedly lend themselves to this conclusion, given their parodic flaunting of various types of learning. Yet even in this context nonsense also reflects other concerns, not least about language learning. Rabelais himself is a badge of learning for English wits but also imaginatively a means of access to other social dimensions, as suggested by the adventures of the likes of Panurge. In a sense, his writings predict their own reception, both among scholarly types and others from different social backgrounds, hence it is no coincidence to find allusions to him in the main practitioner of English nonsense verse, John Taylor (1578–1653), the water poet, who, for example, lists the unlikely prospect of 'catch[ing] *Gargantua* through an augor-hole' among a list of impossibilities.[54] Rabelaisian nonsense plays out in highly learned, self-conscious settings, including the *Ortho-Epia Gallica* and the 'Panegyricke Verses', but even in these contexts it is has an energy that is always to spill out of footnotes into ways of reimagining various things, including encounters with speakers of other languages.

The English works discussed above appear strenuously unserious, especially when compared to others that discuss related issues in different contexts, especially in terms of religious conflict. To pick just one example among many, an anonymous *Remonstrance à Ronsard* (1563/4) accuses the great poet and Catholic polemicist Pierre de Ronsard (1524–85) of being someone 'Qui devant [le peuple] jargonne en langaige incogneu, | Qui luy caches du ciel le commun revenu' ['Who talks an unknown jargon in front of the poeple and hides from them heaven's shared bounty'] whereas this

Protestant author 'ne parle en Latin ny en langue Gregeoise, | Aincois publicquement en parolle Francoise' ['I never talk in Latin or Greek, but rather speak publicly in French'].[55] In contrast, Eliot's concerns about English 'hibber-gibber' and the 'jargon of France' or the mock footnotes to Coryate seem strangely reassuring. That may be part of their point. Even so, their more or less implicit concerns about language learning are not trivial and shed an unexpected light on attempts to come to terms with burgeoning trade, voyages of discovery, and ensuing multilingualism. While some aspects of Rabelais went too far – Eliot stops short of embracing his obscenity – at the same time the French author offered vital ways of thinking about language and culture. There is an ambivalence to such English works that show a certain fascination with Rabelais and other French authors, combined with a distrust of the foreign, whether it is in the form of professional language teachers in London or the mockery of a man who had travelled around Europe. They use nonsense as a means of acknowledging, but not resolving, this tension, while also advocating good fellowship combined with an appreciation of everyday nonsense in multilingual Renaissance London.

Notes

1. On Rabelais's influence on early modern English literature, see above all Anne Lake Prescott, *Imagining Rabelais in Renaissance England* (New Haven: Yale University Press, 1991); on Rabelaisian nonsense among London wits, see Noel Malcolm, *The Origins of English Nonsense* (London: HarperCollins, 1997), pp. 14–15.
2. François Rabelais, *Pantagruel*, Chapters X–XIII, and *Gargantua*, II; all references to the French will be to François Rabelais, *Œuvres complètes*, ed. Mireille Huchon and François Moreau (Paris: Gallimard, 1994); unless otherwise stated, English translations will be from Sir Thomas Urquhart's extraordinary mid-seventeenth-century translation, reprinted in *Gargantua and Pantagruel* (London: Everyman, 1994). Urquhart's version is the closest to Rabelais in spirit but not always accurate. For example, 'Baisecul' and 'Humevesne' are more properly 'Kissarse' and 'Suckfart', which the latest English translator, M. A. Screech, convincingly renders as 'Bumkis' and 'Slurp-ffart' (Randle Cotgrave's Rabelaisian *Dictionarie of the French and English Tongues* (London: Adam Islip, 1611) gives 'A sucke-fist; one that lays his nose on his next fellowes bumme' for 'Hume-vesne'; Cotgrave's translation is the only source cited for the *Oxford English Dictionary*'s entry for 'suck-fist', meaning 'a toady'); in contrast, M. A. Screech gives 'Antidoted Bubbles' for the 'Fanfreluches antidotées' (*Gargantua and Patagruel* (London: Penguin, 2006), p. 211), but Urquhart's choice not to translate a probably invented or at any rate highly unusual term in French is doubtless a more faithful option. The 'Antidoted Fanfreluches: or, a Galimatia of extravagant Conceits found in an ancient Monument' are also included in *The Chatto Book of Nonsense Poetry*, ed. Hugh Haughton (London: Chatto & Windus, 1988), pp. 70–3.
3. Malcolm, *Origins*, pp. xvii–xviii.
4. For example, the 'Fanfreluches antidotées' contain some transparent allusions amidst their overall obscurity, including the second stanza's '*Aulcuns disoient que leicher sa pantoufle | Estoit meilleur que guaigner les pardons*' ['To lick his slipper, some told was much better, | Then to gaine pardons and the merit greater'], which is clearly satirical of the Pope, his slipper, and the trade in pardons (*Gargantua*, II, *Œuvres complètes*, p. 11; *Gargantua and Pantagruel*, p. 27).
5. For a recent account of satire in nonsense writing by Rabelais and Marot, see Bernd Renner, '"*Difficile est saturam non scribere*": L'Herméneutique de la satire rabelaisienne', *Études Rabelaisiennes*, 45 (Geneva: Droz, 2007), pp. 146–53, pp. 171–99.

6. See Grégoire Holtz, 'Illogic and Polemic: The *coq-à-l'âne* during the Wars of Religion', *Gossip and Nonsense*, ed. Hugh Roberts and Emily Butterworth, (special issue of *Renaissance Studies* 30.1 (2016)), 73–87.
7. For recent work on such troubling, often demotic, language, see *Gossip and Nonsense*, ed. Roberts and Butterworth, and Emily Butterworth, *The Unbridled Tongue: Babble and Gossip in Renaissance France* (Oxford: Oxford University Press, 2016). This chapter emerges out of this work on gossip and nonsense in France and England.
8. Although this is Malcolm's main thesis (see p. 88), he also acknowledges the wider implications of nonsense in the context of what he calls the 'galloping linguistic self-consciousness' of the sixteenth and seventeenth centuries, p. 107.
9. Thomas Coryat, *Coryats Crudities* (London: W. S., 1611), sig. e6[r]; repr. in Malcolm, *Origins*, pp. 127–8 (see also pp. 12–19). For a discussion of Hoskins and similar contemporary English and French material, see my 'Comparative Nonsense: French *Galimatias* and English Fustian', in *Gossip and Nonsense*, ed. Roberts and Butterworth, 102–19.
10. Rabelais, *Pantagruel*, IX, *Œuvres complètes*, p. 246; the association between Panurge and his predecessor, the more illustrious trickster, Ulysses, already suggested by Pantagruel's questions, is made explicit later in the chapter (p. 249).
11. Rabelais added to the languages over successive editions, there are ten in the first edition of 1532, fourteen in the 1542 edition that is the base text for most modern editions. For a helpful table of Panurge's languages and a recent study of the episode, see Paul J. Smith, 'Les langues de Panurge: une relecture', *Rabelais et l'hybridité des récits rabelaisiens*, ed. Diane Desrosiers, Claude La Charité, Christian Veilleux and Tristan Vigliano, *Études Rabelaisiennes*, 56 (Geneva: Droz, 2017), 607–16.
12. Rabelais, *Œuvres complètes*, p. 249.
13. See Malcolm, *Origins*, pp. 106–7, citing Émile Pons, 'Les langues imaginaires dans le voyage utopique. Les jargons de Panurge dans Rabelais', *Revue de littérature comparée* 11 (1931), 185–218.
14. Peacham's poem, *Coryats Crudities*, sig. lir, and Taylor's gibberish poems are all included in Malcolm's anthology of nonsense verse, pp. 129, 139–41, 149; see also Haughton, *Chatto Book of Nonsense*, pp. 96–7.
15. Thomas More, *Utopia*, in *Three Early Modern Utopias*, ed. Susan Brice (Oxford: Oxford University Press, 1999), p. 127.
16. Jacques Bouveresse, *Dire et ne rien dire: L'illogisme, l'impossibité et le non-sens* (Nîmes: Jacqueline Chambon, 1997), p. 261.
17. On some of the myriad of often contradictory readings of *Pantagruel*, IX, see Paul J. Smith, *Las Langues de Panurge*, pp. 613–14, who sensibly talks of the perplexity of the modern reader faced with trying to find an overall meaning to the episode. For another instance of the tendency of scholarship to ascribe meaning to nonsense, see, for example, Myriam Marrache-Gouraud, '"Hors toute intimidation": Panurge ou la parole singulière', *Études Rabelaisiennes* 41 (Geneva: Droz, 2003), 23–44, who argues that the apparent incomprehension of Pantagruel and his companions points to an understanding of a different order (p. 39), although quite what this different order of understanding is remains something of a mystery.
18. On ultimately undecidable meaning in Rabelais, see Jean Céard, 'Introduction', *Rabelais et la question du sens*, ed. Jean Céard and Marie-Luce Demonet with Stéphan Geonget (Genève: Droz, 2011), 7–12, p. 8.
19. Rabelais, *Pantagruel*, VIII, *Œuvres complètes*, pp. 243–4.
20. The intertextual reference to Pathelin is made explicit in the text, Rabelais, *Œuvres complètes*, p. 248.
21. Rabelais, *Pré-histoires II: langues étrangères et troubles économiques au XVIe siècle* (Geneva: Droz, 2001), 25–101, pp. 75–80.

22. As M. A. Screech points out in his translation and edition of Rabelais, *Gargantua and Pantagruel*, p. 50, Latin would have been the main language spoken in the Latin Quarter but equally many other modern European languages would have been heard from foreign students studying in Paris.
23. Rabelais, *Pré-histoires II*, pp. 79–80.
24. Ibid. pp. 44–53.
25. For examples of nonsense and Dutch and recent scholarship in this area, see Adam Zucker, '*Twelfth Night* and the Philology of Nonsense', in *Gossip and Nonsense*, ed. Roberts and Butterworth 88–101, pp. 93–4.
26. John Eliot, *Ortho-Epia Gallica [. . .]* (London: John Wolfe, 1593); for recent scholarship on Eliot, see Carla Mazzio, *The Inarticulate Renaissance: Language Trouble in an Age of Eloquence* (Philadelphia: University of Pennsylvania Press, 2009), pp. 156–8 and pp. 166–7. For Eliot's very extensive borrowings from Rabelais, see David H. Thomas, 'Rabelais in England: John Eliot's *Ortho-Epia Gallica* (1593)', *Études Rabelaisiennes* 9 (1971), 97–126. This part of the current chapter builds on the introduction to in *Gossip and Nonsense*, ed. Roberts and Butterworth 9–16.
27. See Frances Yates, 'The Importance of John Eliot's *Ortho-Epia Gallica*', *The Review of English Studies* 7 (1931), 419–30 and *John Florio: the Life of an Italian in Shakespeares's England* (Cambridge: Cambridge University Press, 1934), pp. 139–73. The Huntingdon Library copy of the *Ortho-Epia Gallica*, available on EEBO, is signed and probably annotated by Harvey, available at <http://gateway.proquest.com/openurl?ctx_ver=Z39.88-2003&res_id=xri:eebo&rft_id=xri:eebo:image:22826> (last accessed 3 May 2021); the annotations, especially on the first part of the 'The Parlement of Pratlers', including one which notes Eliot's borrowing from Florio's *Firste Fruites* (1578) to praise Elizabeth I and her mastery of eight ancient and modern languages (see n. 37 below), sig. L1r, available at <http://gateway.proquest.com/openurl?ctx_ver=Z39.88-2003&res_id=xri:eebo&rft_id=xri:eebo:image:22826:40> (last accessed 3 May 2021). The British Library copy, C.33.b.43 (repr. Menston: The Scolar Press, 1968), also contains contemporary annotations, especially to the section on pronunciation (sigs C1r-C2v), indicating that the reader took the book seriously, at least at first. Both sets of annotations diminish as the volume progresses, doubtless because it becomes ever more idiosyncratic.
28. See, for example, the condemnation of Machiavelli and Aretino at an early stage of Eliot's dialogues, sig. D2v.
29. On the design of manuals for modern language learning, which Eliot also adopts for parodic purposes, see Guyda Armstrong, 'Coding continental: information design in sixteenth-century English vernacular language manuals and translations', *Renaissance Studies* 29.1 (2015), 78–102.
30. Eliot may have had Dudley's illegitimate son in mind, 'a wild and rather mysterious youth' according to Yates, *John Florio*, pp. 153–4.
31. Eliot, *Ortho-Epia Gallica,* sig. B2v; Mazzio, p. 280 n. 91. John Palsgrave already establishes the connection between jargon and 'pedlar's French' in *Lesclarcissement de la langue francoyse* (London: Johan Haukyns, 1530), fol. 368r; see 'French *Galimatias* and English Fustian', in *Gossip and Nonsense*, ed. Roberts and Butterworth, p. 107, n. 18.
32. See David H. Thomas, 'Rabelais in England', p. 120.
33. Eliot, *Ortho-Epia Gallica*, sig. d1v; see 'Introduction', in *Gossip and Nonsense*, ed. Roberts and Butterworth, p. 15.
34. Rabelais, *Œuvres complètes*, pp. 247–8.
35. See Cave, *Pré-histoires II*, pp. 56–62 and, for example, Meurier's bilingual guide to French and Flemish, the *Colloques, ou nouvelle invention de propos familiers* (Antwerp: Christofle Plantin, 1557).

36. See Adam Zucker 'Twelfth Night and the philology of nonsense', in *Gossip and Nonsense*, ed. Roberts and Butterworth.
37. 'Shee speaketh Greeke, Latine, Italian, French, Spanish, Scottish, Flemish, and English: al these tongues shee speaketh very wel, and eloquent', *Florio his firste fruites which yeelde familiar speech, merie proverbes, wittie sentences, and golden sayings. Also a perfect induction to the Italian, and English tongues [. . .]* ([London]: Thomas Dawson, for Thomas Woodcocke, [1578]), fol. 11v (dialogue 13).
38. Coryat, *Coryats Crudities*, pp. 64–5.
39. Mazzio, *The Inarticulate Renaissance*, p. 157.
40. The mock learned reference to 'the two egges of Proserpina', Eliot, sig. s1v-s2r; comes from Rabelais, *Gargantua*, II, *Œuvres complètes*, p. 13.
41. Rabelais, *Œuvres complètes*, p. 107; *Gargantua and Pantagruel*, p. 116.
42. See the accompanying endnote to Rabelais, *Œuvres complètes*, p. 107.
43. Stephen Booth, *Precious Nonsense: The Gettysburg Address, Ben Jonson's Epitaphs on His Children, and 'Twelfth Night'* (Berkeley: University of California Press, 1998), pp. 6–8.
44. Yates, *John Florio*, p. 168.
45. Rabelais's and Urquhart's terms are linguistic borrowings from the Italian 'cazzo', a standard way of more or less veiling obscenity, by putting it in another language.
46. For recent work on the *Crudities*, see, for example, Katharine A. Craik, 'Reading *Coryats Crudities* (1611)', *Studies in English Literature, 1500–1900* 44 (2004), 77–96; Andrew Hadfeld, *Literature, Travel, and Colonial Writing in the English Renaissance 1545–1625* (Oxford University Press, 2007), pp. 58–68; Michelle O'Callaghan, *The English Wits: Literature and Sociability in Early Modern England* (Cambridge: Cambridge University Press, 2007), pp. 128–52; Melanie Ord, 'Textual Experince in Thomas Coryat's *Crudities* (1611): Reading, Writing, Traveling', *Travel and Experience in Early Modern English Literature* (New York: Palgrave Macmillan, 2008), 123–54. On the seminal role of these verses in the history of English nonsense writing, and about the Mitre Tavern, see Malcolm, *Origins*, pp. 11–19.
47. Coryat, *Coryats Crudities*, sig. d6r-v.
48. Eliot, *Ortho-Epia Gallica*, sig. G4v.
49. See Malcolm, *Origins*, p. 114.
50. Ibid. p. 12.
51. See my 'Previously unnoticed annotations to Jonson's copy of Rabelais', *Notes & Queries* 61 (2014), 270–3.
52. Coryat, *Coryats Crudities*, sig. l2v; Malcolm, *Origins*, p. 15.
53. Malcolm, *Origins*, p. 114.
54. John Taylor, 'Sir Gregory Nonsence His Newes from No Place', included in Malcolm's anthology, p. 163.
55. The *Remonstrance* was collected in a manuscript by the Huguenot surgeon François Rasse des Noeux (?–1581), cited and translated by Butterworth, *The Unbridled Tongue*, p. 115.

14

Musical Foundations of Nonsense

Michael Heyman

For while Sense is, and must remain, essentially prosaic and commonplace, Nonsense has proved not to be an equally prosaic and commonplace negative of Sense, not a mere putting forward of incongruities and absurdities, but the bringing out a new and deeper harmony of life in and through its contradictions [. . .] [It is] a true work of the imagination, a child of genius, and its writing one of the Fine Arts.

Edward Strachey (1888)[1]

And what is the purpose of writing music? [. . .] the answer must take the form of paradox: a purposeful purposelessness or a purposeless play. This play, however, is an affirmation of life – not an attempt to bring order out of chaos nor to suggest improvements in creation, but simply a way of waking up to the very life we're living [. . .]

John Cage (1957)[2]

Much of the trouble critics have had in defining 'literary nonsense' has arisen from the latter half of the term, especially considering that we tend not to regard the canonical 'nonsense' of Edward Lear, Lewis Carroll and their artistic descendants to be 'meaningless' or 'worthless', as would be demanded by the word's literal, rather than literary meaning. As the nineteenth-century critic Edward Strachey argues, non-sense is *not* non-sense, and he struggles, as we critics have tended to do since then, to articulate exactly how this 'child of genius' functions within competing fields of language and logic. How strange, then, that John Cage articulates, in describing music, a directly comparable paradox. Then again, Strachey's words, written to eulogise and canonise the recently departed Edward Lear, also loop back around to claim nonsense as 'one of the Fine Arts', implying it goes beyond the literary. From different angles, Cage and Strachey seem to arrive at a similar destination: the relationship of meaning-making to paradox and performative play, in both music and the 'music' of words, the result being nothing less than revelatory. Perhaps, in this unlikely aesthetic confluence, the problems with the word 'nonsense' may be mitigated by questioning that which had been thought safe, the 'literary' element.

Strachey and Cage are tapping into discrete, often isolated, aesthetic critical traditions. Nonsense, after all, has frequently been defined ostensively, using the 'literary' works of its two 'fathers', Edward Lear and Lewis Carroll. More recently, Noel Malcolm unearthed another model, a poem from 1611 by John Hoskyns, but the assumption that nonsense is exclusively 'literary' has often remained; consequently, many critics since Strachey have focused on the genre being, as Vivien Noakes puts it, a 'universe of words'.[3] Limiting the focus to words and their sounds has not, however, stopped many critics from waxing lyrical about nonsense's 'musicality' and its relationship, as Strachey notes, to the 'Fine Arts', but almost always in an untutored, metaphorical or cursory manner, almost as if this musicality were an ideological obviousness unworthy of more than a nod.[4] Angus Davidson, for instance, writing in 1938, speaks of the sounds of words having a close relationship to music, where the overall effect is sonic rather than semantic, in the works of Edward Lear, who 'had an ear that was exquisitely sensitive to verbal music. Many of his lines – quite irrespective of their content – have a great beauty of sound.'[5] The focus on the literary has also limited the discussion of the 'musical' to the phonemes within neologisms and literary sound devices.[6] The height of this approach is Marnie Parson's *Touch Monkeys* (1994), which dives deeper, by way of Derrida, Deleuze and Orlov, into the semiotic implications of sound.[7]

While it is useful to discuss the 'music of words' metaphorically or phonemically, it happens that music, *real* music, has always played a much larger role, even in the 'literary' models of Lear and Carroll, as a few studies have recognised. Dealing specifically with Lear's work in relation to the piano and vocal music he composed, both for his nonsense texts and other more 'serious' pieces, are brief studies by Randall Thompson (with Philip Hofer, in 1967), Anne Henry Ehrenpreis (1979) and I. A. Copley (1980).[8] My own chapter in *The Aesthetics of Children's Poetry* (2017) and Richard Elliott's *The Sound of Nonsense* (2018) venture further in this area, recognising the fact that Lear's longer poems (the 'nonsense songs') are true songs, though little of the actual music survives.[9] Cecily Raysor Hancock (1988) has written in a similar vein on the music in Carroll's books and Saville Clarke's operatic version of *Alice*.[10]

For literary critics of nonsense this consideration of 'fine arts' performance, hinted at by Strachey, may be seen as a modern, 'progressive' step, but ask a musician, and the answer has long been more obvious. Towards the end of a long career Alfred Brendel, the respected pianist and poet, mocked one of the early proponents of nonsense, G. K. Chesterton, whose starry-eyed adoration betrayed his ignorance of its history. Brendel writes:

> When Edward Lear discovered Nonsense Poetry, Chesterton greeted him as a new Columbus. But nonsense poetry had been around, in one form or another, since the Middle Ages, and not just in England. The minnesinger Reinmar the Old had cultivated it already, and it is a nice thought that nonsense poetry, or *Lügendichtung*, may have been invented by a practitioner of love songs.[11]

There may have been reasons why Chesterton, no fool, might have thought Lear 'a new Columbus',[12] but the fact is that some critics outside of the field of literature like Brendel recognise the musical origins of nonsense, reaching back to the love songsters of medieval Germany, the Minnesingers.

What these critics recognise is that literary nonsense is often much more than literary, and if we take Lear's, not to mention the Minnesingers', performative song model ostensively, the door is not only open to new critical approaches but also to consideration of a host of texts that have not traditionally been included in the nonsense genre. We do not have to look far to see nonsense lyrics set to a fairly comfortable notion of musical genre in works from many eras. Folk songs often follow this tradition, songs like 'Nottamun Town', a musically simple tune which portrays in the lyrics an unstructured, upside-down world. African diasporic discords and native blues conspired to create the American form of jazz, which employed scat, or gibberish vocalised syllables, as heard from Louis Armstrong and Slim Gaillard. The mid-century ushered in a new wave of nonsense lyrics over structurally sound music, with neo-folk songs like Bob Dylan's 'Bob Dylan's 115th Dream' (1965) and the psychedelic pop of the Beatles' 'I Am The Walrus' (1967). Nonsense exists in hip hop, with artists like freestyling rapper Serengeti and wizards of absurd sampling, the Avalanches; in the oddball amphigory-rock of They Might Be Giants, and in the Sun Ra-meets-Tolkien-meets-Dalí-meets-Barfing Song God mythological worlds of Rushad Eggleston, master cellist and mad nonsense goblin of Snee.[13]

In all of these works, from 'Nottamun Town' to Eggleston's song actually and accurately titled 'Barfing Song God' (2015), the most common modus operandi is one in which music provides an element of stability, a kind of 'sense' against which the words may play more freely, just as in most nonsense verse where strict poetic form scaffolds the wild play of language and logic, creating the requisite 'balance between form and content'.[14] But the experience of this kind of music and word combination creates further nonsense effects. Norman Cazden, an aesthetic theorist and composer, argues in his collection *A Book of Nonsense Songs* (1961) that when

> words or the sounds of words are made to follow musical patterns rather than their own, the meanings of the words come out funny. Yet our habits of thinking in words lead us to seek their normal references and meanings just the same. The result is that special kind of imaginative humor called nonsense.[15]

To demonstrate word-music nonsense mechanics, Cazden points us towards 'Peter Gray', a folk song of thwarted love, wherein both the protagonist and his love Luciana perish tragically. The song begins traditionally, with four-line verses, regular metre and rhyme, and a simple melody. As the tune progresses, the verses begin to exploit the melodic pattern to force a change in the sounds of certain key words, sometimes creating nonsensical effects. The most radical sound and meaning shifts come in the bathetic fifth verse, where Peter, having been prevented from marrying Luciana, leaves his native 'Pennsylvane-eye-ay', only to find his bloody fate:

> But he went trading to the West
> For furs and other skins,
> Where he was caught and scalp-eye-ed
> By several in-jy-ins.[16]

The Burl Ives version of the same song has, in this verse, the variant 'blood-eye in-dye-yans' to rhyme with the 'fort-aye-yan' (for 'fortune') that Peter is seeking. The altered words in both versions all have the odd 'rhyme or extra syllable' Cazden mentions, so that they fit in the melody,[17] but the meanings also change. To be 'scalp-eye-ed', for instance, is not only less frightening than being 'scalped', but, oddly, funnier, all the more so because of the mispronounced, half-rhyming antagonists. The stereotype humour may be lost on us today, but that seems to have been the intended effect.

In 'Peter Gray', as in many of the folk songs in Cazden's collection,[18] the music provides a solid structural backdrop, a kind of 'sense' that is so persuasive, in a way, that the words, which create meaning differently from music, get swept up in its current. In Cazden's words, the 'musical logic of a good tune makes any incongruities in the sense of the words seem natural and right'.[19] Of course, words like 'scalp-eye-ed' and 'in-jy-ins' are *not* 'natural and right' but the nonsensical effect is not just in the semantic and logical phenomena in the language; it is also in their relationship to the music. That is, the 'sensical' music forces us to impose meanings unnatural to the naked, music-less words, while at the same time providing a formalistic smokescreen of familiarity. This is so of the folk music in Cazden's volume, and it is so in most of the music genres in which nonsensical lyrics appear.

If we expand the field of music and nonsense a little more, to include musical notation, another set of texts rushes in: nonsensical scores, inspired, perhaps, by John Cage, an originator of alternative music notation, and others who followed, such as Brian Eno and Krzysztof Penderecki.[20] In these experimental works, the relationship between traditional notational rules and the riotous liberties taken in dramatic flourishes and visual games lays the ground for what would come next, what we might call notational nonsense. John Stump, a reclusive American composer, is a master of this type of nonsense, as can be seen in his 'Love Theme from Prelude and the Last Hope in C and C♯ Minor' (1971), 'Faerie's Aire and Death Waltz' (1980), and *String Quartet No. 556(b) for Strings In a Minor (Motoring Accident)* (1997). Worthy of the pyrrhic challenge of musical analysis, these pieces are cyclones of mostly unplayable music notation, with overly dense clusters of notes that evoke infinitude and the rule-breaking employment of most elements of music notation. Akin to Erik Satie's humorously noted compositions, but magnified in intensity, Stump's pieces also employ bizarre directions to the musician on how they are to be played, including 'Like a Dirigible', 'add bicycle', 'rests are imaginary' and 'Have a nice day' ('Faerie's'). Like the best so-called literary nonsense, these scores brim with simultaneity, inversions and arbitrariness, and, importantly, much of their content makes sense: some notation rules are followed, some of the runs are playable, some of the directions are possible – even some of the more nonsensical ones.[21]

Notational chaos would be easy, but this is something else. As the excerpt in Figure 14.1 shows, Stump's work follows, for the most part, the basic conventions of music notation, such as the correct groupings of notes and staff and bar lines. Many of the dizzying runs and leaps here are *theoretically* playable (though often not on a violin). And yet, within the (mostly) rule-bound staves is careful linguistic, graphic and notational nonsense.

The directional notes alone demand a full-length study, but a few examples will have to serve. Instruction such as 'Pass the chicken, please' and 'in the frog' are out of context and absurd – though the 'frog' does leap up many times throughout the score, implying some consistency and meaning. 'With pesto' and '*Credenza*' are Italianesque misappropriations, and 'Slippery when wet', to most musicians at that time, almost certainly would refer to Jon Bon Jovi's 1986 twelve-time platinum album, incongruously mixing eighties glam metal with Western classical music. Stump's articulation signs are often decorative rather than functional, as the arbitrary auroral slurs in the first measure show. Another visual joke, the dense cluster of notes in the lower section creates in the negative space '1:21' (for some reason,

Figure 14.1 from John Stump's *String Quartet No. 556(b) for Strings In A Minor (Motoring Accident)* (1997).

perhaps a musical allusion). The time signatures 54/32 and 5/16 are ridiculous – though not impossible. But Stump's nonsense is even more devious, and the intrepid obsessive will discover that the upper 54/32 measure is a mere one 32nd note short of the metre, while the lower stave, though impossibly dense, has *precisely* twenty-seven 16th notes, the equivalent of the requisite fifty-four 32nd notes. Sense and non-sense are kept in careful balance in a similar manner throughout, creating a type of musical travesty since imitated by others such as Yamasaki Atushi and Andrew Fielding. This kind of composition occupies a unique position in terms of potential critical approaches, as it is notated music, weighted also with words, that is not meant to be heard but still could be, at least partially. Many of the tools of literary nonsense criticism can be brought to bear, in particular because, as we have seen, the nonsense functions partly by way of notational semiotics, which is much closer to written language than the ostensible product, the sounds in the air.[22]

Music *matters*, in other words, but the heart of the matter here, going back to the unlikely camaraderie between Cage and Strachey, is the manipulation of meaning-making through the overlapping, messy relationship between word and music. The study of this kind of relationship requires a revised approach to the nonsense models that accepts Cazden's and other music critics' forays, and goes further, to help us question, and perhaps move beyond, the *literary* in 'literary nonsense'. Providing a theoretical base for this effort, Calvin S. Brown, whose pioneering aesthetic theory marries the studies of music and literature, begins with the recognition that language and music, as 'auditory arts', share a unique connection, being 'dynamic and hav[ing] their extension, development, and relationships in time'.[23] He goes on to make distinctions, of course, primarily using the semiotic differences between the corresponding units of meaning: phonemes and words, in the case of language, and notes, chords, rhythms or melodic phrases, in the case of music. The distinctions notwithstanding, Paja Faudree, a linguistic anthropologist, has more recently expanded on this useful, even necessary, muddying, to account for a greater 'field' of meaning: 'The musical and linguistic signifiers making up this field compose an integrated expressive system whose components are differing, sometimes competing, overlapping, mutually influencing signs essential to human societies.'[24] To propose music as 'signifier' brings it into the field of semiotics, but doing so does not imply that *sense* is made; on the contrary, to have various codes and systems playing on the same 'field' often exposes the mechanics of meaning-making as problematic. That is, showing the necessary connections between words, music, and sound destabilises them.

This is the muddiness I would like to embrace, following Marnie Parsons, who defines nonsense as a 'converging, intermingling, transliterating that moves in and out of various sign systems and, in doing so, takes with it the residues of those systems'.[25] Parsons writes specifically of musical, visual, verbal, mathematical and philosophical systems, and argues that language 'laden with all these elements, must radically alter its movement',[26] or as Cazden might say, the words 'come out funny'. Because Parsons is dealing with such varied elements, she keeps them, conceptually, more separate, but as we have seen, music and language, especially language as it is used in nonsense, are more closely related. As Faudree states, music and language are 'variably constructed distinctions in a total semiotic field'.[27] In other words, the lines are disappearing between the systems of signs – and this new, bigger field is where nonsense loves to play.

But play requires a player. The last element to add to my approach here is the performative model of nonsense criticism in which nonsense becomes not just words which have 'come out funny', but our *experience* of their doing so, the result of a continual performative process, a kind of play. Alan Levinovitz takes up this thread, calling nonsense the 'experience of rewarding sense juggling' and acknowledging, as we have seen in Brown's work, the crucial element of time: 'Nonsense is something more than the quality of a symbol or set of symbols: it is the nexus of connection between ambiguous semantic elements, a reader, and a context, which together determine a particular and rewarding experience.'[28] The 'context' he mentions also brings in Susan Stewart's definition of nonsense as a textual, but also potentially extra-textual, act that exposes ideology as cultural construction.[29] Levinovitz's 'rewarding experience' is articulated by Richard Elliott, whose definition of nonsense, in a way, *is* this experience. He calls this the 'nonsense moment': 'a moment in perception when one is beyond, between or ahead of the moment of ascertaining sense. It is a glitch moment, a temporary period of blurring, the point in the process of code-switching where the codes are muddled.'[30] The 'codes' he refers to, I would argue, are best seen as the various elements that flourish on Paja Faudree's 'total semiotic field' where 'music and language are socially determined constructs that arbitrarily divide, in fundamentally cultural ways, a communicative whole'.[31] The goal is to embrace the 'whole' of nonsense, which includes, it would seem, far more things than have been dreamt of in our philosophies.

* * *

Cracking the concept of nonsense open to include performative processes in a wider semiotic field creates a jumbled tide of words and music that might seem to drown the distinctions of nonsense so carefully built by critics like Tigges, in an extra-literary flood. But at our darkest moments in nonsense definition, when the sheer array of words and music and notation and sound and critical confounding of it all threaten to beach us on the Chankly Bore, there is a way out. Despite the panoply of theories, most critics seem to agree, after all, on an ostensive approach – that Lear and Carroll's nonsense corpora define by example what we now call nonsense literature.[32] In terms of music and performance, Lear and Carroll would once again suit this role, as they have done in the few studies that incorporate actual music, but Noel Malcolm's scholarship offers an earlier example, a nonsense urtext, whose musical elements, by design or not, have been suppressed, but which, brought to light again, may bring us back from the brink.

Malcolm's *The Origins of English Nonsense* (1997), in part an anthology of nonsense literature from the seventeenth century, fills a significant gap in the intellectual history of nonsense while making a rather bold argument, that it is possible 'to attribute the origins of this genre to one poet in particular, and to explain how, when and why he created it'.[33] The originator, he claims, is the early seventeenth-century 'lawyer, rhetorician, minor poet and wit, Sir John Hoskyns'.[34] Not only does Hoskyns's poem 'Cabalistical Verses' exhibit the formal requirements of literary nonsense long before Lear and Carroll, but through this text (and as we shall see, his editorial elisions) Malcolm also makes a statement about the fundamental aesthetics and politics of literary nonsense.

Malcolm is responding to scholars who have seen nonsense as coming from a split background, allowing for the 'literary' side, but also noting the folk influence – and importantly, its connection to sound and music. Susan Stewart, for instance, has shown 'the study of nonsense literature forces a consideration of the literature as indebted to popular practice and that literature's populism is often best expressed by its reliance on, and experimentation with, sound'.[35] Likewise, when Kevin Shortsleeve exposes the near-ubiquitous mystical resonances of nonsense, his examples by and large come from Mother Goose, playground rhymes, and other bubblings-up from the oral folk tradition and Bakhtin's 'carnivalesque'.[36] Roderick McGillis also connects nonsense's 'incantatory force', its musical sonic rituals 'to nursery rhyme and fairy tale'.[37] In all of these cases, the sonic aspect is associated with the 'low' cultures of childhood, folklore or the people's popular carnival tradition, and this is exactly what Malcolm argues against:

> [F]ull-scale nonsense poetry as an English literary phenomenon is not a timeless thing, springing up here, there and everywhere of its own accord; still less is it something that wells up from folk culture. It is, rather, a literary genre with a particular history or histories, developed by individual poets and possessing a peculiarly close relationship [. . .] to the 'high' literary conventions of its day.[38]

Reflecting Tigges's strict theory, Malcolm argues for the 'high' culture origins of nonsense rooted in the *literary*, in 'individual poets', as opposed to multi-modal 'low' cultural readings. While this argument may indeed balance other studies that, perhaps, tilt too far in the 'folk' direction, its insistence on an exclusively '"high" literary' derivation comes, it seems, at the cost of ignoring the actual *music* integrally connected to Hoskyns's piece, music that has aesthetic and cultural resonance.[39]

Malcolm's argument is based on Hoskyns's poem, 'Cabalistical Verses', which appeared in *Coryat's Crudities* (1611), a travel journal by the infamous Thomas Coryate, a member of the 'Fraternity of Sireniacal Gentlemen' that met in the London's Mermaid Tavern and was populated by revered artists and intellectuals like Ben Jonson, John Donne and, probably, John Hoskyns.[40] Coryate's infamy began with his travel book documenting his peregrinations, mostly on foot, through Europe. Opening the volume was a section common at the time: a set of verses from literati in praise of the author. Coryate's book, however, went down a stranger path, in that it became the fashion for the wits of the day to write *mock*-panegyrics, blasting in fustian fullness what they reckoned to be Coryate's oversized ego and exaggerated travel exploits.

Among this set of fifty-six of the most distinguished intellectuals of the day we find Hoskyns and his 'Cabalistical Verses', making merry with the risible Coryate. The poem begins with the culinary and wild piscine pranks now familiar in modern nonsense:

> Even as the waves of brainlesse butter'd fish
> With bugle horne writ in the Hebrew tongue,
> Fuming up flounders like a chafing-dish,
> That looks asquint upon a Three-mans song [. . .][41]

This poem sparked a fad within the fad of mock-panegyrics, with contributors like John Taylor (the ablest nonsense successor to Hoskyns) joining in – and unwittingly helping to define what we now call the genre of nonsense literature. And yet, as I have briefly mentioned, when we look to Hoskyns's work, we find more nonsense flora than the one piece Malcolm plucked. In fact, Hoskyns's 'section' includes *eight* parts: after the aforementioned poem comes a grotesquely ornate description of impossible song lyric metre, a scansion chart that is and is not a representation of the described metre, two long measures of annotated and notated music, lyrics and a Latin semi-pseudo-quasi-translation of the lyrics. Lastly, there is a longer mock-heroic tribute verse and a postscript, mostly in Latin. Not only is there nonsense of various kinds in these pieces, but, more significantly for our purposes here, at least six of the eight sections are related to, or simply are, music. If we accept Malcolm's argument that the nonsense genre, in a way, 'sprang, almost fully armed, out of Hoskyns's head'[42] we should consider *all* of Hoskyns's nonsense, which includes music.

Contrary to how they are printed in the Malcolm volume, the verses are not titled, but rather begin with a description:

> Cabalisitical Verses, which by Transposition of Words, Syllables, and Letters, make excellent Sense, otherwise none.[43]

Malcolm argues convincingly that these verses are a model of the nonsense genre over two hundred years before Lear's *A Book of Nonsense* (1846). He cites the absurd linguistic excesses stemming particularly from the 'fustian' mode common at the time, which used overblown scholarly verbiage against itself. Of course, what sets this verse apart from other parodies and travesties common in contemporary 'drolleries' is the extremes to which Hoskyns takes his mockery, the code-switching and leaps of logic. Malcolm also observes that these are purported to be, of course, 'Cabalistical', thus placing them ostensibly in the tradition of Jewish mystic thought and inviting us into an arcane process of meaning-making.[44] Engaging the performative challenge of this invitation evokes further levels of meaning that play along the borders of word and music. In fact, this 'spiritual' element proves to be pivotal to the nature of nonsense, as shall be discussed more fully below.

Malcolm's recognition of the poem's arcane formulae argues well for the 'high-literary' origins of nonsense, but now, finally, to address the musical elements, beginning with the more conventional references. Making an incongruous appearance is a 'Three-mans song' (a 'part-song for three male voices'),[45] which is somehow disdained, or looked at 'asquint', by the likes of a 'chafing-dish', of all indignities. The code shift from aesthetic to cooking categories (not to mention the ambiguous syntax) creates the nonsense moment, something that also may happen with the mention of squeezing the 'spheares', mixing, potentially, the famed celestial music with lowly 'dust'. The most telling musical reference, however, connects to the linguistic: the 'bugle horne' incongruously adorning the 'waves' of fish, or possibly the fish themselves (again, the syntax is unclear). Rather than simply a 'horn', which might imply any animal's accoutrement, this is a 'bugle' horn, a musical protuberance and quite possibly a reference to the *shofar*, the ram's horn played bugle-like in Jewish religious services. This horn is immediately linked, cross-disciplinarily, with linguistic output, as it is (somehow) 'writ in the Hebrew tongue'. Orality aside, this 'tongue' of course stays within the titular description involving Kabbalah, which in turn evokes myriad possibilities concerning music and language within that tradition – a world evoked and discarded – fulfilling the typical nonsense function of implying meanings while denying their certitude. The mystical implications, however, are amplified by the parts that follow and the success we will have in making partial sense, by nonsense methods, of what appeared to be merely non-sense.

The references to music in this poem still bound the semiotic field with words; that is to say, words *about* music are not the same as words, or symbols, meant to *represent* music. Next in the original we find a series of interconnected sections that begin to do just that: just below the 'Cabalistical verses', on the far left of a vertical dividing line, is a scansion chart; on the right, what appears to be a description of lyric metre (Figure 14.2). The next page has a description of the music, and then two notated measures, with the beginning of the lyrics beneath (Figure 14.3). What follows is the full set of lyrics, starting with 'Admired Coryate [. . .]', as confirmed within the notation, and then an eight-lined section labelled 'The same in Latin'. It is these parts, restored here to complete Hoskyns's full work in the volume, that add more sonic and musical dimensions to nonsense.

Immediately, there is some confusion as to what, exactly, the scansion chart and rhythm description reference. Beyond the succession of texts on the page, the concept of 'Cabalistical Verses' jibes with what follows, especially knowing the arcane complexities behind Kabbalistic hermeneutic traditions, roughly summarised in the opening description, of the necessary 'Transposition of Words, Syllables, and Letters'. There is no reason to believe that these structural elements are *not* associated with

---vv--vv-vv
---vv--vv-vv
---vv--v-v-v
---vv-v-v-v

Encomiological Antispasticks,

Consisting of Epitrits, the fourth in the first syzugie, which the vulgar call Phaleuciac hendecasyllables; trimeters Catalectics with Antispastic Asclepiads, trimeters Acatalectics consisting of two dactylicall commaes of some learned named Choriambicks, both together dicoli distrophi, rythmicall and hyperrythmicall, amphibologicall, dedicated to the undeclinable memory of the autarkesticall Coryate, the only true travelling Porcupen of England.

Figure 14.2 John Hoskyns, *Coryat's Crudites*, ed. Thomas Coryat (Glasgow: James MacLehose and sons, [1611] 1901), p. 58.

Also there is this tune added to the verses, and pricked according to the forme of Musicke to be sung by those that are so disposed.

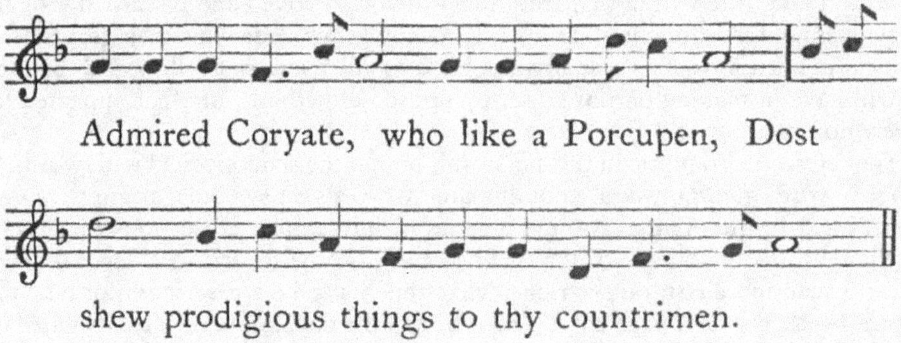

Admired Coryate, who like a Porcupen, Dost

shew prodigious things to thy countrimen.

Figure 14.3 John Hoskyns, *Coryat's Crudites*, ed. Thomas Coryat (Glasgow: James MacLehose and sons, [1611] 1901), p. 59.

the opening verses, except, of course, once we turn the page and get to the notation, with lyrics within, where it becomes clear we may have been duped. The verses beginning 'Admired Coryate [. . .]' (also twelve-line iambic pentameter), an amusing mock-heroic comparison of Coryate to a porcupine, are the true lyrics, which makes things easier until we realise that these lyrics are actually quite clear in their meaning: there is nothing 'Cabalistical' about them, and yet the metre chart and description are in the obscurantist vein, creating an irreconcilable conundrum, a 'nonsense moment', as Elliott would call it, when we are caught between the lyrics *before* or *after*, nonsense or sense.

With the scansion chart and rhythmic description, we arrive at the point where Hoskyns's nonsense jumps the rails into sonic realms represented by differing, sometimes non-lingual semiotic systems. A full analysis of the musical implications is not possible within this space, but a few telling examples should prove more than adequate, given the technical, multimodal complexity, to begin mapping a larger semiotic field. Let's begin with the 'Encomiological Antispasticks' section, which, contrary to its appearance, is far from gibberish. This section is a wild, seemingly impenetrable, sesquipedalian, logorrheic concatenation of what are actually legitimate terms relating to the metrical analysis of classical Greek and Latin poetry, a subject that would have been quite familiar to Hoskyns and the educated audience of the day. And while it might have been easy for Hoskyns simply to jumble these terms together to create a fustian, gibberishy mix, as we'll see, his mash-up was far more clever: a cross-disciplinary virtuoso act of nonsense with sonic, musical, linguistic, and even spiritual, implications.

The section starts with 'Encomiological Antispastics', typographically larger, in what appears to be a title but is just the beginning of a serpentine sentence that describes the lyrics' metre within what we soon learn to be a 'tune'. In this sentence are three subsections, each describing one metrical subset of the 'Antispastics'. In other words, the 'Encomiological Antispastics' consist, so the sentence implies, of (1) epitrits, (2) 'trimeters Catalectics, with Antispastic Asclepiads', and (3) 'trimeters Acatalectics consisting of two dactylicall commaes', with each of these subsections containing further technical elaboration. The terms, as has been noted, are all legitimate in themselves; the only flaw is that most of this is quite impossible.

The passage begins with what appears to be the blanket lyrical form on which everything that follows is an elaboration, but even in these two words is a direct impossibility: an 'Encomiological Antispastic'. *Encomiological* refers to a compound metre, consisting of two-and-a-half dactylic feet, added to two-and-a-half iambic feet, creating: (– ∪ ∪ – ∪ ∪ –) + (∪ – ∪ – ∪). An *antispastic* is one metrical foot consisting of an iamb and a trochee, back to back (∪ – – ∪). Whether we look at only one unit of these, or line them up to see if a chain of them might bring out connections, it becomes clear that antispastics simply can't be encomiological; antispastics do share one of the basic encomiological feet, the iamb, but this is trivial considering all of the other basic differences relating to duration and pattern. This kind of irreconcilability is compounded within this section as each archaic term hops on the wordpile.

The rhythmic impossibilities quickly mount to dizzying heights, reminding us of Hoskyns's initial challenge, as to whether the words make no sense at all or if, through active manipulation, we can make them make 'excellent Sense'. In other words, is this simply, as the contradictory 'Encomiological Antispasticks' seem to show, rhythmic gibberish, a fustian fulsomeness that functions to negate sense entirely? My argument here is that it is not. Hoskyns's qualification '*excellent* Sense' [my emphasis] may be a sly wink to signal that his entire exercise is different from, and more clever than, what we might call utilitarian, 'normal' sense; it exists between the poles of non-meaning and sense, a rhythmic, aural type of *nonsense* that hearkens back to our definitions involving time, 'nonsense moment'-making, code-switching, and a tension between mystical meaning and lack of meaning. To verify this, we need to prove at least partial logical connections that tie word to symbol to sound via the suggested 'Cabalistical' process.

Diving deeper into the labyrinthine and mathematical-linguistic machinations of pseudo-Kabbalah reveals that the 'Encomiological Antispastics', contrary to the prior analysis, are not exactly impossible. 'Encomiological' is an adjective, after all, and even though, as we have seen, an antispastic can't *be* encomiological, it would not be so unreasonable to try to follow the syntactic 'instruction', to *make* antispastics 'encomiological', or at least more so. The most logical method to do this would be to apply the 'encomiological' metrical *process* to the antispastics. Thus, we replace the encomiological (dactyl/iamb) feet with antispastic feet (iamb/trochee) but still follow the rule of multiplying the foot by two-and-a-half. The result is this:

∪ – – ∪ (+) ∪ – – ∪ (+) ∪ –

Classical scholarly eyebrows may rise at this impossible exercise, but the effort is rewarded when we compare the result to the scansion chart positioned on the page next to the descriptive paragraph, in a kind of visual simultaneity that implies equivalency. When we line up our retooled 'Encomiological Antispasticks' with the first line of this chart, we make a startling discovery:

Our retooled version (repeated twice):
∪ **– – ∪ ∪ – – ∪ ∪ – ∪** – – ∪ ∪ – – ∪ ∪ –

The chart's scansion of line one:
– **– – ∪ ∪ – – ∪ ∪ – ∪** ∪

The bold portions of the scansion above show the exact match, revealing that with our half-true, 'Cabalistically' derived 'encomiological' antispastic, we actually arrive at something startlingly close to the scansion chart. The trick is to start on the *second* beat; the following *ten* syllables match the original foot of Hoskyns's scansion exactly, making a surprising ten out of twelve total. What appeared to be non-sense has turned out to be nonsense: the pattern of resemblance and lack thereof, over and over again, creates a kind of balance to the impossibility, the kind of unresolved tension nonsense thrives on. We experience Elliott's 'nonsense moment' in the constant shifting back and forth between sense and nonsense, between systems of sound, metrical representation, and linguistic semantics, all in the service of a quasi-spiritual 'method' validated by the method's partial success.

The joke is not just on poor Thomas Coryate, but also on us. In addition to the metre description and the scansion chart, Hoskyns has carefully built up three more layers of rhythms, including the bars of music notation, the actual English song lyrics, and the pseudo-Latin 'translation'. Each has a kind of coherence within itself, in addition to possible internal contradictions. Likewise, in relation to each other, some points align, and some do not, creating a rhythmic palimpsest of sorts. The nonsense is, in part, our experience in moving between musical and linguistic systems which never allow us to resolve the tensions. These 'nonsense moments' are themselves what end up revealing the significance of how music and nonsense intertwine in this (according to Malcolm) first example of what might now seem (half) a misnomer, 'literary nonsense'. Perhaps, as Elliott suggests, we can now finally 'attend more dutifully to those "funny noises" which are so crucial to nonsense',[46] to mind the music within and without. In doing so, we begin to account for what this wider field of meaning-making signifies.

The kind of juggling Hoskyns's texts invite may sound familiar, as it brings us back to his initial description (and invitation), the 'Cabalistical Verses, which by Transposition of Words, Syllables, and Letters, make excellent Sense, otherwise none'.[47] If such play is all baroque nonsensical fantasy, blame Hoskyns: he teases us into attempting the arcane, technical procedures of Kabbalah with systems of music and language – and he provides plenty of coherence that rewards (though never fully) such manipulations. In other words, he makes mystics of us – and of nonsense.

While spirituality within nonsense has been noted from the start, going all the way back to Strachey's 'deeper harmony of life', a more common critical stance has been to observe how the 'fastidious and concrete' nonsense world, crowded as it is with a decidedly earthly host of owls, household utensils and plum pudding, eschews spirituality. Elizabeth Sewell, one of the most influential critics of nonsense, writes, 'Far from being ambiguous, shifting and dreamlike, it is concrete, clear and wholly comprehensible.'[48] In a similar vein, Jacqueline Flescher comments on Carroll's work, where 'Meaning is often purely physical or factual. [Nonsense] leaves no room for speculation or suggestion and therefore refers to nothing beyond itself.'[49] Still, a mystical nonsense underground has always been around, highlighted, oddly enough, by Sewell herself, whose last chapter of *The Field of Nonsense* consciously reverses, in a way, her prior claims (in the same book) of nonsense being exclusively a closed circle of logical play. She likens our playing nonsense games to Plato's concept of a playful God, and also to the Hindu god Shiva and his consort at dice, 'For words and play together fringe out into liturgy and magic.'[50] Kevin Shortsleeve has given the fullest accounting of this 'hidden' mysticism, noting its contradictory nature. He argues that, while nonsense is known to manifest

> an overt mistrust of all that is spiritual, magical, or divine – a deeper look reveals that [it] has been consciously or unconsciously cribbing from occult traditions for ages and, more specifically, that in the impossible spaces that nonsense occupies and promotes, there are profound echoes of an intimate ancestral connection to the spiritual and supernatural.[51]

This is not to say that nonsense and spirituality are necessarily the same, of course, but that they seem to 'echo' similar ways of meaning-making – and that such echoes are intrinsic to nonsense.

Perhaps the most famous proponent of nonsense spirituality was G. K. Chesterton, who noted, 'This simple sense of wonder at the shapes of things, and at their exuberant independence of our intellectual standards and our trivial definitions, is the basis of spirituality as it is the basis of nonsense.'[52] Chesterton argues that nonsense invites us to expand our critical apparatus beyond logic to embrace the hidden nature of reality, its surprising 'exuberance'. Just as Sewell turned to the East for spiritual parallels, we may also witness a similar line of thought in fifteenth-century Indian mystic, Kabir, who was known for poetry exhibiting impossibilia and logical wild goose chases. Kabir's nonsensical poetry became known as 'twilight verse', implying existence between states, between day and night. Hess and Singh have related this 'in-betweenness' to Kabir's leading us to see beyond *maya*, the illusory world that we take for reality, by making us aware of our own position between truths, between systems of belief like Hinduism and Islam.[53] In other words, enlightenment is existing in the nonsense moment. Indeed, we are brought back to John Cage, who, though in a more secular manner, reflects the desires of Kabir by using music as a 'way of waking up to the very life we're living'. Roderick McGillis furthers the quasi-mystical discourse in literary studies, arguing that the sonic devices of nonsense 'do more than add sound patterns to a rhythmic scutter; they draw attention to language itself as both a communicative and an incantatory force'.[54] Nonsense becomes all the more tenebrous and 'incantatory' (leaning on the 'singing' in the Latin *cantare*) when we add *music* to the linguistic sound devices McGillis discusses.

In a postscript to his volume of nonsense poetry and song, iconic Zen philosopher Alan Watts writes, '*Life is a kind of nonsense* in the same way that music is a kind of nonsense, because music isn't usually supposed to mean anything other than itself.'[55] Either music can or cannot mean, but, regardless, a thing that means 'itself' still has to contend with the nature of that self – not a bad start to philosophical rumination. Even Watts, whose own nonsense marries nursery rhyme, folk tale, koan and music, while trying to deny meaning, betrays the possibilities nonsense offers in treading upon wider semiotic fields. Whatever 'meanings' may arise, however, may be less important than what we do to arrive at them, and thus, the spirituality of Chesterton, Kabir and Watts, and the 'spiritual' mock-Kabbalah of Hoskyns's set of palimpsestic texts, can operate as metaphor for the processes of experiencing nonsense, moving in the 'nonsense moments' of medial states. And even with more strictly 'literary' nonsense like that of Mervyn Peake, Edward Gorey or Carl Sandburg, the music within the ostensive nonsense models of Lear, Carroll, and now, Hoskyns, may yet reverberate.

Notes

Many thanks to: Kevin Shortsleeve, Joseph T. Thomas, Jr, Jodie Tesoriero, Mark Simos, Mark Sylvester, Marti Epstein, Rebecca Marchand, James Revell Carr and Emily Petermann.

1. Edward Strachey, 'Nonsense as a Fine Art', *Quarterly Review* 167 (1888), 335–65, p. 335.
2. John Cage, *Silence* (Middletown, CT: Wesleyan University Press, 1967), p. 12.
3. Vivien Noakes, *Edward Lear: The Life of a Wanderer*, revised edn (Stroud: Sutton Publishing 2004), p. 193.
4. Full disclosure: I am equally guilty of such waxing.
5. Angus Davidson, *Edward Lear: Landscape Painter and Nonsense Poet* (London: John Murray, 1938), p. 198.
6. More recent critics, discussed below, have invited music back into the discussion. Even Vivien Noakes found it necessary to emend her original assertions about strict linguistic 'purity'. In the revised 2004 edition of her authoritative Lear biography, she includes, in several places, Lear's musicianship as a part of his nonsense, and she even adds a footnote relating nonsense to the 'oral and dramatic inheritance' of classical roots, including music and dance (p. 276).
7. Marnie Parsons, *Touch Monkeys: Nonsense Strategies for Reading Twentieth-Century Poetry* (Toronto: University of Toronto Press, 1994), p. 134.

8. Phillip Hofer and Randal Thompson, 'The Yonghy Bonghy Bò', *Harvard Literary Bulletin* 15.3 (1967), 229–37. Ann Henry Ehrenpreis, 'Edward Lear Sings Tennyson's Songs', *Harvard Literary Bulletin* 27.1 (1979), 65–75; I. A. Copely, 'Edward Lear: Composer', *Musical Opinion* 104 (1980), 8–9.
9. Michael Heyman, 'That Terrible Bugaboo: The role of music in poetry for children', in *The Aesthetics of Children's Poetry*, ed. Katherine Wakely-Mulroney and Louise Joy (London: Routledge, 2018), 162–81. Richard Elliott, *The Sound of Nonsense* (London: Bloomsbury, 2017).
10. Cecily Raysor Hancock, 'Musical Notes to *The Annotated Alice*', *Children's Literature* 16.1 (1988), 1–29.
11. Alfred Brendel, 'On Humour, Sense, and Nonsense', *Music, Sense and Nonsense: Collected Essays and Lectures* (London: Robson, 2015), 431–6, p. 433.
12. Brendel's definition of nonsense is fairly loose, and these German 'lying-songs', while related to modern nonsense, are quite different from what Lear created.
13. See Elliott's chapter 'Pop Hearts Nonsense' in *The Sound of Nonsense* for a survey of these types of musical nonsense. Note, also, that not all of the lyrics mentioned here fit perfectly into the genre. They fall into the nonsense 'spectrum' in various ways. Scat singing, for instance, is usually just melodic gibberish, lacking enough 'sense' to make us question the semantic meanings of the lyrics.
14. Wim Tigges, *An Anatomy of Literary Nonsense* (Amsterdam: Rodopi, 1988), p. 74.
15. Norman Cazden, 'Introduction', *A Book of Nonsense Songs*, ed. Norman Cazden (New York: Crown Publishers, 1961), p. iii.
16. Cazden, *Nonsense Songs*, p. 67.
17. 'Indians', of course, would have worked in Cazden's version, as it contains the required three syllables, but the word being used is the slang and offensive (and two-syllable) term 'Injins'.
18. For tamer, more traditional versions, also see *The American Songbag*, ed. Carl Sandburg (Chicago: Harcourt Brace, 1927).
19. Cazden, *Nonsense Songs*, p. iii.
20. Jimmy Stamp, '5 1/2 Examples of Experimental Music Notation', *Smithsonian Magazine* (5th June, 2013)<https://www.smithsonianmag.com/arts-culture/5-12-examples-of-experimental-music-notation-92223646/>(last accessed 10th February 2017).
21. After all, one *could* 'add bicycle' to music, an idea that may have come about from Frank Zappa's bicycle-playing debut on the Steve Allen Show in 1963.
22. Music and nonsense meet in myriad other ways, of course. In *The Sound of Nonsense* Richard Elliott also takes on, among other texts, Kurt Schwitters's sound poetry, the experimental music of Cage and the sound experiments of the Fluxus movement.
23. Calvin S. Brown, *Music and Literature: A Comparison of the Arts* (Hanover and New England: University Press of New England, [1948] 1987), p. 10.
24. Paja Faudree, 'Music, Language and Texts: Sound and Semiotic Ethnography', *Annual Review of Anthropology* 41 (2021), 519–36, p. 520.
25. Parsons, *Touch Monkeys*, p. 137.
26. Ibid. p. 137.
27. Faudree, 'Music, Language and Texts', p. 520.
28. Alan Levinovitz, 'Slaying the Chinese Jabberwock: Toward a Comparative Philosophy of Nonsense', *Comparative Literature* 69.3 (2017), 251–70, p. 255. This is a term partly from Michael Heyman, 'A New Defense of Nonsense; or, "Where then is his phallus?" and other questions not to ask', *Children's Literature Association Quarterly* 24.4 (1999), 187–94, p. 193.
29. Ibid. p. 49.
30. Elliott, *Sound of Nonsense*, p. 3.

31. Faudree, 'Music, Language and Texts', p. 520.
32. Hugh Haughton, for instance, dubs Lear and Carroll the 'godfathers of nonsense [. . .] whose names are almost synonymous with nonsense, and whose work stands at the centre of the eccentric "nonsense canon"', ('Introduction', *The Chatto Book of Nonsense Poetry* (London: Chatto and Windus, 1988), p. 7).
33. Noel Malcolm, *The Origins of English Nonsense* (London: Fontana, 1997), p. 4.
34. Ibid. p. 5.
35. Elliott, *Sound of Nonsense*, p. 12.
36. Kevin Shortsleeve, 'Nonsense, Magic, Religion and Superstition', *Bookbird* 53.3 (2015), 28–36.
37. Roderick McGillis, 'Nonsense', *A Companion to Victorian Poetry*, ed. Richard Cronin, Alison Chapman, Anthony Harrison (Oxford: Blackwell, 2002), 155–70, p. 167
38. Malcolm, *Origins*, p. 4.
39. The punchline, it seems, is that the music referenced in the Hoskyns texts is actually quite clearly not from the folk tradition; rather, it is based on classical Greek and Latin rhythmic terms and scansion, as well as epic (rather than lyric) metre within the lyrics, as the following analysis shows.
40. Malcolm, *Origins*, p. 12.
41. John Hoskyns, 'Incipit Joannes Hoskins', *Coryat's Crudites*, ed. Thomas Coryat (Glasgow: James MacLehose and sons, [1611] 1901), p. 58.
42. Malcolm, *Origins*, p. 5.
43. Ibid. p. 58.
44. Hoskyns and his audience probably knew little of Kabbalah, but they 'may have had some knowledge of [its] techniques of verbal and numerical analysis' (Malcolm, *Origins*, p. 16).
45. Malcolm, *Origins*, p. 127.
46. Elliott, *Sound of Nonsense*, p. 11.
47. Hoskyns, p. 58.
48. Elizabeth Sewell, *The Field of Nonsense* (London: Chatto and Windus, 1952), p. 23.
49. Jacqueline Flescher, 'The Language of Nonsense in *Alice*', *Yale French Studies* 43 (1969–70), 128–44, p. 137.
50. Sewell, *Field of Nonsense*, pp. 183–4.
51. Shortsleeve, 'Nonsense, Magic, Religion', p. 35.
52. Chesterton, 'Defence', p. 49.
53. Kabir, *The Bijak of Kabir*, trans. Linda Hess and Sukhdeo Singh (Oxford: Oxford University Press, 2002), p. 146.
54. McGillis, 'Nonsense', p. 167.
55. Alan Watts, 'On Nonsense', in *Nonsense* (New York: E. P. Dutton [1967] 1977), 41–2, p. 41.

15

Doubtful Girls and Silly Women: Nonsense and Gender

Anna Barton

Charles Dickens disapproved of no-nonsense women. At the beginning of *Hard Times*, Mr Gradgrind, a character who embodies the evils of patriarchal utilitarianism unmitigated by a sympathetic imagination, singles out Mrs Gradgrind as a desirable spouse because she has 'no nonsense' about her: 'Mr Gradgrind in raising her to her high matrimonial position, had been influenced by two reasons. Firstly, she was most satisfactory as a question of figures; and, secondly, she had "no nonsense" about her. By nonsense he meant fancy.'[1] In *Great Expectations* Estella, the victim of Miss Havisham's misguided parenting, mourns the lack that Gradgrind celebrates: '"Oh! I have a heart to be stabbed in or shot in, I have no doubt," said Estella, "[. . .] and of course, if it ceased to beat I should cease to be. But you know what I mean. I have no softness there, no – sympathy – sentiment – nonsense"'.[2] These two examples propose nonsense, fatally missing from these two damaged or deficient women, as a crucial feminine quality, a quality that Dickens associates with fancy and with feeling. In both cases, Dickens brings up the question of feminine nonsense when he writes about marriage. A lack of nonsense is of particular note when it comes to considering a woman's ability to perform her role as a wife and mother. For Dickens, then, nonsense begins at home. It is part of the private, domestic realm that balances and sustains public, social life: the feminine other of rational masculinity.

Writing about gender binaries, Caroline Levine observes that masculinity and femininity, 'do [. . .] not emerge out of given or prior sex distinctions, but [are] repeatedly asserted and reasserted through attention to norms and deviations'.[3] Likewise, nonsense, as its name suggests, is instinctively understood as a deviation from sense that reaffirms its norms. Levine also argues that the relative nature of gender identity is created in order to assert power: 'gender is an organising principle by which social groups come to be organised in a hierarchy, one high and one low, one wielding power and the other coerced into service'.[4] Although we may not wish to go so far as to say that nonsense is coerced into the service of sense, nonsense has been identified as the means by which sense patrols and asserts its own boundaries. As Jean-Jacques Lecercle puts it, nonsense 'enables the subject to construct a world of values around her, to establish the boundaries of her world, of the possible and of the acceptable'.[5] In this way, nonsense, like femininity, can be understood as a negative category, a condition of lack, or a space beyond. By extension, nonsense literature becomes a means to inhabit and experience that space and to expose as false the divisions and hierarchies that create it. Beginning with a brief discussion of Wonderland, a space that is both the dreamscape of a young girl and the fantasy of a male author, this chapter moves on to look at two women writers, Christina Rossetti and Stevie Smith, who return to Wonderland and the Looking-Glass World and find new ways to navigate, lay claim to, or escape from these feminine underworlds. The final section looks to Smith's affinity for Edward Lear's silliness, and proposes silliness as a quality that might disturb the boundaries by which gender constructs itself.

Doubtful Girlhoods

Like Dickens's cautionary sketches of bad wives, Carroll's *Alice* books propose nonsense as a kind of writing that might have something to say about femininity and, more broadly, about the relationship between sense, nonsense and gendered identity. During Chapter 5 of *Alice's Adventures in Wonderland* a caterpillar and then a pigeon ask Alice to identify herself. Their requests cause Alice some difficulty because, as she says to the Caterpillar, she 'has made several changes' since she got up this morning and so her identity is now uncertain.[6] But eventually, in order to refute the pigeon's accusation that her long neck and her penchant for eggs identify her as a serpent, she 'doubtfully' asserts that she is 'a little girl' (*AW* p. 41). Alice may well doubt her littleness. By this point in the novel she has gone through five changes in size. However, Alice has no cause to doubt her girlishness. Although the inhabitants of Wonderland and the world beyond the looking-glass frequently mistake Alice for something or someone else, they consistently recognise her femininity. The Lion and the Unicorn, who think Alice is a 'monster' and refer to her as 'it', are the two exceptions to this rule, but even they have reverted to the feminine pronoun by the end of their chapter. Likewise, when Alice wonders at her own identity, the possibilities she considers never trouble her gender. Whether she is worrying that she might have become Mabel, considering whether she will ever become 'an old woman', or hoping that she might become queen, Alice's femininity remains a stable characteristic in the midst of the various fluctuations she undergoes.

Nina Auerbach observes that the Alice, who 'explodes out of Wonderland hungry and unregenerate', is a uniquely complex representation of Victorian femininity.[7] Driven by appetite, prone to violence, Alice's dream-self represents a femininity that is both post-Darwinian and proto-Freudian.[8] At the same time Wonderland becomes a space in which to satirise the conventions of Victorian femininity and to explore transgressive possibilities for alternative ways of being female. Carroll's achievement in this regard relies, in part, on nonsense literature's intentional irresponsibility: the way nonsense asks to be dismissed as mere child's play, 'stuff and nonsense', 'nothing but a pack of cards'. Hugh Haughton captures this aspect of nonsense when he calls it 'a dialect of innocence, a language associated with childhood, but somehow divested of the burden of meaning'.[9] However, the innocence of Carroll's nonsense is only ever temporary and so Alice's errant femininity cannot exist outside her dream. The beginnings and endings of both *Wonderland* and *Through the Looking-Glass* include more conventional, less interesting sketches of Alice that frame and moderate the nonsensical extremes of Alice's dream-self. At the end of *Wonderland*, Alice's elder sister re-dreams Alice's dream, transforming her little sister into a girl with a 'simple and loving heart' (p. 111). Likewise, a prefatory poem to *Through the Looking-Glass* addresses Alice as 'Child of the pure unclouded brow | And dreaming eyes of wonder!'

(p. 116). Here Carroll both asserts the virgin purity of Alice's inner life and chooses the gender-neutral 'child', which might be read as both an acknowledgement and a denial of Alice's troubling girlishness.[10] Both Alice's sister and Carroll himself appear deliberately forgetful of Alice the serpent and Alice the monster, who remain safely contained within Wonderland.

But Alice's rich literary and cultural afterlife disturbs the boundary between sleeping and waking that Carroll's text insists upon. From the late nineteenth century onwards writers, especially women writers, have adopted Alice into their works via direct reference or allusion, allowing her to inhabit a huge range of different texts and contexts. At the end of the nineteenth century, Mary E. Coleridge's poem, 'The other side of a mirror' (1896) reimagines Alice's looking-glass self becomes 'a woman wild | with more than womanly despair'.[11] Riding the crest of second-wave feminism, Angela Carter's short story, 'Woolf Alice' incorporates Alice's latent bestiality into her postmodern feminist fairy tale, while her novel *The Magic Toyshop* weaves allusions to Alice into its magic-realist-feminist *Bildungsroman*.[12] In the early decades of the twenty-first century, Siri Hustvedt's playful, allusive novel, *The Blazing World*, tells the story of a sculptor, Harriet Burden, who, posing as a man, exhibits a sequence of 'story boxes' that employ a Wonderland iconography as part of their representation of monstrous, mythic femininity: a 'female figure, disproportionately large for the room, [who] must bend her head to fit under the ceiling'; and a 'disturbing fuzzy mammal, something like a rabbit, but not a rabbit'.[13] Of this handful of examples, taken from a large and growing list of Alice's literary offspring, none sits easily with the description 'nonsense literature'; but, by incorporating Carroll's dream child into their work, Coleridge, Woolf, Carter, Hustvedt and many others carve out space for the subversive gender-play of Victorian nonsense. The remainder of this chapter explores the work of two writers, Christina Rossetti and Stevie Smith, who likewise employ their nonsensical inheritance to reflect upon and challenge their position within a gendered hierarchy.

Christina Rossetti and the Nonsense of Female Authorship

Christina Rossetti, a poet whose lyric and devotional work has been important for the developing understanding of nineteenth-century feminine poetics, was also an aspiring nonsense writer. She could claim a direct connection to the tradition via her acquaintance with Charles Dodgson, whom her brother commissioned to photograph the Rossetti family in 1863. In 1865 Dodgson sent a copy of *Wonderland* to Christina, her mother and her sister. Rossetti responded to the gift with a letter, offering 'a thousand and one thanks – surely an appropriate number – for the funny, pretty book you have so kindly sent me. My mother and sister as well as myself made ourselves quite at home yesterday in Wonderland.'[14] Nearly a decade later, Rossetti published a second response to Carroll's book: *Speaking Likenesses* (1874), a collection of three linked stories, narrated by an irritable nurse to the children in her charge, in which three young girls find themselves in dream worlds that resemble distorted reflections of the world they leave behind. In the first and longest of the three tales, Flora, a girl who behaves badly at her eighth birthday party, falls asleep during a game of hide-and-seek and finds herself in a nightmare version of her own festivities, encountering a magnified version of her brattish manners, a red-faced girl with a tinsel crown. The queen is accompanied by a group of companions, Hooks, Sticky, Slime and Quills, each named for a peculiar physical disfigurement, who terrorise her, sticking her with pins and pelting her with glass bricks, until she wakes to find herself back at home and just in time for tea.

Speaking Likenesses is full of direct allusions to the *Alice* books: descriptions of flowers that 'rang without clappers' recall the 'garden of live flowers' in *Through the Looking-Glass*,[15] and Flora enters her wonderland by following the written instruction, '"Ring also" printed in black letters on the brass plate; all as plain as possible in the lamplight' (*SL* p. 16), just as Alice's progress through Wonderland begins when she follows written instructions that command her to 'Eat me' and 'Drink me'. The nurse-narrator also makes a number of self-conscious references to the 'wonderful' nature of her story: replying to a request from one of her charges that she must 'be wonderful', she says, 'Well, Laura, I shall try to be wonderful; but I cannot promise first-rate wonders on such extremely short notice' (p. 71). Rossetti's allusions to Carroll invite us to understand *Speaking Likenesses* as what U. C. Knoepflmacher describes as an 'antagonistic work', a jaded mirror image of Looking-Glass World that blurs the distinction between nonsense literature and the moral tales that nonsense appears to satirise.[16]

This story and the other two in the collection are an uncomfortable mixture of Carrollian nonsense and the kind of moral tales written by earlier authors such as Maria Edgeworth and Mary Martha Sherwood. Popular in the eighteenth century, the moral tale for children is a genre that has been recognised by feminist criticism for its role in the development of a female literary tradition. In the mid-1980s, Mitzi Myers made the case for the significance of this previously overlooked body of work, identifying a 'matrilineage of nursery novels' that 'comprehends an undervalued and almost unrecognised female literary tradition, the more revelatory because it *is* didactic, because it accepts and emphasises the instructive and intellectual potential of narrative'.[17] By openly satirising the kind of didactic children's literature that, like his child-abusing, croquet-playing duchess, looks for the moral in everything, Carroll dismisses this kind of feminine authority. By contrast, Rossetti's disturbing, violent, nonsensical surreal appears to be put to instructive use. The nurse-narrator, a figure borrowed from Sherwood's *The Governess* (1820), models the didactic work of storytelling that imparts both 'wonder' and ethical guidance. It is a balancing act that perhaps seeks to claim nonsense as part of a feminine tradition of writing for children, rather than (as in Carroll's work) a departure from it, reasserting the authority of the woman's voice within the domestic space of the nursery.

Carolyn Sigler also argues that questions of gender and authorship can be brought to bear on an interpretation of this generic oddity. She suggests that, along with other female-authored Alice spin-offs published in the last decades of the nineteenth century, *Speaking Likenesses* employs Carroll's characters 'to dramatise the incongruous status of female authorship, trapped in a middle ground between private and public, simultaneously enacting the ideals of domestic ideology while reacting against those ideals'.[18] In other words, Rossetti's stories suggest that the woman writer is herself a nonsensical figure because the published word is a breach of femininity, properly understood as a condition of domestic confinement. For Rossetti, then, nonsense is not simply the feminine other to rational masculinity, but is instead a kind of writing that gives voice to aspects of identity that refute the binary categorisations of gender.

In a letter to her publisher Rossetti refers to an early draft of *Speaking Likenesses* as 'Nowhere', a working title that seems further to suggest that Rossetti's nonsense tales are concerned with the displaced gender identity of Rossetti as female author, caught between the private realm of femininity and the public realm of authorship.[19] A later letter from Rossetti to her publisher explains her final choice of title:

> And then I really must adopt 'Speaking Likenesses' as my title [. . .] Very likely you did not so deeply ponder upon my text as to remark that my small heroines perpetually encounter 'speaking (literally speaking) likenesses' or embodiments or caricatures of themselves or their faults. This premised, I think my title boasts some point and neatness.[20]

This rather laboured account puts Rossetti's book in touch with a nonsense tradition in a way that might disrupt the instructive encounter between the heroine and her 'embodied faults' that Rossetti's letter describes. As Rossetti points out, the wordplay of the title relies on taking literal meaning from an idiomatic expression, a trick that Rossetti borrows from Carroll (think of the drawing of 'muchness' in the Dormouse's tale). The point about a speaking likeness, of course, is that it is *not* 'literally speaking'. A portrait might be so vivid that we can imagine it stepping out of the frame and engaging us in conversation, but the sense of the phrase rests on, and therefore might be said to emphasise, the certain knowledge that paintings *do not* speak.[21] If *Speaking Likenesses* is a nonsense text that stages the conundrum of female authorship, the punning wordplay of its title brings related questions of speech and silence to the fore.

Christina Rossetti, artist's model and unofficial sister-member of the Pre-Raphaelite brotherhood, was uniquely positioned to appreciate the silence of the visual image. Her sonnet, 'In an Artist's Studio' (1856) describes a room full of paintings as a hall of looking-glasses, each projecting a new iteration of the same female figure:

> One face looks out from all his canvasses,
> One selfsame figure sits or walks or leans;
> We found her hidden just behind those screens,
> That mirror gave back all her loveliness.[22]

But, as the sonnet concludes, the likeness is false, reflecting the unnamed woman, 'not as she is [. . .] but as she fills his dream'. Like Alice, the model, 'queen', 'saint', 'angel' is a dream-girl, figment of the male artist's imagination.[23] In *Speaking Likenesses*, Rossetti returns to this hall of mirrors, employing allusions to the *Alice* books to reframe her interest in the way female identity is reflected and refracted within the cultural imagination. The walls, floor and ceiling of the room where Flora first encounters the red-faced queen are 'lined with looking-glasses' (*SL* p. 18). The narrator comments that, 'at first this did not strike Flora as any disadvantage, indeed she took a long look at her little self at full length' (p. 18). Flora is initially able to take pleasure in the fact that she is the complete subject of her own confident gaze. But Flora's pleasure and confidence are short-lived. She soon discovers that, whereas in *Through the Looking-Glass*, the mirror is a portal into and out of Wonderland, the mirrors in this post-Carrollian dreamland keep her trapped against her will:

> If she could only have discovered the door, she would have fled back through it to the yew-tree walk and there have moped in solitude, rather than remain where she was not made welcome; but either the door was gone, or else it was shut to and

> lost among the multitude of mirrors. The birthday Queen, reflected over and over again in five hundred mirrors looked frightful, I do assure you: and for one minute, Flora's fifty million fold face looked flushed and angry too. (p. 18)

As Flora loses herself within the near-infinite repetitions of her own image it becomes difficult to distinguish between her and her speaking likeness. The passage recalls Alice's own attempts to get into the garden that she spies through a small door at the beginning of *Wonderland*, attempts that are repeatedly frustrated by her dramatic shifts in size. But in Rossetti's text questions of identity and agency are put at risk by the uncertain status of the female image, rather than by the transformation of the female body. Rossetti is concerned with femininity as construct, rather than as essential physiological fact. Like 'In an Artist's Studio', *Speaking Likenesses* appears to be informed by a deep unease about the visual representation of femininity, suggesting that a likeness can only ever speak in a disciplinary capacity, identifying and magnifying aberration in order to enforce conformity.

Whereas *Speaking Likenesses* employs allusions to Victorian nonsense in order to expose the vexed position of the woman writer, Rossetti's poetry draws on nonsense stratagems to evade the constraints that gender imposes on creative ambition. 'Winter: My Secret', a poem that Rossetti originally titled 'Nonsense', is a gleeful lyric experiment that makes its feminine privacy public by transforming poetic form into an inaccessible, deliberately inarticulate space:

> I tell my secret? No indeed, not I;
> Perhaps some day, who knows?
> But not to-day; it froze, and blows, and snows,
> And you're too curious: fie!
> You want to hear it? well:
> Only, my secret's mine, and I won't tell.[24]

Rossetti levels a teasing accusation at the reader that places us back in the company of Carroll's dream-child. Like Alice, we are '[too] curious'. In the *Alice* books, Alice's curiosity leads her and her readers through Wonderland: female interiority is laid bare via Alice's intrepid exploration of her own dreaming mind. By contrast, Rossetti's lyric signals interiority, but denies the reader access. Her speaker simultaneously incites and resists curiosity. As a number of critics have observed, 'Winter: My Secret' can be understood as an intervention into a lyric tradition that is often associated with direct and intense emotional expression (taken literally to mean a 'pressing out', a transference from interior to exterior, from private to public).[25] Rossetti's poem practises deliberate restraint, drawing attention to the give and take of lyric transaction and inviting reflection on the (implicitly gendered) power dynamics of an exchange between a female poet and her audience.

As Rossetti's original title suggests, her refusal to satisfy the reader's curiosity is also a refusal to make sense. The poem's riddling discourse, which has something in common with Alice's frustrating conversations with the Mad Hatter, the Duchess, Humpty Dumpty and any number of the other characters she encounters in Wonderland, breaks the social rules of engagement and in so doing exposes the social assumptions that predicate meaningful speech. The speaking silence of its secrecy is antisocial in the way that it demarcates and defends a space of private knowledge or sensation. Rossetti's speaker conflates this secret with her body and her home:

To-day's a nipping day, a biting day;
In which one wants a shawl,
A veil, a cloak, and other wraps:
I cannot ope to every one who taps,
And let the draughts come whistling thro' my hall;

These corporeal and domestic allusions point towards the possibility that the privacy of nonsense might offer particular opportunities for feminine discourse in a world where the rules that determine social (sensical) utterance are part and parcel of patriarchal systems and structures.

If nonsense provides a means to ward off unwelcome curiosity, it also sanctions and facilitates a different kind of curiosity, one that leads the feminine subject both beyond and further into herself. A review of *Speaking Likenesses* in *The Athenaeum* commented that 'Miss Rossetti's are pretty, fanciful stories, which would have been more original if Alice had never been to Wonderland.'[26] Rossetti made no secret of her debt to Carroll, describing the work in a letter to her brother as, 'merely a Christmas trifle, would-be in the Alice style, with an eye to the market'.[27] However, the line of influence runs both ways. Just as *Speaking Likenesses* draws directly on the looking-glass, Red Queen and talking animals of Carroll's text, Carroll's Alice is drawn from a literary tradition of curious girls that must include 'Goblin Market', which Rossetti published three years earlier. Like *Wonderland*, Rossetti's most famous poem tells the story of a pair of sisters, one of who is inclined to wander/wonder. Just as Alice is led to Wonderland by a talking rabbit wearing a waistcoat, Laura is led astray by an encounter with a band of human-animal hybrids:

Curious Laura chose to linger
Wondering at each merchant man.
One had a cat's face,
One whisk'd a tail,
One tramp'd at a rat's pace,
One crawl'd like a snail,
One like a wombat prowl'd obtuse and furry,
One like a ratel tumbled hurry scurry.[28]

Here again it is Laura's curiosity and her capacity for wonder that motivate her adventure; and, like Alice, whose dream-world is structured around encounters with various kinds of food and drink, Laura's curiosity awakens her appetite. Rossetti's poem expresses its anxieties about the cost of satisfying that appetite more directly than do Carroll's nonsense works: after tasting the goblin fruit, Laura falls into a mortal decline; whereas for Alice, who remembers to check that the little bottle from which she drinks is not marked 'poison', eating and drinking pose no threat to life. But in both texts consumption also provides the means to salvation or transformation. When Laura's sister Lizzie returns from her violent encounter with the goblin men, covered in juice from the fruit they have attempted to force into her mouth, she instructs her sister to 'eat me, drink me, love me', making of herself a Eucharistic offering that translates bodily sacrifice into spiritual sustenance.[29] After falling down the rabbit hole, Alice eats a cake labelled 'Eat me' and drinks from a bottle labelled 'Drink me' while standing on the wrong side of a door to a beautiful garden. The redemptive promise of this second Eucharist proves false when Alice finds herself, not back in Eden, but splashing around in a Darwinian pool with a collection of other animals. Nevertheless, imbricated allusions to Genesis and to the Gospels in both 'Goblin Market' and *Wonderland* allow both texts to claim Eve as the archetypal curious child and to suggest the broader application of the paradoxical femininity that nonsense exposes. This, and Rossetti's other intertextual exchanges with Carroll, demonstrate her alertness to the connections between the different literary traditions in which they worked and propose nonsense as both a critical expression of conventional femininity and a space within which the woman writer might begin to re-author her gender.

Stevie Smith: Awkward and Silly

In her 1937 essay 'How to read books', Stevie Smith recalls her first encounter with Alice:

> To come back to children's books proper – and you will see how the habit of rambling grows upon one, it is one of the pleasures of reading – those two great children's books, *Alice in Wonderland* and *Alice Through the Looking Glass* [*sic*] were read aloud to me when I was too young to read for myself. I remember the feel of that hot summer sultry day when Alice, sitting beside her grown-up sister, complained that the book her sister was reading was dull because it had no pictures and no conversation. And at that moment along came the White Rabbit – 'Oh my whiskers and waistcoat', and off went Alice to some of the most extraordinary conversations and picture-scenes that anyone has ever thought of.[30]

Smith's description of Alice's reading and rambling blends with her memories of hearing Carroll's books read aloud, or, as Will May puts it, 'the naïve reader-rambler hovers between the receiver of the text and its subject'.[31] In the same way that Rossetti's letter to Dodgson describes herself, her mother and her sister making themselves 'quite at home in Wonderland', Smith's recollections imply that she accompanied Alice in pursuit of the White Rabbit and that they witnessed the 'extraordinary conversations and picture scenes' together. In figuring Alice as a model reader, Smith characterises reading as a process of both participation and interpellation. Her essay employs this early encounter with nonsense to celebrate the capacity literature has to take us beyond ourselves.

Elsewhere in Smith's work, allusions to Alice suggest a greater unease about the dissolution of discrete (specifically feminine) subjectivity. In *Novel on Yellow Paper* (1936), Pompey, the novel's heroine, is persuaded to try on the clothes of her '*chic*' friend, Lottie.[32] Regarding herself in the 'long glass', she feels uncomfortable: 'And there was something that I didn't like, that I couldn't think, and then I thought: It's the gloves are wrong. So I threw them down and took up the goblet, that was Fifi's drinking goblet' (*YP* p. 62). Perhaps it is the long glass and Lottie's gloves, which recall the White Rabbit's white kid-gloves that Alice slips on absent-mindedly before realising she is shrinking down to rabbit-sized proportions, that lead Pompey to think of Alice:

> Oh how glad I am I am not Lottie Beit [. . .] I often think of Alice, and how she was glad she was not Mabel, and how for one dreadful moment she thought she was going to be Mabel. But that is just one thing we don't have to worry about. In our calm and reasonable moments we don't have to worry about that. There are hazards enough in life and death, but Alice can never be Mabel. (p. 63)

Smith alludes to the identity crisis that Alice suffers shortly after her arrival in Wonderland: '"I'm sure I'm not Ada," she said, "for her hair goes in such long ringlets, and mine doesn't go in ringlets at all; and I'm sure I can't be Mabel, for I know all sorts of things, and she, oh, she knows so very little"' (*AW* p. 18). Pompey declares, 'that is just one thing we don't have to worry about'. But then she repeats and qualifies her assertion: 'in our calm and reasonable moments we don't have to worry about that'. Here, Smith's heroine worries at her own worry. She suggests rational thought and a placid emotional state as the mutually dependent conditions for stable identity, while at the same time both performing and implicitly alluding to an opposite state of affairs. We sense that there are moments (and perhaps this is one of them) when Pompey is neither calm nor reasonable and that it is within these instants of emotional tempest and unreason that her identity is placed at risk by the possibility that, as Romona Huk puts it, 'she *is* a reflection of not only the figures that appear in her looking-glass world, but also the figures of language that shape her supposedly separate "individual" self'.[33] It is worth noting that although 'calm and reasonable' feels like a familiar or natural pairing, one that recapitulates a set of implicitly gendered assumptions about rational masculinity and hysterical femininity, Alice herself often reacts quite calmly to the unreason of her dream.

The logical endpoint of this fragile feminine individuality is the utter obliteration of the self in death. This is something Carroll understood, of course. From his morbid observation that it was 'very likely true' that Alice "'wouldn't say anything about it, even if I fell from the top of the house!"' (p. 10), to the death sentences handed out willy-nilly by the Queen of Hearts, the threat of death hangs over Wonderland. Carroll's nonsensical morbidity seems to have appealed to Smith. *Me Again: The Uncollected Writings of Stevie Smith*, includes a brief poem called 'Mabel':

> In her loneliness Mabel
> Found the hiss of the unlit gas
> Companionable
> And in a little time, dying
> Sublime[34]

The lyric imagines a tragic end for Alice's ignorant acquaintance, offering the sublime annihilation of suicide as the heroic fulfilment of feminine nonentity. The same collection includes a sketch of a figure, lying naked and prone on a bed. Three shelves line the wall behind the figure, holding a disordered selection of briefly rendered books and boxes. On the top shelf is a bottle with the word 'POISON' written on it. The sketch reimagines the opening chapter of *Wonderland*, in which Alice checks to see whether the little bottle with the label instructing her to

> 'DRINK ME' [is] 'marked "*poison*" or not;' for she had read several nice little stories about children who had got burnt, and eaten up by wild beasts, all because they would not remember the simple rules their friends had taught them: such as, that [. . .] if you drink from a bottle marked 'poison,' it is almost certain to disagree with you, sooner or later. (pp. 13–14)

Smith's sketch might illustrate one of the 'nice little stories' that Alice has read, providing a kind of cautionary tale after the fact and imagining a different outcome for Alice, one that haunts Carroll's dream-child, who runs the constant risk of losing herself completely in Wonderland's sequence of reflections and language games.

A second of the handful of looking-glass allusions included in *Novel on Yellow Paper* also understands the life within or behind the glass as a kind of death. Considering the woman's passive role within conventional courtship rituals, which she describes as a feminine capacity to 'linger' in expectation of their suitor, Pompey draws on the example of 'that White Girl that Whistler painted' (*YP* p. 148). She writes, 'She is lingering now, but not hopefully, I think that one is lingering now like they say, the relatives say, of someone who is very sick – She is lingering. And it is death that is going to come up out of that mirror, and I think she will be glad.' The 'White Girl' in question is the subject of James Whistler's 'Symphony in White, no. 2' (1864), also known as 'The Little White Girl'. In the painting a woman stands, one arm resting on a mantelpiece, her gaze directed towards her own reflection in the mirror. Whereas Pompey's uneasy response to the sight of her own mirror image posits the encounter between self and reflection as a moment, not of Lacanian self-recognition, but of self-alienation, her interpretation of Whistler's girl reframes that same encounter as one that offers an escape from what Pompey sees as a diseased femininity. Smith's poem, 'Persephone' returns to this idea, figuring Persephone, death's bride, as another Alice:

> Oh can you wonder can you wonder
> I struck the doll-faced day asunder
> Stretched out and plucked the flower of winter thunder?[35]

Smith's lyric implies that it is little wonder that Persephone chose to leave behind the stifling idyll of her girlhood to join her king in Hades; but in invoking wonder, Smith invokes Persephone's Victorian descendent (she would have known that an early draft of *Alice's Adventures in Wonderland* was called 'Alice's Adventures Underground'), including Carroll's text as part of a mythography that understands burgeoning feminine sexuality as a kind of death.

As well as employing wonderlands and looking-glass worlds to explore the contingent and fragile aspects of feminine subjectivity, Smith's poetry also proposes alternatives to a patriarchal dream of girlhood. Smith's 1968 review of an anthology of poetry by women (including some of her own work as well as poetry by Christina Rossetti) expresses her impatience with the idea of women's writing: 'Why have poems by women only? Or any group poems, come to that (really the regionalists are as bad as the women) [. . .] good poets of either sex are above these squabbles, at least one hopes they are.'[36] The anthology is, she writes, 'awkward. Very awkward indeed'. Smith's sense of the anthology's awkwardness characterises the book as something akin to a social faux pas, clumsily achieved and likely to cause embarrassment. Squabbling about questions of sex and poetry is, Smith implies, the height of bad manners. Her review has been taken as evidence of Smith's ambivalence about feminism more generally (Christopher Ricks rightly cautions against co-opting Smith 'into a feminism for which she felt some sympathy but also some distaste').[37] But by identifying the anthology's awkwardness, Smith might also be said to recognise a characteristic aspect of her own poetry, a deliberate clumsiness that pushes back against the precarious version of feminine subjectivity that Smith takes from Carroll.

Smith's poetry frequently describes embarrassing, unresolved encounters between oddity and social convention. 'Lady "Rogue" Singleton', for example, records an unsuccessful marriage proposal:

Come, wed me, Lady Singleton,
And we will have a baby soon
And we will live in Edmonton
Where all the friendly people run.

I could never make you happy, darling,
Or give you the baby you want,
I would always much rather, dear,
Live in a tent.

I am not a cold woman, Henry,
But I do not feel for you,
What I feel for the elephants and the miasmas
And the general view.[38]

Whereas Rossetti's nonsense teases our curiosity only to deflect it, Smith's appears more indifferent or obdurate in the face of our interpretive advances. Lady Singleton's awkwardness is bodied forth in the poem's metre. The unnamed suitor speaks his part in regular iambic tetrameters, which match the humdrum conformity of his offer of a suburban marriage. The Lady's refusal is a metrical mishmash of lines that go on for too long, or finish too quickly, describing unsuitable aspirations and unaccountable affections (what is it, we are forced to wonder, that she feels for miasmas?). The poem looks and feels like doggerel, which Chris Baldick defines as, 'clumsy verse, usually monotonously rhymed, rhythmically awkward, and often shallow in sentiment', adding that, 'some poets, like Skelton and Stevie Smith have deliberately imitated doggerel for comic effect'.[39] However, Baldick's account does not quite do justice to Smith's doggerel. As Ricks has observed, her verse (sentimental or otherwise) contains shallows in which a person is likely to sink, or even drown.[40] By the same token, Smith's doggerel, though deliberate, is not an imitation: its comedy effects an awkwardness that is a fundamental aspect of her poetic style. Its metrical faux pas express a lack of regard for the rules and resist easy assimilation into conventional systems of value and knowledge.

Ian Gregson suggests something similar when he identifies the metrical irregularity of Smith's poetry as part of her contribution to 'a female tradition in which poetic sound and rhythm are privileged and so wielded as to disrupt routine patterns of meaning'.[41] Gregson draws here on post-Freudian feminist theorisation of the feminine voice that originates with Julia Kristeva and Helen Cixous and that associates the somatic, unmeaning aspects of language with the maternal body. The division Kristeva makes between the (paternal) 'symbolic' and (maternal) 'semiotic' functions of language (which I have discussed in greater detail elsewhere)[42] categorises 'nonsense effects' as part of the 'heterogeneous signification' of the semiotic, which 'operate[s] through, despite and in excess of' the symbolic.[43] Likewise, Cixous theorises an *écriture feminine* that uncouples writing from phallocentric reason and relocates it within the body.[44] Cixous and Kristeva celebrate women's voices in ways that might be understood to reassert the kinds of division between masculine and feminine, women writers and male writers, which Smith's remarks on women's poetry appear to resist. Rather than simply giving prominence to the (implicitly feminine) body, Smith's awkward rhythms remind us of the ways that bodies (of women, of men, of poetry) are also produced by and subject to the disciplining work of language.

Smith inherits her awkwardness from that second founding father of nonsense literature, Edward Lear. As Will May has pointed out, Smith's work is full of indirect allusions to and echoes of Lear. Her work 'attempts, like the questing misfits of his limericks, to start off on the island of Lear and get to somewhere else'.[45] Smith wrote that she admired Lear's sketches of his cat, Foss:

> We all know Lear's drawings of his fat cat Foss. There is true cathood here, though much, too, of course, of Mr Lear, so 'pleasant to know'. [. . .] Why I particularly like Edward Lear's drawings of cat Foss, is one peculiar character they have that the cats of ancient Greece and Egypt and our own Christian cats as shown by master painters do not have. I mean that impression he gives of true cat-intransigence, of the cat in its long drawn-out 'love-affair' with the human race – loved, mocked, cross and resisting, Why should we not mock our cats a little? We know we cannot understand them.[46]

Here, Smith identifies in Lear's work a quality that might be regarded as a near neighbour of awkwardness: if awkwardness results from a failure to conform or to fit, then intransigence describes a more deliberate refusal to give way to the demands and expectations of others. The drawings that Smith celebrates are a series of sketches of Lear's cat, Foss, published as 'The Heraldic Blazons of Foss the Cat' in *Nonsense Songs and Stories* (1895), which represent the animal in a number of characteristic poses: 'Foss Couchant', 'Foss, rampant', 'Foss, a untin' and so on.[47] Foss's 'cat-intransigence' is conveyed through a combination of the cat's ungainly physicality and the saucer-round stare of his eyes, which defy our laughter while at the same time making the images funnier. We may mock the cat because we do not know how else to respond to it, but we do so on the understanding that he will not yield to our mockery. As May puts it, Smith 'praises [Lear] for capturing the unknown without attempting to decipher it'.[48] Her brief critique suggests that Foss's intransigence is also Lear's. If Lear is 'so pleasant to know', the echoes in Smith's prose raise questions about the nature and extent of such knowledge. Perhaps our pleasure in knowing

Lear is, in part, a pleasure in knowing that we cannot understand him. This baffled knowledge is, Smith writes, a kind of love, one that perhaps offers an opportunity to refigure the binary dynamics of self/other, male/female, sense/nonsense that I outlined at the beginning of the chapter.

The poetry of both Lear and Smith is populated by awkward bodies. Lear's limericks sketch characters that often exhibit a Foss-y intransigence in the face of attempts to comprehend them. Take, for example, 'The Old Person of Wick':

There was an Old Person of Wick,
Who said, 'Tick-a-Tick, Tick-a-Tick,
Chickaabee, Chickabaw.' And he said nothing more,
That laconic Old Person of Wick.[49]

Or, 'a Young Lady in blue':

There was a Young Lady in blue,
Who said, 'Is it you? Is it you?'
When they said, 'Yes, it is,' – she replied only, 'Whizz!'
That ungracious Young Lady in blue.[50]

The accompanying illustrations to both these examples show the Old Person and Young Lady as fairground mirror images of their companions: slightly too large, a little oddly shaped. Whereas the figure on the left-hand side of the sketch leans in, in a gesture of engagement, the Old person and the Young Lady draw back, while still staring straight ahead, neither entering into the proffered interaction, nor retreating or giving way. In a similar vein, an early poem by Smith, 'The Songster', describes a woman who sings on in the face of an uncomprehending audience:

Miss Pauncefort sang at the top of her voice
(Sing tirry-lirry-lirry down the lane)
And nobody knew what she sang about
(Sing tirry-lirry-lirry all the same).[51]

Miss Pauncefort's nonsense-song, given in parentheses, resists complete incorporation into the slight lyric that it also helps to create: its rapid iambs jar against the lilting dactylic lines that it punctuates and the last three words provide a final punning interjection that appears to both encourage the singer's eccentricity ('all the same' as in, 'nevertheless') and describe the monotony of her song ('all the same' as in, 'unchanging'), leaving us uncertain of its value. This means that, as readers, we are disappointed to find that we have more in common with the uncomprehending 'nobodies' than we do with the songster herself.

Philip Larkin also identified an affinity between Smith and Lear, writing that in Smith, 'as in Lear, the silliness was part of the seriousness'.[52] In the same essay, Larkin describes Smith's poetry as 'feminine', enclosing the designation in scare quotes that imply its clichéd inadequacy and perhaps acknowledge Smith's own stated distaste for squabbles about gender and poetry. But Larkin's sense that Smith is both 'feminine' and silly suggests how her Leary inheritance might allow her to rewrite just those stereotypes that uphold the version of 'femininity' for which he appears to feel disdain. The *OED* identifies the 'silly woman' as one such stereotype. The term derives from a now obsolete sixteenth-century usage (also commonly applied to infants and animals), which employs 'silly' to denote 'weakness, vulnerability, or physical incapacity'. If a sense of physical silliness has fallen out of use, the silly woman remains, though somewhat transformed. Her physical vulnerability is mistaken for foolishness, a foolishness that might still hold trace associations with the female body. Lear's poetry, by teaching Smith how to be seriously silly, enables her to effect a further transformation of feminine foolishness and to redefine an account of femininity that has been employed to oppress and silence.

A limerick from *A Book of Nonsense* (1861) demonstrates Lear's appreciation that silliness might have a serious side:

There was an Old Person of Chili,
Whose conduct was painful and silly;
He sate on the stairs, eating apples and pears,
That imprudent Old Person of Chili.[53]

Whereas the silliness of the old person's conduct is self-evident and, following the logic of the limerick's rhyme scheme, inevitable, its painfulness is more puzzling. The fact that 'painful' could be substituted for almost any other two-syllable adjective (happy, naughty, stupid, etc.) means that it is both the most arbitrary and the most deliberate word in the limerick. We understand neither its cause nor its object: the expression of the old person in Lear's illustration does not appear to be one of suffering, but nor does the limerick point towards any other characters who might experience pain as the result of his conduct. Pain and silliness, the limerick suggests, simply come as a pair, like the apples and pears that make up the Old Person's cockney rhyming snack. The same pairing is also implicit in the story of the 'old person so silly', who 'poked his head into a lily; But six bees who lived there filled him full of despair, | For they stung that old person so silly'.[54] This has a more straightforward cause-and-effect narrative than many of Lear's limericks. To be stung by bees for getting too close to a flower might be judged a fair comeuppance, one that is reiterated by the double use of silly: silly (unwise) behaviour results in being stung silly (excessively). All of which suggests that 'pain' might in fact be a better pair-word than Larkin's 'seriousness' for thinking about the import of silliness in Lear and Smith. 'Painful and silly' avoids the re-inscription of an implicitly gendered binary that can only appreciate the irrational or silly in so far as it speaks to or within rational, serious, masculine discourse. It allows us to think instead about nonsense as a kind of expression that does not seek to provide a rational account of itself, and that instead expresses the double edge of affective experience.

Painful and silly describes the experience and behaviour of any one of a number of Lear's nonsense creations: the Dong with the Luminous Nose, the Yonghy-Bonghy-Bò, the Family Discobolos, or Lear himself who 'weeps by the side of the ocean | He weeps on the top of the hill; | He purchases pancakes and lotion, | And chocolate shrimps from the mill'.[55] Sometimes, as in the limericks, silliness appears to result in pain; in other examples, as in 'How pleasant to know Mr Lear', pain engenders silliness. Mutually producing, mutually dependent, pain and silliness offer a dialectic binary that sits within what we might call the feminine realm, one that in some way releases femininity from the oppressive dialectics of gender.

'Everything is Swimming' addresses the question of feminine silliness head-on by imagining a conversation between two speakers in response to peculiar female utterance:

Everything is swimming in a wonderful wisdom
She said everything was swimming in a wonderful wisdom
Silly ass
What a silly woman
Perhaps she is drunk
No I think it is mescalin
Silly woman
What a silly woman
Yes perhaps it is mescalin
It must be something
Her father, they say . . .
And that funny man William . . .
Silly ass
What a silly woman

Elle continua de rire comme une hyène.[56]

'Silly woman' has a complacent ring to it. The poem repeats it ad absurdum in a way that gives the lie to the speaker's doubtful assertion that 'it must be something': that the woman's silly behaviour must be made answerable to something beyond itself. Despite the dialogue's attempt to undermine the woman's visionary declaration and to make sense of her behaviour by finding a serious reason for her silliness: alcohol, hallucinogens and, finally, her relationship with men (her father and 'that funny man William'), the final line, which switches from English to French and from the present to the future tense, signals that the woman's experience is inexplicable and inviolable. We are told that her laughter, not mentioned until now, 'will continue', the implication being that it provides an unheard and invisible counter-text to the discussion between the two speakers, one that outlasts the frame of the poem.

Ian Gregson talks about 'the silliness and shrillness of the music of Smith – which', he writes, 'turns feminine self-parody into satire of masculine assumptions of its own rational authority, and derisive questioning of masculine dismissiveness towards what it regards as feminine inchoateness'.[57] But this poem goes beyond satire, taking ownership of the term and exploring its potential power. To return to Caroline Levine's account of gender as a category brought into being by the repeated assertion of a set of norms and deviations, Smith's poem dramatises a deviation so extreme that it cannot be coerced into the service of the norm. The laughter of her 'silly woman', like the unnerving smile of the Cheshire cat, or the laugh of Cixous's Medusa is non-linguistic, affective, animal, appetitive. Like Rossetti's lyric poetry, it simultaneously wields and withholds its expressive force, gesturing towards a private language in a way that both signals the double bind experienced by the woman writer and makes good its escape.

Notes

1. Charles Dickens, *Hard Times* (Harmondsworth: Penguin, 1994), pp. 24–5.
2. Charles Dickens, *Great Expectations* (Harmondsworth: Penguin, 2003), p. 237.
3. Caroline Levine, *Forms: Whole, Rhythm, Hierarchy, Network* (Princeton: Princeton University Press, 2015), p. 94.
4. Levine, *Forms*, p. 94.
5. Jean-Jacques Lecercle, *The Philosophy of Nonsense* (London: Routledge, 2012), p. 221.
6. Lewis Carroll, *Alice's Adventures in Wonderland* and *Through the Looking-Glass*, ed. Peter Hunt (Oxford: Oxford University Press, 2009), p. 41. Hereafter referenced in the main text as *AW* and *TLG*.
7. Nina Auerbach, 'Alice in Wonderland: A Curious Child', *Victorian Studies* 17.1 (1973), 31–47, p. 35.
8. James R. Kincaid, for example, describes Alice's deepest impulses as ones that involve 'power and aggression' ('Alice's Invasion of Wonderland', *PMLA* 88.1 (1973), 92–9, p. 95).
9. Hugh Haughton, 'Introduction', *The Chatto Book of Nonsense Poetry* (London: Chatto and Windus, 1988), p.4.
10. An alternative interpretation of Carroll's use of 'child' might take into account the older use of the word to mean 'girl'. See, for example, the Shepherd's question on discovering Perdita in *The Winter's Tale*: 'A boy or a child, I wonder'. (Shakespeare, *The Winter's Tale* III. 3. 75).
11. Mary E. Coleridge, 'The Other Side of a Mirror', *Mary Coleridge, Selected Poems* ed. Simon Avery (London: Shearsman Books, 2010), p. 33.
12. Angela Carter, 'Wolf Alice', *The Bloody Chamber and Other Stories* (London: Vintage, 2006), p. 140; *The Magic Toyshop* (London: Virago, 1993).
13. Siri Hustvedt, *The Blazing World* (New York: Simon and Schuster, 2014), pp. 44–5.
14. *The Letters of Christina Rossetti, A Digital Edition*, ed. Anthony H. Harrison (Charlottesville: University Press of Virginia, 2006). <https://rotunda.upress.virginia.edu/crossetti/> (last accessed 10th January 2021).
15. Christina Rossetti, *Speaking Likenesses* (London: Macmillan, 1874), p. 15. Hereafter referenced in the main text as *SL*.
16. U. C. Knoepflmacher, 'Avenging Alice: Christina Rossetti and Lewis Carroll', *Nineteenth-Century Literature* 41.3 (1986), 299–328, p. 311.
17. Mitzi Myers, 'Impeccable Governesses, Rational Dames and Moral Mothers: Mary Wollstonecraft and the Female Tradition in Georgian Children's Books', *Children's Literature* 14 (1986), 31–59, p. 33.
18. Carolyn Sigler, 'Authorising Alice: Professional Authority, The Literary Marketplace, and Victorian Re-Visions of the Alice Books', *The Lion and the Unicorn* 22.3 (1998), 531–63, p. 352.
19. Rossetti to Macmillan, 20 March 1874. *Rossetti Letters*.
20. Rossetti to Macmillan, 27 July 1874. Ibid.
21. The *OED* entry for 'speaking', 'of likeness, etc.', meaning 'striking, true, faithful' takes two of its three examples from nineteenth-century texts that use the term with reference to portraiture.
22. Christina Rossetti, 'In an Artist's Studio', *The Complete Poems*, ed. R. W. Crump (Harmondsworth: Penguin, 2005), p. 79.
23. For a discussion of what is at stake for the male artist in the construction and idealisation of girlhood, see Catherine Robson, *Men in Wonderland: The Lost Girlhood of the Victorian Gentleman* (Princeton: Princeton University Press, 2001). Robson argues that 'the little girl represents, not just the true essence of childhood, but an adult male's best opportunity of reconnecting with his lost self' (p. 3).
24. Rossetti, 'Winter: My Secret', *The Complete Poems*, p. 41.

25. See, for example, Isobel Armstrong, *Victorian Poetry: Poetry, Poetics, Politics* (Oxford Blackwell, 1995), pp. 338–9.
26. Review of *Speaking Likenesses*, *The Athenaeum*, 27 December 1874, pp. 878–9.
27. Rossetti to Dante Gabriel Rossetti, 4 May 1874. *Rossetti Letters*.
28. Rossetti, 'Goblin Market', *The Complete Poems*, pp. 5–20.
29. Emma Mason writes, 'The juice [the goblins] force on Lizzie becomes a symbol of Christ's remissive body and blood in the sisters' Eucharistic kiss.' (*Christina Rossetti: Poetry, Ecology, Faith* (Oxford: Oxford University Press, 2017), p. 100.
30. Stevie Smith, 'How to Read Books', in *Discovery and Romance for Girls and Boys*, II (London: Jonathan Cape, 1937), 267–72, p. 270.
31. Will May, *Stevie Smith and Authorship* (Oxford: Oxford University Press, 2010), p. 59.
32. Stevie Smith, *Novel on Yellow Paper* (London: Virago, 1981), p. 61. Hereafter referenced in the main text as *YP*.
33. Romona Huk, *Stevie Smith: Between the Lines* (London: Palgrave, 2004), p. 106.
34. Stevie Smith, 'Mabel', *Me Again: The Uncollected Writings of Stevie Smith*, ed. Jack Barbera and William McBrien (London: Virago, 1981), p. 221.
35. Stevie Smith, 'Persephone', *The Collected Poems of Stevie Smith*, ed. James MacGibbon (Harmondsworth: Penguin, 1985), p. 248.
36. Smith, 'Poems in Petticoats', *Me Again*, 180–1, p. 180.
37. Christopher Ricks, 'Steve Smith: The Art of Sinking in Poetry', *The Force of Poetry* (Oxford: Clarendon, 1984), p. 255.
38. Smith, 'Lady "Rogue" Singleton', *Collected Poems*, p. 194.
39. Chris Baldick, *The Oxford Dictionary of Literary Terms* (online), (Oxford: Oxford University Press, 2015).
40. Ricks writes that Smith's poems 'sound like child's-play, but are inimitable' ('The Art of Sinking', p. 200).
41. Ian Gregson, 'Post/Modernist rhythms and voices: Edith Sitwell and Stevie Smith to Jo Shapcott and Selima Hill', in *The Cambridge Companion to Twentieth-Century British and Irish Women's Poetry*, ed. Jane Dowson (Cambridge: Cambridge University Press, 2011), 9–24, p. 9.
42. See Anna Barton, 'The Sense and Nonsense of Weariness: Edward Lear and Gertrude Stein read Tennyson', in *Edward Lear and the Play of Poetry*, ed. James Williams and Matthew Bevis (Oxford: Oxford University Press, 2016), 243–60.
43. Julia Kristeva, *Desire in Language: A Semiotic Approach to Literature and Art*, trans. Thomas Gora, Alice Jardine and Leon S. Roudiez (Oxford: Blackwell, 1980), p. 133.
44. Hélène Cixous, 'The Laugh of the Medusa', *Signs* 1.4 (1976), 875–93.
45. Will May, 'Drawing Away from Lear: Stevie Smith's Deceitful Echo', *Edward Lear and the Play of Poetry*, 316–39, p. 337.
46. Smith, 'Cats in Colour', *Me Again*, 134–48, p. 142.
47. Edward Lear, 'The Heraldic Blazons of Foss the Cat', *The Complete Nonsense and Other Verse* (London: Penguin, 2006), p. 444.
48. May, 'Drawing Away from Lear', p. 338.
49. Lear, *The Complete Nonsense*, p. 338.
50. Ibid. p. 346.
51. Smith, *Collected Poems*, p. 30.
52. Philip Larkin, 'Frivolous and Vulnerable', in *In Search of Stevie Smith*, 75–82, p. 78.
53. Lear, *Complete Nonsense*, p. 160.
54. Ibid. p. 112.
55. Ibid. p. 428.
56. Smith, *Collected Poems*, p. 429.
57. Gregson, 'Post/Modernist rhythms and voices', p. 9.

16

Queer Nonsense: Query?

Hugh Haughton

The founding Victorian texts of nonsense thrive on what is queer. They also give a strange currency to the word itself. Edward Lear, for example, noted that 'some think him ill-tempered and queer' and described the Old Man of Cashmere as 'scroobious and queer'.[1] Meanwhile, the heroine of Lewis Carroll in *Alice's Adventures in Wonderland*, fanning herself in an underground hall, reflects on how queer 'everything' is:

> 'Dear, dear! How queer everything is to-day! And yesterday things went on just as usual. I wonder if I've been changed in the night? Let me think, was I the same when I got up this morning? I almost think I can remember feeling a little different [. . .]'[2]

Alice's sense of queerness signals a crisis of identity, a disoriented relationship to normality, a different relationship between self and world. Later in her adventures she observes a 'queer-looking party', finds that 'queer things' happen, and discovers that words are sometimes 'very queer indeed'.[3]

In *The Pickwick Papers*, a text which did much to shape the comic culture of Victorian England and its new literature of nonsense, Dickens reports Mr Weller in full flow:

> 'He's a queer customer, the vun-eyed vun, sir,' observed Mr. Weller, as he led the way. 'He's a-gammonin' that 'ere landlord, he is, sir, till he don't rightly know whether he's a-standing on the soles of his boots or the crown of his hat.'[4]

To 'gammon' is to 'talk volubly', 'hoodwink' or 'flatter', and here queerness, inversions and nonsense are once more in cahoots in a topsy-turvy moment involving a 'queer customer'. Dickens's works are peppered with people who dismissively exclaim 'Nonsense', of course, including Betsy Trotwood, who retorts 'Bah! Stuff and Nonsense' when Mr Murdstone threatens her.[5] Nonetheless, Dickens's works and words repeatedly trespass across the border with nonsense, playing with names, puns, linguistic tics and idiosyncrasies in protean comic ways.

Taking our cue from Alice, we could say queer words and uses of words go to the heart of nonsense. Indeed, the word 'queer' provides a clue to think about the pursuit of defiantly deviant forms of absurdity from the period of Dickens, Lear and Carroll to the present – a period in which, after Wilde, the word came also to refer to an unorthodox form of sexual identity and the 'nonsensical' was given a new momentum in the wake of the writings of Freud, Joyce and the modernists. Taking off from Lear, Carroll and Wilde, this chapter pursues the trail of post-Learical nonsense in the work of twentieth-century writers with investments in both aesthetic and erotic queerness, focusing on James Joyce, Gertrude Stein, W. H. Auden, Elizabeth Bishop, Edward Gorey and the Joe Orton of *What the Butler Saw*.

The *OED* defines 'queer' as an adjective originally meaning 'Strange, odd, peculiar, eccentric', but also 'of questionable character; suspicious, dubious'. It traces it to the late Middle Ages, giving an example from Gavin Douglas's Virgil: 'Heir cumis our awin queir clerk' ('here comes our own queer clerk') while explaining that later it also came to mean 'Out of sorts; unwell; faint, giddy', as in 'I came over all queer.' It is presumably in these senses that Lear, Carroll and Dickens use the word. In the early twentieth century, however, the adjective came to mean 'of a person: homosexual', and hence 'of or relating to homosexuals and homosexuality'. The dictionary's first example as a noun is in a letter by Wilde's accuser, the Marquis of Queensbury, referring to 'Snob Queers like Roseberry'. For its earliest uses as an adjective in this sense, *OED* cites the *Los Angeles Times* of 1914 and an entry in Arnold Bennett's journal the following year. The US newspaper recorded that 'the Ninety-six Club' was 'composed of the "queer" people' and 'At these "drags" the "queer" people have a good time.' In similar vein, Bennett reported: 'An immense reunion of art students, painters, and queer people. Girls in fancy male costume, queer dancing, etc.' These 'queer' parties, full of gay metropolitan bohemians having fun, are a far cry from Alice's 'queer-looking party'.

Reviewing subsequent usage, the *OED* says that:

> Although originally chiefly derogatory (and still widely considered offensive, esp. when used by heterosexual people), from the late 1980s it began to be used as a neutral or positive term (originally of self-reference), by some homosexuals [. . .] in place of *gay* or *homosexual*, without regard to, or in implicit denial of, its negative connotations.

It cites 'Queer Nation' and notes the arrival of 'Queer Theory' after the landmark conference with that title organised by Teresa de Lauretis in February 1990, and the resulting special issue of *Differences: A Journal of Feminist Cultural Studies*. This appeared a hundred years after Wilde's *Intentions* (1890), a work that arguably laid the foundations for a 'queer' aesthetic. In 'The Decay of Lying', for example, Wilde advanced the apparently nonsensical but revolutionary claims that 'all bad art comes from returning to Life and Nature' and that 'Life imitates Art far more than Art imitates Life.'[6] Like Wilde, nineteenth-century nonsense did artful things to Nature: Carroll's gardeners painting white roses red in *Alice's Adventures in Wonderland* and the 'bread-and-butter-fly' in *Through the Looking-Glass*; Lear's flowers with faux-Linnean names such as 'Manypeeplia Upsidownia' and 'Pollybirdia Singularis' (*CN*, pp. 252–3). As Darwinian zoology focused on speciation, nonsense specialised in the singular, the 'upside-down' or 'inverted' in every sense (the *OED* records that Aubrey Beardsley told André Raffalovich in 1895 'I think your study of inversion is quite brilliant'). Nonsense thrives on parodying 'the natural order' and its taxonomies, as when Joe Orton and Kenneth Halliwell created a spoof cover for a library copy of the *Collins Guide to Roses* with a picture of a monkey pasted over the centre of a rose, quietly subverting another English version of pastoral.[7]

Like 'queer', 'nonsense' acquired a new currency in the period of Gertrude Stein's *Tender Buttons*, Joyce's *Finnegans Wake*, the sound poems of the Russian *zaumniks*, the linguistic pranks of the Dadaists and the post-Freudian experiments of the French

Surrealists. These, along with Freud's revisionary accounts of the apparent nonsense of dreams, hysterical symptoms and slips of the tongue, had a retroactive effect on people's understanding of Lear, Carroll and Victorian nonsense, as well exerting as an active impetus on later writers.[8] So now has the arrival of Queer Theory, with its emphasis on what Annamarie Jagose calls 'mismatches between sex, gender and desire', and its claim that 'by refusing to crystallise in any form, queer maintains a relation of resistance to whatever constitutes the normal'.[9]

The fairy godmother of Queer theory, Eve Kosofsky Sedgwick, suggests the term 'queer' refers to 'the open mesh of possibilities, gaps, overlaps, dissonances and resonances, lapses and excesses of meaning when the constituent element of anyone's gender, or anyone's sexuality aren't made (or *can't* be made) to signify monolithically'.[10] There is a parallel here with nonsense, which, as I have argued elsewhere, 'rejoices in the misfit of language and the world, allowing words [. . .] a freer rein than usual, favouring puns [. . .] neologisms, inversions, twinnings, formal elaboration, *double entendres*, secret codes and private languages'.[11] Though Carroll, Lear and Mr Weller might find Sedgwick's argument implausible, their nonsense also depended on 'lapses and excesses of meaning'. Sedgwick offers a brilliant analysis of the 'avunculate' in *The Importance of Being Earnest*, the great nineteenth-century contribution to theatrical nonsense, but curiously Wilde himself steers clear of the adjective 'queer' (a digital search suggests he rarely if ever used it, despite his love of the related term 'strange').[12] Nonetheless, the play renders absurd the structures of heterosexual romance, the 'normal' family, and patriarchal identity (as in the revelation of 'the name of the father' in its farcical denouement). In their stead it advocates 'Bunburying', a queer neologism that enables each of the characters to lead a double life and represents, as Sedgwick says, 'the nonfamilial alibi in the play', potentially suggesting the 'buried' (or concealed) life of the Victorian homosexual.[13] When Jack tells Algernon 'you never talk anything but nonsense' and Algernon replies 'Nobody ever does', nonsense is queered by being impossibly universalised, with the play rendering all the norms of sense and sensibility seductively absurd.[14]

Nonsense and theatre go as far back as Aristophanes, but in *The Importance of Being Earnest* Wilde gave theatrical nonsense a new inflection, involving parodic redefinitions of romance, gender, class and personal identity. In Gilbert and Sullivan's *Patience*, one of the characters, travestying Wilde and other aesthetes, when enthusing over a poem exclaims 'Nonsense, yes, perhaps – but oh what precious nonsense!'[15] *The Importance* turns that serious Victorian word 'Earnest' into a nonsensically over-determined pun. Name-play, often associated with the queering of naming itself, reaches its apotheosis in this play where the two girls claim they can only fall in love with a man called Ernest and, since neither male actually bears that name, both principal men seek to be rechristened while the already doubly-named Jack turns out already to have been christened Ernest (after his father) without knowing it. This name-play is a sign of the play's determination to make a mockery of everything that is usually taken in earnest – including heterosexual romance and social hierarchy.

* * *

Edward Lear was posthumously associated with a book called *Queery Leary Nonsense* (1911) and, rather than being leery of it, positively relished the rhyme of

'Lear' and 'queer'. Indeed, he was deeply invested in both 'queer' beings and being 'queer', as we can see in his late self-portrait 'How Pleasant to Know Mr Lear':

> 'How pleasant to know Mr Lear!'
>   Who has written such volumes of stuff!
> Some think him ill-tempered and queer,
>   But a few think him pleasant enough. (*CN*, p. 428)

The rhyme of 'queer' and 'Lear' sets up the poem's ambivalent keynote, bracing the negative and bilious-sounding 'ill-tempered' against the more positive 'pleasant enough'. 'Ill-tempered' and 'pleasant' seem straightforwardly antithetical, but 'queer' could go either way, depending on the observer's attitudes towards difference and otherness.

Eccentricity and peculiarity, like queerness, are Lear's forte, and his sense of being 'queer' in some way is intimately related to his gravitation towards nonsense. In 1881, writing to his friend Chichester Fortescue, Lear said 'I know you would not blow me up about my political maunderings, because you are of the few who understand this queer child.'[16] Writing from Turin in 1870, he observes 'I live the queerest solitary life here, in company of seventy people' (*LL*, p. 122). Earlier still, he described himself as 'a very queer beast to have so many friends' (*LL*, p. 81), observing that 'Very happily for me, my queer natural elasticity of temperament does not at all lead me to the morbids' (*LL*, p. 86). 'Queer elasticity' suggests something of the elastic dynamism of the adjective in his hands. A letter written towards the end of his life was 'all confused and indicative of my mucilaginous and morose mind – all more or less queer and upside down as the mouse said when he bit off his grandmothers tail, having mistaken it for barley straw' (*LL*, p. 334). With the last twist in the tail of that Wellerism – literally the last straw – Lear commits himself to playing his self-invented role as a nonsense virtuoso who specialises in what is 'more or less queer and upside down'. 'Confused and indicative' are indeed indicative, suggesting the marriage of a 'morose' mind and his 'more or less queer' nonsense art.

The adjective also crops up in one of Lear's limericks:

> There was an old man of Cashmere,
> Whose movements were scroobious and queer;
> Being slender and tall, he looked over a wall,
> And perceived two fat ducks of Cashmere. (*CN*, p. 352)

The poem is important for aligning 'queer' with 'scroobious', Lear's absolutely indicative self-coined adjective, and it situates them both by a wall like Humpty-Dumpty's in *Through the Looking-Glass*. If the wall embodies the vertiginous feeling for boundaries typical of nonsense, the elasticity of the term 'scroobious' shows its potential to cover opposite kinds of extremity (Lear portrays himself as 'spherical' as well as 'queer' in his self-portrait while the man of Cashmere is queer but 'slender and tall'). Another limerick reports that 'There was an old person of Grange, | Whose manners were scroobious and strange' (CN, p. 359), aligning 'scroobious' to the key related term 'strange' (the *OED* defining 'queer' as primarily meaning 'strange, odd, peculiar, eccentric'). The protagonist of his early poem 'Miss Maniac', for example, suffers

'Strange feelings, such as none but maniacs ever know' (*CN*, p. 38), while in an early 'Journal' letter Lear describes his family's 'strange wanderings' (*CN*, p. 13). In the 'The Dong with a Luminous Nose', a comparably disturbed wanderer materialises as a 'A Meteor strange and bright', which we learn is the effect of his decision to weave himself 'a wondrous Nose, – | A Nose as strange as a Nose could be' (*CN*, p. 424). Here 'strangeness' operates as a kind of florid defence, a meteoric creative response to melancholy, a clown-like assertion of luminous idiosyncrasy that distracts him from his romantic feelings towards his lost Jumbly Girl. Lear's limericks and longer lyrics form a narrative encyclopedia of strange behaviour and desire, which, while dwelling on solid geographical place names, disturbs cultural and psychological norms.

In drawing – and drawing attention to – what is curious and queer, Lear insists on the inspiration of the strange and 'scroobious', his ineffably screwball adjective. The word can be used with a certain pejorative implication, as when we are told 'There was an Old Person of Philæ, | Whose conduct was scroobious and wily' (*CN*, p. 167) or more positively, as in 'The Scroobious Snake, | who always wore a Hat on his Head for | fear he should bite anybody' (*CN*, p. 266). It also names the protagonist of Lear's nonsensical Pindaric ode, the queer apotheosis of the *sui generis* taxonomically anomalous creature who is not 'Beast or Bird or Fish or Fly' but whose 'only name is the Scroobious Pip' (*CN*, p. 388). The nominal sign of Lear's creature is pure anomaly or singularity, unaligned with any zoological category. He could be said to be the queerest of the queer.

Since Angus Davidson's 1938 biography, Lear's biographers have generally identified Lear himself as homosexual, living a life shaped by passionate same-sex feelings towards younger men, particularly Franklin Lushington.[17] Peter Swaab, in a psychologically nuanced review of the biographical evidence, concludes that 'It is impossible to say where Lear's sexuality, his queerness, begins and ends.' He adds that 'a critical account of Lear needs to come to terms with his entire mode of apprehension of the world, alive with the sense that all is not as it might be and that normality can be troubling.'[18] Offering just such a critical reading of the anomalous relationships played out across the lyrics and limericks, Swaab concludes, in a play on Empson's reading of the *Alice* books, that 'His poems are so frankly about social nonconformity and romantic love that there is no great discovery in seeing them as part of queer writing; it seems the proper exegesis.'[19]

This alerts us to the fact that Lear's longer lyrics celebrate numerous queer couples. These include the eternally coupled male duo of 'Mr Daddy Long-Legs and Mr Floppy Fly', the eloping enigmatically gendered trans-specific couple of 'The Owl and the Pussy-Cat' and the equally unlikely trans-species couple of 'The Duck and the Kangaroo'. Such trans-specific romances align unlikely couples with the transgressive idea of the 'trans' itself. The Dong, the Jumblies, the Pobble, are all marginalised figures defined by their defiant or deviant relationship to biological, physiological or psychological norms. In this sense, Lear's nonsense creates mis-fitting forms for misfits, developing a captivating lyrical space in which to explore psychological and physiological difference in a world of what I have called 'pairing and despairing'.[20] This may be one reason for his magnetic appeal to later queer writers.

Though Carrollian nonsense is a bird of a different feather, the adjective 'queer' features regularly in the *Alice* books as a key barometer of the strange climate of nonsense, where the 'natural' order is subjected to the rules of card games, chess, logical contortionism and dreams. As with Lear, the eccentric world through the Looking-Glass reflects something of the attitude of its author, Charles Lutwidge Dodgson, towards the adult world, in his case Victorian Oxford. Carrolian nonsense, like his life, is organised around the author's hyper-investment in the image of the young girl – Alice in the first instance as dedicatee and protagonist of his two fantasy novels, but also the hundreds of girls he photographed and made friends with across his life. The question of Carroll's sexuality remains a riddle, akin to the riddles which obsess his egg-headed Humpty-Dumpty, perched precariously on his wall, where Alice confronts him:

> 'Why do you sit out here all alone?' said Alice, not wishing to begin an argument.
>
> 'Why, because there's nobody with me!' cried Humpty Dumpty. 'Did you think I didn't know the answer to *that*? Ask another.'
>
> 'Don't you think you'd be safer down on the ground?' Alice went on, not with any idea of making another riddle, but simply in her good-natured anxiety for the queer creature. 'That wall is so *very* narrow!'
>
> 'What tremendously easy riddles you ask!' Humpty Dumpty growled out.[21]

Humpty-Dumpty, like Carroll, is obsessed by names and riddles and is a virtuoso interpreter of nonsense poetry, offering Alice a lexical guide to 'Jabberwocky'. There is a sense in which the 'queer creature' Alice feels anxious about is a mirror of the author as well as a fragile embodiment of the precariousness of nonsense. Later, when told by Alice he is holding the book upside-down, he says 'To be sure I was!', as she turned it round for him, 'I thought it looked a little queer.'[22] This is one of two inverted books in the text (the other includes 'Jabberwocky'), and it suggests the connection between nonsense, inversion and things looking queer – a queer creature and a queer book.

In Carroll's later nonsensical mock-epic *The Hunting of the Snark*, we're told the Butcher also 'felt queer', suggesting the adjective continues to carry a lot of weight, if not any implication of sexuality, in this book's nonsensical quest:

> Then a scream, shrill and high, rent the shuddering sky,
> And they knew that some danger was near:
> The Beaver turned pale to the tip of its tail,
> And even the Butcher felt queer.
>
> He thought of his childhood, left far far behind –
> That blissful and innocent state –
> The sound so exactly recalled to his mind
> A pencil that squeaks on a slate!
>
> ''Tis the voice of the Jubjub!' he suddenly cried.
> (This man, that they used to call 'Dunce.')
> 'As the Bellman would tell you,' he added with pride,
> 'I have uttered that sentiment once.'[23]

The 'voice of the Jubjub' – a creature as unclassifiable as Lear's Scroobious Pip – evokes fear, 'feeling queer' and childhood for the Butcher, and this configuration of feelings is characteristic of Carroll's universe. It turns up again later when we are told that the Beaver 'brought paper, portfolios, pens | And ink in unfailing supplies', and 'strange creepy creatures came out of their dens | And watched them with wondering eyes.'[24] These lines associate the whole process of writing with 'strange' creatures, mirroring Carroll's own compositional process in this warped ballad, whose last line ('For the Snark was a Boojum, you see!'), with its equation of two different unknown neologistic creatures, was, he said, its dream-like inspiration.[25] As in Lear, the 'strange' and the 'queer' are natural bedfellows in the anomalous order of the quasi-Darwinian geographical expedition described in Carroll's quasi-Tennysonian epic. Soon after its publication, Carroll's publisher reported that, while sales of the poem weren't comparable to those of the *Alice* books, it was by no means a 'failure', though 'It is no doubt very *Queer*!'[26]

The dazzling and perverse nonsense machinery of the *Alice* texts and *The Hunting of the Snark* has the effect of undoing the authority of the figure Auden calls the 'goddess of bossy underlings, Normality'.[27] One of the stranger features of Wonderland and the world through the Looking-Glass is the absence of overt sexuality (though we sense it may be working covertly underground). There are game-style kings and queens but no princes or princesses (as there are in George MacDonald's contemporary romantic fantasias), and no romance. Carroll creates a world palpably made up out of language and culture (a corridor becomes a pool, a shop a river, flowers get painted different colours, the landscape is a chessboard, and a butterfly is displaced by a 'bread-and-butter fly'). This is a world of rules (but nonsensical rules), of nature (but artificially constructed nature), and of jokes that interrupt the authority of 'sense' and 'logic'. If this is comic, it also involves a proliferation of dangerously destabilising meanings and references to appetites that are never overtly erotic but skirt its borderline. It is reported of the crew of Snark-hunters, 'They knew that some danger was near', and this is true of the whole story, like the *Alice* books, where the heroine thinks Humpty-Dumpty would be 'safer' on the ground, and we encounter innumerable jokes about death, the food chain, growing up and 'vanishing away'. It is the nearness of danger which makes the electrically asexual comedy of Carrollian nonsense so edgy.

* * *

I want to suggest then that an interest in nonsense is implicitly related to a pleasurable investment in anomalous, 'abnormal' and 'un-natural' feelings. After the Wilde scandal and Freud's sexualised interpretations of apparently nonsensical dreams, slips of the tongue, jokes and hysterical symptoms, nonsense became more overtly aligned with the expression of erotic anomaly (as in limericks after Lear). This is particularly the case for writers and artists who are gay or sceptical about normative accounts of sexuality and identity, as I hope to show.

Joyce is a case in point. In *Finnegans Wake*, the post-Freudian nonsense text par excellence, Joyce calls up the ghosts of Carroll, Lear and Wilde, in his Rabelaisian dreamscape, associating all of them with his principal protagonist HCE, who is regularly associated in turn with perverse sexuality.[28] Writing in the wake of Freud's account of polymorphous and perverse infantile sexuality,[29] as well as psychoanalytic interpretations of *Alice* by William Empson and others, Joyce speaks of 'All old Dadgerson's dodges' and 'wonderland's wanderlad' (*FW*, 374.1). He also exclaims, 'Now, listen, Mr Leer! And stow that sweatyfunnyadams Simper' (*FW*, 65.4–6). When he goes on to speak of 'we grisly Sykos who have done our unsmiling bit on alices, when they were yung and easily freudened' (115.21–3), Joyce's nonsense reflects on the transformation of both nonsense and childhood in the era of Jung and Freud. Alice becomes 'Alicious', for example, and is seen Lolita-like 'through alluring glass or alas in jumboland' (*FW*, 528.17). Likewise, as Adam Piette suggests, Lear is turned into a 'leering "old geyser" rather than the innocent Old Man of the limericks', and as a result of the 'transferential transformation of dream and child by psychoanalysis [. . .] the nonsense of Lear has also fallen under the penumbra of a Carroll-like procuring'.[30]

Finnegans Wake is an open sesame of polymorphous and perverse sexual and linguistic high jinks and kinks, building upon the nonsensical wordplay pioneered by Lear and Carroll. Like them, Joyce revalues the queer, describing its heroine, Anna Livia Plurabelle, for example, as 'the queer old skeowsha anyhow' and its guilty male father figure HCE as 'the quare old buntz too, Dear Dirty Dumpling' (*FW*, 215.12–13). The text's choric washerwomen 'Queer Mrs Quickenough and odd Miss Dodd-pebble' (the latter clearly a refugee from the world of Lear) have more than enough scandalous 'dirty clothes to publish', including the child-love of Carroll ('Lewd's Carol', *FW*, 501.34) and the accusations against Wilde, which surface when the exhibitionistic HCE is accused of 'at its wildest, a partial exposure' (*FW*, 34.26). By the close, Joyce says that his constantly renamed 'Alma Luvia, Pollabella' – his 'princeable girl' (*FW*, 626.27) – is 'about fetted up now with nonsery reams' (*FW*, 619.16–18) – suggesting the intimate continuity between the text, nursery rhymes, pantomime and nonsense. Being 'fetted up with nonsery reams' might mean his heroine is 'fed up with nursery rhymes' or 'fêted' with 'reams of nonsense', capturing the inherently ambivalent – or, to use Joyce's word, 'ambiviolent' (*FW*, 518.2) – nature of what he calls 'an artful of outer nocense' (*FW* 378.33). The text makes us question the relationship between artful 'outer nonsense' and whatever is inner (whether inner sense or nonsense).

If nonsense and queerness show 'ambiviolent' affinities in *Finnegans Wake*, they also proved attractive bedfellows for twentieth-century gay writers. In one of W. H. Auden's clerihews, Wilde figures briefly as part of a queer couple when we are told that 'Oscar Wilde | Was greatly beguiled, | When into the Café Royal walked Bosie | In a tea-cosy.'[31] Another reports that 'Edward Lear | Was haunted by a fear | While travelling in Albania | Of contracting kleptomania', associating Lear with fear and random criminality, and suggesting kleptomania shares the same infectious quality commonly attributed to homosexuality by the homophobic.[32] It reminds us that Auden's great sonnet about Lear interprets his nonsense art in primarily biographical terms, viewing it in terms of his 'Terrible Demon', the word Lear used to name his lifelong epilepsy but could also represent his homosexuality. The octet records the effect of that 'Terrible Demon' in the life of 'A dirty landscape-painter who hated his nose' as well as the persecuting presence of the 'legions of cruel inquisitive They' conjured in Lear's limericks. The sestet goes on to celebrate his art in terms of a carnivalesque triumph of nonsense travel:

How prodigious the welcome was. Flowers took his hat
And bore him off to introduce him to the tongs;
The demon's false nose made the table laugh; a cat
Soon had him waltzing madly, let him squeeze her hand;
Words pushed him to the piano to sing comic songs;

And children swarmed to him like settlers. He became a land.[33]

The effect is to ground the escapist ballet of the 'comic songs' in Lear's experience of his 'Terrible Demon', which forced him to assume a 'false nose' like a clown (or the Dong). Drawing on Angus Davidson's biography, the poem quietly queers Lear's geographically oriented nonsense, portraying a journey 'guided by tears' to a 'land' – not unlike the 'land where the Bong Tree grows' – where he can perform in comic freedom for children who are naturally attracted to this way of escaping the painful anomalies caused by unrealisable desires. Auden deploys nonsense effects elsewhere in many poems, including in *The Orators*, his disturbing cryptic study in queerness and cultural anomaly, or his early poem, 'Roar, Gloucestershire', where in the context of a 'piss-proud prophet, that pooty redeemer, | That bugger magician with his Polish lad' he invokes the complex word 'queer' in all its queerness when he speaks of someone 'Queer to these birds: yes, very queer, | But to the tryers such a dear.'[34] In his Lear poem Auden helped transform the ways we might understand the queerness of nonsense, complimenting his seductive argument in *The Oxford Book of Light Verse* that 'nonsense poetry [. . .] appeals to the Unconscious', and is 'an attempt to find a world where the divisions of class, sex, occupation did not operate'.[35]

The writing of Gertrude Stein also foregrounds formal queerness, subliminally aligning her aesthetic practice with her lesbianism but also, as Anna Barton notes, with the nonsense art of Edward Lear.[36] Though using the most everyday vocabulary and objects, Stein projects a drastically strange view of the world which dances acrobatically on the edge of the nonsensical. Indeed, towards the start of *Tender Buttons*, she briefly invokes nonsense:

> What is the use of a violent kind of delightfulness if there is no pleasure in not getting tired of it [. . .] In any kind of place there is a top to covering and it is a pleasure at any rate there is some venturing in refusing to believe nonsense. It shows what use there is in a whole piece if one uses it and it is extreme and very likely the little things could be dearer but in any case there is a bargain and if there is the best thing to do is to take it away and wear it and then be reckless be reckless and resolved on returning gratitude.[37]

Whether writing of everyday objects or about everybody's autobiography or her own, Stein brought a weird and unconventional ordinariness to everything she wrote, as when, writing of herself in the third person in *The Autobiography of Alice B. Toklas*, she said: 'She always says she dislikes the abnormal, it is so obvious. She says the normal is so much more simply complicated and arresting.'[38] That said, she took great pleasure in embodying an avant-garde queer domesticity and overtly lesbian identity in her émigré life as well as in her experimental writings. There's a sense in which her life and art both involved a complex and often comic recalibration of the relation between the normal and abnormal. When the publication of *Tender Buttons* unleashed a flood of parodies in the newspapers, Stein reports writing to the editor of *Life* to say that 'the real Gertrude Stein was as Henry McBride had pointed out funnier in every way than the imitations, not to say much more interesting'.[39] 'Funny' is a word in the same Janus-faced family as 'queer', suggesting both 'funny peculiar' and 'funny ha-ha' as well as the possible bridges between them.

In *The Making of Americans*, Stein writes about having 'funny' tastes in a way that reflects on her own writing. Beginning by asserting 'It is a very strange feeling when one is loving a clock', suggesting a strange kind of love, she goes on to talk of 'a handkerchief that is very gay', and then of writing a book that you fear people will think you are a 'silly or a crazy one' for writing, so that 'you have a queer feeling and you are not very certain and you go on writing'.[40] The sentence suggests that the 'strange' taste Stein is talking about can be viewed as 'ugly', 'foolish', 'funny', 'childish', 'dirty', 'silly' and 'crazy'. In other words, this is writing that is potentially fearful and shameful, involving a 'feeling of being afraid and ashamed' which she defiantly embraces: 'you have a queer feeling and you are not very certain and you go on writing'. Stein is not talking explicitly about her identity as a lesbian here, but all the terms – 'strange', 'gay,' 'queer' and 'dirty' (as in Lear's 'dirty landscape-painter') – hover around it.[41] As in nonsense, the text 'ambiviolently' embraces anomaly. As Stein wrote in *Everybody's Autobiography*, 'identity is funny being yourself is funny as you are never yourself to yourself except as you remember yourself and then of course you do not believe yourself'.[42] What is 'funny' is a halfway house to an acknowledgement of both the queerness of identity and of a queer identity ('It is funny this knowing being a genius, everything is funny').

Judith Halberstam discusses the historical association of queer subjects 'to negativity, to nonsense, to anti-reproduction, and to unintelligibility', and, though Stein may not have signed up as a nonsense writer, her texts play with just these issues.[43] They certainly juggle words, rules, games and names in ways reminiscent of Lear and Carroll with the effect of questioning normal taxonomies and normative assumptions. Take this passage in 'Patriarchal Poetry', for example:

> Was it a fish was heard was it a bird was it a cow was stirred was it a third was it a cow was stirred was it a third was it a fish was heard was it a third. Fishes a bird cows were stirred a bird fish were heard a bird cows were stirred. A third is all. Come too.[44]

Like the best nonsense, this is both anarchic and highly patterned. It offers a sequence of eight questions ('was it' this, 'was it' that), harps on one reiterated verb (there are twelve waspish instances of 'was' here), plays on three apparently random zoological nouns (bird, cow and fish), and conjures a bouncy sequence of nursery-style rhymes ('heard', 'bird', 'third' and 'stirred'). A few paragraphs later, she reports on things being 'Patriarchal in investigation and renewing of an intermediate rectification of the initial boundary between cows and fishes', suggesting an attempt to rectify the boundaries after 'stirring' them. Later, she does something even closer to Lear:

> Day-light and wishes apples and fishes, dedicated to you all the way through day-light and fishes apples and wishes dedicated to all the way through dedicated to you dedicated to you all the way through day-light and fishes apples and fishes apples and fishes [. . .][45]

We might set this against the nonsense pairings of the poems of Lear's 'Ribands and Pigs' sequence, such as these: 'Lobsters & owls, | Scissors and fowls, | Set him a howling & hark how he howls!' (*CN*, p. 139). Stein's double-pairing of 'day-light and wishes' and 'apples and fishes', underscored by the rhyme of 'wishes' and 'fishes', invokes something like a cubist still life but, despite being cast in prose, has the luminous lyric oddity of Lear's bagatelles. Taking pleasure in odd couples and couplings is a feature of queer nonsense writers, and Stein's interventions in sense-making and sentence-making decouples subjects and objects in innumerable ways that alert us to the arbitrariness of grammatical norms and linguistic constructions as well, subliminally, of gender norms and constructions.

* * *

Elizabeth Bishop observed that Stein's 'characters are turned slowly on an enormous wheel, like so many St Catherines' so that 'they and the readers are fooled into thinking they're getting somewhere'.[46] Though less 'avant-garde' than Stein, Bishop, like many other gay poets, has her own taste for nonsense and the queer, as we can see in 'Insomnia', a lesbian love poem that gets somewhere new by playing with Carroll-style inversions:

So wrap up care in a cobweb
and drop it down a well
into that world inverted
where left is always right,
where the shadows are really the body,
where we stay awake all night,
where the heavens are shallow as the sea
is now deep, and you love me.[47]

A graceful, nonsensically inflected lyric like this plays with *Looking-Glass*-style inversions as a trope for sexual inversion. The same is true of 'The Gentleman of Shalott'. Its title conjures a comic male mirror image of Tennyson's Arthurian heroine in front of her medieval looking glass and triggers a game in the manner of Magritte, as Bishop imagines 'his person was | half looking-glass', with one half visible beyond the mirror and the other reflected in it. As a result, she says, 'The glass must stretch | down his middle, | or rather down the edge. | But he's in doubt | as to which side's in or out | of the mirror.'[48] With its asymmetrical form and syncopated couplets, the poem makes a case for an impossibly bifurcated life with poignant dignity, not unlike Lear's parodic response to Tennyson in 'The Dong with the Luminous Nose'. The protagonist of Bishop's 'The Manmoth' is a Manhattan reincarnation of Lear's Dong, born of a newspaper misprint for 'mammoth' (which Bishop described as 'an oracle' that 'spoke from [. . .] the *New York Times* [. . .] explaining New York City to me').[49] It opens with his portrait:

The whole shadow of Man is only as big as his hat.
It lies at his feet like a circle for a doll to stand on,
and he makes an inverted pin, the point magnetized to the moon.
He does not see the moon; he observes only her vast properties,
feeling the queer light on his hands, neither warm nor cold,
of a temperature impossible to record in thermometers.[50]

The wandering outsider responding to the 'queer light' of the moon has a disproportionate inverted shadow and huge nocturnal hat which makes him irresistibly Lear-like, as does his solitary tearfulness when 'one tear, his only possession, like the bee's sting, slips'. One of Bishop's pupils at Harvard records her telling the class to 'memorize "How Pleasant to Know Mr. Lear"', recalling that 'she liked the nonsense, a kind of brainteaser'.[51]

'The Manmoth' is a comparable 'brain-teaser'. In Bishop's unpublished 'Keaton', the speaker says 'I was made at right-angles to the world | and I see it so. I can only see it so. | I do not find all this absurdity people talk about.'[52] She would not want to have this identified with her lesbianism, but, like Lear and others whose ideas of romance are homosexually oriented, she was naturally drawn to the apparent 'absurdity' of nonsense. This is equally true of other gay American poets I have no space to discuss here, particularly the New York poets Frank O'Hara, James Schuyler and John Ashbery, the last of whom published a cento with Lear's title, 'The Dong with a Luminous Nose'. Indeed, readers such as Adam Phillips, Stephanie Burt and Stephen Ross have read Ashbery as a fully fledged 'nonsense poet' – with Ross, in a fine essay on Ashbery's debt to Lear, claiming that 'Typical late Ashbery is free verse nonsense.'[53] Stephanie Burt entitled her brilliant study of contemporary American poetry *Close Calls with Nonsense*, and much of the most inventive and challenging of recent US poetry, like Ashbery's, situates itself on or near the border of nonsense.[54] In an interview, Ashbery said he thought his recent poetry was 'Maybe too funny. Maybe silly', before noting that 'like so much light verse, like Edward Lear or Lewis Carroll, it has a pathetic, plangent side to it', and admitting 'How Pleasant to Know Mr. Lear' is one of his favourite poems.[55] Whereas T. S. Eliot acknowledged 'How Unpleasant' it was to meet Mr Eliot, Ashbery's readers know how pleasant it is to know the incorrigibly polymorphous and pleasure-seeking Ashbery, whose 'homotextual' poetry keeps opening up anomalous and often surreal worlds beyond the looking glass.[56]

It seems appropriate that Ashbery and Frank O'Hara met at a party of Edward Gorey's, since, as a nonsense poet and professional illustrator, Gorey is the most direct contemporary inheritor of Edward Lear's two-pronged nonsense. Gorey has done his own quirky illustrations for 'The Jumblies' and 'The Dong with a Luminous Nose' – the only ones that compare to Lear's own – as well as written a series of macabre limericks that cross Lear and Edgar Allen Poe. He has also written numerous Lear-style narratives about singular, unknown creatures, including the infuriating protagonist of *The Doubtful Guest*, who is described as 'something standing on top of an urn, | Whose peculiar appearance gave them quite a turn' and in the illustration is depicted as a shapeless, shoe-wearing creature between a tall bird and small bear.[57] Another poem tells the story of 'An osbisk bird' which 'flew and sat | On Emblus Fingby's bowler hat', reporting that 'It had not done so for a whim | But meant to come and live with him.'[58] A Lear-like tale about an odd couple, told in couplets, it records their shared domestic life ('On Fridays when Emblus played the flute; | The bird now joined him on the lute'), reporting finally that 'when at last poor Emblus died | The osbick bird was by his side.' Gorey has also produced many virtuosic Lear-style alphabets, including the gruesome *The Gashlycrumb Tinies*, which recounts the fate of twenty-six children (including 'M is for Maud who was swept out to sea | N is for Neville who died of Ennui') and a number of nonsense bestiaries such as 'The Utter Zoo'. This last features twenty-six imaginary creatures in alphabetic order running from the Ampoo ('The Ampoo is intensely neat; | Its head is small, likewise his feet') to the Zote, about whom we are simply told: 'About the Zote, what can be said? | There was just one, and it is dead.'[59]

As poet and illustrator, Gorey is an 'intensely neat' reinventor of the nonsense tradition. In an interview, he said he had 'been influenced a lot by Lewis Carroll and Edward Lear and the whole tradition of English nonsense verse'.[60] Like the Zote, however, he also chose to represent himself as single and singular. Asked about his sexual preferences in another interview, Gorey replied:

> I've never said that I was gay and I've never said that I wasn't [. . .] What I'm trying to say is that I am a person before I am anything else [. . .] I realize that homosexuality is a serious problem for anyone who is – but then, of course, heterosexuality is a serious problem for anyone who is, too. And being a man is a serious problem and being a woman is, too. Lots of things are problems.[61]

This recalls Stein's remark that 'identity is funny being yourself is funny', but also clarifies his elegy for the Zote ('There was just one, and it is dead'). Such remarks illuminate the convergence in Gorey's work of enigmatic or problematic identity and the nonsense to which he devoted himself. There is only one exception to the rampant Carrollian asexuality of Gorey's comic repertoire, however, *The Curious Sofa: A Pornographic Work by Ogdred Weary*, written under one of his many anagrammatic pseudonyms.[62] Set in an Edwardian country house, it euphemistically describes a series of genteel orgies, gracefully conjuring up an impressive menu of perversions with po-faced decorum. Beside a picture of two balletic bare-chested young men in striped Edwardian swimwear tossing another in the air, for example, we read the caption: 'Looking out the window, she saw Herbert, Albert, and Harold, the gardener, an exceptionally well-made youth, disporting themselves on the lawn.' The effect is of a convergence of Balanchine, Wilde and Ronald Firbank, 'disporting themselves'.

The queer innuendoes of *The Curious Sofa* are the exception that proves the rule. Generally, in the nonsense narratives collected in Gorey's three *Amphigorey* compendia, Gothic innuendo displaces the erotic, and the threat of murderous or accidental violence becomes the source of their uncanny comedy (rather on the model of Hilaire Belloc's *Cautionary Tales*, which he also illustrated). Gorey tells us that the title *Amphigorey* comes from 'amphigory, or amphigouri, meaning a nonsense verse or composition'. This follows the *OED*'s 'composition without sense, as Latin "nonsense verse"' but smuggles in his own signature ('Gorey'). Gorey's narratives depict a world of nonsensical perversity, not unlike that of *The Hunting of the Snark*, conjuring a sense of omnipresent violence which threatens the stable Edwardian-style social order which Gorey invokes in his graphic idiom and genteel lexicon. Lear-style nonsense meets American Gothic. With 'Utter Zoo' Gorey exploits the fact that the intensifier 'utter' is usually associated with 'nonsense', renovating the conjunction between nonsense and queer zoological life forms that Lear and Carroll pioneered. Gorey's 'Mork', 'Humglum' and Zote' join the Pobble who has no Toes, The Dong with the Luminous Nose, the Snark and Boojum in the Nonsense Zoo. Whether these represent unknown forms of animal life or hitherto unnamed forms of human life is unclear.

* * *

Nonsense and the queer are nowhere more spectacularly allied than in Joe Orton's *What the Butler Saw*, which looks back in both anger and hilarity at the tradition of English comedy. First performed in 1969 after Orton's murder by his partner Kenneth Halliwell, it represents the young English dramatist's post-Freudian take on Wildean comedy. Set in a psychiatric clinic, it works with the normal conventions of farce to make a farce out of normal conventions. Indeed, it represents the world of Auden's 'Goddess of bossy underlings, Normality' – the middle-class marriage of Dr and Mrs Prentice, the medical institution, and the visits of a government inspector and policeman – as a mirror of every conceivable sexual transgression and perversion. It begins with Dr Prentice inveigling Miss Barclay, a candidate to be his secretary, into undressing for a medical examination. Interrupted by his wife and then a health inspector Dr Rance, Prentice attempts to cover up his indiscretion with each desperate attempt to 'normalise' things leading him into more bizarrely incriminating situations. As a result, Miss Barclay is certified as a mental patient, Dr Prentice viewed as a transvestite, bisexual, fetishist and everyone else caught up in comparably scandalous sexual situations, with Geraldine Barclay, Nicholas Beckett and a police constable at one time or another dressed as members of the opposite sex or stalking the stage in their underwear. The result is a comedy of diagnostic errors, which ends, rather as *The Importance of Being Earnest* does, with the revelation that the young man and woman are twin children of Dr and Mrs Prentice, conceived after the rape of the latter by the former (prior to their marriage) in the linen closet of the Station Hotel, the place where Mrs Prentice is later photographed and blackmailed by the page Nicholas (who turns out to be her son).

At one point, Mrs Prentice asks Rance, 'Does any of this make sense to you?'[63] This is the classic nonsense query in the style of *Alice*, but the play is not only a post-Freudian farce but satirises Rance's increasingly bizarre attempts to make sense of things in Freudian terms. It simultaneously spoofs psychiatric diagnoses and generates a nonsensical comedy out of Oedipal fantasy, confirming Orton's view that 'the actual material of tragedy is equally viable in comedy'. (*CP*, p. 7). Introducing himself, Dr Rance says 'I represent Her Majesty's Government, your superiors in madness', explaining that 'My brief is infinite. I would hold sway over a rabbit-hutch, if the inmates were disturbed' (*CP*, p. 376). In this hierarchical political world of 'superiors in madness', where everyone is 'disturbed' (not least the psychiatrist holding sway 'over a rabbit hutch), the distinction between 'normality' and 'abnormality' dissolves. At one point, for example, Rance asks Prentice 'Were your relations with your secretary normal?', and being told 'Yes', answers 'Well, Prentice, your private life is your own affair [. . .] I find it shocking, nonetheless' (*CP*, p. 381). In similar vein, when the unfortunate Miss Barclay is asked 'Did your step-mother know of your love for your father?' she replies, 'I live in a normal family, I have no love for my father' (*CP*, p. 382).

The play might have been called *What the Psychiatrist Saw*, bringing together as it does the world of a smutty end-of-the-pier show and that of a mental hospital. In doing so, it comically breaks down the opposition between the 'normal' and 'abnormal', 'sane' and 'insane', and any stable notion of sexual or familial normality. Rance, who claims to be 'a representative of order' (*CP*, p. 417), boasts that 'I once put a whole family into a communal straightjacket', before admitting it was his 'own family' and noting he'd sent a picture of the scene to Freud and got 'a charming postcard in reply' (*CP*, 442). As things wind towards the apocalyptically farcical denouement, Rance anticipates writing it up as a psychiatric bestseller, saying 'The final chapters of my book are knitting together: incest, buggery, outrageous women and strange love-cults catering for depraved appetites. All the fashionable bric-a-brac' (*CP*, pp. 427–8).

There is a sense in which Orton's play is also made out of the 'fashionable' 'bric-a-brac' of the late 1960s in the wake of the Profumo affair, the decriminalisation of homosexuality, the vogue for satire and the movement of 'sexual liberation' in America. It flaunts Orton's overt homosexuality as well as pleasure in cocking a snook at the establishment, bringing both queer sexuality and polymorphous heterosexuality (a word Rance deplores as 'Chaucerian') out of the closet onto the stage. Like the theatre of Wilde, Orton's farce makes a nonsense of the most cherished values of English culture, and, like much gay writing, thrives on the pleasures of nonsense. *What the Butler Saw* may seem a far cry from *Alice's Adventures in Wonderland*, but Prentice's exclamation that 'I've been too long among the mad to know what sanity is' (*CP*, 419) recalls the Mad Hatter's Tea-Party where the Cheshire Cat tells Alice 'We're all mad here. I'm mad. You're mad.'[64] When Dr Rance asserts sternly, 'I am a representative of order, you of chaos', he foregrounds the dizzying questions about order, normality, logic and identity, which the queer nonsense relay race I have been tracing plays with and upon.

Notes

1. Edward Lear, *The Complete Nonsense and Other Verse*, ed. Vivien Noakes (London: Penguin, 2006), pp. 428, 352. Hereafter referenced in the main text as *CN*.
2. Lewis Carroll, *Alice's Adventures in Wonderland and Through the Looking-Glass*, ed. Hugh Haughton (London: Penguin, 1998), p. 17.
3. Ibid. pp. 24, 58, 91.
4. Charles Dickens, *The Pickwick Papers* (London: Chapman & Hall, 1894), p. 543.
5. Charles Dickens, *David Copperfield* (London: Chapman & Hall, 1894), p. 168.
6. Oscar Wilde, *The Artist as Critic: Critical Writings of Oscar Wilde*, ed. Richard Ellmann (Chicago: University of Chicago Press, 1969), pp. 319–20.
7. Joe Orton said the pair were given a prison sentence for defacing the books 'because we were queers', Simon Shepherd, *Because We're Queers: The Life and Crimes of Kenneth Halliwell and Joe Orton* (London: Gay Men's Press, 1989), p. 14.
8. For a fuller discussion of this see my introduction to *The Chatto Book of Nonsense Poetry* (London: Chatto and Windus, 1988), 1–32.
9. Annamarie Jagose, *Introduction to Queer Theory* (New York: New York University Press, 1996), pp. 3, 99.
10. Eve Kosofsky Sedgwick, *Tendencies* (London: Routledge, 1994), p. 8.
11. Haughton, *Chatto Book*, p. 8.
12. In the Victorian web's online concordance to Wilde, there is no record of his using 'queer' in the fiction, plays and essays. In *Intentions* (1890), there are thirty-three uses of 'strange' and none of 'queer', <http://victorian-studies.net/concordance/wilde/> (last accessed 20 April 2021).
13. Sedgwick notes: 'The highly cathected noun and verb "Bunbury" itself, the non-familial alibi in the play, as distinct from the term "brother", alludes (as several critics note) to the surreptitious sexuality in terms of a particular genital practice: anal sex as "burying in the bun"', *Tendencies*, p. 67.
14. Oscar Wilde, *The Importance of Being Earnest*, ed. Russell Jackson (London: Ernest Benn, 1980), p. 40.
15. Gilbert and Sullivan, *Patience*, Act 1, l. 318, in *The Complete Annotated Gilbert and Sullivan*, ed. Ian Bradley (Oxford: Oxford University Press, 2016), p. 357. Richard Ellmann argues that Wilde is a model for both Bunthorne and Grosvenor: see *Oscar Wilde* (London: Penguin, 1988), pp. 129, 130–1.

16. Edward Lear, *Later Letters of Edward Lear*, ed. Lady Strachey (London: Unwin, 1911), p. 253. Hereafter referenced in the main text as *LL*.
17. Angus Davidson, *Edward Lear: Landscape Painter and Nonsense Poet* (Harmondsworth: Penguin, [1938] 1950), p. 67.
18. Peter Swaab, '"Some think him . . . Queer": Loners and Love in Edward Lear', in James Williams and Matthew Bevis (eds), *Edward Lear and the Play of Poetry*, ed. Matthew Bevis (Oxford: Oxford University Press, 2016), 89–114, p. 96.
19. Ibid. p. 114.
20. Hugh Haughton, 'Edward Lear and "The fiddlediddlety of representation"', in *The Oxford Handbook of Victorian Poetry*, ed. Matthew Bevis (Oxford: Oxford University Press, 2013), 351–69, p. 354.
21. Carroll, *Looking-Glass*, p. 182.
22. Ibid. p. 186.
23. Lewis Carroll, *Jabberwocky and Other Nonsense*, ed. Gillian Beer (London: Penguin, 2012), p. 248.
24. Ibid. p. 250.
25. Lewis Carroll, 'Alice on the Stage', in *Alice's Adventures in Wonderland and Through the Looking-Glass*, p. 295.
26. Morton N. Cohen and Anita Gandolfo (eds), *Lewis Carroll and the House of Macmillan* (Cambridge: Cambridge University Press, 1987), p. 135.
27. W. H. Auden, *The English Auden*, ed. Edward Mendelson (London: Faber and Faber, 1977), p. 193.
28. See James Atherton, *The Books at the Wake* (London: Faber and Faber, 1959), pp. 124–36; Franklin Walton, 'Wilde at the Wake', *James Joyce Quarterly* 14.3 (1977), 300–12; and Sam Slote, 'Wilde Things: Concerning the Eccentricities of a Figure of Decadence in *Finnegans Wake*', in *Probes: Genetic Studies in Joyce*, ed. David Hayman and Sam Slote (Amsterdam: Rodopi, 1995), 101–22. Main text references are to page and line numbers in *Finnegans Wake* (London: Faber and Faber, 1939), abbreviated *FW*.
29. For Freud on 'polymorphous and perverse' sexuality in infancy and adulthood, see *The Psychology of Love*, ed. Jeri Johnson (London: Penguin, 2006).
30. Adam Piette, '"Now listen, Mr Leer!": Joyce's Lear', in *Play of Poetry*, ed. Williams and Bevis, 281–99, pp. 294, 289.
31. W. H. Auden, *Academic Graffiti* (London: Faber and Faber, 1971), p. 58.
32. Ibid. p. 32.
33. W. H. Auden, *Collected Poems*, ed. Edward Mendelson (London: Faber and Faber, 1991), p. 183.
34. Auden, *English Auden*, p. 105.
35. *The Oxford Book of Light Verse*, ed. W. H. Auden (Oxford: Oxford University Press, 1938), p. xviii.
36. Anna Barton, 'The Sense and Nonsense of Weariness: Edward Lear and Gertrude Stein read Tennyson', in *Play of Poetry*, ed. Williams and Bevis, 243–59.
37. Gertrude Stein, *Writings: 1903–1932* (New York: Library of America, 1998), p. 314.
38. Ibid. p. 743.
39. Ibid. p. 828.
40. Gertrude Stein, *The Making of Americans* (London: Dalkey Archive, 1995), p. 485.
41. Hannah Roche notes that Stein's 'Miss Furr and Miss Skeene' of 1922 is 'celebrated as a pioneering work providing the first recorded instance of the semantic shift of "gay" from "happy" to "homosexual"', *The Outside Thing: Modernist Lesbian Romance* (New York: Columbia University Press, 2021), p. 56.
42. Gertrude Stein, *Everybody's Autobiography* (Cambridge: Exact Change, 1995), p. 70.

43. Jack Halberstam [published as Judith Halberstam], 'The anti-social turn in queer studies', *Graduate Journal of Social Science* 5.2 (2008), 140–52, p. 141. See also Prudence Bussey-Chamberlain's chapter '"He Cannot Understand Women. I Can": Gertrude Stein and the Camp Butch' in *Queer Troublemakers: The Poetics of Flippancy* (London: Bloomsbury Academic, 2019), 33–68.
44. Stein, *Writings 1903–1932*, p. 571.
45. Ibid. p. 579.
46. Elizabeth Bishop, 'Time's Andromedas', in *Poems, Prose, Letters*, ed. Robert Giroux and Lloyd Schwartz (New York: Library of America, 2008), p. 656.
47. Ibid. pp. 53–4.
48. Ibid.
49. Ibid. p. 715.
50. Ibid. p. 10.
51. Robert Boucheron, 'Elizabeth Bishop at Harvard', 'talking writing', 21 January 2013, <http://talkingwriting.com/elizabeth-bishop-at-harvard/> (last accessed 20 April 2021).
52. Bishop, *Poems, Prose, Letters*, p. 243.
53. Stephen Ross, 'Edward Lear, John Ashbery and the Pleasant Surprise', in *Play of Poetry*, ed. Williams and Bevis, pp. 347–65.
54. Stephanie Burt [published as Stephen Burt], *Close Calls with Nonsense: Reading New Poetry* (Minneapolis: Graywolf, 2009).
55. Craig Burnett, 'A Kind of Musical Space: An Interview with John Ashbery', *Frieze* 185 (2004), quoted by Stephen Ross, 'Pleasant Surprise', in *Play of Poetry*, ed. Williams and Bevis, p. 351.
56. For Ashbery and 'homotextuality', see John Shoptaw, *On the Outside, Looking Out* (Cambridge, MA: Harvard University Press, 1995), p. 4 and *passim*.
57. Edward Gorey, *Amphigorey Also* (New York: Congdon and Weed, 1983), n.p.
58. Edward Gorey, *Amphigorey Too* (New York: Perigee, 1980), n.p.
59. Gorey, *Amphigorey Also*, n.p.
60. Interview with Christopher Steufert, <https://www.youtube.com/watch?v=444lf0a0ot0> (last accessed 20 April 2021).
61. Edward Gorey, *Ascending Peculiarity: Edward Gorey on Edward Gorey* (New York: Harvest Books, 2002), p. 102.
62. Edward Gorey, *Amphigorey* (New York: Berkley Windhover Books, 1975), n.p.
63. Joe Orton, *The Complete Plays* ed. John Lahr (London: Methuen, 1976), p. 424. Hereafter referenced in the main text as *CP*.
64. Carroll, *Wonderland*, p. 57.

17

Humans, and Other Nonsense Animals

Cassie Westwood

'Every great literature has always been allegorical – allegorical of some view of the whole universe', wrote G. K. Chesterton in 1902. 'If, therefore, nonsense is really to be the literature of the future', he continued, 'it must have its own version of the Cosmos to offer; the world must not only be tragic, romantic, and religious, it must be nonsensical also.'[1] This is another way of saying what Anthony Burgess put in more colloquial terms eighty years later: nonsense 'is a playful pragmatic way of interpreting the universe'.[2] Taking these quotations as springboards, this chapter suggests some ways in which nonsense allows us to see the world – and particularly our cohabitation of it with other animals – in a nonsensical light. Rather than offering a survey of the representation of other animals, this chapter proposes that nonsense enables us to understand our own relations to and with them differently.

Nonsense revivifies our perception of a world that exceeds our ability to apprehend it rationally or imaginatively, and stirs a feeling that our understanding of life, such as it is, cannot exhaust life itself. It does so through the creation of different, often unexpected, perspectives on life, for the sense of wonder that Chesterton finds in nonsense is not a property of the things in themselves but rather a function of how we look at them. 'So long as we regard a tree as an obvious thing', Chesterton explained,

> naturally and reasonably created for a giraffe to eat, we cannot properly wonder at it. It is when we consider it as a prodigious wave of the living soil sprawling up to the skies for no reason in particular that we take off our hats, to the astonishment of the park-keeper. Everything has in fact another side to it, like the moon, the patroness of nonsense. Viewed from that other side, a bird is a blossom broken loose from its chain of stalk, a man a quadruped begging on its hind legs, a house a gigantesque hat to cover a man from the sun, a chair an apparatus of four wooden legs for a cripple with only two.[3]

The examples offered by Chesterton handily furnish forth the objects of this chapter's attention, constituting as they do an unlikely menagerie of a giraffe, a bird and a familiar hairless creature hovering inelegantly between bipedality and quadrupedality. This bestiary, odd as it looks, is nonetheless of a piece with those found in the nonsense about which Chesterton spoke, and similar bestiaries constitute one of its ubiquitous aspects: the presence of animals (human or otherwise).

Perhaps this parenthesis snags on the ear, either as redundant ('of course the word "animals" includes humans') or fallacious ('"animal" and "human" are mutually exclusive terms'). In fact, though, the relations between what I will be referring to in this chapter as 'humans and other animals' have been the subject of increasing scrutiny over the last three decades or so, across the humanities, social sciences and biological sciences. These diverse studies have grown, unevenly, into a field known as 'animal studies' or 'human-animal studies'.[4] In the next section of this chapter, I outline some of the main avenues of inquiry within this field. For now, though, consider how the phrase 'animals (human or otherwise)' raises two different possibilities: first, that we can consider humans to be united with other animals by something like a common animality or creatureliness;[5] and secondly, that we humans necessarily speak and think about ourselves as a special case – animals, yes, but a species that is exceptional or anomalous within the animal kingdom. Both are true in their own way, and lead us on to further questions, which have formed a major part of the conversations within the field: to what extent, and in what ways, are humans similar to other animals? To what extent, and in what ways, are non-human animals similar to each other? And what are the ramifications – philosophical, ethical, political and cultural – of our responses to these questions?

Animal studies interrogates what we often think of as the human/animal binary, and many critics have argued that the absolute separation entailed by this dichotomy is an inadequate, even iniquitous, description of the nature of our relations with other animals – that it is, moreover, supportive of an ideology which devalues the natural world so as to render it more fully exploitable.[6] On both sides of the binary, critics have found fault with its terminology and assumptions. 'Animal' corrals an enormous variety of different organisms into one word, which tends to simplify and essentialise the differences between humans and all other animals – when, in fact, the similarities between, say, humans and dolphins seem far more significant than those between dolphins and fleas.[7] And on the other side, the coherence of the 'human' itself has been scrutinised in ideological, conceptual and political terms.[8] In other words, animal studies in all its guises refuses to take the ideas of 'the human' and 'the animal' as givens, but treats them rather as constructed and unstable ideas with a history of their own.

In its own way, nonsense literature often complicates this binary vision: it introduces 'personages' that are 'both more and less than an ordinary person',[9] like Edward Lear's 'Jumblies', whose 'heads are green, and [. . .] hands are blue';[10] it multiplies the kinds of living form and then draws those categories into polymorphous choreographies, like in another of Lear's poems, 'The Quangle Wangle's Hat', with the 'Fimble Fowl', the 'Golden Grouse', the 'Blue Baboon' and the 'Orient Calf' coming together to dance under the eponymous hat.[11] Such instances illustrate some of the ways in which nonsense interprets and responds to a world that humans cohabit with other animals. What follows in this chapter addresses two aspects in particular of this relationship: first, the traditional conception of humans as uniquely in possession of language; and secondly, the inaccessibility of animals' private experience from a human's perspective. Following each of these sections are ones that consider how nonsense literature might fruitfully come to bear on these questions, by complicating our understanding of 'the human' and by enriching our responses to questions of animal subjectivity. These readings are interlaced with arguments for the hitherto-unrealised importance of nonsense for animal studies, showing how nonsense enables a new perspective on humans' imaginative relations with other animals.

If we think of nonsense as Chesterton did – as a kind of attitude or disposition towards life (particularly towards the elements of experience that are strange or obscure) – then it becomes clear that the study of nonsense can make legible a fuller range of our responses to, and thoughts about, other animals. Nonsense cultivates another perspective, one of messiness and fecundity, 'pierc[ing] us with strange relation', in Wallace Stevens's words.[12] Looked at in this way, animals are principal parts of this world view, for they have long held both a privileged and a precarious place in the cultural imagination. They are at once familiar and strange, part of our everyday interactions and yet evidently subjects of a life of their own; as such, they remind us that the world is a living and crowded stage, rather than a static backdrop. And it is this quality of the world, the fact of its alive-ness and of its independence from the determination of human will, that is so often the springboard for nonsense; its living objects, its animals acting like humans, its humans acting like machines, the recalcitrance of language – these are all (il)logical extensions of the perception of a peculiarly animated nature.

On Language

Since Aristotle, the capacity for language has been thought to represent a decisive border separating humans from other animals. That is to say, in the popular imagination, 'man' was (and still to an extent is) considered to be the 'speaking animal'. The conventional position held by scientists and philosophers alike was this: whereas other animals could make noises, and signal pain or pleasure through those vocalisations, only humans were capable of organising those sounds into a systematic, structured grammar. In Aristotle's *Politics*, he describes it in the following way:

> Nature, as we often say, makes nothing in vain, and man is the only animal who has the gift of speech [*logos*]. And whereas mere voice [*phōnē*] is but an indication of pleasure and pain, and is therefore found in other animals (for their nature attains to the perception of pleasure and pain and the intimation of them to one another, and no further).[13]

It is, therefore, supposed to be the unique quality of human language that it is capable of abstract conceptual thought. This link between speech and abstract thought has meant that the myth of an exceptional human capacity for language also fed directly into the Aristotelian idea that humans alone were capable of rational speech – that is, both the capacity for rational thought and the means of expressing it verbally.[14] This notion is one of the most enduring in Western philosophy:[15] Descartes, for instance, put this idea in its most familiar form when he contended that animals lacked reason and therefore also the ability to speak: 'the reason why animals do not speak as we do is not that they lack the organs but that they have no thoughts'.[16] Three centuries later, the influential nineteenth-century Oxford philologist Friedrich Max Müller put it in similar terms:

> thought, in one sense of the word, i.e. in the sense of reasoning, is impossible without language or without signs. [. . .] Animals and infants who are without language, are alike without reason; but the difference between animal and infant

> is, that the infant possesses the healthy germs of speech and reason, only not yet developed [. . .] whereas the animal has no such germs or faculties, capable of development.[17]

Reason and speech are linked, moreover, in the Greek word *logos* ('λόγος'), meaning both speech and reason.[18] Conveniently joining these two concepts in a single word, *logos* became a kind of shorthand for the defining excellence of humanity, denoting what humans 'had' that all other animals did not.

The philosopher Mary Midgley argues convincingly in *Beast and Man* that the idea that there could be a 'single, simple, final distinction' between one species and all others is too simplistic. If we think about how we might define another species, she notes, 'We can certainly find marks that will help us to classify and understand them. But we had better not claim that by doing so we have finally expressed their true nature in a simple formula.'[19] Yet, in spite of this philosophical good sense, the notion that there is some single characteristic excellence that separates 'man' from the 'animals' has endured in a wide variety of spheres of thought and discourse. Thomas Hood, for one, saw some comic potential in such attempts, facetiously proposing in 'A Recipe – for Civilization' that man was not the rational animal, but rather 'The only COOKING ANIMAL!'.[20] Were human distinction to be based on the former, he mused, 'parrots [might] claim affinity, | And dogs be doctors by latinity'.[21] Sealing it with a groan-inducing clincher, he points out that '*Nay*, no one but a horse would forage | On naked oats instead of porridge'.[22]

In addition to Midgley's objection, two significant strands of inquiry in animal studies have further complicated the idea that the capacity for language is the defining difference between humans and other animals. In the second half of the twentieth century, particularly the 1960s and 70s, a body of scientific evidence developed showing apes and birds to be capable of varying degrees of linguistic proficiency. The most famous example was Washoe the chimpanzee, who acquired a considerable degree of fluency in a sign language called Ameslan.[23] More recent research has instead explored the vast array of non-verbal communication systems used by other species. Although in general, the eminent primatologist Frans de Waal suggests, it is now admitted that humans do have a unique way of using their particular linguistic system, it is also now widely recognised that thought is not dependent on, nor does it necessarily take the form of, speech.[24] This is a fact which we may learn as clearly from nonsense literature as from scientists.[25] Language, as a poem like Edward Gorey's 'The Utter Zoo Alphabet' illuminates, might as much be shaped by arbitrary ordering systems as by rational thought:

> The Crunk is not unseldom drastic
> And must be hindered by elastic.
>
> The Dawbis is remote and shy;
> It shuns the gaze of passers-by.[26]

And poems like those of John Ashbery's show how thought itself can deform, overspill, or chafe against what we conventionally recognise as rational speech.

The disarticulation of speech from reason points to the efforts of a second, philosophically inclined body of thought, which has argued for an alternative understanding of language itself. Drawing from the poststructuralist theories of language first articulated in the 1960s and 70s, what has become known as 'posthumanism' (particularly that version of it formulated by Cary Wolfe) argues that the nature of language is such that it gives the lie to the humanist ideal of people as independent, coherent and autonomous beings – sovereign over themselves and the world of mere 'things'. If language is an essentially arbitrary semiotic system, it is argued, in which the conventional relations between the elements in that system are operative independent of humans' use of language, then language should be considered not simply a tool for communication, but a semiotic phenomenon that exists apart from human intention. Linguistic systems, Wolfe argues, 'are always radically other, already in- or ahuman'; and human language itself is 'a diacritical, semiotic machine [. . .] in the broadest sense that exceeds any and all presence, including our own'.[27] This 'technicity' of language, as Wolfe terms it, with which humans are 'prosthetically entwined', bears witness to a 'subjection to and constitution in the materiality and technicity of a language that is always on the scene before we are, as a precondition of our subjectivity'.[28] Intuitively, we might be inclined to reject this account as philosophical high-mindedness, but the theorist of nonsense Jean-Jacques Lecercle points out that this 'ahuman technicity' is a familiar part of everyday speech:

> the speaker is always torn apart between the two poles of the contradiction of language, 'language speaks' (it is language, not I, that speaks, the words come out of my mouth 'all wrong') and 'I speak language' (I am in full control of my utterance, I say what I mean and mean what I say).[29]

In this account, language cannot be considered the characteristic achievement of human beings, but rather evidence that the idea of the human itself is constitutionally compromised by something inhuman at its core.

Nonsense literature relishes moments when the structuring logics of language renders speech nonsensical, where it is undone by its own structure, and as such it stands as one of the most recognisable examples of the 'technicity' described by Wolfe. It has an inherent tendency to knock humans off of their exceptionalist perch with spoonerisms, malapropisms, excessive alliteration and parapraxes. These moments give us a hint that language is not completely under human control, and nonsense delves deeply into these phenomena for its materials. It shows how language cannot be thought of as domesticated or tamed, or how it cannot be thought of simply as a tool for communication. In Hugh Haughton's words, nonsense gives us 'a salutary and savoury sense of the saving incongruity between our language mastery and all it does not and can never master'.[30]

'Hum! quoth the Bee'

This section will consider some of the ways in which nonsense evinces a similar scepticism about the idea that humans are paradigmatically and uniquely in possession of *logos*, complicating the picture of humans as 'the rational or speaking animal'. As William Empson would have put it, nonsense 'blows the gaff' on the idea of language as an instrument of pure reason.[31] We humans are creatures of sound as well as speech, expressing ourselves as much by noise and oracular accident as by reasoned propositions. Nonsense gives voice, as it were, to those properties of speech that need to be suppressed in order to define the human as the *zōon logon echon*.

First of all, nonsense reminds us that there is an important part of our development as individuals in which we are not able to speak. Müller's oversimplification that 'Animals and infants who are without language, are alike without reason', in the passage quoted above, is meant to distinguish the two by citing the latter's capacity to learn language (what we might call the idea of 'human perfectibility'). But nonsense gives the lie to the idea that that developmental process is one of clear progression with discrete stages. As both Adam Phillips and Hugh Haughton suggest, the Babel of nonsense has much in common with the babble of infants as they learn to imitate the words they hear around them.[32] It stands, Haughton suggests, as 'the most conspicuous surviving monument of the earliest play with – and play of – language in our lives'.[33] Children learn first to imitate the sounds of a language, before they become familiar with its semiotic conventions, by playing about with the rhythm of sentences and the tone and cadence of particular words or phrases. The extra-linguistic and gestural supplements to communication need to be acquired as well as, if not before, the referents of individual words.

Nursery rhymes learned by children tend to stress sound more than sense, coining nonce-words out of repeated units of sound, such as 'Humpty Dumpty' and 'Wee Willy Winky'. This formula is often repeated in nonsense: for instance, in Lear's the Yonghy-Bongy-Bò or Carroll's Tweedle-dee and Tweedle-dum.[34] Much of the pleasure we take in refrains such as 'Hey nonny nonny' or 'fol-de-rol' is closely related to our delight as infants in repetitious, musical sound. It is derived from these early language games, in which we play with sounds, words and phrases as though they were blocks of Lego, piecing together infinite variations with finite resources.[35] Found also in popular songs and ballads, these coinages constitute an important resource in nonsense's verbal repertoire, and they signal the enduring importance of a pre- or non-rational element in human language. 'The truth is', Haughton rightly says, 'that word formation and word deformation are closely allied.'[36] We learn to speak by playing with speech, and this play transports us back aurally and emotionally to a much earlier developmental stage – one in which, traditional wisdom has it, we are much more closely aligned with other animals.[37]

Exclamations such as 'fiddle-de-dee'[38] or 'fara diddle dyno'[39] are a kind of supplement for ordinary language, at once exuberant musical overflows of speech and evidence of a perceived deficiency in its expressive range. As well as constituting survivals of childhood verbal play, they signal the meaningfulness of, and in, sound; this is another way in which nonsense complicates the idea of language-based human exceptionalism. 'Fiddle-de-dee', for instance, can be found in the *Oxford English Dictionary* – albeit attached to the tautologous definition: 'Nonsense!' As both a synonym for, and an example of, nonsense, the phrase exhibits an anomalously direct relation between the sign and what it denotes; in a way, it short-circuits the conventional structure of symbolic language by closing the gap between signifier and signified. This is also one way in which we might think of nonsense's interest in rhyme, whereby the sound rather than the sense of words is the determining factor of their pairing. By 'savour[ing] the clatter' of 'patently arbitrary rhymes',[40] nonsense shifts the significance of words away from their semantic content and towards their phonic make-up – just as in Gorey's 'Utter Zoo Alphabet', the Crunk's 'drastic' behaviour necessitates the use of 'elastic' to restrain them. In Edward Lear's limericks, for instance, his characters' behaviour or possessions are determined by the necessity of rhyming with the final word of the first line – which is itself arbitrarily determined. Lear's frequent preference for animal rhymes means that someone from Dunluce is almost certain to consort with a goose.[41] In this way, nonsense uncovers a tendency or potentiality in language that has little to do with human will or reason, a kind of logic of linguistic accidents.

One of the chief pleasures of nonsense verse derives from this play with the arbitrariness of a chance phonic convergence. In a nonsense verse like the popular nineteenth-century ballad 'Old Mother Hubbard and her Dog', rhyme determines what the two titular characters do, in a recursive structure that is reminiscent of childhood playground games. In each stanza, Mother Hubbard attempts to respond appropriately to the dog's behaviour, only to find on her return that the dog is now doing something completely different. This new action is determined by the necessity of rhyming with Mother Hubbard's behaviour, as in the following:

Old Mother Hubbard
Went to the cupboard,
To fetch her poor dog a bone;
But when she came there
The cupboard was bare
And so the poor dog had none.

She went to the baker's
To buy him some bread;
But when she came back
The poor dog was dead.

She went to the undertaker's
To buy him a coffin;
But when she came back
The poor dog was laughing.[42]

Part of the pleasure in this verse, I think, is in perceiving the tension between chance and predetermination which the role of rhyme in the poem introduces. In the artificial orderliness of its language – in its tendency, too, to order the characters around – this kind of nonsense stages a relinquishing of human control. It invites a submission to an external force, but in a way that cultivates a pleasurable susceptibility to that submission.

The poetic artificiality of some nonsense can undermine the sense that language is a possession or instrument of human reason, but other, less ordered kinds of nonsense suggest the possibility that the language of unreason might itself open up new spheres of experience. The twentieth-century Russian Futurist Velimir Khlebnikov's work shows how nonsense could transform language into an instrument capable of blurring the border between humans and other animals, rather than establishing it. In his work, and in other Futurist and *zaumnik* (Russian: 'trans-sense') work from the early twentieth century, both the signs and the structure of conventional speech are abandoned.[43] Consider the birds' speeches to the dawn from Khlebnikov's utopian 'supersaga', *Zangezi*, which – like Aristophanes, Lear and others before him – senses an affinity between birdsong and nonsense:

> *Chaffinch (from the very top of the fir tree, puffing out its silver throat)*
> Peet *pate* tveechan! Peet pate tveechan! Peets *pate* tveechan!
>
> *Yellow Bunting (quietly, from the top of a walnut tree)*
> Kree-tee-tee-tee-*tee*-ee-tsuey-tsuey-tsuey-*ssue*yee.[44]

In this kind of writing, there is no sense of an underlying syntax or structural order. In fact, it stretches the limits of human language to breaking point, for this is both a phonic transliteration of birdsong, and a translation of it into a kind of improvised pidgin – much like the 'Tio, tio, tio, tiotinx' in Aristophanes' *The Birds*, or 'Twikky wikky wikky wee' in Lear's 'Mr and Mrs Spikky Sparrow'.[45] Such experiments show how nonsense literature can be a kind of linguistic thought experiment about the limits of the human itself. A 'supersaga', Khlebnikov wrote, is a structure composed of independent sections or 'planes', 'each with its own special god, its special faith, and its special rule'; composed, as it is, of many different kinds of language (established and invented), *Zangezi* is a text that enacts an idea of independent but intersecting forms of life – what he described elsewhere as a 'one-dimensional manifold' in which one cannot perceive a 'distinction between human and animal species'.[46] It proposes that nonsense (like the speech of the gods: 'Rapr, grapr, apr! Zhai! | Kaf! Bzuey! Kaf!')[47] is both the production of non-human life, and a means of representing it to other humans. But while the birds' chorus is necessarily a kind of representation of the language of birds using a human speech system (it uses an existing alphabet; or rather two, in Russian and its English translation), our inability to recognise it as syntactically or semantically meaningful attenuates the extent to which we may regard it as a translation from an avian into a human register. Elsewhere in *Zangezi*, the titular prophet refers to a 'speech that frees you from the fetters of words',[48] and indeed the speech of the birds embodies a kind of intermediate position between human speech and natural sound.

Nonsense literature's playful depiction of the intrinsic irrationality within speech threatens to undermine one of the pillars of human exceptionalism, teasing apart the conjunction of language and reason that is symbolised in the word *logos*. Nonsense tends to reveal the frequency with which language slips the leash of reason and human will. One way in which it has done so is by imagining what forms human speech would take if uttered by non-human mouths. For instance, in Ben Jonson's 'A Catch', a fly and a bee obligingly give voice to the human approximation of their respective sounds:

> Buzz! quoth the Blue-Fly,
> Hum! quoth the Bee;
> Buzz and hum! they cry,
> And so do we.[49]

This reminds one of the stories about crows that have learned to mimic not just human speech, but humans' imitations of crows: exclaiming 'caw!'[50] It also calls to mind several of Lear's limericks: the 'Young Lady of Troy, | Whom several large flies did annoy' (*CN* p. 88); the 'old man who said, "See! | I have found a most beautiful bee!"', which bee also buzzes (p. 111); the 'silly' old person who was 'filled [. . .] full of despair' by 'six bees' (p. 112); the 'Old Man in a tree, | Who was horribly bored by a Bee', which, like the 'old man who said "See!"', also includes a resonant and rhyming 'buzz' (p. 161); not to mention several more such limericks.[51] Jonson's poem treats the sounds of the insects like reported speech ('quoth the Bee'), and the stanza ends with a kind of chorus: 'And so do we'. Whatever else the poem is doing, that last line offers a half-serious proposition about a shared language between humans and other animals. 'Buzz' and 'hum', being transliterated approximations of a sound, are at once speech and sound, and their ambiguous status is what permits that affirmation of communality in the final line; both bees and humans can, as it were, cry 'hum!' That we ought not to take this too seriously, however, is suggested by the second of poem's two stanzas, which collapses into nonsense, and in which pronouns have no clear referent:

In his ear! in his nose!
Thus, – do you see?
He eat the Dormouse –
    Else it was he.[52]

It is as though the assertion of commonality in 'And so do we' precipitates this prosodic and semantic confusion. Who, in this stanza, is the 'he' of the last line, into which the 'we' of the previous stanza's corresponding line appears to have resolved? Nonsense seems here to permit a thought experiment about the possibility of a shared language, which it can just as quickly abandon or dissolve.

This kind of experimentalism, in which an animal is imagined as speaking an approximation of human language that is both recognisable and strange, is a consistent feature of nonsense. Witness, for example, Paul Klee's 'Der Herr weis was der wil', which is written 'in the style of Klee's favourite cat, Bimbo':[53]

The Master knows what he want.
he can.

But he has one vice, not smoking.
He skrattches on his fiddle with a hairwhip.
It make Bimbo's ears go tingle.[54]

Bimbo's feline 'style' is signalled by the unorthodox spelling ('skrattches') and syntax ('It make'), but, perhaps fittingly for the imagined speech of a domesticated animal, its general structure is decipherable, recognisably human. 'It make Bimbo's ears go tingle', moreover, gives its readers its own tingle of consonants which conveys a bodily sensation not dissimilar, we are to imagine, from Bimbo's imagined physical sensation (a distaste that could be the result of his master playing on what is known in English and German as 'catgut' – violin strings that are usually made, in fact, from sheep intestine).[55] Elizabeth Sewell described this effect astutely when she said that nonsense, 'by [a] re-patterning of letters in a word or of objects in a seemingly given universe', produces a 'dislocation of that given and then a re-location which, slight as it is, may yet permit glimpses of [. . .] other orders beyond and through our usual perspectives'.[56] And it is able to offer these glimpses of 'other orders' because the patterns of language, 'of letters, sounds, grammatical categories, syntactical organization', 'pattern the universe'.[57] Changing the ordinary arrangements of language changes our perception of the world, and much of the significance of nonsense literature for animal studies resides in this ability to manipulate language in order (partially) to transcend or transform it. Nonsense develops in us a sense of community that exceeds language, yet which is experienced through it.

On the Minds of Animals

Bimbo, Descartes would have said, could have had no such thoughts – ungrammatical or otherwise – only the 'tingle', unaccompanied by reflective thought.[58] His reasoning has often been juxtaposed with Michel de Montaigne's equally strident, but contradictory, scepticism regarding human exceptionalism in his 'Apology for Raymond Sebond':

> The natural, and original distemper of Man is presumption. Man is the most blighted and frail of all creatures and, moreover, the most given to pride. This creature knows and sees that he is lodged down here, among the mire and shit of the world, [. . .] yet, in thought, he sets himself above the circle of the Moon [. . .]. The vanity of this same thought makes him equal himself to God; attribute to himself God's mode of being; pick himself out and set himself apart from the mass of other creatures; and (although they are his fellows and his brothers) carve out for them such helpings of force or faculties as he thinks fit. How can he, from the power of his own understanding, know the hidden, inward motivations of animate creatures? What comparison between us and them leads him to conclude that they have the attributes of senseless brutes?
>
> When I play with my cat, how do I know that she is not passing time with me rather than I with her?[59]

In this, we can see the outlines of a knotty question concerning the minds of animals, and our ability to confirm or know them, which has continued for centuries. Montaigne's point is not simply that animals are our 'fellows and brothers', but rather that the assumptions about the mental capacity of other animals are just that – assumptions. The debate has been, and continues to be, a long one, and much of the reason for this lies in the particular inaccessibility of animals' intentions and thoughts, compared with our access to those of other humans.[60] Contemporary animal studies has thus paid considerable attention to this 'alterity' of other animals, their otherness.[61] In a famous essay, Thomas Nagel argues that, while most people would agree 'that there is something that it is like to be a bat', the fact that they 'perceive the external world primarily by sonar, or echolocation' makes the nature of their experience 'fundamentally alien' to our own, so that 'there is no reason to suppose that it is subjectively like anything we can experience or imagine'.[62] This is not only the case with bats, Nagel suggests, but with all other forms of conscious life also. This epistemological impasse has been described in different ways since the publication of Nagel's essay, but the idea of other animals as unknowable continues to be influential; as John Berger put it, humans and animals 'scrutinize' each other 'across a narrow abyss of noncomprehension'.[63]

More recently, though, numerous works of popular science have sought to redress the balance, arguing that there are significant aspects of the lives of other species of which we can claim a kind of knowledge.[64] The success of such works (at least commercially speaking) indicates that, in spite of the dilemma that Nagel describes, we continue to be intrigued by the possibility that other animals experience the world subjectively in ways that are recognisable to us. We continue to seek confirmation, in Montaigne's terms, that our cats and ourselves are engaging in something that we both understand as 'play'. This question matters because our responses to the ethical questions raised by our treatment of other animals – both the formalised philosophy of it, and our more instinctive, everyday decisions – ordinarily rest on whether or not we judge animals to be subjects of a life in ways that are similar to humans. (Not that there isn't room for contradiction and inconsistency in this matter.) In important senses, of course, advocates of an 'alterity' approach to ethics are right: there are, epistemologically speaking, more significant gaps between the consciousness of humans and of other animals than between that of most humans. But epistemology or philosophy is not the only way we deal with this fact, or the only realm in which it affects us. In the next and final section of this chapter, I suggest that one of nonsense's fundamental concerns – with non-sequiturs and inscrutability – represents a creative response to the everyday manifestations of these questions of subjectivity and animal minds.

'How I Wonder What You're At'

The sense of incongruity we feel in reading nonsense has a lot to do with people behaving inexplicably, though with a kind of parodic rationality. As is the case, for instance, in the following rhyme, collected in an eighteenth-century anthology:

> There was a Man so Wise,
> He jumpt into
> A Bramble Bush
> And scratcht out both his eyes.
> And when he saw,
> His Eyes were out,
> And reason to Complain,
> He jumpt into a Quickset Hedge,
> And Scracht [*sic*] them in again.[65]

What about the man's wisdom made him jump into the bramble bush in the first place, we might ask? The initial motivation notwithstanding, however, once the rhyme has established that scratching out one's eyes is a consequence of jumping into hedges, it makes a kind of sense that leaping into a different bush might have the equal and opposite effect. Along with verbal play, behavioural non-sequiturs like this are the very stuff of nonsense. As T. S. Eliot famously observed, nonsense is not 'a vacuity of sense; it is a parody of sense',[66] and, in this, its characters mirror its grammar. In the most ticklish examples, there is often a hint or a tenuous thread of logic linking things together. So, for instance, in Lear's limerick about the Young Lady of Lucca, it may strike a reader as at once unusual and understandable that she should run up a tree upon being forsaken by her lovers; it represents both an escape and a dead end.[67]

The feelings engendered by these parodies of reasonableness are not, though, unique to nonsense. Each of us, almost every day, bears witness to behaviour for which we do not (or cannot) have any explanation. Illustrator Grant Schaffer's series of vignettes of life in New York, *NYSEE*, is exemplary of how this partial or fleeting glimpse into the life of another can have the kind of incongruous comedy that we find in nonsense. Each panel in the comic illustrates a moment overheard or glimpsed by Schaffer, without explanation or context. This snapshot effect consequently gives us such absurd non-sequiturs as: 'Overheard on 8th Avenue: "In the cupboard with the wigs"'; or 'Overheard on West 57th Street: "She scratched her retina on a lace curtain."'[68] Taken together, the panels of Schaffer's comic pay homage to the kaleidoscopic and episodic character of life in a major city – to that sense of myriad lives momentarily intersecting above, below and around one. On their own, though, they are little models of the psychic strangeness of a much broader phenomenon, one that is not limited to metropolitan life, but rather is intrinsic to social existence as a whole: the problem of other minds. Loosed as these scenes are from their respective contexts, the events depicted in *NYSEE* vividly (and often humorously) remind us of the fact that our access to the thoughts, feelings and intentions of others is always limited, always partial. Many everyday encounters are, strictly speaking, nonsensical.

Often, this fact has been met with either resignation or despair; Stanley Cavell, for instance, explored the recurrent tendency for scepticism to be understood as an engine of tragedy.[69] In nonsense, though, readers are confronted with an experience that is representative of our limited access to the minds of others – seeing the actions of an individual without understanding their motivation – but which tends to reveal the comic, rather than the tragic, aspects of it. Indeed, one of the more peculiar tropes of nonsense is that this bafflement might be turned into something like a refrain, rather than an obstacle. In Carroll's poem, '"You are old, Father William," the young man said', for instance, which appears in *Alice's Adventures in Wonderland*, the eponymous young man concludes most of the four-line stanzas with an expression of puzzlement at Father William's surprising antics: 'Yet you turned a back-somersault in at the door – | Pray, what is the reason for that?'; 'Yet you finished the goose, with the bones and the beak – | Pray, how did you manage to do it?'[70] Or we might think of Lear's poem, 'The Scroobious Pip', in which the different species of the animal kingdom are confounded in their attempt to classify the titular Pip – each stanza concluding with a variation of 'Flippetty chip – Chippetty flip – | My only name is the Scroobious Pip'.[71] In these instances – as in other less familiar ones[72] – a characteristically Learical compound of curiosity, marvel and confusion is transformed into a poetic refrain; what might be thought ordinarily to impede discourse in fact renews it.

All this is to say that nonsense offers a pragmatic, rather than a philosophical, answer to the question of other minds. (Indeed, Anthony Burgess suggested that pragmatism and nonsense are curiously aligned: 'Stupidity, or illogicality, can be termed pragmatism. Pragmatic people will accept nonsense, hoping that experience will prove there is a sense in it.')[73] If existential despair and intellectual inquiry are two possible responses to this question, laughter or song are others. In this way, nonsense opens up a new angle from which to consider the question of animal minds outlined above – not in terms of the existence (or not) of something we would call consciousness in other animals, but rather in terms of our repertoire of intellectual, aesthetic and linguistic responses to the impression that they have private lives. The experience of bafflement, after all, is an essential part of our everyday interactions with other animals. How often, I am tempted to ask, might one see an animal going about its business and not know quite what it's doing, or why? How often – on seeing the mad fluttering of bats overhead at dusk, without any apparent purpose but nonetheless purposive – might we be prompted to echo Carroll's Mad Hatter and exclaim 'Twinkle, twinkle, little bat! | How I wonder what you're at!'[74] Lear's description of his encounters with the 'Maned Geese' at the Earl of Derby's private menagerie captures this sense of comic bewilderment at the antics of other creatures:

> On the approach of a stranger they have the habit of raising their bodies nearly erect, swelling out their breasts, and flapping their wings against the legs of the intruder. They sometimes bend themselves backwards to such an extent, that they appear as if they would fall on their backs.[75]

The sensation of witnessing purposive action, the intention of which is unclear to us, is inextricable from our experience of living alongside other animals. It reveals a more striking gap between outward expression and conjectured private experience than we are habituated to with other human beings, and nonsense is a development of the more absurd possibilities suggested by this feeling.

Consider a more understated example. The twentieth and twenty-first centuries produced many poems that dwell on the alien nature of an encountered animal.[76] Often, though, the strangeness of the encounter is depicted as enigmatic, even mystical. Think, for instance, of D. H. Lawrence's impression of bats, 'Hanging upside down like rows of disgusting old rags | And grinning in their sleep.'[77] For other poets of the same period, though – in particular Marianne Moore – the apparent unreason of the behaviour of other animals could provoke a different kind of response. In 'Critics and Connoisseurs', she fondly recollects the example set by an ant – though quite what the example suggests remains appealingly ambiguous:

> I have
> Seen a fastidious ant carrying a stick north, south,
> east, west, till it turned on
> itself, struck out from the flower-bed into the lawn,
> and returned to the point
>
> from which it had started.[78]

This 'fastidious' ant has more than a hint of nonsense about its repetitious and apparently objectless meandering.[79] Its determination and its apparent failure to go anywhere are like those of the characters in Lear's limericks, who end up exactly where they began. In this instance, a nonsensical sensibility discloses the problem of other (animal) minds, but at the same time the writer finds a poetic or emotional consolation for it. 'What is | there', Moore asks of the ant's behaviour, 'in proving that one has had the experience | of carrying a stick?' – as though something of value might be recuperated from the ant's enigmatic behaviour. That 'something', in Moore's poem, is a recognition of the value of 'ambition without understanding', the 'poetry in unconscious | fastidiousness' described in its first lines. In more obviously nonsensical literature, however, what tends to be recuperated is a sense of fun, of the comic incongruity between action and supposed intention.

In other words, while nonsense verse may appear far removed from the fastidious descriptiveness of Marianne Moore or Elizabeth Bishop (though the latter, famously, was a devoted reader of Lear),[80] there is a common source for their depictions of animals: the sensation of visible action and invisible consciousness that has been described above. In nonsense, this strangeness is exaggerated and transposed into a more absurd register. The first appearance of the Beaver in Carroll's poem 'The Hunting of the Snark', for instance, is a particularly entertaining example of this phenomenon, in which inscrutability becomes comic incongruity, and it is with it that this chapter concludes:

> There was also a Beaver, that paced on the deck,
> Or would sit making lace in the bow:
> And had often (the Bellman said) saved them from wreck
> Though none of the sailors knew how.[81]

The poetic logic of the stanza implies a causal relation between the beaver's lace-making and boat-saving, but, just like the ship's crew, its readers are left with a blank. The lines do, though, make a kind of partial sense; although making lace is an unlikely occupation for a beaver, they do nevertheless build dams. They are not the most unlikely animal to be found making intricate, interweaved structures. In this, the beaver's lacework parodies the industrious construction for which it was often celebrated by naturalists,[82] and it does so by giving us the sailor's perspective of the beaver: from this, what we see is purposeful activity without a purpose, industry without intention.

Beavers are a special case, at least they were at the time at which Carroll was writing. 'There is no animal, below man', wrote the American anthropologist Lewis Henry Morgan, 'which offers to our investigation such a series of works, or presents such remarkable materials for the study and illustration of animal psychology.'[83] So remarkable was its natural history, thought Morgan, that 'no other animal will be allowed to entrap the unambitious author so completely as he confesses himself to have been by the beaver'.[84] Carroll owned and read Morgan's pioneering study of *The American Beaver and His Works*, published three years before *Through the Looking-Glass, and What Alice Found There* (1871),[85] and, paradoxically perhaps, this detailed natural history of the beaver can help explain its appearance in 'The Hunting of the Snark'. It does not seem surprising that, on reading about 'whole groves of pine-trees cut down within a few inches of the ground and carried off bodily' by these busy rodents,[86] Carroll should have been struck with wonder and amusement; or that, faced with an amphibious creature that built sophisticated lodges with three storeys, mated in pairs, and exhibited exceptional 'intelligence and sagacity',[87] they might have seemed at once familiar and alien. It is as though a more thorough knowledge of the beaver in fact augmented its wonderfulness rather than diminishing it.

When the Butcher asks for 'paper and ink' in Carroll's poem, the Beaver answers the request handsomely, bringing 'paper, portfolio, pens, | And ink in unfailing supplies'.[88] And while its readers know the reason for this abundance of stationery, the poem momentarily shifts perspective, and implicitly remarks the oddness of the scene as it might appear to an outsider: 'While strange creepy creatures came out of their dens, | And watched them with wondering eyes.'[89] Nonsense literature is full of wanderers, but the 'wondering eyes' usually belong to its readers; in this stanza, the perspective of the 'strange creepy creatures' fleetingly converges with our own habitual position in our encounters with other animals.

Susan Stewart suggests that nonsense 'gives us a place to store any mysterious gaps in our systems of order',[90] and this is well said, for nonsense is indeed a way of managing the parts of the world that confound us. But the implication that nonsense is a form in which we squirrel away those mysteries does not seem quite right. We might think of it instead as a way of acknowledging, and engaging with, the world's strangeness by exaggerating it. Nonsense gives us a place to confront what is exorbitant about our responses to those 'mysterious gaps'. It is 'a playful pragmatic way of interpreting the universe', as the quotation from Anthony Burgess at the beginning of this chapter put it – 'Not that anyone can make sense of the universe', Burgess astutely added.[91] Both the humans and other animals alike in nonsense gleefully resist the imposition of order or sense, and in this they reflect back to us a foundational condition of our own everyday lives: a 'playful pragmatic' way of failing to interpret those of others.

Notes

1. G. K. Chesterton, 'A Defence of Nonsense', *The Defendant* (London: J. M. Dent, 1902), 61–70, pp. 68–9.
2. Anthony Burgess, 'Nonsense', in *Explorations in the Field of Nonsense*, ed. Wim Tigges (Amsterdam: Rodopi, 1987), 17–22, p. 21.
3. Chesterton, 'Defence', p. 69.
4. For an older, but still useful, account of the growth of the field, see Cary Wolfe, 'Human, All Too Human', *PMLA* 124.2 (2009), 564–75.
5. On the idea of 'creatureliness' and embodiment, see Anat Pick, *Creaturely Poetics: Animality and Vulnerability in Literature and Film* (New York and London: Columbia University Press, 2011). The term is often used to denote a shared embodiment, and all the attendant exigencies and vulnerabilities entailed by this.
6. The most influential of these critiques have been those by Donna Haraway, in *Primate Visions: Gender, Race, and Nature in the World of Modern Science* (London: Routledge, 1989), and *When Species Meet* (Minneapolis and London: University of Minnesota Press, 2007); and Cary Wolfe, *Animal Rites: American Culture, the Discourse of Species, and Posthumanist Theory* (Chicago: Chicago University Press, 2003) and *What is Posthumanism?* (Minneapolis and London: University of Minnesota Press, 2010). This is, of course, a tradition of thought that owes a strong debt to Charles Darwin, particularly in *The Descent of Man* (1871).
7. For an important critique of this, see Jacques Derrida, *The Animal That Therefore I Am*, trans. David Wills (New York: Fordham University Press, 2009), pp. 31–5.
8. For an overview of such critiques, see Pramod K. Nayar, *Posthumanism* (Cambridge: Polity, 2014).
9. '*Not* characters, but something both more and less than an ordinary person'. Anne Stillman, 'T. S. Eliot Plays Edward Lear', in *Edward Lear and the Play of Poetry*, ed. James Williams and Matthew Bevis (Oxford: Oxford University Press, 2016), 260–80, p. 273.
10. Edward Lear, *The Complete Nonsense and Other Verse*, ed. Vivian Noakes (London: Penguin, 2006), p. 254. Hereafter referenced in the main text as *CN*.
11. Ibid. p. 392. Matthew Bevis and James Williams discuss this moment in their introduction to *Play of Poetry*, 1–15, p. 10.

12. Wallace Stevens, 'Notes Towards a Supreme Fiction', *Collected Poems* (London: Faber and Faber, 2006), p. 333. James Williams notes Stevens's line in *Edward Lear* (Liverpool: Liverpool University Press on behalf of Northcote House, 2018), p. 5.
13. Aristotle, *The Politics*, ed. Stephen Everson (Cambridge: Cambridge University Press, 1988), p. 3. For a discussion of the significance for animal studies of this and Descartes's writing on animals and language, see Derek Ryan, *Animal Theory* (Edinburgh: Edinburgh University Press, 2015), pp. 5–9.
14. Aristotle, *Problems, Books 1–19*, ed. and trans. Robert Mayhew (Cambridge, MA: Harvard University Press, 2011), pp. 313–15.
15. For a nuanced discussion of this, see Richard Sorabji, *Animal Minds and Human Morals: The Origins of the Western Debate* (Ithaca: Cornell University Press, 1993), pp. 80–6.
16. Letter to the Marquess of Newcastle, 23 November 1646, *Descartes: Philosophical Letters*, ed. and trans. Anthony Kenny (Oxford: Clarendon Press, 2006), p. 206.
17. *Lectures on the Science of Language*, 2 vols (London: Longmans, Green, 1871), II, pp. 66–7.
18. Ibid. p. 67.
19. Mary Midgley, *Beast and Man: The Roots of Human Nature* (Brighton: Harvester, 1979), p. 204.
20. Thomas Hood, 'A Recipe – For Civilization', *The Complete Poetical Works of Thomas Hood*, ed. Walter Jerrold (London: Oxford University Press, 1906), p. 38.
21. Ibid.
22. Ibid. p. 39.
23. This is discussed by Midgley (p. 215), whose source is Eugene Linden, *Apes, Men, and Language* (London: Penguin, 1974).
24. Frans de Waal, *Are We Smart Enough to Know How Smart Animals Are?* (London: Granta, 2016), pp. 95–118, 101–2.
25. For a history of the debate on animal language, see Greg Radick, *The Simian Tongue: The Long Debate about Animal Language* (Chicago and London: University of Chicago Press, 2007).
26. *The Chatto Book of Nonsense Poetry*, ed. Hugh Haughton (London: Chatto and Windus, 1988), p. 453.
27. Cary Wolfe, 'Exposures', in *Philosophy and Animal Life*, ed. Stanley Cavell, Cora Diamond, John McDowell, Ian Hacking, and Cary Wolfe (New York: Columbia University Press, 2008), 1–42, pp. 27, 30.
28. Ibid. p. 27.
29. Jean-Jacques Lecercle, *Philosophy of Nonsense: The Intuitions of Victorian Nonsense Literature* (London: Routledge, 1994), p. 3.
30. Haughton, *Chatto Book*, p. 8.
31. I take this phrase from his essay on 'The English Dog' in *The Structure of Complex Words*, (Harmondsworth: Penguin, [1951] 1995), p. 166.
32. In his essay, 'Winnicott's Lear', Phillips discusses the importance of Lear's nonsense to the pioneering child psychoanalyst Donald Winnicott's thought. *In Writing* (London: Hamish Hamilton, 2016), 218–30.
33. Haughton, *Chatto Book*, p. 4.
34. Ibid. pp. 4–6. See also Lecercle on the morphology of nonsense words, *Philosophy of Nonsense*, pp. 38–51.
35. This idea is discussed in Midgley, *Beast and Man*, p. 239.
36. Haughton, *Chatto Book*, p. 5.
37. There is a growing body of scholarship considering the relation of children and animals. For an early theoretical articulation of this idea, see *Human, All Too Human*, ed. Diana Fuss (London: Routledge, 1994); for a literary study of a particular genre, see Tess Cosslett, *Talking Animals in British Children's Fiction, 1786–1914* (Farnham: Ashgate, 2006);

for a more recent take, see Kathryn Bond Stockton, *The Queer Child, or Growing Sideways in the Twentieth Century* (Durham, NC and London: Duke University Press, 2009), pp. 89–118.

38. Lear, *Complete Nonsense*, p. 169.
39. Anonymous, 'Song', *Chatto Book*, ed. Haughton, p. 87.
40. Haughton, *Chatto Book*, p. 2.
41. Edward Lear, *Complete Nonsense*, p. 335. I'm grateful to James Williams for reminding me of Lear's fondness for animal rhymes.
42. *Old Mother Hubbard and Her Dog* (London: J. Harris, 1805), p. 1.
43. For an influential account of this tradition, see Vladimir Markov, *Russian Futurism* (London: Macgibbon and Kee, 1969). See also Haughton's introduction to *The Chatto Book*, pp. 25–7.
44. *The Collected Works of Velimir Khlebnikov*, trans. Paul Schmidt, 3 vols (Cambridge MA: Harvard University Press, 1987–98), II: *Prose, Plays, and Supersagas*, ed. Ronald Vroon (1989) p. 332. See also Paul Scheerbart's 'Monologue of the Crazed Mastodon' in Haughton's anthology for another excellent example of this tradition's attempt to find a new language for other creatures.
45. Aristophanes, *The Birds and Other Plays*, trans. David Barrett and Alan H. Sommerstein (Harmondsworth: Penguin, 1978), p. 179; *The Complete Nonsense*, p. 274.
46. 'Let them read on my gravestone', *The Collected Works of Velimir Khlebnikov*, I: *Letters and Theoretical Writings*, ed. Charlotte Douglas (1987) p. 196
47. Ibid. p. 334.
48. Ibid. p. 344.
49. *Chatto Book*, ed. Haughton, p. 92.
50. I have not been able to find a reliable source for such stories, and so they remain, perhaps appropriately, in the realm of folklore and hearsay.
51. *The Complete Nonsense*, pp. 88, 111, 112, 161.
52. *Chatto Book*, ed. Haughton, p. 92.
53. Ibid. p. 359.
54. Ibid.
55. Thanks to James Williams for noticing this.
56. Sewell, 'Nonsense Verse and the Child', in *Explorations*, 135–48, pp. 144–5.
57. Ibid. p. 144.
58. For a concise outline of Descartes's views on animal consciousness and feeling, see Peter Harrison, 'Descartes on Animals', *The Philosophical Quarterly* 42.167 (1992), 219–27.
59. Michel de Montaigne, 'An Apology for Raymond Sebond', *The Complete Essays*, ed. and trans. M. A. Screech (London: Penguin, 2003), p. 505.
60. For a detailed discussion of the present state of research, see Colin Allen and Michael Trestman, 'Animal Consciousness', *The Stanford Encyclopedia of Philosophy* (2017 Edition), ed. Edward N. Zalta. Available at <https://plato.stanford.edu/archives/win2017/entries/consciousness-animal/> (last accessed 23 August 2018).
61. On the inaccessibility of animal consciousness, see Thomas Nagel, 'What Is It Like to Be a Bat?', *The Philosophical Review* 83.4 (1974), 435–50; Emmanuel Levinas, 'The Paradox of Morality: An Interview with Emmanuel Levinas' (conducted by Tamra Wright, Peter Hughes, Alison Ainley), trans. Andrew Benjamin and Tamra Wright, in *The Provocations of Levinas: Rethinking the Other*, ed. Robert Bernasconi and David Wood (London: Routledge, 1988), 168–80); John Berger, *Why Look at Animals?* (London: Penguin, 2009); and Jacques Derrida, *The Animal That Therefore I Am*. For a helpfully schematic overview of this question in literary studies, see Laura Brown, *Homeless Dogs and Melancholy Apes: Humans and Other Animals in the Modern Literary Imagination* (Ithaca and London: Cornell University Press, 2010), pp. 1–21.

62. Nagel, 'What Is It Like to Be a Bat?', p. 438.
63. Berger, *Why Look at Animals?*, pp. 2–3.
64. For academic work on this, see *Experiencing Animal Minds: An Anthology of Human-Animal Encounters*, ed. Julie A. Smith and Robert W. Mitchell (New York: Columbia University Press, 2009); and Vinciane Despret, *What Would Animals Say If We Asked the Right Questions?* (Minneapolis and London: University of Minnesota Press, 2016). For popular examples of this trend, see Sy Montgomery, *The Soul of an Octopus: A Surprising into the Wonder of Consciousness* (New York and London: Atria, 2015); Peter Wohlleben, *The Inner Life of Animals: Surprising Observations of a Hidden World* (London: Random House, 2017); and Rosamund Young, *The Secret Life of Cows* (London: Faber and Faber, 2017).
65. *Chatto Book*, ed. Haughton, p. 148.
66. T. S. Eliot, *On Poetry and Poets* (London: Faber and Faber, 1957), p. 53.
67. 'There was a Young Lady of Lucca, | Whose lovers completely forsook her; | She ran up a tree, and said, 'Fiddle-de-dee!' | Which embarrassed the people of Lucca.' Lear, *Complete Nonsense*, p. 169.
68. *NYSEE*, <http://grantshaffer.com/comics> (last accessed 20 March 2019).
69. Stanley Cavell, *Disowning Knowledge in Seven of Shakespeare's Plays*, 2nd edn (Cambridge: Cambridge University Press, 2003).
70. Carroll, *Jabberwocky and Other Nonsense: Collected Poems*, ed. Gillian Beer (London: Penguin, 2012), p. 90.
71. Lear, *Complete Nonsense*, p. 388.
72. See, for instance, William Blake's 'The World Turned Upside Down; or, No News, and Strange News', which features many stanzas ending with the refrain, 'But to see *x* is strange indeed!': 'To see a cat steal milk from a pan, | is no news; | But to see a buck hunting a man, | is strange indeed!', *Chatto Book*, ed. Haughton, p. 183.
73. Burgess, 'Nonsense', in *Explorations*, 17–22, p. 17.
74. Carroll, *Jabberwocky and Other Nonsense*, p. 91.
75. J. E. Gray, *Gleanings from the Menagerie and Aviary at Knowsley Hall* (Knowsley, 1846), unpaginated. For a detailed and astute account of Lear's time at Knowsley, see Jenny Uglow, *Mr Lear: A Life of Art and Nonsense* (London: Faber and Faber, 2017), pp. 66–73.
76. On the 'animal encounter' poem, see Onno Oerlemans, *Animals and Poetry: Blurring the Boundaries with the Human* (New York: Columbia University Press, 2018), pp. 119–53.
77. D. H. Lawrence, *Selected Poetry*, ed. Keith Sagar (Harmondsworth: Penguin, 1972), p. 134. Or think of the 'curious' seal listening to Elizabeth Bishop sing hymns in 'At the Fishhouses', who 'would disappear, then suddenly emerge | almost in the same spot, with a sort of shrug', *Poems* (New York: Farrar, Strauss, and Giroux, 2011), p. 63.
78. *The Poems of Marianne Moore*, ed. Grace Schulman (New York: Viking, 2003), p. 106.
79. On the place of animals in Moore's comic imagination, see Clifford Mak, 'On Falling Fastidiously: Marianne Moore's Slapstick Animals', *ELH* 83.3 (2016), 873–98.
80. Robert Lowell wrote to Bishop on 4 January 1960, 'I have rereading Lear (Edward) whom you like so much.' *Words in Air: The Complete Correspondence Between Elizabeth Bishop and Robert Lowell*, ed. Thomas Travisano with Saskia Hamilton (New York: Farrar, Strauss and Giroux, 2008), p. 307.
81. Carroll, *Jabberwocky and Other Nonsense*, p. 238.
82. Georges Buffon, for instance, saw the beaver as exemplifying the capacity for social intelligence among other animals. Georges Louis Leclerc Buffon, *Buffon's Natural History, containing A Theory of the Earth, A General History of Man, of the Brute Creation, and of Vegetables, Minerals, &c*, 10 vols, trans. J. S. Barr (London: H. D. Symonds, 1797), IV, p. 287.

83. Lewis Henry Morgan, *The American Beaver and His Works* (Philadelphia: J. B. Lippincott, 1868), p. 18.
84. Ibid. p. ix.
85. Charlie Lovett, *Lewis Carroll Among His Books: A Descriptive Catalogue of the Private Library of Charles L. Dodgson* (Jefferson, NC and London: McFarland, 2005), p. 217.
86. Morgan, *The American Beaver*, p. 184.
87. Ibid. p. 133.
88. Carroll, *Jabberwocky and Other Poems*, p. 250.
89. Ibid.
90. Stewart, *Nonsense: Aspects of Intertextuality in Folklore and Literature* (Baltimore and London: Johns Hopkins University Press, 1989), p. 5.
91. Burgess, 'Nonsense', p. 21.

18

Nonsense Among the Philosophers

Michael Potter

Sense and Meaning

Let us distinguish first between sentences we do not understand and ones we do understand that express something absurd or impossible. Philosophers tend to use the word 'nonsense' and its cognates only for the former case. So, for instance, 'The table penholders the book' is nonsense, whereas 'The square is round' makes sense but is impossible. This philosophical usage is plainly at variance with ordinary language, which routinely uses 'nonsense' for both sorts of case. The reader would be entitled to ask, therefore, what the point is of discriminating among the cases. A short answer would be that the philosopher's distinction tracks a logical fault line: arguing about what is nonsensical is importantly different from arguing about what is impossible. This chapter will be largely concerned with filling out the contours of that short answer.

Within the category of the impossible philosophers further distinguish something's being *logically* impossible (contrary to the laws of logic), *conceptually* impossible (contradicting our understanding of the concepts involved), *nomologically* impossible (contrary to natural laws), *practically* impossible (not feasible), and *epistemically* impossible (contrary to what we already know). It is, for instance, logically possible but conceptually impossible for water not to be H_2O. It is conceptually possible but nomologically impossible to travel faster than light. In ordinary language 'possible' very often means 'epistemically possible' ('It's possible I didn't lock my car') or 'practically possible' ('It won't be possible for me to be there next Tuesday').

Much science fiction is nomologically impossible, but there is a significant difference between this and logical impossibility, at least psychologically. We seem to find it fairly easy to imagine (or at least to think we are imagining) a situation that is contrary to natural laws. For many of us, though, this is closely related to a point about epistemic possibility: the more we know about the relevant laws, the harder we find it to imagine their infringement.

Most of what goes by the name of nonsense poetry is not nonsense on the taxonomy just proposed but exhibits various kinds of impossibility (sometimes in the same passage). There is, for instance, nothing impossible about an owl and a pussycat going to sea in a boat, pea-green or otherwise; that they should then have a conversation is conceptually possible but nomologically impossible. Yet however much we try to suspend disbelief, we cannot picture the conceptual impossibility in which

> One fine day in the middle of the night
> Two dead men got up to fight,

Back to back they faced each other,
Drew their swords and shot each other.[1]

Interestingly, though, it is much rarer to find straightforward examples in the canon of nonsense poetry of logical impossibility.

There is a widespread view according to which grammar is in a certain sense prior to meaning. Noam Chomsky famously coined 'Colorless green ideas sleep furiously' as an example of a sentence that is grammatical (because the bare categories which the surface syntax of English recognises – noun, verb, adverb, etc. – are respected), but nonsensical (because the meanings of the words clash).[2] No meaning had been given to an idea's sleeping or having the colour green. (Of course, language moves on, and nowadays any environmentalist worth their salt will have come up with plenty of green ideas, but that is irrelevant to Chomsky's point.) Now, by way of contrast, consider 'Jabberwocky':

'Twas brillig, and the slithy toves
  Did gyre and gimble in the wabe:
All mimsy were the borogoves,
  And the mome raths outgrabe.[3]

The Chomskian grammarian will want to distinguish this from the 'green ideas' sentence, because it is not a case of meaning-clash: the poem seems to respect grammar but many of the words have been given no meaning. (I say 'seems to' because, not knowing the meanings, I cannot be sure. What if, for example, 'wabe' is in fact a verb?) Then there is a further class consisting of sentences which do not obey even the crude syntactic rules. Chomsky himself is reported[4] to have used an e. e. cummings poem, as a case where even the crude grammatical rules are disobeyed:

Me up at does

out of the floor
quietly Stare

a poisoned mouse

still who alive

is asking What
have i done that

You wouldn't have[5]

(Notice, though, that as ungrammaticality goes, this poem is rather tame: apart from word order, it is quite conventional.) Finally, one might also wish to distinguish the extreme case of mere noise, where there is neither grammar nor meaning in the conventional sense. (This is not to deny, of course, that noises can be evocative of meaning or that their rhythms can have a kind of 'grammar', but only to recognise the distance between that and the previous cases we have been considering.)

This whole way of presenting the matter suggests, though, that grammar is one thing, semantics quite another. An alternative view would deny this distinction, and hold instead that the true grammatical categories are much more finely grained (e.g. not 'adjective' but 'colour adjective'). The Chomskian 'syntax first' view might also be called the 'container theory', because it conceives of syntactic categories such as *noun* or *verb* as containers waiting for us to put words in them. The container constrains meaning, in the sense that it will refuse any word I attempt to put in it with the wrong kind of meaning. Some philosophers (e.g. Wittgenstein in the *Tractatus*) have proposed an alternative view according to which the container a word belongs to depends on its meaning rather than the other way round. In their view the notion of an empty container does not make sense, since the 'container' is simply a way of referring to the word's possibilities of combination with other words to form sentences, and these are a function of the possibilities of the meanings to combine to form facts. To some extent, this is an instance of a dispute, familiar to metaphysicians, between Platonic and Aristotelian conceptions of properties: a Platonic property is like a container; an Aristotelian property is immanent in each of its instances. What interested Wittgenstein, however, was the order of explanatory priority between the container and its contents. He thought that a word has some particular grammatical type because of the meaning it has, not the other way round.

Those who study children's language acquisition sometimes mention that the 'vocabulary spurt' takes place several months before the 'grammar spurt'.[6] (What would it be like for the order to be reversed? How could children exhibit their grasp of grammar without knowing many words?) But Wittgenstein's point is *not* a conjecture about language *learning*, nor is it a piece of advice to scientists devising artificial intelligence systems for language. After all, it would be perfectly possible to teach someone the grammar of German while withholding almost all information about individual words: they could learn the standard endings of nouns and verbs without knowing any examples of stems to add them to. Wittgenstein himself published an Austrian spelling dictionary for primary school children, which listed only words, not their meanings.[7] His point is not about whether this is a good way for someone who already knows English to learn German, but about the conceptual relationship between syntax and semantics. For one thing, the grammar-first method is intelligible only for teaching a *second* language, and therefore tells us very little in itself about the conceptual relationship between syntax and semantics. On Wittgenstein's view, the fact that one can know the grammatical category of a word without knowing its meaning, but not the other way round, wrongly encourages the container view.[8]

In his later work Wittgenstein diagnosed the container view as an instance of the mistaken tendency (which he ascribed, somewhat questionably, to Augustine) to regard every language as in effect a second language. Augustine, he suggested,

> describes the learning of human language as if a child did not understand the language and came into a strange country and did not understand the language of the country; that is, as if it already had a language, only not this one. Or again: as if a child could already think, only not yet speak. And 'think' would mean here something like 'talk to himself'.[9]

The Augustinian view has us approaching the world with a set of categories and then acquiring meanings that fit those categories. An alternative view has the world supplying the categories. Wittgenstein attempted to defuse this dispute between grammar-first and world-first views by conceiving of syntax and semantics as being in a sort of necessary harmony. But he was not trying by a priori means to arrive at a conclusion about how the part of the brain responsible for language operates.

Nonsense Parading as Sense

Why should philosophers be interested in nonsense? One reason is because they are interested in sense, hence are interested in the contrast class. This has some truth as far as it goes – quite often in philosophy studying a contrast case can prove illuminating – but it cannot be all that is going on. After all, a chef who tried to learn about the edible by studying the inedible might thereby acquire a working knowledge of health and safety practices but would be unlikely to achieve a Michelin star.

Where the issue becomes specifically philosophical is in the claim that some distinctive kinds of philosophical claim are actually nonsense. This was the mantra of the logical positivists of Schlick's Vienna Circle in the 1920s, popularised in English by Ayer's *Language, Truth and Logic* (1936). The logical positivists emphasised two sorts of case: metaphysics and religion. Their reasons were broadly the same in both cases; indeed, they generally regarded religious claims as metaphysical. Their argument consisted in a test for meaningfulness which, they said, these claims fail to meet. Others, such as Kant, had previously argued that we cannot know these metaphysical and religious claims to be true. The positivists went further by holding that they do not even make sense.

Prima facie this looks absurd. Surely, one might say, a metaphysical claim such as 'Numbers are real' makes *sense*, even if it is in some way mistaken. Not according to the positivists, who held that this is another case of green ideas sleeping furiously: we have not explained what it is for something such as a number to be (or not be) real.

In the case of religious discourse, what the logical positivists claimed was that it is nonsense according to the classification adopted earlier, so not that it is patently absurd but rather that some of the words have not been given meanings that operate in the context. In assessing this claim, one difficulty that arises immediately is the tendency of religion to make use of words that have a meaning already. At one time it was common to contrast the literal with the metaphorical meanings of these words. Nowadays linguists tend to frown on this contrast, suggesting instead that almost all meaning is more or less metaphorical. Guy Deutscher, for instance, calls language 'a reef of dead metaphors'.[10] Notice, though, that there is a difference between calling some distinction a matter of degree and rejecting it altogether as incoherent (consider the distinction between night and day). A usage may now count for ordinary purposes as literal, even if it was originally a metaphor. It is important not to throw a useful baby out with the bathwater and hence let uses of words outside their usual homes go unchallenged. Consider the Apostles' Creed, for example: to descend is to move downwards, but those who claim to believe that the Creed is literally true, and hence in particular that Christ literally 'descended into Hell', do not really believe that a carelessly drilled North Sea borehole might break through into the Underworld.

The literal/metaphorical distinction, rough though it is, at least offers one explanation of how it might come about that a nonsensical sentence gives the illusion of sense: words that have meaning in one context are used in another, superficially similar context where they have none. (Wittgenstein's unimprovable example is 'It is 5 o'clock on the Sun', whose nonsensicality takes most people a while to see.)[11] The distinction therefore gives us one kind of reason to demand a further explanation from our interlocutor: what they mean by descending into Hell, in the former case; by its being 5 o'clock on the sun, in the latter.

The logical positivists' argument that metaphysics and religion are nonsense was closely tied to their verificationism: sentences were supposed by them to be meaningful only if there was in principle a way of verifying whether they were true or false. The subsequent history of logical positivism consisted largely in a struggle to reformulate this principle so as not to rule out implausibly many cases (e.g. arithmetical generalisations such as Goldbach's conjecture, or statements about the past). Verificationism died because of the failure to find a plausible version of it that would cope with such cases. Perhaps as a result, the idea that metaphysics or religion are nonsense is not so much discussed by philosophers nowadays. It is perhaps worth noting, though, that there are arguments for nonsensicality that do not go via an implausibly narrow verificationist premise. For instance, if we resist metaphor, it is quite hard to explain the meanings of many religious words in terms that will not appear question-begging to the non-believer.

The logical positivists' treatment of ethics was interestingly different from their treatment of metaphysics and religion. They agreed that ethical claims are problematic if interpreted straightforwardly as their surface grammar suggests. (What kind of evidence would verify or refute the claim that killing babies is wrong, for instance?) However, they argued that ethical claims should not simply be abandoned but should instead be translated into reports of our mental states of approval or disapproval – the 'boo, hooray' theory, as it came to be known. It would of course be perfectly possible (and have some initial plausibility) to apply this sort of expressivist translation to religion as well ('God loves us' means 'Hooray for us!', for instance), but for some reason this route was less popular.

One difficulty in having a sensible discussion of this question is that calling something nonsense is pejorative in ordinary language. Some of this pejorative character no doubt involves the confusion between nonsense and impossibility mentioned earlier. It is a distinct question what point there might be in uttering nonsense. We need to remember that it is not prima facie absurd that there might be such a thing as important nonsense.

It is worth noting, incidentally, that Wittgenstein, in contrast to most of the positivists, regarded ethics and religion as two sides of a single coin – two attempts to express absolute value. Ethics, he wrote, 'is a document of a tendency in the human mind which I personally cannot help respecting deeply and I would not for my life ridicule it'.[12] Nonetheless, he thought that absolute value, despite its importance to us, is nonsensical because non-factual. The conception of religion that emerges from his writings, both early and late, is radically non-metaphysical. Not only did he dismiss the metaphysical roles that have often been ascribed to religion (e.g. as explaining the existence of the world as a whole) as a misconception, but he also held that no particular fact in the world has a genuinely religious explanation.

He suggested, indeed, that the point of a religious explanation was that it marked the *end* of explanation:

> So people stop short at natural laws as at something unassailable, as did the ancients at God and Fate.
>
> And they both are right and wrong. But the ancients were clearer, in so far as they recognized one clear terminus, whereas the modern system makes it appear as though everything were explained.[13]

He thus hinted at the intriguing idea that the role of religious explanation might be to signal that explanation in the ordinary sense has come to an end.

Logic and Sense

The idea that some of what purports to be philosophy might really be nonsense did not originate with Wittgenstein; but, by making it a lynchpin of his *Tractatus* (1922), he was largely responsible for popularising it far beyond the bounds of professional philosophy. What unfortunately got lost in this diaspora, however, was the Fregean source of Wittgenstein's distinctive use of the word 'sense'. Frege inaugurated modern logic in 1879 by inventing the notation of quantifier and variable. One of the reasons for his success in this endeavour was that he recognised the limited character of the goal he had set himself of devising a conceptual notation sufficient to capture the logically relevant structure of a sentence. Because the logicians' goal is narrower than the grammarians', it follows that the notion of content they work with is correspondingly more limited. For the part of content which logicians discard as irrelevant to their concerns Frege used different words in different places – colouring, scent – but modern philosophers of language generally call it 'tone'. For the part that remains when tone is ignored, he used 'conceptual content'[14] or, from 1891 onwards, 'sense'.[15]

What, then, is the criterion for sameness of sense? Frege held that logic is characterised by its distinctive concern with unfolding the properties of truth: other sciences have truth as their goal, but only logic has truth as its subject matter. It follows that two words will have the same sense just in case they make the same contribution to determining the truth-conditions of sentences in which they occur. He therefore held, for instance, that the pairs 'and' and 'but', 'horse' and 'steed', 'dog' and 'cur' differ only in tone, not in sense. He also held, more problematically, that differences of tone may arise at the level of whole sentences because of differences in grammatical structure. For instance, the sentences

> The Greeks defeated the Persians in the Battle of Platea

and

> The Persians were defeated by the Greeks in the Battle of Platea

differ only in tone, not sense, because they have just the same truth-conditions and just the same inferential power.[16]

The article 'On Sense and Reference' (1892) in which Frege expounded his notion of sense is one of the most read in analytic philosophy.[17] Even so, it should be conceded that in that article he did himself no favours by downplaying the notion's origin in his concern with grounding logic; instead, he suggested that he was somehow drawing a distinction between the public and private parts of content. This is just a mistake: the differences in tone may be harder for a non-native speaker to learn than differences of sense, but they belong just as much to the public language, nonetheless.

Frege himself left the exact contours of the notion of sense a little vague, but Wittgenstein imported the notion into the *Tractatus*, attempting to resolve the ambiguity in the process by holding that sentences have the same sense just in case they are true in all the same possible worlds. In his mouth as in Frege's, then, the word 'sense' has a technical meaning rather different from the one it has in ordinary discourse. It follows that 'nonsense', as its contradictory, equally has a technical meaning. If a sentence is Tractarian nonsense, a further argument is needed if we wish to claim that it is also ordinary nonsense. The *Tractatus* itself does indeed claim that 'all propositions of everyday language, just as they stand, are in perfect logical order',[18] but unfortunately omits to explain why this should be so. Anyone who does not share Wittgenstein's intuition on this point is therefore left wondering why the role of language should be restricted in the manner that identifying Tractarian with ordinary nonsense would entail.

When philosophers in the analytic tradition used the word 'sense' or its contradictory, 'nonsense', they usually take themselves, rather vaguely, to be doing so in something like Frege's way. Too many of them, though, have paid no attention to the extent to which his interests were logical, not linguistic: for him, the sense of a word is that part of its content that is relevant to inference; all the rest is tone. So to call a sentence nonsensical is to impugn only its logical credentials, not its linguistic ones. In the normal case a sentence has both sense *and* tone. Frege held that tone is more important in poetry than in scientific discourse (which is why he was not greatly interested in it). Perhaps we should not expect this to give us a precise taxonomy, though. Most of us would agree, no doubt, that it makes no sense for an idea to sleep. But what about a flower? Or a fungus?

On Frege's categorisation, then, nonsense in the strict sense consists of sentences that have only tone but no sense. So most of what is usually thought of as 'nonsense' poetry would not count as such, since it tends to be absurd rather than incomprehensible. Perhaps, though, Kelly Roper's 'At the fireworks' comes close to being 'all tone':

> Whoosh . . . Boom!
> Crackle, crackle, crackle.
> Ooo! Ah!
>
> Whoosh . . . Boom!
> Sqeal, squeal, squeal.
> Ha, ha, ha, ha, ha![19]

Notice, too, that 'Jabberwocky' resists easy classification for a different reason. We find ourselves tempted to read it as if the words do have perfectly comprehensible senses, but we happen not to know what they are. We might therefore be happy to draw logical inferences from it (e.g. that something slithy was gimbling somewhere) on the assumption that it made sense to its author, if not to us.

Arguing to Nonsense

Why does it matter whether a sentence that seems to make sense really does? The most plausible answer is that the rules of logic were developed to apply to sentences that really do make sense, so there is a risk that we will be led astray if we apply them in the nonsensical cases too. For instance, if it is not fully senseful to say that God exists, we are entitled to ask whether standard logic is applicable in reasoning about the claim that He does. So even if, for instance, we could formulate a version of the ontological argument that is correct by the standards of conventional logic (a tall order), the appearance of correctness would be deceptive, because an argument with a nonsensical conclusion is not really an argument at all.

We may contrast this sort of radical attack on theological arguments with Kant's more moderate critique. He sought to show that any argument for the existence of God would have to be of one of three familiar sorts – ontological argument, cosmological argument, argument from design. He then tried to demonstrate that none of these three has any chance of working. He famously hoped thus to 'deny *knowledge*, in order to make room for *faith*',[20] but he did not hold that the very *idea* of a proof of God's existence is incoherent. If the conclusion is nonsensical, on the other hand, this shows straightaway that no argument for it could be valid. The positivists' dismissal of arguments for God is thus more thoroughgoing, and potentially more robust, than Kant's.

There is a particular problem about arguing against nonsense, however. If I think that you have said something nonsensical, how do I respond? If I argue against you in your own terms, then I seem to be accepting that what you have said at least makes sense, which is precisely what I dispute. If I try to persuade you to give up sexist or racist language, I may face structurally similar difficulties. If 'you can't say things like that' does not suffice, will I have to use the very words I disapprove of in order to explain to you what is wrong with them? Sometimes, of course, I can get away with mentioning rather than using – putting the offensive words in quotation marks – but that technique only goes so far. Partly this is because the use-mention distinction is not nearly as binary as some logic books would have you believe; but it is also because tone has a tendency to leak through quotation marks (as you will find if you recount in polite company an offensive conversation you have overheard). This is why, in addition to the general device of naming a word by putting it in quotation marks, we have a few extra expressions ('the C-word', 'the N-word') which attempt to insulate us from the tone of the words they name. If all that concerned us was logic, so that we were wholly indifferent to tone, we would have no need for these extra names.

In the nonsense case, one possibility is that arguing on your terms may be successful, in that your position collapses under its own weight: the assumption that your words make sense is internally inconsistent. What, though, if that is not the case? What if your language game is internally consistent? Is there anything I can then do to persuade you to give it up? Rudolf Carnap tried to argue that the answer is no, saying that all there is to choose between consistent languages is pragmatic considerations such as usefulness. He called this the 'principle of tolerance' and epitomised it eye-catchingly in his claim that 'in logic there are no morals'.[21] Others (including Carnap's later self) have been less tolerant, however. There is plainly *something* right about the idea that my conceptual scheme should be assessed relative to its capacity to meet my needs, but that is not enough to immunise it to external criticism altogether, not least because if I want to use it to communicate with you, you had better have some sympathy with the needs that led me to choose it. This problem of finding a neutral position from which to assess incommensurable conceptual schemes without question-beggingly privileging one or the other continues to receive much attention from philosophers, particularly following a discussion of the scientific case by Thomas Kuhn,[22] but has not achieved anything close to a satisfying resolution.

Notice, too, that tolerance concerning conceptual schemes is not at all the same as relativism concerning truth. Even if I am free to choose my conceptual scheme according to my own interests, once it is chosen the world will then constrain which sentences are true, provided only that it contains *some* empirical vocabulary with which to talk about the world at all. Some have tried to insulate religious language from this constraint by developing a 'fideistic' conception according to which it forms a self-contained discourse with no empirical vocabulary; but this then invites the converse difficulty of explaining what the point is of engaging in a discourse that floats free of the world in this fashion.[23]

Arguing from Nonsense

The logical positivists were known for the general principle that there are no non-trivial a priori truths. The standard refutation of this principle is supposed to be the observation that the principle itself is, if true, a non-trivial a priori truth, and hence self-refuting. Is this a compelling argument? This is an instance of a split in philosophical attitudes: some think that the argument is compelling; others that it makes a mistake over levels. The 'two-levellers' think that philosophy occupies a distinctive position outside the practices which it critiques and hence not straightforwardly susceptible to its own arguments. This is sometimes known as the 'side-on' view, presumably because we are conceived of as confronting the world with language much as one might hold up a picture in front of what it depicts, while the philosopher attempts to examine the relationship between the two, side-on as it were, without being party to the depiction.

The *Tractatus* famously advances a particularly striking version of a one-level view – striking because it ends up applying the criterion of nonsensicality developed in the book to the book itself. As a consequence, it enjoins the reader to throw it away before lapsing into a kind of quietism.

> 6.54 My propositions are elucidatory in this way: he who understands me finally recognizes them as senseless, when he has climbed out through them, on them, over them. (He must so to speak throw away the ladder, after he has climbed up on it.) He must surmount these propositions; then he sees the world rightly.
>
> 7 Whereof one cannot speak, thereof one must be silent.[24]

The interpretation of this reflexive claim has attracted far too much attention from *Tractatus* scholars in the last three decades (by deflecting their interest away from a lot else in the book that is of interest). Nonetheless, there is plainly something interesting about an argument that collapses under its own weight in this manner. Logicians are familiar with proof by *reductio ad absurdum* (*P* and *Q* are being used here schematically, to stand in place of suitable declarative sentences):[25]

> assume *P*;
> deduce *Q* and not-*Q*;
> conclude not-*P*.

Here, though, we have *reductio ad alogiam*:

> assume *P*;
> deduce that *P* is itself nonsense.

We do not then conclude not-*P*, since the negation of nonsense is nonsense; rather we merely withdraw *P*, like a bad penny, from circulation. Now, though, as we look back, how are we to regard our argument with *P* as a premise? That whole argument was nonsense, hence not really an argument at all. So how did it persuade us to reach a substantive conclusion (namely that *P* is nonsense)?

This suggests two broad conclusions. First, even if making Tractarian sense is an all-or-nothing matter, making ordinary sense is not. Many things count as moves in a language game that are not the utterance of sentences with a Tractarian sense. It is often said, rightly, that this was one of the points on which the later Wittgenstein laid stress. It is also often said, less plausibly, that on this point he was disagreeing with his own earlier self.

The second conclusion is that logical argument is not the only effective form of linguistic persuasion. Let us call a sequence of sentences that do not make Tractarian sense a 'pseudo-argument'. What we have seen is that some pseudo-arguments are capable of changing our minds. So far, that is merely a psychological observation. What turns it into a philosophical problem is that in response to some pseudo-arguments we are *right* to change our minds. We are therefore owed an explanation of *why* we are right, and this explanation cannot be wholly psychological, since psychology is descriptive, whereas what we are now seeking is normative. It is surely more than a little odd that logicians, who have been so successful in explaining the mechanics of arguments proper, have until now had so little to say about the mechanics of how pseudo-arguments actually work.

Notes

1. This popular piece of folk nonsense can be found in, among other places, *The Chatto Book of Nonsense Poetry*, ed. Hugh Haughton (London: Chatto and Windus, 1988), p. 481.
2. Noam Chomsky, *Syntactic Structures* (The Hague: Mouton, 1957), p. 15.
3. Lewis Carroll, *Alice's Adventures in Wonderland and Through the Looking-Glass*, ed. Hugh Haughton (London: Penguin, 1998), p. 132.
4. By Irene Fairley, 'Syntactic deviation and cohesion' (1973), in *Essays in Modern Stylistics*, ed. Donald Freeman (London: Methuen, 1981), 123–37, p. 123.
5. e. e. cummings, *73 Poems* (New York: Harcourt, Brace & World, Inc., 1963), p. 12.

6. See e.g. Florence Labrell et al., '"Speaking volumes": A longitudinal study of lexical and grammatical growth between 17 and 42 months', *First Language* 34.2 (2014), 97–124, p. 118.
7. Ludwig Wittgenstein, *Wörterbuch für Volksschulen* (Vienna: Hölder-Pichler-Tempsky, 1926).
8. Note that knowing the grammatical category does not mean being able to say what the category is called. Throughout this discussion, 'knowing grammar' means a practical ability to use words more or less correctly in sentences, not being able to explain it. (Compare, for example, knowing how to play a topspin backhand in tennis with explaining how it is done.)
9. Wittgenstein, *Philosophical Investigations*, trans. G. E. M. Anscombe, P. M. S. Hacker and Joachim Schulte, rev. 4th edn (Oxford: Blackwell, 2009), §32, p. 19[e].
10. Guy Deutscher, *The Unfolding of Language: the Evolution of Mankind's Greatest Invention* (London: Arrow, 2005), p. 115.
11. Wittgenstein, *Philosophical Investigations*, §350, p. 118[e].
12. Wittgenstein, 'Lecture on ethics' (1929), reprinted in *Philosophical Occasions, 1912–1951*, ed. A. Nordmann and J. C. Klagge (Indianapolis and Cambridge: Hackett, 1993), p. 44.
13. Wittgenstein, *Tractatus Logico-Philosophicus*, trans. C. K. Ogden and F. P. Ramsey (London: Kegan Paul, Trench, Trubner, 1922), 6.372.
14. Gottlob Frege, *Begriffsschrift* (1879), trans. T. W. Bynum as *Conceptual Notation* (Oxford: Oxford University Press, 1972), §3.
15. See Frege, 'Function und Begriff' (1891), trans. Peter Geach, with revisions by Michael Beaney, as 'Function and Concept', in *The Frege Reader*, ed. Michael Beaney (Oxford: Blackwell, 1997), 130–48, p. 138.
16. Frege, *Conceptual Notation*, §3.
17. Frege, 'Über Sinn und Bedeutung' (1892), trans. Max Black as 'On Sense and Reference' in *Frege Reader*, ed. Beaney, 151–71.
18. Wittgenstein, *Tractatus*, 5.5563.
19. Kelly Roper, 'At the Fireworks', available at <https://childrens-books.lovetoknow.com/Onomatopoeia_Poems_for_Children> (last accessed 14 September 2020).
20. Immanuel Kant, *Kritik der reinen Vernunft* (A edn 1781, B edn 1787), trans. Norman Kemp-Smith as *Critique of Pure Reason* (London and Basingstoke: Macmillan, 1929), p. 29.
21. Rudolf Carnap, *Logische Syntax der Sprache* (1934), trans. A. Smeaton as *The Logical Syntax of Language* (London: Kegan Paul, 1937), p. 52.
22. In *The Structure of Scientific Revolutions* (Chicago: University of Chicago Press, 1962).
23. For a discussion of this position, see Bernard Williams, (1964) 'Tertullian's paradox', in Antony Flew and Alasdair MacIntyre (eds), *New Essays in Philosophical Theology* (London: SCM Press, 1955), 187–211.
24. Wittgenstein, *Tractatus*, 6.54–7.
25. For a specific example, consider the standard proof that √2 is irrational. Suppose that √2 is rational. So it can be expressed as a fraction m/n in its lowest terms. So $m^2=2n^2$. So m^2 is even. So m is even. So n^2 is even. So n is even. So m/n is not in its lowest terms. Contradiction. Therefore √2 is irrational.

19

'Word beyond Speech': Nonsense and the Sacred

James Williams

Near the end of G. K. Chesterton's metaphysical detective thriller, *The Man Who Was Thursday*, the novel takes another in a long series of strange turns. Our hero, Syme, in pursuit of a group of anarchist conspirators, finds himself in 'a vast carnival of people', and time seems to slow down suddenly as the narrative pauses on a naïvely dream-like dance:

> For a long time – it seemed like hours – that huge masquerade of mankind swayed and stamped in front of them to marching and exultant music. Every couple dancing seemed a separate romance; it might be a fairy dancing with a pillar-box, or a peasant girl dancing with the moon; but in each case it was, somehow, as absurd as Alice in Wonderland, yet as grave and kind as a love story.[1]

The allusion to *Alice* is, perhaps, a subtle acknowledgement that the whole novel up to this point has possessed a dream-like quality (as one might expect from the subtitle: *A Nightmare*). At the same time, this moment represents something new: we are taken deeper and more steeply into the realm of nonsense, and Chesterton seems to have a particular Carrollian moment in mind.[2] In Chapter 4 of *Through the Looking-Glass*, Alice reaches out to shake simultaneously the hands of Tweedledum and Tweedledee and finds herself 'dancing round in a ring' to music that 'seemed to come from the tree under which they were dancing, [. . .] by the branches rubbing one across the other, like fiddles and fiddle-sticks'. Later, when the dream is over, Alice tells her sister:

> But it certainly *was* funny [. . .] to find myself singing '*Here we go round the mulberry bush.*' I don't know when I began it, but somehow I felt as if I'd been singing it for a long long time![3]

Chesterton was always suspicious of the circle, which he saw as the symbol at once of reason and of madness which, for him, is the excess, not the absence, of reason.[4] Perhaps for this reason *The Man Who Was Thursday*'s discrete pairs, 'swaying and stamping', are slightly different from Carroll's dance in a ring, yet the scene is, in other respects, strikingly similar: the sudden slowing of time ('[f]or a long time – it seemed like hours'), the sharp falling away of the main plot, and the artfully absurd conjunctions – the fairy and the pillar box, the girl and the moon – bring us squarely into the imaginative territory of Victorian nonsense even before Chesterton's narrator name-checks Carroll by calling the sight 'as absurd as Alice in Wonderland'.

This suddenly heightened foregrounding of the novel's most nonsensical tendencies arrives just at the point at which Chesterton's religious vision is also most clearly on display: 'I am the Sabbath [. . .] I am the peace of God'.[5] The impulses of the dance and the dream, of nonsense and a kind of metaphysical religious vision, are, in this moment, one and the same. An insight is being offered, we cannot help but feel, both about 'Alice in Wonderland' and about the divine, in which the 'absurd' and the 'grave and kind' are two sides of the same coin. Something very similar, and undoubtedly indebted to Chesterton, takes place at the conclusion of Elizabeth Sewell's classic study *The Field of Nonsense*. Like *The Man Who Was Thursday*, *The Field of Nonsense* is an extended meditation on the competing claims that order and anarchy might stake upon the imagination, and throughout the book Sewell presses the case for order as the primary underpinning of nonsense, downplaying 'poetry' and 'the dream' in favour of a vision of nonsense as a strictly formal, excessively logical game that plays with words as if with chess pieces. Her final chapter, however, takes the reader up to and beyond the limits of her own argument:

> Any game, no matter how logical, sets one by the mere fact of playing it in the position of make-believe and divination. Logic cannot deal with such a situation. It has nothing to say outside the little closed circuit of its own activity, and could not by itself grasp such a situation – that the pursuit of a logical end could automatically lift one straight out of logic and into the world of unreason and magic.[6]

'We thought we were on safe ground with these logical games, so numbered and orderly', Sewell writes, and yet 'need some way of moving from the circle of logic to the world outside the circle, from manipulation to make-believe'.[7] Sewell finds the best way to describe this 'way of moving' in the figure of the dance which, as she points out, is everywhere in Carroll and Lear:

> Dance is half a game, but only half. Games are a manipulation of things, but this is what we were looking for just now, a kind of thinking with the body, freedom and mobility combined with the experience of some intuitive make-believe way of understanding things by dancing them [. . .] It is not rational, yet it is not out of control, and best of all, it has an immeasurably ancient right of entry into the world in which logic has landed us defenceless, the world of ritual, magic, and religion [. . .][8]

On this view nonsense, however orderly and logical its internal structure, is always in some way cumulatively, feelingly, dancing into the sphere of non-rational. And for Sewell, as for Chesterton, nonsense understood as a kind of dance – controlled and measured, but ultimately unanswerable to the demands of reason – serves as a port of entry into the realm of the sacred.

Chesterton himself had theorised this connection between nonsense and the sacred in his 1901 essay 'A Defence of Nonsense'. '[W]e fancy that nonsense will', he writes, 'come to the aid of the spiritual view of things. Religion has for centuries been trying to make men exult in the "wonders" of creation, but it has forgotten that a thing cannot be completely wonderful so long as it remains sensible.'[9] What nonsense and religion have in common, for Chesterton, is a fundamental resistance to the more absolutist and totalising claims of reason and logic, and a shared investment in 'wonder' as an experience that both cuts across, and yokes together, the categories of reason and emotion. He recognises, of course, that the claim 'religion is nonsense' is more often and more readily on the lips of the sceptical atheist than the believer, but in a characteristic apologetic manoeuvre seeks to turn this point of resistance into a point of persuasive traction:

> The well-meaning person who, by merely studying the logical side of things, has decided that 'faith is nonsense', does not know how truly he speaks; later it may come back to him in the form that nonsense is faith.[10]

In this chapter I am interested neither in pressing home the view that faith is nonsense in the sense that Richard Dawkins might mean that, nor in persuading the reader to arrive at a position of faith via the attractions of literary nonsense. Those who want pro- or anti-religious polemic can find plenty of both elsewhere and are unlikely to be looking for it within these pages. Rather, I want to explore some of the explicit affinities and connections between nonsense and religious traditions of thought, belief, and practice and, in the process, to say something about the spiritual life of nonsense as a literary and artistic mode.

That spiritual life, it should be acknowledged, is often tricky to pin down. Literary nonsense with an overtly religious agenda is rare: the conclusion of *The Man Who Was Thursday* is unusual in the extent to which it puts itself forward as a moment of Christian allegory (though this might not surprise us when we consider how far all nonsense is, by its nature, resistant to allegorical paraphrase). The *Alice* books, though written by a man in holy orders, are, partly for that very reason, fastidious in avoiding any mention of holy things, to the point of omitting the Bishops from the chess game in *Through the Looking-Glass*.[11] We needn't be doctrinaire Freudians, however, to suspect that anything so rigorously repressed is bound to find a way back in. When Alice protests that she can't believe the White Queen's age to be 'a hundred and one, five months, and a day', the Queen replies:

> 'Ca'n't you? [. . .] Try again: draw a long breath, and shut your eyes.'
>
> Alice laughed. 'There's no use trying,' she said: 'one *ca'n't* believe impossible things.'
>
> 'I daresay you haven't had much practice,' said the Queen. 'When I was your age, I always did it for half-an-hour a day. Why, sometimes I've believed as many as six impossible things before breakfast [. . .]'[12]

The theological position known as 'fideism' – that is, belief based on faith, with an explicit disregard to 'reason or the intellect' (*OED*) – is part of the cloud of ideas stirred up by Carroll's joke. (So, it must be said, are a lot of other things, including the sudden literalisation of a polite social platitude: 'Oh, *I can't believe* you're that age!') It may or may not be overreach to assume that this joke casts the White Queen in the role of Cardinal Newman, good-naturedly rationalising the recently defined doctrine of Papal Infallibility,[13] but more imaginative editors of *Alice*, such as Martin Gardner and Hugh Haughton, have connected this moment to Carroll's own discomfort about abstract theological argument, and seen in it a tacit affirmation of the paradoxical nature of certain Christian doctrines. Gardner references the popular nonsensical credo attributed to the early Latin theologian Tertullian, 'I believe it *because* it is absurd!',[14] and Haughton tracks down its correct form, *certum est quia impossibile est*, in the Latin Father's *De Carne Christi*: 'And he was buried, and rose again; the fact is certain, because it is impossible.'[15]

For the true fideist the disregard of reason is an essential feature, even the defining and authenticating feature, of religious belief. On the basis of this comment (often taken out of context) claims have been made for Tertullian as a proto-fideist that stretch the evidence and downplay the significance attached to reason elsewhere in his thought. Nonetheless even as a moment of rhetorical flourish, Tertullian's *certum est quia impossibile* offers a moment of striking alignment between the claims of faith and the limits of reason. To affirm belief in the impossible appears to violate the logician's most sacred law, that of non-contradiction, and even to violate the syntax of the word 'impossible' in a way that risks being not simply false, but, in the strict philosophical sense, nonsense (incapable of being either false or true, because expressing nothing). As in the White Queen's claim to have believed 'six impossible things before breakfast', faith and nonsense each appear to be revealed and illuminated in the light of the other, or perhaps simply reduced to one and the same thing.

Even from within a position of reasoned faith, however, it makes sense to ask how far the truth-claims of religion can be made to make sense in human language which, by definition, is formed and shaped by a limited human perspective. Religious thought has long queried how far natural language can meaningfully describe the supernatural, and the architect of this line of thought in the Christian tradition is the fifth- or sixth-century Neoplatonist and theologian known to history as 'Pseudo-Dionysius the Areopagite'. In his discourse on *The Divine Names*, Pseudo-Dionysius writes:

> Indeed the inscrutable One is out of the reach of every rational process. Nor can any words come up to the inexpressible Good, this One, this Source of all unity, this supra-existent Being. Mind beyond mind, word beyond speech, it is gathered up by no discourse, by no intuition, by no name.[16]

The believer, in Pseudo-Dionysius' view, may appear, like the White Queen, to be a denizen of the world of nonsense: 'The man in union with truth knows clearly that all is well, even if everyone else thinks he has gone out of this mind.'[17] Yet this is because the language at the believer's disposal is framed and delimited by a natural world which is incommensurate with, and inadequate to articulating, a higher and inaccessible reality.

That natural language is inadequate to describe the Divine is a widely accepted belief across many religions, and with it comes the perpetual risk that religious language might always topple into – or simply be – nonsense. Something is needed to differentiate this position, born out of faith, from the externally similar position of the logical positivist philosopher for whom, in the words of A. J. Ayer, 'all utterances about the nature of God are nonsensical'[18] because lacking any criteria by which they might be verified or falsified. A range of responses to this problem are possible, of which a couple deserve attention here. The first is to incorporate the insight in some way into one's method of doing theology. Pseudo-Dionysius's short treatise *The Mystical Theology* offers a way forward, albeit by groping in the dark:

> Since it [the Divine nature] is the Cause of all beings, we should posit and ascribe to it all the affirmations we make in regard to beings, and, *more appropriately*, we should negate all these affirmations, since it surpasses all being.[19]

Although the Godhead is beyond the reach of any speech act, nonetheless negation is to be preferred as 'more appropriate', less likely to mislead the seeker after truth into false pictures of God. The effects of this view, known as 'negative theology' or 'apophaticism', are far-reaching in a range of religious contexts. It may be objected, of course, that the *via negativa* attributed to Pseudo-Dionysius fails by its creator's own lights, since elsewhere in the *Mystical Theology* it is made clear that 'There is no speaking of it, nor name nor knowledge of it. Darkness and light, error and truth – it is none of these. It is beyond assertion and denial.'[20] Negation, then, is scarcely better than affirmation: merely 'more appropriate', and one might ask in what this appropriateness consists. The hope of the negative theologian must be for a way of discriminating between more and less inadequate forms of language, or perhaps a way of separating out the better and more illuminating forms of nonsense from the worse and more misleading.

The notion of a 'useful nonsense' finds a more developed form in the modern school of theology known sometimes as 'Grammatical Thomism', an attempt to harmonise the theology of Thomas Aquinas with the method of Ludwig Wittgenstein in which doing philosophy is to a large extent a matter of uncovering and exposing the forms of nonsense generated by previous attempts to do philosophy. The Grammatical Thomists are a loose group, but as Stephen Mulhall points out (in an important defence of their approach which also serves as a useful introduction to it):

> One central point of resemblance between them lay in their willingness to characterize discourse about God as nonsensical – more specifically, their willingness to take as a touchstone of theological insight the awareness that language was essentially incapable of putting us in touch with the reality of God, given the fact that (as mainstream Christianity has always averred) he is utterly transcendent with respect to the world we users of language inhabit, and in relation to which our words attain and maintain whatever meaning or sense they possess.[21]

In such a view, then, nonsense is seen to be not the fatal problem that exposes the bankruptcy of theology but its essential currency, its 'touchstone of insight'. One way of putting this might be that the persistent nonsense generated by statements about God is precisely what guarantees that God is indeed what Christians (and other theists), have always claimed him to be: entirely transcendent of, and standing utterly beyond, the realm of created reality, which includes natural language.

This union of Aquinas and Wittgenstein has been controversial, both among more conservative Thomistic theologians – for whom it has sometimes seemed too much like dissolving real metaphysical questions about God into abstracted quibbles about grammar[22] – and among Wittgensteinians. The latter group have tended to divide over the question of what use, if any, can be found for nonsense. On a traditional account,

Wittgenstein's early work represented by the *Tractatus Logico-Philosophicus* 'allowed that certain kinds of violation of the limits of sense were nevertheless ways of gesturing towards ineffable insights',[23] an idea foreclosed by the later thought of the *Philosophical Investigations*, in which 'nonsense is not a peculiar (say, a peculiarly mysterious or ungraspable) kind of sense – it is the plain and simple absence of sense'.[24] Yet this is hardly the end of the matter, since for Wittgenstein the encounter with nonsense, however we understand it, is central to the philosophical enterprise, and for the theologian the arrival at the limits of sense may itself be the point, rather than any claim that meaningful insights into God lie 'beyond' or 'outside' sense. As Mulhall writes:

> In both cases [Aquinas and Wittgenstein] we find the human imagination committed to the construction of a form of words that extrapolates everyday speech patterns to the point at which they become utterly severed from their original contexts, and to valuing the result of that construction process precisely because of its lack of sense.[25]

Theology, on this view, is a discourse that works by subjecting natural language to forms of extreme intellectual pressure and noting the points at which, and the ways in which, it breaks down.

In debating the role of nonsense in religious statements, theologians and philosophers of religion have not, generally speaking, taken examples of *literary* nonsense as their starting point.[26] All the same, nonsense writing can be read afresh in the light of these debates, as richly abundant in religious intuitions, and pregnant with suggestions of sacred riddles. In the *Alice* books, for instance, the motif of the unanswered riddle, or 'the great puzzle'[27] runs through both narratives with the suggestion that the books' careful logical paradoxes might be repeatedly taking us to the edge of what reason and logic can do for us. Or we might look elsewhere, for instance to the poetry of that great Anglican atheist Stevie Smith, to find matters of belief dramatised as nonsense:

> Our Bog is dood, our Bog is dood,
> They lisped in accents mild,
> But when I asked them to explain
> They grew a little wild.
> How do you know your Bog is dood
> My darling little child?[28]

'Bog' is Russian and Polish for 'God', which may or may not be important, but it is also English for a swamp. Smith's 'they', represented by the 'darling little child', in professing 'Our Bog is dood!' can be imagined both as saying 'Our God is dead!' and at the same time as not saying this, but something that resists paraphrase, drawing us into a treacherous and swampy intellectual morass. The poem becomes an exasperated attempt to make 'them' make sense, in which we find ourselves sinking further into nonsense:

> Then tell me, darling little ones,
> What's dood, suppose Bog is?
> Just what we think, the answer came,

Just what we think it is.
They bowed their heads. Our Bog is ours
And we are wholly his.

As so often in Lewis Carroll, a riddling speaker is pressed for an explanation which they persistently refuse to offer. Read as a poem about religion (and this interpretation is clearly suggested) 'Our Bog is Dood' casts believers as childish, incoherent and muddled: yet at the same time the poem itself pointedly, elusively, declines to be a poem 'about' anything at all. The conversation begins and ends in exasperating nonsense and the poem carries the suggestion, without much joy, that it is only by talking nonsense that we talk about sacred things at all, and at the cost of perplexity or unhappiness (it is ambiguous, in the end, whether 'They bowed their heads' in prayer or despair).

Literature might find ways to make us hear the nonsensical status of religious statements, but it can also come close to evoking or instantiating forms of religious experience that evade reason or sense. Edward Lear, whose religious convictions ran deep and included, towards the end of his life, an increasing rejection of organised religion,[29] often seems to carry us into the affective territory of the divine encounter:

There was an Old Person of Tring,
Who embellished his nose with a ring;
He gazed at the moon, every evening in June,
That ecstatic Old Person of Tring.[30]

Critics of nonsense have often insisted that true nonsense is pure nonsense: if it can be seen as 'about' anything at all, or has any ulterior purpose, no matter what nonsensical elements it may possess, a text it is not really nonsense at all.[31] This insistence on purity, which itself has a religious ring to it, has always been a statement of aspiration as much as a clear-sighted description of the texts. The resistance to sense is, of course, at the heart of nonsense, but it has always been possible to see this resistance as offering a kind of plausible deniability, which allows nonsense to be about all kinds of things while ostensibly not being 'about' anything. Nothing in this poem is about religion, and yet as so often in Lear, it is the 'how' as much as the 'what' of the verse that does the imaginative work: it presents us with a kind of religious experience which it invites us to feel rather than to understand, an 'ecstasy' of contemplation the meaninglessness of which is, paradoxically, its most religious element insofar as it appears to be orientated towards nothing meaningfully describable. In Lear's illustration the moon gazes back, suggesting that it is not the moon, or the Old Person of Tring, that is the poem's subject so much as the ecstatic gaze that passes between them, a kind of love that eludes sense.

This kind of nonsense, like Chesterton's absurd dance with which this chapter began, takes us into the territory of mysticism, the second of the two outworkings of Pseudo-Dionysian apophaticism that I indicated earlier. If any text demonstrates that there is no hard line between mysticism and theology, it is the *Mystical Theology*: and yet it makes sense to draw a rough and ready distinction. If our language is incapable of making sense about God, we might accommodate paradox and nonsense, not by trying to find a place for it within an overarchingly rational theology, but by embracing it as a way of communicating a subjective encounter with the sacred. Medieval Christian mysticism grows out of the tradition of Pseudo-Dionysius: the tradition is especially clear in a text like *The Cloud of Unknowing*, in which negation, obscurity and darkness mark the approach to the Divine, but it is hard not to see elements of a divine nonsense in less obviously indebted texts, such as the *Revelations* of Julian of Norwich:

> And in this vision [our Lord] showed me a little thing, the size of a hazel-nut, lying in the palm of my hand, and to my mind's eye it was as round as any ball. I looked at it and thought, 'What can this be?' And the answer came to me, 'It is all that is made.'[32]

Something dazzlingly non-literal and contradictory is visualised here – are not Julian, her palm, her viewing eye, part of 'all that is made'? – and pressed into the service of communicating a more profound and unattainable truth. Something beyond human comprehension is literalised and made accessible to us as luminous paradox. It seems like a mistake to call the *Revelations* a work of 'nonsense', but its effects are worked in part by incorporating elements of vigorously suggestive nonsense imagery into its account of a mystical encounter that exceeds rational, naturalistic description.

This dynamic has always been potentially dangerous, insofar as the visions of the mystics offer an alternative set of spiritual symbols and images, beyond the control of official religion. The mystic, at least in the Abrahamic traditions, has always been an outsider figure whose visions have often been the foundation of a 'secret' tradition. To this extent the mystic can be read as a kind of avant-garde figure, a comparison developed by the Syrian poet Adonis in his study *Sufism and Surrealism*. For Adonis, the insights of Islamic mysticism bear fruitful comparison with the French surrealists who, inspired by Freud, sought to make literal in absurd or nonsensical ways the deeper realities of the unconscious mind. In doing so, Adonis argues, they abandoned the fundamental rationalist principle of non-contradiction, bringing them into line with ancient traditions of occult religion:

> They believe that, 'Everything is in everything.' The Surrealists subscribe to this irrational way of thinking, which is close to the view held by Pythagorists and members of secret religions, and seek to release the secrets that lie behind logical speech . . .[33]

Adonis's Sufis are like the surrealists insofar as both offer a critique of visible reality in the contradictory and seemingly nonsensical language of a higher reality (or a deeper – the spatial metaphor does not matter much either way). Both place themselves outside the norms of their prevailing religious and intellectual cultures: 'as the Sufis work to go beyond the *shari'a* and orthodox religion in order to arrive at the truth, the Surrealists work on going beyond the social, cultural and moral establishment, to make man disappear, to enable him to discover his true essence and true existence and true life'.[34] Both are, in other words, kinds of eccentric.

Pseudo-Dionysius observed in *The Divine Names* that 'The man in union with truth knows clearly that all is well with him, even if everyone else thinks that he has gone out of his mind.'[35] Mystical or religious experience, in other words, is from the outside confusable with folly or madness. In the Christian tradition this idea has always drawn scriptural sanction from St Paul's first letter to the Corinthians, in which the contrast between an elevated divine foolishness and a reductive human wisdom is an important point of paradoxical rhetoric. Paul's boast that 'We are fools for Christ's sake'[36] may be intended as to mean no more than that Christians, by rejecting the standards and mores of the surrounding pagan culture, must wear their eccentricity in the eyes of others as a badge of pride, but certain individuals, including canonised saints of the church, have taken this injunction much further, living radically at odds with the behaviour even of their fellow Christians, and acting in apparently foolish or even insane ways.[37] Yet Holy Fools, despite their Pauline warrant, are in no way unique to Christianity, and include among their number many prominent Sufi saints who, like their Christian counterparts, are of various historicity. One figure, around whom a great many tales have accumulated, is the jester 'called by the Arabs Si-Djoha or Joha, and by the Persians "Juha" or "Juhi", who is regarded by most scholars', writes the historian of folly, Enid Welsford, 'as a completely unhistorical figure'. Welsford notes that 'these Jests of Si-Djoha, which had penetrated orally into the West, travelled probably in a more literary form to Turkey and were there translated and attributed to a certain Nasr-ed-Din Hodja or Khoja [. . .]'.[38] The Khoja is often presented as a holy man, a kind of Mullah or Imam, though of a rustic kind more akin to a country parson than a sophisticated religious scholar.

In a characteristic and often-told story, the Khoja goes to preach a Friday sermon:

> One day he stood up in the pulpit and said to the congregation, 'O Moslems, do you know what I am going to say to you to-day?' 'No', replied they. 'And no more do I', said the Khoja; and hastily left the mosque. The next Friday he asked the same question, but this time the congregation answered, 'Yes.' 'If you know, then I needn't tell you', said the Khoja, and again made off. The next week, when the Khoja asked his usual question, the congregation, thinking to display great cunning, said, 'Some of us do, but some of us don't.' 'Then let those who know tell those who don't', said the Khoja, and once more the congregation were outwitted.[39]

The Khoja does not so much speak nonsense as act nonsensically, subverting the expectations and conventions of sermon-giving and of communication more broadly. The comedy of the tale is in the Khoja's skilful evasion of his duty, and his evading the congregation's best efforts to get the better of him. Taken as a whole, the story reads like the frustrated non-communications of nonsense writing. There is, for example, the crucial piece of evidence at the trial of the Knave of Hearts, which concludes:

> My notion was that you had been
>   (Before she had this fit)
> An obstacle that came between
>   Him, and ourselves, and it.
>
> Don't let them know she liked them best,
>   For this must ever be
> A secret, kept from all the rest,
>   Between yourself and me.

'This is the most important piece of evidence we've heard yet',[40] says the King of Hearts, yet of course the particular form of nonsense game being played in this moment is that the 'evidence' is nothing of the sort: it fails to meet the standards of evidence, much as the Khoja's sermon fails to meet the requirements for a sermon, even as his twisting position, from one Friday to the next, dances a dance with its own internal logic.

The possibility always remains that the Khoja merely puts on a show of foolish behaviour in order to teach some profound lesson. More conservative, or perhaps merely cautious, religious writers have often preferred to take this sort of line with the Holy Fool, as in for example the rather po-faced gloss on St Simeon Salus ('Simeon the Mad') in *Butler's Lives of the Saints* that 'by *affecting* the manners of those who want sense, he *passed for* a fool'.[41] Perhaps the Khoja merely passes for a fool: by denying he knows what to preach, he teaches us something about our speechlessness before God; by refusing to reveal his message again and again, he teaches his brethren that the message of God is already within them, and so on. If this seems like too much of a stretch, consider that the stretching may be part of the point: we should both feel that a lesson of this kind is possible, as well as feeling how far we have to reach to make it work. Stories of the Khoja as a pastor have a similar ring, frustrating and comic, to some of the anecdotes about famous rabbis preserved within the Hasidic tradition in Judaism, as for example this exchange featuring the great Rabbi Menachem Mendel of Kotzk:

> A hasid came to the rabbi of Kotzk. 'Rabbi,' he complained, 'I keep brooding and brooding, and don't seem to be able to stop.'
>
> 'What do you brood about?' asked the rabbi.
>
> 'I keep brooding about whether there really is a judgment and a judge.'
>
> 'What does it matter to you!'
>
> 'Rabbi, if there is no judgment and no judge, then what does all creation mean!'
>
> 'What does that matter to you!'
>
> 'Rabbi, if there is no judgment and no judge, then what do the words of the Torah mean!'
>
> 'What does that matter to you?'
>
> 'Rabbi! "What does it matter to me?" What does the rabbi think? What else could matter to me?'
>
> 'Well, if it matters to you as much as all that,' said the rabbi of Kotzk, 'then you are a good Jew after all – and it is quite all right for a good Jew to brood: nothing can go wrong with him.'[42]

As in many of Alice's conversations with the creatures of Wonderland or the Looking-glass world we can ask whether this a maddening failure to understand or take seriously an interlocutor's concerns, or a piece of inspired psychotherapy. Might it even be both? The Kotzker Rebbe, as Mendel was simply known, takes a piece of sincere religious doubt and transforms it into a piece of inspired paradox: that you brood shows you have no need to brood; that you are racked with doubts shows you are a good Jew.

It may be in the pedagogical and pastoral sphere that nonsense finds its most fruitful interplay with the sacred. Teaching, from the time of Socrates (a great prototype of the wise fool) has involved the teacher adopting strategies of deliberate folly or nonsense to provoke the disciple into forms of questioning, or of realisation. The Kotzker Rebbe takes an experience of spiritual angst and, by a performance of apparent obtuseness as vexing as a hookah-smoking Caterpillar, turns it into a piece of circular riddling the purpose of which is to release the disciple from his worries by piercing through them 'with strange relation' (in Wallace Stevens's phrase).[43] It is precisely the rabbi's non-engagement with the terms of 'sense' on which the anxious Hasid presents his problem that makes possible the rewriting of the dilemma in a newly liberating, translated form. The religious tradition that has put nonsense to most extensive didactic use in this way is surely the tradition of Buddhism known in the West by the Japanese form of its name: Zen. The two forms of Zen writing in which teaching practice has been preserved are the dialogue, or *mondō*, and the meditation text or test-case, the *kōan*. *Mondōs* record the dialectical methods of Zen masters in the form of interaction; *kōans* preserve the problems they set for their disciples to meditate upon. Both employ forms of nonsense, as M. Conrad Hyers observes in his study of *Zen and the Comic Spirit*, to play off against one another two forms of knowledge identified in the Indic corpus of early Buddhism: 'the clarity of *prajñā*, or direct, intuitive knowledge, in contradistinction to *vijñāna*, or discriminating, analytical knowledge'.[44]

For Hyers, as for any writer formed within a Western literary tradition, to read Zen *mondōs* and *kōans* is 'as if one were suddenly plunged into the world of Lear's nonsense rhymes or of Alice in Wonderland'. To grapple with Zen, in other words, is to grapple with the question of nonsense, and Hyers offers some useful reflections:

> Nonsense does not mean totally without sense, but without sense in the customary view of the sensical, and beyond rationality in the ordinary understanding of reason [. . .] Nonsense is the question-mark placed after the supposedly firm reality of the 'real' world of intelligibility, the irrefutable logic of rationality, or the categories and dichotomies of any system. It is this maieutic play upon irrationality in order to move beyond rationality that is expressed in Hakuin's familiar *kōan*, 'What is the sound of one hand clapping?' or in Yün-Mēn's reply to the question, 'What is a sermon that surpasses the teaching of the Buddha and the Patriarchs?' 'Cake!'[45]

Yün-Mēn's cry of 'Cake!' has the familiar ring, both exasperating and joyous, of the nonsense non sequitur:

> There was an Old Person of Sestri,
> Who sate himself down in the vestry;
> When they said, 'You are wrong!' – he merely said, 'Bong!'
> That repulsive Old Person of Sestri.[46]

No doubt Lear would have been baffled to see his 'nonsenses' compared to Zen *mondōs* (though by the lucky accident of rhyme this little tale takes place in a vestry, and hence becomes a tiny fable of religious nonconformism).[47] It is irresistible to note, however, how many of the limericks are dialogic in form; in how many a frustrated 'they' seeking clarity or reassurance are met with a sheerly nonsensical response; and how far the poems carry us along into the feeling that these nonsense exchanges are a kind of liberating relief from the norms of sensible communication. We might reasonably raise an eyebrow at attributing the possibility of *satori* – 'awakening' or 'enlightenment' – to such nonsense, but we might equally reasonably think that it is the situation of the text within a wider culture, religious tradition, or what Wittgenstein called a 'form of life', that is the real difference between the 'Bong!' of the Old Person from Sestri and the 'Cake!' of the Zen master.[48]

The Zen tradition is willing to go perhaps even further than the Christian *via negativa* in its willingness to give up on words entirely. There are, as Hyers observes, Zen parables of masters who consign their own books to the flames: it is hard to imagine this gesture gaining much cultural traction in the logocentric cultures of the 'religions of the book'. 'But in a very real sense', he writes, 'in Zen, as in mysticism generally, inner illumination implies the burning of all words.'[49] And here we encounter a final paradox, since Zen, like the mysticisms and theologies of the Abrahamic faiths, has never ceased to generate an endless flow of words in the service of provoking or generating its moments of 'wordless Dharma', its encounters with a sacred reality which evades the capacities of natural language. In this sense there is a deep affinity with the view of Christian theology suggested earlier, as a repeated subjection of natural language to forms of pressure that generate instructive nonsense. Despite its own reverence for wordlessness, Zen too, it would appear, has often felt that, as Mulhall puts it:

> [t]he best way to appreciate the transcendence of God to human language is thus not to fall into silence, avoiding even the assertion that nothing is assertible of him [. . .] it is rather endlessly to employ that language in relation to him, and endlessly to experience its inevitable collapse upon itself.[50]

That this endless linguistic interrogation of the divine has been played out for centuries at the limits of sense is reason enough to take seriously the idea that the creativity of literary nonsense might contain, intentionally or otherwise, authentic intimations of the sacred.

Notes

1. G. K. Chesterton, *The Man Who Was Thursday* (London: Penguin, [1908] 2010), pp. 199, 201.
2. There may be a more subtle allusion to Lear there, too, recalling the Owl and the Pussy-cat 'dancing with the moon'; see Edward Lear, *The Complete Nonsense and Other Verse*, ed. Vivien Noakes (London: Penguin, 2006), p. 239.
3. Lewis Carroll, *Alice's Adventures in Wonderland and Through the Looking-Glass*, ed. Hugh Haughton (London: Penguin, 1998), p. 158.
4. In *Orthodoxy* (1908); see *The Everyman Chesterton*, ed. Ian Ker (New York: Alfred A. Knopf, 2011), p. 283.
5. Chesterton, *Thursday*, p. 203. My account of plot is deliberately thin on details, to avoid spoilers.
6. Elizabeth Sewell, *The Field of Nonsense* (Dalkey Archive Press, [1952] 2015), p. 187.
7. Ibid. pp. 186, 188.
8. Ibid. p. 192.
9. Chesterton, 'A Defence of Nonsense', in *The Defendant* (London: Dent, 1901), p. 69.
10. Ibid. p. 70.
11. Tenniel shows us a Bishop with his back to us, reading a newspaper, in his fifth illustration to Chapter 1 of *Through the Looking-Glass*.
12. Carroll, *Looking-Glass*, p. 174.

13. In the dogmatic constitution *Pastor Aeternus* (1870), the product of the First Vatican Council which concluded in that year. See Jo Elwyn Jones and J. Francis Gladstone, *The Red King's Dream or Lewis Carroll in Wonderland* (London: Pimlico, 1996), pp. 208–21 for an example of this kind of reading.
14. See Martin Gardner, *The Annotated Alice: Definitive Edition* (London: Penguin, 2001), p. 210.
15. Tertullian, *De carne Christi*, Ch. 5; English translation by Peter Holmes (1885), available at <https://www.newadvent.org/fathers/0315.htm> (last accessed 24 April 2021).
16. Pseudo-Dionysius, *The Divine Names*, in *The Complete Works*, trans. Colm Luibheid (New York: Paulist Press, 1987), 47–131, pp. 49–50.
17. Ibid. p. 110.
18. A. J. Ayer, *Language, Truth and Logic* (London: Penguin, [1936] 2001), p. 121.
19. Pseudo-Dionysius, *The Mystical Theology*, in *The Complete Works*, 133–141, p. 136. My emphasis.
20. Ibid. p. 141.
21. Stephen Mulhall, *The Great Riddle: Wittgenstein and Nonsense, Theology and Philosophy* (Oxford: Oxford University Press, 2015), p. 5.
22. An important critique here is Francesca Aran Murphy, *God is Not a Story* (Oxford: Oxford University Press, 2007).
23. Mulhall, *The Great Riddle*, p. 5.
24. Ibid. p. 46.
25. Ibid. p. 58.
26. One recent exception is Josephine Gabelman, *A Theology of Nonsense* (Cambridge: Lutterworth Press, 2017), which uses the work of Lewis Carroll to refocus positive attention on the 'paradoxical', 'anarchic' and 'childlike' elements of Christian belief.
27. Carroll, *Wonderland*, p. 18.
28. *Collected Poems and Drawings of Stevie Smith*, ed. Will May (London: Faber and Faber, 2015), p. 302.
29. The best account of the evidence for Lear's religious beliefs is Sara Lodge, 'Edward Lear and Dissent', in *Edward Lear and the Play of Poetry*, ed. James Williams and Matthew Bevis (Oxford: Oxford University Press, 2016), 70–88.
30. Edward Lear, *The Complete Nonsense and Other Verse*, ed. Vivien Noakes (London: Penguin, 2006), p. 170.
31. See Anna Barton's and my remarks in our 'Introduction: Companionable Nonsense', pp. 3–4 above.
32. Julian of Norwich, *Revelations of Divine Love*, trans. Elizabeth Spearing (London: Penguin, 1998), p. 7.
33. Adonis, *Sufism and Surrealism* (1995), trans. Judith Cumberbatch (London: Saqi, 2005), p. 25.
34. Ibid. p. 59.
35. Pseudo-Dionysius, *The Divine Names*, in *The Complete Works*, p. 110.
36. 1 Corinthians 4.10 (King James Version).
37. For an overview of the subject, see John Saward, *Perfect Fools: Folly for Christ's Sake in Catholic and Orthodox Spirituality* (Oxford: Oxford University Press, 1980).
38. Enid Welsford, *The Fool: His Social and Literary History* (London: Faber and Faber, [1935] 1968), pp. 29–30.
39. Sir Harry Luke, *An Eastern Chequer-Board*, qtd in Welsford, *The Fool*, pp. 30–1.
40. Carroll, *Looking-Glass*, p. 106.
41. *Butler's Lives of the Saints*, 2nd rev. edn, ed. and rev. Herbert J. Thurston, S. J. and Donald Attwater, 4 vols (London: Burns and Oates, 1956), III, p. 4. My emphases.

42. Martin Buber, *Tales of the Hasidim: The Later Masters* (New York: Schocken Books, 1948), p. 280.
43. Wallace Stevens, 'Notes Towards a Supreme Fiction', *Collected Poems* (London: Faber and Faber, 2006), p. 333.
44. M. Conrad Hyers, *Zen and the Comic Spirit* (London: Rider and Company, 1974), p. 159.
45. Ibid. p. 148.
46. Lear, *Complete Nonsense*, p. 372.
47. The description of rhyme as 'lucky accident' is Wittgenstein's in *Culture and Value*, ed. Georg von Wright and Heikki Nyman, trans. Peter Winch, rev. edn (Oxford: Blackwell, 1998), p. 93. I have more to say about the relationship between chance, rhyme and nonsense in Lear's limericks in my *Edward Lear* (Liverpool: Liverpool University Press on behalf of Northcote House, 2018), pp. 27–34.
48. The phrase is used, among many places, in *Philosophical Investigations*, trans. Elizabeth Anscombe et al., 4th edn (Oxford and Malden, MA: Blackwell, [1953] 2009), §19, p. 11/11[e].
49. Hyers, *Zen*, p. 149.
50. Mulhall, *The Great Riddle*, p. 59.

Notes on Contributors

Anna Barton is Reader in Victorian Literature and Co-Director of the Centre for Nineteenth-Century Studies at the University of Sheffield. She is the author of *Nineteenth-Century Poetry and Liberal Thought: Forms of Freedom* (2017).

Sara Chiarini is Principal Investigator at the Cluster of Excellence *Understanding Written Artefacts* of the University of Hamburg. She is the author of *The So-called Nonsense Inscriptions of Ancient Greek Vase Painting. Between* Paideia *and* Paidia (2018).

Martin Dubois is Associate Professor in the Department of English Studies at Durham University. He is the author of *Gerard Manley Hopkins and the Poetry of Religious Experience* (2017).

Rebecca L. Fall is Program Manager of the Center for Renaissance Studies at the Newberry Library, Chicago. She has published on literature, book history, and the surprising social functions of nonsense writing in early modern England.

Alessandro Giammei is Assistant Professor of Italian Studies and Comparative Literature at Bryn Mawr College. He co-edited books on Pasolini and Art History (2022) and on Virginia Woolf and Lytton Strachey (2021), authored books on Fitzgerald and Central New Jersey (2018) and on Toti Scialoja and Italian Nonsense (2014), and is completing a monograph on Ludovico Ariosto's modern afterlife.

Hugh Haughton is Professor of Modern Literature at the University of York. He is the editor of *The Chatto Book of Nonsense Poetry* (1988) and Lewis Carroll, *Alice's Adventures in Wonderland and Through the Looking-Glass* (1998) and author of a forthcoming study of *Second-Hand Poetry*.

Michael Heyman is Professor of English at the Berklee College of Music, Boston. He publishes on nonsense literature, music, and poetry, and is the head editor of *The Tenth Rasa: An Anthology of Indian Nonsense* (2007), and editor of *This Book Makes No Sense: Nonsense Poems and Worse* (2012).

Freya Johnston is University Lecturer and Tutorial Fellow at St Anne's College, University of Oxford. She is general editor of The Cambridge Edition of the Novels of Thomas Love Peacock (2016–) and co-editor of Jane Austen's *Teenage Writings* (2017).

Jordan Kirk is Associate Professor of English at Pomona College. He is the author of *Medieval Nonsense: Signifying Nothing in Fourteenth-Century England* (2021).

Alexandra Lukes is Assistant Professor of French and Translation Studies at Trinity College Dublin. She is the editor of the special issue 'Nonsense, Madness, and The Limits of Translation' (*Translation Studies*, 2019) and has published in *Romanic Review*, *Modernism/modernity*, *MLN*, *Translation and Literature*.

Noreen Masud will be Lecturer in English at the University of Bristol from January 2022. She is the author of *Hard Language: Stevie Smith and the Aphorism* (2022).

Adam Piette is Professor of Modern Literature at the University of Sheffield. He teaches and researches Irish modernism and poetry and poetics, and is one of the series editors for Oxford University Press's Mid-Century series.

Michael Potter is Professor of Logic at the University of Cambridge and a Life Fellow of Fitzwilliam College. Most of his publications are on the history of analytic philosophy (especially the work of Frege, Russell, Wittgenstein and Ramsey) or the philosophy of mathematics (especially set theory).

James Rann is Lecturer in Russian at the University of Glasgow. His research focuses on early twentieth-century Russian literature and he is the author of *The Unlikely Futurist: Pushkin and the Invention of Originality in Russian Modernism* (2020).

Hugh Roberts is Professor of French Renaissance Literature at the University of Exeter. He has published on nonsense, obscenity and the reception of ancient Cynicism in early modern France.

Sumanyu Satpathy is former Professor and Head of the Department of English at the University of Delhi. He is co-editor of *The Tenth Rasa: An Anthology of Indian Nonsense* (2007), and his most recent publication is *The Will to Argue: Studies in Late Colonial and Postcolonial Controversies* (2017).

Peter Swaab is Professor of English Literature at University College London. He was the editor of *'Over the Land and Over the Sea': Selected Nonsense and Travel Writings of Edward Lear* (2005) and has written the entry on Lear for Oxford Bibliographies Online.

Cassie Westwood is a teacher and writer. Her work on Edward Lear has appeared in *Essays in Criticism*, *Victorian Studies*, *RES*, and the *TLS*, and she co-edited a book of essays on *Thinking Veganism in Literature and Culture* (2018; paperback 2019).

James Williams is Senior Lecturer in Nineteenth-Century Literature and Culture at the University of York. He is the co-editor, with Matthew Bevis, of *Edward Lear and the Play of Poetry* (2016; paperback 2019) and the author of *Edward Lear* (2018).

Index

Note: Page numbers in *italic* refer to illustrations

EU representative:
Easy Access System Europe
Mustamäe tee 50, 10621 Tallinn, Estonia
Gpsr.requests@easproject.com

www.ingramcontent.com/pod-product-compliance
Lightning Source LLC
Chambersburg PA
CBHW081401090726
47908CB00012B/2756

* 9 7 8 1 3 9 9 5 5 7 3 8 2 *